From
Rationalism
to
Existentialism

From
Rationalism
to
Existentialism
The Existentialists and Their Nineteenth-Century Backgrounds

Robert C. Solomon
Queens College *of* The City University of New York

Harper & Row, Publishers
New York, Evanston, San Francisco, London

†

From Rationalism to Existentialism:
The Existentialists and Their Nineteenth-Century Backgrounds

Standard Book Number: 06-046344-9

Library of Congress Catalog Card Number: 76-174531

For Elke

Contents

Preface

My purposes in writing this book can be stated very briefly without explaining why I should suppose that one more book in an already overpopulated literary field should be necessary. First, my students have demonstrated their desire for an introductory yet detailed discussion of the various "existentialist" philosophers, and I have attempted to provide one. Second, I have found even among professional philosophers a general disinterest in what I believe to be a profoundly exciting school of thought. Some philosophers dismiss existentialism because it is too uncritical and too literary; others, more favorably disposed to it, divorce it from traditional philosophical enterprises because of several all-too-common claims about its "radical departure" from traditional thought. Against both of these attitudes, I wish to demonstrate the continuity and identity of projects between "traditional philosophy" and existentialism. It is partly to this end that I have begun the discussion with Kant, whose respectability as a thinker is undisputed in all camps. To serve both of these purposes, I have attempted to capture, or more accurately allow myself to be captured by, the ebullient flow of the exciting mainstream of European thoughts of the past 180 years. Allowing myself to be submerged makes it difficult to be entirely critical, and finding myself faced with a choice between sympathetic exposition and detached criticism, I chose the former as being more compatible with my central purposes. In most cases, I have allowed the philosophers discussed to criticize each other. I have tried to restrain myself as much as possible to allow each philosopher to appear most persuasive. This restraint has its amusing drawbacks, for I find myself going out of my way to defend doctrines I find obscure or unacceptable and to allow myself the luxury of a sarcastic remark only against those philosophers whom I most admire.

Each chapter is intended to serve as an independent study. My choice of authors has been designed to provide a smooth flow of development. This necessitated neglect of some excellent philosophers who might have been included (for example, Schopenhauer and the "religious existentialists": Marcel, Jaspers, Buber, Tillich, Bultmann, Barth), and only a brief summary of others, such as Fichte, Schelling. Moreover, I have focused my attention selectively on those authors whom I do treat in detail. For example, it is the early Hegel (the *Phenomenology*), the early Kierkegaard (before 1845), the early Heidegger (*Being and Time*), and early Sartre and Merleau-Ponty (before 1945) that will receive the bulk of our attention.

The overwhelming problem with the authors treated in this text is their penchant for obscure terminology and a "systematic" presentation of ideas. To the other extreme, Nietzsche and Kierkegaard are so unsystematic that it is equally difficult to characterize their beliefs. I have attempted to break their philosophies out of the difficult idiom—largely derived from Kant—in which they are presented, but I have spent several sections of the book defending these obscure formulations as philosophically significant in themselves. Enough of the original terminology is employed to allow the reader to use these chapters as introductions to original sources, but sufficiently little unexplained terminology is included so that the reader who is not ready to attack the forbidding originals will have little trouble understanding the discussion.

The main credit for the inspiration of this book must go to my students at Princeton, University of Pennsylvania, and UCLA, whose interest in existentialism fired my own and whose perplexities encouraged me to undertake this project. My own interest in the topic is a product of the inspiring guidance of my teacher, Frithjof Bergmann, who is not responsible for the directions I have taken with it. Many people have helped in many ways, but deserving of special mention are Isaac Miller and Susan Smith, Ann Garfield, Malcolm Diamond, Walter Kaufmann, Diana Levine and a bevy of secretaries from New Zealand to Philadelphia. I am especially grateful to my editor, Frank Tillman, who has been helpful and sympathetic since we first discussed this project and who has rescued the manuscript several times from the author's despair with it. My debt to the brilliant philosophers whose work is the subject matter of this book can only be demonstrated in the text itself. Most importantly, I am grateful to my wife, Elke, who not only helped with the text itself, but maintained the mobile environment within which such a prolonged project could be developed. It is to our joint search for 'authenticity' that these studies are devoted: it is to her unpublished part in that search to which this book is dedicated.

Robert C. Solomon

From
Rationalism
to
Existentialism

Introduction

An introduction to a book on the development of existentialism ought to begin with a brief characterization of "existentialism," but, as Sartre has pointed out, "this word has been so stretched and has taken on so broad a meaning that it no longer means anything at all." Authors as diverse as Socrates, Kafka, Dostoevsky, Leroi Jones, St. Thomas Aquinas, Pascal, and Norman Mailer have been described as "existentialists": on the other hand, such central figures as Camus, Jaspers, and Heidegger have denied their affiliation with this movement. Broadly interpreted, "existentialism" is another name for Western thought: narrowly interpreted, it reduces to the philosophy of Jean-Paul Sartre. For this reason, we shall not be concerned with a delineation of existentialism or with the identification of existentialists. A reasonable interpretation of existentialism would surely include Sartre, Kierkegaard, and Heidegger (in spite of his own rejection of the title), but the differences among these three figures are so great that there is no set of doctrines common to them that also distinguishes them from many other influential groups of philosophers. When we add Nietzsche, Camus, and Jaspers to the list, we find that we no longer know what "existentialism" signifies.

What we do find in our study of recent European philosophy is a more or less smooth development of a number of themes which reach their most explicit statement in the philosophy of Jean-Paul Sartre. Yet the variations on these themes isolate each philosopher from the others as each stamps his own indelible mark on his thoughts. Few of these philosophers would have tolerated the thought of their participation in a movement: the name "existentialism" was not even applied to this philosophy until after every work we shall discuss had been published. Kierkegaard and Nietzsche despised the philosophy of the "schools," and Heidegger has commented that the notion "school of philosophy" is a contradiction in terms. Kierkegaard, Nietzsche, Heidegger, and Sartre are often treated as the central figures of existential philosophy, but even a superficial look at their thought shows the diversity of this group. Kierkegaard was a devout Christian and the other three were atheists; Heidegger was a Nazi, Sartre a Communist, and Kierkegaard and Nietzsche antipolitical. Kierkegaard insisted the meaning of life could be found only in God, Nietzsche found it in art, Sartre in political commitment, and Heidegger in philosophy itself. Nietzsche was an ethical "naturalist," while the other three were resolutely antinaturalists.

It is generally agreed that the beginning of existentialism is to be found in the 'untimely' works of Søren Kierkegaard, and that existentialism as a movement— and the philosophy of Kierkegaard in particular—is to be distinguished as a radical break with traditional Western philosophy. Both are distinguished by a "passionate individualism," an "integration of philosophy and life," and "antirationalism." However, it takes little study to ascertain that this is precisely *not* what existentialism is, even the "existential" philosophy taught by Kierkegaard. Existentialism does not begin with a radical break from traditional philosophy, but with a more or less careful reconsideration of traditional philosophy and a continuation of that philosophy (in spite of dramatic announcements of "radical new beginnings") in surprisingly traditional directions. Existentialists may pride themselves on their "passion" and make frequent remarks against "reason," but we shall find that the existentialist authors make good use of reason themselves. They attack only a peculiar notion of "reason" in post-Kantian philosophy. "Irrationality" is a dangerous category of little help in understanding the subtleties of existentialist reasoning. On the other hand, it is commonly said that the existentialists *have* passion whereas other philosophers have only talked *about* passion (compare Kierkegaard, "*The two ways:* one is to suffer; the other is to become a professor of the fact that another suffered.") It is true that the existentialists insist that a man must put his philosophy to work in his own life, and that philosophy is not a detached academic endeavor. However, it is doubtful that this would distinguish the existentialists from a great many other philosophers: religious philosophers, linguistic philosophers, most political philosophers, and especially the American pragmatists, who hold the "livability" of a philosophy to be as crucial as would any existentialist. Moreover, to write about passion is to write *about* passion, whether it is written passionately or not, and whether the writer has experienced the passion or not. Granted, we may distinguish between knowing passion and knowing *about* passion, but we shall find no such distinction of use in understanding existentialism. Kierkegaard's personal description of despair in *The Concept of Dread* and Freud's elaborate theory about anxiety in *The Problem of Anxiety* are on a logical par. As for the existentialists' celebrated passionate writings, we shall find more of it in the *Phenomenology* by Hegel, who is surely not an existentialist, than we shall find in Heidegger and Sartre's philosophical works.

It is also popularly held that the existentialists differ from other philosophical movements in their intense "individualism." Again, this characterization turns out to be inadequate because it is too inclusive or too limiting. If it is said that the existentialists were themselves individualistic, this hardly serves to distinguish them from many other practitioners of a discipline known since Diogenes for its eccentrics. It also makes it hard to include Heidegger, who joined the Nazi party because it was the current stage of the public *Zeitgeist,* and it is a matter of serious debate whether Sartre and Merleau-Ponty's Communism, whether personally reformulated or not, fits within the characterization of existentialism as an individualism. If this characterization is supposed to refer only to the fact that the existentialists wrote *about* the individual, then there is scarcely a philosopher in the Western tradition (even Hegel) who is not an existentialist. P. F. Strawson, on this account, ought to be the foremost existentialist writer. We similarly hear that existentialism is concerned with *existence* (rather than *essence*). We need not bother with the obvious point that existence and the nature of existence have been focal points of Western philosophy since the later pre-Socratic Greeks. It is countered that these philosophers worried only about the *concept* of "existence" and not existence itself. We shall see that this criticism relies on the same misunderstanding as the claim that existentialists know as opposed to know *about* passion. To talk about existence is to employ and worry about the concept of "existence." Thus we find that Kierkegaard is as concerned with the concept "existence" as Hegel. Critics, notably Kierkegaard, have long argued that Hegel and philosophers before him 'neglected existence'. This is often defended in the ridiculous sense that they did not implant their selves somehow *in* their philosophy. Of course, on a more sympathetic interpretation, their concern for existence ought to have been manifested in writings akin to autobiography rather than philosophy's "universal" concern. Notice, however, that the difference between autobiography and universal philosophy (or between uninteresting autobiography and fascinating autobiography) is not a difference between existence and the concept of "existence," but only a difference in the scope of talk *about* existence. We shall find more to complain about in these traditional much-too-easy accounts of existentialism as we proceed in our study. For now, we may be wary of all such accounts, and guard ourselves against the gross misunderstanding of existentialism which they encourage.

If we look for the radical break with traditional philosophy which sets existentialism in motion, we shall find it not in Kierkegaard, but in Immanuel Kant. It is Kant's "Copernican Revolution" which begins the supposedly existentialist attack on the pretensions of Reason to give us Absolute Truth, marking a truly radical break with the Enlightenment (with which Kant is customarily associated). It is also Kant who rejects the omnipotence of the sciences, marking a new separation of philosophy from science and the "natural attitude." Most importantly, it is Kant who forces us to look at philosophical truths not as necessary truths about the world but as descriptions of our way of structuring *our* world. With Kant's revolutionary move from rationalism and the enlightenment to the anthropocentric view of man's "synthesis" of the world, the paths to romanticism and then to existentialist subjectivism are clearly laid open. It is often thought that Kant is the ultimate adversary of such authors as Nietzsche and Sartre, but the dependence of nearly every nineteenth- and twentieth-century philosopher on the genius of Kant marks this battle as a family quarrel. The break from the traditional philosophy by the existentialists is actually a working out of the very serious break engineered by Kant. The "existentialist revolt" is anything but a rejection of traditional Western philosophy: the recurrent existentialist hero is Socrates. Existentialism is, to a large extent, an attempt to return philosophy to its historical foundations.

To establish this thesis, we shall have to trace in detail the development of existentialism (and phenomenology) from Kant's philosophy. The problems examined are the oldest in philosophy—questions concerning the belief in God, the justification of morality, the existence of the "external" world and other people, the "free will" problem, and the problem of validating certain foundation principles of scientific knowledge. We might have presented our study by tracing the movement of various philosophers on each of these problems, but this would have been unwise for several reasons. It is virtually impossible to separate a philosopher's treatment of one problem from his answer to another. For example, we shall see that Kant's attempted justification of Christianity relies heavily on his conception of morality which in turn relies heavily on his critique of Reason which in turn depends on his conception of knowledge. Similarly, we shall see that Kierkegaard's conception of Christianity depends on Hegel's conception of Logic, that Nietzsche's rejection of Christian morality grows from his Darwinian epistemology, and that Heidegger's rejection of ethics and politics depends in part on his philosophical method which he borrows from Husserl. Furthermore, it would be notably unilluminating to prove that there is a smooth transition from Kant to Sartre by selectively discussing just those problems in which there is an obvious transition.

The reader who has heard of existentialism as a moral (or antimoral) philosophy will be surprised to find that most of the writings of the authors we shall study are concerned with metaphysics (broadly conceived) rather than ethics. (Sartre has never written a full-length work on ethics as such; Heidegger denies that there is anything for a philosopher to say in ethics.) From the interrelatedness of philosophical problems, we should see that this stress on metaphysics does not exclude moral considerations. We shall see that the very distinction between theory and practice, between metaphysics and ethics, is a source of controversy through the nineteenth and early twentieth centuries. The philosophies of Kant, Hegel, and the existentialists are not only metaphysics, but rather attempts to provide a world-view within which an ethical framework is already provided. When Sartre and Heidegger do "ontology," they are not neglecting problems of "life." Quite to the contrary, and even against their own occasional protestations, their ontologies are at the same time very definite conceptions of man from which certain views on morality and religion follow.

A common objection to existentialism is its focus on the gloomy and perverted aspects of human reality: its constant talk of dread, anguish, despair, abandonment; its obsession with the questions of loneliness, death, and suicide; and its often perverted view of sex, marriage, and human institutions in general. Consequently, existentialism is often accused of picturing man at his worst, and presenting this degrading portrait as if it were the only possible perspective.

It is true that existentialism does not give us the simple but optimistic view of human beings that we gain from the British utilitarians with their focus on maximizing human happiness. But we must take seriously Sartre's claim that "Existentialism is the only philosophy which gives man dignity, for it is the only theory that does not make man into an object." Freud told us that human dignity had experienced three insufferable blows in modern times: from Copernicus, from Darwin, and from himself. What should become evident in the writings of the Continental philosophers discussed in the following pages is a strong sense of dignity and human worth which begins by upstaging just such "scientific" threats to man's primitive anthropocentric world-view. If existentialists are worried about death, suicide, loneliness, and despair, this does not indicate a gloomy picture of human reality or a loss of feeling of human dignity; perhaps it is an accurate portrait of the only possible direction in which the support of human dignity can proceed.

We shall make no attempt in our exposition of the following authors to minimize the "abstract" elements in their philosophy and maximize the "ethical implications" because no such separation is possible without distortion. In our need to work through some very trying obscurities, therefore, we must keep in mind the overall project which depends upon these obscurities. Sartre, for example, is not a moral philosopher, he is an ontologist, but the results of that ontology are to yield the most revolutionary changes in our conceptions of our own moral codes.

In what follows, I have attempted to construct a detailed outline of the development of classical existentialism from its rationalist origins. But because I have tried to demonstrate a single line of development, certain restraints must be made explicit. For example, I have said nothing of the work of Marcel, Jaspers, and many other religious existentialists who do not provide an essential link (if there be such) in this line of development. The scope of our subject is also limited to what I am calling "classical" existentialism—culminating before 1945 in Sartre's monumental *Being and Nothingness*. After 1945, Sartre turns increasingly towards Marxism and away from his 'classical' position. I have said nothing of this change of thought and attitude here. More important still is the fact that Sartre's existentialism is largely eclipsed after 1945 by the brilliant work of Maurice Merleau-Ponty. In Chapter 7 I have treated Merleau-Ponty as not much more than a critical student of Sartre within this pre-1945 perspective. Were I to write a book on "Existentialism Today," his philosophy would rather be the starting point.

The Nineteenth-Century Backgrounds: Kant, Hegel, and Existentialism
PART ONE

Kant and Hegel are to the Enlightenment and modern European philosophy as Plato and Aristotle are to Classical Greek philosophy. Like the ancients, both are rationalists—they believe that reason is capable of providing us with absolute ideals. Consequently, both Kant and Hegel are idealists, both in the ethical sense that they defend absolute moral and religious ideals, and in the strict philosophical sense that they argue that reality must ultimately be described in terms of the forms of thought. Superficially, they seem far away from the "irrationalism" of Kierkegaara and the "nihilism" of Nietzsche. However, it is Kant who destroys the traditional arguments in defense of morality and Christianity, and who culminates the Enlightenment ideal of the rational autonomy of the individual. It is Hegel who, despite his celebrated notion of "The Absolute," makes respectable a historical approach to philosophy which makes possible the philosophies of cultural relativity and Nietzsche's *Genealogy of Morals* later that century. From the strength of the attacks on Kant and Hegel by Kierkegaard and Nietzsche, it is all too easy to forget that, without the background of the Enlightenment, existentialism would have lost its primary source of philosophical support.

7

Immanuel Kant:
The Problems of
Metaphysics and Morals
CHAPTER 1

We begin our study of contemporary existentialism and phenomenology with an examination of a philosophy that is diametrically opposed to the doctrines of Nietzsche, Heidegger, and Sartre. Both the antimoral and antireligious attitudes of these more recent thinkers would have horrified Immanuel Kant. The often antirational celebration of Dionysian passions and "existential commitments" would surely have struck the very conservative German philosopher as the antithesis of responsible philosophical activity.

Despite the profound differences between Kant and the existentialists, we shall demonstrate a continuous development from Kant's critical philosophy to Sartre's existentialism. This is not to say that these authors and the figures connecting them are in general philosophical agreement or that they could sensibly be linked in a single school or movement. The conceptual path leading from Kant to Sartre is most akin to a path modeled after the Hegelian dialectic, strewn with warring oppositions each of which play their necessary role in the final results. Kant's philosophy could not be further removed from existentialism in the doctrines it defends, in the view of philosophy it employs, and in the personality of the author whose views it expresses. Yet it is Kant who creates the peculiar perspective and novel philosophical images that spawn the growth of the ambitious systems of philosophy of Fichte and Hegel. It is in reaction to these systems and their conservative outlook that Kierkegaard, Nietzsche, and Marx initiate radically new conceptions of philosophy. Again, it is Kant, whose faith in Christianity and whose rigid adherence to the Protestant ethic never weakened, who raises the problems concerning the va-

lidity and rationality of Christianity and Christian morality on which Nietzsche and Sartre will establish their atheism and antimoral postures. Kant would no doubt find the philosophical styles of the existentialists irresponsible; he would find its doctrines morally reprehensible; and he would very likely consider its proponents madmen rather than thinkers in the tradition established by his own philosophy. However, we shall see that it is Kant who defines the conceptual atmosphere within which the generation of existentialism becomes possible and perhaps even inevitable, where it will develop to become the most influential of contemporary philosophical movements.

By way of introduction to Kant, however, it would be deceptive and offensive to display him merely as a precursor of Nietzsche, Heidegger, and Sartre. In fact, there is virtually no indigenous philosophical movement in contemporary Western thought that cannot be traced directly to Kant. Each of the following has its origins in Kantian thought: the analytic or linguistic philosophy currently dominating English and American philosophy, the pragmatism that pervades American thought, and the many varieties of idealism from among which phenomenology and existentialism have developed. In addition to this tremendous influence, Kant holds a very special place in the history of philosophy as the synthesis of the diverse threads of modern philosophy following Descartes. In Kant's philosophy, the conflicts of doctrine and method among the empiricists and rationalists become synthesized into a unified system of thought. In Kant's philosophy, the hardheaded science of the Enlightenment and the traditional values of faith and moral duty of Christianity find themselves side by side (if not always comforta- bly, at least agreeably) after centuries of unyielding antagonism. Even Hegel, who is by no means humble about his own im- portance in the synthesis of previous Western thought, praises Kant as a giant among intellects, and accords him a place in his history of philosophy equalled only by Plato and Aristotle.

The staggering brilliance of Kant's in- tellect and the revolutionary effects of his thought is in such marked contrast with his notoriously routine and unexciting life that we shall find it not only possible, but almost necessary to treat Kant the philosopher in isolation from Kant the academic professor. Kant the philosopher set in motion an intel- lectual upheaval paralleling (and coincid- ing with) the French revolution in its far- reaching and profound influence on all future thought. Kant the professor is most often characterized by his punctual three o'clock strolls through the neighborhood in which he spent his entire adult life. The German poet Heine tells us that "The his- tory of the life of Immanuel Kant is hard to write, inasmuch as he had neither life nor history, for he lived a mechanically or- dered and abstract old bachelor life in a quiet retired street in Königsberg. . . . I do not believe that the great clock of the ca- thedral there did its daily work more dis- passionately and regularly than its com- patriot Immanuel Kant."[1]

Kant the philosopher mercilessly de- stroyed the traditional foundations of Protestant piety and bourgeois morality; the professor faithfully maintained the or- thodox belief and rigid ethics in which he had been disciplined as a child. In Kant, we can see that ultimate in philosophical detachment; the revolutionary passion he evidently held for philosophy is com- pletely self-contained. Kierkegaard, Nietz- sche, and Sartre all resigned public posts to avoid any possible restriction on their philosophies. Kant taught for over forty years in the conservative state-controlled University of Königsberg, whose authority he never challenged. The philosophies of the existentialists frequently manifest the agony and frenzy of men for whom the search for a way of life *is* the philosophical enterprise. Kant's philosophical enterprise leaves no room for experiments in life- styles and psychotherapy, and Kant him- self apparently experienced none of the emotional tortue and turmoil that plagued the lives of Kierkegaard and Nietzsche. If we compare the passionate and involved "living thoughts" of the existentialists to the almost bizarre divorce of philosophical reflection from the practices of life in Kant, we can understand the popular but mis- leading image of existentialism as a per- sonal, nonphilosophical revolt against tra- ditional "academic" philosophy. Later we shall see that the existentialists retain a great deal of "academic" philosophy. First, it is our task to show that Kant's writings also are 'alive' and 'relevant', and that his "academic" philosophy shares with exis- tentialism an attempt to provide us with the Socratic wisdom and enlightenment that we have always demanded of philosophy. If we find ourselves unconvinced by his con- servative conclusions, at least we shall recognize that those we reject have been given their most able defense.

Despite the passionless and ponderous complexion of his writings, Kant was clearly tormented by perplexities whose scope extended far beyond professional or theoretical interests. His philosophy is depicted as the 'critical' synthesis between two rival schools of philosophy led by the arch-rationalist Leibniz and the superem- piricist David Hume. Kant's replies to these authors were but passing notes in a pas sionate and monumental effort to resolve a much more universal and profound di- lemma inherited from the Enlightenment. Kant was a man of science, firmly endors- ing the universality of the techniques of physical sciences to disclose truth and bit- terly attacking all doctrines that could not be defended by an appeal to human reason and experience. Kant was also a devout Christian and a firm believer in the objec- tive validity of Christian morality. In that age of science, the authoritarian founda- tions of religion and morality were in seri- ous trouble, and it is to their defense that Kant directs his brilliant and laborious philosophical efforts.

Science and religion had confronted each other irreconcilably throughout medieval history, and the problem of their noncompatibility was not new. What dis- tinguished the problem since Descartes was the privileged position of science. Be- fore the Renaissance, science and auton- omy of investigation, of action, and of val- ues, were always on the defensive, being forced, if they were to survive, to recon- cile themselves with the unyielding au- thority of the church. Rene Descartes,[2] and Sir Isaac Newton[3] are prototypes of the turning of the favors of history to science. In 1780, it is the church and its doctrines which are called upon to justify themselves against the equally unyielding demands of scientific rigor. The modern period of philosophy, if we were to characterize it in a single description, is a new set of attitudes towards oneself and authority. One no longer looks to the church for truths and values he cannot grasp for himself. One puts a new confidence in his own powers to reason and observe, and one refuses to allow himself to believe in, to value, or to act upon any principle which cannot pass the most ruthless and rigorous investigation.

It is a mistake to think of Cartesianism as simply a new set of solutions for old problems; it is a new method, but even more, it is a new philosophical *attitude* towards philosophical problems. Similarly, it is a mistake to think of Newton's physics as simply a set of theories of motion and gravitation; it is rather the manifestation of an entirely new kind of perspective for understanding oneself and the world. According to the Newtonian world-view, the universe is no longer *primarily* a manifestation of God (although many scientists —notably Newton himself—spent much of their efforts in an attempt to reconcile Newtonian physics with the orthodox Christian world-view). According to Newton's physics, the universe is a senseless, purposeless attraction and repulsion, collision and rebounding of so many mindless, passive bodies. The world is an all encompassing machine operating according to the natural laws Newton had discovered and given precise formulation. Divine Will has no place in the explanation of the motions of this many-component machine, and, so far as physical science is concerned, the universe is *nothing but* this system of moving bodies. The universe is Godless, deanimated, and purposeless. Man, for all his pretensions, becomes no more than one more body (or aggregation of bodies) obeying Newtonian laws of motion in the same senseless, purposeless fashion as all other bodies.

The laws of motion formulated in simple mathematical terms by Newton became the paradigm of scientific theory, and *every* occurrence, whether it be an apple dropping from a tree, a volcanic eruption, or a young student's defiant act of self-immolation, was to be considered nothing more than the movement of bodies in accordance with

these laws. The cornerstone of Newtonian mechanics was the Principle of Universal Causality: every occurrence can be established in a lawlike connection with some sufficient set of antecedent causes. Each of the above occurrences, the youth's act of protest as well as the falling of the apple, could in principle be explained, and predicted beforehand, as the inevitable outcome of certain antecedent conditions of this mechanistic universe.

Yet the philosophical reaction to this man-diminishing world-view was not in the least pessimistic. To the contrary, the movements following Newton's impact, particularly those that made up the movement of thought known as the Enlightenment, took the Newtonian world-view as a cause for unprecedented optimism.

Cultural historians often use the terms "The Enlightenment" and "The Age of Reason" interchangeably to refer to the period between the late seventeenth century and the late eighteenth century in Europe. So characterized, this period would include such diverse thinkers as Thomas Jefferson, Benjamin Franklin, Jonathan Edwards, Thomas Paine, Herbert Spencer, John Locke, Jonathan Swift, William Godwin, the Marquis de Sade, Jean-Jacques Rousseau, Turgot and Condorcet, Voltaire, Diderot, D'Holbach, Helvetius, Lessing, Goethe, Schiller, and Vico.[4] For our purposes, the Enlightenment is best represented by the French atheistic materialists, Voltaire, Diderot, D'Holbach; the British empiricists, Locke, Berkeley, and Hume; Descartes, who is the central philosophical figure of modern philosophy (which is generally traced to his writings); Goethe, Lessing, and Leibniz in Germany. Since many of these figures are contemporaries, the influences among them are far too complex to be treated here. Common to most of these figures is an unshakable faith in man's abilities to master the traditional problems of science, philosophy, and life, and a strong belief in naturalism and mechanistic explanation (this holds true even of philosophers who would never call themselves materialists and who perhaps even reject Newton's physics, for example, Berkeley and Leibniz).

In spite of the materialism and the specter of mechanism which characterized the Newtonian Universe, there was the promise of complete understanding of this universe and the promise that, following the example of Newton's genius, there was no problem that could not be solved by the correct application of man's reason using the principles and methods of science. That this understanding might neglect all mention of minds, desires, purposes either of God or of Man, did not seem the least cause for concern to the members of the Enlightenment either in England or on the Continent. Rather, these philosophers embraced the Newtonian outlook without reservation, and set about applying its principles without limitation. Throwing off all appeal to the authority of the church and the past, rejecting all reference to transcendental superempirical or supernatural explanation, these philosophers instigated tremendous optimism in the ability of man to understand and improve himself and his situation by the use of his experience and reason alone.

If the principles and methods of science were universally valid, then there were areas of vital human concern which remained outside the realm of knowledge, particularly questions of *morality* (for Kant, the bourgeois morality of provincial eighteenth-century Germany), questions of *religion* (for Kant, the Protestant [specifically Pietist] doctrines of Christianity), and problems of the ancient field of inquiry generally known as *metaphysics*. Philosophers of the Enlightenment, assuming the methods of science to be unlimited in scope and application, attempted to devise scientifically respectable techniques for establishing the truth of religious assertions and discovering the basic principles of the morally good life. They assumed that fundamental doctrines of religion, the existence of God—a certain kind of God, the existence of miracles, the immortality of man's soul and so forth, if they were intelligible at all, could be established in precisely the same rational manner as Newton had established the laws of motion. Similarly, they assumed that the laws of morality were exactly parallel with the laws of nature, to be discovered in exactly the same manner, by observing human nature and applying reason. In short, the philosophers of the Enlightenment assumed that one could find out about the divinity of Christ or the way to the "good life" in precisely the same manner as Newton had established the law of universal gravitation. Ethics and religion were simply special branches of scientific studies in an intellectual world which took Newtonian physics as its only paradigm.

The Enlightenment was eclipsed because of its failure to provide acceptable answers or successful techniques in these important areas of religion and morality. As might be expected, religion fared poorly under scientific interrogation. The articles of faith central to the Christian religion had little 'scientific' evidence in their favor, and more often than not flew in the face of well-established scientific principles. It is not surprising, therefore, that many of the philosophers of the Enlightenment preached atheism, or at least anti-Christianity. The most vocal and best known of the French philosophers of the Enlightenment, Voltaire, is said to have claimed "I am tired of hearing that twelve men were able to establish Christianity; I should like to prove that one is capable of destroying it." There were those philosophers who considered themselves both empiricists and theists (John Locke, for example) but they usually defended their theism at the expense of their empiricist principles.

However, the problem was not simply that religious and moral principles were not adequately supported by scientific investigation; rather the presuppositions of science often seemed to contradict flatly principles basic to religious and moral thinking and the methods and demands of scientific inquiry seemed to eliminate the possibility of any knowledge in these areas before such investigation was even begun. For example, the Principle of Universal Causality which demands that every event has sufficient 'natural cause' and lies at the very foundation of Newtonian science was in conflict with the most basic postulates of religion and morality. If this principle is accepted, it a priori rules ou the possibility of miracles, of the Creation or divine intervention of any sort. Similarly, acceptance of this principle leads to one of the most pervasive problems in philosophy, the problem of free will. If every occurrence is the natural consequence of some set of antecedent natural conditions, then every human action is presumed to be determined completely by antecedent events. This seems to entail that these actions are determined independently of any motives, intentions, decisions, resolutions, or acts of will of the 'agent'. If this is so, if actions are nothing but events determined by previous events, and these determined by other previous events, then humans do not really 'act' at all, they are merely bodies moving in accordance with natural laws. As many philosophers before Kant had noticed, this strikes a death blow to the crucial presupposition of moral thinking, that it makes sense to hold a person *responsible* for his actions. Morality depends on a presupposition directly in conflict with the Principle of Universal Causation, that some occurrences (at least some human actions) are not caused by external factors, but are determined by the agent himself.

It is therefore understandable that the ethical systems propounded by the Enlightenment philosophers had little to say of the notion of responsibility, or of the dependent notions of duty and obligation. They rather favored varied forms of utilitarianism,[5] an ethic which seems to make questions of morality reducible to simple calculations based on empirical data. According to utilitarianism, an action is judged to be right or wrong (good or bad) solely on the grounds that it results in good or bad consequences, and these consequences are in turn evaluated on the basis of their pleasure-displeasure, happiness-unhappiness. The consequences of actions, and the amount of pleasure-pain or happiness-unhappiness resulting from these consequences can be empirically determined, and the outcome of various alternative courses of action may then be tabulated and compared. Right action is determined by a simple decision procedure—the calculation of the amount of pleasure/happiness and pain/unhappiness affected by various courses of action.

To the pious and moral middle-class German professor, atheism and amorality were totally unacceptable, even if they were in accord with the unquestionable methods of Newtonian science. Such conclusions convinced Kant, and many others, that religious and moral questions could not be answered by the methods of Newtonian science although Newtonian science was supposed to be unlimited in its scope. The demands of empiricism and the Enlightenment could not be limited to allow the return of the old church dogma along with any more acceptable tenets of Christianity and morality. This led many philosophers, most notably David Hume in Scotland, to doubt that the problems of these disciplines were amenable to resolution at all.

Of course, there were those who challenged the justification of the basic presuppositions of science as well, particularly the Principle of Universal Causation. Leibniz rejected Newton's theory of motion because he could not accept the notion of 'action at a distance' required by Newton's theories of gravitation. Leibniz replaced it with a complex metaphysical theory in which the notion of causality was eliminated in a model of a universe of elements ("monads") in preestablished harmony. Such a universe may still be deterministic, for one can have valid scientific laws (events still occur in a regular, predictable order), but the Principle of Universal Causality is literally false (these events do not *cause* each other). In spite of Kant's Leibnizian professional background (he was a pupil of Leibniz's disciple Christian Wolff), it was the British empiricist David Hume who most profoundly affected him on the subject of causality, one of the germs from which the entire Kantian philosophy grew. It was Hume's discussion of causality that evinced Kant's celebrated comment that "my recollection of David Hume was the very thing which many years ago first interrupted my dogmatic slumber and gave my investigations in the field of speculative philosophy a quite new direction."[6]

Hume argued that the basic presuppositions of science and therefore of the entire empiricist-minded Enlightenment were quite unjustified. Foremost among these were the Principle of Universal Causality and our assumptions that our ideas in fact correspond to any objects 'external to' our minds, and that the laws we have formulated in accordance with past experience will hold in the future (the "problem of Induction"). Hume argued that none of the philosophically acceptable techniques for justifying knowledge could succeed in establishing these crucial principles as valid. (We shall have more to say of these techniques and Hume's arguments in the following section.) Even Hume did not seriously propose to abandon these principles. The universal validity of scientific method, then the unquestionable starting point not only of all scientific investigation but of Hume's empiricism as well, depended on these principles. If the justification of basic scientific principles was a problem, then Kant presumed it to be a problem for philosophers, not for scientists. The hard earned respectability of modern science was not to be impugned by any philosophical subterfuge.

Kant accepted without question the basic presuppositions and methodology of

Newtonian mechanics, assumed these were unrestricted in scope and application, and charged that no philosophy that either rejected or limited scientific inquiry could be correct. This acceptance of science raised serious paradoxes for a thinker who also accepted the Christian religion and held firm devotion to the notions of duty and moral obligation.

Thus, the overall problem of Kant's philosophy can be expressed in a pair of paradoxical demands:

1. To refute Hume's skepticism with regard to the foundations of science by establishing its basic principles as necesary and universally valid.
2. To limit the pretensions of science to make room for religious faith and moral responsibility.

To satisfy both of these demands, Kant introduced his "Copernican Revolution" in philosophy, a radically new perspective on the nature of human knowledge.[7]

**The *Critique of Pure Reason*
and the Problem of Metaphysics**
The stated theme of the *Critique of Pure Reason* is to "decide as to the possibility or impossibility of metaphysics in general, and determine its sources, its extent, and its limits."[8] Metaphysics traditionally encompassed a large variety of philosophical doctrines, most of which were concerned with ultimate principles of various fields of human knowledge and belief. Philosophy was embarrassed by an indeterminacy with regard to every metaphysical question, and Kant complains from the beginning that,

metaphysics has rather to be regarded as a battle-ground quite peculiarly suited for those who desire to exercise themselves in mock combats, and in which no participant has ever yet succeeded in gaining even so much as an inch of territory, not at least in such manner as to secure him in its permanent possession.[9]

"Metaphysics" has been used to characterize all doctrines which are nonempirical; so used, metaphysics would include all questions of theology, mathematics, logic, and the foundations of science. However, Kant also employs "metaphysics" to apply to a more exclusive set of principles;

These unavoidable problems set by pure reason itself are God, Freedom, and Immortality. *The science which, with all its preparations, is in its final intention directed solely at their solution is metaphysics.*[10]

There are many other metaphysical problems and their solutions with which Kant has little patience; all of those tedious unresolved questions about the details of theology ("How many angels . . .?"), about superphysics and infinity ("Could the universe be divided. . .?"). With regard to these questions, Kant calls for a philosophical purge, a permanent moratorium on philosophical nonsense. Kant is not the first major philosopher of modern times to raise this demand. David Hume had argued,

If we take in our hand any volume of divinity or school metaphysics, for instance, let us ask, Does it contain any abstract reasoning concerning quantity or number? No. Does it contain any experimental reasoning concerning matter of fact and existence? No. *Commit it then to the flames, for it can contain nothing but sophistry and illusion.*[11]

Kant agrees with Hume that metaphysical principles cannot be established either by deductive reasoning nor by experimental inquiry, but he finds Hume's harsh conclusion intolerable. Kant sees some metaphysical questions unavoidable, particularly questions about God's existence, the immortality of the human soul, and of man's freedom and responsibility.

That the human mind will ever give up metaphysical researches is as little to be expected as that we, to avoid inhaling impure air, should prefer to give up breathing altogether.[12]

Furthermore, Kant saw that Hume's rejection of metaphysics must result in a rejection of natural science and mathematics as well. Hume had seen that science was based upon the same sort of nonfactual, nonlogical propositions which were essential to 'school metaphysics'. Hume does not dare suggest that we commit science and mathematics "to the flames."

The first step for Kant's critical philosophy was the recognition of the inconclusiveness of Hume's dichotomy

("Hume's fork") between "relations of ideas" and "matters of fact". Although it is true that most propositions are either necessarily true but trivial (true by virtue of language or "analytic") or else not trivial (or "synthetic") but then only contingently true and empirical, Kant argues that the sort of proposition which is the key to all philosophy is a peculiar hybrid proposition that is both necessary and nontrivial. These *synthetic* (nontrivial) a priori ('universal and necessary') judgments lie at the foundation of every empirical discipline. Kant includes as synthetic a priori propositions all of the propositions of mathematics and geometry, the foundation principles of natural science (for example, the law of induction, the principle of universal causation), the principle that a man is responsible for his actions, the proposition that God exists, and the proposition that a man should treat his fellow men as ends rather than as means. Previous philosophers (Hume, for instance) had treated these principles either as straightforward "analytic" or trivial truths or as straightforward empirical and therefore experiential judgments. Kant argues: they are neither, and they can be defended and justified neither by appeal to the language in which they are expressed, nor by appeal to experimental confirmation or disconfirmation. Neither the rationalist tool of Pure Reason nor the empiricist appeal to experience could succeed in demonstrating these issues. For example, the doctrine that God is the moving cause of the Universe (both its creator and its sustainer) is not verifiable or refutable by any evidence whatever, for any findings (including alleged miracles, mystical experiences) are compatible with both the doctrine and its denial. Moreover, it is not contradictory to suppose that there is no God or that there is a God of whom the Universe is totally independent. The problem of metaphysics thus becomes the problem of justifying synthetic a priori truths.

Metaphysical propositions are synthetic a priori propositions. Accordingly, the stated metaphysical theme of the *Critique of Pure Reason* is recast as the question, "How are synthetic a priori judgments possible?" This is not to ask *whether* they are possible, for Kant begins by assuming that the principles of mathematics and the foundation principles of natural science are both true and synthetic a priori, but neither does

this question demand a single acceptance or rejection of all synthetic a priori principles. Some of these principles must be defended, but others must be destroyed (not refuted). The problem facing Kant is that,

In this domain there is actually as yet no standard weight and measure to distinguish sound knowledge from shallow talk.[13]

Transcendental Arguments

Kant believed that he had discovered a method for justifying synthetic a priori principles. These principles could not be established through Reason alone, for they were neither trivial nor could they be derived from other judgments which were not also synthetic and a priori. Neither could they be established through experience, for experience could, at best, establish it as a matter of *fact* that these propositions were true; experience could never show these propositions to be *necessary* (a priori). There was another way to establish these peculiar principles, Kant believed, through a *transcendental argument*. A transcendental argument justifies a judgment by establishing it as a piece of *transcendental knowledge*.[14] Such knowledge is knowledge of the foundations of knowledge itself, a knowledge of those faculties of human consciousness that make possible any knowledge whatever.

I entitle transcendental all knowledge which is occupied not so much with objects as with the mode of our knowledge of objects insofar as this mode of knowledge is to be possible a priori.[15]

We must be careful to distinguish "transcendental" from "transcendent." Transcendent knowledge is knowledge of the supersensible; Kant denies that any such knowledge is obtainable. Transcendental knowledge, according to Kant, "does not signify something passing beyond all experience, but something that precedes it a priori, but that is intended simply to make knowledge of experience possible."[16]

To say that a transcendental argument shows a synthetic a priori judgment to state a necessary condition for knowledge is *not* to say that it justifies the judgment by demonstrating *some* body of coveted knowledge to rely on it. On this account, for example, commentators have argued the principle that every event has a cause to be justified because it is a necessary presupposition of all natural science. If this were a transcendental argument, Kant would have failed completely to achieve his ends. The challenge issued by Hume was the justifiability of science in general which in turn depends upon the defense of the principle that every event has a cause. To defend this principle by appeal to its necessity for natural science is viciously circular. This interpretation of a transcendental argument as a demonstration that a principle is necessary to the acceptance of *some* invaluable body of knowledge reduces Kant's entire philosophy to a simple *petitio principii.*

Kant's strategy is to show that synthetic a priori principles can be defended as necessarily true if they state the conditions for *any* experience, *any* knowledge, *any* consciousness whatever. To be *conscious,* a being must have experience and must be able to apply concepts to those experiences. For Kant, empirical knowledge is a necessary condition for consciousness, and there can be no consciousness without experience and understanding of experience. This doctrine lies at the very core of Kant's first *Critique;* it is the premise on which the entire *Critique* is founded. The first sentence of the introduction makes this clear;

There can be no doubt that all our knowledge begins with experience. . . .[17]

and again, in the conclusion of the same introduction;

we need only say that there are two stems of human knowledge, namely sensibility and understanding. . . . Through the former, objects are given to us; through the latter, they are thought.[18]

And later,

Without sensibility no object would be given to us, without understanding, no object would be thought. Thoughts without content are empty, intuitions without concepts are blind.[19]

For a being to be conscious at all, to have experience and understanding, certain conditions must obtain. Since these conditions are necessary for there to be any consciousness, and since there is at least one conscious being (myself), the princi-

ples that state these conditions *must* be true, that is, they are necessary truths. For Kant, as for Descartes, my own thinking existence is the premise from which all philosophy proceeds.

Synthetic a priori principles do not just state *a* set of conditions which make possible consciousness; they rather state *the only* such conditions. Kant claims not only that he has found a *sufficient* set of conditions for consciousness, but a *necessary* set as well. If these principles only stated sufficient conditions, they would not be necessarily true, for it would always be possible for some creature to be conscious in a different way than we are. Kant is firmly against such relativism. The principles defended in his *Critique* are necessarily true because they state a unique set of conditions necessary for any conscious creature (human or not) whatever.

It is not altogether accurate to say that synthetic a priori principles, if true, *state* or *describe* conditions for consciousness. Kant insists that his transcendental principles are not proven as facts (*de facto*), but rather proven as *rights* or *legal claims* (*de jure*). These principles are therefore not so much descriptions as *rules* about how the world must be;

The understanding does not derive its laws (a priori) from, but prescribes them to, nature.[20]

Accordingly, concepts and the Understanding are defined in terms of rules;

A concept is always, as regards its form, something universal which serves as a rule.[21]

We have defined the Understanding in various ways; . . . We may now characterize is as the faculty of rules.[22]

The Understanding . . . is itself the lawgiver of nature.[23]

Since these rules are the *only* possible rules for structuring experience, it makes little difference, for Kant, whether he treats them as rules or as structures of consciousness. Philosophers following Kant, however, notably Fichte and Hegel, will give added importance to the interpretation of concepts as rules. Rules, they will argue, can be changed.

How are synthetic a priori judgments possible? A synthetic a priori judgment can be justified by showing that it is a piece of transcendental knowledge, by showing that it states a necessary condition or rule for there being any consciousness whatever. *The Critique of Pure Reason* is divided into three sections, each investigating the synthetic a priori claims for one field of inquiry. Each field of inquiry corresponds to one of three *faculties* of mind, *Sensibility* (Sinnlichkeit), *Understanding* (Verstand), and *Reason* (Vernunft). The *Transcendental Aesthetic* presents and defends the synthetic a priori principles stating the conditions for sensibility; the *Transcendental Analytic* presents and defends the synthetic a priori principles stating the conditions or rules for the employment of the Understanding; and the *Transcendental Dialectic* presents and gives a critique of the pretensions of Pure Reason to give us knowledge of synthetic a priori principles. Thus, the first two sections of the *Critique* are concerned with the exposition and defense of *the* set of conditions under which experience and knowledge are possible. The *Transcendental Dialectic* serves a different purpose, the separation of transcendental knowledge (which is defended in the first two sections) from transcendental Ideals (which will serve as the basis for the *Critique of Practical Reason* and Kant's moral philosophy). Secondly, the *Transcendental Dialectic* is to explode once and for all time certain illusions to which metaphysical thinking has been victim. The *Dialectic* is to separate proper metaphysics from transcendent nonsense; it is this function that makes the work a "Critique of Pure Reason."

The *Transcendental Aesthetic* gives us the conditions for sensibility, "the capacity for receiving representations through the mode in which we are affected by objects."[24] The possibility of having any experience or "intuition" depends on two "a priori forms of intuition," namely, *space* and *time*. The principles of space and time are captured in the a priori principles of (Euclidean) geometry and arithmetic (respectively).[25] The transcendental proof of the a priori necessity of these principles is the demonstration that they describe the necessary form of any experience. The *Aesthetic* argues that every experience must take place in the same three-dimensional space, in one-dimensional time. The a priori structure of space, the form of

which Kant calls "outer sense," requires that every object of intuition must appear in three dimensions (even if it happens to be a one-dimensional line or two-dimensional surface). We can watch a two-dimensional movie in a three-dimensional theater, but we cannot possibly experience a two-dimensional theater. Similarly, the a priori structure of time-consciousness, which Kant calls "inner sense," is the form of every experience. Every experience occurs in time. These two forms of experience pertain not only to 'normal' experiences, but to every possible experience, no matter how aberrant. Kant would insist that 'experiences of time reversal' or experience of the 'collapse of space' are simply *misdescriptions* of experiences which must have temporal and Euclidean form.

In the *Transcendental Analytic*, Kant attempts to discover those a priori principles "without which no object can be thought." The transcendental arguments of the *Analytic* attempt to establish these principles in three steps: first, there is the unfolding of a list—Kant insists that it is an exhaustive list—of the *Concepts* of the pure Understanding or "Categories." Once these concepts have been discovered, it must be shown that they are indeed necessary to the making of any judgment whatever. Finally, a set of a priori principles is derived from the list of categories, and these are proven necessary and universal in the application of concepts to experience.

In the *Prolegomena*, Part II, which corresponds to the *Analytic* of the *Critique*, Kant asks, "How is Pure Science Possible?" The Categories with their corresponding Principles present us with just those foundations of science whose justification Hume had challenged seriously. Most importantly, a set of Principles called "The Analogies of Experience" (based on Categories of "Relation") include the principle that every event has a cause.

The premise of the arguments in the *Analytic* is the fact of human (my) consciousness, specifically, that my consciousness has an essential unity. Kant begins very much like Descartes:

It must be possible for the 'I Think' to accompany all my representations. . . .
All the manifold of intuition has, therefore, a necessary relation to the "I think" in the same subject in which this manifold is found. . . . The unity of this apperception

I likewise entitle the transcendental *unity of self-consciousness, in order to indicate the possibility of a* priori *knowledge arising from it.*[26]

In one sense, this premise might be interpreted to say no more than the analytic principle that "all the contents of my consciousness are *mine*." From this trivial principle, however, Kant forces the interpretation from the unity of consciousness to the unity of the *object;*

The transcendental unity of apperception is that unity through which all the manifold given in an intuition is united in a concept of the object.[27]

To perceive an object is not merely to have an experience or a set of experiences: to perceive an object, there must be a combination of different experiences into an 'objective' unity. To use one of Kant's examples, my perception of a house from various perspectives could not be considered perception *of a house* (or of any *object*) if the several experiences constituting this perception were not unified or *synthesized* as various experiences *of* one and the same object. My perception *of the house* is not merely the sum of my experiences (of the house), but my synthesizing these experiences as experiences of a house. Because experiences alone can never give us objects, there can be no perception of objects unless there is a synthesis of the manifold of experience. Moreover, because we never perceive simply, or have experience simply, but always perceive or experience *something,* and because perceiving or experiencing something depends on synthesis, there can be no unsynthesized experiences. (We shall see this same major thesis become the central principle of Edmund Husserl's *Phenomenology,* the philosophy which will give a major impetus to the methodological innovations of the twentieth-century existentialists.)

Because a synthesis cannot be found in experiences themselves, it must be imposed on them by the Understanding. Kant thus agrees with Hume that our experiences themselves never include experience of a necessary connection between experiences, but that these connections are always added by us.

We cannot represent to ourselves anything as combined in an object which we have not ourselves previously combined.[28]

Kant, however, radically departs from Hume on the nature of this "combining." Where Hume had argued that this "combination in an object" was merely a *habit* and without justification, Kant insists that such "combinations" are *necessary* by virtue of the very structure of human consciousness. In this difference lies the key to Kant's reply to Humean skepticism.

The pattern of argument we have just sketched occupies the most labyrinthian depths of the *Critique* called the *Transcendental Deduction.* The purpose of this *Deduction* is to show that the categories are indeed necessary in every experience and every judgment. It begins with the simple fact that I am conscious and moves to the unity of perceived objects, arguing that this unity is a condition for all perception and that this unity is *synthetic* and produced by the Understanding. The conclusion of the *Deduction* is that it is impossible for a consciousness not to use concepts, that every experience must be synthesized or "gone through in a certain way, taken up and connected" to conform to the concepts of the Understanding. There can be no unconceptualized experience.

Then, in the *Analytic of Principles,* Kant proceeds to argue that the particular concepts called the categories are necessary for every experience. (The *Transcendental Deduction* has established only that *some* concepts must be employed.) To show that these concepts or categories are a priori necessary for Understanding is also to show that the synthetic a priori principles based on these categories are necessarily true.

The proof of the principle that every event has a cause is based on the argument of the *Transcendental Deduction,* that "experience is possible only through the representation of a necessary connection of perceptions."[29] The *Deduction* argued that synthesis of experience is always "successive" in time. While events in the imagination may be arbitrarily ordered (as when, in a daydream, we reverse cause and effect), an experience which is *given* to us does not allow for arbitrary ordering. In Kant's terms, "the order of appearances is determined by the object."[30] Objectivity is necessarily *causal*, and an objective order of events is an order of appearances according to a rule. The difference between a "subjective play of my fancy" and an event of which we can have knowledge is that the latter is "determined";

that is, it presupposes another appearance in time, upon which it follows necessarily, according to a rule.[31]

If an experience is isolated from all other experiences which can be causally related to it, the distinction between reality and fantasy becomes impossible. Knowledge is gained not from isolated experiences but from causally systematic experiences, "successive according to a rule." Consciousness in general, according to Kant, is possible only because we can make this important distinction, and this, he argues, presupposes the applicability of the categories of Relation to every experience and the necessary truth of the synthetic a priori principle that every event has a cause which precedes it in time.

Both the *Transcendental Deduction* and the arguments for the Principles of the Understanding are convoluted and obscure. Philosophers are still struggling just to expose the logic of these arguments,[32] but the philosophers of Europe have been more influenced by the method and conclusion of Kant's *Critique* than by the intricacies of argument. We have seen enough of this method—the transcendental approach to those conditions or rules necessary to any consciousness—and enough of those conclusions—that certain intuitive forms and certain concepts are necessary to any consciousness—to understand the basis of the revolutionary movement that Kant initiates in European philosophy.

The Copernican Revolution

We said in our introduction that Kant calls his *Critique* a 'Copernican Revolution' in philosophy; yet so far, it might seem that Kant's original contributions to philosophy, his introduction of new distinctions, the refutation of Hume's skepticism, the introduction of a new argument type and so on are impressive, but hardly the revolutionary uprooting of all past philosophy. However, our discussion of transcendental arguments has already indicated to us the nature of this revolution which begins

with Kant's transcendental proofs of how the world we perceive *must* be.

Transcendental arguments do not argue what the world is like, but what it *must* be like because of the rules to which any experience, any knowledge, any consciousness must conform. As soon as Kant claims that any world of which we are conscious must have *this* form, he has not simply added a new metaphysical theory to philosophy, but he has changed the entire character of the philosophical enterprise. To understand this, we must quickly review the theory of knowledge preceding Kant's *Critique*. In spite of great differences between various theories, notably between empiricist and rationalist theories of knowledge, one problem was common to every theory: "How can we know whether our ideas of what the world is like correspond to what the world is *really* like?" Underlying this question was a host of assumptions concerning the nature of human understanding, most importantly, that our ideas if correct, conform to the *real* objects to which they correspond, that we have an immediate awareness of our ideas and experiences but only a mediated awareness of the real objects of the world. Thus, the underlying metaphysics of both rationalist and empiricist theories of knowledge recognize two sorts of entities—mental (ideas, experiences) and physical (real and substantial objects of the world).[33] With this metaphysics comes the problem which, more than any other, has plagued philosophers since Descartes' *Discourse on Method*: "How can I ever know that these two correspond?"

Although Kant remained very much a dualist, speaking continuously of "inner" and "outer" experiences, of "subjectivity" and "objectivity," and of the "world-as-it-appears" and "world-as-it-is-in-itself," he succeeds in undermining the dualism on which is founded traditional metaphysics and consequent problems of knowledge. Rather than speak of the conformity of our knowledge to objects, he insists that we speak instead of the necessary conformity of objects to our knowledge. In order to be known, an object has to obey our rules. This is not merely a radical change in perspective, now taking the knower as primary rather than the known; it is a complete change in the very formulation of the problems of knowledge. Kant would no longer ask whether it is true that the world as we know it conforms to the world as it *really* is. Because the world as we perceive it in accordance with the a priori principles of the *Critique* is the *only* world we can know or about which we can intelligibly talk. The world as it *really* is, if by that is meant a world independent of and possibly different from the world we know, cannot be our concern. For us, there *can* only be the world we know, and this world is not passively constituted by our experiences, but actively regulated by our understanding.

In place of the traditional dichotomy between ideas of the world and the real world, Kant substitutes a new dichotomy, between objects as-they-appear-to-us, which he calls *phenomena*, and things as they are 'in-themselves', which he calls *noumena*. Although the two dichotomies appear superficially similar, their differences are profound. First, for Kant, the only sense to be given to the notion of the *real* world is the sense of the world *as phenomenon*. The question of how we can know that our ideas correspond to the *real* world cannot then arise, for the world we perceive *is* the *real* world. Secondly, the question of what the world is like independently of our experiences of it is, for Kant, unintelligible. Because the only world of which we can conceive is the world as it conforms to the principles of the *Critique*, there is no intelligibility, for us, in the suggestion that the world-as-noumenon might have some different form, for example, exist in nine-dimensional space, or have no causal relations. The world-as-noumenon either conforms to the world as phenomenon, in which case we may address our inquiries to the phenomenal world, or else it is different, in which case the very notion of 'noumenon' becomes incomprehensible to us. *Noumenon*, in Kant's terms, is strictly a "*limiting* concept"; we can have no knowedge of noumena. Thus, the Kantian 'Copernican' revolution eliminates the old problems and the threat of skepticism which dominated previous philosophy. Because the only sense to be given to the notion, "the *real world*," is the sense of the world as phenomenon, skepticism regarding the existence of objects (in general) makes no sense. (It is from this principle that the entire movement called 'Phenomenology' will take its departure.) For the same reasons, idealism, the position that only consciousness exists (which threatened Descartes and was openly endorsed by Berkeley) makes no sense either (Kant argues this in a separate chapter of the *Critique*).[34]

The Copernican revolution can be characterized in a slightly different way, using a set of terms which were often used by Kant and became the center of attention in the post-Kantian philosophies. The traditional idea-of-the-world/real-world distinction had often been cast as a distinction between a *subjective* world and the *objective* world. The former consists of the contents of one's own consciousness, the latter consists of objects. The traditional problem of knowledge could then be restated as, "How can I ever obtain knowledge of the objective world, that is, obtain objective knowledge?"

Kant attacks this query by destroying the grounds on which the question is based. Since we cannot have knowledge of objects independent of any possible experience, we cannot *in that sense* have knowledge of an objective world, that is, "objective knowledge." On the other hand, if "subjective knowledge" means knowledge taken from our own experience, there can be no other sort of knowledge we could have. Thus Kant maintains that the traditional subjective-objective distinction, because it rests upon the same inadequate metaphysical dichotomy as the idea-world distinction, must be given up.

Yet, Kant does want to say that we can have objective knowledge, and he sometimes even describes the *Analytic* as a proof that we can have objective knowledge, that is, knowledge of objects. However, Kant's sense of "objective" clearly cannot be the sense in which earlier theorists had taken it, for "objective" in their sense makes objective knowledge (that is, knowledge of objects apart from our experiences of them) impossible. Kant's distinction between subjective and objective is consequently characterized not in terms of mere idea and *real* object, but is rather in terms of *private* vs. *public*, the necessity and universality of objective knowledge.[35] According to Kant, "objective" refers to the possibility of knowledge by every consciousness, while "subjective" refers to experiences had by only individual consciousness. Objective knowledge is knowledge of a public world, a world that must be identical for every consciousness. Knowledge of objects is not a "true" correspondence of our beliefs with transcendent objects; knowledge of objects is recognition of a synthesis of experiences that we have produced.

We must not seek the universal laws of nature in nature . . . but conversely must seek nature, as to its universal conformity to law, in the conditions of possibility of experience. . . .[36]

We have discussed the *Critique* as an exposition of the necessary conditions for consciousness and the *Analytic* specifically as the exposition of the necessary conditions for knowledge. Knowledge, for Kant, can only be knowledge of an objective (phenomenal) world, a world of objects. And a world of objects is a world which is constituted such that these objects must be substantial. To use a phrase that Kant favors in the *Prolegomena,* the concepts of the understanding are the rules for *consciousness in general.* It makes no sense to suppose that our knowledge could be knowledge of a private world, one whose objects were hidden from any other consciousness. Knowledge is necessarily *public,* and necessarily objective. The publicity of objects, while not argued by Kant as one of his famous categories, is a necessary condition for knowledge.

If the world of which we are conscious is necessarily objective and public, it must be the case that all philosophical theories which suppose that the objects in question are nothing other than mere "ideas" or "mental entities" are seriously confused. Accordingly, all the versions of "idealism" which assert such a thesis must be distinguished from what Kant calls his "transcendental idealism" and rejected as philosophically absurd. For the transcendental idealist, (Kant, and, we shall see later, Husserl), the world is not my idea: the world is the phenomenon which must exist independently of my idea of it.

The Transcendental Ego
Among the necessary conditions for there to be experience or knowledge is the existence of a self which has experiences and synthesizes these experiences according to the categories. Kant sometimes restates the premise of the deduction, the unity of consciousness, as the existence of self-consciousness.

This seems clear, and even trivial at first, but a moment's reflection dislodges deep and disturbing problems in this notion of self-consciousness. What is this

self? For Kant, it is an individual, personal subject of experiences which busies itself unifying experience according to its understanding; but what is this subject? A mind? A spirit? A person?

The problem of the *self* can be raised in this way: Are we speaking of the same subject ("I") in each of the following: "I am falling." "I am bleeding." "I am president of my class." "I am thinking." "I am running." "I am hallucinating." "I am signing a contract." "I am dead." Thinking unphilosophically, it seems, of course, that we are speaking of the same subject. Is the "I" that is bleeding the same "I" that does the thinking, or the same "I" that runs? The "I" that bleeds is an organism's living *body,* while the "I" that thinks seems to be my mind, which is more or less independent from the state of my body. The "I" that runs seems to be a curious partnership between my body and my mind. It would seem, therefore, that one can discern three different "I's" or selves in these three examples: a body-self, a mental-self, and a self of action. In addition, of course, one might isolate a social self (president of the class) or a responsible self (upholding a contract) or a purely physical self (I am falling). As soon as we begin to see that the identification of selves is not simply the recognition of persons (John, Mary, Sam), but the recognition of persons as a . . . , the question of the nature of the *self* becomes immensely complicated. Then, when we ask which of these selves is the *real* self, the locus of self-identity, the confusion of the question is equalled only by the importance of answering it. Restricting our interest to Kant, we must ask what is the self which is the subject of experiences and which imposes the conditions for understanding upon these experiences?

In the *Transcendental Deduction,* Kant distinguishes the *transcendental* ego from the *empirical* ego and maintains that only the transcendental ego has these a priori relations with experience. The empirical ego, on the other hand, is the ego or egos of the sciences. The empirical ego is a person's physical body, personality, and all those aspects of a person about which we may formulate empirical laws. Thus, we may generalize in biology about the physiological mechanisms of a person's body, or in psychology we may test his intelligence, or his tolerance for pain, or his tendency to become angry. In each case, the knowledge we receive about the person is strictly empirical. The knowledge we have of the transcendental ego is strictly a priori—it consists solely of necessary laws. In Kant's terms, the transcendental ego is a merely *formal* ego; all the knowledge we have of it is a priori and independent of the characteristics of any particular persons. It is this formal ego about which Kant is talking throughout the *Analytic*. To understand the significance of this ego, it is again necessary to review some of the philosophy preceding Kant.

The question of self-identity confronting Kant has its historical roots in the philosophy of Descartes, who, like Kant, took self-consciousness to be the cornerstone of his philosophy. Descartes' "I think, therefore I am" was meant to be the single, indubitable, and self-evident proposition on which his entire theory of knowledge was constructed. Descartes also posed the question as to the nature of this "I" and methodically rejected interpretations of this self as a physical body, as an organism, or as a person. The "I think" proved the existence only of a *thinker,* not a person or a body. The "I" of the "I think" must therefore be a *thinking substance.* In accordance with his methodological doubt, Descartes argued that it would be possible to doubt the existence of his body, but not that he was in fact thinking.

However, even this limited inference from thought to thinker was called into question. Why must a thought require a thinker? Perhaps, there are just thoughts. This line of skepticism with regard to self-identity was brought to its conclusion, predictably, by David Hume, who argued:

There are some philosophers who imagine we are every moment intimately conscious of what we call our self; that we feel its existence and its continuance in existence; and are certain, beyond the evidence of a demonstration, both of its perfect identity and simplicity. . . . Unluckily, all these positive assertions are contrary to that very experience which is pleaded for them nor have we any idea of self after the manner it is here explained. For, from what impression could this idea be derived? . . . If any impression gives rise to the idea of the self, that impression must continue invariably the same, through the whole course of our lives; since self is supposed to exist in that manner. . . .

But farther, what must become of all our particular perceptions upon this hypothesis? All these are different and distinguishable and separate from each other, and may be separately considered and may exist separately, and have no need of anything to support their existence. . . . I never can catch myself at any time without a perception, and never can observe anything but the perception.[37]

Kant's transcendental twist to this argument can be anticipated by bringing to mind his general mode of reply to Hume's problems. Hume claims that there is no justification for our supposed knowledge of ourselves because we have no experience corresponding to this supposed knowledge. Kant has claimed that one can justify knowledge not only by demonstrating its origin *in* experience, but by demonstrating that it is a *basis* for experience. The self, for Kant, is not to be considered an object for experience, but is to be postulated as one of the necessary conditions for any experience. In the *Deduction,* Kant argues that it makes no sense to speak of an experience *simpliciter,* for every experience is an experience of a consciousness which organizes and unifies experience into a whole. If there were not this unification, according to Kant, there could be no knowledge and no experience. Unification presupposes a principle of unification, and this is the ego. In reply to Hume, therefore, Kant answers that the self is not to be found among the contents of experience but is to be transcendentally found among the conditions for experience. The ego lies 'behind' all our experiences; it is what has these experiences.

Thus far, Kant's reply has been notably Cartesian: our knowledge of the self is derivative of the presence of thought. Descartes then concluded that this self is a *thinking substance,* and here Kant becomes very unCartesian. According to his *Critique,* the self is a *condition* of experience, but as such a condition, it transcends any possible experience. If this self is to be considered as an object in any sense, it must be considered a *noumenal* object. As a noumenon, the self cannot be subject to the categories, which are applicable only to objects of possible experience. Since one of these categories is *substance,* the self cannot be a substance, and all doctrines depending on such a notion, such as the traditional doctrine of the *soul*, must be based upon the fallacious treatment of a noumenal object as phenomenal (Kant's source of concern in the *Dialectic*). Because the transcendental ego is beyond the bounds of possible experience, we can have no knowledge whatsoever about it, but because it lies at the very foundations of the possibility of consciousness, we cannot help but know *of* it. Knowing *that it is* is all that we can know of the ego. This initially seems to have implausible consequences, for it appears that we can speak of self-knowledge as well as knowledge of other selves. For Kant, however, all such discussion is about the *empirical* ego, which is the only self which can be known. The empirical ego is the transcendental ego *as it appears to me*, that is, as phenomenon, and thus it can be conceived of under the categories. The transcendental ego, however, which Kant occasionally refers to as the "self-in-itself" can be the subject of only one piece of knowledge, namely, that it exists.

Kant answers the question of self-identity with a complicated theory of two selves, one of which is the subject of the phenomenal world, the other of which is an object in this world. The complication of this dual self theory is both one of the outstanding contributions and one of the fatally weak doctrines of Kant's philosophy as a whole. It endangers the whole of his moral philosophy and generates problems for other philosophers for the remainder of the nineteenth century.

The *Dialectic*

In our introduction, we indicated that Kant distinguished the synthetic a priori principles of mathematics, natural science, and metaphysics, devoting a section of the *Critique* to each. We then ignored the *Transcendental Dialectic* which deals with the principles of metaphysics, and similarly neglected the third mental faculty, Reason, of which we said only that it, with the understanding, manipulates concepts. In spite of Kant's obvious fascination with parallel triadic structures, the *Dialectic* is very much out of step with the first two sections of the *Critique*. Kant began with the promise that he would give us the conditions for any possible experience and knowledge. In the *Dialectic*, he instead promises the critical destruction of false

ideas, and the exposition of a "Logic of Illusion."

Reason, the third faculty, manipulates concepts, but unlike the understanding, it does not apply these concepts to experience. In his characterization,[38] Kant tells us that the concepts of reason unify the understanding in the same way that the concepts of the understanding unify experience. Consequently, the *logical* employment of reason "endeavors to reduce the varied and manifold knowledge of the understanding to the smallest number of principles and thereby achieve in it the highest possible unity."[39] However, there is also the possibility of a set of a priori concepts and principles of Pure Reason, and Kant tells us that philosophers have long employed such a set of concepts and principles in metaphysics. The concepts of Pure Reason he calls the *Transcendental Ideas*;[40] the principles derived from these Ideas he calls *Dialectical Inferences*, of which there are three sets: *Paralogisms*, *Antinomies*, and *Ideals*. These names hardly share the grandeur of the names of the principles of the understanding. A *paralogism* is a piece of (unconsciously) fallacious reasoning. *Antinomies* are equally valid but contradictory arguments, which contribute to what Kant calls the "euthanasia" of pure reason.[41]

The concepts of Reason are independent of any possible experience, and moreover, unlike the concepts of the pure understanding, they are not necessary for there to be experience. The transcendental ideas are thus necessarily *transcendent*, going beyond any possible experience. The objects posited by these concepts are also transcendent; they are objects of no possible experience.

In the earlier discussion of the *Critique*, we emphasized that knowledge can arise only with the application of concepts to experience. Because the concepts of Reason are independent of any possible experience and thus apply only to objects of no possible experience (noumena), Reason, unlike Sensibility and Understanding, cannot give us knowledge. Metaphysics, the system of principles of pure reason, must, therefore, only *appear* to give us knowledge. Indeed, Kant argues, metaphysical principles are comprehensible to us only because their concepts are parasitic on the concepts of the understanding (for example, we understand "time has a beginning" or "the soul is inside the brain" only because we have an understanding of events having beginnings in time and objects being inside of other objects). Metaphysics, however, is illusory because, in spite of this apparent understanding, its principles misuse concepts by extending them beyond the realm of possible experience.

The fact that Reason cannot give us knowledge is not sufficient reason for doing away with metaphysics, however, for we have a "natural disposition" towards metaphysical thinking. The demand of Reason is the unification of the understanding, that is, the synthesis of all knowledge. Because our knowledge is dependent upon the limitations of our experience and understanding, our knowledge is necessarily incomplete and conditional. Thus, there has always been the urging of reason to find *absolute* principles which are impervious to doubt. Metaphysics is the futile attempt to supply this demand of reason for completeness and certainty, the attempt to push our knowledge beyond any limitation. Even though these attempts are futile, they serve an important, even necessary purpose; they provide a goal for knowledge without which we would be constantly threatened by disillusionment and agnosticism. The principles of Pure Reason will never give us knowledge, yet they will always be indispensable to knowledge.

The discipline of metaphysics needed little defense among the philosophers of the eighteenth century, so the bulk of the *Dialectic* is concerned with the demonstration of the illusory nature of traditional metaphysics and specific metaphysical theses and their proofs. Kant separated these theses into three classes: those principles maintaining the "absolute unity of the conscious subject" (the *soul*), those principles maintaining the "absolute unity of all phenomena" (the *world*), and those principles concerned with an "Ultimate Being" (*God*). Of the many principles of Pure Reason, only three constitute the central concern of metaphysics:

Metaphysics has for the real object of its investigation three ideas only; God, Freedom, and Immortality; . . . Everything else treated by that science is a means only in order to establish those ideas and their reality.[42]

In his study of the metaphysical princi-

ples regarding the Soul (the "psychological ideas"), Kant discusses the possibility of an essential "I" going beyond the contingencies of human existence. He begins by renewing the argument of the *Deduction* concerning the "possibility of the 'I think' accompanying all our experiences." However, this self (the *transcendental ego*), as the transcendental unity of apperception, cannot be an *object* of any possible experience; it is always "behind" experience. Because this ego is not a possible object of experience, it cannot be known under the categories, and cannot even be spoken of as a *something*, for it would be a something without any possible properties. Because the ego of the "I think" is transcendental, we can argue that it *is* by virtue of its necessity for any experience or knowledge; but because it also transcends any possible experience, and therefore is a *noumenal ego*, there is nothing more that we can know about it. The traditional doctrine of the soul cannot give us any knowledge.

Similarly, Kant argues that all previous attempts to prove the existence of God, who is also a noumenal being, must arrive at their conclusion through fallacious reasoning. He offers us brilliant refutations of the traditional ontological, teleological and cosmological proofs for the existence of God,[43] and goes on to argue that no argument by pure reason can succeed in producing a valid proof of His existence. Yet Kant is quite clear that this failure is not a justification for atheism or even religious agnosticism, for the existence of God as a transcendental *ideal* can be proven in other ways (which Kant attempts in the second *Critique*).

It is in his discussion of the "cosmological ideas," however, that Kant demonstrates the most remarkable consequences of the illusory use of pure reason. In a series of principles which he calls the *Antinomies,* Kant shows that metaphysics not only provides theses which cannot be justified in the traditional way, but produces theses whose antitheses can be defended equally well by valid arguments from equally compelling premises. There are four pairs of antinomies, each pair generated by the misapplication of one set of categories beyond the boundaries of experience. For example:

I Thesis: the world has a beginning in time and space. Antithesis: the world has no beginning in time and space.

II Thesis: everything consists of
ultimately simple elements.
Antithesis: everything is composite;
there are no simple elements.[44]

There is no need for us to discuss the arguments Kant provides for these; it will suffice to note that Kant believed all four arguments to be valid. However, he also maintained that the fact that contradictory conclusions could be derived validly proved that both pairs of antinomies are founded on a self-contradictory concept which is essential to Reason itself—the treatment of noumena as if they could be objects of knowledge.

The later antinomies are of more direct interest to us, for they shall lead us into the second Critique:

III Thesis: there are in the world causes
through freedom (in human action).
Antithesis: there is no freedom, but
only natural causes.

IV Thesis: there is a necessary being.
Antithesis: no being is necessary.[45]

These antinomies, according to Kant, are also proven validly, but are quite different from the 'mathematical' antinomies in not being contradictory after all. Rather, the antithesis of each pair is valid of phenomena; the thesis of each pair is valid of noumena. In other words, freedom of action and the existence of God cannot be proven on a phenomenal level as we have already seen, but now Kant gives us the surprising conclusion that as noumena, they can yet be proven.

This surprising promise that the transcendent principles concerning God, Freedom, and the Immortality of the Soul can be justified is not given full proof until the second Critique. What is important for an understanding of the first Critique is that Kant has no desire to eliminate metaphysics, contrary to some of his own misleading statements, but takes at least these three metaphysical principles as central concerns of his entire philosophy. In the first Critique, he is anxious to show that these principles cannot be justified by an appeal to pure reason, and they cannot be taken as knowledge because they are necessarily divorced from experience; but one of the purposes of this Critique is to save these principles from the universal validity of science and its methods; and this it does by taking these principles as central

doctrines of morality, as postulates of practical reason.

Metaphysics does not require these ideas for the sake of natural science, but in order to go beyond nature.[46]

Morality and Metaphysics

Although the Critique of Pure Reason begins by announcing its defense of the three key metaphysical theses of God, Freedom, and Immortality, the first Critique nowhere attempts to justify these principles. Quite to the contrary: the Transcendental Dialectic, which is concerned with metaphysical problems, consists of demonstrations that the methods by which these principles have been defended cannot possibly succeed. Kant does maintain a parallel between his defense of the a priori principles of mathematics and natural science and the a priori principles of metaphysics, but he does not do so until his second Critique. There, although he maintains the claims from the Dialectic that metaphysical principles cannot give us knowledge, he argues with the same transcendental method of the first Critique, the necessity and universality of the above three metaphysical principles. However, because these principles do not concern any possible experience, and because, unlike the principles of the Aesthetic and the Analytic, they do not state the conditions for any experience, they cannot be shown to be a priori knowledge. Rather, these are shown to be necessary postulates of practical reason, that is, statements of the conditions for the application of reason not to the understanding or to supersensible objects but to the 'determination of the will' in right action. Practical reason, as opposed to pure or theoretical reason, is concerned not with what is true but with what is right, and the synthetic a priori principles of practical reason are not necessary truths, but statements of the necessities of duty and obligation.[47] The Critique of Practical Reason, therefore, begins not with a concern for the scope and limits of human knowledge, but with a concern for the a priori rational demands of human action, with a metaphysics of morals.

The postulates of practical reason, God, Freedom, and Immortality, are defended by the demonstration that they lie at the basis of any morality, or, what for Kant is the same, for any rational action. Such principles are not construed as knowledge, but rather are necessary as articles of faith;

their necessity is a moral necessity. Thus, belief in God, in immortality, or in the autonomy of human action is independent of any possible evidence, for they bear no possible relationship to any experience whatever. Yet Kant refuses to take the step that most often follows such a characterization of faith as independent of evidence; namely, he does not go on to claim that articles of faith are *irrational* or at least nonrational and therefore to be grasped subjectively or emotionally. Reason is still intimately involved in the acceptance of these postulates, for they are necessary for rational action. Although there is a sharp cleavage between the principles of the first *Critique* and the postulates of the *Critique of Practical Reason,* Kant intends to establish these a priori principles of morality and religion with as much certainty and necessity as he has already established the Principle of Universal Causation. The second *Critique* may be considered as a parallel to the *Transcendental Aesthetic* and *Analytic,* but instead of taking human consciousness as the given, it is human *moral consciousness* with which we begin. Where Kant has asked, "How is experience possible?" he now asks "How is morality possible?" Where the first *Critique* repeatedly insisted that all knowledge be grounded in experience, the second *Critique* is equally insistent that all morality be grounded in reason. Just as the first *Critique* gave us the conditions for any possible knowledge, the second *Critique* and its companion *Foundations of the Metaphysics of Morals*[48] give us a transcendental exposition of those principles which are the conditions of any possible morality.

A philosophical investigation of morality promises two important results; first, there is always vital need for the formulation of a supreme and unshakable principle of all morality which may serve as an absolute criterion in all moral decisions. Secondly, from what has been said before, we may expect to find a rational justification for the morality-conditioning postulates of God, Freedom, and Immortality.

To serve both of these interests, Kant begins with an analysis of morality, and with an analysis of moral judgments as they are actually made in Protestant bourgeoisie German society. The validity of these judgments, in general, Kant takes as a tentative assumption, although it is not at all clear that Kant in fact ever goes

on to question this assumption itself. He claims that his investigation of morality proceeds in two steps, first by a regressive argument to the conditions necessary *if* ordinary moral judgments are to be valid, and then by a progressive argument to show that these conditions actually obtain. However, it is in his attempt to provide progressive arguments establishing the objective validity of (Protestant bourgeosie) morality that Kant's moral philosophy is notably inferior to analogous attempts in the first *Critique*. He does provide us with a penetrating analysis of the nature of morality, and his arguments for the moral necessity of the postulates, particularly the postulate of Freedom, are brilliant even when they fail. However, it remains unclear throughout his ethical writings how Kant thinks he has justified morality itself. Rather, the ethics argues only that certain principles must be true *if* our morality is objectively valid and that among these are the postulates of God, Freedom, and Immortality.

The distinctive mark of Kant's ethics is its emphasis on *reason* and its subsequent diminution in the importance of inclination, desire, the search for pleasure, self-love, satisfaction, happiness, and the appeal to any sort of conscience or moral sense. The British moral philosophers before him (notably Hume and Hutcheson) had based their entire ethics on appeal to some form of sense; but ethics thus conceived, Kant argues, makes our moral principles merely conditional on the sentiments and inclinations of the individual, whereas it is the very nature of morality that it applies equally to every man, regardless of his personal inclinations or situation. *Duty,* the central concept of morality, is indifferent to situation and to personal inclination. Furthermore, inclination only *advises* us how to act: reason *commands.* Therefore, the principles of morality cannot be derived from subjective principles of individual interest ("maxims"), but must be derived directly from the disinterested, universally-binding dictates of reason ("laws"). The principles of morality are invariant and, because they are derived from the very nature of (practical) reason itself, they are binding on every rational creature.

In Kant's own terms, maxims and resolutions of the will (decisions to act) are of two sorts. Some principles command us to act in certain ways on the condition that we desire certain results. For example, "If you wish to enter politics, then move to a city where no one knows you." This command is binding only on someone who already wishes to enter politics; it has no force on one who is disinterested. Such a command or principle is called a *hypothetical imperative.* It holds only for those agents who have the special interests cited (or implied) in the set of conditions stated. *Moral* principles, on the other hand, do not apply only to a limited special interest group, but apply unconditionally to all men. They are *categorical imperatives* because they admit of no exceptions. One ought to do his duty no matter who he is, where he is, what he wants to do, or what he feels like doing. The very nature of morality is such that its principles are *universal laws,* binding on all rational creatures by virtue of the nature of reason alone.

For those philosophers (Hume and Hutcheson) who based morality on a moral sense, or on a pleasure principle or principle of selfishness (Hobbes), or on the motives of satisfaction or happiness (Aristotle and philosophers of the Enlightenment), all moral principles were no more than hypothetical imperatives since the rightness of certain actions had to be decided on the basis of whether they would give this particular man pleasure, or this particular man happiness. In Kant's ethics, however, *right* is totally independent of individual peculiarities, and moreover, independent of personal pleasure, satisfaction, and happiness. A man will often find his duty to be painful, unsatisfying, and contrary to his personal happiness. Yet, this in no way diminishes his obligation. To act morally is to disregard personal interest and act solely *for the sake of duty.* An action is morally good, therefore, if it is performed for the sake of duty alone[49] and a person has a morally good character or has *moral worth* if he acts not from inclination but from duty.

Here is an insight of immense importance which too few philosophers before or after Kant have appreciated. Kant claims that the justification of morality lies in the fact that its principles are embodied in the very nature of reason and not that its principles lead to personal pleasure or happiness. In stressing this point, Kant sometimes speaks (especially in *Foundations of the Metaphysics of Morals*) as if morality and personal inclination are naturally opposed to each other. The importance of Kant's insistence on the independence of morality from personal interest is evident as soon as we analyze previous attempts to justify the obligatoriness of moral principles. In reply to the question "Why should I be moral?" a great many of Kant's predecessors attempted to show that it is ultimately in one's self-interest to be moral. If, as Kant claims again and again, one's interests are sometimes, or even often, at odds with one's duty, then it is futile to argue that doing one's duty is in his interest, for the very nature of the problem is that one's duty and one's interests conflict. Thus, the defense of morality which can be restated, "act counter to your own interests because it is in your own interests" is clearly unsatisfactory. (However, we will see that Kant will do some serious backsliding on precisely this important point.)

As much as Kant insists on the separation of morality and happiness, it is necessary that we do not accept the popular but unwarranted interpretation that Kant took any act motivated by inclination or personal happiness to be wrong or immoral. To the contrary, Kant insists that it is only natural and right that a man should seek his own happiness, and furthermore, that it is only reasonable to expect that a virtuous man will have happiness accompany his moral goodness. Although Kant sometimes gives the impression that personal motives for personal happiness detract from the moral worth of an action, this assuredly is not his intention; if it were the case that the only truly good acts were those done from duty and *opposed* to all inclination, the only good act would be the act of a wholly miserable man. Kant explicitly rejects this interpretation,[50] most importantly, because he sees that it would exclude a truly good man from his notion of moral worth. A philanthropist, for example, gets personal satisfaction and even joy from helping others, and surely he is to be credited with having moral worth in spite of his personal enjoyment. In the most extreme example, those men whom Kant calls "holy," who act *only* from the motive of duty and no other, are surely the most morally worthy of men, and no less so because they receive great personal satisfaction and happiness from their acts of duty. In fact, Kant tells us that a goodwill is an "indispensable condition for our very worthiness to be happy."[51] Therefore,

Kant's position would be best interpreted as not thinking happiness, pleasure, satisfaction, or any inclinations to be themselves either morally good or morally degrading but rather construing these as simply *irrelevant* to morality. The moral worth of an action is to be decided simply by appeal to whether it was done for the sake of duty, not whether or not the agent achieved, or intended to achieve pleasure or happiness thereby. It is in his attempt to emphasize the irrelevance of inclination to moral worth that he tends to leave us with the impression that inclination detracts from moral worth, but in fact, inclination is simply devoid of moral worth and detracts only insofar as it *replaces* the motive of duty. Later, in his discussion of the *Summum Bonum*,[52] Kant goes yet further and claims that it is unthinkable that a man could act for the sake of duty without the expectation that happiness will follow.[53]

Kant's insistence upon morality as duty for duty's sake leads us to a unique kind of *moral* consideration. Because an action done from duty has its moral worth solely in its having been done for the sake of duty, neither the actual results of that action, nor even the results foreseen in that action are relevant to its moral worth. Because the actual results of action are due to contingencies beyond the person's knowledge and control, these cannot be used in judging either the morality of the action or the moral worth of the agent. This is not to say that an act cannot be judged as 'fortunate' or 'disastrous', but that these judgments are in no way *moral* judgments. In Kant's own terms, the only thing that can be conceived of as good without qualification is a *goodwill*. A person may be morally good even if the consequences of his actions are generally disastrous (if he has good intentions and acts solely for the sake of duty). One is reminded of Dostoevsky's Prince Myshkin who is just such a morally perfect person in spite of his consistent ruination of those around him by virtue of his goodness.

Because only a "goodwill" makes for moral worth, Kant continuously warns us against confusing acting *in conformity with duty* with acting *for the sake of duty*. A man who *happens* to perform good acts for personal reasons is not morally worthy, and his acts are not morally good no matter how exactly they conform to our expecta-

tions of what the moral course of action would be. But neither is a goodwill merely "good intentions" without underlying principles. An act of kindness which is done without regard to principle does not manifest a goodwill. A goodwill must determine action *for the sake of duty*, and because duty means *for the sake of law*, moral goodness and worth depend on action *on principle*. Morality depends solely on action directed to the satisfaction of a moral principle; what other motives or considerations might guide our actions, what our expectations of the results might be, and what actually follows our action is not of *moral* concern.

The central task of the investigation of morality must be, therefore, to discover and formulate those moral principles which are objectively valid and binding for all rational creatures, action for the sake of which is the sole consideration in determination of moral worth.

These moral principles, or categorical imperatives, can be summarized in the single consideration that principles of morality are invariant and apply equally to each and every moral agent. This consideration gives us *the* Categorical Imperative, the supreme moral principle from which all other moral principles, or specific categorical imperatives, are derivative. The first formulation of this categorical imperative is a restatement of the demand for universality in morals:

Act only on that maxim through which you can at the same time will that it should become a universal law.[54]

and alternatively:

Act as if the maxim of your action were through your will to become a universal law of nature.[55]

Because this imperative is a *formal* condition for morality, it does not claim merely that you should act only in those cases when universalization does not lead to disadvantage to myself or even to others, but rather Kant claims that the universalization of the wrong principles leads to *inconsistency,* not merely to disaster. This is an important point in Kant, for if he were arguing only that the test of a moral principle is the consequences of universalization, then the categorical imperative would be merely a "material" and therefore hypothetical imperative telling us what to do *if* we wish to avoid disaster. Because he is arguing that the categorical imperative is nonconditional and derivative of reason alone, a violation of this principle must constitute a violation of reason itself.

However, it is not at all clear what Kant intends by the notion of "inconsistency," and his examples only make the issue more difficult: suppose a man finds himself in a position of needing to borrow money, which he knows he will never be capable of paying back. He is in desperate need, but knows that he will not get the loan unless he falsely promises to return the money within a certain period of time. He thus faces the dilemma of deciding whether it is right for him to borrow money when he needs it by falsely promising to repay the loan. To find out whether such an action is morally right, he applies the categorical imperative and universalizes the maxim that one may make false promises under certain conditions of need. Then,

I see straight away that this maxim can never rank as a universal law of nature and be self-consistent, but must necessarily contradict itself. For the universality of a law that everyone believing himself to be in need can make any promise he pleases with the intention not to keep it would make promising, and the very purpose of promising itself impossible, since no one would believe he was being promised anything, but would laugh at utterances of this kind as empty shams.[56]

Notice that the 'inconsistency' Kant speaks of here is not strictly speaking a logical inconsistency, for there is no breach of logic in the supposition that the institution of promise-making should become meaningless. Rather, Kant seems to have in mind that the universalization of the maxim condoning promise-breaking would result in the destruction of the very institution which allows for the making and breaking of promises. The 'inconsistency', then, is the "self-defeating" consequences of an act which, if universally performed, would destroy the very possibility of anyone's performing that act.

Similarly, Kant replies to the question of the morality of committing suicide by telling us that we should ask whether a principle condoning suicide could (consistently) become a universal law of nature. However,

it is then seen at once that a system of nature by whose law the very same feeling whose function is to stimulate the furtherance of life should actually destroy life would contradict itself. . .[57]

Here again, the notion of "inconsistency" (or 'contradiction') is not a strictly logical notion. Rather, it is the 'inconsistency' of a universalized maxim destroying the very basis of the possibility of the relevant action, in this case, the existence of life which is necessary for anyone to commit suicide.

Although Kant's notion of "inconsistency" is obscure, his purpose in insisting that immoral principles when universalized lead to inconsistency is sufficiently clear. The fault in such universalizations must be a *formal* fault because the categorical imperative must be derivative of a priori reason alone. Otherwise Kant's central claim, that morality is a function of reason and not of personal inclinations (requiring appeal to specific cases), must be a failure.

Kant gives us two further formulations of *the* categorical imperative, which are claimed to be restatements of the same consideration summarized in the first formulation. Most importantly, he tells us that we should

Act in such a way that you always treat humanity, whether in your own person or in the person of any other, never simply as a means, but always at the same time as an end.[58]

If I treat another person as a means to my personal ends, I am placing myself in a privileged position, one which I cannot use in universal legislation. To use another person is to fail to treat him as an independent rational judge, either because of some deception or use of force on my part. From this formulation, Kant introduces his Utopian ideal of a *Kingdom of Ends,* a community of rational beings in which each person is an autonomous moral legislator and judge. Because each member of this community treats himself and every other as an exact equal, individual legislation leads to a single set of principles, allowing for total harmony in which there can be none of the usual human tragedy of conflict of personal interests. Because each man acts out of duty for the universal law, there can be no conflict of interests simply because each man's interest is at one with the interests of all.

Freedom—The First
Principle of Practical Reason

In the above analysis of morality, Kant has unfolded for us the (analytically) necessary conditions for there to be morality, namely, that moral right and moral worth are concerned with a goodwill and not with results or inclinations, and that moral principles must be 'objective' or universally applicable without exception (as summarized in the Categorical Imperative). However, it is possible that morality is an illusion, if for example, men are never capable of acting from reason but are always the slaves of their inclinations. There can only be morality if it is possible for men to act morally, and this possibility can come about only if men can act according to reason, that is, for the sake of duty and not simply as determined by personal inclination.

The first condition of morality must, therefore, be man's possibility of acting either in accordance with or against his moral obligations. If a man cannot possibly perform an act of duty because he is the helpless pawn of his 'passions', or, in the language of the twentieth century, if he is fully determined by unconscious forces beyond his control, then it does not even make sense to claim that he has an obligation to perform that act. For example, under no circumstances can a blind man have an obligation to read, nor a cripple have an obligation to run. Kant's famous catch phrase, " 'ought' implies 'can'," tells us that there can be no obligation unless there is the possibility of fulfilling that obligation. On the other hand, it makes no sense to speak of obligation in cases in which a man cannot help but perform some action. For example, it would be absurd to speak of a man's obligation to obey the law of gravity, for he could not possibly do otherwise.

Suppose that there were *always* a sufficient set of conditions such that a man could never help but do exactly as he does. We might never know this set of conditions, which would include such diverse determinants as early childhood, neurological conditions, certain unconscious mo-

tives and beliefs; but *if* there were such a set, we could never meaningfully speak of obligation, or duty, or responsibility, or morality, for these presuppose a man's freedom to do or not to do those actions which are commanded by the dictates of reason.

According to Kant's first *Critique*, there must be just such a set of sufficient causal conditions for every act a man performs. Because man is a being in the phenomenal world, and because the principle of universal causation must apply to all beings in this world, a man and all of his actions must be considered fully determined by the laws of nature. As such, the most 'free' or 'voluntary' actions are just as much the necessary outcome of some set of natural and 'involuntary' causes as those actions which we now consider wholly involuntary and determined (for example, those 'actions' due to sudden brain disturbances). If all actions are fully determined, then there cannot possibly be morality, for moral principles cannot be binding on creatures who have not the freedom to do or not to do what these moral principles command.

However, the first *Critique* has left open for us the possibility of considering man outside of the natural order of things. In addition to the standpoint which takes man as a natural object, as an empirical ego, the *Transcendental Deduction* introduced to us a perspective of man as transcendental ego, as a self lying 'behind' the natural order of phenomenal objects. As a transcendent(al) self, beyond the possibility of any experience whatever, this being is noumenal. As Kant tells us in the *Deduction,* the transcendent(al) self is the self as it is *in-itself:* the empirical ego is the self as it *appears* to itself, that is, as phenomenon. As noumenon, however, the transcendent(al) or noumenal ego is not subject to the conditions of knowledge disclosed in the first *Critique;* specifically, it is not subject to the category of causality. Therefore, the Principle of Universal Causation does not apply to it. As a noumenal self, man is outside the natural world, and his actions need not be fully determined by antecedent causes. In this way, Kant's distinction between empirical and transcendental ego begins to blossom into one of the most intriguing and possibly most obscure doctrines of modern philosophy. This distinction allows Kant to maintain *both* that man is understandable as a natural object, that is, as an object for scientific study, and that man is free from causal determination and therefore responsible for his actions and bound by the moral law. If coherent, this doctrine of the "two-standpoints" (man as natural object and man as moral agent) may succeed in resolving the very deepest underlying problem of Kant's entire philosophy, namely the defense of the universal validity of science as well as the objective validity of morality.

In the *Transcendental Dialectic,* Kant has already argued that the antinomy of causality[59] demonstrates the a priori truth of both the principle of universal causation (as demonstrated in the *Analytic*) and the possibility of "freedom as a cause" of action. In the *Dialectic,* Kant indicates that causality applies only to phenomena while freedom applies to noumena. The proof of freedom, however, does not occur until the second *Critique,* where, for the first time, Kant attempts to prove something about noumenal objects. Kant still insists that principles concerning noumena cannot give us *knowledge* and that pure or theoretical reason has nothing to say of transcendent objects. He does attempt to provide substantial truths about noumena in this one case, and it will be argued that, in doing so, he lays the basis for the undermining of his entire philosophy:

The idea of freedom is the only concept of the supersensible which . . . proves its objective reality in nature.[60]

Kant's argument for the postulate of freedom, although in some ways the subversion of his entire philosophy, is also the one attempt he makes to justify the original 'tentative' assumption of his entire ethics, namely the objective validity of our (that is, Protestant bourgeois German) ordinary moral judgments. Kant recognizes that any attempt to justify the postulate of freedom by appeal to morality would be circular (since freedom is a necessary condition of morality). In order to defend the postulate of freedom, therefore, Kant reintroduces the noumenal or transcendent world, which hitherto has been a mere *limiting* concept about which we could intelligibly say nothing. Now, in order to defend freedom, Kant attempts to show that man as moral agent is a *noumenal* being and thereby free of causal determination. Freedom from the

laws of nature is not a sufficient condition for rationality, of course. Kant insists that freedom *from* causal laws is only a *limiting* or *negative* freedom. However, man is free also in a *positive* sense, free *to* think and act in conformity with the moral law. Thus, considerations about human freedom and concern for rationality and the moral law are never far apart. Sometimes, in both the second *Critique* and in *Foundations,* Kant tells us that "freedom is the moral law" and a "lawless free will would be contradictory."[61]

The noumenal ego, according to Kant, is the "I Will" (as the transcendental ego was characterized as the "I Think"). The "pure activity" of this "I Will" is Reason in its practical employment. As a noumenal being, man is a willing, rational, free creature.[62] 'Will', 'rationality', and 'freedom' are intimately related in the characterization of man as agent;

Will is a kind of causality belonging to living things so far as they are rational.[63]

Freedom would then be the property this causality has of being able to work independently of determination by alien causes . . .[64]

Freedom Must be Presupposed as a Property of the Will of All Rational Beings.[65]

Thus, freedom is not simply a postulate of morality, but a necessary precondition for rationality. However, Kant often allows himself to move from this position to the considerably weaker stand that rationality presupposes only the *Idea* of freedom;

Now I assert that every being who cannot act except under the idea *of freedom is by this alone—from a practical point of view— really free.*[66]

Thus we shall find that Kant's defense of the postulate of freedom wavers between the defense of metaphysical freedom, which asserts outright that human actions are not determined because the Will is not determined except by itself, and a defense of a much weaker thesis—that acting rationally (morally) presupposes that the agent *suppose* that he is free. The former claim runs head-on into the Principle of Universal Causation which has been argued to be a priori true in the first *Critique;* the second claim allows that the

Idea of freedom which a rational agent must suppose may nevertheless be false, and this claim does not, therefore, conflict with the Principle of Universal Causation.

In Kant's practical philosophy, the dichotomy between noumena and phenomena becomes greatly pronounced. In the *Critique of Pure Reason*, "noumenon" is a 'limiting' concept; in the *Critique of Practical Reason*, Kant maintains that we *must* suppose there to be noumena;

behind appearances we must admit and assume something else which is not appearance—namely things in themselves —although since we can never be acquainted with these, but only with the way in which they affect us, we must resign ourselves to the fact that we can never get any nearer to them and can never know what they are in themselves. This must yield us a distinction, however rough, between the sensible world and the intelligible world, the first of which can vary a great deal according to the differences in sensibility in sundry observers, while the second, which is its ground, always remains the same.[67]

How far removed from the hardheaded 'Critique' in Kant's epistemology is this? The earlier distinction between the world-in-itself and the world-as-we-know-it now becomes a dichotomy of two different worlds. Of course, much of the expression of this "two-world" view is metaphorical, but the metaphor is so pervasive that we are hard put to separate metaphor from philosophical theory;

as regards mere perception and the capacity for perceiving sensations he must count himself as belonging to the sensible world, but as regards whatever there may be in him of pure activity (whatever comes into consciousness . . . immediately) he must count himself as belonging to the intelligible world.[68]

Of course, these two worlds are closely related, for human actions are not simply acts of Will (in the intelligible world), but are also, and result in, movements of one's body and movements and changes in the world (that is, the sensible world). We are tempted to say, of course, that these two worlds are not merely *related*, but are *identical*. Unfortunately, this identification cannot be made for Kant. If the worlds

were identical, the laws valid for one would also be valid for the other. Since the absence of causality in the intelligible world is the purpose of the "two-worlds" view, Kant would most certainly not accept such an identification.

Kant sees this problem, but his insistence on the "two standpoints" forbids him from resolving it:

Reason must . . . suppose that no contradiction is to be found between freedom and natural necessity ascribed to the very same human actions; for it can abandon the concept of nature as little as it can abandon that of freedom.[69]

Is there no contradiction?

. . . while freedom is only an idea of reason whose objective reality is questionable, nature is a concept of the understanding, which proves, and must necessarily prove, its reality in examples from experience.[70]

Kant is evidently uncomfortable with this 'antinomy', and constantly tends to weaken his defense of freedom to a defense of the need for a (perhaps false) *Idea* of freedom.

The concept of the intelligible world is thus only a point of view which reason finds itself constrained to adopt outside appearances in order to conceive itself as practical.[71]

and, more obscurely he argues the *Idea* of freedom, although necessary, to be unintelligible:

Thus the Idea of freedom can never admit of full comprehension, or indeed of insight, since it can never by any analogy have an example falling under it. . . . Nothing is left but defense . . .[72]

The confusion over the nature of *Freedom* causes Kant to have similar concern over his related notions of "Reason" and "Practicality (Will)." He maintains, for example, that "all human reason is totally incapable of explaining this" [how reason can be practical][73] and finds himself unable to understand "how freedom itself is possible as causality of the will."[74] As a result, Kant finds himself ultimately dumbfounded by his entire ethics:

And thus, while we do not comprehend the practical unconditioned necessity of the moral imperative, we do comprehend its incomprehensibility.[75]

All that becomes clear is the necessity of the postulate of freedom for rationality and morality. However, it never becomes clear to what extent real freedom is demanded (an actual breakdown of the Principle of Universal Causality) or to what extent a man must simply *suppose* himself to be free in order to consider himself as a responsible moral agent.

In order to establish the postulate of freedom, in either the strong or the weaker sense, Kant must avoid any support from morality itself, and he must likewise avoid any appeal to a notion of rationality that already assumes the objective validity of morality. Since the objective validity of morality itself presupposes the postulate of freedom, the problem of the second *Critique* is to avoid the vicious circle of defending freedom in terms of morality and morality in terms of freedom. Kant again sees this problem, and the introduction of the two-world view is an attempt to defend the postulate of freedom apart from any reference to morality:

The suspicion which we raised above is now removed—namely that there might be hidden a circle in our inference from freedom to autonomy and from autonomy to the moral law; that in effect we had presumed the idea of freedom only because of the moral law in order subsequently to infer the moral law in its turn from freedom. . . . We now see that when we think of ourselves as free, we transfer ourselves into the intelligible world as members and recognize the autonomy of the will together with its consequences— morality. Whereas when we think ourselves under obligation, we look upon ourselves as belonging to the sensible world and yet to the intelligible world at the same time.[76]

The last sentence of the quotation indicates to us once more that the relationship between the sensible and intelligible worlds remains a very serious problem, but it is not clear how the two-worlds view can solve the problem of circularity which here concerns Kant. Introduction of the intelligible world to defend freedom and escape the circle seems to be a failure from the outset, since the notion of the 'intelligible world' is introduced as a product of Reason and, more specifically, of practical reason. Similarly, in the *Critique of Practical Reason,*[77] it again looks as if Kant assumes rationality (and the moral law) in order to prove the postulate of freedom. Thus, Kant's overall attempt to prove the reality of human freedom of action runs aground on several counts. First, it is not clear that Kant ever escapes the vicious circle of arguing from rationality to freedom to rationality, and, if he does not escape this circle, he has succeeded in proving only that *if* morality is objectively valid, then the postulate of freedom must be true. Secondly, Kant's radical claim that man must be considered differently as an object of nature and as agent (a claim to be considered by every author we shall study) is coupled with his equally radical but more problematic claim that man is a 'member' of two different 'worlds'—a sensible (phenomenal) world and an intelligible (noumenal) world. Given what Kant has argued in the first *Critique,* namely, that we cannot know the noumenal world, is not the notion of 'membership in the noumenal world' incoherent? Furthermore, is the identification of man as agent with man in the intelligible world necessary for Kant's purposes? Is it not possible to interpret freedom of action within a phenomenal framework? Future authors, notably Hegel and Sartre, shall attempt to do so. Thirdly, Kant supposes that the two standpoints are *independent,* and that it is possible that the Principle of Universal Causation is true universally in the sensible world, and false or meaningless in the intelligible world. If it is a priori true that every event has a sufficient cause, then in what sense could a man's action be undetermined? It would seem that we must either give up the Principle of Universal Causation or give up our belief in human freedom of action. Or, if we return to the "two-world" or "two-standpoints" view, then we must clarify the distinction between these two worlds in such a way that we can make sense of the fact that an action seems to span both worlds at once. The choice is not a pleasant one; either we maintain belief in two contradictory but equally necessary theses, or we invoke the obscure if not incomprehensible notion of "two worlds" to save both theses and avoid contradiction. Or, we may take the route along which Kant sometimes directs himself and weaken the postulate of freedom to the need to *think* of oneself as free in order to consider oneself as a responsible agent. If it is only a need to think one is free, and not be free, and if there are independent grounds for thinking one is never in fact free (the Principle of Universal Causality tells us this), then the idea of freedom is only a *delusion* of freedom: the incomprehensibility of which Kant complains is that sort of incomprehensibility which results from the attempt to prove a false doctrine true at any cost.

God and Immortality

In Kant's proof of the postulates of God and immortality, there is no doubt but that the objective validity of morality is accepted as given. These proofs, which together constitute a demonstration of the necessity of the Christian faith, prove only what must be accepted *if* we are to be bound to the moral law. There is no attempt whatever to establish the postulates of God and immortality independently of their necessity for morality. On the contrary, Kant insists throughout all three *Critiques* that there is no legitimate possibility of doing so.

Kant's treatment of God as a postulate of practical and not pure reason marks a major departure from other philosophers who had attempted to link morality and religion. Judeo-Christian theology had long been made the basis for morality, and God had been cited as the source of moral values, as their justification and as their enforcer. (For example, St. Augustine's *City of God* is such a defense of God as the source of moral values. More obviously, the Old Testament is an elaborate assertion of this claim.) In other words, morality had its basis in religion, and morality could thus be justified by appeal to religion, which had its justification in the truths of Pure Reason. With Kant, however, we find the dependency of morality upon religion turned on its head; morality is supported by appeal to reason alone, while religion, for its support, requires an appeal to morality. This is not to say, of course, that Kant would allow that we could keep morality and dispense with religion. Even if we ignore Kant's personal religious temperament, it is evident that to interpret belief in God as a postulate of practical reason is to retain the traditional theological doctrine that without God, there can be no morality. Morality still requires belief in God as its presupposition,

but the proof of God can only proceed by beginning with morality. God is necessary for morality, but, apart from moral considerations, God is without philosophical importance. Thus, in spite of Kant's personal piety, it is already evident how his philosophy will contribute to the rapid diminution of the philosophical importance of religion which, after a brilliant but desperate attempt at salvation by Hegel, will end in the irrationalism of Kierkegaard and the vicious atheism of Nietzsche.

Kant's justification of the postulates of God and immortality can be separated into two very different sets of arguments. The first of these, the best known and historically most important, are formulated in the last two *Critiques* and in his increasingly recognized *Religion Within the Bounds of Reason Alone*. Central to his arguments is the notion of the 'Summum Bonum', with which we shall be concerned in this section. However, there are convincing reasons for supposing that this notion of *Summum Bonum* makes Kant's ethics inconsistent, and Kant, in recognition of this, dispensed with it in his very last writings[78] and attempted to justify his religious beliefs without appeal to a *Summum Bonum*. However, we shall not pay much attention to these later writings, not because they are unimportant, but simply because they had little effect on the later writers with whom we shall be concerned.

Although action in accordance with the moral law is the crux of Kant's ethics, he does appreciate, as we have already noted, that happiness plays a necessary role in the ideally good life. Although a life of duty may be morally good, a life of duty which has more than its due share of misery could hardly be called a good life. In most earlier moral philosophies, the connection of happiness and the good life was never considered problematic, for happiness was nearly always recognized as a necessary component of the good life, or even as the good life itself. Where virtue was also necessary for the good life, it was usually subsumed under happiness (and virtue and duties were analyzed in terms of the happiness they procured). For Aristotle, for example, it was inconceivable that a virtuous man not be happy, for happiness (*eudaimonia*) was defined as "activity of the soul in accordance with virtue."[79] For Kant however, there is a problem. By insisting that happiness and the search for happiness are irrelevant to morality, he seems forced to concede that a man has an unconditional obligation to do his duty even if it turns out that his duty brings him nothing but disaster and misery.

Kant does not accept this consequence of his ethics, but rather agrees with the classical picture of the good life as consisting of both virtue and happiness. The *Summum Bonum,* the highest good for man, is the rational ideal in which virtue and happiness always go hand in hand:

In the Summum Bonum *which is practical for us, i.e., one which is to be made real by our will, virtue and happiness are thought of as necessarily combined, so that the one cannot be assumed by a practical reason without the other belonging to it.*[60]

Kant recognizes the problem of incorporating happiness into his conception of the good life, and refers to the problem of doing so as the "antinomy of practical reason." Namely, how can the *Summum Bonum* necessarily include happiness if action for the sake of happiness is devoid of moral worth?

If, therefore, the Summum Bonum *is impossible according to practical rules, then the moral law which commands that it be furthered must be fantastic, directed to empty imaginary ends, and consequently inherently false.*[61]

If the *Summum Bonum* requires virtue, which is action for the sake of duty alone, but also requires happiness, it seems therefore that action for the *Summum Bonum* is impossible, for it requires acting both for happiness and without the expectation of happiness.

However, it would seem that the most primitive observation of our world demonstrates that virtue and happiness are not commensurate, and Kant expresses amazement that so many philosophers have argued so:

It must appear strange that philosophers of both ancient and modern times have been able to find happiness in very just proportion to virtue in this life.[62]

Kant, however, sees no reason to suppose that this world should reward virtue with happiness, but rather, because man as moral agent is not of the sensible world,

the *Summum Bonum* need not be of this world either.

Expectation of immediate reward for virtuous action is the most serious threat to morality, for if men believe that their doing good does not make them happier, they will abandon their duty for immediate happiness. Therefore, if morality is to be binding upon men, belief in the *Summum Bonum* must be maintained as well. This can be done, claims Kant, by adopting the postulates of God and immortality, for if we believe in a God who is himself a moral (that is, rational) being and is also the ground or ultimate cause of the universe, then we can easily justify our belief in the harmony between the moral and the natural order. If we believe in an afterlife, then we can justify our belief in the just distribution of happiness, though not in this life. God and immortality are thus necessary for the *Summum Bonum,* which is in turn necessary for morality. The postulates of God and immortality are therefore necessary as conditions for morality.

At this juncture, it is convenient to mention a philosophical disposition which runs through all three of Kant's *Critiques,* the disposition to interpret phenomena *teleologically,* as if they have an ultimate purpose. The notion of "teleology", which appears in the *Dialectic,* is implied throughout the discussion of the *Summum Bonum* and lies at the very core of Kant's aesthetic theory, but it does not receive sustained attention until the second half of the *Critique of Judgment.* In that discussion, Kant claims that we have a natural tendency to look for purposive explanations, even though the Principle of Universal Causation tells us that mechanistic or causal explanations are always available. Kant himself manifests this tendency quite often. For example, he argues that the existence of *reason* in man is sufficient to prove that its purpose and therefore the purpose of man cannot be to achieve happiness[63] simply because man already has an 'organ', namely *instinct,* which has this purpose. In his discussion of the *Summum Bonum,* the notion of a teleological universe is central, for it is only because the universe has an ultimate direction (the direction of God) that we may expect that the amoral natural world and the rational world of ideals and values will coincide. Because we may believe that the world, as noumenon, is teleological, we may therefore act for the sake of duty with the full expectation that our good deeds will be ultimately rewarded by happiness.

However, once we have established that the only justification of religious belief is its necessity for morality, the exact content of our religion is still in question. Because the objects of religious devotion are noumenal, and therefore not objects of any possible knowledge, we are only entitled to attribute to these objects those properties which are necessary for morality. Such morally justifiable beliefs Kant calls "natural," because they can be derived from (practical) reason alone; a religion consisting only of natural beliefs is a natural religion. Against this, most religions are based on dogma derived solely from authority; such a religion is said to be "statutory" or "learned."[84] Of those beliefs of a natural religion, Kant has thus far mentioned two, belief in God and belief in immortality. There are many conceptions of God, and a great many appendages to belief in God which the Christian faith had also accepted. A major task of a critique of religion must be to separate those beliefs which are natural from those which are merely learned. However, Kant cannot be judged to have performed very satisfactorily in this respect, and his few arguments are not nearly adequate to support the huge amount of traditional Christian theology that he accepts as natural.

With regard to the nature of God, Kant is quite specific but hardly threatening to orthodox Christian thought. Because a God which supports morality must be capable of understanding both the natural and the moral law, He must be intelligent, but since He is supreme, Kant stipulates that He must be omniscient. Since He must be capable of acting in accordance with the moral law, He must be powerful, but since He is supreme, omnipotent. Since the moral law and its obeyance must be eternal, He must be eternal, and since the moral law is binding at all times, He must be omnipresent. In short, Kant almost routinely characterizes the traditional Christian God without any serious attempt to question the legitimacy of this conception of God, and uncritically announces Christianity in its entirety as the one religion which successfully fulfills the demands of morality:

The doctrine of Christianity, even when not regarded as a religious doctrine, gives at this point a concept of the Summum Bonum (the Kingdom of God) which is alone sufficient to the strictest demand of practical reason.[85]

`Kant's discussion of the postulate of immortality occupies only a few pages demonstrating the necessity of the postulate for the Summum Bonum. Although several previous discussions allow us to confidently fill in Kant's views on the possibility of immortality, it is not at all evident that his theory could be made coherent. In the Transcendental Deduction, we have already been introduced to the notion of a transcendental or limiting ego which lies beyond the scope of the categories. Because one of the categories is substance, this limiting ego cannot be a substance. It is on this ground that Kant rejects the traditional doctrine of the soul as substance (the "paralogism of psychology" in the Dialectic). However, as noumenon, the self is timeless. Not being an object of experience, it need not conform to the temporal a priori form of experience. Immortality of the soul is thus comprehensible for Kant because the self as noumenon is timeless (just as God as noumenon is beyond space and time). However, beyond this general outline, Kant's doctrine of immortality is most likely incoherent. The immortal soul needed for the postulate of morality would have to be capable of being happy, and of continuing to exist as precisely the same person who in life has earned this happiness. However, the transcendental ego, as we have discussed it so far, is not the ego which has a personality, which is a property of the empirical or phenomenal ego. Yet the phenomenal ego, because it is subject to the a priori forms of experience and the categories, cannot be what survives the death of the body. Unfortunately, Kant spends no time discussing these problems, and his postulate of immortality remains a hopelessly obscure but necessary corollary of his postulation of Christianity as necessary for morality.

In basing his entire justification of religion on the notion of the Summum Bonum, Kant opens his ethics to very serious objections. Because his analysis of morality demands that only action in accordance with and solely for the sake of the moral law has moral worth, he is committed to excluding actions done for happiness as morally worthy. Yet the notion of the *Summum Bonum* commits Kant to the incompatible doctrine that a man is bound to the moral law only insofar as he has the expectation of happiness as a consequence of his good acts. Kant makes several attempts to render these two theses compatible; for example, by insisting that the necessity of accepting the *Summum Bonum* is only a *subjective* necessity,[86] and by insisting that the causation of happiness by virtue is not 'phenomenal causation', but "indirect, mediated by an intelligible Author of nature."[87] Kant ultimately gives up the notion of the *Summum Bonum* altogether and replaces it with a notion of the moral law itself as Divine and the moral experience itself as a bit of revelation of the Divine.

In his ethical writings, Kant promises that he will establish the validity of morality, and thus show us why the moral law is binding on all men. In fact, at the very best, he does no more than show us that, *if* we are free (which he may or may not have proved), and *if* we accept his other postulates of God and immortality, and *if* we accept his analysis of morality (as universality as stated in the categorical imperative), *then* we will accept the obligation to be moral. If, however, one refuses to accept any of these conditions, then the question, "Why should I be moral?" remains without an answer. For example, suppose someone refused to accept the categorical imperative, but did acknowledge that the categorical imperative is presupposed in all our ordinary moral judgments and then claimed that this is not in itself a proof that we should continue to take these judgments as binding. If we question the legitimacy of morality to make categorical demands of us, what reply has Kant given? Those principles which Kant identifies as "categorical" or moral have surely not been given the unshakable a priori justification promised by Kant.

Whatever failings might be found in Kant's philosophy, they are the failings of a unique genius who dared a brilliant deflection from contemporary rationalist and Enlightenment thought, but yet refused to join forces with Rousseau and the Romantics on whose behalf he was continuously warring. With the Romantics, Kant was willing to transcend the demands of science and to reject the abstractions of pure reason to enter the realms of action and faith. Also with the Romantics, Kant emphasized above all respect for the human individual as an end in himself. However, unlike the Romantics, Kant never left the embraces of reason, and, as a result, his emphasis on the individual never led to the Romantic disrespect for universal law and rigorous *rational* morality. Yet, even though Kant held his rationalism as central to every aspect of his philosophy, his rationalistic doctrines were a major step into the Romantic-inspired ideology of the nineteenth century and the 'nihilist' doctrines of the twentieth-century existentialists. His attempt to justify Christianity as a set of rational beliefs is the point of departure for both Kierkegaard and Nietzsche, who not only deny Christianity its claims to rationality, but deny the whole of morality its claim to a priori validity as well. Similarly, it is Kant's Copernican revolution which makes possible the phenomenology of Husserl, which, in the hands of Heidegger and Sartre, once again undermines the foundations of traditional knowledge of good and evil.

Bibliography

There are literally hundreds of good books and articles on the background of Kant's philosophy. Most essential, of course, are the original writings of Descartes and David Hume: *The Philosophy of Descartes,* translated by Haldane and Ross, London, 1967. Hume, David. *Enquiry Concerning Human Nature,* La Salle, Ill., 1963.

Brief analyses of the Enlightenment with selections from original works can be found in:

Berlin, I. ed., *The Age of Enlightenment.* New York, 1965.

Hampshire, S. *The Age of Reason.* New York, 1956.

Every text in the history of philosophy deals extensively with this period; the following are particularly recommended:

Brehier, E. *The History of Philosophy.* Vol. VI. Chicago, 1969.

Copleston, F. *A History of Philosophy.* Vols. IV, V, VI. New York, 1963–1966.

Jones, W. T. *History of Western Philosophy.* Vols. III and IV. New York, 1952.

O'Connor, D. J. *A Critical History of Western Philosophy.* New York, 1964. Essays on Descartes, Locke, Leibniz, Hume, and eighteenth-century materialism.

Also recommended are relevant articles

in Edwards, P., ed. *Encyclopedia of Philosophy*. New York, 1967.

Anchor, R. *The Enlightenment Tradition*. New York, 1967.

Kant's Works in English
The Critique of Pure Reason. Translated by N. Kemp Smith. New York, 1966.

The Critique of Practical Reason. Translated by L. W. Beck. New York, 1956.

The Critique of Judgment. Translated by J. C. Meredith. Oxford, 1952.

The Prolegomena to Any Future Metaphysics. Translated by L. W. Beck. New York, 1950.

The Groundwork (Foundations) of the Metaphysics of Morals. Translated by H. Paton, *The Moral Law*. New York, 1964.

Religion Within the Limits of Reason Alone. Translated by T. M. Green. New York, 1960.

Perpetual Peace. Translated by L. W. Beck. New York, 1939.

Idea of Universal History. Translated by W. Hastie in *Theories of History*. Edited by P. Gardiner. New York, 1958.

Metaphysics of Morals, Part I; Metaphysical Elements of Justice. Part II. Translated by J. Ladd. Indianapolis, 1956.

The Metaphysical Principles of Virtue. Translated by M. J. Gregor. New York, 1949.

Lectures on Ethics. Translated by L. Infield. New York, 1949.

Philosophical Correspondence, 1759–99. Translated and edited by A. Zweig. Chicago, 1967.

Books about Kant's Philosophy
Good works about Kant's philosophy are also plentiful; particularly recommended are the following:

Beck, L. W. *Commentary on Kant's Critique of Practical Reason*. Chicago, 1962.

Bennett, J. *Kant's Analytic*. Cambridge, 1966.

Heidegger, M. *Kant and the Problem of Metaphysics*. Translated by J. Churchill. Bloomington, Ind., 1962.

Jones, W. T. *Morality and Freedom in Kant*. London, 1940.

Kemp Smith, N. *Commentary on Kant's Critique of Pure Reason*. (London, 1958.)

Körner, S. *Kant*. Baltimore, Md., 1967.

Paton, H. J. *The Categorical Imperative*. Chicago, 1948.

Ross, Sir W. D. *Kant's Ethical Theory*. Oxford, 1954.

Sellars, W. *Science and Metaphysics*. London, 1968.

Strawson, P. F. *The Bounds of Sense*. London, 1966.

Weldon, *Introduction to Kant's Critique of Pure Reason*. Oxford, 1958.

Wolff, R. P. *Kant's Theory of Mental Activity*. Cambridge, Mass., 1965.

———, ed. *Kant: A Collection of Critical Essays*. Garden City, N.Y., 1967.

G. W. F. Hegel: Spirit and Absolute Truth
CHAPTER 2

Hegel has been called "the Aristotle of our Post-Renaissance World." Georg Wilhelm Friedrich Hegel is one of those figures in terms of whom an entire conceptual age can be summarized. It is fair to say that he brought to a climax a philosophical and cultural attitude only partially evident in Kant, an attitude which is definitive of nearly a century of European thought. For Hegel, philosophy was not merely philosophy, but the thought and feelings of an age made self-conscious. That age—Germany at the end of the eighteenth century—was a period of apocalyptic consciousness culminating in a period of unprecedented 'high-culture' and conservatism. This was the period of the French Revolution, with the upheaval of war, the self-aggrandizement of an exaggerated sense of history, a fear mingled with respect for the ideals of revolution, but also a passion for the comfort of the *status quo*. It was an age of conflict and the forced illusions of painful progress. It is no wonder that the Heraclitian concept of "contradiction" becomes the central theme of Hegel's philosophy, and it is no less surprising that the present-glorifying dialectic should become his method. Within this philosophy, Hegel attempts the most ambitious philosophical project of modern times, the synthesis of all human knowledge and culture into a single system, to show where it has been, how it has progressed, and to find the underlying purpose of it all.[1]

The Early Theological Writings
Because of the emphasis so often placed upon Hegel's famous 'system', his concern with logic and the nature of conceptual thought, he is frequently approached as a logician-metaphysician, whose concern is primarily the problem of knowledge as presented by Kant. With this emphasis (adopted by generations of English scholars, notably Stace and McTaggart), Hegel's frequent insistence that the "Truth is the whole" and that he seeks Absolute Truth simply refers to the epistemological thesis that there is some underlying or unifying Truth which is inadequately expressed by the partial truths of science and previous philosophy. However, Hegel, like Kant, was not primarily concerned with epistemological problems, but with religion and morality. But while it is easily possible to isolate Kant's great epistemological work and treat it separately from his moral and religious concerns, it is virtually impossible to separate Hegel's epistemology and logic from his moral and religious doctrines, for even his *Logic* has religious underpinnings.

If the later works were all that we had of Hegel's writings, the approach to his system would be far more difficult than it is. Luckily we have in our possession a series of early essays written by Hegel as a student, which he never published and evidently never intended to publish.[2] Perhaps the most striking difference between these essays and the later works is their clarity. They are written in an unprofessional style which is a pleasure for anyone who has struggled with the terminology of the *Phenomenology*. These essays are products of youthful enthusiasm and rebellion more than serious scholarship, and at least one of these manuscripts seems to have been a source of embarrassment to the older Hegel. However, the thematic concern of these essays with the opposing religious philosophies of Kant, the Romantics, and the Orthodox church continues to drive Hegel's philosophical enterprises throughout his mature works.

These manuscripts were written before 1800 and have been traditionally referred to as Hegel's "theological writings." However, a more fitting label has been supplied by Kaufmann, who refers to them as the "antitheological writings," as they consist for the most part of a brutal attack on Christian theology, on the Christian church, and even on Christ himself. In these attacks, the youthful Hegel surpasses even the bitterly anti-Christian Nietzsche in acrimonious and blasphemous sarcasm. Hegel's condemnation of Christianity, like that of Nietzsche and also like the defense by Kant, was inextricable from a concern for morality. All three thinkers insist that the only possible justification for any religious beliefs must be a *practical,* or a *moral* justification. Christianity is rejected by Hegel because it fails to fulfill the demands of morality, and, in its place, Hegel attempts to formulate a new religion which will satisfy these demands. Even in these early writings, there is evidence of Hegel's tremendous pretentiousness in his consideration of himself as a philosophical prophet and his attempt to found a new religion. This tendency to regard himself as an intermediary between man and God, or as a spokesman for universal Spirit, is never lost in Hegel's intellectual maturity.

His early manuscripts are four in number: "Folk Religion and Christianity" (1793), "The Life of Jesus" (1795), "The Positivity of the Christian Religion" (1795), and "The Spirit of Christianity and Its Fate" (1799).

In the fragments of "Folk Religion and Christianity," we already find the central threads of Hegel's philosophical development. We find him in alliance with Kant in the attack on theology (religion based on pure reason) and the demand for a 'natural' religion, one founded on the demands of morality and practical reason. We find him dissatisfied with the authoritarianism of traditional Christianity, but still seeking a religion, even if he finds it necessary to formulate one for himself. We find the attack on the traditional Judeo-Christian notion of a *transcendent* God, and the attack on the antagonism of Reason and passion in traditional thought and, specifically, in Kant's ethics. We find the notion of the historical development of religion, in which each religion contributes to the truth.

In this early essay, Hegel draws a distinction between "objective" and "subjective" religion (later expressed in the distinction between "positive" and "negative"). However, "subjective" religion is contrasted not with what is valid, or rational, or demonstrable, but is contrasted with what is merely objective, or merely theoretical, or divorced from action. In other words, "subjective" here means "practical," while "objective" means "theoretical," or, in this context, "impractical." "Subjective" carries with it no connotation of 'individual' or 'eccentric', but refers only to the relation of a set of religious doctrines to practice. A religion, because it is defensible only by appeal to practical reason, must therefore be subjective.

In this same essay on "Folk Religion," we see Hegel's departure from Kant, who so sharply separated reason from inclination and the passions (which were overpowering inclinations). Because of this separation, Hegel claims Kant's ethics to be unworkable, for the reason that morality must consist of these two factors working together. Without much argument, Hegel simply applies the commonsense reaction to Kant that one cannot condemn a man's actions because he *wanted* to do what was also his duty. Hegel, therefore, formulates an ethics in which duty and inclination are not in conflict—an ethics of love, "which though it is a pathological principle of action, is unselfish.[3] Morality must be authorized by reason but must also conform to the passions, which are not universal but rather specific to a particular people at a particular time. Passions as well as Reason are necessary to produce right action. In his immature reaction to Kant, we may discern an attack which is recurrent in Hegel's mature works. Hegel's unsophisticated attempt to reply to Kant unfolds a most important attitude in his philosophy, the emphasis on the importance of local custom (*Sitte*) as well as universal reason, which here manifests itself as an admiration for folk society, but later manifests itself as a generous tolerance for the eccentricities of particular societies.

In the fragments of this first essay, Hegel manifests an intense hostility to Christianity as a whole, not only to theological doctrine, but to the church and even Christ himself. These passages, like passages from Nietzsche's anti-Christian writings, are gems of sarcasm and condensed vitriol. Most often, and like Nietzsche,

Hegel compares the Christians unfavorably to the Greeks:

Not only does one train the Christian mob from childhood on to pray constantly; one also tries continually to persuade them of the supreme necessity of prayer by promising its sure fulfillment. And one has piled up such a heap of reasons for comfort in misfortune . . . that we might be sorry in the end that we cannot lose a father or a mother once a week . . . It might be very interesting to compare all this with the faith of the Greeks. For them, misfortune was misfortune, pain was pain.[4]

Hegel contrasts Christ with Socrates, who fares the better, and Hegel sardonically comments that for Socrates, "the number of his closer friends was indeterminate . . . he had no mind to polish for himself a small corps that might be his bodyguard, with the same uniform, drill, passwords—a corps that would have one spirit and bear his name forever."[5] Even Christian morality is attacked, marking a major departure from Kant, who assumed that Christianity was necessary for morality. Hegel argues that Christian ethics provides us with impossible social norms. At most, these norms are workable for a group as small and as closely knit as a family, never for an entire society; but elsewhere,[6] Hegel comments that the teachings and principles of Jesus are really suitable only for lone hermitic human beings. He calls Christianity a provider of "debasing monuments of human degradation."

Hegel's intention is evident even in these early fragments. He is concerned for morality, and he is concerned for religion insofar as it serves morality, as was Kant. Where Kant simply supposed, with too little argument, that orthodox Christianity fit this role, Hegel claims that Christianity is far from moral. As illustrated by the comparison with the Greeks, Christianity's founder is not the exemplary human being (as was Socrates), and the ethics derived from Christianity is simply unworkable and therefore certainly not conducive to supporting morality. The problem, then, is to find a religion which does support morality. Beginning with an idealization of folk religion, and, specifically, attempting to reinterpret Christianity as a folk religion in which subjectivity (practice) and not doctrine is the essence, Hegel attempts to make Christianity into what Kant simply assumed that it was, morality.

In "The Life of Jesus," Hegel makes his first attempt to reformulate Christianity as a religion which will serve morality, and he begins by defining the Deity as Reason itself. The "Life of Jesus" is a popularized presentation of the categorical imperative presented by a very human Jesus in a clever but yet simple-minded attempt to equate historical Christianity with a religion whose *only* beliefs are those necessary to morality (that is, *Kant's* morality).

In "The Positivity of the Christian Religion," we have, for the first time, an extended discussion of Hegel's position vis-à-vis Kant concerning morality and Christianity. Again, we find them in essential agreement on the main problem—the nature of religion—and Hegel, like Kant, begins by affirming that:

the aim and essence of all true religion, and of our religion included, is human morality.[7]

The question now explicitly examined is whether Christianity, or the contemporary or early Christian church, or even Christ himself adequately serves this end.

At this point, Hegel reintroduces two notions found in Kant's discussion of religion, the notions of "authoritarian" or "positive" and "natural" religions—*positive* religion again being that which is founded on authority and not Reason (that is, practical reason)[8]—*natural* religion being that which is founded on morality (and therefore Reason) alone. Only a natural religion is a justifiable religion. It is obvious that the contemporary Christian church, in all its divisions, fails to meet this criterion, but furthermore, Hegel argues, even Christ himself taught a positive religion, one founded on authority and not on reason. He argues, then, that the Christian religion, from its very inception, has been unnatural and therefore unjustifiable according to the standards laid down by Kant. The church, "a system of contempt for human beings," cannot be, as Kant supposed, argued *in toto* as a postulate of practical reason in support of morality.

The last and longest of Hegel's theological essays, "The Spirit of Christianity and Its Fate," marks a prominent departure from Kant, who thus far has more or less guided the young Hegel through his attacks on Christianity. In this essay, we meet for the first time the precursors of Hegel's later notion of 'alienation' in the form of 'disharmonies' or 'separations.' We also find fully explicated for the first time those failings of Christianity which, positivity aside, make it incapable of meeting the requirements of morality. We have a return to Gotthold Lessing's notion of the partial truth of all religions:

Why shouldn't we rather see in all
positive religions nothing but the way
in which the human understanding
everywhere could not but develop
and shall continue to develop, instead
of either smiling at one of them or
getting wroth? This our scorn, this
our indignation nothing should
serve in the best world, and only
religions should deserve it? God's hand
should be involved everywhere, only not
in our errors?[9]

As Hegel's sharp criticism of Christianity begins to soften, he takes up the constructive task of looking for what is profound in Christianity rather than what is base.

The turn from Kant takes the form of two 'disharmonies' (*entzweiungen*) which lie at the very base of Kant's ethics and its supporting religious postulates. However, neither of these disharmonies can be attributed to Kant, for they are said to permeate all of Christian morality, and merely become explicitly formulated in Kant's writings. First, there is a disharmony between man and God arising from the traditional notions of the Divine. Secondly, there is a disharmony within man between reason and inclinations, making morality, as conceived by Kant, impossible. The first of these disharmonies is not adequately overcome until the *Phenomenology*, but the second is partially resolved even in these very early writings.

The disharmony of God and man is involved in any religious doctrine which teaches of a *transcendent* God, a God whose existence is somehow independent of men. A special case of such transcendence, of particular interest to Hegel, is found in traditional Christianity, where God transcends all possible experience. Kant, of course, adopts such a religious attitude in postulating a *noumenal* God in his sys-

tem, but it is clear that this postulation is nothing more than a formal statement of the belief in a God "out there" which has always been the focus of Western religion. Hegel's objection to this conception of God begins, as we ought to expect, with a demonstration of its moral inadequacy. A view of God as transcendent moral judge takes moral autonomy and responsibility out of the hands of man and places it beyond him. Man is reduced to a 'slave', and his morality is not, as it must be, derived from his own reason, but is instead imposed on him from an outside source. In fact, Hegel explicitly refers to Christianity and Judaism as "slave religions," a phrase usually attributed to Nietzsche a full century later. In this essay, however, Jesus escapes blame for this attitude, and the burden of guilt passes in full to the Jews, whom Hegel, like Nietzsche, blames for the introduction of this slavelike attitude.

Because Kant endorses and formalizes this conception of a transcendent God, his ethics is attacked as inconsistent. Kant had argued that God was a necessary postulate for morality, but he had also argued that freedom was such a postulate. Hegel argues that these two postulates conflict with each other; a transcendent God makes human moral autonomy impossible.[10] Even in these early essays, "freedom" is a key concern in Hegel's writings. In fact, this 'contradiction' between God and freedom may be taken as one of the central themes of the *Phenomenology*, which is characterized not only as the "development of Spirit," but also as the "realization of Freedom" (in the second and third parts of the *Phenomenology*, the first and third parts of the *Encyclopedia*, the third part of the *Logic*, and the entire *Philosophy of Right*). In the essay on the "Positivity," freedom is referred to as the "source of morality,"[11] and we are already given a clear indication of the nature of Hegel's perceived 'disharmony' of man and God:

But this the character (Freedom), *the*
source of morality, has been wholly
renounced by the man who has subjected
himself to the law only when compelled
by fear of his Lord's punishment; hence
when he is deprived of the theoretical
faith in this power on which he is
dependent, he is like an emancipated
slave and knows no law at all. The law
whose yoke he bore was not given by

*himself, by his reason, since he could
not regard his reason as free, as a master,
but only as a servant; . . .*[12]

Hegel's attack on this disharmony does
not contain any reference to the various
metaphysical problems of 'transcendence,'
and, specifically, contains no reference to
any problems with a postulate of a *noumenal* God. His only objection to this long-
standing Christian tradition is its contradiction with moral autonomy. This initial and
total concern for religion as a moral problem must be kept in mind throughout the
later, apparently 'metaphysical', writings
as well.

The second disharmony between reason
and the passions is given less space but far
more critical philosophical attention than
the first disharmony. Hegel argues that a
morality of formal principles (*moralität*),
a morality of practical reason which ignores the importance of the passions effects not right action but rather an internal personal war of one part of the self
against another. This bifurcated ('alienated') soul is not, as Kant had argued in
his formal statement of such a morality,
the man of true moral worth, but rather
a pathetic creature suffering from a bad
conception of morality. To make man harmonious (as his idealized early Greeks),
Hegel argues that we must replace this
conception of morality (*moralität*) with a
'higher' conception. This more advanced
notion of morality he refers to as *Sittlichkeit*, a morality which depends not only on
the universal dictates of reason, but on the
provincial dictates of *custom* (*Sitte*) as well.
Moralität is viewed here as simply a passing stage to *Sittlichkeit*, and the movement
is an early example of the sort of conceptual movement with which Hegel is occupied in all of his later works. Here we have
two opposing *conceptions* of morality, one
of which is a passing stage to the other. Of
particular interest in this essay is the fact
that it is Jesus who is said to preach
Sittlichkeit (and not *moralität* as he did in
the "Life of Jesus"). Jesus once again becomes a favored figure in Hegel's writings.

Hegel's observation of the schism between reason and passion was not original
with him. It was explicit in Kant, who did
not view it as a problem but as a given to
be considered by any moral theory. It was
of equal concern to nearly all of Hegel's
illustrious German contemporaries, most

notably, Schiller and Goethe, who contrasted fragmented modern men to the
healthy, harmonious Greeks. Given that
the separation existed, Kant had simply
attempted to work with it, but his more
literary compatriots rather cursed the lot
of modern man and looked beyond and
even worshipped the pre-Hellenic Greek.

Hegel, siding with the Romantics, condemns Kant's acceptance of the separation,
and assaults his moral philosophy as the
explicit statement of what is wrong with
contemporary morality as well as contemporary religion—an irresolvable separation between "reason and heart." (It must
be repeatedly emphasized that Hegel did
not, with the Romantics, take Reason from
its exalted position. He did emphasize,
against Kant and the Enlightenment, that
reason *alone,* without the passions, is life-
less, and Hegel, again like Nietzsche, was
adamant about assuring a proper place for
them in morality and in religion.)

It is interesting that, although both of
these philosophers looked to pre-Hellenic
Greece as an ideal of harmony between
reason and passion, Hegel is usually taken
as an extreme rationalist, in whom passion
plays no role, and Nietzsche is interpreted
as an antirational romantic, who treats
reason as "pathological" in the same way
that Kant treated the passions. Hegel insists that it is passion that propels reason,
and, in the midst of his well-known demonstration of the rationality of history, he
comments that "nothing great was accomplished in the world without passion."[13]
Similarly, both Hegel and Nietzsche turn
against *Moralität* in favor of a different
form of morality, but Nietzsche is taken
to be immoral, or at least amoral, while
Hegel is pictured as a rigid authoritarian.

According to Hegel, a man divided
against himself cannot have moral worth.
Kant's ethics only adds "rigid conceit" to
this division. According to Kant, an act or
a person has moral worth only if the act
is performed out of respect for duty alone,
and here, Hegel interprets Kant in the familiar way (which we argued against in
Chapter 1), namely, that such acts must
be performed *in contradiction to* the inclinations. Hegel argues that:

*To act in the spirit of the laws could not
have meant for him "to act out of respect
for duty and to contradict inclinations;
for both [parts of the spirit] . . . would*

have been not in the spirit of the laws but against that spirit . . .[14]

In other words, to act for the 'spirit of the laws' means to have a passion for the law, but supposedly Kant has demanded that such a will cannot be good because its respect for the law corresponds to a passion for the law. As we have seen in Chapter 1, this may be based on a serious misinterpretation of Kant, who would certainly wish to include these 'holy' persons as morally worthy. Kant himself was hardly blameless in promoting this interpretation. Much of nineteenth-century philosophy takes as a point of departure Kant's alleged treatment of the passions as "pathological" and demeaning.

Hegel does not merely argue here that Kant's ethics is therefore wrong, or, in the twist given the same charge by Nietzsche, that Kant's morality (*moralität*) is *immoral*. Instead, he argues that Kant's ethics is a phase in man's moral development, a natural and even necessary phase which began with Judaism and culminated in Kant. Such a phase must be transcended, argues Hegel, just because it undercuts its own aims. It begins with the demand that man be treated as rational, free, and morally autonomous, but then makes man a slave of himself. A man cannot be truly free unless he is free not only to obey the law (Kant's *positive* notion of freedom), but also free from the necessary frustration of his own passions. Thus morality, properly conceived, transcends *moralität* (duty to law) and becomes *Sittlichkeit*, passion for the law. Law and passion are in agreement, and moral worth is not obeyance to reason *against* the passions, but obeyance with the passion to be rational.

At this point, it is useful to compare Hegel's *Sittlichkeit* with Aristotle's "good life" (or *eudaimonia*) which Hegel would say provided a more advanced conception of "morality" than Kant's *moralität*. According to Aristotle, virtue, happiness, pleasure and the passions coalesce in the good (moral) life. It is not a sign of the virtuous man that one must act counter to passion. The virtuous man, to the contrary, has his passion in agreement with virtue. Hegel even insists that inclination and law in the good man are so closely intertwined that no longer is it "suitable" to speak of the "agreement" between them.

In a later (published) essay (1803, still before his *Phenomenology*), Hegel goes on to argue that Kant's first formulation of the categorical imperative, on which he rested the burden of adequacy of the categorical imperative in general, cannot work as a principle whose function it is to produce moral laws. Because it is a formal principle, and moral laws are principles whose importance is in their content ("What *specifically* should I do?"), the categorical imperative cannot succeed in moral legislation. In those cases in which it does seem to work, the imperative can be used just as easily to prove the contrary principle. As we noted in Chapter 1, Kant himself gives us only a few abbreviated examples of the workings of the imperative. Hegel provides us with his own examples which, remaining faithful to Kant's obscure notion of 'contradiction', prove that the categorical imperative, although it may work for a few examples which tend to prove Kant's point, will not work for many other cases. Hegel's counterexample is the universalization of the maxim to help the poor. This argument might be compared with Kant's example concerning promise keeping.[15]

When one thinks that the poor would be helped universally, then there would be either no poor at all any more or only poor people; so none would remain who could help, and in both cases help would become impossible. The maxim then, universalized, does away with itself.[16]

In order to correct this fatal flaw in Kant's ethics, Hegel reintroduces his notion of *Sittlichkeit*, and in a fashion typical of early Hegel, he returns to the Greeks as an example. *Moralität*, Kant's more or less technical notion, referred morality to formal principles, principles derived from reason alone. For all practical purposes, Hegel felt the problem of Kant's formalism —lack of content and emphasis on reason —and his denial of the relevance of the passions to moral worth were closely related if not identical problems. *Sittlichkeit* is not related only to principles or to the dictates of reason but is dependent on *custom* (*Sitte*). Morality is not universal for all time but is always tied to a *people*, to a particular stage of ethical development; the universality of morality applies only at particular places at particular times. At this stage, Hegel occasionally speaks of "absolute morality" (Absolute

Sittlichkeit), and regards the manifestation of spirit in ethical community life as the highest realization of spirit. Here "absolute" refers not to one single *correct* morality for all people, but to the correctness of a morality for a given people. Hegel has not yet turned to religion or philosophy as the highest endeavors of man, but takes as his highest ideal the Greek folk society. However, Hegel realizes that the realities of modern life make realization of this ancient ideal totally impossible, and one of the personal confusions in his philosophy, not fully resolved until the *Phenomenology,* is the reconciliation of this ideal with the demand that philosophy should not be wishfully idealistic. When he did resolve this confusion, it was by removing *Sittlichkeit* from its exalted position and replacing it with the higher realizations of Spirit in art, religion, and philosophy.

The Purpose of Hegel's System
Hegel does give us a straightforward statement regarding the goal of his system, but this statement is as unenlightening as it is misleadingly simple. The purpose of philosophy is to find the *truth.* This goal is reiterated in the same superficially simple claim in the Preface and Introduction to the *Phenomenology,* in the Introduction to the *Science of Logic,* and in the comprehensive *Encyclopedia.* However, it would seem that every intellectual discipline would have an equal claim to the truth as its goal, and Hegel states that 'truth' is the goal of not only every intellectual discipline, but of every human activity. The truth which is searched for by philosophy (and, Hegel adds in the *Encyclopedia,* by religion) is not the limited, 'conditioned', 'nonsystematic' truths searched for by science, mathematics, and the practical disciplines of ethics and politics, but *truth* itself, the Absolute Truth. The purpose of Hegel's system is to give us knowledge which is absolute, of a truth which is absolute.

However, this characterization of Hegel's goals in terms of truth is not only too simplified to serve as an adequate summary of Hegel's philosophy, but it is seriously misleading. The "search for truth" sounds very much like a host of disciplines which are clearly not of interest for systematic philosophy. For example, "the search for truth" is so characteristic of empirical science that it is all to easy to think that Hegel takes philosophy to be a science differing from physics only in its scope. Because Hegel speaks of his own philosophy as 'science', and because of his fascination for detail in filling in his system, we are often confronted with interpretations to the effect that Hegel foolishly thought that philosophy can give us empirical truths (for example, some of the specific scientific theories mentioned in the first part of the *Phenomenology,* or some of the historical data mentioned in his many lectures on history). However, it must be clear from the outset that Hegel expects of philosophy only one sort of truth, that which is absolute, and makes no attempt to derive, in fact explicitly denies the possibility of deriving, specific nonphilosophical truth from his system. By 'science', Hegel means nothing like 'empirical' or 'natural' science, and science of that sort occupies only the initial and therefore least mature stage of the development of consciousness. Furthermore, the search for truth sounds too much like a purely theoretical endeavor, but Hegel emphasizes throughout his mature as well as his early works the *practical* aspects of his philosophy. For Hegel, the truth is the goal of ethics, politics, and religion as well as for science and mathematics.

Most importantly, the stress on the notion of *truth* makes the system look as if it is primarily an epistemological enterprise, which, at best, is an only partially adequate interpretation of Hegel's philosophy. We said above that Hegel's philosophy has an important practical aspect, and this aspect is constantly with us in Hegel's discussion of morality and religion (objective and absolute spirit). Christianity, the penultimate stage to the highest (philosophical) truth, remains from the very earliest writings the focal point of Hegel's philosophical activity. However, like Kant, Hegel found that his ultimate interests in morality and religion required a preliminary investigation of the possibility of knowledge in these areas. So, like Kant, Hegel begins his philosophy with an investigation of knowledge and the examination of the faculties of knowledge in order to defend morality and Christianity against their detractors from the sciences.

In the early 'theological' writings, we have already identified several concerns that Hegel carries with him throughout his mature philosophical writings. In subject matter, his interests are religious and moral, and in this sense, Hegel's lectures on Religion and his *Philosophy of Right* may be thought of not so much as particular applications of Hegel's metaphysics, but as the culmination and *raison d'etre* of his entire philosophy. In his earliest writings, Hegel is concerned with the 'rationality' of the Christian religion, the extent to which its teachings and practices can be justified by appeal to reason alone. In these early essays, we have seen that Hegel first argues that Christianity fits this rational ideal insofar as it coincides with Kant's morality,[17] but then turns upon Christianity for its "positivity' and its failure to adequately support Kant's morality. Because Christianity and Jesus himself make constant reference to authority of God and to miracles, the religion is far from rational. Because the religion puts such emphasis on man as God's servant and on reward and punishment, it fails to meet Kant's ideal. In the earliest writings, we already see Hegel's immature attempts to reinterpret Christianity as a natural 'folk religion'; in the *Phenomenology,* we see the same kind of attempt in full maturity, where Hegel reintroduces Christianity as the 'revealed religion' whose rationality is demonstrated by its place in Hegel's system.

From these earlier works, we have identified two crucial 'disharmonies' or 'separations' which lay at the basis of Hegel's departure from Kant and from traditional Christianity. First, traditional *moralität* contains a fatal disharmony between Reason (duty) and passion (personal interest). Second, the 'disharmony' between God and man, based on the notion of a transcendent God, produces an irresolvable disharmony in Christianity and in any morality which seeks to support itself with the postulate of a transcendent God. According to Hegel in the essay on "Positivity," if we take the notion of a transcendent God seriously, we have a conflict with Kant's postulate of freedom; one cannot have both an omniscient, omnipotent being and maintain the postulate of autonomy. The problem here lies with Kant's central notion of the *Summum Bonum,* and Hegel points out, ineptly in the early writing, that such a notion undermines the support of Christianity by making God into an authority figure and inconsistent with autonomy of human action. This 'disharmony' becomes a key problem in each of the mature writings; the resolution of the 'disharmony' between God and man is the overall goal of the entire *Phenomenology,* of the entire *Encyclopedia*, and even of the entire *Logic*. This disharmony is only resolved in the final realization of "spirit," and in fact, is responsible for the notion of "spirit" in Hegel's philosophy. It is the driving force behind the movement in all Hegel's works from the particular (individual men, individual moralities) to the universal and is the simple motivation for Hegel's philosophically complex attempts to "make one" or synthesize the subjective and the objective. It is this 'disharmony' arising from the traditional notion of a transcendent God which leads Hegel to reject this notion and demonstrate the reality of an *immanent* God. This God is *Spirit* and the Hegelian system the demonstration of its realization.

To understand the mature Hegel is to comprehend the connection between the early religious-moral concerns and the later concern with 'truth', Kant's *Critique,* and the peculiar expository form of the mature system. If Hegel is interested in reinterpreting and justifying Christianity and in correcting certain inadequacies in Kant's moral philosophy, why could he not simply have written an essay on Christianity, as he once intended to do with his essay on the "Positivity"? Or he might have written a short book based on Lessing's very short "Education of Mankind." Or why could he not have written a brief pamphlet on Kant's morality extending the ideas of his essay on "Natural Right" of 1803? Why need these concerns be dealt with in systematic works the shortest of which (the *Phenomenology*) is over 800 pages in length? Why need a system dealing with the problem so simply stated in the earliest essays include not only religion and morality but all of philosophy, religion, history, and, in fact, all human culture in its broadest possible conception? To understand this need, we must return not only to Kant's ethico-religious philosophy, but to his critique of metaphysics as well.

Summarily, Hegel is interested in the subject matter of Kant's second *Critique—* the nature of morality and its supporting postulates of God, freedom, and immortality. Hegel's early attacks on Kantian morality and traditional Christianity had made no appeal to the Kantian *Critique of Pure Reason*. It is possible that Hegel had not even read the first *Critique* before he wrote his early essays. Hegel's knowledge of Kant at this time may have been limited to the *Religion Within the Bounds of Reason Alone,* which was published while Hegel was studying for his theology degree and in the same year that he wrote the first of his 'theological' essays. Hegel's objection to the notion of a transcendent God thus far had no reference to Kant's piercing *Critique of Pure Reason* and demonstration of the impossibility of knowing noumenal objects. Hegel's objections had been strictly religious and moral, without the reference he later makes to the origins of these problems in Kant's first *Critique.* In the period preceding the writing of the *Phenomenology,* Hegel takes increasing concern with Kant's *Critique of Pure Reason.* The *Phenomenology,* far from being a simple tract on religion and morals, finds itself confronting the whole of Kant's *Critique* of metaphysics.

In Hegel, as in Kant, we have found the demand that religion must be *rational* and justified by demonstration of its necessity for practical reason or morality. In Kant's second *Critique,* this demand was argued to be satisfied by appeal to a *Summum Bonum,* a *rational universe* in which virtue and happiness were commensurate. This notion of a rational universe in which the real and the ideal are identical might be interpreted quite plausibly as the defining philosophical attitude of nineteenth-century thought. Underlying the philosophies of both Kant and Hegel, and also Fichte, Schelling, and the many lesser figures of the German Enlightenment is the demand for order and rationality, and the business of philosophy is taken to be the explication and proof of this order and rationality. In Kant's philosophy, this took the form of the postulates of practical reason, but in Hegel's thought, the rationality of the development of spirit was not simply a necessary presupposition of morality, but the highest and absolute philosophical truth. For Hegel, the recognition of this rationality of spirit meant that the story of mankind need not be viewed as a meaningless history of atrocities and stupidity, but might be viewed as *progress.* With the realization of this ideal of rationality, the present could be viewed not simply as a new time period, but as a result of and an improvement on and even a culmination of the centuries of the past.

The demand for *teleological* explanation is continuously implicit throughout Kant's

works, but is often defended by him only as a form of explanation of secondary importance. In the first *Critique* Kant argues the universality and necessity of the Principle of Universal Causation, and thus takes causal explanation to be explanation proper. In the *Critique of Judgment,* where we receive a detailed analysis of teleological explanation, Kant argues that teleological explanation is demanded when causal or mechanistic explanation is not available. Kant insists that there are kinds of situations in which causal explanations are not available, most importantly, in situations where the event to be explained is the action of a moral agent, but Kant's generally scientific bent makes it unquestionably clear that teleological explanation should be used cautiously and sparingly. Against this Kantian caution, Fichte came to take teleological explanation as the highest form of explanation, and Hegel, borrowing from Fichte, took teleological explanation as the central methodology of his entire philosophy. In Hegel, teleological explanation is not to be reserved for those cases in which causal explanations fail; teleological explanation is explanation, and the business of philosophy is to explain, or to *rationalize* its subject matter by relating it to its ultimate *end* or *purpose.*

However, Hegel's divergence from Kant does not consist solely in the scope and primacy which he allotted to teleology, but also in Hegel's insistence that teleological explanation must be *demonstrated.* Kant had defended the *Summum Bonum,* the ultimate rationality of the universe, as a necessary presupposition of morality and argued that one could not justify morality unless the seemingly purposeless mechanism of natural law and the rationality of justice and virtue coincided. Kant proved only that the *Summum Bonum* was a necessary presupposition of morality, not that this presupposition was *actual.* As we argued in Chapter 1, the proof of the necessity of the *Summum Bonum* for morality demonstrates neither the actuality of the *Summum Bonum* nor the objective validity of the morality it is needed to support. Rather, Kant proves only that *if* morality is objectively valid, *then* the postulates of God, freedom, and immortality must be true. This, however, does not constitute a proof of these postulates, and it is possible that the postulates are false and morality not valid. Unless there is some independent justification of these principles, in short, some proof of the *Summum Bonum,* we have no proof of the objective validity of morality.

Kant does not offer us any such demonstration, and therefore his entire moral philosophy fails in its central ambition, to demonstrate the rationality of morality. He further fails, however, to demonstrate the rationality of the religious postulates (of Christianity), for their necessity for practical reason is a rational justification of them only if it can also be shown that practical reason itself is objectively valid. Because of the circular defense of morality in terms of God and immortality and the postulates of God and immortality in terms of morality, Kant has failed to demonstrate both the validity of morality and the rationality of religion.

Hegel clearly recognizes this deficiency in Kant's moral philosophy, and a crucial problem for his philosophy is the demonstration not simply that the postulates of practical reason are necessary for moral consciousness, but also that they are *true.* The task of the *Phenomenology of Spirit,* Hegel's first systematic work, is the demonstration of the necessary truth of these postulates which Kant had only assumed.

The problems involved in such a demonstration, however, had been made explicit in Kant's *Critique of Pure Reason.* These postulates pretended to give us knowledge of noumenal objects, of the world-as-it-is-in-itself. Kant argued that the demand for rationality of the world-in-itself was a demand not only of practical reason, but also a disposition of theoretical (or pure or speculative) reason. However, this disposition was necessarily to be frustrated by the very nature of reason. The *Transcendental Dialectic* had supposedly dealt a death blow to any pretensions of reason to such knowledge. The *transcendent* objects of God and noumenal self (or Soul), because they are beyond the bounds of sensibility, are 'unconditioned', can be conceived of only through a misuse of the categories, and therefore cannot be known at all. Consequently, Kant argues that the disposition of reason to know the unconditioned or the "absolute" (a term occurring in Aristotle and Kant as well as in Hegel) is necessarily illusory. Knowledge of ultimate reality or ultimate purpose cannot be gained from pure reason, but, as we have seen, neither can it be gained by appeal to prac-

tical reason as Kant supposed, for practical reason itself requires the presupposition of such knowledge.

The purpose of Hegel's system may thus be related to Kant's critical philosophy in two ways: first, Hegel, like Kant, wishes to prove those principles of God, freedom, and immortality to be true, but, unlike Kant, argues that showing these principles to be mere postulates does not constitute such a proof. Secondly, Kant has argued that these principles cannot be *known* by us because of the limitations on reason argued in the first *Critique.* Hegel argues that if we cannot know that the world has an ultimate purpose, that is, is rational, and that there is an unconditioned Supreme Being responsible for this purpose, and that the human soul can survive its earthly body to share the rewards of the Kingdom of God, then it makes no sense to speak of the rationality of religion. Therefore, Hegel must prove that Kant's critique of knowledge is not correct, and that we can have knowledge of unconditioned things as they are in-themselves. The peculiar expository form of the system is largely due to the necessity of refuting Kant's critique of knowledge.[18]

The Phenomenology of Spirit

The Phenomenology of Spirit[19] is Hegel's first attempt to present his 'system' of philosophy. Far from being merely a system of philosophy, the *Phenomenology* is an attempt to provide *the* system of philosophy, to absorb the whole of Western thought in a single linear development. For this ambition alone, the *Phenomenology* deserves its place in Western philosophy. The conception of the book, in spite of its great difficulty, its often seemingly arbitrary or tedious inclusion of materials, is itself a remarkable feat of philosophizing. Hegel refuses to begin with basic undemonstrable propositions, as did Descartes, Spinoza, and Fichte, to name a few, for this would make the entire philosophy dependent or "conditioned" by this first principle. Rather, Hegel claims that his philosophy has 'no beginning', for his philosophy is not simply the presentation of a philosophical position, but is the presentation of *philosophy* itself, and the mature Hegel constantly refers to his works as simply 'philosophy'. Rather than begin with a premise, Hegel begins by taking up all the philosophies of the past, and (his) philosophy is shown to grow from these as their fruition. Hegel's inclusion of all previous philosophies is not a gratuitous display of scholarship, but the very essence of the system.

The stated goal of philosophy is Absolute Truth, the attainment of absolute knowledge. The philosophies of the past, Hegel complains, have given us only partial truths. However, philosophy is not conceived as an isolated intellectual effort but as spiritual development made explicit. More general than various philosophies, there have been various *stages of consciousness,* of which philosophy is the explicit conceptual manifestation. These have also given us truths which were not absolute, but limited or conditioned. The purpose of the system, therefore, and the *Phenomenology* in particular, is to examine these inferior forms of consciousness with their partial truths to find out how we will be forced to progress to the Absolute Truth. The *Phenomenology* makes no less bold a claim than its own significance as the culmination and fulfillment of all previous thought.

Hegel often tells us that he is doing "speculative philosophy." This is most often interpreted as a return to speculative metaphysics—the fare of Spinoza and Leibniz—the investigation of transcendent objects or 'noumena'. However, this interpretation fails with the most superficial investigation of the actual contents of Hegel's works. By "speculation," Hegel does not mean 'speculation about noumena', but rather something closer to 'reflection and rationalization'. Philosophy, as a purely 'reflective science', always looks back on and tries to understand a set of already given material. Philosophy is the attempt to derive *meaning* from material, and because philosophy is the most general quest for knowledge and value, its function is to find meaning in or attempt to understand the whole of human intellectual and cultural development. In other words, philosophy as a reflective science makes it nothing like our ordinary concept of 'science'. It does not formulate hypotheses about why something happens or try to subsume one event under a general class of events. It rather *reinterprets* a past series of phenomena in such a way that it can be demonstrated that this series led up to some end. In other words, the business of philosophy is *post hoc* teleological explanation. Thus, philosophy, unlike the natural sciences, does not claim

predictability as one of its results. The Hegelian dialectic, as Hegel himself repeatedly insists, can be used to predict nothing (compare Marx for whom prediction is the primary use of historical 'Dialectical' understanding).

An understanding of this attitude towards philosophy is of the utmost importance in understanding the mature system. By "rationalization," a term which Hegel uses, he does not intend to suggest an imaginative but false causal or pseudo-causal accounting of past phenomena, as connoted by the recent Freudian use of "rationalization" to refer to a mildly pathological ego-defense mechanism. Rationalization in philosophy is not a personal rationalization, but in Hegel's terms is *objective* and will become evident to anyone who works his way through the system, that is, who traces the development of culture, or concepts, or art through the hierarchy in which Hegel has arranged them. However, the sequence of events or 'stages' in the various forms of the dialectic are often not in proper historical order at all. In the *Phenomenology,* the stages of Spirit include modes of thought unmistakably identifiable as Kantian before modes of thought of the Roman Stoical philosophers, and these before modes of thought clearly attributable to the pre-Socratic Greeks. In the *Logic,* there is little reason to suppose that the acquisition of concepts in young babies, or the acquisition of these concepts for mankind as a whole, follows anything like the sequence marked by Hegel. Hegel's *Logic* is nothing like the psychology of logic as developed by Piaget or as carried out by other learning theorists which hypothesizes how people *in fact* learn to use concepts. Hegel's sequences are arranged a priori, and not on the basis of any experimental-empirical basis. Similarly, Hegel arranges the various stages of art in a manner which cannot conceivably be interpreted as a strict historical interpretation.

Yet, it is clear that the historical presentation of this system cannot be ignored. The system is not merely a historical interpretation, is not in any way an attempt to show causal accounts between stages (although this can be found in some works, for example, the philosophy of history), and in no way attempts to predict the future. In this sense, Hegel's philosophy is 'timeless' or outside of time, not in the sense usually argued to the effect that

Hegel argues the unreality of time, but rather in the sense that Hegel's philosophy consists of nothing more than this *post hoc* rationalization. Philosophy is concerned with understanding the past, and the present as an end to the past. It is this view of philosophy, more than any particular theses within it, that will force Kierkegaard to denounce the Hegelian foundations of early nineteenth-century thought.

Knowledge of Things-in-Themselves[20]

With Kant's distinction between noumena and phenomena, it becomes impossible for us to know anything as it is in-itself. Once the distinction is made between the world-for-us and the world-independent of us, there can be no escape from the conclusion that we can know only the world as it is for-us. Hegel's search for absolute knowledge depends on a rejection of this distinction. In the introduction to the *Phenomenology*, Hegel begins his attack on Kant's theory of knowledge by attacking just this distinction, which he claims is based on an unanalyzed and undefended metaphor in which knowledge is considered a "tool with which one masters the Absolute." If knowledge is a tool, there must be a certain necessary distortion due to the operations of knowledge on reality, and therefore we can never know reality (the Absolute) itself but only as it has been manipulated and distorted by the instrument of knowledge. We can, therefore, have only mediated knowledge of the absolute, and never know the absolute itself. This is Kant's problem in the first *Critique*, and his solution to it is the critical doctrine that we never know reality independent of the distortions imposed on it by knowledge. The best that can be done by the philosopher is an exploration of the nature of this tool of knowledge and the necessary distortions it imposes on reality. Kant's *Critique*, therefore, abandons the search for absolute reality and simply investigates the tool by which we come to know (in a distorted way) reality. In short, Hegel argues that the premise of the whole of Kant's philosophy is

before one attempts to know God, the essence of things, etc., one must first investigate the capacity of knowledge itself, to see whether it is able to accomplish such tasks. One must first become acquainted with the instrument, before one undertakes the work which is to be accomplished by means of it.[21]

But why should we accept this metaphor? Kant never examines or defends this metaphorical starting point, and Hegel even ascribes not very commendable motives to Kant's adoption of it:

It [the fear of error in Kantian philosophy] starts with ideas of knowledge as an instrument, and as a medium; and presupposes a distinction of ourselves from this knowledge.[22]

By beginning with the investigation of the faculties of knowledge, Kant has already determined the critical outcome of his first *Critique*. Once the distinction between things as known and things in themselves or between reality-for-a-subject and absolute reality are introduced, one must conclude that we cannot have any but conditioned knowledge and that the demands of traditional metaphysics are utterly impossible. However, Kant, according to Hegel, offers no justification for this starting point and, more importantly, fails to see fatal problems inherent in this approach. First, the metaphor simply plays on the notions 'truth', 'reality' and 'knowledge', and, given Kant's distinctions, Hegel argues that what he ought to have concluded was that we can have no knowledge at all, that our cognitive faculties are such that we can never know the truth. Secondly, Hegel argues that one cannot begin by investigating the faculties of knowledge before one attempts to gain knowledge in philosophy, for the investigation itself already utilizes these faculties and their concepts. Any such analysis is covertly circular.

The first criticism is that Kant, on the basis of this metaphor, distinguishes between two different sorts of knowledge, two different kinds of truth. There is limited or conditional knowledge giving us truth limited by the conditions of our cognitive faculties, and there is absolute or unconditioned knowledge of things as they are in themselves which human consciousness cannot have. This distinction is of a piece with the noumena-phenomena distinction, for absolute 'knowledge' of noumena would be of a very different sort than our conditioned knowledge of phenomena.

Kant claims that we cannot have knowledge of noumena, but we can have genuine knowledge of phenomena—limited knowledge. What is such limited or conditioned knowledge? According to Hegel:

... pointless talk like this leads in the long run to a confused distinction between an absolute truth and a truth of some other sort. ... [23]

This limited truth is indeed truth only if it is in accordance with reality—with the way things really are—in other words, with Absolute Truth. If it is a limited truth that all events must be temporally ordered (for us), then this limited truth is a truth only if it is true that all events really must be ordered. If events are not really so ordered, but rather we order them, then this limited truth is a falsehood, even if it is *necessary for us*. (Nietzsche will argue that *all* of our necessary truths are such 'falsehoods'). Similarly, our conditioned or limited knowledge is really knowledge only if it is in agreement with what is really true. If we have conditional knowledge that there exist objects 'outside' us due to the nature of our cognition, this knowledge is true knowledge and not false (but necessary) belief only if there truly are such objects. In other words, truth is Absolute Truth; knowledge is Absolute Knowledge; the 'real' world is the world as it is in itself, whether that is the world of our experience or not. The whole point of Kant's 'transcendental idealism' is to shift the significances of 'knowledge', 'truth', and 'reality' from the notion of a world-in-itself to a "real world of appearances." Hegel argues this shift is nothing but an absurd play on words, for as long as we hold to the possibility of a world-in-itself different from the world we know and experience, we *must* talk only of the noumenal world as the real or true world, and speak of knowledge only with relationship to this noumenal world. The world as it appears is the 'real' world only insofar as it conforms to the *real* world, and our knowledge of it is knowledge only insofar as it conforms to the *real* world. In other words, because of his dualist metaphor of knowledge as tool and reality as that which is to be known, Kant is ultimately committed to the same skepticism as Hume. To know something is to know it as it is, to know the truth, but to know something only as it appears—as it is experienced—is not knowledge at all. Thus, this dichotomy between noumena and phenomena leads one to the intolerable skeptical conclusion that we can never know the world as it is in itself, and that it is possible that we have no knowledge of reality at all. In order to avoid this conclusion, Hegel, like many prominent American philosophers in this century, becomes a violent antidualist, attempting to rid philosophy of these dualisms and their conclusions.

Hegel's reason for rejecting this dualism is not simply its skeptical conclusions; the preliminary investigation of knowledge, which is part and parcel of the Kantian "knowledge as tool" metaphor, is logically ill-conceived. Kant argues that philosophy must begin by examining those faculties which purport to give us knowledge, but with what do we examine these faculties? The investigation of the understanding must itself be carried out by the understanding; Kant demands that we use our instrument on itself before it is used at all. A preliminary investigation of the tool of knowledge is already a use of that tool. Hegel agrees with Kant that philosophy must begin with an investigation of knowledge, but unlike Kant he recognizes that this investigation cannot be independent of the use of the faculties of knowledge. The investigation of knowledge by itself cannot be thought of as a preliminary investigation which leaves its subject matter untouched, since its subject matter is itself. Kant believed that we could first investigate knowledge, find out what it can do, and then use these faculties in appropriate ways. Hegel argues that the investigation of knowledge changes that very knowledge, and that such an investigation can never be preliminary, but constitutes the whole of philosophical investigation. The critique of knowledge is the development of knowledge as well.

Once we appreciate this problem as Hegel perceived it, we are in an excellent position to understand the necessity for the peculiar dialectical structure of his work, particularly of the *Phenomenology*. Knowledge *develops* with our conceptual sophistication. This is not to say merely that as we learn more, our knowledge increases; rather, the *kind* of knowledge changes (compare Marx's derivative claim that changes in quantity become changes in quality). Specifically, knowledge changes *in kind* when we come to question the faculties of knowledge, when we question not the world, but ourselves. For Kant, self-knowledge was either empirical knowledge of ourselves as objects or transcendental knowledge which could disclose only the necessary *forms* of our consciousness. But, according to Kant, we could not have *knowledge* of ourselves in any other sense (e.g., as moral agent or as immortal soul). Neither could we have *knowledge* of things-in-themselves. For Hegel, knowledge of objects and transcendental self-knowledge are but two stages in the attainment of further kinds of knowledge, knowledge of oneself as *Spirit,* and knowledge of objects as they are in-themselves.

Ultimately, one can have knowledge which is neither limited to an 'objective' world nor to the sphere of consciousness but in which these two kinds of knowledge are unified into a single form of knowledge. In other words, Hegel argues that knowledge progresses not simply in its content, but that the *form* of knowledge progresses as our conception of 'knowledge' becomes more sophisticated. Kant saw the more sophisticated levels, but was caught with an inadequate conception of knowledge that prohibited him from seeing the consequences of his *Critique.* This unsophisticated conception of knowledge has now been surpassed by Kant himself, although unintentionally, in his self-conscious *Critique.* One must cease to take 'objective' knowledge as paradigm of knowledge, and see as the ultimate end of all knowledge the highest or Absolute Truth. One must move beyond this kind of knowledge to a level on which philosophical problems, such as the skeptical conclusions of Hume and Kant, may be surpassed. The traditional conception of knowledge utilized by Kant gives rise to paradoxes which can be overcome only by developing a more adequate conception of knowledge. The *Phenomenology* is just this development, starting with the lowest forms of knowledge, showing how these are inadequate to other forms, and culminating in Absolute Truth in which all of the problems, paradoxes and inadequacies of the lower forms disappear.

Philosophy, for Hegel, is the demonstration of the 'becoming' of absolute knowledge. Such a becoming *need* not be the pattern of development of any particular individual consciousness, and the development of knowledge in the system is not the psychological development of an individual. The "forms of consciousness" or forms of knowledge derived in the *Phenomenology* lead to absolute knowledge, that level of conceptual development where all conceptual (philosophical) problems disappear. This stage of knowledge eliminates traditional philosophical dichotomies, and is not one-sidedly oriented either toward the natural world (as is science) nor towards the knowing subject (as in Kant's self-analysis), nor towards dogmatism (the ultimate consequence of the first one-sided conception), nor idealism (the ultimate consequence of the second). This stage of knowledge recognizes the inadequacies of traditional theories of knowledge, and replaces them by demonstrating how the rejection of traditional dichotomies solves the problems inherent in them. The development of the system is simply the ordering of these stages in a hierarchy of more sophisticated forms. The purpose of this ordering is to demonstrate how each level corrects inadequacies of the previous conceptual level and how it is possible to correct all these inadequacies in a final step. This step is the realization of the Absolute (absolute truth) in the *Phenomenology.*

Spirit

No notion is more central to Hegel's mature philosophy than the notion of *Geist,* sometimes translated as "Mind" (for example, by Baillie in his often-used translation), but better translated as the more vague and religious-tinged notion of "Spirit." Spirit is the 'subject' of Hegel's *Phenomenology,* and it is the development of Spirit with which the entire book is concerned. It is also Spirit, as the *Idea,* which is the subject of the *Science of Logic.* Spirit, however, is not simply the subject *matter* of these books, but the subject in the special sense of being He whose thoughts are recorded in this book. We have said that the *Phenomenology,* and the system as a whole, may be considered something very much like an "autobiography of God." In fact, it becomes very clear from the way that Hegel talks about Spirit that Spirit is equivalent to the Divine. Although Hegel rarely uses the term "God," it is clear that his notion of Spirit occupies the same position in his philosophy that the established vocabulary of Christianity plays in traditional philosophy. It is also clear that Spirit is something very human, for the development of Spirit we find in the *Phenomenology* is clearly the development of human thought. From our initial considerations of Hegel's early religious interests, specifically his concern with the 'disharmony' of God and man, we may already surmise that Hegel's attempt to reinterpret the traditional Christian notion of God as Immanent God is to be performed through the notion of Spirit, which is both human and divine.

Spirit is also referred to as "The Truth," with which it is identical (the entire *Phenomenology* is the demonstration of this equivalence) and thus is also referred to as the Absolute Truth or simply the Absolute. In the *Logic,* this same Spirit is referred to as the "Idea" or the "Notion" (*Begriff,* sometimes translated as "The Concept"). As Hegel expresses it, the culmination of the development of Spirit is its becoming the Idea, or Absolute Idea, which is sometimes expressed as "absolute Spirit" ("The Absolute" again). In Hegel's terminology with regard to Spirit, we find a simple, but easily confusing ambiguity. Spirit and Truth are (is) the subject of the system, specifically the *Phenomenology,* from the very beginning. Yet we do not really have Spirit and Truth until the end of the system. Thus, we find initially perplexing statements such as:

Of the Absolute it must be said that it is essentially a result, that only at the end is it what it is in very (sic) truth.[24]

Although we cannot fully explain this ambiguity until we discuss the detailed development of Spirit, we may simply state the problem. Hegel sometimes uses "Truth" or "Spirit" in a 'conditioned' or qualified sense. This is the sense in which Spirit has not yet reached its full development but is only *potentially* spirit or truth (such as manifested in traditional philosophy). When it fulfills its development, it is Spirit or Truth absolutely and unconditionally. To illustrate with a metaphor of which Hegel is fond, one can speak of the development of a 'tree', although the tree in question is only an acorn or a small twig. We speak of the development of the tree, but the tree is a tree only in the sense of its potential to be a tree. It is *really* a tree only when it has completed this development. Similarly, Hegel's notion of the development of Spirit leads to the same sort of 'ambiguity' in discussing "Spirit." Spirit is not really Spirit until the completion of its development. Thus, when Hegel implies that Spirit is not always Spirit or that "spirit is becoming," or that "spirit becomes in the end what it always has been in reality," this is not at all confusing if we keep the tree metaphor in mind.

Hegel is fond of speaking of Spirit as the Whole or the Totality. In some of his interpreters (notably, Royce), Spirit is identical to the Universe (Hegel does use the term "universal," but rarely "the universe"). Because of the popularity of this interpretation, which is correct only in a very qualified sense, Hegel has often been taken to be a pantheist, an interpretation which is reinforced by his well-known admiration for Spinoza. However, one of the most important characteristics of Spirit, which Hegel claims is also one of the key points to be demonstrated by the system, is the existence of Spirit as "subject as well as substance." Spirit, as we find at the end of the *Phenomenology* and the *Logic,* is the "merging of the subject and the ob-subject" and "the universal subject." Most important in Hegel's insistence on Spirit as subject is his denial of Spinoza's pantheism. For Hegel, following Kant (for reasons we shall soon see), Spirit is not merely a *substance,* either mental or physical. For Descartes there is physical substance and mental substance. For Spinoza, these were two *modes* of God. For Hegel, these are God but God as subject as well as (physical) substance. It is debatable how great the alleged difference is between Hegel and Spinoza. Surely there are differences: for example, Spinoza is a determinist, Hegel is not. But Hegel's peculiar theism is remarkably similar to that of Spinoza, but cast in a Kantian mold.

The problem in understanding the meaning of Spirit and its many related terms is due to Hegel's own insistence and the insistence of so many of his commentators that his terminology cannot be understood until the system as a whole is understood. Thus, the tendency is to go through the entire development of Spirit before attempting to understand what it is that is developing. Of course, we carry some vague notions with us; for example, we see that it is a religious concept, that it is a world Spirit not an individual human spirit, but yet it is somehow 'in' humanity. All this vagueness is unnecessary, for Hegel's notion is a clear derivative of a notion we have already discussed which is central to Kant's philosophy, namely the *transcendental ego.* Although this connection is often recognized, most commentators treat Hegel's notion of Spirit as a sort of bastardization or pilfering of Kant's notion or else a serious misunderstanding. Hegel, in fact, considers himself as improving on certain inconsistencies in Kant's notion which we have already discussed. For Kant, the transcendental ego is a pure ego, the "self itself," and not the self as appearance (empirical ego). Therefore, it cannot be understood under the categories, for it is not phenomenon. The status of this ego is purely as a postulate, argued to exist transcendentally from the facts of empirical consciousness. Therefore, whatever can be said about this transcendental ego can be argued only transcendentally, but Kant provides many such arguments. His entire set of categories and the pure forms of perception can be said to be properties of the transcendental ego, for these have been shown transcendentally to be necessary for experience and understanding. Furthermore, Kant argues in his second *Critique* that we must ascribe certain other properties to this ego, such as freedom of action and moral sensitivity. However, key to all these transcendental arguments is the requirement of *universality,* that what has been argued to be true for the transcendental ego must be true of all transcendental egos. In other words, the transcendental deduction is thought to be valid just because its categories are necessary for any human consciousness. Similarly the argument in the second *Critique* is thought to be valid because the postulates of practical reason and the moral law itself are thought valid for any rational being whatever.

This requirement of universality for any ascription to the transcendental ego is precisely what destroys Kant's thesis. Kant continually talks of transcendental egos and in such a way that it is clear that there is a one-one correspondence between transcendental egos and persons. This becomes most clear in his second *Critique* where he speaks constantly of other moral selves, other free agents. Kant never seemed to doubt that such an assumption was consistent with the rest of his theory. A preliminary objection might be simply to question Kant's supposition that there are other minds. This would not be an inconsistency in Kant for the problem of other minds does not seem to be any more difficult for him than for any philosopher attacking this same problem. (With reference to this second *Critique,* he could argue the existence of other conscious beings simply as a postulate of practical reason, on the grounds that doing one's duty to others is not rational unless there are other conscious beings.) Kant's dilemma is much more serious. His problem is not whether there are other minds, or

even other transcendental egos, but what sense it makes to say even that I have an ego, or what it could even mean to say there is another ego or another three billion egos in the world. The reason for this is simply that Kant's concept of the transcendental ego makes individuation of transcendental egos impossible. The transcendental ego, being transcendental, is not subject to the categories of unity and multiplicity, and Kant's requirement of universality precludes the possibility of ascribing any property to 'one' transcendental ego that cannot be ascribed to all. There is nothing to differentiate any 'two' transcendental egos, and therefore no grounds to say they are different in any property except number. Kant never questioned the assumption of a one-one correlation between egos. He simply differentiated them by differentiating persons, or perhaps persons' bodies. However, there is no basis for this assumption in Kant; the transcendental ego cannot be argued to require a body within Kant's system for it is necessary only for experience. The experience of having a body is not one which requires a body and certainly does not require one body per ego.

In short, Kant has no way of individuating transcendental egos; by his own admission they have no distinguishable properties. The problem is just beginning, however, for it does not even make sense to ascribe numerical identity to them. On the one hand, since they are transcendental, the categories of unity and plurality and the category of substance do not apply, so that the principles of the understanding cannot even say whether there is one transcendental ego per man. Secondly, the fact that the transcendental ego is simply necessary for experience, and the experience for which it is necessary itself is unified by the ego, that is, identified as the experiences of that subject, the only possibility of differentiating experiences would seem to be the possibility of differentiating experiences of a particular ego. Then our only recourse is to go back to the assumption that subjects can only be differentiated by differentiating persons. Yet this currently acceptable conclusion is clearly closed to Kant, because his very characterization of the transcendental ego makes it impossible for him to assume that it has any properties, for example, location 'within' a body, which can differentiate it from any other ego.

If it makes no sense to speak of "my transcendental ego" as opposed to "your transcendental ego," then how can we talk about the transcendental ego consistently with Kant's derivation of it? The answer is that we can still speak of categories of experience and forms of perception and even of a moral ego and an ego with freedom of action. We can no longer make any commitment as to the number of such egos or the differentiation of them. We can simply speak of "transcendental ego" without thereby indicating individuality.[25]

But this notion of transcendental ego without the possibility of individuation is precisely Hegel's notion of Spirit. For Hegel, the transcendental ego is literally a general or universal consciousness, as it *ought* to have been for Kant. Hegel's *Spirit* is Kant's transcendental ego without commitment concerning its number or individuation. Spirit is simply the general postulated unifier of experience and understanding. Hegel does sometimes speak as if there is *one* general transcendental ego, which of course is equally inconsistent with its basic meaning, but these slips are not frequent and most often are due to Hegel's insistence upon personifying transcendental ego into a divine subject. This is not serious. Because Spirit is simply subject, Hegel can speak of it as subject without ever committing himself to any sort of differentiation. The mistake Kant made is only duplicated if one attempts to differentiate subjects, and this Hegel does not do.[26]

Consciousness and the Dialectic

The *Phenomenology* may be considered as the introduction to the system as a whole. Hegel once considered it as a mere introduction, but he became so involved in its detail that the *Phenomenology* became impossibly long and was published as a more or less autonomous work. The explicit goal of the *Phenomenology* is to show us the way to Absolute Knowledge, and in doing so, it is a reinterpretation and defense of Christianity, a correction of Kant's ethics and epistemology. As a vehicle for the Absolute Truth, it absorbs within it natural science, ethics, and aesthetics as well as metaphysics.

The problem is how this ambitious work is to be interpreted. It is presented as the historical development of Spirit, but does this signify the actual historical conceptual development of mankind, or the stages of development necessary for any individual or is it an hypothesis about the 'normal' development of consciousness? How literally is the historical form of the dialectic to be taken?

Secondly, we must understand the relationship between the various stages. Hegel greatly emphasizes the transitions between these, and it is clear from the developmental structure that there is some sense in which one stage 'leads into' the other, by which this *dialectic* proceeds. Sometimes Hegel speaks of "necessity" in this context, and often, particularly in the *Logic* and the *Encyclopedia,* he speaks of a "deduction." From such talk, many commentators, notably an entire generation of logic-minded British interpreters, took Hegel to be claiming necessary connections in the sense of deductive logic. Given this interpretation, it was easily discovered that Hegel failed to make such claims good. In reaction to this much too strong interpretation, some authors[27] have given up the notion of 'deduction' and taken Hegel to claim only that the connections are "not arbitrary", that one can give "some reasons" for the progression. This extraordinarily weak interpretation is too weak, for Hegel's grand system depends not only on the availability of *some* reasons. Rather, there is a single set of reasons given for each stage, namely, the self-realization of spirit.

The problem is the movement from one stage to another. The most currently accepted view is that Hegel discovers a process "hidden behind the back of consciousness." Findlay, for example, argues:

Hegel further maintains that the full inevitability of the process which leads consciousness from one inadequate view of things to another more adequate must be in a measure hidden from consciousness; . . . and will be evident only to the phenomenological observer or in the phenomenological retrospect. (Phen 79–80 footnoted) (In a meta-language, we should say, one can say things about a given language which that language is unable to say of itself.) Thus the scientist will be led on from the things of sense-perception to the non-sensuous things of the scientific understanding, but he will not know exactly why he is thus led. It is we, the phenomenological observers, practicing our external reflection, who can understand the whole transition. What is

*for him a merely factual discovery can
be seen by us to be an inevitable
revolution in consciousness.*[28]

But it is not clear whether this dialectic
is a process actually 'inherent' in this sequence of events, or rather whether it is
to be considered *only* an interpretation.

In this same context, one questions the
necessity of the system's following this
particular dialectic. The *Phenomenology*
traces a route to the realization of Spirit
or Absolute Truth, and one wonders
whether there might be alternative routes.
The consensus of opinion is that Hegel
claims that this is *the* way to the Truth,
and that alternative routes are not open.
Even Findlay, who provides the interpretation closest to that of this chapter, argues *against* Hegel that he ought not to
have made this claim. Hegel did not make
this claim; first of all, his various statements of the system do show very different progressions to the same end (compare the *Phenomenology* to the *Logic,* or
the various *Lectures*). Most importantly,
an adequate understanding of the teleological and 'reflective' nature of Hegel's
system makes it quite clear that no such
uniqueness claim is involved, for another
sequence of past events might be similarly
rationalized.

I shall argue that the *Phenomenology*
must be considered more akin to an extended historical and philosophical metaphor than to an actual historical account,
and that the purpose of this metaphor is
to demonstrate by way of an incredibly
complex counterexample to Kant, the way
Spirit may achieve the Absolute Truth.
This is not to say that Hegel does not intend it to be historically significant, or that
he believes that the history of Spirit does
not closely resemble this development, but
it is clear that a literal interpretation is
necessarily a failure. Kant's philosophy appears, for example, in the first section of
the *Phenomenology;* the early Greeks appear in the third. The ordering of stages
of Spirit is by levels of 'maturity', not strict
chronology, and there is no claim to strict
historical necessity here. In the *Phenomenology,* the point is to order, in metaphorical form, the stages of development of the
maturity of Spirit, and to show how this
maturity is a progression towards absolute
knowledge. This ordering need not follow
an actual historical sequence, and its purpose is not to provide an accurate intellectual history of man.

The *Phenomenology* is divided into
three uneven parts, each representing one
'form' or 'level of consciousness' in ascending order of sophistication. The first and
shortest section is called "Consciousness,"
which deals with relatively naive epistemological consciousness. The second is
called "Self-Consciousness" and traces the
beginnings of the awakening of the consciousness of Spirit in its early form of
simple antagonistic recognition of other
people. Finally, there is a long section on
"Reason," which traces the ultimate development of Spiritual-Rational consciousness
from a simple sense of community to the
penultimate realization of Spirit in art and
primitive Christianity and its ultimate realization in Hegel's philosophy. We shall not
trace this impressive *Phenomenology* in
detail, but must limit ourselves to brief outline of its method and its most influential
chapters.

The first section of the *Phenomenology*
discusses the most primitive stages in the
development of spirit. Because it encompasses many of the traditional problems
of philosophy, it can be partially viewed
not only as the development of the understanding from mere experience, but as an
analysis of the entire movement in modern
philosophy including such central problems as the nature of substance, the necessity of concepts for understanding experience, and the nature of connections
between experiences and the synthesis of
objects; in other words, the subject matter
of Kant's first *Critique* (and the *Transcendental Aesthetic* and *Analytic*), and the
major epistemological work of Locke,
Berkeley, and Hume. The stages of *Consciousness* are three, which Hegel designates *"sense-certainty," "perception,"* and
"understanding."

The stage of consciousness referred to
as "sense-certainty," the very beginning of
consciousness or knowledge, is "knowledge of the immediate."[29] It is "what is
presented before us," "what is given." It
is "pure apprehension" without yet any
"conceptual comprehension."[30] It is raw
experience, without any trace of understanding of this experience, the experience
of a passive sensitive receptacle. As such,
this stage is not truly consciousness or
knowledge at all, but merely "knowledge
implicit." This is the pure data of the
senses which so many philosophers, of this
century as well as the past, have taken to
be the indubitable, secure foundation of
human knowledge. It is pure experience,

uninterpreted and thus unadulterated by us in any way. Many philosophers have argued that errors in human knowledge, when they arise, must arise after this level. For on this level, our knowledge is certain and becomes fallible only when we attempt to conceptualize or to understand our experiences.

Although this section is among the shortest of the *Phenomenology* (ten pages), it provides us with some vital clues for understanding the nature of Hegel's dialectic. Hegel's argument against this form of 'knowledge' as certain knowledge, or even as knowledge at all, is brilliantly clear and to the point and has far-reaching consequences for epistemological theory even in this century. Briefly, Hegel argues that this knowledge, which he describes as a mere "this, here, now," far from being, as so often is argued, 'authentic' knowledge, knowledge which is complete, from which all other knowledge is abstraction and limiting, is "really and admittedly the abstractest and poorest kind of truth." It is what we 'mean' only in sense of pointing (*this*) and not really meaning at all. (Again, the implicit distinction here between *meaning* and denotation has had a profound influence on contemporary analytic philosophy—compare Frege on 'sense' and 'reference'.) In fact, it is no knowledge at all, but simply *is*. Knowledge *requires* concepts, and the supposed certainty of this 'knowledge' is certain only insofar as it is not knowledge at all; it asserts nothing. The infallibility of sense-certainty, of pure experience, lies in its failure to give us any claim to knowledge which might be taken as wrong. This knowledge which "is called unspeakable, is nothing else than what is untrue, irrational, something barely and simply meant."[31]

From this argument, a great many puzzles of the *Phenomenology* and Hegel's work in general become clear. For example, the celebrated late nineteenth-century criticism of Hegel as a *negative* philosopher by Schelling and Kierkegaard is explained—Hegel is interested in knowledge and knowledge is conceptual. Mere confrontation, or in Russell's terms, "acquaintance," is not knowledge at all. The heavy emphasis on *The Concept* in Hegel's system and his constant interrelating of the Concept and Spirit, Consciousness and Knowledge, can be easily understood from this initial characterization of knowledge as necessarily *conceptual*.

From this characterization we may also see clearly that Hegel essentially agreed with Kant (in his *Transcendental Deduction*) that there can be no unconceptualized knowledge, that knowledge is essentially a product of the understanding. (It is not altogether clear whether Hegel further agrees with Kant that there can be no unconceptualized experiences). From this agreement, however, we have one of the keys to the Hegelian works, that knowledge is essentially an *active* process, that mere experience can never give us knowledge, that synthesis of experience by rules or concepts is necessary. To use the frequent Hegelian-Kantian term, knowledge is necessarily *universal*, it comes about by use of concepts in a language that always apply to not one particular case but to an indefinitely large number of cases. This initial insistence on universality as the essence of knowledge is already a reply to the Schelling-Kierkegaard criticism which gathers momentum after Hegel's death.

Even in this section we can see that many of the prominent interpretations of what Hegel is doing with his dialectic cannot succeed. The interpretation of the *Phenomenology* as a running autobiography of Spirit should have to explain how Spirit, at a stage in which it has no concepts and no knowledge, is capable of describing itself, which is what such an interpretation must take this section to be. As it is evident that no such description is possible on this level, it is clear that Hegel does not intend the *Phenomenology* as such a running developmental report, but rather as a retrospective of the development of Spirit. Hegel's own insistence (in the preface and elsewhere) that he is looking back on development to see how it got to the present is confirmation that the *Phenomenology* is retrospective. More importantly, Findlay,[32] most prominently, but other commentators as well, treat the transitions between sections as if they are a demonstration of a development, showing the causes or the necessity of transition from one stage to the next. In Hegel's argument for the inadequacy of sense-certainty, however, there is nothing that could even be interpreted as a *mechanism* which pushes this stage to the next, nor does the inadequacy of sense-certainty act to push the dialectic along. Hegel simply points out that this *conception* of knowledge is an *inadequate* conception, and that knowledge does not exist at this stage.

There is no argument for the evolution of a consciousness that does have knowledge.

If Hegel is not explaining a transition from one stage to the next, what is he doing? We have already answered this in our introduction, but the section on sense-certainty will allow us to demonstrate our interpretation. Hegel claims that there are two stages of consciousness (again we need not, but in this case probably should, take them as chronologically ordered), one of which is more mature than the other, "more mature" meaning closer to absolute knowledge. The transition from sense-certainty to perception is a step closer to the truth, by bringing us from knowledge implicit to knowledge of at least a primitive sort. This transition is not *explained* in the sense of showing why (causally) one step moves to the next, but is explained only in the sense that the transition is *rationalized* as bringing us one step closer to the truth. The work of the dialectic is thus not to show us how spirit developed (in the causal or evolutionary sense), but to rationalize this development, to show us a pathway to Absolute Truth by juxtaposing various stages of knowledge according to their approach to Absolute Truth. Of these many stages, the very lowest, which can only barely be called conscious at all, is that stage at which we have only experience. Sense-certainty is inadequate as knowledge because it is not knowledge at all. Therefore, *we* move along the dialectic to a more adequate form of consciousness, which is that of *Perception.*

Perception is the first appearance of knowledge, for this stage is the beginning of comprehension of our experiences. We now interpret our experiences by applying concepts. In Hegel's short description, the object of consciousness is now the *thing.* As a thing, this object is characterizable and characterized by ascription of properties, in other words, by the application of universally applicable concepts to this particular *thing.* Our experience is therefore no longer 'pure' experience but experience *of* something. In an argument which is still piercing to many philosophers of this century, Hegel notes that many of these properties, which only come about with the application of concepts to our experiences, are mistaken by philosophers to be inherent in the sense-certainty stage. However, the very nature of sense-certainty is to be without knowledge, and knowledge, even of this primitive sort that simply recognizes things, requires the application of concepts to exist.

The problem (inadequacy) that arises in the level of sense-certainty is one familiar to all readers of modern empiricist philosophy. How do we see, not experiences, but *things?* According to the perceptual consciousness, objects, things, have a unity, in fact, exist as a unity of properties. In other words, our perception of a tree is a certain unity of color experiences, of certain shapes, and perhaps consists also of certain tactile sensations, sounds, and smells. Over and above this, there is *the tree,* that which 'lies behind' all of these experiences and ties them together. In traditional philosophical terms, there is the tree as *substance* which is responsible for the unity of the tree-perceptions. The problem is, then, why we should be led to think anything beyond the tree-perception, for any substance 'behind' these perceptions is itself not the object of any possible perception.

In the history of philosophy, this line of questioning sent Berkeley to idealism, but idealism does not yet appear in the Hegelian hierarchy of knowledge. In his terms, this substance, which is an "unconditioned universal," cannot be part of perception. However, perception itself does not recognize the extra-perceptual, so that, if we are to understand this unity of objects, we must move to the next stage of consciousness, not yet idealism, which does help us explain this unity.[33]

The solution to the problem of unity is provided by the level of consciousness which is the *understanding.* The concept of 'understanding' here is clearly taken from Kant's use of the term, and like his use, refers to the application of concepts to experience. However, like Kant's use, there is the reference here not to just *any* concepts (for this is not the subject of discussion in Kant's *Analytic*), but rather those special sets of concepts to which Kant refers as the *Categories.* Among these categories is the category of substance, which is the solution to the problem of unity. The tree-perceptions have a unity of a tree because of the substantial tree that lies behind them. Similarly, problems such as the coexistence of various objects, the reality of causal interconnections between perceptions, as well as successions of perceptions, all appear at this level of the dialectic, to which one might refer as the Kantian level, for it consists primarily of the conclusions of the *Transcendental Analytic* of the first *Critique*. Of central interest in this section is Hegel's analysis of the world of the understanding as culminating in a dual world-view. On the one hand, there is the world as perceived, and the laws intrinsic to that perception. On the other hand, there is the world in itself, which is postulated 'behind' this world to 'explain' it.

In the Understanding, we postulate 'unconditioned universals' behind our experiences as objects in themselves. However, Hegel does not adopt the traditional notion of 'substance' for those objects, but begins by referring to them as 'forces' or 'powers'. This is then related to the "kingdom of laws" which is Kant's vision of a necessarily unified and ordered (phenomenal) world.

While the chapter is essentially Kantian (although it contains a powerful critique of Kant's *Critique*), the implication is still clearly that the laws of which one speaks at this stage are not yet imposed laws, but laws *inherent in the world itself*. A few brilliant insights into the nature of science may be found here, for example, Hegel's discussion of whether laws are to be conceived of as laws in nature or as *concepts* (that is, provided by us), and his discussion of the nature of scientific explanation, which Hegel claims consists of a *redescription* of phenomena. The most important section of this chapter for our purposes is Hegel's peculiar argument in attack of Kant's theory of knowledge. What he argues, basically, is that Kant's noumenon-phenomenon distinction is fundamentally wrong; that if there is any sense to be made of the notion of "thing-in-itself" it must be part of the thing-as-phenomenon (that is, noumena are not transcendent to phenomena, but are immanent in them).

The argument itself consists of one of Hegel's long and peculiar counterexamples in which he provides a postulation of a noumenal world which happens to be an inverted (*verkehrte*) world. According to Kant, the world-in-itself, that is, as noumenon, is at once a necessary supposition of the conditions of knowledge, but by its very nature cannot be known. Because knowledge depends on the human faculties for knowledge, and because we cannot know that our knowledge is not therefore some distortion of things as they exist independent of our experience of them, we must, while supposing our knowledge

to be valid, resort to *noumenon* which very possibly might have its own principles, different from the world as perceived and known by us. Hegel then goes on to suggest what the world-as-it-is *might* be like by suggesting that everything in this world is 'unlike' that in the other. "What is there black is here white, what by the first law (of phenomena) is in the case of electricity the oxygen pole becomes in its other supersensible reality the hydrogen pole."[34] The two-worlds doctrine is carried to the realm of morality, where Hegel argues that the two-worlds view destroys the very concept of morality it is invoked to protect. For, according to him,

an act which in appearance is a crime would in its inner nature be capable of being really good—a bad act may have a good intention; punishment is only in appearance punishment; in itself or in another world it might well be, for the criminal, a benefit.[35]

Here we have the first reference to Kant's morality, which begins with the crushing criticism of Kant's *Summum Bonum* and his entire two-world view. The problem, as stated here, is that the *Summum Bonum* and Kant's morality in general require man and his actions to be considered as noumenon. A man and his actions are also part of the phenomenal world where they are evaluated, and Hegel is here briefly pointing out the problem in applying the phenomenon-noumenon distinction to a man acting. Or, as we questioned in our brief criticism, why suppose that what we consider punishment to the phenomenal man will have any such effect to man as noumenon. Here, even in this first section, we have a clear indication of the continuing attack on Kant's moral-religious philosophy that we have claimed is the core of Hegel's mature writings.

The inverted world passage is essentially an argument by ridicule, for what becomes evident is that, if we take Kant's notion of noumenon seriously, any sort of nonsense becomes equally intelligible. Either the noumenal world is just like the phenomenal world, or, not only does it not make sense to talk about it, but it does not even make sense to suppose that there might be one. It might be argued that Hegel takes the two-world view as literally consisting of two worlds instead of simply as one world as it is and as it might not be subject to conditions of human understanding. Of course, Hegel's criticism applies as well to the latter interpretation. The inadequacy in the section on *Consciousness*, considered in its entirety, therefore, is the inadequacy of Kant's philosophy, which Hegel considers the culmination of all modern philosophies before it. The inadequacy of understanding is a signal to a new move in philosophy, a move which is not simply new knowledge or a new progression in consciousness, but which is an entirely new *kind* of knowledge—one that Kant did not consider as such—and a new kind of consciousness. Insofar as one wishes to interpret the progress of the *Phenomenology* along philosophical-historical lines, one might say that this new stage was initiated, implicitly, by Kant, and made explicit by Fichte. Again, the *Phenomenology* is not intended to be a history of philosophy.[36]

Self-consciousness: Master and Slave

Consciousness becomes self-consciousnes when it realizes *itself* as the source of the forces and laws of the understanding. Kant is the culmination of that particular stage called "consciousness" in his postulation of an underlying world (though not Kant alone, of course; nearly all traditional metaphysics supplied some such postulate). Kant, however, is also, in his recognition that the application of these transcendental concepts is actually carried out by consciousness itself, the mark of the turn to "self-consciousness."

The confrontation of two consciousnesses is the key to the most celebrated stage of the *Phenomenology*, the section called "Master and Slave," which Marx takes up as a model for his social theory and Sartre borrows as a paradigm for his analysis of "Being-for-Others" in *Being and Nothingness*. Hegel tells us that "self-consciousness attains its satisfaction only in another self-consciousness,"[37] and that,

Self-consciousness exists in itself and for-itself, in that, and by the fact that it exists for another self-consciousness; that is to say, it is only by being acknowledged or recognized.[38]

These cryptic sentences are the crux of "self-consciousness"; they spell out for us the first appearance of Spirit—the recognition of the existence of a universal consciousness still in the primitive form of the recognition of other consciousnesses than one's own. What is Hegel trying to argue here? First, there is the suggestion that the *concept* of "self-consciousness" or "self-identity" can only arise in confrontation with others. Hegel's thesis might thus be construed as the claim that a person has no concept of 'self', cannot refer to himself, and cannot say things about himself (for example, ascribe states of consciousness to himself) until he is *taught* by someone else. This thesis has remarkable affinities with Ludwig Wittgenstein's claim that psychological predicates can only be learned through learning to apply them to someone *else*. (Findlay has claimed the two theses to be virtually identical.)

Secondly, there is a more modest thesis that one can only develop self-consciousness, that is, a *particular* concept of himself, through confrontation with other people. This thesis does not claim that one cannot have concepts of self-reference before social confrontation, but rather that the particular image one has of himself is acquired socially, not in isolation. It is this sort of thesis which occupies much of Sartre's quasi-psychological efforts in *Being and Nothingness*. The first claim, that concerning the concept of self-reference, is hardly treated by Hegel, for he considers self-reference "merely formal" and "entirely empty," hardly worth the title of "self-consciousness" at all. (Compare his discussion of the 'knowledge' of *sense-certainty*. An extended discussion of this empty self-reference can be found in Part III of the *Encyclopedia*.) The second thesis, however, seems to fit well into the overall direction of the system, and a discussion of the 'parable' of master and slave should make this clear.

The first part of the parable is quite simple and straightforward: two self-consciousnesses encounter each other and struggle to "cancel" each other in order to "prove their certainty of themselves" (prove their independence and freedom) against the other, who appears as an independent (and therefore limiting) being. Each self-consciousness originally tries to treat the other as object, but finds that the other does not react as an object, which demands that each recognize the other as an independent consciousness. However, recognizing another as independent limits one's own independence, and, moreover, one then becomes determined to prove his own freedom and independence not simply to himself, but to the other as well. (As Hegel says, they wish to bring their self-certainty (autonomy and independence) to the "level of objective truth.") Hegel adds that it is solely by risking one's life that such objective freedom is obtained, and "one attains the truth of this recognition as an independent self-consciousness."[39] The other must be 'cancelled' because his otherness contradicts one's view as self-conscious (free and independent as well as self-aware). However, it becomes clear that the role of the other in this life-and-death struggle is not only that of a threat or purely destructive. The recognition by the other of one's self is at the very crux of the conflict. Thus obtaining the recognition of the other as a self-consciousness is the point of the battle, not the extinction of the other. Hegel says that "trial by death cancels both the truth which was to result from it [that is, the recognition of self-consciousness by the other] and therewith the certainty of self altogether."[40] This passage seems to show that Hegel did hold the second thesis above, that self-consciousness requires the presence of another for one's own self-image. In fighting for recognition, each tries to save his own life, but each tries also, if possible, to preserve the life of his opponent. If one consciousness is victor, and neither loses his life, then one becomes a consciousness "for-itself," independent, a master, while the other becomes a consciousness "for-another," a slave (whose essence, Hegel mysteriously comments, is "life," indicating that it is perhaps he who arranged this relationship to save his life).

The master "is a consciousness existing on its own account which is mediated with itself through another consciousness."[41] The master is "self-existence," but he too is a being-for-itself existing only through another. The master, although self-sufficient in the sense of having the slave dependent on him, is also dependent on this dependence. Because the master maintains the power, he is the master, and thereby self-sufficient. Because he is now self-sufficient only through the industry of the slave, he is also dependent on the slave. Hegel here speaks obscurely of a relationship to "the thing," which the slave has im-mediately ("he labours upon it") but "the master only mediately, except that he gets the enjoyment of it."[42] In the course of development, the slave, because of his direct relation to the thing, becomes self-sufficient while the master, because of his dependence on the slave, becomes wholly dependent. (From this reversal Marx is to take his central theses of class struggle and the ultimate degeneration and self-destruction of the economic master classes.) Furthermore, the problem of the recognition of the other breeds a further instability into this relationship. The master, who depends on the servant for the 'recognition' that he is autonomous, finds the servant a totally dependent creature without an independent will, incapable of giving him the recognition of an independent other.

In the master-slave relationship, we first see the striving for freedom of Spirit, the *truth* for self-consciousness. In the master-slave relationship, where this striving begins, we see the inadequacy of the attempt to derive this truth from human relationships which treat persons as independent and opposed consciousness. The way to freedom, the goal of this stage of consciousness, lies not in such relationships, but in the direction of increased socialization. The explicit recognition of Spirit does not appear in the section on "self-consciousness." The master-slave relationship gives way to the explicit rejection of the master-slave situation, denying all 'external' reality and rejecting all action as meaningless *(stoicism)*. In a more extreme form, "self-consciousness" attempts to take *everything* as meaningless *(skepticism)*. Ultimately, the 'contradictions' or 'disharmonies' of all forms of self-consciousness become explicit in an alienated soul, a consciousness whose inconsistent state is 'unhappy'. The master-slave relationship, introduced as a relationship between two people, becomes internalized in a single schizoid individual. This 'unhappy' soul is the primitive Christian ascetic who believes himself to be *both* a part of this world and an essentially Divine consciousness, but the "creature of the flesh" and the "soul before God" cannot coexist. Kierkegaard will return to this disharmonious Christian for the material for his "knight of faith." Where Kierkegaard will insist that this incomprehensible schizophrenia is a necessary condition for Christianity, Hegel insists on going beyond this internalized master-slave relationship with its self-flagellation and self-denial. In Christianity, and in the figure of Christ, Hegel finds the first explicit concept of Spirit,

the idea of Reason, of the certainty that consciousness is, in its particularity, inherently and essentially absolute, or is all reality.[43]

Reason

Rational consciousness is the end of the *Phenomenology*, a final "unification of the diverse elements in its process." Reason resolves by harmonizing *(aufheben)* the 'disharmonies' between God and Man, and between morality (Practical Reason) and personal inclination. The Spirit of Absolute Knowledge is both Immanent God and human society. There is no separating God from man or morality from custom. Reason in the *Phenomenology* also marks the synthesis of a number of disharmonies that have been introduced in the dialectic of the *Phenomenology itself:* the inadequacies of traditional epistemological thought (the "opposition of subject and object"); the resolution of the master-slave relationship and interpersonal conflict (including the internalized conflict of the 'unhappy' consciousness); and, most ambitious of all, the *Phenomenology* is Hegel's first attempt to 'harmonize' all human efforts and, in an Aristotelian way, find the proper conceptual place for each of them.

The stages of Reason move from philosophical idealism (Fichte's "ethical idealism" more than Berkeley's epistemological idealism), the first conception of the autonomy of consciousness, and through scientific idealism, in which man becomes confident in his ability to fathom the secrets of nature, not as an alien object (as in "Understanding"), but as objects inextricably tied to human consciousness. (A fuller understanding of this notion will have to wait for our discussion of Hegel's *Logic;* we shall see it developed in Nietzsche's epistemology and in Husserl's phenomenology as well.) Reason then moves through Spirit becoming explicitly formulated, through the custom-bound folk morality of the family, the tribe, and the small community to "Spirit certain of itself," that is, Kant's *moralität,* through religion to "revealed religion," Christianity, and finally to Absolute Knowledge.

The Reason of the *Phenomenology* is primarily concerned with early religious-ethical disharmonies. The epistemological 'opposition' between subject and object will become the central theme of the *Logic.* Ethics is the recognition of man's moral autonomy, a recognition for which Kant is primarily responsible. Kant's "moral world-view" recognizes this autonomy, however, only at a terrible cost, the one-sided picture of man as separated from nature, from his own desires and happiness, and concerned only with the imperatives of duty. Hegel argues (as he had in his early manuscripts) that morality and happiness cannot be separated: "enjoyment lies in the very principle of morality." Hegel restates the *Summum Bonum* as a necessary condition for morality:

The harmony of morality and nature, or . . . the harmony of morality and happiness, is thought of as necessarily existing . . .[44]

This "harmony of morality and objective nature" Hegel refers to as "the final purpose of the world."[45] Postulation, however, is not proof, and the vital belief in a Divine moral Legislator[46] and the Kingdom of Heaven cannot be left to mere postulation. The dialectical movement from Kant's ethics to religion is such a 'proof', an attempt to demonstrate the conceptual inadequacy of Kant's thesis. In a nasty critique of Kant's ethics, Hegel calls his basic notion of duty "dishonest" and a "perfect nest of thoughtless contradictions." Kant's morality is said to be "hypocrisy," for it pretends to take duty as absolute, but takes constant if devious recourse to appeals to inclination and Divine reward. In the *Phenomenology,* as in the early writings, Hegel suggests that a more sophisticated and harmonious conception of morality can be found in *Sittlichkeit,* the morality of custom. Conceptually, *Sittlichkeit* is bettered by the early Christian ideal of Conscience, in which, Hegel argues (after Fichte) the command of duty and the incentive of inclination are synthesized. Conscience acts on implicit principle, yet is specific to particular situations. It is derivative of reason, but also involves inclination; it is individual yet derivative of a person's upbringing in society. Conscience finds its living ideal in the figure that Hegel identifies as the "beautiful soul," a holy figure whose "pure goodness" makes him "lose contact with social reality." One immediately thinks of Dostoevsky's Prince Myshkin (*The Idiot*). More aptly, it is the conception of the historical Jesus that best characterizes the beautiful soul and the perfect voice of conscience, and it is Jesus who moves the dialectic to that penultimate level of consciousness known as religion.

"The concept of Religion," according to Hegel, "is the consciousness that sees itself as Truth." After a brief excursion through primitive and 'artistic' religious consciousness, Hegel brings us back to Christianity, whose Judaic origins have already promoted the conception of God as Spirit, but an 'objective' or substantial Spirit, "out there." What Christ represents, according to Hegel, is not a concrete manifestation of God "out there" in the form of *one* man; Christ is rather the symbol of the conception that God and all men are a unity. Spirit is "substance and subject as well" means that the Christian Spirit and we ourselves are the same. Here is the resolution of the 'disharmony' between man and God which had caused Hegel to renounce Christianity in his early writings, but it is not to be thought that this is a simple endorsement of traditional Christianity either. Christianity has failed to become Absolute Truth, according to Hegel, because it has become obsessed with figurative thinking in stories and pictures. To become Absolute Truth, Christianity must reject such thinking and become wholly *conceptual*. Needless to say, this entailed a rejection of many of the teachings and most of the ritual story telling of the Christian church. In secularized Prussia, this did not seem to seriously affect Hegel's enormously powerful appeal. The Absolute Knowledge of the *Phenomenology* is thus a reconceptualization of the basic themes of Christianity. The insistence that Christianity thus become totally conceptual does not mean that it must dispense with any *content*; its content, the content of the *Phenomenology*, and the content of contemporary Prussian culture, was *everything* that had gone before it. Consciousness had its identity in its past, that is, in it rationalization of its past. The content and the justification for Hegel's revised Christianity was everything that had gone before it. The end and purpose of the *Phenomenology*, and the justification and end of all human activity ("Absolute Truth") rested in Hegel's revised Christianity, which, as Kierkegaard bitterly points out, is far more Hegelian than Christian.

The *Logic* and Absolute Knowledge[47]

Philosophy is the search for Absolute Knowledge—the search for rationality—for Reason in the world. In the *Phenomenology,* Hegel has shown that such absolute or nonconditioned knowledge is possible, namely it is possible if we understand that all knowledge and experience serves the ultimate purpose of our realization of ourselves as Spirit. The *Phenomenology* has demonstrated this important philosophical perspective by showing how the only adequate conception of ourselves and of our knowledge under intense philosophical scrutiny is that position in which we cease to distinguish real selves (transcendental ego) from each other, and we cease thinking critically (in Kant's sense) as if knowledge of things as they are in-themselves is impossible to us.

The *Phenomenology* is only the beginning of the system; it proves that systematic Absolute Knowledge is possible. On the Continent, this has proven to be the most influential of Hegel's works, so we have allotted most of our space to a discussion of it. However, the system as Hegel conceived of it is constituted by those books written *after* the *Phenomenology*. They are the systematic application of the philosophical perspective and method established in the *Phenomenology*. In them, Hegel investigates and demonstrates the rationality of many different manifestations of consciousness and shows how they lead to the same goal of Spiritual self-realization as do the cultural stages of the *Phenomenology*. In the *Logic*, this is done in the realm of "pure thought": the most formal concepts (those which Kant referred to as the Categories) are shown to be ordered in levels of sophistication leading to Absolute Truth. In the *Philosophy of Right*, ethical and political institutions (that is, ethical and political concepts) are similarly ordered according to sophistication. In the *Lectures,* the same is done for religion, the arts, the history of philosophy, and history itself. We may note from the outset that the only system which follows a strict historical pattern is the history. All of these vital human endeavors are ordered as their various conceptions approach the Spiritual climax of the *Phenomenology*.

Of these works, the most important is the *Logic,* which exists in two separate but similar versions. The *Logic* can only come after the *Phenomenology,* and Hegel clearly considered the *Phenomenology* a prolegomena to his work in *Logic.* The *Phenomenology* sets up the goal and methodology, and the *Logic* is the execution of the ordering of a priori concepts— those most basic concepts which we use to establish a general framework within which to understand all experience. Kant had given us a more or less arbitrary list of twelve such concepts and made no distinctions among them as far as conceptual sophistication. Hegel complains that this list *is* arbitrary, but more importantly, that Kant treated these concepts as concepts of the understanding while insisting they could only be misused by Reason. Against this, Hegel treats these concepts as concepts of Reason, not understanding (their employment in the understanding being a less adequate use of them) and asks, as he did in the *Phenomenology,* which of various antithetical sets of a priori concepts is most sophisticated, that is, can give the Absolute Truth. Unlike Kant (and like Fichte), Hegel argues that there are alternative sets of a priori concepts (that is, alternative conceptual frameworks for viewing the world), and that the job of philosophy could not be simply to show the a priori necessity of one set of categories (which Hegel felt that Kant had *not* succeeded in doing), but rather in showing the consequences and inadequacies of these various concepts, and then ordering these with regard to their adequacy.

Among the most startling and most often misunderstood of Hegel's claims is the claim that Kant had taken the antinomies[48] as a repudiation of the use of a priori concepts by Reason instead of recognizing that these antinomies are a natural and more adequate use of these concepts than understanding can give them. In other words, Hegel claims that antinomy is good, that contradiction of that sort is a more adequate, not an impossible use of concepts. To this end Hegel complains that Kant did not find enough antinomies (but limited himself to only four) and did not appreciate the true importance of what he himself considered his greatest discovery. Furthermore, Hegel makes the startling and frequently attacked claim that the *Logic* (concepts and their relations) are not merely embodied in a language or in a mode of thought but are *in the world.* In other words, logical relationships do not hold because of certain rules of thought, but because the world itself contains these relationships. Consequently, logical contradictions, as manifested in the antinomies, are properties of the world itself, not simply of the mode of thought that produced them. To understand these radical theses, we must return to the conclusion of the *Phenomenology,* which is there, and in our exposition, left obscure. In the *Phenomenology,* we moved from one form of consciousness to a more adequate form until we reached the highest form in which we realized that all of our various modes of experience and thought were part of a process of *self*-discovery. In the *Logic,* the notion or the concept of self-conscious Spirit which was introduced in the *Phenomenology* is shown to be the highest purely conceptual truth. In other words, the conception of the world which is most adequate is the conception of Spirit.

In *Logic,* Spirit is that conception of the world in which subject and object (subjective and objective) are not distinguished, in which various 'subjects' are not *distinguished either,*

it is only when absolute knowledge has been reached that the separation of the object of knowledge *from* subjective certainty *is complete resolved, and truth equated to this certainty, and this certainty equated to truth.*[49]

Because it makes no sense to distinguish subject from object, neither does it make sense to distinguish the abstract formal modes of thought in logic ("certainty") from the objects or content of knowledge ("truth"), and therefore it makes no sense to speak of "logic" independently of "truth."

On the contrary, the necessary forms and characteristic determinations of thought are the content and the supreme truth itself.[50]

In other words, *logic is metaphysics.* Again, God enters as the supreme principle.

This content (of the Logic) *shows forth God as He is in His eternal essence before the creation of nature and of finite spirit.*[51]

The "before" here is clearly a 'conceptual' not a temporal "before." Hegel frequently insists that the *Logic* precedes the *Phenomenology* as bare form precedes experience, but also insists that experience and understanding (concepts) are inseparable. This leaves in considerable confusion exactly what is the relationship between concepts and experiences, the *Phenomenology* and the *Logic*.

Although it is generally recognized that the attack on the subjective-objective distinction is the final step of Hegel's systematic works, few Hegelians have been able to make sense out of this notion. The corollary to this attack—the existence of logical properties in things—the operation of the dialectic in the world, so often attacked as serious confusion in Hegel, makes much better sense once the former is understood. First of all, Hegel does not mean, as his worst disciples would claim, that one cannot draw *any* distinction between subject and object. Clearly, I do not confuse myself with the table in front of me, and it makes perfectly good sense to speak of me (the subject) perceiving the table (the object). More seriously, Hegel does not deny the possibility of drawing the distinction between "subjective" and "objective" in the sense in which we speak (and Kant speaks) of "objective reality" (that experienced by any conscious being) and "subjective reality" (that which is experienced by a single peculiar consciousness and cannot be duplicated for another consciousness). Hegel does not even deny the possibility of a philosophical distinction between subject and object, such as that continually used by Kant. It is clearly the purpose of the early *Phenomenology* and the first two sections of the *Logic* (the "Objective Logic") to show exactly how such distinctions can be drawn. What Hegel does maintain is that such a philosophical distinction *applied to the foundation of experience and knowledge* is inadequate and leads to serious dilemmas—notably the skepticism explicit in Hume and implicit in Kant.

What Hegel claims is that an entire set of questions on which traditional philosophy has been based must be discarded. He does not claim that there is no "subject-object" distinction, but argues that this distinction has made advancement in philosophy impossible. Therefore, we ought to replace the "subject-object" conceptual scheme with one which contains no such distinction. Furthermore, the conception of *Spirit* (and the Notion) tells *us* that the problem is not *my* knowledge of reality but *our* knowledge. Concepts and reality itself are *socially* discovered. We must not ask whether our experiences are in accord with reality, or whether we can know things as they might be entirely different from the way we can know them. We must not ask whether some particular basic framework in which we view the world is in the world-in-itself ("objective") or imposed on the perceived world by *us* ("subjective"). In other words, philosophy for Hegel must proceed only by considering *everything* as a manifestation of ourselves, and by not asking whether there is any world beyond this (Kant's noumenal world). For Hegel, philosophy investigates the world (for *us*) and ceases to question the status of this world. One can already see the germ of the Phenomenological Movement to be initiated a half-century later by Edmond Husserl, who similarly argues that philosophy must begin by "bracketing existence," and who investigates only the world as it appears to *us* as phenomenon. (Husserl also comes to insist on the "Intersubjectivity" of all knowledge.[52]) Questions about the world-in-itself, if by this is meant a world which we do not or cannot know, have no part in philosophy. Similarly, one might consider J. L. Austin's[53] criticism of the modified two-world view of logical positivism, in which he argues, like Hegel, the common-sense position that we do have knowledge of objects-or-things in-themselves and that no other view can result in fruitful philosophy.

When Hegel maintains that the dialectic, that logic, is inherent in things-in-themselves, he is thus not making the absurd claims that we cannot ever distinguish objectivity from subjectivity or that logic exists in-the-world *as opposed to* in thought. What he is arguing is rather that traditional metaphysics, which investigates the world as rational or 'logical', is much closer to the truth than Kant's critical philosophy which denies the possibility of understanding things-in-themselves.

The older metaphysic had in this respect a loftier conception of thought than that which has become current in more modern times. For the older metaphysic laid down as fundamental that which

*by thinking is known of and in things,
that alone is what is really true in them.
. . . Thus this older metaphysic stands
for the view that thinking and the
determination of thinking are not
something foreign to the objects of
thought, but are rather of the very
essence of those objects.*[54]

Hegel's radical claim thus comes down to a very old and commonsense dictum, but one which was in ill-repute in post-Kantian philosophy. Namely, he insisted that philosophy could tell us the way things really are, but to do so it had to give up those less adequate conceptual frameworks which lead us into philosophical impasse. (We might compare this modest view with Marx's version of it which literally placed the dialectic in history and in objects with no such conceptual revisionism in mind. We might also contrast Hegel's view with that which Kierkegaard attacks.[55] Had he better understood Hegel, Kierkegaard might have realized that his notion of 'subjective truth' is less incompatible with Hegel than he supposed.)

Hegel's love of contradiction and 'dialectic' is well known but usually misinterpreted so as to make his brilliant theses impossibly obscure if not absurd. Hegel praises Kant's *Transcendental Dialectic* and his 'antinomies' (but not his execution of them) as disclosing important characteristics of Reason which Kant himself did not appreciate.

*Kant set dialectic higher, and this part
of his work is among the greatest of his
merits, for he freed dialectic from the
semblance of arbitrariness attributed
to it in ordinary thought, and set it forth
as* a necessary procedure of reason. . . .
*When Kant's dialectical expositions in
the* antinomies of Pure Reason *are
looked at closely . . . it will seem that
they are not indeed deserving of any
great promise; but the general idea upon
which he builds and which he has
vindicated is the objectivity of appearance
and the* necessity of contradiction *which
belong to the very nature of
thought-determinations; primarily
indeed in so far as these determinations
are applied by reason to* things in
themselves.[56]

Hegel's love of antinomy is intimately connected to his glorification of the 'fluid-ity' of Reason in contrast to the 'rigidity' of the Understanding.

*The battle of Reason consists in this,
to overcome the rigidity which the Understanding has brought in.*[57]

What Hegel objects to is the dogmatism with which Kant defends one 'correct' conceptual framework. "Understanding" (that is, Kant's *Analytic*) refuses to recognize what Kant himself demonstrates in the antinomies, that there are other conceptual schemes equally valid. Kant tries to get rid of the antinomies, notably the latter two 'dialectical' antinomies, by arguing that one set refers to noumena. This is defensible only by *practical* reason, and is therefore not *knowledge* at all. Hegel has continuously pointed out that this use of "knowledge" is akin to sophistry on Kant's part. What Kant ought to have recognized is that the antinomies demonstrate the impossibility of a transcendental deduction, and that philosophical truth lies in the realm of reason, not that of understanding or critique.

A modern way of putting Hegel's thesis of the 'fluidity' and necessary dialectical nature of Reason is to compare Kant's *Analytic* to a variety of currently accepted absolutist theories of meaning and Hegel's *Logic* to an opposed school of *contextualists*. Kant argues as if his key a priori concepts "being," "freedom," "causality," and so on, have a single fixed meaning which remains invariant in different philosophical contexts. Hegel argues to the contrary, that these concepts vary in meaning depending on context, and that no analysis of these concepts can disclose one 'proper' mode of thinking. Rather, different philosophical theories use these terms in different ways, with different meanings, but no single use is correct. (Compare Locke's and Lenin's use of "liberty," for example.) The movement of the *Logic* discloses to us various conceptions of the world demonstrating the changes of meaning in a priori philosophically important concepts. Finally we reach the highest conception of these concepts, which, to put the Absolute in very different terms than before, consists in the recognition of this conceptual fluidity and of the role which these concepts have played in various conceptual modes. The Absolute from this perspective is the realization of the variance of meaning of philosophical terms, and the covalidity of very different, even contradictory, philosophical theses. Absolute Truth, or the Notion, far from being the pretentious dogmatic concept it is so often accused of being, is the most tolerant of philosophical positions. It says that many philosophical theses are equally valid, and that the job of the philosopher, above all else, is to realize this, and to be tolerant of them. Perhaps, no philosopher has been less dogmatic than Hegel, his own pretentious utterances to the contrary. This is not to deny, however, that Hegel thought his own philosophy of superhistorical tolerance to occupy an exalted place. He calls philosophy,

the finest flower, it is the conception of its whole forms, it is consciousness and the spiritual essence of the whole situation, the spirit of the time, present in the spirit of comprehending itself.[58]

It should be evident what self-glorification must follow for the man who has finally articulated—for all mankind—this self-realization. Needless to say, it is this self-aggrandizement that will, more than any specific thesis or general methodology in Hegel's philosophy, fuel the antagonism of a century of anti-Hegelian, anti-Rationalist philosophers.

Bibliography
Hegel's Works in English

Early Theological Writings. Nos. III and IV. Translated by Knox. New York, 1961.

The Phenomenology of Mind (Spirit). Translated by J. B. Baillie. New York, 1964.

The Philosophy of Right. Translated by Knox. Oxford, 1967.

The Science of Logic. 2 vols. Translated by W. H. Johnston and L. G. Struthers. London, 1929.

" 'Lesser' Logic." Translated by W. Wallace. In *Encyclopedia.* Part I. Oxford, 1874.

"Hegel's Philosophy of Mind." Translated by W. Wallace. In *Encyclopedia.* Part III. Oxford, 1894.

Hegel's Philosophy of Nature. Translated by J. N. Findlay. In *Encyclopedia.* Part II. New York, 1970.

Hegel's famous *Lectures* are edited together from students' notes and lecture notes, and so are less dependable than the above works. Most are available only in expensive editions, but they are beginning to appear in paperback selections:

Lectures on the Philosophy of History. Translated by J. Sibree. New York, 1956. "Introduction" to the *Lectures.* Translated by R. S. Hartman in *Reason In History.* New York, 1953.

Philosophy of Fine Art. Translated by F. Osmaston. London, 1920.

On the Philosophy of Religion, 3 vols. Translated by Spiers and Sanderson. London, 1895.

On the History of Philosophy. Translated by E. Haldane and F. Simson. London, 1892–1896.

Selections from these last three are now available in paperback:

Hegel on Art, Religion, and Philosophy. Edited by J. Glen Gray. New York, 1970.

Many of Hegel's letters are available in W. Kaufmann's *Hegel: A Reinterpretation* (New York, 1965), which also contains a superior new translation of the "Preface" to the *Phenomenology.*

Books about Hegel's Philosophy

There are no truly introductory books on Hegel's philosophy, but for the more advanced philosophy student, four books are particularly recommended:

Findlay, J. N. *Hegel: A Re-examination,* newly reprinted as *Philosophy of Hegel.* New York, 1962.

Kaufmann, W. *Hegel: A Reinterpretation.* New York, 1962.

Marcuse, H. *Reason and Revolution.* Boston, 1960.

Soll, I. *An Introduction to Hegel's Metaphysics.* Chicago, 1969.

Also:

Copleston, F. *History of Philosophy.* Vol. VII. New York, 1963–66.

Croce, B. *What Is Living and What Is Dead in the Philosophy of Hegel.* Translated by D. Ainslie. New York, 1969.

Foster, M. B. *The Political Philosophies of Plato and Hegel.* Oxford, 1935.

Heidegger, M. *Hegel's Concept of Experience.* New York, 1970.

Hook, S. *From Hegel to Marx.* Ann Arbor, Mich., 1962.

Kaufmann, W. *From Shakespeare to Existentialism.* Boston, 1959. (See chaps. 7, 8, and 9.)

Löwenberg, J. *Hegel's Phenomenology.* La Salle, Ill., 1965.

Löwith, K. *From Hegel to Nietzsche.* Translated by D. Green. New York, 1964.

McTaggart, J. M. *Studies in the Hegelian Dialectic.* and *A Commentary on Hegel's Logic.* New York, 1964.

These two books are more important for understanding British Hegelianism than for understanding Hegel.

Marx, K. "A Critique of Hegel's Philosophy of Right." Translated by T. Bottomore in *Economic and Philosophical Manuscripts of 1844.* New York, 1964.

Mure. *Introduction to Hegel.* Oxford, 1940.

Popper, K. *The Open Society and Its Enemies.* Vol. II. Princeton, 1963.

Royce, J. *The Spirit of Modern Philosophy.* New York, 1962; and *Lectures on Modern Idealism.* New York, 1964.

Stace, W. T. *The Philosophy of Hegel.* New York, 1955. For many years this was the primary American textbook on Hegel.

Søren Kierkegaard: Faith and the Subjective Individual
CHAPTER 3

Kierkegaard had received little attention in philosophy until the recent popularity of the 'existentialist' movement in Europe and the United States. Then, because of the respect bestowed on him by such influential thinkers as Heidegger, Jaspers, and Sartre, he became generally recognized as the founder of this movement although he preceded it by a full century. Existentialism is often characterized as a break with traditional Western philosophy, taking as its point of departure and as its goal (its Truth) the crisis-ridden isolated existence of an individual. So characterized, this 'movement' is nowhere given a more poetic or more explicit statement than in the writings of Søren Kierkegaard.

Kierkegaard insists on the importance of the individual thinker first of all as a reaction to an attitude which he took to be the mark and the shame of the nineteenth century, a period that he characterized as "essentially one of understanding and reflection, without passion."[1]

"Each age has its own characteristic depravity. Ours is perhaps not pleasure or indulgence or sensuality, but rather a dissolute pantheistic contempt for individual man.[2]

It is an epoch in which every human endeavor is marred by an "unhappy objectivity" (an "absence of personality"), and the individual and the personal have become smothered in the mechanical "leveling" processes of the mediocrity of the "masses" (alternatively characterized as "the group," "the crowd," and "the public"). This mediocrity with its stress on the concept of the group and its denial of individuality is at one with the tendency to passionless reflection.

In order that everything should be reduced to the same level, it is first of all necessary to procure a phantom, its spirit, a monstrous abstraction, an all-embracing something that is nothing, a mirage—and that phantom is the public. It is only in an age which is without passion, yet reflective, that such a phantom can develop itself.[3]

The 'present age' is characterized by the fact that "there are no longer any human beings," for a human being is an individual and this "age has forsaken the individual in order to take refuge in the Collective Idea."[4] (The notion of the "Collective Idea" comes directly from Hegel.) A human being is not an organ of a larger body but a *person;* but, Kierkegaard complains, nothing is *personal* in this age of the "crowd." A human being ought to be passionate and committed, but no one now is willing to commit himself or allow himself to succumb to what Kant called the "pathology of passion." This is an age in which men have given up the dangers of passionate commitment and assertive individuality and have turned to the comforts of 'understanding' and 'reflection.' Men reflect on great happenings, but nothing ever happens. Men understand greatness, but no great deeds are performed. Men have become superbly rational, "Absolutely rational," but they have, in turn, forgotten "how to live."

The age is characterized, or caricatured, by its scholars and intellectuals. They are the embodiment and the culmination of a public dedicated to busy reflection and passionless inactivity. Scholars have mastered the art of reflection and have obtained the Absolute Truth of total lack of involvement and devotion. Scholars *under-*

stand life, but they do not know *how* to live:

*Like Leporello, learned literary men
keep a list, but the point is what they
lack; while Don Juan seduces girls and
enjoys himself—Leporello notes down
the time, the place, and a description
of the girl.*[5]

In their writings on Christianity, and their constant apologetics for making Christianity conveniently compatible with the non-religious life, the scholars once again have shown their great ability at reflection, and their greater disability to live. To be Christian, according to Kierkegaard, is to *suffer* before God. The theologians know little of suffering, but a great deal *about* suffering:

*The Two Ways. One is to suffer; the
other is to become a professor of the
fact that another suffered.*[6]

The intellectual literary giant of Kierkegaard's youth was, of course, Hegel, and the great philosopher as well as his philosophy were the explicit manifestation, the prime example, of the Spirit of the age. With this characterization, Hegel would, of course, be in complete accord. In Hegel, philosophical reflection had become the highest virtue of man, and the present realization of Absolute Spirit viewed through the eyes of the historical past had been shown to be the ultimate in Spiritual development. There was no serious talk or concern for the future in the Hegelian philosophy, only an adoration of the present. There was no mention of the failings of the present, and therefore no attempt to generate ideals according to which we might commit ourselves to a better future. The reflective, rational understanding of the present in view of the past was absolute knowledge; the immediate future was simply not of philosophical concern.

Kierkegaard stressed the importance of the immediate future, however, and conceived of the job of philosophy not as a detached search for knowledge and understanding, but as an involved, even desperate quest to find out what to *do*.

*What I really lack is to be clear in my
mind what I am to do, not what I am
to know, except insofar as a certain
understanding must precede every*

*action. The thing is to understand
myself, to see what God really wishes
me to do; the thing is to find a truth
which is true for me, to find the idea
for which I can live and die.*[7]

Hegel does not mention the individual except for those early portions of the *Phenomenology* and the *Philosophy of Right* where he explicitly rejects the concept of the individual in favor of the Collective Idea—the concept of Spirit.[8] Individual self-realization apart from collective Spiritual self-realization was out of the question for him. The best that one could do was to be the particular manifestation of collective Spirit, and to realize oneself in bringing about the realization of Spirit. This, of course, is precisely Hegel's own role in the development of his system, which is not merely to be considered as the development of *his* philosophy but rather the explicit development of Spirit (God) by Spirit using Hegel as a mere instrument for this realization.

In Kierkegaard, collective self-realization is not realization at all:

*The way of objective reflection makes
the subject accidental, and thereby
transforms existence into something
indifferent, something vanishing. . . .
The way of objective reflection . . .
always leads away from the subject,
whose existence or non-existence . . .
becomes infinitely indifferent.*[9]

Since Kierkegaard's concept of individual self-realization is entirely "subjective," it carries with it no guarantees of objective truth, no criterion of general applicability or universality.

*However, the objective way deems
itself to have a security which the
subjective way does not have . . . it
thinks to escape a danger which threatens
the subjective way, and this danger
is at its maximum: madness. In a
merely subjective determination of the
truth, madness and truth become
in the last analysis indistinguishable . . .*[10]

In other words, self-realization, the search for "subjective truth," is equivalent to personal expression, without regard for "objectivity". Philosophy is *not* the abstraction of universal truths from the idiosyncrasies and errors of any particular individual. Philosophy cannot be separated from the philosopher; one's philosophy is truly "his."[11] However, this repeated insistence on the "personal" aspect of philosophy must not lead us to miss the importance of several truly universal ("objective") truths that emerge from Kierkegaard's philosophy.

Given the embodiment of the depravity of the age in Hegel, it is not in the least surprising that Kierkegaard's rage should begin with a devastating attack on systematic philosophy. Despite the frequently *ad hominem* character of his arguments, Kierkegaard's objections reach far beyond Hegel, as partially evidenced by the **enormous** influence of Kierkegaard's criticisms on several generations of European thinkers. Kierkegaard objected not just to Hegel's peculiar variety of 'systematic' philosophy, but to the entire Western philosophical tradition which took the medium of philosophical enquiry to be "The Concept" (conceptual thought and analysis) and objective conceptual truth as its goal. This search for universal, impersonal truth was the defining mark of virtually every major Western philosopher from Plato until Kant and Hegel. Only those truths which held for "every rational creature," regardless of situation and psychological peculiarities, were acceptable as philosophical truths. A philosophical truth could be disclosed by a Greek philosopher of three centuries B.C., and, if true, must be valid for a Chinese philosopher of the same period as well as for an American philosopher of the twentieth century. A philosophical truth, for example, the Principle of Universal Causation or the Law of Induction, was not indigenous or peculiar to any particular philosophical style, or to any particularly endowed philosophers. These laws hold for every man, and the philosopher takes it upon himself to do nothing other than to formulate and prove these universal principles. The philosopher is explicitly concerned with these principles, but he has no privileged relationship to them.

Whether the demand for universality manifests itself as the postulation of truths existing in themselves (as in Plato's *Ideas*), or as the demands of pure universal Reason (as in traditional rationalist philosophies), or as the necessary conditions for any consciousness whatever (as in Kant), or as the peculiar notion of universality that accompanies Hegel's notion of Spirit, this demand effectively excludes everything personal or 'subjective' from philosophy. Kierkegaard's objection to this tendency to insist on universality as the mark of philosophical truths is not, as his critics maintain, a result of the desire to include his autobiographical writings in the corpus of traditional Western philosophy. The brunt of his objection is not simply that there should be room for 'subjective truth' in philosophy, but that those central issues which philosophers have been discussing in these 'objective' philosophies *cannot* be resolved in an objective way. Rather, there are truths, "essential philosophical truths," which *cannot* be determined as valid for all men, or even for a group of men, but can only be determined by the "individual subjective thinker." These truths, of which the 'highest' is the realization that the human soul is rooted in God, are expressions of individual commitment rather than of an objective detached truth which can be established by any rational impartial observer. Belief in God, in the peculiar Kierkegaardian sense which we shall discuss, is a matter of passion, not knowledge. Kierkegaard compares this 'truth' to the 'truth' embodied in a lover's declaration. The "truth" of "I love you" is a passionate commitment; a third disinterested party could never 'understand' (that is, feel himself) the intensity of the relationship, and his demand for 'justification' or 'proof' would simply be inappropriate. Similarly, one cannot *prove* that God exists; one must simply commit himself to God in the face of the absence of such a proof:

To stand on one leg and prove God's existence is a very different thing from going on one's knees and thanking him.[12]

For Kierkegaard, it is the *manner* and *intensity* of one's belief, and not the object or objective necessity of belief, which determines truth. In those issues in which no objective (universally valid) solution is possible, it can only be the degree of commitment which is philosophically relevant. From this equivalence between truth ('subjective' truth) and commitment and involvement, we may already understand the basis of Kierkegaard's departure from Hegel with regard to religious questions.

An objective uncertainty held fast in the approximation-process of the most

passionate inwardness is the truth,
the highest truth attainable for an
existing *individual.*[13]

Behind the Hegelian jargon lies a very clear statement of Kierkegaard's objectives in philosophy; to free us from the illusion that certain problems can be finally and disinterestedly settled by use of clear reflection and understanding, and to confront us with the demand that the most important philosophical questions are ultimately choices of commitments. They are problems of what to do, not conceptual dilemmas. Philosophy can clear away the old illusions from these difficult problems, but ultimately, it is only each isolated individual who is capable of supplying philosophically appropriate answers.

Kierkegaard's Life as Related to His Thought

Because of Kierkegaard's personal 'subjective' approach to philosophy, we are forced to suspend the usual insistence that we completely separate the character of the philosopher from his philosophical writings. This does not mean that an adequate psychological explanation of how he came to believe or write some particular thesis is sufficient to invalidate that thesis. Notably, one cannot argue away Kierkegaard's general thesis of the incompatibility of the secular ethical life with the life of religious devotion as a *post facto* rationalization of his youthful unexplained breaking of an engagement to be married. But because Kierkegaard so often insists on the "personal subjective validity" of his works, and because he fails to appreciate just this distinction between validity and personal expression in his frequent use of *ad hominem* arguments (towards his own writings as well as towards the writings of others), some brief consideration of the philosopher himself is necessary for an appreciation of his philosophy.

Kierkegaard was born (in 1813) into a devoutly Pietist family in which religious guilt was considered to be the definitive emotion in life. His father, in spite of considerate attention to his family in its material and intellectual needs, neglected them emotionally because of his nearly crippling state of despair over his sins before God. The despairing confrontation with personal guilt, and the anxiety and suffering accompanying the awareness of personal Sin became deeply engraved in the brooding and unhappy spirit of the young Kierkegaard. From his earliest writings in his *Journals,*[14] it is all too evident that this despair and suffering had become the defining marks of his life and his thought, and that he would never be free from the anxiety and desperation of one seeking salvation from a dread which had no object, a guilt which had no cause. The philosophical concepts of *dread* and *guilt* which play a central part in Kierkegaard's thought are universal extensions of these personal experiences.

The emotional upbringing which Kierkegaard suffered did not, however, interfere with his intellectual life. His father was insistent on intellectual acuity, and Kierkegaard became familiar with the world of scholarship at a very early age. In the University, he first confronted the philosophy of Hegel, largely through his Danish disciples and reacted strongly against the 'reflective' and impersonal attitude of the systematic philosophy. The philosopher Schelling (with whom Kierkegaard studied) also reacted strongly against Hegel, and in the years after Hegel's death he repeatedly emphasized the 'negative' aspects of Hegelianism, that is, the neglect of *existence*.

Kierkegaard became progressively disillusioned with the philosophy at the University and the empty Christianity of the Lutheran church. He dropped out of the University and out of the church and indulged in a youthful spree of sensuousness that he never enjoyed because of the guilt and despair which had never left him from his early home life. Kierkegaard returned to the University and entered the ministry as a Lutheran pastor. He became engaged to Regina Olsen, whom, from all available evidence, he loved very deeply. However, the respectable social life as pastor and husband would not fit the eccentric and troubled genius whose emotional energies were securely tied to the resolution of his religious despair. In the definitive acts of his life, Kierkegaard broke the engagement to marry, left the church, and withdrew himself from public life and began to write dozens of philosophic-religious treatises, many of which were published under pseudonyms. His works often contradicted and even explicitly attacked each other. The insistence on subjectivity and personal expression in all of his works, with his deliberate and frequent use of paradox and a refusal to legislate between two conflicting issues, combine to demonstrate his conscientious avoidance of any interpretation of his writings in the terms of the systematic philosophy so prevalent at the time.[15]

Of course, Kierkegaard's withdrawal from public life did not remove him from the public view. His contempt for contemporary mass-society and church often surfaced in vicious public denunciations of the most powerful institutions, notably the Danish press and the Lutheran church. These attacks made Kierkegaard quite well known, and frequently attacked, so that he spent considerable portions of his secluded life in open controversy.

Kierkegaard on Christianity

Kierkegaard considered his own task to be the explication of what it is *to become a Christian*. "We are all Christians—without having so much as a suspicion what Christianity is."[16] Like his predecessors Kant and Hegel, he felt the present dangers to Christianity in an increasingly secular and mass-oriented society. However, unlike the many defenders of Christianity before him who had struggled to show that the doctrines of the religion were reasonable and that philosophy, as the embodiment of reason, could show these doctrines to be objectively valid, Kierkegaard claimed that such a defense could not be successfully carried out. Christianity, far from consisting of a set of reasonable doctrines, was the paragon of absurdity. Philosophy or Reason and Christianity were absolutely irreconcilable, for the very essence of Christianity was paradox and irrationality.

To be a Christian, according to traditional religious thought, was to accept a particular set of doctrines as true. To justify Christianity, or to justify one's being a Christian, therefore, consisted in the demonstration that these doctrines were plausible and worthy of belief. Kant before him had argued that the central doctrines of Christianity were necessary postulates of (practical) reason, and that the very concept of morality required Christianity as its presupposition. Before Kant, many philosophers and theologians had constructed elaborate logical proofs of the basic tenets of Christianity, demonstrating to their own satisfaction at least that the doctrines of the Christ were defensible by appeal solely to the laws of reason. Following Kant, Hegel had attempted to show that the doctrines of Christianity, in modified form, were the logical consequence of the whole movement of Western thought.

Of course, there was the vulgar conception of "being a Christian," which also accepted the notion that Christianity was a set of true doctrines, but primarily accepted a person as a Christian if he had been born of Christian parentage and occasionally succeeded in barely consciously performing several ritual actions, such as going to church, mouthing the phonetic sequences that constituted the sentences which stated these doctrines and nodding acquiescently to their assertion from the pulpit. All of this was intimately connected, of course, with a warm satisfied feeling of holiness and self-righteousness that one got from the idea of being in the grace of God (or from winning the approval of the community). Thus, for the masses of Christians, to be a Christian was not even so deliberate as suggested by the philosophers, for the doctrines involved were never brought into question, nor were they nor need they be thought about to see whether they even make sense. To be a Christian was to be born into, or laboriously work oneself into, a mass of Christian soldiers, indistinguishable from each other, in a community before God. To be a Christian, ultimately, came to little more than identifying oneself with the Christian public—those who also considered themselves as Christians. All of this was conveniently institutionalized in the concept of the state-Church.

Thus it was established by the state as a kind of eternal principle that every child is naturally born a Christian. As the state obligated itself to furnish eternal bliss for all Christians, so, to make the whole complete, it also took upon itself to produce Christians. . . . so the state delivered, generation after generation, an assortment of Christians: each bearing the manufacturer's trademark of the state, with perfect accuracy one Christian exactly like all the others, . . . the point of Christianity became: the greatest possible uniformity of a factory product.[17]

From our introduction to Kierkegaard, it should be evident how he reacts against this state-Church (the Lutheran church of Denmark). First, there is his recurrrent insistence on individuality, which permeates his religious writings and becomes the very foundation of being a Christian:

'The individual'; now that the world has gone so far along the road of reflection, Christianity stands and falls with that category.[18]

Secondly, Kierkegaard's childhood confrontation with the despair and suffering inherent in his father's Christianity leads him to reject, with a bitterness excessive even in his works, any notion of "being a Christian" which provides men with happiness and self-satisfaction. "Christianity is suffering,"[19] and to be a Christian is to be forever conscious of the unhappy passions of dread and guilt.

Thirdly, Christianity, because it is defined by suffering and the feelings associated with Sin, is not a set of doctrines to be accepted or rejected except insofar as some minimal doctrine is required in suffering and feeling. In short, Christianity is not a mode or a body of knowledge, but it is a way of life.[20]

Fourthly, Christianity is not to be achieved easily by the individual who sets himself off from the masses, as if any man who decides to become a Christian might do so. Because of the overwhelming demands of suffering, a Christian could be only the most spectacular of men. One could not lead a successful secular life *and* be a Christian. One could only be a Christian. In fact, Kierkegaard takes as his model of Christianity the asceticism of the monastery.

Back to the monastery out of which Luther broke—that is the truth— that is what must be done. . . . The fault with the monastery was not ascetism, celibacy, etc.; no, the fault was that Christianity had been moderated by making the admission that all this was considered to be extraordinarily Christian—and the purely secular nonsense to be considered ordinary Christianity.[21]

Kierkegaard takes it upon himself to change the conception of Christianity. In the face of eighteen hundred years of attempts to change Christianity to make it reasonable, Kierkegaard responds that what must be changed is not Christianity but only our conception of Christianity, that is, what it is to be Christian.

My only analogy is Socrates. My task is a Socratic task—to revise the conception of what it means to be a Christian.[22]

In the traditional interpretation of Christianity as a set of purportedly true doctrines, the problem of justification of Christianity, that is, of justifying one's own Christianity, consisted in proving that these doctrines were plausible. Unfortunately, the rise of science and the resultant sophistication of thought had cast serious doubt about the truth, even the intelligibility, of several central Christian doctrines. To meet this challenge arose the science of *apologetics,* whose task it was to amend the Christian doctrines so as to be compatible with secular belief. "If one were to describe the whole orthodox apologetic effort in a single sentence, but also with categorical precision, one might say that it has the intent to make Christianity *plausible."* Christianity is not plausible, and its doctrines can be made convenient only at the sacrifice of Christianity.

if this effort [to make Christianity plausible] were to succeed, then would this effort have the ironical fate that precisely on the day of its triumph it would have lost everything and entirely quashed Christianity.[23]

Insofar as Christianity involves doctrines at all, becoming a Christian is accepting a set of essentially absurd doctrines, particularly the doctrine that a man was God, which Kierkegaard insists is absolutely paradoxical.

Because of the essential absurdity of key Christian doctrines, one cannot possibly bring Christianity into alignment with reason (that is, with philosophy). Acceptance of Christianity is not at all reasonable, and belief in Christ can never constitute a piece of *knowledge.* "The problem is not to understand Christianity, but to understand that it cannot be understood."[24] What this means is that although Christianity contains a set of doctrines as its foundations, to be a Christian cannot be merely the acceptance of these doctrines. The doctrines of Christianity are absurd, and an absurd doctrine is not one which one can accept as true. Since Christianity is not something that can be known at all, "acceptance" is not appropriate to it. "Christianity is not a doctrine."[25] What is required is *passion*—the passion of *faith*.

Faith is traditionally (and somewhat cynically) characterized as believing anyway what we have insufficient evidence to know. Faith, so conceived, is cognitive. It purports, if not to give us knowledge, at least to provide us with hopefully true belief in spite of a lack of warrant for that belief. But Kierkegaard relates faith to what is *absurd,* to what *cannot* be known not simply because of lack of warrant but because it is unintelligible. For Kierkegaard, faith is passion, and so he is using the notion of 'faith' in a very special sense.

Shortly after his famous definition of his peculiar notion of truth as 'passionate inwardness',[26] Kierkegaard tells us that "The above definition is an equivalent expression for faith."[27] This means that the central doctrine of Christianity is not to be *believed* in any literal sense at all, but is rather to be used as a foil, as a cause for passion, for feeling. The 'acceptance of Christianity' is in fact an acceptance of a way of life, a life of suffering, but suffering, *from a secular (third person) standpoint,* for no reason whatsoever. At the basis of this suffering is the doctrine of one's relationship before God, as signified by Christ. This doctrine is not something true or known or even literally believed. It is a *feeling* one has of constant guilt and despair, but whose object (one's Sin before God) must forever remain, not only a "mystery," but simply incomprehensible. To be a Christian, therefore, is to embark upon this 'irrational' way of life.

One might well wonder how this conception of Christianity aided Kierkegaard in overcoming his childhood suffering of dread and guilt. The obvious answer is that it was not meant to *overcome* his suffering, but that it rather constituted a *meaning* or *justification* for that suffering.

Christianity is certainly not melancholy; it is, on the contrary, glad tidings—for the melancholy.[28]

One must not conclude from this plausible explanation of Kierkegaard's acceptance of Christianity, of this dreadful life of suffering, that his philosophy is simply "subjective" in the sense in which he so often insists. Kierkegaard's own acceptance of

Christianity may well be for these very personal and even pathological reasons, but he quite consistently emphasizes the irrationality of this choice, and never, in all of his writings, misleads us by claiming that there are plausible and objectively valid reasons for making such a choice. Kierkegaard never argues or forces Christianity upon his readers, for he realizes his position could not allow such argument. Rather he simply *presents* to us the Christian way of life, considering himself only an *"occasion"* to allow others to find in themselves the faith which he has found.

With this conception of Christianity, it is clear why Kierkegaard so adamantly rejects all attempts at apologetics—all attempts to make the doctrines of Christianity "plausible." A plausible doctrine can be simply accepted, one need expend little passion in assimilating a belief that is reasonable and has been proven to him. On the other hand, it takes great emotional expense to maintain an absurd belief.[29] Because Christianity is a way of life, and its essence lies in feeling, nothing could be more inimicable to it than the success of apologetics. If one could accept the doctrine of the Trinity as one could accept, for example, the law of universal gravitation, one would have a true or at least plausible belief, but hardly a way of life. The attempt to rationalize Christianity is nothing other than the attempt to make being a Christian emotionally empty. The many attempted proofs of the faith are nothing other than aids to digestion for the emotionally lazy and the passionless.

When faith . . . begins to lose its passion, when faith begins to cease to be faith, then a proof becomes necessary so as to command respect from the side of unbelief.[30]

Of all of the follies of traditional theology, the most damaging and the most insulting is the long sequence of attempts to prove the existence of God. Kierkegaard lauds Kant's refutation of the traditional arguments, complaining only that Kant himself should not have gone on to attempt to prove in a different way that belief in God was rational. On the one hand, because God (the Christian God of the Trinity) is an absolute paradox, the very notion is antithetical to Reason, and therefore clearly not conducive to proof by Reason. However, Kierkegaard's favorite objection

to the notion of a 'proof' of God's existence lies not in the contradictoriness of
key religious doctrines, but in the impossibility of any proof of *existence:*

*Generally speaking, it is a difficult
matter to prove that anything exists;
and what is still worse for the intrepid
souls who undertake the venture, the
difficulty is such, that fame scarcely
awaits those who concern themselves
with it. The entire demonstration
always turns into something very
different from what it assumes to be,
and becomes an additional
development of the consequences that
flow from my having assumed that
the object in question exists. Thus I
always reason from existence, not
towards existence, whether I move in
the realm of palpable sensible fact or
in the real of thought. I do not, for
example, prove that a stone exists,
but that some existing thing is a
stone.*[31]

Kierkegaard is arguing an important
logical point, one which is taken more or
less directly from Kant's refutation of the
ontological argument. The claim of those
who seek to prove the existence of God is
that one can get an existential conclusion
(one asserting the existence of some 'x')
from a set of premises which do not include the assertion of the existence of 'x'.
The problem is that one cannot derive
existence unless that existence is already
given, for there is no valid inference to the
existence of 'x' from any set of statements,
no matter how complex, about 'x' (for
example, no set of statements about the
nature of unicorns, or of God, is sufficient
to show that there are unicorns, or God).
The Kantian defense of this argument lay
in the claim that "existence is not a predicate"; it is not one of the properties which
can be named in the characterization of
a thing and therefore the existence of 'x'
cannot be concluded from the characterization of 'x' (as, for example, the white-
ness of 'x' might be concluded from the
characterization of 'x' as white). One cannot say "x exists" or "x has the property of
existing". One can only say, of some existing x, that it has certain properties.[32]

However, Kierkegaard's usual lack of
regard for logical points leads him to attack the attempted proofs in a far less
rigorous but, it must be admitted, far more

touching manner. He argues that such
proofs of God's existence are nothing less
than impudent blasphemy.

*So rather let us mock God out and
out, this would always be preferable
to the disparaging air of importance
with which one would prove God's
existence. For to prove the existence
of one who is present is the most
shameless affront. . . . The existence
of a king or his presence is commonly
acknowledged by an appropriate
expression of subjection and
submission; what if, in his presence,
one were to prove that he existed.*[33]

We have emphasized that the basis of
Kierkegaard's reformulation of the conception of what it is to be a Christian is his
rejection of any attempt to prove the
rationality of Christianity. However, we
must note that Kierkegaard, like Hegel,
distorted the concept of Reason virtually
beyond recognition, and used this concept
to refer simultaneously to a faculty of the
mind and to the providing of *good reasons
for* something. When Kierkegaard claims
that Christianity is irrational and incompatible with Reason, he is claiming that
there are *no good reasons* for being a
Christian. (We shall see that even this
claim must be amended, however). He
does not claim that the *faculty* of Reason
is antithetical to the paradox of Christianity, but to the contrary insists that paradox
is the very essence of Reason (a view
clearly taken from Hegel's notion of 'dialectic').

*the paradox is the source of the
thinker's passion, and the thinker
without a paradox is like a lover
without feeling; a paltry
mediocrity. . . . The supreme paradox
of all thought is the attempt to
discover something that thought
cannot think. This passion is at bottom
present in all thinking, even in
thinking of the individual, in so far
as in thinking he participates in
something transcending himself. . . .
The paradoxical passion of the
Reason is aroused and seeks a
collision; . . . But what is this
unknown something with which the
Reason collides when inspired by its
paradoxical passion, with the result*

of unsettling even man's knowledge of himself? The Unknown.[34]

Thus, Reason is not only relevant to Christianity, but is *necessary* for an adequate acceptance of the faith.

Kierkegaard's defense of Christianity, as the whole of his thought, firmly rests on his celebration of the Individual and his rejection of collectivity and the "crowd." To be a Christian, as to be an authentic human being, is to isolate oneself and *choose* one's own mode of life with a passionate commitment, as Kierkegaard himself felt that he had done. It is this celebration of the individual and the emphasis on commitment and subjectivity that marks the major breach between Kierkegaard and Hegel and the whole of traditional Western Rationalism.

The Attack on Hegelianism

The central concerns of Kierkegaard's writings are not precisely what many would consider philosophy so much as social criticism and (anti-)theology, for he was more concerned about the degradation of society and religion by the Church and philosophers than about the problems facing the Church and philosophy. However, it must never be forgotten that Kierkegaard is very much a philosopher. The subject matter of his writings consists of traditional philosophical problems (though couched in an unusual philosophical style), and the most frequent target for attack is the rampant Hegelianism which tyrannized the philosophical world of the early nineteenth century. Taking Hegelianism to be the expression of the spirit of these times, Kierkegaard's attacks were directed towards philosophical as well as social and religious reforms. Kierkegaard simply cannot be appreciated fully unless he is studied within this philosophical context.

The reformulation of the concept of Christianity and the unnerving denunciation of the mediocrity and bourgeois complacence of a pseudoreligious pseudomoral society depended on a revitalized conception of the individual, and this in turn depended on a rejection of the foundations of German idealism and rationalism. Of course, Kierkegaard did not propose to change the spirit of the times by attacking the symptoms of Hegelianism, but he did feel that the Hegelian contempt for the individual was so deeply engraved in the institutions he was attacking that his ultimate purposes required a philosophical polemic. Apart from his concern with Hegel, Kierkegaard was very much an intellectual, never losing contact with current scholarship no matter how 'passionate' his writings. Much of the obscurity in his works can be traced to his attempts to be unscholarly, anti-intellectual and 'impassioned' while writing what cannot be considered other than very scholarly treatises.

In his frequent and often *ad hominem* attacks on Hegel, Kierkegaard never loses respect for his antagonist, and it must be remembered that in spite of his radical break with Hegel, he was yet deeply indebted to him philosophically. To begin with, his fundamental purpose was the same, the defense of Christianity. Kierkegaard's 'existential dialectic', while in many ways a repudiation of Hegel's historical dialectic, derives many of its insights and even its basic categories from Hegel. In his straightforward philosophical essays, Kierkegaard's vocabulary and philosophical manner are strikingly Hegelian,[35] although always with the addition of the sarcasm, stylistic flair, and conscientious lack of system ("fragmentation") which established Kierkegaard's fame as a writer long before his acceptance as a serious philosopher. Kierkegaard is known to display openly his admiration for Hegel, although always with characteristic reservations:

If Hegel had written his whole Logic *and in the Preface disclosed the fact that it was merely a thought experiment (in which however at many points he had shirked something), he would have been the greatest thinker that has ever lived; as it is he is merely comic.*[36]

Most importantly, Kierkegaard credits the great system builder with the culmination of all previous attempts to rationalize Christianity, enabling him to show the absurdity and inappropriateness of *any* such attempt.

Kierkegaard's opposition to the Hegelian system does not take the form of a scholarly critique, and there is not the least bit of "internal" criticism in his scathing attacks. Kierkegaard objected to the very idea of the systematic philosophy, and his attacks were lodged against the presuppositions and not the detail of the system.

Kierkegaard repeatedly guards against any interpretation of his work as one more attempt to "go beyond" or to improve upon Hegel, the widespread philosophical challenge of the day (for example, as manifested in the work of Kierkegaard's contemporary, Hans Martensen).[37]

Kierkegaard's opposition to the system can be simply summarized; philosophy, under Hegel, had left no room for *wisdom*, for *'ethics'*. "One thing has always escaped Hegel, and that is how to live." Hegel may have achieved absolute knowledge of reality, but,

The only reality that exists for an
existing individual is his own ethical
reality. What would be the use
of discovering so-called objective
truth, of working through all the
systems of philosophy . . . to construct
a world in which I do not live but
only hold up for the view of
others.[38]

Hegel, in his occupation with the backward-looking world-historical point of view, had completely ignored the living human being, who lives in a world in which history is not yet completed, and in which personal decisions yet to be made *will* be history.

It is perfectly true, as philosophers
say, that life must be understood
backwards. But they forget the other
proposition, that it must be lived
forwards. And if one thinks over that
proposition it becomes more and more
evident that life can never really be
understood in time, simply because
at no particular moment can I find
the necessary resting place from
which to understand it—backwards.[39]

Hegel gives us a system of 'Absolute Knowledge' only at the cost of excluding *practical* wisdom, the 'ethical', as part of philosophy. Yet this practical wisdom, knowledge of how to *live* and what to *do*, is precisely what Kierkegaard demands of philosophy ("thinking").[40] If Hegel's philosophy (that is, "philosophy") cannot give us this wisdom then it is of no use. This philosophy can be substituted for ethical or practical wisdom only as a *distraction* from the need to make ethical or practical decisions. The general disagreement between Hegel and Kierkegaard is

thus Kierkegaard's demand that philosophy provide us with just those edifying 'truths' which Hegel explicitly denies that it is the business of philosophy to give us.

Because this disagreement about the very purpose of philosophy is so basic, there is little communication between Kierkegaard and Hegelianism on specific issues. Much of Kierkegaard's critique takes the form of parody and *ad hominem* argument against those people who would expend the effort to do systematic philosophy:

Usually the philosophers (Hegel
as well as the rest), like the majority
of men, exist in quite different
categories for everyday purposes from
those in which they speculate, and
console themselves with categories
very different from those which they
solemnly discuss. That is the origin
of the mendacity and confusion
which has invaded scientific
(philosophical) thinking.[41]

Hegel's failure, as the failure of all of traditional rationalistic philosophy, was its avoidance of the 'subjective viewpoint', the "existence of the individual."

The way of objective reflection
makes the subject accidental, and
thereby transforms existence into
something indifferent, something
vanishing, . . . It leads
to abstract thought, to mathematics,
to historical knowledge of different
kinds, and always it leads away
from the subject whose existence or
non-existence, and from the objective
point of view, quite rightly, becomes
infinitely indifferent. Quite rightly,
since, as Hamlet says, existence
has only subjective significance.[42]

This failure comes not from an oversight on Hegel's part, or from a conscious attempt to ignore the subject and to neglect 'subjective truth', but comes from a basic "flaw" in the very conception of the systematic philosophy. The medium of the system is *The Concept,* and, in its development every aspect, every conception, of human existence is given expression. Isolated individual human existence, that is, the *concept* of individual existence, is included as one of the stages in the conceptual development of spirit. However,

*What confuses the whole doctrine
about being in Logic is that people
[i.e. Hegel] do not notice
that they are always operating
with the concept of existence . . . the
difficulty is of course whether
existence can be reduced to a
concept.*[43]

Kierkegaard complains that it cannot be so reduced. A concept is a mere possibility (or in Kant's terms, a rule), but existence requires an instantiation of that possibility (an application of that rule). The Hegelian system does attempt to capture individual existence in the logical development of concepts, but it captures only the *concept* of the individual, and not the individual. "Subjectivity" (the existence of an individual human being) can never be captured in logic for it is forever "irreducible to a concept."

According to Kierkegaard's (and Schelling's) critique, the system can speak of only what is logically *common* to all 'existents', that is, all instantiations for *x* in the ill-formed formula, 'x exists' (Heidegger's *Being* and not actual *beings*). Thus, Kant's *Transcendental Logic* exposes those concepts which are necessary conditions for "consciousness in general" while Hegel's *Logic* traces the development of the concepts of a literally 'general consciousness' which are necessary for Spiritual self-consciousness in "The Idea." In both of these philosophies, the concern is only for the Universal, the a priori, and the analysis of those fundamental concepts or Categories in logic. Logic, however, cannot capture the peculiarities of an individual person—his feelings, particular thoughts, emotions, dispositions—in short, all of those nonuniversal aspects of a person to which we refer as his *personality*. The kind of 'understanding' Kierkegaard demands of philosophy is just this sort of understanding, of psychological differences rather than logical similarities. The business of philosophy is the recognition of oneself as unique and peculiar, and not the recognition of oneself as an instance of the concept of 'humanity'. It is on the basis of such self-knowledge that we base our most fundamental commitments, and it is the understanding of the nature of such commitments which constitutes the central problem for Kierkegaard's philosophy. Philosophy for him is primarily concerned with the individual and his way of life,

not with concepts and conceptual knowledge. This objection to logic, however, is typically expressed as a logical complaint. As we have seen in the previous section, the argument begins with the point that there is a crucial distinction between the actual existence of something (for example, a human being) and the concept of that thing ("human being"). In fact, we shall see, Kierkegaard's own philosophy can be best understood as a kind of conceptual analysis ('logic') no less than the philosophy of Kant and Hegel. This logical rejection of 'logic', or, more properly, the rejection of certain claims of a logic in a *meta*logical analysis, will be a point of continuous confusion in those twentieth-century philosophers most influenced by Kierkegaard.

To exist, according to Kierkegaard, is not to be a knowing subject but to be a moral agent, and philosophy is not to answer the question "How or what can we know?" but the question "What should I do?" To answer this latter question, however, one must bring into philosophy just those nonuniversal factors which logic cannot include—one's personal fears, desires, crises, neuroses, and personal commitments. Philosophical "truth," at least the "truth" sought by Kierkegaard, is the truth of a commitment ("a wife who is true") rather than anything like knowledge ("truth" and "knowledge" are virtually interchangeable in Hegel and Kant).

In contemporary terms, one might wish to compare Kierkegaard with J. L. Austin.[44] To find the *truth* in philosophy for Kierkegaard is to make a commitment, just as to say something for Austin might constitute *doing* something (for example, promising, committing oneself) rather than describing something. Austin argues that to say "I promise you that . . ." or "I pledge allegiance to . . ." or "I love you" is not to describe some state of affairs (whether this be a worldly state or some state of mind) but to perform an action the nature of which is to be committed or pledged. Thus, "I promise . . ." does not describe a state of affairs which corresponds to the swearing of the oath: saying "I promise . . ." is itself the act of promising. We might reinterpret Kierkegaard's "objective" as contrasted with "subjective truth" as the difference between "truths" that describe some state of affairs and are thus true or false for different speakers at different times and "performative" or "subjective truths" which hold only for a particular individual just because they do not describe but rather constitute an action by the individual. Thus "I love you" or "I commit myself" are subjective truths because they are performances of the agent and not descriptions of states of affairs. There is no point in pushing this comparison at this stage of our discussion, but it may succeed in making somewhat plausible some of Kierkegaard's superficially most unpalatable claims.

Philosophy, as practiced by Kierkegaard, is directly contrary to Hegel's warning against using philosophy for edification:[45] philosophy must be edifying: "only the truth that edifies is the truth for thee."[46] Its criteria for success are not its objective validity (conformity to fact or rules of logic) but rather its ability to incite our passions. Appropriately, Kierkegaard sees his own philosophy as far more akin to religious pornography than to the cool-headed philosophical search for universal truth.

Kierkegaard distinguishes between a "cognitive reality," to which logic is appropriate, the reality *known* by men, and the very different "ethical reality" of a *moral* agent. In doing so, Kierkegaard leaves the company of Hegel (and Fichte) for a return to Kant. Reaffirming the practical-theoretical distinction in a form even more rigid than that of Kant, Kierkegaard bases his entire attack on Hegel on the claim that all systematic philosophy (and the bulk of Western philosophy) is *merely* theoretical. There is no indication, however, that Kierkegaard even once considered the reasons behind Hegel and Fichte's rejection of this very distinction. Furthermore, it is not at all clear that Kierkegaard's affirmation of two different 'realities'—one known and one acted on —is to be taken literally. (Although, as we indicated in Chapter 1, there is reason to suppose that Kant sometimes held a similar thesis. However, Kant's 'two-world' thesis had the virtue of being sufficiently obscure so as not to obviously commit him to what is *prima facie* an absurd thesis; that the world we know is ontologically not the world in which we live.)

Kierkegaard's objections to the detached and 'collective' nature of Hegel's system may be illuminated by contrast with the unsystematic philosophy of Socrates, to whom Kierkegaard frequently appeals. Wisdom, and not indifferent truths—practical guides for living and not reflective understanding—are the goals of Socratic inquiry. Wisdom, however, is not a property of a group or a society, but that of an individual, a property which manifests itself in wise *reaction to* the group. Nowhere in history is such wisdom better displayed than in the individuality of Socrates' own life and thought. Of course, Socrates (at least the Platonic Socrates) differed from Kierkegaard in believing these ethical guides to be objective and universal and virtue to be a form of knowledge. However, the Socratic virtues were not merely "abstract universals" (that is, mere principles) but were dispositions to act virtuously in the few men who would attain such wisdom. Kierkegaard has no use for Hegel's "Universal in action," which he (misunderstandingly) claims is a purely conceptual notion. The only universal (principle) of importance is that which is manifested in action and, Kierkegaard adds, that need not be universal at all in the sense of holding for all people at all times. (Kierkegaard adopts a formal notion of universalizable principles in his characterization of the "ethical mode of Existence." His attack on the universal in Hegel is thus an attack upon Hegel's rationalizing method and not universal principles as such.) Philosophical inquiry for Socrates and Kierkegaard has its beginnings in an individual's confrontation with an ethical dilemma. Knowledge is knowledge only with reference to the demand of that individual to know what to *do*. Socrates, like Kierkegaard (and unlike Plato and Kant) considers mathematics and the abstract sciences as pointless; to know *thyself* is the end of all inquiry. Hegel, quite to the contrary, left no room for the future in his system, and therefore no room for the question "What should I do?" The concept of the individual, for him, was an inadequate and outmoded concept which had been surpassed (*aufgehoben*)[47] in the dialectic of the system, and preserved only in the abstract notion of "Spirit," which, according to Kierkegaard, is the very negation of the concept of the "existing individual." For Hegel, Socrates could only represent an inferior sort of knowledge, and possess an inadequate conception of himself; that is, the conception of himself as an individual *alienated* from his society. A modern day Socrates would not require hemlock, but only a copy of the *Phenomenology* (or the *Philosophy of Right*) to make him realize that the truth lies not in individual rebellion, but in reconceptualizing one's self-image as an integral part of the group. The moral conflict facing Socrates could arise only with an inadequate conception of oneself, and could be resolved only by a reflective mediation of this conception. Of course, Socrates, as an expression of his age and the group against which he rebelled, could not have conceived the matter so. The reflective Hegelian perspective shows that Socrates' sacrifice was only an historical necessity, and that no Hegelian could be faced with the same irresolvable dilemma today.

In Hegel's *Logic,* no paradox was absolute, that is, unresolvable. A paradox or contradiction, an opposed set of ideas, could always be resolved by finding a "higher synthesis" or a further idea which embraced the central principles of the opposed theses. According to Hegel, such "oppositions" were not always literal contradictions, but included such oppositions as his earlier "disharmonies," between God and man, between the individual and society, and between morality and inclination. It may be that these various oppositions could be stated in the form of logical contradictions, for example, "Morality is duty for duty's sake" and "morality is not duty for duty's sake but a satisfaction of inclinations," but Hegel himself did not take the notion of contradiction in this strict form. Thus, the contradiction between man and transcendent God is not a breach in logic but rather a source of spiritual discomfort for the Christian believer, who feels alienated from his God and imposed upon by His moral laws. *Paradox* ("contradiction," "opposition"), thus broadly conceived, exists between various conceptions—the conception of God as transcendent and of man as separated from God. Conceptions could be *mediated* in Logic in the movement of conceptual thought to the resolution of such oppositions. Thus, the contradictory conceptions of God and man are mediated in the 'higher' conception of 'Immanent God' or 'Spirit'. Similarly, the contradictory conceptions of morality as reason and duty and the conception of man as a creature of passion, can be mediated in the conception of *Sittlichkeit*—the morality which is rational, but according to reason embodied in the customs and mores of a particular society. In Hegel, all such paradoxes or contradictions, including those of morality and religion as well as those of

traditional Logic (narrowly conceived) could be so mediated.

It is important to note that Kierkegaard agreed with Hegel that such mediation of paradox was possible, and that Hegel had succeeded in doing so in his *Science of Logic.* However, such mediation was possible only between concepts, and Kierkegaard complains that Hegel once again has confused concepts—that is, what is universal—with existence—that is, what is particular to an individual. Logic, properly conceived as the science of concepts, was amenable to Hegel's treatment, but existence proper, namely, the existence of the individual, was not reducible to a concept, and the paradoxes which existed for an individual could not be mediated. Kierkegaard is referring not to the logical paradoxes which might plague an individual studying Logic (for example a student who is not able to understand the "liar" paradox). These can be mediated—solved without reference to that particular individual. However, the paradoxes of morality and religion, and here 'paradox' refers not to an opposition of concepts but an opposition of courses of action, are not part of logic and so cannot be mediated. These paradoxes are *Absolute,* and cannot be resolved through the reflection of logic.

The paradoxes of ethics—the paradoxes of 'living'—consist in the daily confrontation of the individual with *choices,* with alternative courses of action. A paradox of ethics is a crisis in living, and truth, in ethics, is the resoluton of crisis through action and commitment. A choice of one course of action, however, is not only that but is also a choice of an entire way of life implicit in that choice. For example, to choose a moral course of action over a selfish amoral course of action is to choose a moral way of life over a selfish way; it is to tacitly adopt a *general* principle that one should choose the moral over the selfish. Similarly, one who acts in the name of God instead of in the name of society or personal desire has implicitly committed himself to a religious way of life and tacitly adopted a general principle regarding the ultimate importance of God's word. Of course, one can change principles and ways of life, frequently perhaps, but one can never make a choice against the personal and for the moral without endorsing morality. One cannot act in God's name without endorsing piety. One does not act morally because he is moral; one is moral because he acts morally. Kierkegaard's notion of committing oneself to principle in acting, as opposed to acting strictly on the basis of principle, will become, in the philosophy of Jean-Paul Sartre, a cornerstone for a revolutionary theory of value.

The claim that ethical paradoxes are *absolute* is the claim that ethical decisions are ultimately based on a choice between incompatible ways of life. It is the view that ultimate ethical choices—the choice of ultimate standards or a way of life—are choices "either/or"; one cannot compromise to have the best of both ways or 'mediate' between choices as Hegel believed one could in the realm of logic. As Kierkegaard states the problem, concepts are mediatable, courses of action are not. This does not mean, of course, that one can *never* find a way of compromising between alternative courses of action or that *any* two courses of action are incompatible. Clearly my choice 'between' wanting to run for parliament and wanting to get my opponent out of government are not only compatible but complimentary. It is commonly supposed that Kierkegaard proposes that all choices are of the crisis sort and that every choice is directed to a choice of a way of life. As we shall see, this is a serious misunderstanding. The absolute paradoxes of ethics arise in one important context, in the choice between ultimate principles, or between the choice between courses of action in which different ways of life are uniquely implicit.

Choice of a way of life must always involve a *commitment* to act in certain ways in the unknown future (in the face of *"objective uncertainty."* This is the "ethical paradox"). In a choice of immediate action, one cannot wait until the crisis of the moment is passed to gain Hegelian reflective insight. Action requires immediate decision, and cannot wait until the outcome of the action is known. Action is always 'objectively uncertain'; it is always 'projected toward the future'. Ethical wisdom, unlike 'absolute knowledge', always requires *risk.* In ethics one must act before the results are in, for it is the action itself that brings about the results. Thus, the paradoxes of practical wisdom cannot be viewed reflectively and disinterestedly. They always must be viewed in the 'passion' of crisis, and their solution always demands commitment to a way of life. Only later, perhaps, can the luxury of reflective understanding of what one has done be enjoyed.

The notion of choice in Kierkegaard cannot be separated from his notion of 'freedom', for it is the freedom of the existing individual to make choices, together with the demand that he make choices, which define the 'paradoxical' nature of ethical existence, that is, the continuous confrontation of the individual with alternative and exclusive possibilities of action. Freedom is also one of the key notions of Hegel's system. It is the concept of 'freedom' that has developed and 'realized' along with "The Idea" in *Logic* and "Spirit" in the *Phenomenology*. Hegel's Spirit is freedom (as Kant's moral ego "is Freedom"), and the development of Spirit is the development of freedom, that is, the continuous opening of new possibilities from the inadequate conceptions of the past. The progression of the dialectic has been considered as a breakdown of imposing conceptual systems—imposing in that they posit some opposition for Spirit—and the system culminates in absolute freedom, that is, a conception of (absolute) Spirit which recognizes no limitations other than those which it imposes upon itself.

For Hegel, *freedom* is not merely the *negative* freedom *from* constraint or imposition, however, and his notion of 'freedom' does not exclude the notion of 'necessity' to which the concept of freedom is ordinarily opposed. Hegel's doctrine of freedom was emphatically a doctrine of *positive* freedom, the freedom of Spirit *to* realize itself. Freedom thus requires constraint, the constraint of the senses, the constraint of the understanding, and finally the constraints of reason which are self-imposed, for example, the constraints of the moral law, and ultimately, the constraints of religious belief.

Freedom, as Hegel develops it through the *Philosophy of Right* and the *Lectures on History* is not the freedom of an individual, but the freedom of Spirit developed over the course of human history. Of course, individuals of any single period manifested the conception of freedom of that particular age, but freedom is ultimately the conforming of the individual to the rational ideals of his age. His freedom consists only in this and not in the freedom to escape from these constraints. Freedom of the individual is not freedom to choose between alternative possibilities, such as to obey or not to obey the laws of one's state or church. Here, it is clear that Kierkegaard must once again reject a basic conception of the Hegelian system. Whereas Hegel insists that freedom is a property of the collective idea and freedom for the individual is the freedom to act according to the ideals of the group, Kierkegaard would insist that this is just the antithesis of individual freedom. Freedom has meaning *only* with regard to the individual, and freedom to submit one's will to the dictates of the group is the very opposite of an expression of freedom, not a manifestation of it.

In Hegel's treatment of positive freedom as a property of the group and only derivatively of the individual, the notion of choice is clearly not essential or even relevant. The individual is free only insofar as he acts with the group, and therefore it does not even make sense to speak of his freedom to rebel from the group and go his own way. Similarly, the notion of *responsibility* plays a small role in Hegel's philosophy, for a man can be held responsible only for his failure to conform to society's dictates, because one has the freedom ("positive freedom"), to make only one set of choices, that is, to go along with the group. Although Kierkegaard is not often involved in politics, his few political writings make it unmistakably clear that he is opposed to any such group evasion of responsibility through a notion of 'collective freedom'. Thus he criticizes the tendencies towards democracy and socialism in Europe at mid-century on the basis that these are essentially manifestations of this escape from responsibility.

Along with the responsibility of one's choices, without any idealization of the group to give one a safe standard from which to choose, comes the personal equivalent of Hegel's feared 'reign of terror'—*despair*. With the responsibility for one's choices, without the group to comfort one that he did the right thing, freedom of choice becomes the *despair* of freedom, and then the *guilt* of responsibility—an unhappy combination well-suited to the morbid demands of Kierkegaard's suffering-ridden conception of Christianity.

Kierkegaard's personal contempt for Hegelianism lay in the system's treatment of Christianity. For Hegel, as for a long tradition of European thought, Christianity consisted of a set of doctrines to be believed by Christians; to be a Christian was to believe these doctrines. In its attempts to make Christianity palatable, philosophers (that is, Hegel) had removed everything Christian about it. Philosophers had given new and totally alien meanings to central Christian concepts, and replaced the need to have faith with the need to read philosophy:

No human being can ever have been in such distress as Christianity of late . . . The entire Christian terminology has been appropriated by speculative thought to its own purposes, under the assumption that speculative thought and Christianity are identical. . . . The concepts have gradually been emasculated and the words have been made to mean anything and everything.[48]

According to Hegel, the contrast between faith and reason is in our time a contrast within philosophy itself, but faith has nothing to do with reason or philosophy.

"The idea of philosophy is mediation: Christianity is the paradox,"[49]

and proof and reflection have no part in the conception of Christianity.

Faith does not need it; aye, it must even regard proof as the enemy.[50]

Christianity is not a set of doctrines, and therefore not a set of doctrines that can be proved to be true or made reasonable. The problem of Christianity is not the truth of Christianity, but the relation of the individual to Christianity, the concern of the "infinitely interested individual."

Becoming a Christian is not a result of philosophical ('scientific') inquiry, but a question of deep personal involvement or "faith":

Faith does not result simply from scientific inquiry; it does not come directly at all. On the contrary, in this objectivity one tends to lose that infinite personal interestness which is the condition of faith.[51]

In Hegel, Christianity is the *result* of his system; that is, it is the absolute knowledge consisting of realization of oneself as Spirit. Argues Kierkegaard,

If inwardness is truth, results are only rubbish with which we should not trouble each other.[52]

The doctrines of Christianity are not important, except as objects of *faith*, not knowledge. Faith, as subjectivity,[53] can *not* be had by a doctrine, or by a religion, or by a church, but only by an individual who "chooses the path of faith." Hegel's understanding of Christianity as a doctrine of the Spirit, that is, spirit's conception of itself ("making 'God' a public word"), is fundamentally at odds with Kierkegaard's conception of Christianity as a way of life which is chosen not because it is true or even plausible, but simply because one *personally* commits himself without appeal to reasons or Reason at all.

The Meaning of Existence
Although Kierkegaard's attack on Hegel's treatment of "existence" begins with a point of Logic borrowed from Schelling— namely, that actual existence can never be reduced to a concept which signifies only the possibility of actual existence—it is quite clear that Kierkegaard is concerned only with a particular kind of existence, namely, individual human existence. His attack on Hegel's 'negative philosophy' (Schelling's characterization) for its neglect of actual existence is merely an initial support for his more personal concern for Hegel's failure to value the individual human being standing apart from the 'crowd'. In actuality, Kierkegaard is as worried about the *concept* of human existence as was Hegel, for in spite of all his insistence on subjectivity, it is the *defining* characteristics of individuality which he seeks to disclose in his writings. His attack on 'negative philosophy', along with his overreaction to the notion of *objective truth,* therefore, can be considered somewhat of a facade. Kierkegaard's true objection to Hegel is simply his failure to appreciate the seriousness of ethical dilemmas facing the individual, that is, to appreciate that the concept of 'individual existence' involves the notions of 'choice', 'individual freedom', 'responsibility,' and, with these, the concepts of 'commitment', 'despair', and 'guilt'.

This is a point rarely appreciated by defenders of Kierkegaard's notion of 'subjectivity', that Kierkegaard is blinded by his insistence on valuing the subjective or personal individual so as to thoroughly confuse (as he accuses Hegel of confusing) existence with the concept of existence. Kierkegaard, as much as Hegel, is concerned to show the nature of the concept of 'individual existence', but he differs radically in his *analysis* of 'existence'. Accordingly, much of what Kierkegaard

claims, for example, the (logical) *necessity* of choice and commitment, is to be interpreted just as much as a conceptual claim as Hegel's discussion of the concept of 'Being' in the beginning of the *Logic.*

This is not to deny, however, that it still makes sense, in a way, to speak of Kierkegaard's writings as 'subjective'. While he endeavours to show us what the concept of 'existence' means ("the meaning of existence"), unlike Hegel and the rationalists before him, Kierkegaard leaves the correctness of the ways of life to which one commits himself an open question to be settled only by the individual. In other words, Kant and Hegel had attempted to prove the objective necessity for believing in God, and, as such, to prove that every rational being ought to believe. Kierkegaard denies that any such objective necessity can be demonstrated, and then, in the face of this 'objective uncertainty' (the existence of God neither proven or disproven), it is the choice of the individual whether to believe or not. This is the subjective truth of which we hear so much— that some decisions cannot be made rationally. This notion of 'subjectivity' is very different from the doctrines attributed to Kierkegaard to the effect that he rediscovered or 'rescued' the 'subjective individual' from the 'concept'. If this is supposed to mean that Kierkegaard ceased to talk about the *concept* of *individual existence,*[54] then it must be an incorrect interpretation of Kierkegaard. Whether Kierkegaard *admits* that he is doing conceptual analysis or not, nothing can be clearer from his writings than the claim that the very *concept* of 'the individual' entails the notions of 'passion', 'choice', 'commitment', and 'freedom'.

The idea that Kierkegaard dispensed with the concepts in favor of a renewed attention to the individual can only be a gross misunderstanding of his philosophy (one which even he shares with his commentators). Kierkegaard does construct a conceptual system and does conceptual analysis; it is *on this basis* that he makes room for subjectivity. If the emphasis on 'subjectivity' seeks only to stress the ultimate necessity to settle these philosophical issues of ultimate criteria on a strictly personal level, it must be understood that this claim of subjectivity cannot be extended to Kierkegaard's writings as a whole; otherwise the 'objective' framework within which he proves the subjectivity of choices of ultimate values collapses. One can say "all values are arbitrary; I choose 'x'." One cannot say "I choose that all values are arbitrary," and expect that he has done anything intelligible. On the other hand, it has often been supposed that Kierkegaard argues that "all values are arbitrary for me," but nothing could be further from Kierkegaard's intentions; how much of his writings are the demonstration of his personal *necessity* for belief in God; how much is the purpose of his writings (as stated in his *Point of View*) an attempt to get others to see *the truth,* that is, the *necessity* of commitment.

It is not sufficient, however, to characterize Kierkegaard's approach as an analysis of the ordinary concept of 'individual existence', for Kierkegaard was not particularly concerned with stating what it is to be a man (what is involved in the concept of 'man' if this means a humanoid more-or-less conscious creature). Kierkegaard speaks of 'individual existence' in a very special sense, a sense in which a man is not simply a biological, psychological, or social animal, but in which a man is a *'human being'* an *'existent'* which is something far more exciting than the 'mere' existence of a particular organism. This notion of 'existence' is reserved for those who live as individuals, not biologically, but individually in their thought and their values. It is a term specially designed for those who are personally committed, who feel their freedom in despair, who recognize their responsibility for their actions (which for Kierkegaard means resultant guilt more than pride). The *human being,* who merits this special designation of his life as *existence,* is the passionate antisocial or at least asocial individual who is master of his own life, the author of his own values.

It is impossible to exist without passion, unless we understand the word 'exist' in the loose sense of a so-called existence.[55]

And it is just this that it means to exist, if one is to become conscious of it. Eternity is a winged horse, infinitely fast, and time is a worn-out jade; the existing individual is the driver. That is to say, he is such a driver when his mode of existence is not an existence loosely so called; for then he is no driver but a drunken peasant who lies asleep in the

wagon and lets the horses take care of themselves. To be sure, he also drives and is a driver, and so there are many who—also exist.[56]

This play between two senses of 'exists' and 'existence' (and occasionally 'being') permeates all of Kierkegaard's writings (as well as the writings of later 'existentialists'). Kierkegaard, unlike the many philosophers after Descartes for whom personal existence was simply self-evident, insists that *existence* is something *to be striven for.* In this sense, therefore, the standard and worn existentialist cliché "existence precedes essence" does not apply literally to Kierkegaard (or to Heidegger). Given Kierkegaard's special use of "existence," a man *exists* only after a despairing struggle to separate himself from the 'so-called' existence of the collective idea. If one wishes to consider one's essence those defining roles or commitments which he accepts (which is the characterization used by the later existentialists), then we might say that "existence comes only with essence" for Kierkegaard, for it is only by passionately committing, or defining oneself that one can *exist* at all. The meaning of *existence,* therefore, is the significance which one provides for his own life, through realization of one's personal freedom and autonomy, through passionate commitment, through responsibility and the feelings accompanying freedom and responsibility. The unthinking bourgeoisie and even the reflective professional philosopher (for example, Hegel) have only a 'so-called' existence in the uninteresting sense that they take up space, breathe, digest, excrete, and perform sufficiently sophisticated behaviors that we might call them 'men'. This humanoid, "so-called" existence is distinguished by the capacity for abstract thinking, but this, according to Kierkegaard, still leaves man far from *true existence.* The problem of philosophy for Kierkegaard is how to transcend this *mere existence;* and the starting point of his philosophy must be, therefore, the analysis of real or *authentic*[57] existence.

Kierkegaard complains that Western philosophy (after Socrates) has ignored 'individual existence,' but this objection at first must appear grotesque in the light of the almost fanatic attention philosophers of "modern" times have focused on Descartes' *"Cogito, Ergo sum."* On the contrary, it would seem more likely that the crucial problems in Western philosophy *began* with Descartes' unfortunate starting point—his own personal 'subjective' existence. Affirmation of personal existence has dominated philosophy from Descartes' "I think, therefore I am," as reiterated with modifications in Kant's notion of the "I think" which must be capable of accompanying all our representations, and once again in Fichte's initial positing of the ego, in Schelling's Absolute, and even Hegel's system—in Spirit. It is clear, therefore, that Kierkegaard cannot be intelligibly interpreted as simply complaining that it is the idea of the subject that has been ignored in philosophy.

The subject that has been the starting point of philosophy from Descartes through Kant and Fichte has not been the subject from which Kierkegaard demands philosophy begin. For Descartes, as for Kant, the subject of philosophical inquiry is the "I think," the 'cognitive subject' whose reality is a 'cognitive reality'. The reality of the "I think" is that which it thinks—and the starting point of modern Western philosophy has been—"I think; I have thoughts; now what is the reality to which these thoughts correspond?" The subject of philosophical inquiry is the thinking subject; Descartes claims that the subject is a thinking substance that has thoughts, and Kant argues that one must presuppose a thinking subject (although not a thinking substance) and that this subject is the real (as opposed to the empirical) subject. For Kierkegaard, however,

The real subject is not the cognitive subject, ... the real subject is the ethically existing subject.[58]

The Cartesian *cogito* and the Kantian "I Think" (as well as Hegel's "Spirit") provide us with only the *idea* of a subject— the 'mere' understanding of a concept yet to be instantiated. Kierkegaard's emphatic separation of the 'Concept' and 'existence' is nowhere more important than in our alleged 'knowledge' of our own existence. The individual subject is not an idea, he tells us, and thus is not something 'merely' known:

A particularly existing human being is surely not an idea, and his existence is surely something quite different from the conceptual existence of the Idea. An

existence as a particular human being is doubtless an imperfection in comparison with the eternal life of the Idea, but it is a perfection in comparison with not existing at all.[59]

The Cartesian *cogito ergo sum* is confused, according to Kierkegaard, because the *cogito* presupposes one's existence and does not prove it.

"Because I exist and because I think, therefore I think that I exist ... I must exist in order to think.[60]

It should be evident from this critique of the *cogito* that Kierkegaard has misunderstood or at least ignored the role of the *cogito* in traditional philosophy. That personal existence is a *presupposition* of thinking is just what Descartes and Kant wish to establish. Moreover, if Descartes and Kant (and Hegel) treat the *cogito* as a piece of propositional knowledge in their philosophies, this does not in the least indicate that they consider the *cogito* to constitute all of one's personal existence. Once again, we see that Kierkegaard's attack, although apparently focusing upon a specific philosophical claim, is an attack on an entire attitude towards philosophy, not on specific claims.

Kierkegaard again scores the traditional stress on knowledge, and then insists that the *cogito* has been wrongly construed as a piece of (a priori) knowledge. We do not simply *know* that we exist:

The only reality to which an existing individual may have a relation that is more than cognitive is his own reality, the fact that he exists: this reality constitutes his absolute interest. Abstract thought requires him to become disinterested in order to acquire knowledge; the ethical demand is that he became infinitely interested in existing.[61]

Kierkegaard's attack on the "I Think" presupposes a sharp distinction between the theoretical and the practical,[62] and argues that there is only a practical (living or *existing*) self and no theoretical (transcendental) self. Kant had postulated two selves, a transcendental and a moral (willing) self, but had argued that only the former could be known. Why this emphasis upon the *knowing* self?, asks Kierkegaard. Why not begin with the willing, striving, living, existing self, "I suffer, therefore I am" or "I get married, therefore I am?" Why are these not considered the self-evident truths of philosophy instead of the celebrated *cogito?* In reaction to this traditional starting point, Kierkegaard diametrically opposes traditional Cartesian viewpoint by denying the existence of the thinking subject altogether:

But if the "I" in the Cogito *is interpreted as meaning a particular existing human being, philosophy cries: "How silly; here there is no question of yourself or myself, but solely of the pure ego." But this pure ego cannot very well have any other than a purely conceptual existence . . ."*[63]

To attempt to infer existence from thought is thus a contradiction.[64]

As we have seen, a "purely conceptual existence" is no existence at all.

As Kierkegaard draws apart the *cogito* or transcendental ego and the moral or ethical ego, the *cogito* becomes lost altogether. Kierkegaard tells us that only our ethical reality is reality, that the "abstract thinker," the *cogito,* does not even exist:

What is abstract thought? It is thought without a thinker.[65]

An abstract thinker exists, to be sure, but this fact is rather a satire on him than otherwise. For an abstract thinker to try to prove his existence by the fact that he thinks is a curious contradiction; for in the degree that he thinks abstractly he abstracts from his own existence. Insofar his existence is revealed as a presupposition from which he seeks emancipation; but the act of abstraction nevertheless becomes a strange sort of proof for his existence, since if it succeeded entirely his existence would cease.[66]

Behind the attack on Cartesianism, we can clearly discern the very significant agreement with Hegel which leads Kierkegaard to these extreme conclusions. Hegel had argued that the concept of Spirit could not be adequately understood in terms of *individuals;* Kierkegaard agrees with this claim, but so much worse for the conception of Spirit. Kierkegaard is interested in the *concept of the individual,* and if nei-

ther the *cogito,* nor Kant's "I think", nor Hegel's Spirit provides us with such a concept, then they must all be rejected. It is not just these concepts which must be rejected but rather the way of thinking which leads to them. We recall that Hegel attacked Kant's critique of knowledge with the objection that it led to an unrecognized skepticism at least as insidious as the skepticism growing from Descartes' *Meditations.* Kierkegaard also sees the problems of a critique of knowledge in the style of Descartes or Kant, but disagrees with them as well as with Hegel that such an enterprise is even possible:

A skepticism which attacks thought itself cannot be vanquished by thinking it through, since the very instrument by which this would have to be done is in revolt. There is only one thing to do with such a skepticism, and that is to break with it.[67]

Kierkegaard's "break" is a return to 'subjectivity', a refusal to even ask the question about our *knowledge* of our world and focus attention only on our intentions and attitudes towards this world. For Kierkegaard, the traditional problems of epistemology and metaphysics are dismissed out of hand; the commonsense answers to the questions that had plagued Descartes and Kant are simply and naively assumed without doubt.

Subjectivity is truth, subjectivity is reality.[68]

The meaning of human *existence* according to Kierkegaard lies in its constant and conscious inner striving *(strebend),* parallel to the fundamental notion of *conatus* in Spinoza and the *Will* in Schopenhauer. However, these latter two philosophers took the task of philosophy to be the *suppression* of this irrational force through the contemplative calm of philosophy. Kierkegaard took as his philosophical task the glorification and maximization of this striving (at the expense of contemplation). For Kierkegaard, as for most philosophers of the Western tradition, to exist as a man is to desire, to fear, to be, if not the slave of one's passions, at least passionate. Few philosophers would adopt Hume's doctrine that "Reason is and ought to be the slave of the passions," for the great philosophies of the West have had a prominent goal, the victory of reason over the passions through philosophical reflection. Kierkegaard would go further still, and Reason for him cannot even occupy the degraded status afforded it by Hume, namely, to direct the will to the fulfillment of the passions. According to Kierkegaard, the ultimate demands of the passions must be outside the scope of Reason. One's choice of a way of life, as opposed to one's choice of a specific course of action within a well-established value framework, has no reasons to support it. Departing from nearly every philosophy in the Western tradition, therefore, Kierkegaard has Reason play virtually no role whatever in answering the most pressing question of philosophy, that is, "What is the good life for man?"

Paradoxically, this is not to say that Reason plays no part in coming to the conclusion that Reason has no part to play in answering this question. To the contrary, Kierkegaard's arguments to the effect that ultimate choices are 'irrational' constitute the central contribution of his philosophy to the existentialist movement. It is his doctrine of 'choice' and 'freedom of choice', and his analysis of these concepts, which sets the stage for the entire existentialist movement away from traditional rationalism.

To achieve authentic individual existence is to commit oneself, deliberately and passionately, to a way of life. Existence is a continuous confrontation with emergencies, competing desires, situations in which choices must be made. The ultimate meaning of existence is not an a priori given, but one's ultimate commitment, the choice not of *this* or *that* course of action, but of a "mode of existence" within which all more particular choices may be determined.

A young student wishes to know whether to heed his father's advice and study business in college or whether he should "drop out" altogether with the encouragement of many of his friends. Assuming the student is not willing (as Kierkegaard demands that he not be) to simply follow advice or encouragement of others, what he seeks is a criterion or standard by which to choose. What is clear in this now-familiar case is the enormous 'gap' of irreconcilability between the two choices and the 'styles of life' consequent with them. Now if the student ultimately wants the community respectability consequent on a business career, his choice is

clear. Similarly, if he has no sympathy for the often grueling demands of the bourgeois business life, his choice is also clear. In other words, once the style of life is known, the particular choices follow from certain rules concerning what is needed within that life.

Given a "mode of existence," the decision can be made by appeal to what Kant called a *hypothetical* imperative; given that one ultimately wants 'x', then the choice between 'y' and 'z' can be made strictly on the grounds of which best leads to 'x'. Given that one knows what he ultimately wants, all more particular choices can be made more or less mechanically, by appeal to the efficacy of one alternative over another in obtaining the desired ultimate end. Thus, if one has chosen a way of life (for example, has chosen to be a respected member of the community), his choice between business studies and 'negative freedom' can be made easily. The only *arbitrary* decision within such a framework is in those cases in which it really does not matter for purposes of one's ultimate goals, whether 'y' or 'z' is chosen.

How does one come to have an ultimate set of goals or a way of life? Because these are ultimate, one cannot appeal them to some more ultimate consideration. These are what Kant referred to as *categorical* imperatives, those which cannot be defended on the basis of some further imperative. Kant attempted to justify one set of these ultimate values by an appeal to pure practical reason; by showing that these values are (transcendentally) *necessary* for any morality. However, one can still ask, as Hegel sometimes points out, why one ought to be moral. In a Kierkegaardian vein, even if one were to agree that those principles Kant identifies as categorical imperatives are necessary for any morality, any particular individual might ask why *he* should have to follow Reason's dictates. In other words, even if we grant that certain principles can be defended by appeal to Reason, one can then turn about and challenge the value of Reason itself. "Granted I *ought* to do 'x' because it is the moral thing to do, but why should I do the moral thing? If I ought to do the moral thing because it is the reasonable thing, why should I be reasonable?" What can the Kantian answer to this?

Kierkegaard claims that no answer can be given, for the value of Reason can be challenged as any more particular ethical principles might be challenged. How then, does one decide whether to be reasonable, to follow the dictates of reason and be moral? There is no way, for any further suggested criterion, for example, "living reasonably will result in living more happily," "living reasonably is necessary for a stable society," or "living reasonably is necessary for mental health," can be challenged in precisely the same way. "Why should I be happy?" "Why should I care about society?" "Why should I want to be healthy?" can always be raised in reply, as can similar challenges for any suggested 'ultimate' ethical criterion.[69]

We now face a serious problem, if the choice of ultimate criteria, of a way of life, cannot be made by appeal to some set of criteria, how can we go about choosing at all? Kierkegaard's answer is that we simply have to choose, without appeal to further standards, without reasons, without justification. We simply have to decide, 'irrationally'—that is, without Reason— how we are going to live, by what ultimate standard we are going to make decisions.

Reason, that is, the capacity to give reasons and justify our choices, can play no part in this ultimate decision, for here we have the need for 'pure' commitment, without appeal to any supporting principles, and therefore without reasons or Reason. "Choice is ultimately *irrational*," means that one cannot ultimately give reasons for his choices, as all choices are founded on one's fundamental choice of criteria and that ultimate choice is itself unjustifiable.

Because our fundamental criteria are unjustifiable, all our choices, which depend on these criteria for their justification, are also ultimately unjustifiable. Yet, we must choose, must "leap to" a way of life if we are to *exist,* for the only alternative (apart from suicide or a total retreat to inactivity) is to refuse to acknowledge the absence of ultimate justification (what Sartre later refers to as "bad faith") or, what is worst, to abstain from choice of existence altogether and simply follow the 'crowd.'[70] Because our ultimate choices are unjustifiable, an unhappy spirit such as Kierkegaard can easily find that the demand for choice becomes a crucifying demand; for the burden of choice is entirely on one's own shoulders; no other support, whether it be from society, from one's religious teachings, or from Reason itself can be made responsible for one's decisions. Because no criteria can be used in ultimate decisions, one cannot blame these criteria

for the choice that one makes. The incredible responsibility of having no one and no value to which to turn leads Kierkegaard to cite *despair* as an essential ingredient in freedom of choice, to cite *guilt* as an essential component of responsibility, and to identify *dread,* the dread of an indefinitely large range of possibilities which it is one's own responsibility to choose between, as the defining passions of human existence.

There is a great deal said of the 'irrationalism' which lies at the core of Kierkegaard's philosophy and the existentialist movement as a whole. However, from what we have said thus far, it should be evident that such bandying about of terminology must be carefully guarded. Kierkegaard is an irrationalist in at least one important respect, he claims that Reason is inappropriate as an aid to the most important choices of our lives. However, the *reason* for this inappropriateness is the absence of any objective standard for making these choices, by virtue of the fact that they themselves are ultimate. Irrationalism refers simply to this absence of ultimate standards of value. However, overzealous enthusiasts of modern existentialism have delighted in stretching this irrationalist claim even beyond Kierkegaard's too-liberal use of it. They say that Kierkegaard dispenses with Reason altogether, and his writings are writings of pure passion. However, from what we have said, it is clear that Kierkegaard does not deny Reason its place in human thought, but denies only its relevance to the specific problems of *existence;* a choice of values. Moreover, it is only through a more or less carefully reasoned argument that Kierkegaard is able to conclude that ultimate objective standards for value are not available. It is only through an impressive exercise of Reason that Kierkegaard comes to the conclusion that Reason is inadequate in certain contexts.

The most horrifying misinterpretation of Kierkegaard's doctrine of irrationalism is the too popular thesis that all values, and therefore all decisions, are arbitrary. Therefore, it *does not matter* which value system, which way of life one chooses. However, if there is any feature of Kierkegaard's philosophy which cannot be missed by the most distracted reader, it is Kierkegaard's almost pathological concern with how much the choice of ultimate values *must* matter to us. It may well be the case that these choices are ultimately unjustifiable, but they are our responsibility, and the "arbitrariness" of choice, far from alleviating us from concern, imposes on us the most terrifying burdens.

It would also be a serious mistake to leave the reader with the impression that these ultimate choices are *totally* without reason or justification, even though this is the strong claim that Kierkegaard often stresses. The absence of ultimate justification is, in fact, an absence of ultimate *objective* justification; in other words, an absence of any justification which would justify a single way of life for *all men*. However, this is where 'subjectivity' plays its most important role in Kierkegaard's philosophy, for there are *subjective* considerations which do argue for one way of life rather than another. These considerations are the personal desires, hopes, fears, eccentricities, and habits of the individual person. There is no ultimate justification for leading a moral life, that is no justification which would show that anyone at any time ought to be moral (in Kant's terms, "any rational creature"); however, some people are simply morally inclined. For these people, the justification, the *only* justification available to them for living morally, is the fact that they are so inclined. However, not everyone is so inclined, and some people find that they desire the life of pleasure, or the life of art, or, with Kierkegaard, the life of religious passion. "Truth is subjectivity," in the last analysis, means that the choice of a way of life can be made only by and on the basis of the person who has to live it.

The Dialectic and the Spheres of Existence

Kierkegaard's breach with Hegel is nowhere better exemplified than in his own 'existential' version of the dialectic. Like Hegel's 'historical dialectic', the existential dialectic is the formulation of various opposed *conceptions,* and the "stages on life's way" or "modes of existence" in Kierkegaard's dialectic are in many ways identical to the "forms of consciousness" found in Hegel's *Phenomenology of Spirit.* Both consist of opposed conceptions of 'life', of oneself and of different systems of values. In Hegel, the most primitive forms of consciousness are mere "consciousness" and then consciousness of oneself as an individual opposed to other individuals. In the stages of Reason, one recognizes one's oneness with others, first

through ethics, and ultimately through religion and philosophy, which are the highest conceptions of Spirit, the Absolute Truth, the rational goal of human existence. In Kierkegaard, we first meet the "aesthetic stage," in which man is already self-conscious and opposed to, or at least independent of, other men. (Kierkegaard is simply not concerned with the epistemological forms of Hegel's "Consciousness.") We then meet the "ethical stage," which, as in Hegel, constitutes a societal and 'moral' way of life. Finally, we are introduced to the "religious stage," in which Christianity is introduced as a crowning conception of life.

The difference between the two dialectics is not their content, but rather the relations between the various stages or forms of life. Kierkegaard and Hegel agree approximately on the same delineations of conceptions; and they order them the same. For both, the aesthetic life is unsatisfactory and Christianity is the most adequate conception of life. How are these dialectics ordered? In Hegel, they are ordered according to the "movement of reason," according to the sophistication of these concepts in rectifying conceptual inadequacies. The various forms are opposed to each other, but only because each gives a 'one-sided' view of life. A reflective mediation of the opposition can absorb what is true from each and find a new, and therefore 'higher' form in which opposition and one-sidedness do not occur. By means of such 'mediation', the inadequacies which develop in the conception of oneself as an individual are corrected in the conception of oneself as a rational and moral being, as a member of society. The inadequacies with such 'ethical' conceptions of self are corrected in the religious stages in which the conception of oneself as Spirit, as part of the Absolute (God) becomes fully explicit. At the completion of this stage—the conceptual reformulation of Christianity without its pictorial myths—one's conception of oneself is 'absolute'; it is without inadequacies, for it opposes oneself to nothing.

Although Kierkegaard accepts the validity of such a 'system' of concepts with its mediation of 'paradox' (by which Kierkegaard liberally designates any apparently opposed ideas), he insists that such systematization can be applied *only* in logic, in the study of concepts, and not to *life* itself. Logic aside, such a system is of absolutely no use to the "ethically existing individual," who wants to know *how* to live. This individual faces 'paradoxes', that is, opposed ways of life or alternative courses of action which *cannot* be 'mediated', but have to be chosen between. These 'paradoxes' are unresolvable by Reason; they are *absolute paradoxes,* and one can choose *either* one *or* the other, but not have the best of both. These choices are beyond the scope of Reason, for the mediating powers of Reason have no use in an absolute paradox. Choice is here not guided by rational principle but by a *leap of faith*. Reason plays the part of disclosing these choices for us and showing us that they are uncompromisingly opposed; in other words, Reason shows us that we have a choice, but not what to choose. Here Kierkegaard is in the company of both Kant and Hegel in his insistence that the production of paradoxes is characteristic of Reason, and on the side of Hegel, but not Kant, in his insistence that the production of paradoxes is not a problem of Reason but its chief virtue. In this sense, therefore, Kierkegaard is very much a rationalist. Where he ceases to become a rationalist is in the resolution of these paradoxes, in which reason is impotent and 'passion' or 'subjective truth' or 'faith' (in a religious context) or, more straightforwardly, individual logically-gratuitous choice provides the only possible resolution.

Kierkegaard's development of the dialectic is often couched in characteristically misleading language. He speaks of his dialectic as "qualitative" as opposed to Hegel's "quantitative" dialectic of "pure being" (that is, conceptual truth) and claims that his dialectic is the dialectic of "actual existence" rather than the "concept of existence." As we have argued, however, Kierkegaard is equally concerned with *conceptions* of existence, and his difference with Hegel lies in the value he places on the conception of oneself as an individual over the conception of oneself as "collectivity" (Spirit), and in the manner in which one moves from one conception to another.

In the existential dialectic, we confront three alternative ways of life, three fundamental commitments, or as Kierkegaard elsewhere titles them, "views of life," "existential categories," "spheres of existence," "modes of existing," and "stages on life's way."[71] These three different conceptions of life, each with its own value system and principles, are fundamentally incompatible in that one can only choose among them, not compromise between them by use of Reason. Because each "sphere of existence" contains its own system of values, there can be no further criterion for choosing between spheres, and, therefore, the choice must be made without a criterion, without a guiding principle, without Reason, by a "leap," a commitment which cannot be further defended. Thus, there is no *rational* way of life, no one conception of life style which is more reasonable than others. One's choice of fundamental values is "irrational" because there is no reason for choosing one style of life rather than another, nor is there the possibility that one can compromise to find the best of each. Kierkegaard, like Hegel, will celebrate the religious life as the "best" form of life, but, for Kierkegaard, the adoption of this life is not the Absolute Truth but his own unflinching *commitment*. It is not chosen because it is most rational, but chosen *in spite of* its lack of defense by Reason.

We have already mentioned that Kierkegaard's objection to Hegelianism is based not only on philosophical grounds, but on personal and moral grounds as well. He objected to Hegel's glorification of the possibilities of reflective reason not only because he felt that Reason was not adequate to rationalize ultimate choices, but because Reason gave the illusion that choice and commitment were unnecessary. If Reason could systematize and order all forms of life, then the *rational* way to live could be discovered in the system. Reason, because universal, would therefore dictate that every rational creature choose a single mode of existence, the moral Christian life (for Kant), the reflective intellectual Christian life (for Hegel); in other words, there would be no room for choice. Once Reason is given ultimate authority, the dictates of Reason are absolute and it makes no sense to ask whether one should be reasonable or not. If reason is not given this authority, and is open to challenge by the individual (who can ask "Why follow reason's dictates?" "Why be rational?"), then choice is reintroduced, and the 'rational' way of life (that discovered by the system) is just *one* conception of life among others. The system is not only philosophically inadequate because of its glorification of Reason, but is morally insidious as well; it gives men the illusion that the choice and therefore responsibility for a system of values is out of their hands.

It is evident from Kierkegaard's attack on Reason that he glorifies freedom of choice in precisely the same way that Hegel glorifies Reason:

The most tremendous thing which has been granted to man is: the choice of freedom.[72]

For Hegel, as for Aristotle, man is essentially rational; for Kierkegaard, man is essentially the chooser of his own values. For Hegel, everything lies in being rational, objective, and reflectively understanding; for Kierkegaard, everything lies in the act of choosing, in being subjective (passionate and committed). This freedom of choice is itself the most basic of values, what makes a man a *human being* or an *existent individual,* and the recognition and use of this freedom is far more important than the *object* of choice.

According to Hegel, freedom consists simply in following Reason; but for Kierkegaard, *following* anything is to give up one's freedom.

In making a choice it is not so much a question of choosing the right as of the energy, the earnestness, the pathos with which one chooses.[73]

Of course, there is a serious problem in the use of "right" (and "wrong") here, and Kierkegaard frequently uses these terms. Once he has argued the 'objective uncertainty' of all 'existential' decisions—the impossibility of justifying any one value system—he cannot then refer to any of these as "right" or "wrong." However, Kierkegaard's point, although once again misleadingly stated, is quite clear: *how* one chooses—that is, whether he has chosen freely and passionately committed himself to his choice—is all-important.

The objective accent falls on WHAT is said, the subjective accent on HOW it is said.[74]

What particular sphere of existence has been chosen is not important, for all are equally unjustified. A man has exerted his freedom and proven himself an *individual*

by virture of his choosing, not by virtue of the object of his choice.

The spheres of existence are alternative value systems or ways of life which are mutually incompatible. The choice among these spheres cannot consist in compromise, but yet there is no further criterion for choice. Thus, unlike Hegel's dialectic, there is no transition from one sphere to the next, no compromise or 'mediation' between spheres, and no rational resolution with their 'opposition'. However, these spheres do represent stages in a *hierarchy* of values in Kierkegaard's writings, with the religious or Christian stage the chosen ('highest') sphere. Similarly, Kierkegaard sometimes treats the ethical and religious spheres not as incompatible, but as a single system to be contrasted only with the aesthetic sphere. These ambiguities persist throughout Kierkegaard's writings, and the consistency of the existential dialectic thus becomes a key issue in the interpretation of Kierkegaard.

The spheres are often presented as equally valid (invalid) possibilities for choice, and as such, Kierkegaard can show no preference among them. His favorite technique employed to maintain this neutrality is the use of dialogue and pseudonymous characters to represent alternatives without the need to resolve the conflict between them. This is illustrated in *Either/Or,* in which two figures of an old man (Judge Wilhelm "B") and a young Aesthete (Johannes the Seducer "A") for whom the pleasures of life have soured[75] argue the virtues of the ethical and aesthetic spheres, exposing the values and problems of each. There is no attempt at resolution, and the alternatives are presented only as alternatives; the choice between them is left entirely to the reader.

However, at other times, Kierkegaard presents the stages as an actual progression from aesthetic to ethical to religious, and argues in almost Hegelian fashion the inadequacy of each stage which leads us to the next. The aesthetic sphere leads to despair, and then leads to the ethical sphere, which also ends in despair, which in turn leads one to the religious sphere. In his later and most religious writings (*Philosophical Fragments, Concluding Unscientific Postscript,* and *Sickness unto Death*), Kierkegaard leaves no doubt that he thinks the aesthetic and ethical spheres are inadequate and inferior while the religious way of life is, in some sense, the 'right' way of life.

These very different uses of the dialectic can be resolved, we shall suggest, because Kierkegaard, unlike Hegel, never argues that the movement from stage to stage is *necessary* or that it can be demonstrated systematically (that is, by reference to Reason alone). The movement of the dialectic always requires a *leap*, and, regardless of the inadequacy of any sphere, the transition to another sphere must be *chosen*. Yet, in a sense, we shall see that Kierkegaard's critique of the aesthetic sphere does constitute some *reasons* for abandoning that sphere and adopting a new mode of existence.

The Aesthetic Sphere

The aesthetic mode of existence is the life of pure 'immediacy'. The aesthetic is sometimes presented as a life without principles, but this is misleading; its ultimate maxim is not a 'reflective' or a 'rational' principle, one of duty, obligation, or self-discipline. The aesthetic life can be the life of whim, of immediate satisfaction and gratification. It has no *moral* principles, there is no *good* and no *evil,* there is satisfaction and dissatisfaction, fulfillment and frustration, pleasure and pain, happiness and suffering, ecstasy and despair. The aesthetic existence is the life of the Romantic, as celebrated by Byron and Rousseau, and captured by Hegel as the Romantic spirit in the *Phenomenology.*[76] The aesthetic mode's luminary example is Don Juan[77] in his unending quest for "sensual faithless love." Sensual love (unlike "psychical love," which passes into the ethical sphere) is purely "for the moment, in the same moment everything is over, and the same thing repeats itself endlessly." There is no question whether the union will be a happy one, for it is a union with no possibility of lasting. Don Juan does not know the anxiety of developing a relationship, for "he makes short work of it, and must always be regarded as absolutely victorious." Every woman is simply "woman in the abstract"; at most there is a sensual difference between them, not a *personal* difference. Don Juan is without principle, or faithless, in that there is only an arbitrary difference between his loves. He *seduces* women, which means that each is to be enjoyed for the moment, and, in that moment, is indistinguishable from every

other woman, and that "moment is indistinguishable from all other moments."

The principle of the aesthetic is satisfaction with the immediate, with whatever is arbitrarily chosen as an object of immediate concern.

The whole secret lies in arbitrariness. People usually think it easy to be arbitrary, but it requires much study to succeed in being arbitrary so as not to lose oneself in it, but so as to derive satisfaction from it. . . . You go see the middle of a play, you read the third part of a book. By this means you insure yourself a very different kind of enjoyment from that which the author has been so kind as to plan for you. You enjoy something entirely accidental; you consider the whole of existence from this standpoint; let its reality be stranded thereon. . . . You transform something accidental into the absolute, and, as such, into the object of a wager, and so forth. The more rigidly consistent you are in holding fast to your arbitrariness, the more amusing the ensuing combinations will be. The degree of consistency shows whether you are an artist or a bungler; for to a certain extent all men do the same. The eye with which you look at reality must be constantly changed.[78]

The aesthetic life need not be confined to the seduction of women, of course, but, as the above passage indicates, will consist in the enjoyment of the moment regardless of what that moment consists. One can enjoy good health or beauty, in himself or others, or riches and honor or talent in the arts as well as sensuous pleasure. The aesthetic life, although essentially unreflective, need not be unintelligent, for it may consist in the enjoyment or even creation of music (Mozart) or poetry, or even philosophy, as long as these are enjoyed purely for their immediate satisfaction.

There is, however, a negative component to this attractive Dionysian life; there is not only pleasure, but the constant threat of pain and suffering; not only satisfaction but frustration, and, what is worst of all, *boredom.* For the aesthete, nothing is more damaging than being bored, or recognizing the *repetition* of his life of the 'immediate'. The aesthetic life, once it first recognizes the threat, becomes obsessed with escaping boredom and repetition, and subsequently becomes a slave to the demand for new experience. Don Juan comes to live not for pleasure and gratification, but to escape boredom and the staleness of repetition.

The aesthetic life is essentially the life of the immediate, and as such, rejects any reflection concerning the *significance* of that moment. One does, however, come to reflect on his life and the significance of his actions, and this is disastrous to the aesthete. On reflection, the immediate loses its value, and the life of absorption in the moment is seen as a mere 'emptiness', a series of repetitions which are ultimately meaningless. One becomes increasingly restless, attempting to find continuous novel experiences to suppress the feeling of meaninglessness. The presence of reflective Reason stultifies this attempt, for the moment can never again regain its spontaneity and autonomous importance.

With reflection, an *aesthetic dialectic* is initiated. Don Juan represents the first stage of this dialectic, that in which the aesthetic life can be said to be satisfying. As one reflects on the futility of trying to satisfy the human spirit through immediate gratification, he tends to become skeptical about all gratification and about all desires. At this stage of the aesthetic, typified by Faust, one refuses to seek gratification for his desires and comes to deny those desires themselves. His existence is pure *pride*, coupled with cynicism for the worth of anything. From this lack of self-assertion, passionless cynicism lays the foundations of the anonymous character of modern life.

In the third stage of aesthetic dialectic, exemplified by Ahasuerus—the wandering Jew—the once happy aesthete falls into total despair.

So it appears that every aesthetic view of life is in despair, and that everyone who lives aesthetically is in despair, whether he knows it or not.[79]

Facing the prospect of death and the meaninglessness of life, the aesthete, in silent despair, desperately attempts to escape from reflection altogether. The natural way of doing so, Kierkegaard suggests, is to stop all self-appraisal and self-assertion, and to lose oneself in the crowd and the hustle and bustle of everyday Collective life. Or, for those few who are suffi-

ciently strong to maintain their individuality, there is the ethical life. The aesthetic sphere has degenerated to a life of meaningless despair; can the ethical sphere provide the meaning that the aesthetic life lacks?

The Ethical Sphere

Kierkegaard's presentation of the ethical sphere is not as much the formulation of an ethic as such as the contrast of a life lived according to ethical (secular) standards with the whimsical personal life of the Aesthetic and the religious life whose highest ideals are not of this world or of Reason. The basic feature of the Ethical would be expected to be the employment of universal rational principles that transcend and leave no exception for the individual but yet remain secular principles. The ethical life is the societal life, the life of a man who considers himself part of a community of men and lives according to principles which treat every man as an end in himself and subsume self-interest to moral duty. The ethical life, with its emphasis on universality, rationality, and duty, in short, *morality,* signified for Kierkegaard, as for Hegel, the ethics of Kant. Although Kierkegaard does not deny the inclusion of a non-Kantian ethics within the ethical sphere, it is clear that the system of values which concerns him is that of the *Critique of Practical Reason.* The ethical sphere thus consists of living for the good of men in community (in a "Kingdom of Ends"), and personal interests are always to be subsumed under the interests of morality.

The central feature of the ethical is universality (rationality), and a necessary condition for a set of principles to be ethical principles is the impartial applicability to every person at every time:

The ethical as such is the universal; and as the universal it applies to everyone, which may be expressed from another point of view by saying that it applies every instant.[80]

It should be clear that the ethical life with its value on community is *not* equivalent to 'crowd morality', and 'social concern' does not imply anti-individuality or unquestioning obedience to society. Kierkegaard, like Kant, considers morality to be *autonomous* and *rational.* Every man produces these principles for himself, and must, insofar as he is moral, uphold these principles even against the opposition of society.

Of course, Kierkegaard does not fully adopt Kant's moral philosophy to his dialectic, because the thesis from which Kant maintains that every rational creature will recognize these principles (that is, the categorical imperatives) in himself is identical to his characterization of Reason (that is, practical Reason). Because Kierkegaard rejects this characterization in his denial that Reason can give us justification of ultimate moral principles, he cannot hold with Kant that the principles of morality can be autonomously derived by every 'rational creature'.

However, we can separate this Kantian thesis regarding the justification of moral principles from those moral principles themselves. Kierkegaard's ethical sphere consists in the acceptance of the categorical imperative(s) as ultimate values (as "dictates of practical reason"), but acceptance of these moral values as ultimate does not entail their ultimate justifiability. (Thus, according to Kierkegaard, to demonstrate the *rationality* of a moral principle is not sufficient to justify it.) It is the requirement of universality that is central to the ethical life, and not the claim to justifiability of these universal principles. The ethical life takes individual interest to be subservient to the demands of principle, but the origins or justifications of these principles, or even the specific content of these principles, is not provided by the existential dialectic.

Although the ethical stage is distinguished from the religious stage, it might be suspected that Kierkegaard's acceptance of Kantian ethics will lead him to favor the religious support that Kant gives for his ethics. Kant and Kierkegaard's ethics are both Christian ethics, and the sanctions of Damnation and Paradise are implicit in them. It is in Kierkegaard's acceptance of Kant's arguments to the effect that morality cannot be justified without the postulates of Christianity that we find the tendency to speak of the ethical life as a transition to and part of the religious life. Yet the two stages are importantly distinct, for the two central religious concepts of Sin and Faith do not appear in the ethical conception of life. These two concepts mark a drastic dif-

ference between the two "spheres", so drastic that any attempt to treat them as a single system of values must end in confusion.

The model for the ethical life, however, is not the formality of Kant's ethics, but the historical example of Socrates. In Socrates, we find a clear representation of not only the values but the living adherence to the values of morality. Where could we find a clearer example of the subordination of personal interest to the demands of principle and the interests of community? It is Socrates who not only taught, but *lived* the principles that man is of the highest value, that "the good is in every man," and that love of man is the ultimate good. Again, we find Kierkegaard carefully distinguishing between the life and principles of Socrates and his justification of those principles. Socrates, like Kant, argued that the good which is in every man has absolute justification and that subjectivity does not serve as justification of these principles. It is the self-reflection and life of principle which marks Socrates as the paragon of ethical existence.

It would follow from the Socratic example that the virtues of the ethical life would be *social* virtues, and one need only turn to either Plato or Aristotle to get an enumeration of these. Friendship and ("psychic") love are all-important, and finding one's proper place in the social order is an ethical necessity. To this end, courage, temperance, kindness, and generosity acquire the status of virtues. Marriage is of central importance to the ethical life, for it contains within it all of the central demands of morality, commitment to others, acceptance of duty and obligation, submission of personal interest to community (family) interests, the stability of community through stability of the family. One can, of course, trace Kierkegaard's emphasis on the importance of marriage to his own experience with Regina Olsen, but what he has to say about the decision to marry has far more than 'subjective' (biographical) importance.

Unlike the aesthetic life, the ethical life is characterized by reflection and self-appraisal, and with reflection one can appraise the meaningfulness of his life. Deliberate and principled choice, as opposed to action on whim, is the mark of the ethical, and actions have significance not according to immediate gratification, but with regard to their accordance with moral principle. This long-term significance and regard for principle rather than satisfaction, allows the ethical life to give a *meaning* (a coherence to (moral) principles) to existence that the Aesthetic cannot give; but is the ethical life therefore adequate?

According to Kierkegaard, the secular reflection of the ethical life is adequate to disclose the meaninglessness (lack of principle) of the aesthetic life and disclose the moral principles which define and give meaning to this life. As long as one remains in this secular state of reflection, guilt is a result of failure to fulfill ethical demands and can always be overcome by the performance of good acts. If one's self-reflection moves from the secular to the religious and one just once perceives the revelation of his personal, yet nonethical *Sin* and its unavoidable personal guilt, the despair of the aesthetic dialectic returns, for the good ethical life is not sufficient to escape the despair of the revelation of Sin. (We find the same despair in Camus' character Clemence, as soon as he sees his "public service" and "good character" from a quasi-religious perspective.) Once one has this terrifying revelation, which it is the business of Kierkegaard's writings to produce in him, he has little recourse but to "leap into the arms of God."

The Relationship Between the Aesthetic and the Ethical

In our descriptions of the aesthetic and ethical stages, we have already indicated the nature of the differences between the two and the 'existential dialectic' that brings us from one stage to the next. However, we have also indicated that there is a serious problem in the movement of the dialectic from one stage to the next; if the choice between spheres of existence is really 'irrational' or 'arbitrary', then there cannot be any *movement* of the dialectic at all. Yet the aesthetic dialectic does give us *reasons* for moving to the ethical stage, namely, the despair confronting the aesthete as soon as he comes to reflect on the ultimate meaningless of his existence. Given that both the dialectic, with its progression to the religious life, and the ultimate 'irrationality' of choice are central doctrines in Kierkegaard's philosophy, must we conclude that his philosophy is fundamentally inconsistent? Does Kierkegaard claim there are no reasons for committing oneself to a way of life which he then proceeds to give us reasons for adopting?

This question most often arises in the transition from the ethical to the religious sphere, primarily because Kierkegaard's claims regarding the 'leap of faith' to Christianity is the best known and most influential of his doctrines. However, Kierkegaard's very personal concern with Christianity often leads him to drop his insistence on merely presenting positions and, when he speaks of Christianity, makes it impossible for us to distinguish between *his* reasons for accepting Christianity and *the* reasons (valid for anyone) for choosing Christianity. In addition to this problem, there is the already mentioned question concerning the distinctness of the religious and ethical stages. We shall, therefore, concentrate our efforts to defend the 'existential dialectic' in the more clear-cut distinction between the aesthetic and ethical stages.

To begin the defense, it must be clear that Kierkegaard never claims that the reasons he gives for the transition are *logically sufficient* conditions, and denies, therefore, that the transitions are logically *necessary*. (He claims this as a central difference between his dialectic and Hegel's dialectic. However, we have seen that this is a misinterpretation of Hegel, who is not claiming *logical* necessity, but rather *teleological* necessity for the transitions of his dialectic.) The reasons which Kierkegaard gives for moving from one stage to the next are not logical but *psychological;* they are not logically compelling, but they may be compelling for some individual. One might compare this sort of reason to an argument by appeal to sympathy, or fear, or anger. The argument itself makes no claim to validity—to the contrary, such arguments are often the clearest cases of fallacious reasoning—yet they may be persuasive nonetheless. If someone argues that we ought to accept social inequality by appealing to our fear of social unrest, the question of validity may not come seriously into question, but the argument may be successful nonetheless.

Kierkegaard is thus not claiming to be giving us a valid argument for accepting one stage over another, and, therefore, the question of the logical compulsion of the choice of one stage rather than another does not arise. Kierkegaard is appealing to our feelings, primarily our feelings of despair and guilt. If one feels these emotions as Kierkegaard does, he will feel attracted to Kierkegaard's conclusions, independent of any logically compelling arguments (of which there are none, according to Kierkegaard). Kierkegaard is not giving *reasons* in the sense of *logically compelling reasons,* therefore, but reasons only in the degenerate sense that they are personal *considerations* which might persuade us to accept his position. Furthermore, it should be clear that no claim for universality need be made for these reasons either, for Kierkegaard, like Nietzsche and very unlike Kant and Hegel, writes for "the Few" who can "understand him." "Understand" in this context refers to sharing feelings—for Kierkegaard, the feelings of dread, despair, guilt, and suffering—and not to the more intellectual understanding appealed to by Kant and Hegel in their claims that they are writing truths holding for "any rational creature."

The 'movement' of the existential dialectic does not constitute an inconsistency in Kierkegaard's philosophy, for his denial of rationality is of a very different category than the reasons he offers for moving from stage to stage. The 'reasons' of despair that push one from the aesthetic sphere to the ethical sphere are not logically compelling reasons but personal or 'subjective' reasons, and because these consist of feelings and not of propositions, one might argue that these 'reasons' are not even relevant to considerations of rationality.

Kierkegaard's apparent inconsistency stems from the ambiguous use of "reason" and "rational" that he inherits from Hegel. On the one hand, 'reason' and 'rationality' are strictly logical notions (although Hegel's notions are broadened to include the notion of 'teleological necessity' as well), and it is this sense in which Kierkegaard denies that one can demonstrate the rationality or give reasons for choice of one sphere rather than another. There is another sense of 'reason', also utilized by Hegel, in this other sense a 'reason' is anything (a feeling as well as a consideration) that makes one more likely to accept some conclusion. In Hegel, this use of 'reason' and the use of 'reason' in the sense of 'logically compelling' are joined together in the central notion of teleological explanation so that the senses need not be distinguished. In Kierkegaard, the play on "reason" and "rationality" becomes impossibly confusing, and failure to distinguish these very different uses threatens his entire philosophy with confusion.

However, we again find Kierkegaard much closer to Hegel than his intense anti-Hegelian instincts would allow. If we return to the operation of Hegel's dialectic, we see that the transitions between stages in the *Phenomenology* are sometimes identical in kind to Kierkegaard's 'existential' transitions. For example, the transitions in the stage of "Self-Consciousness" come about not as a result of any *logical* inadequacy, but because the persons who hold certain conceptions of themselves find they cannot *live* with these conceptions (compare the transitions to Stoicism and Skepticism). Similarly, the rejection of Kantian *moralität* depends upon the inability of real people to live in accordance with merely formal doctrines when their passions are ignored. The difference between Hegel and Kierkegaard is not, therefore, a difference between logic and choice; rather, Hegel looks back and reflects over the ultimate purpose of such transitions (resulting in his conception of teleological necessity), while Kierkegaard asks what justification one can adduce for making certain choices *now.*

The relationship between the aesthetic and ethical spheres is best illustrated by the example to which Kierkegaard himself gives much weight. In *Either/Or,* Judge Wilhelm argues that only the man who is married can "thoroughly fathom the depths of life" and that marriage is the greatest end of human existence. Marriage, (the culmination of 'psychic love') is contrasted with mere 'sensual love' or infatuation; it is not for the moment, but a commitment for the future; it is not aimed at personal gratification, but the interests of others. Sensual love requires only a given momentary feeling; psychic love and its culmination in marriage requires a decision to commit oneself.

Suppose one is deciding whether to commit himself to a relationship; that is, commit himself to an ethical mode of existence. He might go about weighing all the immediate satisfactions and dissatisfactions to be derived from a union, and, according to the criteria inherent in the aesthetic life, the decision would be made on the basis of the greatest personal satisfaction. One might also weigh the moral principles and good for society and other people, and decide, on the basis of purely universal 'rational' principles, whether he ought to marry or not. Given these two very different sets of considerations, how does one make a decision, that is, to decide which kind of consideration is the more important (assuming that they are in conflict)? According to Kierkegaard, (like Kant) considerations of personal inclination are totally independent of moral (ethical) considerations. Unlike Kant, the choice between the two does not necessarily go to the Ethical, but, in the absence of any further criterion, one has no (logically compelling) reasons for choosing either the Aesthetic or the Ethical.

However, this is not to say that there are no reasons in the less-than-rigorous psychological sense. If the aesthete begins to reflect on the repetition of love affairs he has had and gets the feeling of despair at the pointlessness of it all, this may well move him into marriage, that is, into the ethical life. However, there is no (logical) necessity for this move, unless the psychology of that particular individual happens to be such that he *feels* compelled to grasp at a new way of life. Despair is capable of pushing one to change his way of life, but there is no (logical) necessity that it do so, nor is there any necessity that one feels despair when reflecting on his present way of life. Thus, the claim in Kierkegaard that everyone who leads the aesthetic life is in despair does not entail or even causally necessitate that everyone leading an aesthetic life will move to the ethical life. It is possible that one remain indefinitely in the aesthetic sphere in spite of his despair, and it is even possible that he be immune to Kierkegaard's indirect preachings and stay indefinitely in the Don Juan stage, successfully resisting the reflectiveness that would push him through the rest of the dialectic.

Kierkegaard's dialectic and his analysis of despair are more akin to a selectively directed psychoanalysis than to a logical analysis. He attempts to find those who can be made to feel the despair that he describes, and to lead these people to tell them how to find the way to escape this despair;

Becoming a Christian— The Religious Way of Life

A man who cannot seduce men cannot save them either.[81]

The religious stage is that sphere of life defined by the conception of the individual *in relationship to God.* There is no doubt that Kierkegaard personally considered this his chosen mode of existence and that the central purpose of his writing, as he admits in his *Point of View of My Work as an Author,* is to arouse the religious view of life in his readers. "Religious" for Kierkegaard is to be taken in a very restricted sense—to be religious is to be a Christian, but a Christian in Kierkegaard's very special sense.[82] To be a Buddhist, a Jainist, or a Jew, or to be a worthy, nonsuffering Church-going doctrinaire Protestant is not to be religious in this sense. In fact, the sense of religious here is so restricted that it is questionable whether anyone who has not had a background in Kierkegaard's pathologically guilt-ridden Lutheran upbringing could qualify as the religious "Knight of Faith." Membership in the Christian church is the very antithesis of being a Christian. In fact,

it is easier to become a Christian when I am not a Christian than to become a Christian when I am one.[83]

Hegel and Kierkegaard (and more subtly, Kant) take the Christian conception of existence to be the 'highest', but yet Kierkegaard's conception of Christianity is diametrically opposite to the rationalist conception. For Kant, Christianity was rationally justified by its necessity for practical reason, and God is a *postulate* in support of morality. Christ enters into Christianity as a corollary of belief in God, for belief in Christ can be rationally justified only so far as this belief is necessary for morality. For Hegel also, belief in God is rational, but the Hegelian God is of a radically different sort, and the *rationality* of this belief is defended in a very different way. For Hegel, God is not transcendent as for Kant, but *immanent.* God for Hegel is that subject which is common to all men, and Christ is the symbol of that 'incarnation', that is, the fact that God or Spirit is man, and man is God. Kierkegaard rejects not only the reinterpretation of the Christian conceptions of God, Christ, and the incarnation by Hegel, but the entire rationalist approach to Christianity. God is not immanence—such a concept is 'hypocritical atheism'—but transcendence, in Kant's terms, *noumenon,* and essentially unknowable and incomprehensible. God is not only separated from man, but forever unknowable by man. God cannot be an object of knowledge, but simply an object of faith, and here Kierkegaard is in complete agreement with Kant. He also shares some of Hegel's views, for he insists that God must be viewed as a *subject,* and therefore Kant's notion that we must have *faith that God exists* is inappropriate. What is needed is faith *in* God, for the question of His existence, once one is within the religious viewpoint, cannot be intelligibly raised.

The central tenet of Christianity is the historical existence of God in the form of man. In rationalist thought, this doctrine had been variously interpreted in order to make it reasonable, for the literal interpretation of a transcendent eternal God existing and dying as mortal man seemed absurd. Hegel is typical of such attempts in his interpretation of Christ as a symbol for the doctrine of the immanence of God. Kierkegaard, however, complains that such imposed plausibility is the destruction of the very doctrine to be rescued. The notion of God as man is not that sort of paradox which can be resolved through the mediation of the Hegelian dialectic. Here we have an *Absolute paradox,* one which cannot be resolved. The idea that God is at once eternal and temporal, is like a man but not at all like a man, is utterly and fundamentally absurd. Because this doctrine is *the* central doctrine of Christianity, the religion is absurd and paradoxical at its very foundations.

As we stressed before, Christianity is not a set of doctrines, but a way of life, a set of values. The absurd doctrines of the Incarnation, the Trinity, and so on are not important in themselves; it is the *attitude* of the religious toward these that is important. The appropriate attitudes for Kierkegaard are fear, dread, and even terror, before an almighty yet unknowable God, despair and suffering at one's personal weaknesses, and overpowering guilt in the face of Sin before God because of these weaknesses.

Yet, Christianity is also the love of this God, confidence in His goodness and justice, as well as the fear and despair of Him. The life of a Christian is to be totally and passionately *before* God, and to be the Christian "Knight of Faith" is to drop every vestige of skepticism and rationality with regard to religious questions and simply exist in the presence of God.

The believer differs from the ethicist in being infinitely interested in the reality of another.[84]

One can be rational only to the extent of recognizing the absurdity of the doctrines of Christianity and discovering the utter irrationality of accepting the Christian way of life. Reason thus having completed its functions, what is left is the choice, the unquestioning acceptance, the *leap* to Christianity.

It by now must be evident that there are two senses in which Christianity can be said to be 'irrational' for Kierkegaard, and these senses must be kept distinct. First, the choice of the Christian way of life is irrational because, as one of the autonomous spheres of existence, there are no external standards for choosing it, and the choice must be a simple leap of faith. However, in this sense, the religious way of life is no more irrational than the ethical way of life which is also autonomous and requires a leap for its acceptance. In the sense that Christianity is irrational here, all ways of life are equally irrational. The too-common interpretation of Kierkegaard's plea for the irrational acceptance of Christianity—that one not attempt to prove its truth—is highly misleading if it is taken as a contrast to the rational acceptance of the other spheres. The choice of Christianity as a way of life is irrational only so far as any choice of a way of life is irrational.

In another sense, however, we may say that Christianity is irrational not only because Reason is incapable of determining choice, but Reason cannot even comprehend the doctrines of Christianity. God, as necessarily unknown, cannot be reasonable understood, and the basic doctrine about God, namely, that "in his timelessness he existed in time on earth as man," is incomprehensible.

Knowledge of God is past the limits of Reason, but yet a product of Reason insofar as it results from Reason's being pushed to its ultimate limits. Christianity is irrational in the sense that it is absurd, in the sense that it must be accepted even though it cannot be understood. In this sense, Kierkegaard is a strict antirationalist, in that he attacks any possibility of *rationalizing* Christianity. Contrary to Hegel, Christianity cannot be grasped by the development of Reason, for Christianity is not a set of doctrines to be understood, but only to be accepted and lived by. This is in sharp contrast to the ethical sphere, in which the use of Reason is sufficient to derive ethical truths, for Kierkegaard accepted Kant's notion of a priori ethical truths attainable by Reason alone. Being moral consisted not simply in acting in accordance with morality, but with *understanding* morality as well. In the religious stage, no comparable understanding and no comparable employment of Reason is possible. In this sense, Kierkegaard does speak of the ethical sphere as rational (in that it depends upon the employment of Reason), but the religious sphere is not. The ethical life is the life of Reason; the religious life is the unreasonable life of faith.

Because the doctrines of Christianity are paradoxical or absurd, acceptance of Christianity comes about in a manner somewhat different from acceptance of the other spheres. Once one has committed himself to the ethical mode of existence, Reason is capable of telling him what is good and what is evil. Kierkegaard's appeal here is again to Kant but perhaps more directly to Socrates. The teacher of good and evil, as Socrates in the *Protagoras,* acts only as an "occasion" to bring out the knowledge of good and evil. In the *Philosophical Fragments,* Kierkegaard refers to Socrates' dialectic method of teaching and the ethical aspect of the Theory of Recollection as the defining characteristic of the ethical or 'rational' way of life. The doctrines of the ethical sphere are comprehensible and acceptable to any rational creature who is brought to recognize them; once one is within the ethical sphere, he needs no external source to explain or to justify these 'rational' principles.

In the religious sphere, however, Reason cannot show us the Truth, nor can it even allow us to comprehend the Truth. The teachings of Christianity, therefore, *cannot* be based on Reason but must be based on *authority.* Kant and Hegel's insistence on *natural* religion is, according to Kierkegaard, to reject what is fundamental to the religious way of life. *'Positive'* religion is the only possible religion.[85]

Because religion rests on authority, the teacher, namely Jesus, is not simply an 'occasion' for learning, but himself constitutes the Truth that "God exists in and with his own Existence."[86] In other words, it is not a matter of indifference that Christ is the teacher of religion, for he himself is the 'truth' which he is teaching. Again, there is the emphasis on Christianity as a *relationship* between oneself and God, and not as a set of doctrines. To 'learn' Christianity, one must feel himself *confronted* with God, and this confrontation is not the sort of 'learning' which could be prompted

by an 'occasional' teacher. Similarly, the 'Moment' of learning, that is, the time of revelation, is all-important, in contrast with the Socratic method of teaching. It is the historical existence of Christ-in-time which constitutes the miracle (absurdity) that is the Truth for Christianity, and the Moment of his existence is the Moment of God's revelation to us. Of course, those of us who were not present at this original presentation of the Truth are forced to learn it "second-hand," but the Moment of revelation is still vital to religious faith. It is only by feeling oneself in the actual presence of God that one can become a Christian.

At that Moment, the Eternal, which
hitherto did not exist (for us), came
into existence.[87]

It is this conception of the eternal which most clearly differentiates the religious sphere from the other two. In the aesthetic sphere, "time" refers only to the immediate; in the ethical, "time" refers to more than the immediate, but only to secular (worldly) existence. In the religious sphere, however, there is no concept of time; our recognition of God places us "beyond the this-worldly and the temporal."

In Christianity, everything rests on the *authority* of God and His presentation of Himself in the person of Christ as the Truth of Christianity. Acceptance of the teacher is acceptance of His teachings but, more importantly, it is the recognition of the teacher as a personal God (the Truth). Being in the presence of God unavoidably brings one to the recognition of his own relative "incompleteness," which Kierkegaard, attempting to carry on a parallel with Socrates, refers to confusingly as "error":

The teacher is then the God himself,
who in acting as an occasion
prompts the learner to recall that he
is in error, and that by reason
of his own guilt. But this state, the
being in error by reason of one's
own guilt, what shall we call it? Let
us call it Sin.[88]

The central teaching of God, therefore, is that man is in Sin; acceptance of God is the acceptance that one is sinful. Facing this Sin, which need involve no specific transgression, feeling guilty about it, despairing at the impossibility of erasing it, and earnestly repenting is the Christian way of life,

the way of suffering, of fear and trembling, of infinite resignation.[89]

Christianity begins with the doctrine of Sin, and therefore with the Individual.[90]

It is the presence of Sin that distinguishes the religious from the ethical, for Sin is "irrational." In ethics, a man feels guilty (justifiably or needlessly) because he believes he has transgressed some specific moral principle. In religion, the Believer feels guilty for a transgression against no principle in particular. By his very being he has Sinned against God where no amount of reasoning could disclose how such a Sin is possible. In ethics, one is responsible for his own errors, but this is not true of the doctrine of Original Sin. Moral transgressions, even if not remediable, can be absolved by God Himself, Who, because He is not concerned with the temporal but with salvation, makes it a point not to provide such absolution during a man's worldly existence. Rather, this existence must be one of continuous guilt and suffering—the permeating recognition that one is basically incomplete and as such constitutes a virtual insult to God. Therefore, Sin is not one of the corollary doctrines of Christianity, but is the inevitable consequence (not logical consequence) of recognizing oneself in God's presence.

The breach between the religious and the ethical is best illustrated in the story of Abraham and Isaac.[91] In his choice between obeying the command of God and saving his son, Abraham was faced with an unenviable choice between the central precepts of the religious and the ethical. What could be more blasphemous for a religious person than to fail to obey a direct imperative of God? Yet what could constitute a more heinous crime in the moral sphere than the murder of one's own son? The choice itself shows beyond any doubt that secular morality and religious duty may be in Absolute conflict in that there is no criterion for making this horrible choice; one must simply choose between God and morality. Kierkegaard, of course, encourages a broader conception of morality in which one's first duty is to God, the "teleological suspension of the Ethical"[92] or the "individual (before God) becoming higher than the universal."[93] However, few of us are confronted with such a direct imperative in religion, and for those people (including Kierkegaard, who in spite of his "mystical" tendencies, never claimed that his confrontation with God included the Lord's speaking to him) who do not have such direct access, the religious way of life consists basically in the adoption of religious attitudes of "inwardness" and suffering, guilt, and the like. In the absence of a Divine countermand to morality there is no normal contradiction between the religious life[94] and the ethical life, in that the latter does consist in part in following the Lord's Commandments. Abraham provides a special case (showing him to be a true *knight of faith*) just because he confronts even his grotesque test with unflinching faith in God. In these Commandments, the ethical can be considered God's expression of His commands to all men, and it is belief in God that gives sanction and ultimate meaning to morality (an obviously Kantian point). However, the Abraham example should be sufficient to keep us from ever attempting to deny the distinctness of the two spheres.

Freedom and Subjectivity

We have presented Kierkegaard's philosophy as he develops it with the conceptions of the "existent individual," the "freedom of choice" of the individual, the absence of ultimate justification of values, the importance of 'subjective truth' in accepting a set of values, and Kierkegaard's own choice of Christianity (in his special sense) as a way of life. These central notions have all been subjected to severe criticism, but, unfortunately, not always well-informed criticism. Kierkegaard's philosophy is developed into a well-protected system (although he would not like this characterization) which is difficult to penetrate critically from the outside because of the safeguarding concept of 'subjective truth'; yet the system is equally difficult to criticize internally because of the slippery employment of its key terms, for example "Reason." Most of the criticism that maintains its grip on this viscous philosophy is simply criticism concerning Kierkegaard's failure to defend crucial philosophical positions on which his entire philosophy depends.

Most notably, we find no defense in Kierkegaard of his central value of *free-dom*. Hegel's glorification of Reason is un-justified in his system; it is the presupposition of the powers of Reason which is the basis of the system. It is this presupposition that is attacked by Kierkegaard, who replaces it with a glorification of freedom of choice and 'irrationality'. Suppose we were to question this presupposition as Kierkegaard has challenged that of Hegel: Why is freedom a value? Why even suppose that there is any such freedom of choice?

It is the "existential value" of freedom which determines the worth of one's ac-tions, that is, an action is of "existential value" if it is the result of a freely chosen commitment. Free choice is the mark of the "truly existent individual," setting him off from the "crowd," a clearly derogatory term in Kierkegaard's writings. Why is it valuable to be a truly existent individual as opposed to a member of the crowd? Why should it be better to suffer the de-spair and anxiety which accompanies one's recognition of freedom than to be secure and settled in the comfort of an uncrit-ically accepted set of crowd-derived "rea-sonable" values? Kierkegaard does not fairly consider this question, and he never seems to feel discomfort at holding at one and the same time the denial of any ulti-mate criterion for evaluation and the pos-iting of a single ultimate value according to which every human being is to be mea-sured. Of course, freedom is not a measure of the value of one course of action as opposed to another, but a measure of the value of a *person* in choosing some course of action. Why should we take freedom to be a value at all?

This question of the value of freedom is to become, in later existentialist thinkers, the central problem of their philosophy. Sartre, for example, sees, as Kierkegaard does not, that there is at least an apparent inconsistency in denying the existence of absolute values and maintaining that the only value is freedom. Where Sartre at-tempts to dispel the problem, Kierkegaard does not even recognize that there is a problem. Similarly, there is a multitude of well-established doctrines in philosophy which would deny that there is even a single case of freedom of choice. Kierke-gaard makes virtually no mention of the "free-will problem," but simply *assumes* the reality of the individual freedom he

values. Kierkegaard's most sympathetic interpreters have suggested that his con-cept of freedom does have a basis in his phenomenological description of our expe-rience of freedom, and that this description establishes both the actuality of this free-dom and the value of it. No doubt this is a fitting description of the use to which several later existentialists have put Kierkegaard's brilliant analysis of the dreadful experience of freedom, but Kierkegaard himself does not present a "phenomenological analysis"[95] in this con-text. This is not in the least to deny that Kierkegaard's analyses of "dread" and other passions are among the most per-ceptive essays in psychology in the nine-teenth century. However, the problem of whether one actually has free choice is fully distinct from the question of how we feel when we believe that we have free choice, and Kierkegaard has virtually nothing to say about this problem, nor does he seem to be the least bit interested in it. Similarly, the analysis of one's feel-ings of freedom might and often do incite similar feelings in others, but this does not constitute a justification of freedom as a value any more than Kierkegaard's reli-gious writings constitute a justification of Christianity in their ability to incite the Christian temperament in readers.

Kierkegaard simply avoids these crucial philosophical objections to his system; but again, he can make himself immune to criticism by claiming that he is not at-tempting to *justify* any philosophical posi-tion, but merely to describe a position from within and attempt to draw the reader into that position as well. By in-sisting on the "subjectivity" of his writings, Kierkegaard is capable of simply ignoring the charge that he has begged certain questions, or has failed to justify the posi-tion that he apparently defends. This sort of 'subjectivist' hedging is bound to be a source of annoyance to philosophers, and it explains both the occasional hostility to and the frequent neglect of Kierkegaard among contemporary nonexistentialist phi-losophers. Freedom, for Kierkegaard, is simply 'suggested' as a value in a "per-suasive definition" of the "truly existing individual" or the "authentic human be-ing" as one who recognizes the ultimate value of freedom, choice, and passion.

Despite the apparent immunity Kierke-gaard's philosophy enjoys against attacks from without, there has been a long series of charges from within claiming that his philosophy is simply inconsistent. However, such charges can rarely be fully substantiated because of Kierkegaard's slippery ambiguity in his use of key terms. For example, we have already argued that the objection against his notion of the 'irrationality of choice' on the grounds that he does provide reasons can be avoided once we become clear about Kierkegaard's unannounced use of several different notions of Reason.

There is a long-standing objection to Kierkegaard's defense of Christianity which focuses on his insistence on the 'absurdity' or 'paradoxical nature' of Christian doctrines. First, it is argued that Kierkegaard fails to distinguish between paradox and absurdity, on the one hand, and flat logical contradiction and utter nonsense on the other. This objection is assuredly valid, but loses its force as a criticism when we find that the "paradoxes" discussed by Kierkegaard inevitably fall into the first category. "Paradox" refers to any notion for which the explanations of Reason do not suffice, and his 'paradoxes' of ultimate choice and of Christianity are 'absurd' only in that they cannot be 'rationalized'; they are not logical contradictions in any sense. We may agree with Kierkegaard that the orthodox doctrine of the Incarnation is absurd or incomprehensible without insisting that it violates any laws of logic. It is true that Kierkegaard fails to use logical terms in their accepted ways and that he fails to draw important distinctions; yet it does not follow and is not the case that his paradoxes make his philosophy explicitly inconsistent.

Kierkegaard insists that faith is necessary in religion because of the absurdity of its doctrines, and moreover that it is absurdity which makes faith possible ("there cannot be faith where there is proof"). It often has been argued that there are doctrines other than those of traditional Christianity that are a good deal more absurd than the doctrine that Jesus was God-incarnate, for example, the doctrine that Pontius Pilate was God-incarnate. It is concluded that the absurdity of Christianity does not constitute its justification, for there are other doctrines more absurd.

However, this objection once again misses the force of Kierkegaard's insistence on 'subjective truth'. Kierkegaard does not argue that the justification of Christianity is the absurdity of its doctrines, but rather that the absurdity of its doctrines is a necessary condition for it to be a *religious* way of life. Kierkegaard insists that Christianity is not a set of doctrines, absurd or not, but a life of suffering and religious passion. Christianity is this way of life, and Kierkegaard claims that as such, it cannot be justified at all. The objection that there are more absurd doctrines is therefore to simply miss the point of Kierkegaard's conception of Christianity; it cannot be justified and is not defined by a set of doctrines.

The concept of 'subjective truth' has held a central position in our discussion of Kierkegaard and has been the main defense against standard objections to his philosophy. However, it has often been claimed that this notion is itself incomprehensive, that truth is necessarily objective if it is truth at all. To speak of the 'subjective truth' of mathematics or science is to speak utter nonsense; to speak of the 'subjective truth' of moral or religious commitment is not to speak of "truth" at all.

'Subjective truth' does raise these problems if interpreted as a *general* conception of truth. However, Kierkegaard did not so present it, and reserved talk of "subjective truth" only for cases of 'objective uncertainty'. It is true that in these cases, namely those cases in which choice and commitment are required, we should be hesitant of speaking of Truth and speak rather of "intentionality" or "personal choice." However, this reduces the objection against Kierkegaard to his unfortunate and perhaps misleading choice of words. Whether this choice is a manifestation of a deeper philosophical confusion or an attempt on Kierkegaard's part to deliberately muddy the issues of Hegelianism is open to debate. Kierkegaard evidences the traits of the philosophical sophist and the confused philosophical novice as well as the traits of genius and sincerity which make him one of the great religious philosophers of modern times.

Bibliography
Kierkegaard's Works in English

The Concept of Irony. Translated by L. Capel. New York, 1963.

Either/Or. 2 Vols. Translated by Swenson, Lowrie, and Johnston. New York, 1959 (ed. Victor Eremita). [Parenthesized names are pseudonyms.]

Edifying Discourses I-IV. Translated by D. Swenson and L. Swenson. Minneapolis, 1943–46.

Fear and Trembling. Translated by W. Lowrie. New York, 1954 (Johannes de Silentio).

Repetition. Translated by W. Lowrie. Princeton, 1941 (Constantine Constantius).

Philosophical Fragments. Translated by D. Swenson and H. Hong. Princeton, 1962 (Johannes Climacus).

The Concept of Dread. Translated by W. Lowrie. Princeton, 1957 (Vigilius Haufniensis).

Stages on Life's Way. Translated by W. Lowrie. Princeton, 1940 (Hilarius Bookbinder).

Concluding Unscientific Postscript. Translated by D. Swenson and W. Lowrie. Princeton, 1944 (Johannes Climacus).

The Present Age. Translated by W. Lowrie. New York, 1940.

Purity of Heart. Translated by D. Steere. New York, 1948.

Works of Love. Translated by H. and E. Hong. New York, 1962.

Christian Discourses. Translated by W. Lowrie. New York, 1940.

The Point of View of My Work as an Author. Translated by W. Lowrie. New York, 1940.

Sickness Unto Death. Translated by W. Lowrie. New York, 1954 (Anti-Climacus).

Training in Christianity. Translated by W. Lowrie. New York, 1941 (Anti-Climacus).

For Self-Examination. Translated by H. and E. Hong. Minneapolis, 1940.

Attack Upon Christendom. Translated by W. Lowrie. Princeton, 1946.

Journals (1834–54). Translated and edited by A. Dru. London, 1938. Perhaps the most illuminating philosophical journals written; comparable to Pascal's Pensées.

Books about Kierkegaard

Barrett, W. Irrational Man. New York, 1958.

Blackham, H. J. Søren Kierkegaard. London, 1952.

Collins, J. The Mind of Kierkegaard. Chicago, 1953. Especially recommended.

Diem, H. An Introduction to Kierkegaard. New York, 1951.

Diem, H. Kierkegaard's Dialectic of Existence. Edinburg, 1959.

Geisman, E. Lectures on the Religous Thought of S. Kierkegaard. Minneapolis, 1937.

Heaker, T. Søren Kierkegaard. New York, 1937.

Hohlenberg. Søren Kierkegaard. New York, 1954.

Johnson and Thulstrup, eds. A Kierkegaard Critique. New York, 1962.

Jolivet, R. Introduction to Kierkegaard. Translated by W. Barber. New York, 1946.

Lowrie, W. Kierkegaard. New York, 1938.

———. A Short Life of Kierkegaard. Princeton, 1942.

MacIntyre, A. "Existentialism." In D. J. O'Connor, ed. A Critical History of Western Philosophy. Glencoe, Ill. Free Press, 1964 and "Kierkegaard." In P. Edwards, ed. Encyclopedia of Philosophy. New York, Macmillan, 1967.

Mackey, J. L. "The Poetry of Inwardness." In G. Schrader, ed. Existential Philosophy. New York, McGraw-Hill, 1967, pp. 45–107.

Prince, G. The Narrow Pass. New York, 1963.

Rohde, P. Søren Kierkegaard. New York, 1963.

Swenson, D. Something about Kierkegaard. Minneapolis, 1949.

Thomas, H. Subjectivity and Paradox. New York, 1957.

Thompson, J. The Lonely Labyrinth. Carbondale, Ill., 1967.

Wyschogrod, M. Kierkegaard and Heidegger: The Ontology of Existence. London, 1954.

Friedrich Nietzsche: Nihilism and the Will to Power
CHAPTER 4

When Nietzsche was thirty-five years old, he left the University and the philosophy of the university, and went into the mountains of Switzerland and Italy. For ten years he suffered in body and spirit, pushing himself to a frenzy of philosophic and literary creation. The resultant writings are terse and unsystematic explosions of brilliance, more akin to the ancient teachings of religious leaders than to the scholarly tomes of the nineteenth century. Accordingly, Nietzsche found a spiritual ancestor in the prophet Zarathustra, who becomes the spokesman for Nietzsche's most treasured doctrines. In *Zarathustra,* we cannot help but perceive Nietzsche's projections of his own solitude in this 'wanderer' who is forever distant from the mankind he claims to love, who sought to "teach mankind" but feared that he would be pronounced "holy" for it, and who was never quite certain himself whether he was or would rather be a saint or a buffoon.

Nietzsche's interpreters have not agreed on his significance either; much of his considerable 'influence' has been due to the gross misrepresentation and misinterpretation of his philosophy by the Nazis, who dealt him the ultimate insult of accepting him as their philosopher. He has been worshiped as a saint for the worst of reasons, and celebrated for defending doctrines which he in fact found repulsive. In reaction to the resultant ill-founded enthusiasm for Nietzsche, many serious philosophers have tried to cleanse philosophy of his name altogether, and dismiss him, not even as a buffoon—the fruits of his 'influence' have been far too disastrous for such light treatment—but rather as a madman. Thus, it should not be surprising that Nietzsche is more often the subject for psychoanalytic than serious philosophical

investigations, and his ideas are often dismissed as manifestations of the illnesses discovered in his biography. His vicious attacks on the church are diagnosed as a reaction to his strict Christian upbringing; his sarcastic and sometimes silly attacks on women are attributed to his early life in a family of women and his subsequent sexual failures; his glorification of power and strength is said to be the reaction to his persistent ill health, and the celebration of the *Übermensch* the imaginative projection of his own *Unter*-manly life. His philosophy as a whole has not infrequently been discounted as the product of the tragic madness which ultimately caused his death.

No doubt the origins of many of Nietzsche's most radical ideas can be better understood by appeal to his biography (as we found in our study of Kierkegaard), and his dreadful influence can be understood only if we go beyond his writings to the techniques and prejudices of his interpreters. In our survey, however, we shall be concerned only with Nietzsche's philosophy. The gruesome details of his unhappy life are sufficiently well-known that they need not be reviewed here. We shall discuss Nietzsche's notorious 'influence' only as a preliminary to understanding what Nietzsche really did believe.

So distorted were Nietzsche's doctrines that any adequate historical treatment of Nietzsche as philosopher would perhaps require two separate studies, one of his writings, and the other what he has been said to have written. The two lists would have little in common except for familiar catch phrases. Nietzsche despised politics and nationalism and referred to himself as "a good European"; yet his editor-sister celebrates his great love for Germanism and his enthusiastic patriotism during the Franco-Prussian War. Nietzsche predicted with horror that Germany of the twentieth century would be racked with dictatorship and disastrous wars; yet his alleged celebration of a German-dominated Europe is well known. Nietzsche hated the new German racism which accompanied the new nationalism[1] and mercilessly attacked anti-Semitism, particularly in his sister;[2] yet we find short fragments taken from Nietzsche's works used to support Aryan racism as the central doctrine of his philosophy. (This is not to deny that Nietzsche held some very strong opinions concerning the inequality of men. Men are, according to Nietzsche, unequal *by nature,* and Nietzsche leaves no doubt that he admires the stronger men. His "master-race" is not constituted by any race, creed, or nationality.) The 'power' celebrated by Nietzsche was very close to the 'power' of the religious ascetic, the great artist, the great philosopher; the power celebrated in his name is the military *Reich* which he despised as the most despicable exercise of power. The *Übermensch* celebrated by Zarathustra is more similar to Zarathustra himself—in his tolerance for loneliness and suffering, in his love for humanity—than to the gregarious, sensual, and violent heroes of military history; but the *Übermensch* of recent German history is the "blond beast" of the German *Reich* off in conquest. (The expression "blond beast," incidentally, is a recurrent metaphorical image referring to the lion, the symbol of autonomy for Nietzsche. In no context does the expression refer to the Aryan image.) Nietzsche took intellectual honesty and the courage to attack the powers that be as his highest values (his criticism of Kant is that "in his relation to the State he was not great"),[3] and he resigned his own university post, in part, in order to escape any demand to fit his philosophy to official doctrines; yet Nietzsche is pictured as an early proponent of the "big lie," the reduction of *Truth* to political expediency.

This remarkable set of contrasts can be explained by noting that Nietzsche's sister, Elizabeth, who was married to and was herself a proto-Nazi anti-Semite, took upon herself the responsibility for distributing (and withholding) and interpreting her brother's works. It was only when Nietzsche was near death and near fame that Elizabeth seems to have discovered her

'life-long' closeness to him. Her control over some of his most important writings and her extensive "memories" of her brother's conversations established her as his 'authoritative' interpreter and biographer, and established Nietzsche as an unwilling and popular instrument of the brutal forces which had already begun their terrible rise to power in the German state. Under the extensive distortion of Nietzsche's official Nazi interpreters (Bäumler, for example),[4] the twisted fragments and pre-'interpreted' works yielded the required endorsement of the Hitlerian specters of the 'master-Aryan race', anti-Semitism, the glory of the *Reich,* and the Germanization of Europe. If we ignore Nietzsche's writings and look only at this history, we should not be surprised that Hitler accepted Elizabeth Forster-Nietzsche's invitation to visit the *Nietzsche-archiv* during his fast climb to power.

Although Nietzsche's antipathy to these Nazi doctrines can be amply demonstrated by appeal to his works,[5] it must not be pretended that Nietzsche is in no way responsible for his subsequent misinterpretation. He does make frequent overstatements about the Jews, Truth, inequality, Power, and overly dramatic metaphorical claims mentioning the military and traditional military heroes (for example, Napoleon and Caesar). One can, by selective editing, paint a picture of Nietzsche's thought similar to that defended by the Nazis, and the disjointedness of much of Nietzsche's writing certainly encourages that sort of selectivity. Like Kierkegaard, Nietzsche was a stylist, and clear philosophical exposition and argument are often sacrificed to literary interests. The brilliant 'dithyrambs' of *Thus Spake Zarathustra* yield their philosophical insights only in subsequent and less popular works. One easily grasps the significance of a terse aphorism at the expense of the meaning of the entire work. In our discussion, therefore, it is of the utmost importance that we avoid the temptation to reemphasize the popular fragments which have been so abused and stress the total context in which these appear and the overall concerns which develop through Nietzsche's philosophy.

Nietzsche's Writings
Nietzsche's works have been divided into three more or less distinct periods, although certain key conceptions and con-

cerns recur throughout. (It is suggested, even by Nietzsche himself, that these three periods are not to be opposed to each other, but rather considered to be progressive stages in spiritual (and stylistic) development, as in the "camel, lion, and child" stages in *Zarathustra*.[6]) In what is popularly referred to as his "Romantic period", Nietzsche wrote his famous *Birth of Tragedy*[7] (*Die Geburt der Tragödie*) in 1872, manifesting the intense preoccupation with philology and aesthetic values as well as the brilliant antiacademic style characteristic of all his works. In *Birth of Tragedy*, Nietzsche proclaims that,

Only as an aesthetic phenomenon is the world justified eternally.[8]

It is this concern with the "primacy of art" (in which Nietzsche agrees with Schelling) and his celebration of the *Dionysian* elements in Greek life that are responsible for the "Romantic" flavor of this period. In fact, however, we find that Nietzsche is bitterly opposed to the Romanticism of Rousseau and the German Romantics (Schlegel and Schelling) even at this stage. Furthermore, as we have already indicated in the introduction, the concern for aesthetics will remain through Nietzsche's last works, occupying a key position in his conception of the *Übermensch* and the *will to power*. The prescription to shape one's character like a work of art (through Apollonian discipline) and live not only as an artist but as a work of art (through Dionysian "frenzy") in *Birth of Tragedy*[9] is already the characterization of Zarathustra's *Übermensch*.

I am convinced that art represents the highest task and the truly metaphysical activity of this life.[10]

Oh, those Greeks! They knew how to live ... Adorers of forms, of tomes, of words! And therefore-artists?[11]

This period is best characterized, however, by Nietzsche's enthusiasm for Schopenhauer and his dislike for the philosophy of Hegel. In an *"Untimely" Meditation*[12] on "The Use and Disadvantage of History for Life" (1874), Nietzsche begins his long struggle with Darwinism and the relationship between history and the theory of value. Against Hegel's (and Darwin's) "idolatry of the factual," it is argued that

the "goal for mankind" he seeks cannot be simply given in the past. To the contrary, history shows us a panorama of stupidity and suffering which indicates how far man is from this goal; but neither, Nietzsche argues, can we ignore history in our search for values.

Like Kierkegaard, Nietzsche is already concerned only for "the few" who might understand him, and the 'elitist' connotations of the *Übermensch* are already evident in the early *Meditations:*

The goal of humanity cannot lie in the end [of man], but only in its highest specimens.[13]

In these *Meditations,* the concept of "the herd" is introduced, the concern with self-realization ("Be who you are!")[14] and the struggle against Nihilism are apparent, and the later conception of the *Übermensch* is foreshadowed by Nietzsche's concern to show that man can be more than a Darwinian beast. Even in the earliest essays, therefore, we find the central attitudes of Nietzsche's mature philosophy.

The "positivistic" period is so-called because of Nietzsche's introduction of his 'experimental' method. Philosophically, this is perhaps the least significant of the three periods, for the works of this period are mostly aphoristic; arguments are condensed to slogans and no philosophy is worked through. In this period, the brief observations of *Human-All-Too-Human,* (*Menschliches, Allzumenschliches*) written in 1878, *Dawn* (*Morgenröte*) produced in 1881, and *The Gay Science* (*Die Fröhliche Wissenschaft*)[15] in 1882, are the seeds of Nietzsche's mature philosophy. Their presentation is so permeated with attacks on women, current literature, and things in general, that it is to Nietzsche's mature period that we must turn for "his philosophy." The second period is very important, however, in understanding Nietzsche's personal development. Here he breaks with Schopenhauer, begins his famous disillusionment and feud with Richard Wagner, and resigns from the University. Clearly, the daring experimentalism of this period and the escape from old structures is of the same piece. From this period on, Nietzsche marks himself as one of the great rebels of history.

It is the mature philosophy which begins with *Zarathustra*, with which we shall be concerned primarily in our discussion in this chapter, although the earlier works will often help us to study the development of this philosophy. The first book of *Thus Spake Zarathustra (Also Sprach Zarathustra)* was published in 1883, the second and third books within a year. The fourth book, although written in 1885, was not released until 1892. In rapid succession, Nietzsche published *Beyond Good and Evil (Jenseits von Gut und Böse)* in 1886, *The Genealogy of Morals (Zur Genealogie der Moral)* in 1887, *The Case of Wagner (Der Fall Wagner)* in 1888, the *Twilight of the Idols (Die Götzendammerung)* in 1889, the *Antichrist* in 1895, and *Nietzsche Contra Wagner* in 1895 (the last two were submitted for publication after Nietzsche became insane). *Ecce Homo,*[16] Nietzsche's last work (which contains his own reviews of all his other books) was withheld from publication by his sister until 1908. Her motives are apparent, for the autobiographical aspect of the book clearly contradicts many of her own claims about Nietzsche's 'personal' attitudes, particularly towards his sister. Her defense was that Nietzsche was already insane when he wrote it (a major controversy still rages regarding how this book should be considered). In addition, Nietzsche had hundreds of unpublished notes and plans for future writings. Until recently, these have been published selectively, often to prove one interpretation or another. (They are currently published altogether in English under the title *Will to Power (Der Wille Zu Macht).*[17]

The Attack on Systematic Philosophy

Nietzsche presents the same problems to his readers as Kierkegaard. Similarly, he has written many books, all important to an understanding of his philosophy. None of these books contains a clear exposition of his basic philosophical doctrines, and all of them contain an extraordinary amount of fascinating but digressive material. As in Kierkegaard, this lack of systematization is not so much a stylistic fault as it is a deliberate attempt *not* to write systematically. With Nietzsche as with Kierkegaard, this refusal is born of the suspicion and reaction to the 'systematic' philosophy of Hegel and, to a lesser but significant extent, to that of Kant, Schopenhauer, and Spinoza, three philosophers whom Nietzsche most attacks and most respects. (He calls Kant the greatest of philosophers, once took Schopenhauer as

mentor, and calls Spinoza his "precursor."[18])

In reaction to "systematization," Nietzsche is insistent that each proposition be capable of standing independently, without a system for support. This does not mean that he is not systematic in another sense, however, namely, that there is a core of central theses recurring throughout his philosophy. (He does insist, in his later works, that his readers are expected to understand previous works.) Like Kierkegaard, he insists that a philosophical system, like that of Hegel, in which not only the truth of propositions but the meaning of key terms is derived in the system, is not merely bad philosophical method but inherently *dishonest.*[19]

The will to a system, in a philosopher, morally speaking, is a subtle corruption, a disease of character. Amorally speaking, his will to appear more stupid than he is. . . . I am not bigoted enough for a system, not even for my system.[20]
The will to a system is a lack of integrity.[21]

Ironically, Nietzsche accuses Hegel of just that 'one-sidedness' that it was the purpose of his system to overcome. A system, he argues, must proceed from some set of premises which themselves remain unexamined. (We have seen, however, in Chapter 2 that Hegel believes his system to be free from such 'presuppositions'; we have argued that he does make certain *methodological* assumptions, at least, as Nietzsche claims, the value of a *system.*) According to Nietzsche, however, it is the business of philosophy to question all assumptions, all perspectives,

to look now out of this window, now out of that; I guarded against settling down with any of these dogmas, considered them harmful.[22]

The system is nothing but an excuse to stop questioning at some point.

Nietzsche's offensive against this confining effect of systematic philosophy and his demand for seeing all alternatives explains his notably 'unsystematic' style. It also explains how his philosophical hero is one with that of Kierkegaard, namely Socrates. It is interesting, however, that Nietzsche's appeal to Socrates and rejection of *system* is based on very different considerations. Kierkegaard prefers Socrates to the system because of his concern for the subjective *individual* who is ignored by the system. For Nietzsche, systems are one-sided—it is not that they give us only truth (that is, objective truth), and we want *subjective* truth—but that system does not give us *truth* at all, just a systematically distorted and one-sided account. Nietzsche does not claim that the system ignores the individual, but rather that it ignores the truth by failing to question. In fact, Nietzsche claims that the system is the (subjective) expression of the individual in the *guise* of (objective) truth:

They are often all expressions of the humanity of 'great human beings.'[23]

Later,

The different philosophic systems are to be considered as educational methods of the spirit.[24]

Thus Nietzsche's objection to the system is the very opposite of Kierkegaard's indignant grievances. Kierkegaard claims that the system gives us only 'objective truth' and not 'subjective truth' (personal expression). Nietzsche complains that the system gives us only 'subjective truth' and not *truth.*

How does Nietzsche avoid system in philosophy without lapsing into incoherence or inconsistency? An extreme suggestion, argued by Karl Jaspers in his book on *Nietzsche,* is that Nietzsche does not attempt to avoid inconsistency, but rather it is the *basis* of his philosophy. According to Jaspers, Nietzsche must always be read by finding contradictory pairs of theses. Nietzsche does contradict himself, particularly if his earliest and last works are juxtaposed. Consider the same charge of inconsistency leveled against Kant by comparing the second *Critique* with the posthumous works, of Wittgenstein by comparing the *Tractatus* with the *Philosophical Investigation.* There is no evidence that the inconsistency is a conscious attempt to show basic antinomies, and the key theses of the late works are surely without intentional contradiction.

The honorific title of "science" had been applied by Kant, Fichte, and Hegel to their philosophies to praise systematic rigor and scholarly dedication to the

search for truth. Nietzsche, too, insists that philosophy be scientific, but he insists not that a philosophical investigation be systematic, but that it be rigorously empirical. Every meaningful philosophical conception allows a test or an experiment (*Versuch*):

I would praise any skepsis to which I am permitted to reply: 'Let us try it.' But I do not want to hear anything more of all the things and questions which do not permit of experiment . . . for there courage has lost its rights.[25]

One may interestingly compare this radical empiricism to the Logical Positivism of the "Vienna Circle,"[26]

the meaning of a proposition can be given only by giving the rules of its verification in experience.[27]

(Metaphysicians) are compelled to cut all connections between their statements and experience, and precisely by this procedure, they deprive them of any sense.[28]

and also to John Dewey's "Instrumentalism";

Ideas are operational in that they instigate and direct further operation of observation.[29]

Judgments about values are judgments about the conditions and results of experienced objects.[30]

Subjected to this rigorous experimentalism, philosophical investigation becomes the testing of hypothetical solutions to a large variety of more or less separate philosophical problems. As such, philosophy becomes a number of smaller investigations, which may *later* be interrelated, but which are carried out independently. There is no "single stroke," according to Nietzsche, by which all philosophical dilemmas could be resolved, and the ambitions of the "systematic philosopher" were too far reaching;

The small single questions and experiments were considered contemptible . . . To solve all with one stroke . . . that was the secret wish . . .[31]

For Fichte, for Hegel, for Schopenhauer, even for Kant, 'small' philosophical questions were to be considered and answered only insofar as they conformed to the concerns and demands of their philosophy as a whole. The purpose of attacking any philosophical point was to elucidate the whole; the individual problem had no particular interest.

The dissolution of philosophy into a great many separate and less ambitious (but, Nietzsche would insist, more serious) investigations has prominent champions in current philosophy. In England and America, the limited logical investigations initiated after 1900 in professional journals, culminating in the "philosophy by committee" as celebrated by J. L. Austin and his many followers, succeeded in ridiculing traditional ambitions and breaking philosophy into small—some would say too small—pieces. Such has been the success of this disintegrating movement, that one is hard put to name even a single recent philosophical treatise with the scope and breadth of interests of the philosophical work of the seventeenth to nineteenth centuries. This same disintegration is found on the Continent, in the work of Edmund Husserl, whose "Phenomenology" also destroyed expectations of a single philosophical system and replaced these hopes with deep involvement in many more or less isolated problems.[32]

This brief and prophetic comparison with Austin and Husserl provides us with the counter to Jaspers' extreme interpretation of Nietzsche's antisystematic attitude. To refuse to answer any philosophical question other than by appeal to an investigation specific to that question is, according to Nietzsche, dishonest. To systematize, in the sense he attacks, is to base the solution to philosophical problems on the solution to other problems without investigating these independently. However, to insist on the autonomy of each question in no way supposes that the answers to different questions may turn out to be contradictory, nor does it suppose the set of answers to a large number of individual investigations will form a coherent whole. Nietzsche's 'atomistic' philosophy and his attack on the system is ultimately no more than, and no less important than, an insistence on the intellectual rigor and honesty that mark the best in philosophy. Where Nietzsche's philosophy does not add up to a coherent and consistent whole, this is not a conscious attempt on his part to be paradoxical (compare Kierkegaard)

but rather a result of the tragic interruption of his thinking life in his horrible madness and his inability to bring his thought to fruition.

The kind of experiment appropriate to Nietzsche's philosophical investigation, however, was not anything like a scientific experiment, or anything like the conceptual analyses of Austin or the experiential analyses of Husserl. The philosophical prototype of this special philosophical experimenter is Socrates, and the "experiment" involved is an exercise of practical wisdom. Joining forces with Kierkegaard, and thus bringing himself in close kinship with the existentialism of this century, Nietzsche emphasizes the importance of a philosophy which is *lived*. Nietzsche's experimentalism is a series of attempts to find a conception of life which suits him, and here he is very close to Kierkegaard's 'subjective truth'. The experimentation and refusal to "settle anywhere" extends to Nietzsche's style; his notable aphoristic style was just one of many "experiments," and there is no philosophical author who excels Nietzsche in his command of a wide diversity of styles, several of which are incorporated in a single work (compare *Gay Science* and *Beyond Good and Evil*).

The appropriateness of this "Let us try it" (*Versuchen wir*) philosophical method to the practical problems of ethics, art, and religion may be easily recognized. Where Kierkegaard explicitly (but too infrequently) emphasized the limitation of 'subjective truth' to just these areas, Nietzsche claims his method as a *general* philosophical method. How could Nietzsche's experimentalism solve the more theoretical problems of metaphysics, for example, the problems of the existence of universals, or the problem of induction?

With a boldness befitting a progenitor of both American pragmatism and logical positivism, Nietzsche replies that problems which cannot be decided experimentally are not problems at all. These "pseudo problems" (as they are declared in this century) only have the grammatical appearance of intelligible questions. Nietzsche even appeals to language to explain how this is so. He maintains, metaphysical illusions often arise within a correct grammatical formula, but signify nothing. For example, he tells us, "I am afraid we are not rid of God because we still have faith in grammar."[33] The problems of universals or induction are legitimate philo- •

sophical concerns only insofar as they "make a difference" (to use A. J. Ayer's phrase). If there is no *practical* concern involved, there is no need for concern at all. Nietzsche's insistence on the role of *practice* in philosophy is more thorough-going than even Kierkegaard, who reservingly allows that the Hegelian theoretical system has achieved a kind of truth.

Nietzsche's "positivism" is itself as based on epistemological underpinnings as the twentieth-century position is founded on a theory of language. Unfortunately, the theory of knowledge underlying Nietzsche's pragmatism is never worked through by him and constitutes one of the most serious gaps in his philosophy. There is no continued treatment of it and much of the existing discussion is confined to (previously) unpublished notes. However, this existing skeletal discussion is so important to the 'systematic' analysis of Nietzsche's thought that we shall give it attention disproportionate to the small space it occupies in his writings.

Values and Nihilism

Philosophical methods rarely are formed as a preliminary to philosophical concerns. More frequently, as with Kant, Hegel, and Kierkegaard, the methodology is tailored to fit a more or less specific area of interest. With Kant, the reconciliation of science and morality is the *raison d'etre* of his transcendental method, and not simply the consequence of that method. Similarly, Hegel's Absolute Spirit, in spite of the claims of a presuppositionless philosophy, is the incentive for the construction of the system and its "first-principle" as well as the result. In his primary concern for the ultimate justification of morality and religion *for an individual,* Nietzsche closely follows Kierkegaard, and his appeal to the traditional notion of practical wisdom at the expense of purely *theoretical* wisdom is the result of his basic search for the "good life." The nature of values is the core problem of all of Nietzsche's works, and like Kierkegaard, his problem reduces to the relationship between aesthetic, ethical, and religious values and their ultimate justification. However, although Nietzsche followed Kierkegaard in arranging these values in a definite hierarchy, his own "dialectic" was the converse of that of Kierkegaard. For Nietzsche, all values were ultimately *aesthetic,* while the values of morality and religion, particularly Chris-

tianity and Christian ethics, were attacked by him (as once by Hegel in his early writing) as a perversion of the notion of value and as essentially degrading. Nietzsche's concern, therefore, is a rejection ("by instinct") of a traditional hierarchy of values defended by Kierkegaard no less than by Kant, Hegel, and traditional Christian thinkers. Nietzsche's philosophy in its multifold twists and digressions is primarily an attempt to defend this "instinct" which carries him from his first work

existence and the world seem justified only as an aesthetic phenomenon.[34]

to his last.

Have you understood me? Dionysus versus Christ.[35]

Once again, we find the central philosophical problem to be the justification of moral (and religious) values. Like Kierkegaard, Nietzsche concludes that moral and religious values cannot be rationally justified. He does not agree, however, that all values are and must be ultimately justifiable, although this is the interpretation usually given to his "nihilist" philosophy. Nietzsche, as we shall see, is very much a naturalist in his attempted justification of certain values, and very much a rationalist as well. He maintains that there is no *good* and *evil,* that is, *absolute* values of good and evil, and this moral nihilism is indeed the cornerstone of his philosophy. However, this is not Nietzsche's final position but rather its original problem. The notions of 'Good and Evil' as *moral facts* existing in the world is a recurrent set of concepts in Nietzsche, and is most often contrasted with 'Good and Bad', an evaluative contrast which does not carry with it the status of *facts.* (It might be noted that the voice of Zarathustra (Zoroaster) as the exponent of Nietzsche's morality of the *Übermensch* is ironic in that the historical Zoroaster taught that the world was the battleground for the *objective* forces of Good and Evil). Nihilism is the seed from which the philosophy of Power and the *Übermensch* is to grow. It is a 'destructive' philosophy, as so often is charged, *only* in the sense that one destroys a field of weeds to plant a garden.

The doctrine of *nihilism,* made famous by Nietzsche (taking the term from Turgenev's *Fathers and Sons),* is simply the thesis that there is *nothing* of ultimate value. Narrowly conceived, nihilism is the ethical thesis that no moral principle can be ultimately justified, that dishonesty is ultimately as virtuous as honesty, that the Ten Commandments are no more valid than ten contra-commandments (Thou shalt kill, Thou shalt steal, and so on). Nihilism is the rejection of a long tradition of thought in which certain moral (religious) principles (exemplified by the Ten Commandments and Kant's categorical imperative) were thought to be universally valid and binding on all rational or human creatures. Nietzsche and Kierkegaard both argue that morality and reverence for God cannot be rationally defended. Kierkegaard and Nietzsche, however, part company; Kierkegaard maintains that we ought to accept these values *anyway,* even though no values are rationally justifiable. Nietzsche argues that we ought not accept these nonrational values, but that we ought to accept another set of values—those which are referred to as aesthetic—and that these values can be naturalistically defended. As we shall see, Nietzsche is not truly a nihilist. He does not argue that no values have justification, but only that traditional moral and religious (Christian) values have no rational defense. Nietzsche's attack on traditional values ("the revaluation of all values") and his nihilism are based first on the Kierkegaardian (and Humean) doctrine of the insufficiency of reason to resolve questions of value. (Like Hume, he insists that Reason is *necessary* for such resolution.) Secondly, Nietzsche's nihilism and the need for the "revaluation" are based on the very un-Kierkegaardian thesis of the irreversible "death of God."

Nihilism has a broader meaning in Nietzsche's philosophy in which it refers to the lack of ultimate justification for *any* belief, whether it be a belief concerning values or not. It is this *epistemological nihilism* which forms the uncompleted foundation for Nietzsche's all too rare but brilliant insights into the nature of truth and knowledge. The fame and historical importance of Nietzsche's arguments for the narrow ethical nihilism have often eclipsed the 'systematic' relation of his moral philosophy to general philosophical concerns. Most importantly, it is in the treatment of the problem of truth that we can see the basis for Nietzsche's naturalism (much as Aristotle's analysis of human 'function' provides the basis for his ethics).

In the delicate transition from Nietzsche's views on the justification of knowledge to his more elaborate views on the justification of values, we shall see clearly that (moral) nihilism is not the doctrine which he seeks to defend, as is popularly supposed, but rather the *problem* with which his philosophy begins.

Now that the shabby origin of these values [social values] is becoming clear, the universe seems to have lost value, seems "meaningless," but that is only a transitional stage.[36]

Epistemological Nihilism

The *dawn* of Nietzsche's mature philosophy is truly Cartesian in spirit. From what has already been said of Nietzsche's method, it is evident that the primary business of the philosopher is to *question,* to *attack* self-evident suppositions, to treat all "error as cowardice," as the result of the fear of questioning too far. Unlike Descartes, Nietzsche is unwilling to rest on any seemingly self-evident principle, and like Kierkegaard, disclaims the Cartesian *cogito* (and Schopenhauer's "Will") with its consequent distinction between the world of appearance and the 'real' world (as do Heidegger and Sartre a half century later). The general movement of 'modern' philosophy away from Descartes had been an increasing recognition of how few propositions could be shown to be beyond doubt; and philosophy moved from the newly enjoyed critical certainty of the Cartesian *Meditations* to the broad skepticism of Hume's *Treatise.* Kant sought to derive a new certainty for basic philosophical propositions, but even Kant, Nietzsche charges, has refused to question far enough. Nietzsche's epistemology is based on an attack on the world-of-appearance, real world distinction held in one form or another by every major philosopher from Descartes to Kant (and Schopenhauer). Unfortunately, this attack derives its effectiveness only from historical precedence (notably through Fichte and Hegel) and incisive style, for there is no argument to be found against this distinction. In *Beyond Good and Evil,* we are simply told:

The apparent world is the only one, the 'real world' is merely added by a lie.[37]

Thus, the Cartesian question, "How do I know the world is like my experiences?" and the Kantian question, "Can I know that the world-in-itself is like the world I experience?" are dismissed out of hand. Coupled with the rejection of this metaphysical two-world view, however, is rejection of a related epistemological thesis—that, in spite of the variety of perspectives, conceptions, and interpretations of the world, there is a *true* conception of the world—what the world is like in *fact:*

> *. . . against positivism, which halts at phenomena—"There are only* Facts*"—I would say: No, Facts is precisely what there is not, only interpretations.*[38]

> *The true world—an idea which is no longer good for anything . . . an idea which has become useless and superfluous—consequently, a refuted idea, let us abolish it.*[39]

Since there is no true world, philosophers (and everyone else) are mistaken in supposing that philosophy is a search for *truth* in this sense:

> *What is needed is that something must be held to be true—not that something* is *true.*[40]

> *Rational thought is interpretation according to a scheme that we cannot throw off.*[41]

In support of this thesis, it can be argued, with Kant and Hegel, that "there can be no unconceptualized experiences," and that every conceptualization is already an imposition of an interpretation. Nietzsche's arguments are sparse on this subject, but he does give us sufficient ground for supposing that he agreed with this Kantian thesis, and used it in conjunction with an embryonic but original theory of language to give us a "meta-metaphysics" surprisingly similar to that endorsed by many analytic philosophers of this century. According to this theory, it is the language we use (the system of interpretation) which determines our metaphysics, not vice versa. The thesis that there exist objects independent of our experiences, for example, is a 'linguistic fiction';

> the 'thing-in-itself' nonsensical. If I remove all the relationships, all the 'properties', all the 'activities' of a thing, the thing does not remain over; because thingness has only been invented by us owing to the requirements of logic.[42]

The search for truth, for the true world, is thus not a search for a real world behind appearances or a world of facts underlying our interpretation of it. The true world is simply the world of our experiences and our interpretations.

From this beginning, still much in agreement with Kant and Hegel, Nietzsche draws some bold conclusions, so bold that he was not able to formulate them without severe confusion. In agreeing with Kant and Hegel that the philosopher's search for truth could not be a search for a *correspondence* between 'our' world (or experience and our interpretations) and the 'real world', Nietzsche failed to see that the refutation of this particular ('correspondence') theory of truth did not constitute a refutation of *truth* itself. Yet this is the impression we get from Nietzsche's brief writings on this subject.

> *Truth is error.*[43]

> *There is no truth.*[44]

Less ironically paraphrased, these claims state that if any proposition is said to be 'true', its truth cannot be determined by a correct matching with the 'real' world. This does not mean, as Nietzsche is occasionally tempted to assert, that there is no truth. The philosophical conception of "truth" must rather be reanalyzed, and this is precisely what Nietzsche attempts to do—culminating in his "experimental" method.

Why do we believe certain propositions to be true?—and some of these to be *necessarily* true? If it is not because of agreement with *the facts* ("there are no facts"),[45] then what ground is there for saying anything is 'true'? Nietzsche's answer, remarkably paralleling the new "pragmatism" of the Americans (notably James) and the German post-Kantians (for example, Vaihinger), is typically stated in form of a dramatic paradox:

> *What really are mankind's truths? They are the irrefutable errors of mankind.*[46]

and "truth is that sort of error without which a particular class of living creatures could not live."[47]

The influence of Darwin is unmistakable here—and Nietzsche's theory of truth can be summarized—"the truth of a proposition is its survival value—its ability to help us live in the world." However, this is not a theory of truth as such, rather a theory of what we *regard as true*.[48] Since Nietzsche begins by disclaiming that there is any truth, it is a variety of "errors" among which we find those "truths" which will help us survive. The confusion in this terminology is evident, Nietzsche talks *as if* there were a world of fact or world in itself which we cannot know and which is different from the world we do know. Thus his talk of "error" is simply inconsistent with his central point. This is further demonstrated when Nietzsche explicitly talks of truth as *distinct* from survival value or efficiency, thus distinguishing him from the pragmatists for whom utility is identical to truth,

but why must we have the truth at any cost anyway.[49]

There is no pre-established harmony between the pursuit of truth and the welfare of mankind.[50]

There are two different theses here which are confused with each other, and while they are not incompatible, they may be complementary, yet they are decidedly distinct. First, Nietzsche maintains that the only criterion for the "truth" (acceptability) of a proposition is its ability to help us survive. Secondly, he insists that what is *important* in philosophy is the practicality of a proposition, but that there is *truth* as distinguished from practicality. We find here the same sort of confusion usually attributed to Kierkegaard. On the one hand, Nietzsche seems to be arguing for a pragmatic theory of truth; on the other, he simply insists that there is no *point* to discussing what does not have practical value. It is interesting that Nietzsche sometimes supports the epistemological thesis by appeal to the criterion of practicability, for example, when he rejects the two-world view on the basis that the existence of a transcendent world could make "no possible difference to me."[51]

Kant had asked "How synthetic a priori judgments were possible?" but Nietzsche, who takes the very notion of 'a priori knowledge' to be one more obstacle to serious questioning, asks rather "Why belief in such truths should be necessary?" The Darwinian criterion of survival explains how we have come to consider some prop-

ositions as necessary, for these are the "irrefutable errors of mankind, that sort of error without which [man] cannot live." Consider, by way of example, the problematic principle of induction, that the future will be like the past. Suppose one man believes in this proposition, while another believes in the contrary principle "that the future will be unlike the past." Each man drives through a red light and gets in an accident. The first man resolves to stop at red lights hereafter in the belief that accidents are likely to occur if one goes through them. The second man resolves to go through red lights because, having once been followed by an accident, it is highly unlikely it would happen again. The *necessity* of the Principle of Induction is due to the fact that those men who do not believe it are systematically eliminated. Nietzsche's theory of necessary truth is a bizarre combination of Darwin's evolutionary theory and Hegel's reflective philosophy. A proposition is seen to be necessary if only those creatures who believe it survive. A priori truths are necessary only in the sense that one who did not believe them could not survive to refute them; they are "irrefutable" only in the sense that there is no one around to refute them.

Such judgments [synthetic a priori] must be believed to be true for the sake of the preservation of such creatures like ourselves; though they might, of course, be false judgments for all that.[52]

Nietzsche's epistemology *explains* how we have come to hold certain philosophical conceptions, it does not justify these conceptions (in Kant's terms, Nietzsche gives us a 'physiology' (origins) of knowledge, but does not demonstrate our *right* to this knowledge). In fact, Nietzsche has no intention of attempting to justify these claims, for the purpose of his exposition of the origins of these truths is to show the impossibility of any ultimate justification of knowledge. Against Kant's doctrine of a priori knowledge in the "forms of intuition" and the "Categories," Nietzsche argues,

The categories are "truths" only in the sense that they are conditions for life for us: as Euclidean space is a conditional "truth." (Between ourselves: since no one would maintain that there is any necessity

for men to exist, reason, as well as
Euclidean space, is a mere idiosyncrasy of
a certain species of animal, and one
among many.)[53]

A proposition is "true" if it is efficient, "false" if it hinders us, and simply irrelevant ("meaningless") if it does not have any practical import.

Like Kierkegaard, Nietzsche is not interested in mere human survival ('so-called' existence), and Nietzsche, perhaps more than any other Western philosopher, is engrossed in the concept of the *Great Man,* the man who has overcome (*überwinden*) *mere* humanity (the "all-too-human"). It is thus important to stress that Nietzsche does not take survival as a criterion for truth, but rather uses the notion of 'survival' to explain how it is that we have come to believe certain propositions as true. Nietzsche has no theory of truth as such. His entire philosophy is grounded on the impossibility of a general criterion for truth. Philosophy under Nietzsche's direction is to abandon the search for truth and through experimentation find those propositions which 'enhance life'. Yet this notion of 'enhancing life' is not a criterion for truth, but rather what makes Nietzsche give up the search for "truth at any cost." (He refers to Epicurus; "Philosophy as the art of living.")[54]

Nietzsche's epistemology centers around the proposition that "there are no facts, only interpretations." It is the "life enhancing value" of these propositions which determines their acceptability. Thus there is no real distinction for Nietzsche (as for Fichte and Hegel) between 'theory' and 'practice.'[55] Metaphysics, epistemology, and ethics all consist of 'interpretations' whose value is their practicality in making "one's life like a work of art."[56] As a special case of "there are no facts," we find that "there are no *moral* facts,"[57] that the acceptability of a moral proposition depends only on its relevance to our life. Foremost in Nietzsche's mind, of course, is the rejection of one particular moral fact, the moral authority of God. However, the absence of ultimate moral authority is a special case of the absence of any ultimate appeal to "the facts" whatever.[58]

Moral Nihilism: The "Death of God"

Nietzsche did not know of Kierkegaard's writings until after his productive period was at its end (1888), but their remark-

able agreement on the unjustifiability of bourgeois ("crowd" or "herd") moral values and their emphasis on the individual as the source of value has led the two names to be closely linked in recent accounts of the existentialist movement. Nietzsche's appeal to 'instincts' as a source of value, like Kierkegaard's appeal to the 'passions' and his denial of the sufficiency of Reason for the justification of values, has led to his classification as "arch-irrationalist" (Jaspers)[59] and "Romantic" (Bertram).[60] This reputation is due in part to influential accounts of Nietzsche's writings (for example, Jaspers and Bertram) as intentionally self-contradictory, an account we have already rejected. The exaggerated emphasis on the rule of the instincts and the *Dionysian* in Nietzsche's thought will be dealt with in the section on Nietzsche's psychology, but we have already reported how, even in his 'romantic' *Birth of Tragedy,* Nietzsche insists on a *balance* of the Dionysian passion and Apollonian control. We shall argue further that Nietzsche is not an irrationalist in his stress on the instincts any more than is David Hume in his less dramatic celebration of the role of the passions. The charge of irrationalism is often based on Nietzsche's moral *nihilism,* the rejection of the claim of morality to an absolute foundation. On this charge, Nietzsche is even less of an irrationalist than Kierkegaard, whom we argued is not 'irrational' in his denial of ultimate justification either. For both Kierkegaard and Nietzsche, it is *reasoning* which brings us to the 'irrational' conclusion.

The existentialist parallel between Kierkegaard and Nietzsche breaks down completely, however, in their treatment of belief in a divine Being and its relation to morality. For Kierkegaard, the lack of ultimate values demands a 'leap' to values (preferably religious values). For Nietzsche, however, there is no warrant for such an 'irrational leap', which is but another manifestation of the philosophical "cowardice" he so despises. (Compare Albert Camus' criticism of Kierkegaard's "leap" as "philosophical suicide.")[61]

For Nietzsche, as for Kant and many philosophers before Kant, moral and religious values were intimately related. Traditionally, religious values ultimately justified moral values (a position sometimes compatible with Kierkegaard's treatment of the ethical and religious spheres). *Morality,* that is, the accepted values of the Protestant ethic, was absolutely grounded in the Christian (and Jewish) faith, and acceptance of God entailed acceptance of His moral code. However, the entailment might also be formulated conversely, for Kant (and Hegel) had persuasively argued that religious truths were justified only insofar as they were required by morality. Thus, on Kant's account, religious truths were justifiable by appeal to moral truth. For Kierkegaard, the unjustifiability of values is the peculiar validation of the irrational leap to Christian faith; for Nietzsche, morality and religion are *logically* interdependent and stand or fall together. In fact, he argues, they fall together, for religious values have lost their acceptability.

There is serious question whether Nietzsche rejects morality on the basis of a rejection of Christianity, or whether he rejects Christianity on the basis of a moral critique. Some commentators (Morgan)[62] claim that atheism is "the premise of Nietzsche's philosophy." For others, (Kaufmann)[63] the rejection of Christ is a conclusion of Nietzsche's moral consideration. In fact, both arguments can be found, against both sides of the logical equivalence between Christianity and Christian morality. It is, perhaps, the moral critique of religion which is of the greatest interest in Nietzsche, but it is the argument from atheism to amorality which is more simple, more dramatic, and therefore more popular. The first argument will occupy us for the last half of this chapter. The simpler argument from atheism can be simply dealt with here.

The superdramatic slogan of this argument, "God is dead,"[64] is *not* simply an assertion of atheism, as it is not the ridiculous assertion that there was a divine Being who has literally died. Nor is Nietzsche's "death of God" a "fact" to be taken indifferently (as La Place's rejection of God as a "useless hypothesis"). Like Heidegger and Sartre who learned much from him, Nietzsche found the "death" of God to be a matter of morbid concern, and he sometimes presents this idea as one leading inevitably to madness.[65] With the "death of God," "an age of barbarism begins,"[66] the "madness of millenia breaks out in us,"[67] for the entire foundation of Christian morality has disappeared. The contrast with the current "death of God" movement *within* the church is striking, for that is an attempt to *save* Christian ethics by lifting it from its theological foundation.

What is the significance of the "death of God" in Nietzsche's writings? Is it the case that atheism is the "major premise of Nietzsche's philosophy,"[68] and therefore a theological proposal no better supported than the dogmatic theology Nietzsche attacks? These questions are easily answered once we understand that Nietzsche's concern with God has nothing to do with metaphysics—with the actual existence of a supreme being. He is interested in the *belief in God* as a cultural phenomenon, like the young Hegel (and like Dostoevsky), with the *effects* of such a belief on the moral conception of life in a people. In short, it is belief in God that makes morality possible (or, after Kant, the postulate of God is a 'condition' for morality) and Nietzsche is concerned with the status of moral principles once this belief is lost.

If "God is dead" does not refer to *God* at all, but refers to belief in God, then the "death" does not signify the nonexistence of a Being who once existed, but the disappearance of the belief in this Being. It is important to distinguish in Nietzsche, as we did in Kierkegaard, the difference between belief *that* God exists and the belief *in* God. It is clear that the belief concerning Nietzsche, as Kierkegaard, is the belief *in* God. Contrary to the popular conception of Nietzsche (encouraged by contemporary "death of God" theologians) Nietzsche does not argue for atheism (although he describes himself as an atheist "by instinct"), nor does he charge his contemporaries with atheism. It is the *relevance* of belief in God which is challenged, belief that God exists or belief that he does not exist is no longer important, for the God in question is no longer a being who makes any difference to us.

That we find no God—either in history or in nature or behind nature is not what differentiates us, but that we experience what has been revered as God, not as "Godlike" but as miserable, as absurd, as harmful, not merely as an error, but as a crime against life.[69]

Nietzsche's moral nihilism is easily understood in view of his "death of God" thesis. There is no longer belief *in* God, although there is beyond question still a general acceptance *that* God exists. God is no longer felt to be capable of defending his moral dictates, and the "fear of God" is no longer part of Christianity. Again, Nietzsche and Kierkegaard come to close agreement. To be a Christian is not simply to accept a doctrine that there is a God, but it is to feel oneself in the presence of and fear God. Contemporary Christians who are perfectly capable of sinning all week and then righteously going to church are not Christians at all. For them, the belief in God has no power, it has no *practical* (subjective) significance in their lives.

At this point, of course, Kierkegaard goes on to urge a recommitment to God, threatening that the only alternatives are despair or nonexistence. Nietzsche, however, uses the recognition of the un-Christianity of contemporary Christian society as a *beginning* of a long-awaited liberation from the bindings of Christian ethics. For Kierkegaard, the recognition of the "death of God" is a crisis requiring passionate reconfirmation of God and his morality; for Nietzsche, this same recognition is a birth trauma of a new era for humanity, requiring a passionate destruction of that morality which is still clinging to the crumbling supports of an already dying Christianity.

Kierkegaard saw in Christianity the *escape* from this "absurd" and "meaningless" world; Nietzsche despised Christianity for the same reason, and the brunt of Nietzsche's anti-Christianity lies in his attack on the devaluation of "this-worldly" values inherent in any supernatural or mystical value system. It is here, however, that the most common misinterpretation of Nietzsche must be exposed. Nietzsche does not *begin* his philosophy with an assertion of atheism or with a demand for "purely *naturalistic* values";[70] he begins with the *empirical* claim that the supernatural sanctions of Christianity are no longer effective in European culture. His critique of morality is therefore an *internal* one; he does not oppose his naturalistic values to supernatural ones; his claim is rather that supernatural values are simply *irrelevant* to current discussion of morality. God need not be nonexistent; he simply does not matter.

Without belief in God, the Christian ethic which disvalues this world loses its foundations; without God, there is no ultimate court of appeal for any part of traditional morality. Morality (Christian ethics) was ultimately justifiable only so long as it could appeal to Divine law; without any such law (at least without *respect* for any such law), morality is without foundation.

Of course, one could continue the same moral practices in spite of the disappearance of the foundation of those practices. Thus, the "death of God" advocates suggest the continuation of Christian ethics without theological support. Nietzsche, however, is passionately opposed to any such taking of a value system for granted, or to the *rationalization* (for example by Kant and Hegel) of values which are accepted anyway. The job of the philosopher is to "reevaluate all values," to stab "vivisectionally to the very virtues of the time,"[71] to see how much of contemporary morality has as its only *raison d'etre* the now defunct belief in God. The problem here, of course—and the defining problem of Nietzsche's philosophy—is how *any* set of values can be justified in place of the outmoded Christian ethics.

The Nature of Morality

We have argued that *nihilism* is the central problem for Nietzsche's philosophy, and it is the defeat of nihilism, not nihilism itself, which is his goal. Moral nihilism is a special case of the thesis that there is no Absolute Truth, no ultimate court of appeal by which any conception can be justified. We are confronted with a variety of interpretations, all equally unjustified, unfactual. Specifically, we are confronted by a number of moral interpretations—different conceptions of how to live—and no means of deciding among them. At this juncture, Kierkegaard abandons the search for justification and leaves us to "leap" at the alternative of our arbitrary choice. Nietzsche, however, does not yield to nihilism so easily, and the sharp and too often ignored breach between Nietzsche and existentialism is his refusal to admit the unavoidability of nihilism.

The common interpretations of Nietzsche as the arch-destroyer of moral values are inadequate on many grounds. Rather than preach nihilism, Nietzsche's entire philosophy constitutes a passionate *search* for values. As much as Nietzsche may have "philosophized with a hammer," his ultimate purpose is the *construction* of a morality. It is true that Nietzsche is famously negative on a great many moral doctrines; but this negativity is no more than a purging of the moral sphere of those values which have lost their foundation, or have become 'antivalues', detractions rather than ideals. In this sense, Nietzsche's philosophy is negative only in that it builds morality by first ridding itself of the decay of a crumbling Christian ethic.

What is falling, that one should also push.[72]

O my Brothers, break, break the old tablets.[73]

The reconstruction of morality, however, does not consist in the formulation of an entirely new set of values. Contrary to the popular picture of the heretic anti-Christ, Nietzsche's moral values are surprisingly familiar. One should be honest to himself, loyal to his ideals, kind to others, harsh and demanding concerning one's own tasks, understanding and forgiving for the deeds of others. This is not to say that Nietzsche is an extremely delusive defender of bourgeois values. Surely not! However, the values advocated by Nietzsche, in his many aphorisms concerning dealings with other people are far closer to the sentiments of the soft-hearted than to the merciless power-crazed tyrant who has captured the imagination of post-Nietzscheism.

The good Four. Honest with ourselves and with whatever is friend to us: courageous toward the enemy: generous toward the vanquished: polite-always: that is how the four cardinal virtues want us.[74]

The point of Nietzsche's 'revaluation of values" is to question bourgeois values, but it is not to reject them simply because they are bourgeois. The "revaluation" is the questioning of the conception of 'value' and 'morality' rather than the challenging of any particular value or moral principle. The problem, again, is to re-establish values on a new foundation, the old theological foundation no longer being adequate. This new ground for morality will have to be purely *naturalistic;* the problem is how one can find such a ground; how one can find a justification for morality. Of course, it is to be expected that there will be a significant change in moral values given such major relocation of our entire evaluative framework.

[Philosophy] demands that one create values. Those philosophical workers in the noble tradition of Kant and Hegel have to determine and formalize some large reservoir of value-judgments, that is former value-creations which have come to the fore and for a certain length of time are called "Truth". . . . But the real philosophers are commanders and legislators. They say, "It shall be thus!" . . . Must there not be such philosophers? . . . Their instrument, their hammer.[75]

The first and foremost problem is always to establish morality on a naturalistic foundation to escape the nihilism of the "death of God" revelation.

The negative side of this task—the extirpation of the remnant of Christian morality—takes up the bulk of Nietzsche's moral writings, but, it must be emphasized, it is the same considerations which go into these often vicious attacks that will constitute the positive morality envisioned by Nietzsche, the philosophy of the *Übermensch.* Nietzsche's attack on Christian morality is akin to a modification of the thesis of Kant's *Religion* (and Hegel's early writings); any value of Christian morality which cannot be justified by appeal to purely *naturalistic* standards is rejected. Nietzsche's appeal is not exclusively to reason, as was Kant's, and the precise nature of the 'naturalistic' standards for all values remains one of the most important and obscure points in Nietzsche's philosophy. At first, the 'naturalistic' standard is an explicitly aesthetic standard; "one should live one's life like a work of art." As Nietzsche's philosophy matures, this standard becomes more and more derivative of Darwinist biology and psychology. Finally, it is the Will to Power which dictates the "value of all values," and it is the *weakness* of Christianity which causes it to be rejected. As we indicated in the introduction, the aesthetic standard is but a special case—the exemplary case—of the power standard. Christianity is rejected in the 'revaluation' because it is intrinsically *degrading.*

The rejection of Christian ethics is primarily the consequence of the rejection of the absolute foundation of these values in God. Thus the attack on Christianity is first an attack against its claims to absoluteness, and only then against these values which lose their significance once the absoluteness claim gives way to a naturalistic standard. The absolute values of Christianity, "Good and Evil", are not dismissed out of hand, but they are rejected as absolute.

Sin, of course, is central to the Christian concept of *evil.* With the rejection of God as source of values, however, Sin loses its privileged significance as a value.

Let us remove the concept of Sin from the world.[76]

The move of the 'revaluation', therefore, is to deny the absoluteness of every value, and to see which values can stand without theological supports. We have yet to see how Nietzsche can overcome nihilism by finding and justifying naturalistic values.

The attack on absolute foundations of morality is not aimed only at Christian ethics. The "death of God" thesis is but a particular instance of the general thesis of nihilism, and there are many non-theological foundations for morality which make identical claims to absoluteness. Notably, every philosophical theory is an attempt to provide such a foundation. Specifically, Nietzsche isolates Kant, Spinoza, Hegel, and Schopenhauer in this context. What looks like a value-free description of the way "the world *really* is"— in fact turns out to be only a rationalization for a morality.

Gradually it has become clear to me what every great philosophy so far has been: namely, the personal confession of its author and a kind of involuntary and unconscious memoir; also that the moral (or immoral) intentions in every philosophy constituted the real germ of life from which the whole plant had grown.[77]

It is thus that philosophical systems expose the 'humanity' of the philosophers— but it also exposes an inherent dishonesty—the refusal to face the impossibility of providing a nonquestion begging metaphysical justification of values. Nietzsche cites Spinoza's *Ethics* as one such deceptive rationalization of a value system,

How is Spinoza's position explainable ... ? (It was one consequence of his theodicy.)[78]

It is against Kant, however, that Nietzsche directs his most critical efforts. Kant began his moral philosophy with the stipula-tion that moral principles must be derivative a priori, and that moral imperatives must be universally binding categorical imperatives. Nietzsche challenges, *why* must moral values be universal or valid a priori? If universality and necessity are the marks of morality, then why should one be *moral* at all? According to Nietzsche, these questions concerning the possibility of a priori morality are never seriously considered by Kant, who in fact

falsified in his 'morality' his inner psychological tendency.[79]

Kant, of course, would treat the question, "Why should one be moral?" as perverse nonsense, for the necessary conditions of morality are such that this question cannot be asked intelligibly. However, we saw how Nietzsche's perverse philology can lead to serious confusion in his brief discussion of 'truth'; this perversity and confusion is nowhere more evident than in his use of the concept of 'morality'.[80] To begin our discussion, we had best distinguish (as Nietzsche does not) among several very different senses of 'morality'.

Most often, the sense of 'morality' intended is *moralität* as analyzed by Kant. As such, "a 'moral' principle" is one which is distinguished by the *formal* criterion that it is universalizable. A moral principle may also be a principle which is distinguished by its privileged status in a particular society (Hegel's *Sittlichkeit*). A moral principle may also be a principle which has as its concern one's treatment of other persons, one's concern for their happiness. As such, a moral principle is one which has *social* relevance (whether or not it is formally universalizable).[81]

In addition to these three senses, there are three other senses which we can distinguish for Nietzsche. First, a morality may be a supreme set of values not only for a society, but for an individual. Thus, any ultimate values may be considered moral values. Sometimes 'morality' refers to the particular values of *this* (Nietzsche's) society, and a moral principle is distinguished *only* by its current voguishness. Lastly, Nietzsche occasionally uses 'moral' and 'morality' as terms simply indicating approval or disapproval for a value. This use, of course, is evident only in context, but several of Nietzsche's uses of 'immoral', for example, can be related to none of the above, but simply to indicate Nietzsche's own displeasure with the principle in question.

With these distinctions in mind, we may safely discuss Nietzsche's own analysis of 'morality'. When he asks how one comes to adopt a morality, he refers to any ultimate set of values. When he criticizes *morality*, he is criticizing either contemporary morality, or else Kant's formal morality, or more generally, the acceptance of any set of *given* values (whether *given* through a formal procedure (Kant) or from divine authority, or from the customs of a particular society (Hegel's *Sittlichkeit*). None of this critique, however, is an attack on morality as acceptance of some (self-given) set of values,

Morals being understood as the doctrine of the relations of supremacy under which the phenomenon of 'life' comes to be.[82]

The attack on these varied conceptions of 'morality' is all a matter of the attack on given values. The particular attacks can only be sorted out as we proceed to discuss Nietzsche's defense of his own conception of 'morality'.

It is his treatment of the question, "What is a value?" that allows him to both criticize the contemporary Christian values he so despises "by instinct" and to construct a *new* morality on the basis of this analysis. Nietzsche's primary concern is one which can very reasonably be called *analytic* rather than prescriptive moralizing. Nietzsche's own way of putting the question of the nature of value is very much in tune with the philosophical temperament of the twentieth century, for he begins by asking: What is the *function* of a moral principle?

The analysis of morality in terms of *function* is, of course, the outstanding example of Nietzsche's use of his pragmatic method. The rigorous but disjointed experimentation of his middle writings is not present in the later work in which this analysis is developed, but there is the insistence that *truth* must always be displayed in a pragmatic context. One must talk about the *role* of a proposition (in this case a moral proposition) in a person's life.

This question of the *function* of a value *for* people brings philosophy into close alliance with psychology, and Nietzsche took his greatest merit as a philosopher

to be his being "the first who is also a psychologist." This examination of the function of morality turns, in typical nineteenth-century tradition, to an examination of the *history* of morality. In the study of history of values, Nietzsche discovers the escape from nihilism. In spite of the tremendous variety of value systems (Zarathustra's "1001 goals"), there is found to be a single *function* which all these systems serve for those who hold them. In every case, a value is a manifestation of a single psychological function— the *Will to Power*. This function itself is then the single value for which all value systems have created themselves. Thus, all previous value systems can be evaluated according to their efficiency as a means to this ultimate value. Christianity is shown to be impossibly defective. A value system which takes the will to power explicitly as its goal will, therefore, be the most effective; this is Nietzsche's philosophy of the *Übermensch*.

Nietzsche's discovery of a single standard is not, it must be emphasized, a discovery of an *absolute* value, or an absolute justification for values. In his early writings, Nietzsche did not see that he could not assert the claim, "there is no 'truth' is true," and he sometimes sounds as if his values are suggested as absolutes. In his mature period, Nietzsche clearly says that the power of his critique of morality lay in the *de facto* agreement on the power standard, but that there is no justification for this standard beyond the fact that people implicitly accept it. With those who would accuse Nietzsche of himself providing only another interpretation, Nietzsche has no quarrel:

Supposing that this also is only interpretation—and you will be eager enough to make this objection?—well, so much the better.[83]

Morality, Reason, and Passion
Every morality, according to Nietzsche, is a "constriction of passion," a prohibition to impulsiveness, a priority given to reason over the passions. Morality is "restraint," the sacrifice of immediate impulse for rational ideals. This general characterization holds no less of the values of Christianity and Taoism than of the ethics of Plato and Kant. The sole exception to this thesis, that principle which commands

"act only according to your impulses" ("act according to nature"), is not a *morality*, but a rejection of all moralities. Those "stoics" who would argue, for example, that we should act according to nature, Nietzsche dismisses as arguing nothing at all,

for how could one act against nature?[84]

Morality is the commitment to an ideal, a conspiracy of human reason against the passions, of human reason against "nature" (that is, human instincts); it is that which is most fundamentally *human* overcoming that which is *beastly* nature.

In understanding these claims, we must remind ourselves of the several senses of 'morality' which Nietzsche employs. In the argument above, 'morality' is any set of value principles, whether these be formally derived (as in Kant), divinely authored (as in Christianity), or customary (as in Hegel and folk morality), or naturalistically based (as in Mills' utilitarianism, or Nietzsche's *Will to Power*).

Any rule is better than none. (This) is the principle which stands at the beginning of civilization.[85]

It ought to be clear from Nietzsche's juxtaposing the human, the civilized, and the rational with the instinctual and the beastly that he is not entirely rejecting Reason and morality as he is so often interpreted as doing.[86] Unbridled expression of instinct is not a *desideratum* for Nietzsche, but neither is passionless employment of 'rational' principles. For Nietzsche, like Socrates, Kant, and Hegel, Reason is the very essence of morality—a moral principle is a rational principle and any set of values is a product of Reason. However, Nietzsche turns on Kant and Socrates, because for them Reason became a *tyrant*,[87] and they declared "war on passion" because of passion's occasional stupidity:

all the old moral monsters are agreed on this: il faut tuer les passions. *The most famous formula for this is to be found in the New Testament, in that Sermon on the Mount. There it is said, for example, with particular reference to sexuality, "If thy eye offend thee, pluck it out."*[88]

Rational control over the passions is not objectionable, but the rational destruction of the passions is a different matter:

Destroying *the passions and cravings, merely as a preventive measure against their stupidity and unpleasant consequences of this stupidity—today this strikes us as merely another acute form of stupidity.*[89]

Nietzsche's alleged 'irrationalism' is a mythology created by interpreters who did not share Nietzsche's respect for philology. We have seen that Nietzsche does complex juggling with such central philosophical concepts as 'truth' and 'morality'. We ought to suspect the same with the often-abused concepts of 'reason' and 'rationality'. We recall that these terms endured a significant amount of conceptual relocation in nineteenth-century German philosophy from Kant through Hegel. In Nietzsche, the confusions generated by a variety of concepts of 'reason' become evident in a way much more explicit than in the 'rationalism' of Hegel.

First, Nietzsche equates Reason with the practical reason of Kant's philosophy. His most frequent attacks against Kant (and against Socrates) are rejections of the use of formal a priori principles in morality. This conception of Reason, we may recall, is also employed by Kierkegaard in his characterization of the 'ethical' mode of existence which takes Socrates as its hero and Kant as its most articulate expositor. Insofar as Nietzsche is against Reason in 'life', he is against that notion of Reason which celebrates formal principles *to the exclusion* of passion.

Secondly, Nietzsche talks about Reason in epistemological terms, and concerns himself with the claim that *Reason* and *Logic* (which are always linked in this context) give us knowledge of the "real" world. We have already seen that Nietzsche rejects the traditional distinction between the "real" and "apparent" world and argues that there is no real world, only interpretations of this world. As such, Reason and Rationality are names for *falsifications* of the world, *interpretations* which put themselves forward as *The Truth*. Included as a center of focus in this notion of Reason is, of course, the philosophy of Hegel. Hegel had claimed that Reason could give us Absolute Truth, and there is no epistemological claim to which Nietzsche is more strongly opposed. These notions of Reason and Truth, Nietzsche argues, are a product, not of a *Will to Truth,* but of the *Will to Power.* As such, all rationality is an attempt to get "not knowledge but mastery and possession." However, Nietzsche's attitude towards this "falsification of life by reason" is ambivalent and not a simple rejection. There are certain products of Reason (for example, previous philosophies), which Nietzsche does attempt to purge from our lives. But he tells us also that many 'errors' are necessary for human existence. He tells us, for example, that they are already built into the language we speak, and that language is necessary to "distinguish man from the beast." Language is necessary for any thought whatsoever, and that thought which is 'necessary' (leaving the interpretation of this 'necessity' purposively ambiguous) is rationality:

We cease to think when we refuse to do so under the constraint of language. . . .
Rational thought is interpretation according to a scheme that we cannot throw off.[90]

This makes it evident that Reason plays an unavoidable part in our lives, and that the Nietzschean attack on Reason is directed not at Reason itself but at the claims for its absolute grounding. In other words, it is necessary that we believe that logic is absolutely *True* or applicable in a world incredibly different from our own. Thus, it is evident that Nietzsche attacks not rational thought as such, but certain claims made for rational thought.

Behind Nietzsche's attack on Reason lies a single claim which we have met before, the claim that *the world is itself rational,* that our knowledge corresponds to reality, and that our happiness is commensurate with our virtue. Nietzsche comments that Descartes ignored his universal doubts when the question of God's beneficence became applicable, and he blames Socrates for the origin and Kant for the perpetration of the insidious equation between 'reason-virtue-happiness.' Kant's *Summum Bonum* is supposed to be a necessary presupposition of moral thought, and one cannot justifiably be moral unless one believes that his good acts will gain their just reward. The demonstration of the absolute dependability of Reason in the world is left to Hegel, and it is his bloated

glorification of Reason that Nietzsche seeks to puncture.

There is no preestablished harmony between the pursuit of truth and the welfare of mankind.[91]

The world is irrational, Nietzsche claims, because there is no significance, no reward and punishment, no 'facts' and no 'good and evil' except what we have put there ourselves. Reason is necessary insofar as we could not live without these 'falsifications.' Reason is insidious insofar as it presents these falsifications as true independent of our creation of them.

There is a final notion of Reason, evident from what has been said, which Nietzsche wholly endorses. To put it most simply, this Reason is *careful thinking.* One can use his conceptual gifts to attack problems and old prejudices, as Nietzsche does, without making the unwarranted assumptions plaguing those concepts of Reason which Nietzsche rejects. Thus one can think carefully and ruthlessly about morality without claiming that his conclusions have the sanction of a priori reason; one can interpret the world and attack silly or degrading interpretations of the world without claiming that this attack or one's own interpretations have the blessings of a Reason not one's own. If this point seems obvious and hardly worth making, it is noteworthy that a half-century of Nietzschean 'irrationalism' is based on the neglect of just this simple observation. Nietzsche does not urge reason alone as the source of our moral outlook or as the source of a world-view: he is in that sense an 'irrationalist' (or at least a not-wholly-rationalist). Nietzsche does not claim we ought to act on instinct or passion alone, and in that sense he is *not* an irrationalist. Even if Reason is but a "tool of the *Will to Power,*" it is not like passions without 'intelligence.' It is reason that distinguishes the "higher from the lower men" and Reason which is the key to the *Übermensch* and spiritualization.

What is good-heartedness, refinement, and genius to me when the human being who has these virtues tolerates slack feelings in his faith and judgments, and when the demand for certainty is not to him the most inmost craving and deepest need—that which distinguishes the higher from the lower men. Among certain pious ones,

I found a hatred of reason and appreciated it: at least they thus betrayed their bad intellectual conscience.[92]

We are now in a reasonably secure position in which to understand the roles of Reason and Passion (the *Apollonian* and *Dionysian*) in Nietzsche's analysis of morality. We must watch for very different uses of 'reason' as well as very different senses of 'morality'. On the one hand, there is the more technical use of 'reason' which provides us with a priori formal 'moral' principles, as in Kant; on the other hand, there is the careful thinking and ruthless questioning into the origins and supposed 'rationality' of our prejudices and the attempt of the 'new' philosophers to provide us with a new set of values, a new 'morality.' Nietzsche is an anti-rationalist and immoralist in the technical sense; he is a moralist and at least a rational thinker in the nontechnical sense. In the following discussion we shall employ only the nontechnical sense except where the Kantian notions are explicitly mentioned.

For Nietzsche, reason is necessary for morality but certainly not *sufficient*. Reason and the passions are not opposed to each other, and the passions are not an obstacle to morality. The passions are themselves necessary for morality, and Nietzsche would sometimes hint that they are just as much a logical necessity as the use of Reason. One might compare Nietzsche's insistence on both Reason and the passions as necessary components of morality to Hegel's earlier attack of Kant's formal notion of *Sittlichkeit*, in which the objection was also the impossibility of an adequate conception of morality in which Reason and the passions were opposed. Like Hegel, Nietzsche would argue that the role of the passions suffices to make a purely formal morality (*moralität*) impossible, and that an adequate balance between reason and passions could never be decided a priori. However, unlike Hegel, Nietzsche is not willing to reduce passion to a societal phenomenon or custom (*Sitte*), and considers acceptance of a *given* social morality as equally abhorrent as the attempts to derive a purely formal morality. For Nietzsche, the faculty of *reason* is already socially derived; it is our passions which allow us to become individuals, and thus our passions which must determine what values are suitable for us. Hegel noted that "nothing great has been done without passion." For Nietzsche, perhaps, nothing *at all* has been done without passion; for it is the instincts which drive the weak as well as the strong, the cowardly as well as the brave. For Nietzsche, as for David Hume a century earlier, reason is, and ought to be, the slave of the passions.

In his earlier writings (before *Zarathustra*) Nietzsche had struggled with the dualism of Reason and Passion in several related forms. In *Birth of Tragedy*, the dichotomy of Dionysian and Apollonian is introduced, and Nietzsche makes it clear that the greatness of Greek art is the *control* of the Dionysian frenzy by Apollonian Reason. (Although many of his commentators assume that Nietzsche's celebration of the Dionysian, particularly in his late writings, especially *Ecce Homo,* in which the term acquires a new meaning, indicates his *preference* for uninhibited licentiousness.) In the *"Untimely" Meditations* and again in the "middle writings," we find oppositions between one's 'self' and 'true self', between 'nature' and 'man's nature'. These dualisms arise in an ethical context, and the single problem surrounding all of them is the respective roles of Reason and Passion in the conception of morality and, derivatively, what weight one should place upon the dictates of Reason and his passionate impulses when formulating a system of values.

It is at this point that Nietzsche turns to psychology to resolve this problem. In his early works, Nietzsche had given himself a choice between Reason and Passion reminiscent of Kant, and his treatment of the nature of morality remained obscure. He insisted that both Reason and Passion had their place, but he was incapable of moving from that general thesis to a more specific thesis about *how* these two were related in morality. Neither Kant nor Hegel considered psychology relevant to ethics; for Kant, moral principles held a priori; for Hegel, moral principles were ascertained within the context of society. Neither of these great philosophers had asked (or could allow themselves to ask) how to formulate one's *own* morality. Both had argued that individual morality was not morality at all. For Nietzsche, however, the construction of a morality depends on individual psychology. One must look at his instincts to know what is a virtue *for him*. More abstractly, one must look to psychology to determine what the relation is, in general, between Reason and Passion. Both Kant and Hegel had used these notions extensively; neither had attempted to analyze them.

For Nietzsche, it is not at all evident that Reason and the passions are as distinct and as antagonistic as Kantian philosophy insisted. Nietzsche's insistence that *both* Reason and the passions are involved in the establishment of values clearly distinguished him from Kant's formalism and from the irrationalist Romantics (for example, Byron, with whom he is often associated) and aligns him with David Hume. Here Nietzsche differs even from Hume in his analysis of the nature of this 'balance' of Reason and Passion, for he claims, in a precocious display of the 'analytic psychology' so important in this century, that Reason and Passion are compatible and inseparable, and are reducible to one and the same basic drive. Nietzsche's analysis, again scattered and disjointed, tends to fall into three separate but interrelated theories: 1) Reason and Passion are not distinct, 2) both Reason and Passion are reducible to a single fundamental psychological principle, the *Will to Power,* 3) Reason serves to direct the passions, and is not a force in itself.

The first thesis is limited to a few notes which recur throughout Nietzsche's career, for example,

The misunderstanding of passion and reason, *as if the latter were an independent entity and not rather a system of relations between various passions and desires; and as if every passion did not possess its quantum of reason.*[93]

Although interesting as an instance of Nietzsche's frequent attacks on Kantian dualisms, this suggestion is of importance primarily as an aid to understanding the latter two theses. It gives us a hint about the nature of the reducibility of both Reason and Passion to the basic will to power, which is never adequately answered in Nietzsche's published writings. We will return to the second thesis in the following section.

We find the origins of the third thesis as early as the *Birth of Tragedy* in the notions of 'harnessing' and 'channeling the Dionysian', and later in Nietzsche's criticism of Christianity for its attempted *extirpation* of the passions. Nietzsche, like Hegel and Kierkegaard, argued that the

content of any value system must be provided by the passions ("it is the passions which provide the value of values"). The problem is the nature of this cooperation of Reason and Passion in the establishment of values. According to Hume, Reason serves to establish the *means* by which we can fulfill the values established by "sentiment" (passion). According to Nietzsche, this analysis ignores the role of Reason in establishing the values themselves. Contrary again to Nietzsche's popular image, we find his moral philosophy even more rationalistic than that of Hume, in fact quite close to Aristotle, to whom his 'functional' approach to morality is remarkably close.

In his analysis of the relationship of Reason and Passion, Nietzsche introduces a term, later adopted by Freud,[94] which replaces the earlier metaphorical notions of 'harnessing' and 'channeling'. *Sublimation* is a process in which passions are allowed their expression, but in modified *form.* Reason itself has no motivational powers[95] and thus cannot act independently of the passions (as Kant sometimes seems to suggest) and cannot extirpate the passions (as traditional Christianity prescribes). Reason cannot even weaken or change passions, but it can determine their object of expression. Passions (and 'instinct') differ in value, and Nietzsche distinguishes what he calls 'life conditioning' and 'life stultifying' effects:

The function of reason is to allow expression of certain passions at the expense of others: a morality is a set of principles which restricts passions: a successful morality is one which restricts only the life-stultifying passions, which may be fatal, where they drag their victim down with the weight of their stupidity.[96]

Sublimation, therefore, is the censorship by reason of competing passions (the comparison with Freud's "dynamic" model of consciousness with its Ego, Id, and Superego censor is apparent here). We are now prepared to understand Nietzsche's most powerful objection to Christianity—its defense of a morality which urges the extirpation rather than the employment of the passions. Christian ethics attempts to condemn the life-stultifying passions but mistakenly, and tragically, condemns all passions. The saintly ideal of Christianity, according to Nietzsche, is not the powerful man who *controls* and uses well his effects, but the impotent man who is 'moral' only because of a *poverty* of feeling:

the moralists' mania which demands not the control but the extirpation of the passions. Their conclusion is ever; only the emasculated man is the good man.[97]

Instead of employing the great sources of strength, those impetuous torrents of the soul that are so often dangerous and overwhelming, and economizing them, this most short-sighted and pernicious mode of thought, the moral mode of thought, wants to make them dry up.[98]

The key to the operations of Reason in the sublimation of passions and the distinction between life conditioning and life stultifying passions is the *Will to Power*. Morality and Reason, therefore, are nothing other than these mechanisms which serve the ultimate drive, and the analysis of morality thus ultimately depends on the analysis of the *Will to Power*.

The Will to Power

We have maintained that Nietzsche's entire moral philosophy rests on the psychological principle referred to as the *Will to Power*. What Nietzsche means by *der Wille Zu Macht* is not easily understood, first because the notion of 'power' is so often taken in the sense of physical or military power, encouraged by Nietzsche's frequent appeal to military allegories in his writing; secondly, because the role and meaning of the *Will to Power* changed significantly in the course of Nietzsche's career. The interpretation of 'power' as political power by Nietzsche's Nazi interpreter (Bäumler) has resulted in the focus on the will to power in the rejection of Nietzsche's philosophy, although the confusion resulting from Nietzsche's several changes in his conception of the Will to Power has led several commentators to dismiss the notion from the core of Nietzsche's thought. We shall insist that Nietzsche's Will to Power must be considered central to his moral philosophy,[99] however, for the generally celebrated doctrines of master-slave morality, the 'transvaluation of values', the *Übermensch*, and the critique of Christian morality simply do not make sense without the Will to Power as their basis. The interpretation of Will to

Power as a purely political notion is simply inconsistent with demands made by Nietzsche throughout his entire works.

The phrase "will to power" appears late in Nietzsche's writings, and then not at first as the most celebrated principle of his philosophy.

In *Zarathustra*, where the Will to Power is first pronounced as the basis of all morality, it is already clear that the greatest expression of power is to overcome *oneself* and it is the standard of *self-overcoming* which lies implicit in every morality, Greek, Chinese, Christian, or Kantian.

A tablet of the goal hangs over every people. Behold, it is the tablet of their overcomings; behold, it is the voice of their will to power.[100]

Its reappearance in *Beyond Good and Evil*, the *Genealogy of Morals*, and subsequent works, and its frequent appearance in Nietzsche's Notes,[101] firmly establish this concept in the foundation of Nietzsche's later thought.

The notion of 'power', however, makes its appearance long before *Zarathustra*, but Nietzsche first considers a will to power only in order to repudiate it. In the *Birth of Tragedy*, Nietzsche notes that "power is always evil,"[102] and, in his break with Wagner, he comments that it was the corruption of 'success and power' that Nietzsche took to be the key to the *Human-all-too-Human*.[103] Here, Nietzsche equates power with worldly power, and, completely in agreement with his later philosophy, he takes all such power *over others* to be essentially *demeaning*, the very contrary of what Zarathustra's Will to Power means to signify.

In the 'middle' aphoristic period, we find various references to 'power' as a psychological principle, and particularly in *Dawn* and *Human-all-too-Human*, Nietzsche attempts to explain various pieces of behavior by appeal to a power principle. Most striking among these 'attempts' are his explanations of Christian virtues as perverse manifestations of power, and in these we get a clear picture of the considerations that will constitute the critique of Christian morality in *The Genealogy of Morals* and the *Antichrist*. Pity, gratitude, humility, and charity are taken to be expressions of weakness of power rather than pure 'altruistic' or 'good' motives'. In this period, Nietzsche does not make the attempt to formulate the Will to Power as a general psychological principle, nor is it urged as a general ethical norm. Nietzsche's philosophy is still unsystematic in the very bad sense. He uses the motive of power to criticize some moral principles (by using a questionable argument that the *genesis* of these values is in their desire for power), but he does not use this same principle as an explicit standard.

In this period, we find Nietzsche's few comments on 'freedom', a concept Nietzsche strives to avoid throughout his works.

One strives for freedom for the sake of power, not the other way around.[104]

Political freedom finds no forum in his works, except for the repudiation of the specious concept of freedom *'to obey'* in Hegel, and, Nietzsche adds, the freedom *'of mediocrity'* inherent in current brands of democracy and all varieties of socialist thought.[105] Yet we do find[106] that Nietzsche considers 'will to power' and 'instinct to freedom' to be one and the same drive, and much of what he says of 'power' is identical to what so many philosophers have said about freedom: for example, that freedom is tied to the mastery of the impulses by reason (Kant); that freedom is the result of the development of a balanced concept of self and sublimation (Hegel); that freedom is the basic postulate of morality (Hume, Mill, and Kant), and that freedom is primarily moral autonomy rather than political freedom from (over) others. One might be tempted to claim, therefore, that Nietzsche's philosophy of power could be translated into a philosophy of freedom, avoiding the harsh connotations of 'power' and bringing his moralizing into union with the respectable libertarian philosophies of Kant, Locke, and Mill.

There is reason for not doing so, although the difference is perhaps more of emphasis than doctrine. Nietzsche harshly disagrees with the current conceptions of freedom, more often than not denoting civic moral responsibility as well as autonomy (Kant and Hegel) and associating 'freedom' with the comfortable bourgeois moralities he most vehemently hates. Freedom connotes the passive, the unstriving, something that is simply a given (as Kant's postulate of freedom), or something found in conformity and good citizenship (Hegel's positive free-

dom as manifested in Goethe). Will to Power shares neither of these connotations; its forcefulness resides in its connotations of a struggle and fight; connotations much in tune with Nietzsche's remaining Darwinian inclinations. As for freedom as a metaphysical concept, Nietzsche says little of it except to dismiss it as useless. As for the celebrated free will problem, Nietzsche dismisses both free will and determinism as confusion:

but there is no such thing as will.[107]

And,

if there is no will, there is no free will (or unfree will either).[108]

The Will to Power also represents different kinds of principles in Nietzsche's writings. In Nietzsche's experimental works, the Will to Power is clearly intended as an empirical hypothesis, or rather a set of such hypotheses of limited scope, and has no ethical value at all except insofar as it is used as a basis of criticism of those moral principles based on it. Although Nietzsche's Will to Power is often interpreted as a remnant of his Schopenhauerism, it is evident that even in this period Nietzsche had nothing but scorn for the "One Will" as an 'unprovable' metaphysical principle.

From *Zarathustra* on, however, the centrality of the Will to Power does not prevent Nietzsche from often changing his interpretation of this conception. In this period, the Will to Power becomes a general psychological hypothesis, intended to explain all human behavior. At the same time, it begins to conform to its ultimate role as a primary ethical standard, as the basis of every morality and as the end of every human endeavor, including art and the "Will to Truth" of philosophy. However, we also find the Will to Power expanded to be not only a principle of human psychology, but the fundamental drive of all living things:

It can be shown most clearly that every living thing does everything it can not to preserve itself but to become more.[109]

Again the Will to Power replaces the Darwinian concept of survival as the basic *life-striving:*

*Above all, a living thing wants to discharge
its energy; life as such is will to power.
Self preservation is only one of its indirect
and most frequent consequences.*[110]

At times, this employment of Will to
Power as a general principle of life
extends even to a principle of cosmology,
a point dangerously close to Schopenhauer's metaphysical doctrine of will:

*Life as a special case (hypothesis based
upon it applied to the total character of
being) strives after a maximal feeling of
power . . . (Mechanics is merely the
semiotics of the results.)*[111]

The most important employment of Will
to Power, however, is the *dual* role as
psychological theory and ethical standard.
These two are not only compatible but depend on each other. The Will to Power
is argued empirically as the basic human
drive partly on the evidence that every
morality takes the Will to Power as its
implicit foundation. The claim that every
morality is basically a morality of power
is strengthened by as well as strengthens
the general thesis that every human striving (all actions and values) is a striving
for more power. An illuminating comparison can be drawn between Nietzsche's
philosophy of power and John Stuart
Mill's defense of utilitarianism.[112] Mill
was perhaps Nietzsche's main nineteenth-
century rival as a "philosopher who is also
a psychologist," and Mill's ethics derives
much of its support from his psychology.
According to Mill, the ultimate end, with
reference to and for the sake of which all
other things are desirable—whether we
are considering our own good or that of
other people—is "an existence exempt as
far as possible from pain, and as rich as
possible in enjoyment, both in quality and
quantity."[113] Pleasure, as that which all
men ultimately desire, is therefore the
good for man. Mill also wishes to argue
that we ought to act for the pleasure/hap-
piness of *all* men, and here the parallel
with Nietzsche surely breaks down. We
shall be concerned only with the first part
of Mill's thesis, that is, that men ought to
strive for happiness, ignoring further arguments that we ought to strive for the
greatest happiness for the greatest number
of men. (Like Nietzsche's Will to Power,
Mill's "pleasure principle" is sometimes
defended as a general empirical hypothe-

sis and sometimes as a strictly analytical
principle derived from the meaning of
"good.") According to Mill, it is the
general psychological importance of pleasure that justifies its foundation in ethical
theory;

*the sole evidence it is possible to
produce that anything is desirable is that
people actually do desire it.*[114]

Mill identifies pleasure and happiness,
often interchanging the two in his statements of the "ultimate good for man."
Nietzsche also identifies pleasure and happiness, arguing that both are but symptoms of man's true goal;

it is notably enlightening to posit power *in
place of individual 'happiness' (after which
every living thing is supposed to be
striving) . . . pleasure is only a symptom
of the feeling of power attained.*[115]

For Nietzsche,

*The will to power is the primitive form of
affect, that all other affects are merely its
derivatives . . . there is no striving for
pleasure, but pleasure supervenes when
they achieve what they strive for: pleasure
is an accompaniment, pleasure is not
the motive.*[116]

One can favorably compare Aristotle on
pleasure to Nietzsche as opposed to Mill.
"Agreeing with Plato," Aristotle maintains,

*the pleasant life is more desirable with
wisdom than without . . . pleasure is not
the good, for the good cannot become
more desirable by the addition of anything
to it.*[117]

Rather,

*pleasure completes the activity . . . as an
end which supervenes as the bloom of
youth does on those in the flower of
their age.*[118]

Nietzsche will allow that pleasure and
power are closely bound up with each
other, and again we find a remarkable
parallel with Aristotle if we keep in mind
Nietzsche's equation of *Will to Power* and
life. Aristotle claims:

*One might think that all men desire
pleasure because they all aim at life . . .
they seem to be bound up together and
not to admit of separation, since without
activity pleasure does not arise, and every
activity is completed by the attendant
pleasure.*[119]

According to Nietzsche, power is a better explanation of many facts about behavior than pleasure, most importantly, the role of suffering and sacrifice in human history. Even a grotesquely distorted 'pleasure principle' cannot give a convincing account of human suffering self-imposed, but a philosophy of power can explain this quite convincingly when linked with the all-important Nietzschean ideals of self-perfection and *self-overcoming*. It makes little sense to suppose that martyrs (who need not believe in an afterlife) sacrifice themselves for some peculiar pleasure. It is quite plausible that they do so to prove (to themselves as well as others) their *power* for endurance, their self-righteousness, and their ability to remain *significant* even in slavery or death.

Nietzsche's power-principle is more convincing than Mill's pleasure principle, but this is not the only difference between them. Also to Nietzsche's advantage is the manner in which the two thinkers attempted to base an ethics on psychology. Mill's argument from the pleasure principle to utilitarianism has been often attacked as an instance of the 'naturalistic' fallacy, the attempt to argue from a fact (about human nature) to an evaluation (about human obligation).[120] It is important that Nietzsche does not simply found his power-based morality on the psychological principle of Will to Power, but claims that every morality *already* implicitly accepts this power principle. Nietzsche's attack on relativism thus has another striking similarity to Mill's. Mill claims that the utilitarian ethics already lies at the basis of every moral theory, even where not explicitly recognized as such. For example, Mill cites Kant as an (unwilling) utilitarian.[121] Surprisingly, Nietzsche's claim for his power morality, although couched in stronger terms than Mill's pleasure principle, is a logically weaker claim. According to Mill, one cannot entirely accept the pleasure principle and deny utilitarianism; according to Nietzsche, one can accept Will to Power and dismiss his morality. However, the weakness of Nietzsche's claim is also its advantage, for it does not even appear to commit the fallacious inference from psychology to ethics. The psychological thesis provides us with a *good reason* for accepting the power morality, but no more.

Our analysis of the concept of 'power' is still inadequate, for although we have several times insisted that military or physical or political power is not what Nietzsche intends, we have yet to defend this claim against the profusion of such allegories peppering Nietzsche's writings or to state clearly what does constitute Nietzsche's concept of 'power'. Nietzsche, as in Mill's doctrine of pleasure, insists that the *quality* of power is as important as the quantity, and the ultimate end is not brute power for Nietzsche any more than it is gross pleasure which is urged by Mill:

*One should distinguish well: whoever still
wants to gain the consciousness of power
will use any means . . . He, however, who
has it has become very choosy and noble
in his tastes.*[122]

Nietzsche's concept of 'power' is Aristotelian and signifies *potentiality,* specifically the potential to *overcome.* Nietzsche's writings are filled with aphorisms identifying power, like health, as the capability of resistance to disease (of which bourgeois thinking is an instance).

*That which does not overcome me
makes me stronger.*

*An organism is healthy depending upon
what diseases it can survive.*

The notion of power is also (but not primarily) applied to the state:

*A state is strong depending on how many
parasites it can support.*

Power is thus the ability to overcome, the Will to Power is the drive to be strong, to be capable of overcoming. *Power* can refer to physical power to overcome physical obstacles, political power to overcome societal obstacles, health to overcome disease, mental power to solve problems. In short, power is ability to overcome.

What is to be overcome? It is clear that Nietzsche's concept of power is more specific than this. All of these are manifestations of the Will to Power, but all powers are not equal. (Compare Mill: Pleasures differ in quality as well as quantity: "better a Socrates dissatisfied than a pig satisfied.")[123] Physical power and good health are for Nietzsche the lowest manifestation of Will to Power—a healthy man is not an *Übermensch*—and striving for good health and physical strength is not what Nietzsche would call the highest Will to Power.[124] Like Aristotle, Nietzsche considers these 'external' manifestations of power merely as desirable preconditions of true *excellence* (which is the key to Nietzsche's 'philosophy of power' just as it is the conceptual cornerstone of Aristotle's *Ethics*). Similarly, overcoming one's neighbor, although clearly a manifestation of the Will to Power, is a relatively impotent manifestation. However,

there is a long line of degrees of this secretly desired overwhelming and a complete list of these would almost amount to a history of culture from the first still grimace like barbarian to the grimace of . . . over refinement.[125]

The 'striving for excellence' reaches its pinnacle not with those who conquer or overwhelm their neighbors, but with those who overcome *themselves.*

here at the end of the ladder stands the ascetic and martyr.[126]

indeed happiness—taken as the most alive feeling of power—has perhaps nowhere on earth been greater than in the souls of superstitious ascetics.[127]

The highest Will to Power (sometimes called "true power") is 'self-overcoming' (*selb-überwindungen*). From our discussion of his concern for morality, we are already prepared to understand this as the mastery (through sublimation) of the passions by reason. Nietzsche's self-overcoming and Will to Power are ultimately the Socratic pursuit of rationality. So insistent is Nietzsche on the importance of *rationality*, control by reason, that he (like Hegel as well as Socrates and Aristotle) takes philosophy, the 'will to truth' to be

the most spiritual will to power.[128]

and takes strength to be a good only insofar as reason is involved:

When the degree of worthiness of being honored is to be determined, only the degree of reason in strength is decisive.[129]

The German Reich was clearly not the sort of power Nietzsche celebrated, although the passionate philosophy of Socrates clearly was.

There is considerable confusion surrounding Nietzsche's use of the concept of '*Geist*' which he sometimes attacks and sometimes praises (giving extra credence to those commentators who claim Nietzsche to be inconsistent). In fact, it is evident that Nietzsche attacks the concept of Spirit only insofar as it is given a religious 'life-denying' significance, whether this be the traditional concept of a transcendent soul or an immanent 'collective idea' as found in Hegel.

"Spirit" is only a means and tool in the service of higher life, of the enhancement of life; and as for the good, as Plato (and after him Christianity) understood it, it seems to me to be actually a life-endangering, life-calumniating, life-denying principle.[130]

If *Geist* is interpreted as a concept applicable to the *individual*, and is taken to be equivalent to Hegelian rationality (in which reason and the passions are inseparable), it makes perfectly good sense for Nietzsche to speak of one's having spirit and the nature of the spiritual. Thus, we find Nietzsche speaking of "spirit" and of "life" interchangeably with "reason," for these all refer back to the Will to Power, one's mastery over his own impulses. Thus philosophy is the 'most spiritual' (most rational, most life-enhancing) Will to Power, while Christianity—according to Nietzsche's favorite derogation—is for the 'poor in spirit', those who do not live according to Reason and are thereby leading 'unspiritual' (impotent) lives (*vergeistigung*). If self-overcoming (and spiritualization) is the sublimation of impulse by reason, then we can easily understand how the Will to Power underlies every morality, and Nietzsche's 'new' morality is seen to be very much within the traditions of Western philosophy. Whatever their differences, every morality has been an imposition of constraint on the passions—an attempt to overcome one's 'nature'—one's unthinking, even 'stupid' impulses and conform to an ideal. The highest of these ideals is spiritualization itself—complete control of one's self.

From this description of self-overcoming, however, one might well wonder why Nietzsche has caused such a commotion in recent history. If his claim is only that every morality has aimed at self-control in order to approach some ego-ideal, then how does he differ, if at all, from Socrates, Aristotle, and even Kant, with whom he apparently takes himself to be utterly in opposition? The excitement of Nietzsche's philosophy is, ultimately, essentially negative; the Will to Power does not so much give us a new standard, but makes explicit the standard we have always used. The radical conclusions of Nietzsche's philosophy are not so much the result of his offering us a replacement for traditional values, rather, he shows us these traditional values are *inconsistent*. If self-perfection is the ideal, then the Christian self-deprecating 'virtues' are not virtues at all. The only *honest* (consistent) morality is explicit self-overcoming and this might often involve the very antithesis of good Christian behavior. Of course, much too much has been made of Nietzsche's talk of the "need for cruelty" and the "necessity of destroying the herd if necessary," but what is clear is that concern for others is not one's primary concern. Sometimes harming the weak is a necessary *but unfortunate* consequence of self-improvement. Nietzsche clearly does not condone cruelty for its own sake, quite to the contrary, he insists that cruelty is the most impotent Will to Power. Generosity and kindness are marks of nobility (of strong Will to Power),[131] the strong need rarely resort to cruelty. At times, Nietzsche goes so far as to say it is the *duty* of the strong to protect the weak.[132]

Nietzsche's Will to Power is thus far removed from the common imagery of military strength—the most powerful are not the politician and soldier, but the artist, the philosopher, and the aesthete. Will to Power is ultimately control over one's self; it is not license but restraint; not power to hurt or destroy but power to create. The Will to Power manifests itself in just that prescription which we encountered at the very beginning of Nietzsche's philosophy:

Live your life as a work of art.

And this philosophy, not the anti-aesthetic dogmatics of the Deutschreich acting in

Nietzsche's name, is the basis of the doctrine of the *Übermensch*.

Slave Morality and Master Morality

Nietzsche's attack on (Christian) *morality* begins with an analysis of 'morality', in order to show that Christian ethics, *by its own standards,* is inadequate. Its own standard is—like those of every morality—the Will to Power. Nietzsche's most brilliant demonstration of this internal inconsistency is linked with his explanation of *how* this morality has come to occupy such a privileged place in our thought (such that even Kant failed to question its validity seriously). Nietzsche, like Hegel, turns to history to prove a philosophical point, that every morality, including Christianity, has been based on the Will to Power.

Unlike Hegel, Nietzsche does not attempt to demonstrate a progression of moral conceptions, for he is concerned contrarily to show that the seemingly varied conceptions of morality have been identical and that, if one can talk of 'progress' at all here, the history of morals has been a history of degradation of morality, that is, of less adequate expressions of the Will to Power. The purpose of the historical analysis is, consonant with Nietzsche's pragmatism, to find the *function* of morality in history, to discover the function of each morality in the lives of a people. This function will be but a particular case of the general Will to Power, and the special problem of the investigation is to explain how the Will to Power can be the ultimate value of those value systems which would preach just the opposite of power. Of these, Christianity is the most important example, and the key to Nietzsche's attack on Christian values is his attempt to show not only that Christianity is an inadequate expression of the Will to Power (which Christianity itself would be the first to admit), but that Christianity is itself *based* on the Will to Power, and that its inadequacy amounts to internal inconsistency—valuing the Will to Power and rejecting it at the same time.

This historical demonstration is no more a scholarly study of specific societies than we find in Hegel's historical works. As so often in the character of the nineteenth-century temperament, the historical portraits portrayed by Nietzsche are aimed more at proving a point than accurate description, and we often find caricatures of historical figures which are prejudiced to the point of being amusing (or dangerous, as in those caricatures of the Jews which were borrowed by the Nazis from the context in which they were caricatures and used for less philosophical purposes). In that set of essays in which this demonstration is continuously argued, the *Genealogy of Morals* (Nietzsche's only book with *Twilight,* that is a fully coherent, organized philosophical argument), we find verbal cartoons of the Jews and the early Christians, the Greeks and the Romans, and their confrontation in history, but there is notably little detail by which Nietzsche defends his history of morality. Like Hegel, Nietzsche expects us to be sufficiently familiar with the historical details so that we can fill out the overall interpretation he presents.

Although the purpose of the *Genealogy* is to prove the unity of all moralities, Nietzsche bases his argument on the identification of two distinct types of morality: *slave* morality and *master* morality.[133] Both of these are expressive of Will to Power, but they express this *will* in very different ways. Master morality is the explicit recognition of the Will to Power; slave morality expresses its Will to Power in the explicit denial of the value of power. It is in this latter category that we find Nietzsche classifying Christian morality. The problem is to explain how slave-type moralities can express the Will to Power in denying its value, and how such moralities have become so powerful as to now limit the very concept of 'morality' to themselves.

'Master' and 'slave', of course, are not original to Nietzsche in this context even in the critique of Christianity as a slave morality (we find Hegel, for example, utilizing these concepts). The distinction does not appear until Nietzsche's later works, beginning with an aphorism in *Beyond Good and Evil*[134] and becoming fully developed in the *Genealogy.* Master and Slave do not literally refer to a division of social classes (as Hegel is often interpreted) or individual social roles, but refer to types of values (that is, ways of expressing the Will to Power). We do find Nietzsche referring to master and slave, but this must be understood as referring to those who exemplify these moral types. For Nietzsche, the morality one holds depends on what kind of man one is.[135] Again, there is no literal significance to be placed on the master-slave

relationship, although Nietzsche makes reference to a historic master-slave relationship (the Egyptians and Jews). The slave need not be a slave in the literal sense. To the contrary, slave morality, in spite of Nietzsche's frequent appeal to allegory, is most often found in those who would not normally be considered *slaves* at all (for example, the good bourgeois citizens of nineteenth-century Europe).

The explicit acceptance of the Will to Power as an ultimate value—master morality—is historically the primitive morality. Slave morality—as an attack on the Will to Power—only arises against an already established master morality. In master morality, 'good' has a strictly 'subjective' significance: Something is good if it fulfills one's designs. 'Good', therefore, refers simply to the satisfaction of personal expectations; there need be no reference to other persons, to social welfare, to duty, obligation, or any of the superpersonal considerations of Kantian (Christian) *morality.* For the 'master', good things are decided on—what is good is good *for me.* In Nietzsche's terms, masters are 'value-determining.' The values of the master are all expressing the Will to Power, but, as we have shown, the notion of Will to Power is so open to individual differences that the expression of it may be indefinitely varied, one may choose to be a great lover, a great warrior, or a great poet.

Again, the 'subjective' or 'self-determining' factor in master morality does not require egoism or selfishness; dedication to great causes or great artistic projects is very often central to master morality. But the master does take his own goals to be beyond compromise, and cruelty, inconsideration of others, and even inhumanity may be necessary means to satisfying this enterprising and often reckless style of life.

Nietzsche is often classified as an 'egoist,' but it is necessary to see just how far he removes himself from traditional theories of *self-interest.* To begin with, it is perfectly clear that the sorts of goals Nietzsche praises as the 'highest' and 'most spiritual', for example, the values of the artist, the saint, and the philosopher, are not 'selfish' in any meaningful sense. Their *self-imposed* values and disciplines are very different from self-interested values. Secondly, Nietzsche's elitism forces him to distinguish between the value of different persons and, therefore, impose a serious qualification to the value of self-interest in different persons:

Egoism! But no one has yet asked: What kind of ego? On the contrary, everyone unconsciously thinks every ego equal to every other ego. . . .[136]

Nietzsche's position with regard to 'egoism' is confusingly complex. In some of his writings he seeks to "prove that there could not be anything other than egoism,"[137] but even this universal egoism is not simply based on self-interest:

Man is an indifferent egoist; even the cleverest thinks *his habits more important than his advantage.*[138]

Even *life*, which appears as an ultimate value in Nietzsche's early writings, is but a *means* to power. Self-survival, the primary demand of *self-interest*, is but incidental to striving for power. Life is only a means to something; it is the expression of forms of the growth of power.[139] To make the matter much more complicated, he also writes that 'egoism' is a logically incoherent theory, because

The "subject" is only a fiction: The ego of which one speaks when one censures egoism does not exist at all.[140]

Consequently,

there are *no* actions prompted by 'egoism'.[141]

This argument will be repeated in detail by Jean-Paul Sartre in his early essay *Transcendence of the Ego*. He also argues that there is no ego and therefore no egoism. However, Sartre does not deny that there might not be egoism taken up as a matter of principle, and his rejection of egoism is only a rejection of a self-interest ethic as a naturalistically ("prereflectively") justified ethic. We might interpret Nietzsche along similar lines, and argue that egoism is justified naturalistically only so far as the *self-interests* involved are interests in *power*. The interests of power, as should be evident from Nietzsche's examples, are very different and sometimes incompatible with the interests in personal pleasure with which egoism is most often associated.

It is evident that Nietzsche did not consider cruelty and hurting others a desirable part of master morality. In his quest for personal achievement, which will most likely oppose other persons in some way, sacrifice of others is an unfortunate side effect. In the master's search for self-perfection (the Greeks are the model here), the values of self-control but also self-conceit are foremost means to power. (Thus one can view Aristotle's list of virtues and find them remarkably in agreement with Nietzsche—courage, pride, and loyalty.)[142]

For the master, 'bad' refers to failure, defeat, and loss of power. The values and virtues of master morality are determined by an explicit appeal to what serves the Will to Power, to what aids self-perfection, to what is *good*. Acts are 'bad' in such a morality if they are not *good*, resulting in failure, in defeat, in loss of power. The values of master morality are thus primarily the virtues, the way to lead the *good* life (as one determines it). This is in marked contrast to slave morality, and the difference between the two forms of morality is most apparent in the secondary importance of virtue and the primary importance of vice in slave morality.

The 'slave' does not create his own values, but begins by having a set of values forced on him, those values of the master by which he finds it impossible to become virtuous. Master morality tells him to be strong, but he is weak; it tells him to be courageous, but he is cowardly; it tells him to be creative and assert himself, but he is dull and unassertive. Finding himself consistently failing according to the measure of these virtues, the slave (historically, Jews and early Christians)[143] adopts a remarkable strategy for asserting his Will to Power in the face of consistent defeat. He has failed to prove his strength, but why then consider strength a virtue? Consider it rather a vice, and be glad one is not tempted by it. "The meek shall inherit the earth."

One finds himself in poverty, but why take wealth as a virtue? Rather it is the "root of all evil," and one is best rid of it. In order to call himself 'successful' in those same activities in which he has been called 'failure', the slave performs a *transvaluation of values*, and systematically determines as *evil* just those virtues which the master has called 'good.' Thus, one finds himself without pride, without cause for boasting, without desire to succeed, without virility, so humility and modesty, patience and abstinence are said to be 'resisting temptation' rather than failures. The slave finds himself threatened with defeat in battle, so he 'turns the other cheek'; he finds himself incapable of doing great deeds, so he becomes a 'good citizen'.

In short, the slave determines his morality (asserts his Will to Power) in rejecting those values by which he cannot be successful. The fundamental category of slave morality (and Christianity) thus becomes *evil* (and *sin*), and these are just those virtues of the masters which the slave is incapable of practicing.

The *function* of morality—both master and slave morality—has thus been to express the Will to Power. Slave morality, however, can best do this by explicitly denying the Will to Power. There is, for him, more assertion of power in the self-righteousness of abstinence than in constant personal failure. The function of the values of *sin* and *evil* have thus been to increase the power of the weak. The creation of the bland, 'comfortable' world of the bourgeois Christian is the assertion of power by those who are incapable of personal greatness. Evil is the rejection of those values which, if accepted, would make one see how impotent he really is. *Good,* for the slave, is thus the avoidance of evil, that which makes one feel safe, and secure (for example, weakness, humility, kindness, and charity).

Nietzsche has yet to explain how slave morality has come to occupy its present unchallenged position, and how master morality has seemingly disappeared. There is no question but that Nietzsche favored master-type morality,[144] and his philosophy of the *Übermensch,* as we shall see, is primarily an attempt to resurrect the attitudes of master morality.

The domination of slave morality is due to the acceptance of slave values by the masters themselves.[145] This happened mainly through the spread of Christianity —symbolized by the official conversion of the Romans under Constantine—and derivatively through the political-economic doctrines of democracy and socialism which attracted much attention in the revolutionary Europe of Nietzsche's lifetime.

It is the Jews who are responsible for the *transvaluation* (although Nietzsche claims they could not have helped it), and it is early Christianity which is responsible for the spread and eventual domination of slave morals. In the *Old Testament,* one finds many episodes in which the Jews attempt to assert the universal validity of their religion (with the help of occasional Divine intervention). Only the very strong claims of Christianity, threatening unbelievers with an eternal afterlife of damnation, were sufficient to insure the spread of a morality of weakness to the very strong. The conversion of the Roman emperor is a historical event of incredible significance; for with the acceptance of Christianity, master morality appeared explicitly only in isolated and always sinful or evil individuals. The strong were still strong in the Middle Ages, of course, but their strength was considered *by themselves* as something sinful. Nietzsche's elitism never comes out so strongly as in his treatment of the attempts of the strong to become weak:

like an eagle trying not to be an eagle.[146]

The self-hatred or *resentment* of the strong inspired by the values of weakness, Nietzsche comments, is the most spectacular ('most spiritual') feat of *revenge* in history. The punishment of the strong by the weak lasts over ten centuries. While the weak can accept weakness easily, the strong must find it impossible, and the former joy and exaltations of strength by which Nietzsche characterizes the master morality of the Greeks degenerates into the self-destroying 'resentiment' and torture of *bad conscience,* roughly equivalent to Kierkegaard's *recognition of sin* and to Hegel's *unhappy consciousness.* In *bad conscience,* the strong despises his strength and curses his superior intelligence which leads him to doubt the validity of the morality of weakness which constrains him. The strong becomes trapped in failure by Christianity much as the slave was once condemned to failure in master morality. Insofar as he remains a master, he comes to despise himself that much more. As one despises himself more, becomes more aware of his sins, he becomes more and more dedicated to Christianity. (Both Nietzsche and Kierkegaard saw that Christianity thrives on feelings of sinful impotence, but to very different conclusions.)

Nietzsche does not see this slave takeover or the *bad conscience* as entirely bad, however, but rather,

*it is a disease but only as
pregnancy is a disease.*[147]

A necessary condition for the acceptance
of slave morality has always been the
recognition of divine sanctions against
those who dare to be strong, but now,
"God is dead," and those transcendent
sanctions have disappeared. The weak
will continue to be weak, of course, and
Nietzsche predicts that, once they recognize the death of God, they will turn to
new idols of the state.[148] The strong will
now free themselves from the shackles of
Christianity. Their return will not be a
return to the life of the Greeks, for the
long period of *bad conscience* has taught
the new master—the *Übermensch*—a
toleration for suffering and the burden of
self-discipline which even the tragedy-
minded Greeks did not know. For the first
time, Nietzsche proclaims through his
Zarathustra, man is ready to overcome
fully the "human, all-too-human."

The *Übermensch*

*Man is a rope tied between beast and
Übermensch—a rope over an abyss.*[149]

I teach you the Übermensch. *Man is
something that shall be overcome. What
have you done to overcome him?*[150]

With our discussion of Nietzsche's moral
philosophy, the celebrated notion of the
Übermensch can be explained easily. The
Übermensch is the return to the master
morality—the ruthless quest for self-perfection without religious or moral constraints.
The *Übermensch* is Kierkegaard's individual leading an aesthetic mode of existence, glorified in Nietzsche as the best of
the three 'spheres'. The *Übermensch* is the
creator—the ultimate synthesis of Dionysian passion and Apollonian control—the
one who actually does "live his life as a
work of art."[151]

The *"über"* concept plays a complicated
part in Nietzsche's notion of *Übermensch*
as it does in his conception of 'self-*overcoming*'. The *Übermensch* is he who
overcomes himself, he who masters
(through sublimation) all of the beastly,
destructive; especially self-destructive,
drives within himself; the all-too-human
passions and fears would lead him to be
comfortable and secure rather than creative. From his very earliest works, as we

have seen, creativity is inextricably linked
to *rationality*, and the *Übermensch*, contrary to the popular picture of the reckless
warrior, is he who succeeds in the *rational* mastering of his instincts. Not that
there has been much success so far,

*Never yet has there been an
Übermensch. Naked I saw both the greatest
and the smallest man. They are still
all-too-similar to each other. Verily even
the greatest I found all-too-human.*[152]

Yet this is to be expected, given the incredible amount of suffering required to
gain even the smallest increment of independence (that is, rationality or Will to
Power):

*Nothing has been bought more dearly
than that little bit of human reason and
sense of freedom which is now the basis of
our pride.*[153]

There are men, however, who have
stepped far across the abyss toward the
Übermensch. Napoleon, the *man*, not the
conqueror, understood the Will to Power
and self-overcoming, but in the end

*he himself had been corrupted by the
means which he had to employ and lost
noblesse of character.*[154]

Similarly, Julius Caesar is often cited as
an approach to the *Übermensch*, but
again, not because of his political victories
but because of his incredible self-control.
Brutus, ironically, is also mentioned in
this context for the 'independence of soul'
to sacrifice even his dearest friend when
he reasoned it to be necessary. In this
century, T. E. Lawrence perhaps, but certainly none of the *Reichsdeutschen*, approaches the Nietzschean ideal.

The role of aesthetics in Nietzsche's
concept of the *Übermensch* must not be
neglected in our stress of the often under-
emphasized role of rationality. The *Übermensch*, above all else, lives his life as a
'work of art', and *style* of living becomes
far more important than content:

*Giving style to one's character—a great
and rare art! It is exercised by those who
see all the strengths and weaknesses of
their own nature and then comprehend
them in an artistic plan until everything
appears as art and reason.*[155]

This being Nietzsche's conception of the *Übermensch*, it is twice unfortunate that he provides us with so many examples of men whose exercise of power at least partly involved military power. In fact, Nietzsche intended that the *power* and *strength* he lauded were as often as not to be found apart from strength over others. He often argues, as in his analysis of the Will to Power, that power over oneself is always greater than power over others:

I have found strength where one does not look for it; in simple, mild, and pleasant people, without the least desire to rule— and, conversely, the desire to rule has often appeared to me as a sign of inward weakness . . . . The powerful natures dominate, it is a necessity, they need not lift one finger. Even if, during their lifetime, they bury themselves in a garden house.[156]

The clearest vision of the *Übermensch* comes not from the examples of Napoleon or Caesar, but from the examples of Socrates, Mozart, and even Christ. The nobility of the ascetic is always lauded by Nietzsche, and we should not expect his *Übermensch* to be far removed from this ideal. We find Nietzsche, like Hegel and Aristotle, praising the artist, the *truly* religious man (Christ or Buddha, not the Churchmen) and, above all, the philosopher, as the highest specimens of man (Nietzsche occasionally insists they are the only "true human beings").

This rather specific characterization of the ideal of the *Übermensch* does not interfere with Nietzsche's Kierkegaardian insistence on the primary necessity of individuality; in fact, "giving style to one's character" is ultimately setting oneself off as unique. Nietzsche even (questionably) argues (for example, in *Gay Science*) against monotheism in general for its insistence upon a uniform ideal for mankind. The *Übermensch* is best characterized by the ascetic, but only because this image stresses the unimportance of power over others relative to *self*-control. The upshot of Nietzsche's ideal is just that it *cannot* be further prescribed, for the very essence of the ideal is refusal to recognize an ideal other than that which one sets for *himself*.

The notion of *Übermensch* as what man shall become, combined with Nietzsche's earlier enthusiasm for Darwin, has led many commentators (notably the Nazis) to interpret the *Übermensch* as the natural successor of man in evolution. By the time the *Übermensch* is conceived, however (1878), Nietzsche has firmly broken from Darwin, and the struggle for power (independence) has replaced the struggle for existence as the central life-drive. The *Übermensch* is not to come naturally; to the contrary, the nearly total extinction of master-morality at the hands of the weak is ample historical evidence that the survival potential of the truly strong is less than that of the herd. To stress this point, Nietzsche gives us a startling picture of the evolutionary creature which he believed will succeed present mankind, the "Last Man":

The earth hath then become small, and on it there hopeth the last man who maketh everything small. His species is ineradicable like that of the ground-flea; the last man liveth longest. 'We have discovered happiness;—say the last men, and blink thereby.'[157]

The *Übermensch* is a prescribed ideal, something to be striven for:

The problem I thus pose is not what shall succeed mankind in the sequence of living beings (man as an end), but what type of man shall be bred, shall be willed, for being higher in value worthier of life, more certain of a future.[158]

Evidently the Nazis mastered this passage well, tragically without understanding the kind of ideal for which to strive.

In the last section, we mentioned Nietzsche's claim that the great suffering of *bad conscience* was a necessary precondition for the *Übermensch*. The reason for this can be understood if we refer back to the parable Nietzsche offers us concerning the 'three stages' to the *Übermensch* (within which he interprets his own development)—the camel, the lion, and the child. The suffering of the *bad conscience* is the burden of the camel, and such discipline is necessary in order for one to be able to cope with nihilism—the total independence of the 'lion' (the blond beast). (Nietzsche's insistence on *disciplined* freedom is no less intense than Kant and Hegel's demand that freedom be *positive*.) In a sense, the image of the child is unfortunate, for it allows Nietzsche's detractors to equate his *Übermensch* with the irresponsibility of youth. The image of the child, however, is not a celebration of adolescent licentiousness, but rather a symbol of a rebirth, a new found freedom to make oneself *after* one has mastered the disciplines of self control. The great suffering of bad conscience is necessary to the *Übermensch* in very much the same way that the long years of practiced self-control and 'purification of mind' are necessary to the enlightenment of the Buddha. This is not to say, of course, that Nietzsche's philosophy ultimately resembles the ascetic search for peaceful wisdom. The discipline of the Buddha is directed toward an extirpation of passion, and thus shares what Nietzsche considers to be the pathology of Christianity. Nietzsche's 'camel' discipline is directed contrarily toward a heightening of passion coupled with increased self-control. The life of the *Übermensch*, Nietzsche often tells us, is the life of *frenzy*, not peace. It is on this rejection of Eastern thought that Nietzsche most dramatically breaks with his teacher Schopenhauer.

Eternal Recurrence

The doctrine of the *Übermensch* has been taken to be the culmination of Nietzsche's philosophy of power, but Nietzsche himself considered his philosophy completed by a very different although related doctrine—the Eternal Recurrence. The influence of this doctrine has not been extensive—few commentators have even paid attention to it, and the arguments in support of the Recurrence, one of the few completely metaphysical expositions we find in Nietzsche, are so notoriously invalid that one does Nietzsche most credit by not sharing his enthusiasm for this idea.

The doctrine of the Eternal Recurrence is the theory that every event and every sequence of events repeats itself an infinite number of times. The importance of the doctrine for Nietzsche's philosophy as a whole lies in its appropriation as a test for the worth of one's life. The ideal life—the life of the *Übermensch*—is a life which can treat the prospect of eternal repetition with delight:

What if a demon crept after thee into thy loneliness some day or night, and said to thee: 'This life, as thou livest it at present, and has lived it, thou must live it once more, and also innumerable times; and

there will be nothing new in it, but every pain and every joy and every thought and every sigh, and all the unspeakably small and great in thy life must come to thee again, and all in the same series and sequence—and similarly this spider and this moonlight among the trees, and similarly this moment, and I myself. The eternal sandglass of existence will ever be turned once more, and thou with it, thou speck of dust!'—Wouldst thou not throw thyself down and gnash thy teeth, and curse the demon that so spake? Or hast thou once experienced a tremendous moment in which thou wouldst answer him: 'Thou art a God, and never did I hear anything so divine!' If that thought acquired power over thee as thou art, it would transform thee, and perhaps crush thee; the question with regard to all and everything: 'Dost thou want this once more, and also for innumerable times?' would lie as the heaviest burden upon thy activity. Or, how wouldst thou have to become favourably inclined to thyself and to life, so as to long for nothing more ardently than for this last eternal sanctioning and sealing? . . . [160]

Although the central importance of the Recurrence is this ethical (or rather aesthetic) application, the doctrine itself is defended as a physical (metaphysical) theory, and Nietzsche extravagantly praises the scientific foundation of his theory. [161]

Roughly, the argument operates with three premises based on physical mechanics of the time:

1. Amount of energy in the universe is finite and fixed (law of conservation of energy).
2. Number of possible energy states in the universe is finite.
3. Time is infinite. [162]

From these, Nietzsche argues that every event (that is, every configuration of energy states) will recur infinitely many times. Similarly, every (finite) sequence of energy states will be repeated, and one's life—which is a relatively short sequence of energy states will recur and has occurred eternally.

Of course, one might attack the argument by attacking the classical physical model upon which the premises are based —claiming, possibly, that modern physics has rejected both (1) and (3), and would reject (2) as a consequence of rejecting

(1). However, within the classical models of Newton through Poincaré, Nietzsche's simple 'scientific' argument does not fare badly. Danto[163] points out, by way of defense, that Nietzsche's doctrine of Eternal Recurrence closely resembles considerably more sophisticated scientific theories of thermodynamics which evolved after his death. The key notions of 'energy', 'energy-state', and 'finite-infinite' are not developed in Nietzsche, and his brief essay in physics can only be considered as quaint, a clever attempt to toy with a problem far beyond his scientific capabilities (although he clearly was aware of the current state of physics in his time).

We stressed that the importance of the doctrine of recurrence does not lie in its scientific sophistication, but in its ethical implication. The ideal of the *Übermensch* is the ideal of the perfect life, the life which, like a great work of art, has not one detail too few or too many. The Recurrence acts as a test for this perfection; every moment of boredom, of despair, of frustration is magnified infinitely by the application of the doctrine of Recurrence. The test lies in its magnification of faults which might ordinarily be easily ignored. A frustrated student might easily rationalize the painful boredom of professional school by appeal to the relatively short time in school contrasted with the future. If one envisions the same 'short' course of action repeated infinitely, the rationalization loses its force.

The effect of the Recurrence on an ethical standard is the emphasis on the moment, a stress on the immediate rather than an appeal to the indefinite future. The recurrence is Kierkegaard's despair-laden notion of aesthetic 'repetition' (and *Pathos*) reformulated with approval. Interestingly, the test of Recurrence might be compared to Kant's test of universalizability (categorical imperative). Both philosophers test a proposed course of action by applying to it a hypothetical, "What if this action were to be multiplied by *X*?" However, Kant presents his test as a *logical* criterion of adequacy, and the intolerability of an action to conform to universalization to all agents is a conceptual intolerability. Nietzsche's test, on the other hand, is a *psychological* test, and an action is rejected if the hypothetical that it will repeat itself in time is psychologically intolerable.

One must not underestimate the power of Nietzsche's Recurrence. If the defense of the thesis is not questioned, the query

"What if you had to do this *forever?*" is a persuasive reason for rejecting virtually any but the most ideal actions. Again, the image is the work of art, in which nothing can be added or changed merely for the sake of change, but only for the work as a whole.

The doctrine of Recurrence is an alternative to several similar metaphorical doctrines to which we often find Nietzsche opposed. First, of course, there is his opposition to the diminution of this life with an eye to an afterlife, but, according to Nietzsche, this life is the *only* life, and the only after-life will be *exactly* the same. Secondly, Nietzsche is opposed to the Hegelian-Darwinian picture of history as *progress*. Life does not spiral upward, as the diagrammatic representation of the dialectic and evolution often imagine, but simply repeats back on itself. The value of human life is not its consequences or its 'usefulness',

What, after all, is "useful"? One must ask "useful in relation to what?" For example, that which is useful for the long life of the individual might be unfavorable to its strength and splendor.[164]

Powerful arguments are not always valid, however, and although the idea of recurrence may be far more exciting than Kant's categorical imperative, its defense cannot go beyond its psychic effect. The Recurrence argues that every present sequence of energy states will repeat indefinitely, and this is the reason for giving ultimate priority to one's choices of courses of action. But, according to the argument, every possible sequence of energy states will repeat infinitely. This means I will also live all those lives I do not choose an infinite number of times as well. If I must choose, for example, whether to sacrifice myself in a revolution or to remain dedicated to my studies, I find that the doctrine of recurrence tells me that I shall enact both of these courses of action infinitely many times anyway. The 'test' is therefore worthless even as a psychological test if we take the arguments for the Recurrence seriously. Yet we must still conclude that the idea of the Eternal Recurrence has an impact which makes it a valuable *philosophical* metaphor.

Nietzsche's Place in History
Few central figures in philosophy are as difficult to place in their philosophical

heritage as Nietzsche. He conceived of himself as the dawn of a new era in philosophy, but we are hard put to find a generation of philosophers who did conform to Nietzsche's rigorous demands. Many of those philosophers who did claim to be followers were the furthest from the projected 'new philosopher' and perhaps those closest to Nietzsche in spirit would be the least likely to acknowledge the affinity. Nietzsche influenced virtually every major figure in twentieth-century German philosophy (in one direction or the other), but he himself is still very much a part of the nineteenth century against which he rebels.

What does a philosopher demand of himself first and last? To overcome his time in himself, to become timeless . . . . I am, no less than Wagner, a child of this time: that is, a decadent.[165]

Part of the problem with Nietzsche is his style, or variety of styles, which make systematic treatment difficult and detailed exegesis impossible. Much of his writing models the obscurity of religious teachings and seems directed at the same "edifying" effects. The doctrine of the *Übermensch* is as inspiring, and as vague, as the Buddha's teachings of the true self. However we might try to take Nietzsche as a serious philosopher, and respect his denial that he wants to be considered "holy," the mark and ambition of the prophet is always there. This explains why few philosophers maintain a casual attitude toward Nietzsche; they dismiss him or reject him totally or, particularly among the young, they become just the "disciples" that Zarathustra so often repelled. Perhaps that is part of Nietzsche's greatness as well as his chief philosophical failing. He himself lived as the ideal "ruthless questioner." His philosophical and personal failings give us an important model of what a philosopher can be. However, as with Kierkegaard, we are tempted to take "that individual" as one who strayed perhaps too far from the traditional modes of philosophy.

To be the first one here may be a curse: at any rate, it is a destiny.[166]

Bibliography
Nietzsche's Works in English

Birth of Tragedy. Translated by W. Kaufmann. New York, 1966.

"Untimely" Meditations:

I. *David Strauss, Confessor and Writer.* Translated by A. Ludovici. In O. Levy, *Nietzsche's Collected Works,* 18 Vols. New York, 1909.

II. *The Use and Disadvantage of History for Life.* Translated by A. Collins. New York, 1957.

III. *Schopenhauer as Educator.* Translated by J. W. Hillesheim and M. B. Simpson. Chicago, 1965.

IV. *Richard Wagner in Bayreuth.* Translated by A. Ludovici. In O. Levy (op. cit.).

Human, All-Too-Human. Translated by H. Zimmern and P. Cohn. In O. Levy (op. cit.).

Mixed Opinions and Maxims. Part II of *Human, All-Too-Human.* Translated by Zimmern and Cohn. In O. Levy (op. cit.).

The Wanderer and His Shadow. Translated by H. Zimmern and P. Cohn. In O. Levy (op. cit.).

Dawn. Translated by J. M. Kennedy. In O. Levy (op. cit.).

The Gay Science ("The Joyful Wisdom"). Translated by I. Reinhardt. In O. Levy (op. cit.) and in paperback. New York, 1968.

"Thus Spake Zarathustra", Twilight of the Idols; The Antichrist; and *Nietzsche Contra Wagner.* Translated by W. Kaufmann. In *The Viking Portable Nietzsche.* New York, 1964.

Beyond Good and Evil. Translated by W. Kaufmann. New York, 1966.

Genealogy of Morals. Translated by W. Kaufmann. New York, 1967.

The Case of Wagner. Translated by W. Kaufmann. New York, 1966.

Ecce Homo. Translated by W. Kaufmann. New York, 1967.

The Will to Power. Translated and edited by W. Kaufmann and R. Hollingdale. New York, 1968.

Letters. Translated and edited by C. Middleton. Chicago, 1968.

Books about Nietzsche's Philosophy

Two excellent works on Nietzsche's philosophy:

Kaufmann, W. *Nietzsche: Philosopher, Psychologist, Antichrist.* Princeton, 1950.

Danto, A. *Nietzsche as Philosopher.* New York, 1965.

also

Brinton, C. *Nietzsche.* Cambridge, 1941.

Camus, A. "Nietzsche and Nihilism." In *The Rebel.* New York, 1956.

Freud, S. "Nietzsche's *Ecce Homo.*" In *Minutes of Vienna Psychoanalytic Society,* vol. II, 1908–10.

Hollingdale, R. *Nietzsche: The Man and His Philosophy.* Baton Rouge, 1965.

Jaspers, K. *Nietzsche.* Translated by C. Wallraff and F. Schmitz. Tucson, 1965.
———. *Nietzsche and Christianity.* Translated by E. B. Ashton. Chicago, 1961.

Jung, C. G. "Apollonian and Dionysian." In *Psychological Types.* New York, 1959.

Kaufmann, W. *From Shakespeare to Existentialism.* Boston, 1959.

Mencken, H. L. *The Philosophy of Friedrich Nietzsche.* New York, 1913.

Morgan, G. *What Nietzsche Means.* Cambridge, 1941.

Royce, J. "Nietzsche." In *Atlantic Monthly.* March, 1917.

Tillich, P. "Nietzsche and the Bourgeois Spirit." In *Journal of the History of Ideas.* 1945.

The Twentieth Century: Phenomenology and Existentialism
PART TWO

While twentieth-century existentialism is heavily influenced by and in agreement with the essential thoughts of Kierkegaard and Nietzsche, the dominant influence on the writings of Martin Heidegger and Jean-Paul Sartre is the philosophy of Edmund Husserl. Husserl develops a mode of philosophy which he calls "phenomenology," and both Heidegger and Husserl consider themselves "phenomenologists." Husserl's phenomenology is primarily concerned with the foundations of logic and mathematics and the theory of knowledge; it has little to say about freedom, morality, and individual choice and responsibility—themes which come to dominate later French existentialism. In a sense, it is helpful to view the works of Heidegger and Sartre as attempts to supply a very sophisticated philosophical basis through the discipline of phenomenology for the relatively primitive existentialist views of Kierkegaard and Nietzsche. Husserl's philosophy has much in common with Kant's theory of knowledge; it is also rationalistic and a "transcendental idealism." Accordingly, the move from Husserl to Heidegger and Sartre will be interestingly parallel to the earlier move from Kant and Hegel to Kierkegaard and Nietzsche—a move from rationalism and idealism to existentialism.

Edmund Husserl and Phenomenology: The New Way of Philosophy
CHAPTER 5

The turn of the twentieth-century in European philosophy is clearly delineated in the writings of a single figure and by the development of a philosophical method which has virtually defined the philosophical idiom of Heidegger, Sartre, Scheler, and Merleau-Ponty. The publication of Edmund Husserl's *Ideas*[1] in 1913 can be rightly compared with the publication of Russell and Whitehead's *Principia Mathematica* (1910) for its impact on subsequent philosophical thought. No serious study of recent existentialist philosophy can possibly dispense with a preliminary investigation of Husserl's *Phenomenology* and its associated 'phenomenological method'.

Unlike the philosophers of the nineteenth century whom we have studied, Husserl has little interest in the history of philosophy. His efforts are directed towards problems initially contracted outside of philosophy, and he has only tangential concern for their philosophical origins or their treatment by thinkers in the past. Husserl is not even well-read in the history of philosophy. Yet, in true Hegelian fashion, he considers himself not only in direct lineage with the great thinkers of the past, but to have seen more clearly and to have made possible the goals towards which previous philosophers have been groping without success:

phenomenology is as it were the
secret longing of the whole
philosophy of modern times. The
fundamental thought of Descartes in
its wonderful profundity is
already pressing towards it; Hume
again a psychological philosopher
of the school of Locke,
almost enters its domain, but his eyes
are dazzled. The first
to perceive it truly is
Kant, whose greatest intuitions
first became quite clear to us after
we have brought the distinctive
features of the phenomenological
field into the focus
of full consciousness. It then
becomes evident to us that Kant's
mental gaze rested on this field,
although he was not yet able
to appropriate it and recognize
it as the center from which
to work up on his own line a
rigorous science of Essential Being.
Thus the Transcendental
Deduction of the Critique of Pure
Reason, *for instance, already moves*
strictly on phenomenological
ground, . . .[2]

Husserl attempts no less than to start philosophy over again, taking heed of the insights of the geniuses of the past only so far as they allow themselves to be reinterpreted as precursors of what Husserl boldly refers to as the first *true* philosophy.

The pretentiousness of this self-proclaimed revolution in philosophy should not appear novel to us. Kant offered us a 'revolution' of Copernican dimensions. Before him, Descartes and John Locke had clearly jolted philosophical inquiry in new directions. Hegel, however much he may have followed Kantian philosophy, surely gave the Western world an entirely new conception of philosophy. Kierkegaard and Nietzsche both continually stressed their radical break from established philosophical traditions. European philosophy is more like a series of revolutions than a smooth progression of ideas, but behind each of these revolutions lies disagreement not only in substantial doctrine but disagreement in *methodology* and differences of *approach* to philosophical questions.

With each change in philosophical method, we begin to philosophize anew. Old insights must be reexamined in the light of new criteria; old approaches must be redirected to join forces with the new method. It follows, therefore, that the philosophies of previous philosophers cannot be incorporated into a new philosophy until they are 'translated' into the new idiom. It would also follow that, because the older philosophies are not quite at home in this new idiom, they will always be misstated slightly and not fully appreciated by the new perspectives now adopted. Each philosophy begins with a translation and critique of its predecessors, showing how they could be adapted to the new method, and why they are not fully adequate when they are so adapted. Hegel recognized this self-aggrandizing attitude and made it the explicit basis of his philosophizing. We find the same methodological-historical attitudes in virtually every great philosopher whom we have studied or even mentioned. To do philosophy is not only to answer certain questions, but to establish a method for answering these questions. It is this method as well as the philosophical doctrines themselves which determine the characteristic tenor of a philosophy.

Husserl is best known for his methodology, his 'phenomenological method'. It is often suggested, somewhat unfairly, that Husserl's philosophy consists *entirely* in his methodology, and that he was so busy trying to solve problems of method that he never had an opportunity to apply his method to problems. This has an element of truth. Husserl was preoccupied with the clarification of his approach to philosophy and left the applications of his method to the researches of his students (since published in *Jahrbuch*[3]). Much of this impression is due, however, to the illusion that questions concerning philosophical method are themselves not philosophical questions. As we argued for Hegel, it is doubtful that one can separate methodological questions from disputes over philosophical doctrines. Husserl was peculiarly divorced from substantive questions of ethics and religion, particularly considering the period of historical turmoil in which he worked. His questions were almost exclusively epistemological,

problems concerning the foundations of knowledge. Very simply, Husserl concerned himself with the questions of the Aesthetic and Analytic of Kant's first *Critique*. The central questions of Husserl's philosophy are indeed very Kantian. First, a problem of perception,

How can experience as consciousness give or contact an object?[4]

The problem of how we can know and experience *objects* as opposed to the 'contents' of our own consciousness is a problem to haunt Husserl throughout all of his works, and his solution is very much like Kant's "Refutation of Idealism," and shares the same problems. Secondly, there is the problem that brought Husserl into philosophy from his studies of mathematics, the problem of *necessary* (a priori) *truth*. "How is necessary truth, specifically mathematical truth, possible?" To answer this question, he introduces his famous doctrine of *essences*.

These two questions are not simply doctrinal questions, but as Hegel pointed out in his critique of Kant's theory of knowledge, these are basic questions of method. The question whether or not we can know things-in-themselves is not so much a terminus in philosophy as a basic presupposition. Similarly, the question whether there really are (nontrivial) necessary truths is not so clearly a thesis to be proved as a problem which we must *begin* by solving. In a sense, therefore, one might claim that Husserl develops a method to answer these two questions; but it is equally defensible to claim that Husserl builds a method upon his answer to these two problems—a method based on his beliefs that knowledge of things-in-themselves and necessary truths is possible. To formulate a philosophical method which allows for knowledge of the 'real' world and 'essential truth' is, therefore, already to take a firm *doctrinal* stance in philosophy. It is meaningless, therefore, to consider Husserl merely as a methodologist. He is a *philosopher,* and his defense of a method cannot be distinguished, even in principle, from his acceptance of some very substantial epistemological theses.

The Ideal of a 'Presuppositionless' or 'Radical' Philosophy

In our examination of Hegel's philosophy, we encountered the demand that philosophy be 'presuppositionless'. A philosopher, unlike a student of other disciplines, can start from no preconceptions of what his philosophy ought to produce, and he cannot be satisfied to rest his philosophy on any 'self-evident' axiom or set of axioms in the style of Descartes, Spinoza, or Fichte. In Hegel's *Phenomenology*, however, we may easily lose sight of this principle after a few twists of the dialectic, and Hegel's philosophy as a whole looks much like a continuous application of a single preconception of what a philosophical system ought to be. When we find the demand that philosophy be presuppositionless in Husserl, it is an ultimatum forever threatening our confidence in our researches; it is a demand always attacking principles on which we thought we could rely, sometimes bringing to a complete halt what once seemed to be sound and fruitful philosophical pursuits because Husserl leads us to suspect that there is some yet unquestioned element in our thinking. The demand that philosophy be presuppositionless leads Husserl to characterize himself as a 'perpetual beginner'. No thesis was ever sufficiently well-established for him that it could not be called up for reexamination at any point of the investigation. In the diverse but admirable company of Nietzsche, Bertrand Russell, and Wittgenstein, we find Husserl unsurpassed as a 'ruthless' questioner, a brutally intense critic of his own thinking. (Unfortunately, he was not equally receptive to criticism from others; this is reported even by one of his leading admirers, Marvin Farber).[5] The picture of Husserl as totally caught up in his own methodology is largely due to his continuous rethinking of his entire project. This effectively forbade him from embarking on the systematic enterprise of Kant or Hegel. Apart from the specific virtues to be found in Husserl's writings, the intense intellectual honesty of Husserl the man should be sufficient to mark him a paragon of the philosopher in the twentieth century.

Both Hegel and Husserl referred to the ideal of a presuppositionless philosophy as *science*. Their attempted realizations of this science, however, are remarkably different. Hegel's concept of 'science' was inextricably tied to his concept of 'system', and, for him, the demand that philosophy be 'scientific' was identical with the demand that it be systematic. Husserl had no system; on the contrary, his lack of systematization rivals that of Nietzsche, whose vehement criticism of the monolithic Hegelian system he renews (but without Nietzsche's considerable understanding of Hegel's philosophy). The system, Husserl tells us, signifies a refusal to continue questioning. Unlike Hegel, Husserl never arrives at any settled or unquestionable phenomenological truths, for he is ever in the process of redoubting old conclusions and revising older conceptions of his method. This is not to say that Husserl did not propose several purportedly *absolute* truths (for example, his doctrine of the *Ego* and his positing of *essences*). However, there is virtually no proposition or starting point in Husserl's philosophy which was not called into question and seriously revised through the course of his works. One great problem in surveying Husserl's work, consequently, is the problem of distinguishing and at the same time interrelating a series of different phenomenological methods and doctrines. For Hegel, the problem was to present an elaborate system in brief summary form; for Husserl, as for Nietzsche, the danger is that any attempt at systematization will seriously distort fundamentally different strands of thought which can only misleadingly be presented as a single philosophy. Husserl's demand for a philosophy which held every proposition suspect naturally drew him to Descartes, whom Husserl repeatedly cited as his methodological ancestor. Descartes had insisted that every belief be supposed to be false until proven true beyond any doubt. Similarly, Husserl's insistence that philosophy begin without presupposition leads him to go through much the same Cartesian deliberations. It is surely possible to be wrong in our judgments about the world —we 'see' things which are not the case, we generalize about the world in false ways, and we adopt false theories about the world. In fact, it even seems possible to intelligibly question whether there is a world 'out there' at all. With Husserl's 'radical' departure in philosophy, all judgments about the 'external world' or what Husserl refers to as judgments from the 'natural standpoint', must be suspended. Consequently, all judgments about other persons, other persons' experiences, and all judgments about oneself as a person must similarly be suspended or held in doubt. Furthermore, we should have to suspend our faith in the reliability of memory as well, in the existence of ourselves as conscious *persons,* and in all theories we have about the nature of our minds or mental activities. We must even suspend our belief in the laws of mathematics and logic until we have rested them on secure philosophical foundations. (As we shall see, it was an interest in the foundations of mathematics which forced Husserl into philosophy.) The problem, of course, is to seek these philosophical foundations without assuming or presupposing some of these beliefs which must be held in suspension. We must, therefore, establish the validity of our belief in an 'external world', in the existence of other consciousnesses, in the validity of the laws of thought, of mathematics and logic, without appealing to those beliefs for support. Any form of *rationalism* with its confidence in Reason, rational insight, and the validity of clear and distinct ideas or the 'natural light of Reason', for example, as we find in Descartes, must be suspended for our philosophical scrutiny. Failure to do so, Husserl argues, is a failure to carry through the Cartesian ideal, and a resultant unwitting reliance on presuppositions. Husserl's critique of Descartes centers on Descartes' failure to carry through consistently his own program. What we find in Cartesianism, according to Husserl, is a host of unexamined and unjustified assumptions concerning the nature of human thought and the reliability of human reason. Many of these unexamined assumptions had surfaced in those philosophies following Descartes, in Spinoza, Malebranche, Leibniz, Locke, Berkeley, and Hume. Even Hume, however, who was the most persistent questioner of this distinguished group, failed to exorcise philosophy of presuppositions. Kant brought to the surface some of these presuppositions, but Kant again, according to Husserl, failed to achieve that total rigor which is vital to philosophical science.

In questioning (or in attempting to question) propositions which were previously assumed, Descartes had adopted the correct philosophical attitude, Husserl claims, but his rationalism was incompatible with his initial demand for unrelenting doubt. However, if we avoid appeal to Reason in our search for presuppositionless philosophical foundations (and methods), where can we turn? The clear alternative in modern philosophy is *empiricism,* the appeal to experience for

these philosophical foundations. Traditional empiricism, the empiricism of Locke, Berkeley, and Hume, was clearly inadequate for this purpose, again because it failed to adequately question basic methodological principles. For example, Lockean-Humean empiricism presupposed that the mind was a more-or-less passive receptor of experiences, that experiences were caused in the mind by 'external' objects, and so forth. All such questions concerning the nature of experience and human cognitive faculties could not be assumed, for these were the theses that had to be proven. Kant's philosophy is rejected on the same grounds, namely, that his division of the human mind into three *faculties* could not be justified, but was simply borrowed from psychology, and then presupposed for the critique of knowledge. This objection is notably similar to Hegel's objection that Kant's *Critique* is based on the metaphor of consciousness as an instrument (faculty) for gaining knowledge.[6] Husserl's empiricism, therefore, becomes a 'radical' empiricism, beginning from 'pure' experience and looking only to pure experience as a source of philosophical truth.

It must not be thought that the results of this 'radical' empiricist inquiry are to be *empirical* truths. The outstanding feature of Husserl's empiricism—what distinguishes it most markedly from traditional empiricism—is its claim to provide us with *necessary truths.* In the Kantian quest for the a priori foundations of arithmetic, for example, Husserl (much like Kant) tells us that these foundations are to be found in certain necessary structures of experience. A traditional empiricist (for example, John Stuart Mill in *A System of Logic*[7]) would argue that the location of these 'foundations' in experience marks arithmetic as a body of empirical and contingent propositions. It is important to remark that Husserl himself once held this traditional position. His inaugural dissertation on the foundations of arithmetic, for example, borrowed heavily from Mill's argument that the laws of arithmetic are experience-based generalizations concerning our various experiences with counting and related activities. Husserl's 'radical' empiricism becomes primarily a reaction to his own traditional empiricist thinking. We shall begin our study of Husserl, therefore, with a brief study of the position he once held, against which his entire mature philosophy is to test its strength.

The *Philosophy of Arithmetic,* Frege, and Psychologism

Husserl came into philosophy as a mathematician, and his first interests in philosophy naturally fell to the philosophy of mathematics. The dominant influence in Husserl's philosophical development was the psychologist-philosopher Franz Brentano, of whom we shall speak later, who gave him a decidedly psychological perspective on philosophical problems. Husserl's inaugural dissertation (at University of Halle, 1887, where he first became *Privatdozent* under Carl Stumpf) was a psychological analysis of the concept of *number,*[8] an application of Brentano-style psychologizing to one basic problem of the foundations of mathematics. This dissertation became the basis for Husserl's first major work, *Philosophy of Arithmetic* (1891),[9] in which the concept of *number* and the laws of arithmetic were reduced to well-confirmed hypotheses governing the experience of counting. Even in this early work, Husserl speaks of the need to make philosophy into a 'strict science,' but here this signifies the need to reduce philosophy to psychology. The appeal to empiricism here is much like the traditional empiricism of Locke, Hume, and Mill; it is not yet the 'radical empiricism' of the *Ideas,* which, as we shall see, is very different. In Germany the empiricism of Wilhelm Wundt, Carl Stumpf, and Franz Brentano were strong influences on Husserl's *Philosophy of Arithmetic.* A philosophical idea—here the notion of *number*—is clarified by finding the experiential origin of that idea. Thus, in the *Philosophy of Arithmetic,* Husserl argues that the idea of number is derived from the idea of *multiplicity,* which in turn is derived from the idea of *collective association,* which is "observed only through reflection of the psychical act through which totality is realized."[10] The philosophical analysis of "number" thus reduces to an analysis of this mental act. Husserl clearly insists that this same technique, which he takes almost directly from Brentano and Stumpf (both were his teachers and colleagues), will suffice to 'analyze' all symbolic forms—geometry and logic as well as arithmetic.

This effort to reduce philosophical, mathematical, and logical questions to questions of psychology has been called *psychologism.* According to psychologistic theory, all concepts (both those which Kant called 'a priori' as well as 'empirical' concepts) are based upon abstractions from experience. Therefore, according to the psychologist, there is no distinction between empirical truths and so-called "necessary" or "a priori" truths. For example, the psychologist would maintain that our concept of "cause and effect" is no more than a mental habit based on many experiences of "constant conjunction". (Thus, on this question at least, Hume gives us a psychologistic analysis.) He would deny that any special 'necessary' status be attributed to such truths as "every event has a cause" and would maintain that this truth differs from "this event is caused by that" only in its level of abstraction. Similarly, the psychologist would explain the "validity" of the familiar syllogism,

All men are mortal:
Socrates is a man;
Ergo *Socrates is mortal*

not by appeal to rules of logic but by appeal to empirically well-founded laws about what people do in fact think, that is,

If any one believes that All men are mortal and believes that Socrates is a man then he will believe that Socrates is mortal.[11]

We have already discussed psychologism in some detail in previous chapters; it was the psychologistic tendencies of British empiricism which led Kant to his formulation of the notion of 'synthetic a priori' judgments and transcendental arguments to defend them. More recently, Nietzsche's 'epistemological nihilism' is also a psychologism. Nietzsche argues that all knowledge is a kind of 'error' which is necessary for the survival of a species. There is no knowledge, Nietzsche argues, which is 'true' or defensible apart from its survival or 'life-enhancing' value for the knower. In other words, Nietzsche's question, "Why have we come to believe this?" is very much in the spirit of Husserl's early psychologism in which he asks, "How did we come to have this concept of *number?*"

Husserl's enthusiasm for psychologism was destroyed by an assault on all attempted reductions of arithmetic and logic to psychology by the great German mathematician Gottlob Frege. In his forward to *The Fundamental Laws of Arithmetic,*[12] Frege gave a general argument against the psychologistic approach to studies in the foundations of arithmetic, against the "predominance in philosophy of psychological methods of argument, which have penetrated even into the field of logic."[13] Frege argued that

sensations are absolutely of no concern to arithmetic. No more are mental pictures, formed from the amalgamated traces of earlier sense-impressions. All these phases of consciousness are characteristically fluctuating and indefinite, in strong contrast to the definiteness and fixity of the concepts and objects of mathematics. . . .[14]

A psychological generalization depends on the contingent facts about what people happen to think; a mathematical law states what is necessarily true whether or not anyone happens to think it. If the truth of "5x12=60" depended upon the truth of the hypothesis, "everyone has believed and everyone always will believe that 5x12=60," then we should have to admit that the principle demands serious qualification or is proved false every time a doltish school boy confuses his multiplication tables. We might revise the above principle to read "everyone *rational*" or "everyone who knows mathematics believes that . . . " but then we have moved the weight of the justification away from the establishment of the psychological hypothesis toward the characterization of what a person must believe in order to be "rational" or to "know mathematics." This is to say that the validity of the proposition "5x12 = 60" is independent of any inductive evidence in favor of a hypothesis to the effect that anyone or any group of people actually accept this proposition. The laws of arithmetic are not laws of "the connections of ideas in the mind":

Never let us take a description of the origin of an idea for a definition, or an account of the mental and physical conditions on which we become conscious

of a proposition for a proof of it. A proposition may be thought, and again it may be true; let us never confuse these two things. We must remind ourselves, it seems, that a proposition no more ceases to be true when I cease to think of it than the sun ceases to exist when I shut my eyes.[15]

Against the psychologists, Frege argues that the laws of arithmetic are a priori and not empirical: against Kant, however, he also wants to argue that the laws of arithmetic are not *synthetic* a priori. Frege maintains rather that

the laws of arithmetic are analytic judgments and consequently a priori. Arithmetic thus becomes simply a development of logic, and every proposition of arithmetic a law of logic, albeit a derivative one, . . . The laws of number, therefore, are not really applicable to external things; they are not laws of nature . . . They assert not connections between phenomena, but connexions between judgments: and among judgments are the laws of nature.[16]

In 1894,[17] Frege applied this attack on psychologism directly to Husserl's *Philosophy of Arithmetic.* He complained that Husserl's use of the concept of "idea" *(Vorstellung)* confused the ideas or propositions of arithmetic with the ideas people had about arithmetic.

Thus we have a blurring of the distinction between image and concept, between imagination and thought. . . . In order to be able to compare one man's mental images with another's, we should have to have united them into one and the same state of consciousness. . . . It is quite otherwise for thoughts; one and the same thought can be grasped by many men. The constituents of the thought, and a fortiori things themselves, must be distinguished from the images that accompany in some mind the act of grasping the thought— images that each man forms of things.[18]

The concepts of arithmetic, Frege goes on to argue, are not formed through 'abstraction' from particulars as Husserl had maintained. The number 2 is not an abstraction of what is common to all pairs of things, correctly designated by the numeral "2."

On my view, bringing an object under a concept is just a recognition of a relation that was there already; here, objects are essentially altered by abstraction, so that objects brought under one concept become more alike. [19]

By way of conclusion, Frege once again charges that psychology and psychologism can give us only imprecise and probable generalizations, while the principles of arithmetic and logic must be precise and necessarily true. In short, Frege argues that there can be no reduction of philosophy to psychology, for psychology is incapable of clarifying the central notion of *necessity* which is so characteristic of mathematical truths.

Husserl's reaction to this onslaught was admirable. So impressed did he become with Frege's critique that he stopped publication of the projected second volume of *Philosophy of Arithmetic,* and proceeded to give up his entire psychologistic philosophical training. Brentano lost his hold on Husserl, and Husserl's new directions were partially defined by his reaction to his own former psychologizing.[20] Brentano had been strongly anti-Kantian, for his psychologistic methods had little to say about a priori knowledge. We now find Husserl taking a marked return to Kant, and it is illuminating that he lectured on Kant no less than seven times in the period following his traumatic encounter with Frege.

In two volumes of *Logical Investigations* (1900–01),[21] Husserl's 'breakthrough' to *Phenomenology* begins with a lengthy critique of psychologism. Agreeing fully with Frege that natural science could not provide the foundations of mathematics or philosophy, Husserl set out to find a new source of foundations. He did not accept Frege's analysis of the laws of logic as normative, however, for it became increasingly clear to Husserl that the laws of logic and principles of arithmetic were necessarily *true,* and not conventional or normative. The laws of logic and mathematics and the principles of philosophy in general, Husserl suggested, are *ideal laws,* and neither normative nor 'naturalistic' (derived from empirical science). This new realm of truths, it should be evident, occupied precisely the same place in his philosophy as did synthetic a priori principles in the philosophy of Kant. A new science was required to deal with these ideal or a priori laws, and this new science—alternatively designated as "descriptive psychology" or as "phenomenology" in this early work—was the 'radical empiricism' which sought to give a presuppositionless account of the nature of mathematics, logic, natural science, and knowledge in general. This philosophical science must begin, according to Husserl, with pure description (although he soon found the name "descriptive psychology" to be obviously misleading because of psychologistic connotations). This description must be radically distinguished from the sort of description carried out in psychology. The *Logical Investigations* marked the beginning of this new science, and it included essays on just those concepts which Husserl had formerly analyzed psychologistically. In the *Logical Investigations,* Husserl begins his lifelong campaign to defend the *ideality* of the a priori laws of logic, mathematics and philosophy against *skepticism,* the bogey of every philosophy we have studied thus far. Kant had initiated his "Critical method" in order to find a way around Hume's skepticism; Hegel rejected Kant because his rejection of "absolute knowledge" seemed to be just a more subtle form of skepticism; Kierkegaard rejects Hegel because his "dialectic" is still another extension of the inevitable skepticism of the Kantian program; and Nietzsche celebrates his "ruthless" skepticism only to the extent that it is a problem to be overcome. Husserl's attack on skepticism is quite similar to Kant's attack on Hume. Kant rejects Hume because his psychologistic (empirical) approach to the defense of foundation principles of mathematics and natural science leads him to doubt that these principles can be justified at all. Similarly, Husserl rejects psychologism because it leads to the conclusion that the fundamental laws of arithmetic can never be known to be *certainly* true. In *Logical Investigations,* Husserl introduces his phenomenological method in order to provide a new defense for a priori principles. This method quickly moves from the study of the foundations of mathematics to a general concern for "ideal" principles. The central themes of Husserl's philosophy, the a priori or ideal nature of *philosophical* truth, the need for a 'presuppositionless' philosophy and pure description of the 'essential' structure of the acts of consciousness, all grow from a visceral rejection of skepticism which remains the fundamental attitude of Husserl's thought.

Phenomenology and the Foundations of Philosophy

The *Logical Investigations* were succeeded by a flourish of limited investigations into epistemology, few of which are now published. In 1907, Husserl gave a series of lectures, published as *The Idea of Phenomenology,* in which he first introduces his mature ambitions for a "Universal Science" of phenomenology. In the essay, "Philosophy as a Rigorous Science" (1911), Husserl repeats his attacks on psychologism and against any attempts to relativize or 'historicize' truth. The sense in which psychologism is a 'relativization' of knowledge should be evident. If "truth" or the acceptability of propositions is dependent upon the psychology of the knower, then it follows that psychologically different persons or societies will have different "truths." *Historicism* is the application of this same thesis to history; because different cultures in different periods of history were psychologically and culturally different, their "truths" are different. Here, there can be no discussion of "truth" or "knowledge" outside of the context of a particular historical-cultural-psychological context.[22] But what is true is absolutely true, and not simply true in this or that epistemological or historical context. What Husserl needed was a method for getting at (philosophical) truth, a way of utilizing appeal to experience which was indeed presuppositionless and which could assure for us the foundations of our scientific and mathematical knowledge.

In 1913, Husserl published the first volume of *Ideas (Ideas Towards a Pure Phenomenology and Phenomenological Philosophy),*[23] followed by two subsequent volumes written in the same period (but which were not published until 1952). The *Ideas* was the introduction to this new method, this new philosophy, and its publication holds a special place in the history of twentieth-century philosophy. Husserl's writings and publications were prolific between 1913 and 1928. *Formal and Transcendental Logic*[24] was published in 1929, and the more famous *Cartesian Meditations*[52] were derived from a series of lectures given in Paris and published

in 1931 (the Paris Lectures have since been published also [1950]). Also written in this period were *First Philosophy, Phenomenological Psychology,* and *Experience and Judgment,*[26] although none of these were published until after Husserl's death and have still not found their rightful place in current philosophical studies. Husserl's last major work, *Crisis of European Philosophy,*[27] was written between 1934 and 1937. In addition, there are tens of thousands of pages of Husserl's informative essays and notes which are just now becoming available.[28] So extensive are these works that any general treatment of the evolution of Husserl's phenomenology must remain conspicuously tentative.

Husserl's philosophy undergoes a considerable development so any general account must show the changes in such key notions as "essence," "intuition," "ego," "phenomenological reduction," and "reflection." The central doctrines concerning the nature of consciousness and the ego and the relationship of consciousness to the objects of perception change so radically from *Logical Investigations* to *Ideas* to *Cartesian Meditations* to *Crisis* that no single account could possibly capture the important differences in Husserl's philosophy. However, we have already stressed that these differences are at one and the same time differences both in method and in doctrine, and therefore the changes we find are not simply different proposals harvested by a single 'phenomenological' method, but different methods.

This mutual evolution of doctrine and method exhibits a characteristic twentieth-century concern with philosophical method and a peculiarity of the philosophical enterprise which had only gradually emerged from the writings of such early methodologists as Descartes and Locke. Philosophy seeks a basic criterion for truth, knowledge, certainty by which we can scrutinize our more specific beliefs in all areas of human inquiry. What sort of criteria can the philosopher use to tell whether he has found the right criterion? It would seem that the philosophers' method of clarification and justification can proceed only if it can first justify itself, and it can justify itself only by appeal to itself. Husserl was aware of this peculiar situation in the *Logical Investigations* (and even in *Philosophy of Arithmetic,* where he noticed that logic differs from other sciences in that it can and must justify itself only by appeal to its own laws.) For example, the law of noncontradiction, perhaps the most basic law of logic, can justify itself only by the appeal that violation of the law gives us a contradiction. Phenomenology, as the basic 'science', can clarify its concepts and justify itself only by appeal to its own concepts and methods. Phenomenology, therefore, must be circular—it can proceed only so far as it can clarify its own concepts and justify its own basic epistemological doctrines—but it can do this only so far as it already accepts its concepts as clear and its doctrines as valid.[29] The attempt to overcome this problem is to insist repeatedly that phenomenology must be careful to restrict itself to *pure description,* for only the pure description of experience, of "the things-themselves," can allow us to break out of this circle and rest philosophy on what is 'given'. In spite of this insistence on pure description, however, the phenomenologist, notably Husserl, is easily prone to wander away from description and introduce theory into his study: perhaps it is impossible not to do this. At any rate, the frequency with which phenomenology appeals back to its own technical concepts and methods has led to a common objection to phenomenology; that its own concepts and techniques are essentially unjustifiable and intelligible only to those who will uncritically accept its peculiar jargon and starting points.

The problem of circularity is not peculiar to phenomenology, of course, but plagues every philosophical inquiry. Empiricists have always tried to clarify the concepts of "experience" and justify appeal to experience by appeal to experience; rationalists have always tried to clarify their concept of "reason" and justify their appeal to reason by appeal to reason. Where this has not been done, for example, when an empiricist appeals to reason to justify his empiricism, he has simply been inconsistent to his **own** method. In current analytic philosophy, a similar methodological dilemma is encountered in the demand that (at least some) philosophical truths can be discovered by appeal to linguistic *meaning.* The problem then becomes to clarify this concept of "meaning" and justify the appeal to linguistic meaning as a source

of philosophical truth. Thus analytic philosophy, like phenomenology, is conceived as a general philosophical method but spends an enormous amount of its energy and talent in clarifying its own nature and justification. The central concern in continental phenomenology has thus developed into the (phenomenological) analysis of "intuition," "essence," and "phenomenon"; the concerns of Anglo-American 'analytic' philosophy have developed in the analysis of "meaning" and "entailment" and the like. Because a philosophical method is presented as the ultimate mode of justification, it can, in turn, be justified by nothing other than itself. As an alternative, the philosopher tries to *ground* his method in something which appears to be given independently of the method, for example, 'pure experience' in phenomenology, 'ordinary' linguistic usage for some analytic philosophers, 'practicality' for the pragmatists, and the established results of science or established dogmas of religion for others. From the very presentation of the problem, we can suspect that all philosophical methods are going to become circular or inconsistent; circular if the 'given' appealed to can only be clarified or justified by appeal to itself; inconsistent if the 'given' to which it appeals differs from that which the method *says* ought to be the ultimate grounds for knowledge. The only alternative to this unwelcome choice is to give up attempts at justification and simply introduce one's philosophy. Some aspects of Fichte's philosophy conform to this demand, and the historicism of Dilthey is an open recognition of the impossibility of ultimate philosophical justification. However, few philosophers, even the most 'nihilist', such as Nietzsche, are ready to give up all claims that philosophy can give us *truth* (even if only 'subjective' truth). Fichte, Nietzsche, and even Dilthey tend to move towards an attack on relativism when their own philosophy is challenged. Husserl is clearly unwilling to give up the claim that philosophy can give us truth. His constant attacks on all forms of skepticism, relativism, and historicism clearly show us that he expects nothing less of an adequate philosophy than *absolute truth.* The phenomenological method, once clarified, is the true philosophy; there is no question of our having a choice of philosophical methods or doctrines.

To avoid this methodological circle and prove phenomenology to be the *true* philosophy, Husserl becomes a 'radical empiricist', ultimately referring all knowledge back to experience;

If we ask why the statement is justified, and ascribe no value to the reply, "I see that it is so," we fall into absurdity . . .[30]

Unlike traditional empiricism, phenomenology must appeal to experience without theoretical bias or presuppositions. In order to achieve this pure empiricism, phenomenology, as we have said, becomes descriptive. (Heidegger says that "the expression 'descriptive phenomenology' . . . is at bottom tautological."[31]) To characterize phenomenology as pure description based on experience is not even the beginning of an adequate description of a technique which Husserl felt entitled to call "the first true philosophy" or "philosophy as science." "Empirical description" is a characterization of botany and ornithology as well as phenomenology. Ornithology *observes* certain objects, *describes* them carefully and categorizes them according to their described properties. Phenomenology would then differ from ornithology only in the size of the domain of its objects; not just birds, but all objects would be subject matter for observation, description and categorization. This surely is *not* phenomenology. Phenomenology is not simply the empirical examination of objects, at least not at all in the sense in which its objects are birds, plants, and the like. Phenomenology is the examination of the *objects of consciousness*, and by this the phenomenologist does not mean *worldly* objects (birds, plants) of which we are conscious. The phenomenologist takes as a central principle of method that he is concerned with the objects of consciousness *only* insofar as they are conscious, and not at all insofar as they are 'real' objects in the world. The botanist observes and describes a plant; the phenomenologist observes and describes his experience of the plant. The botanist has nothing to examine if there are no plants; the phenomenologist has his objects to study even in the face of a "total destruction of the world." Of course, a phenomenologist can be said, in a sense we shall discover later, to examine the plant itself in his examination of his experience of the plant. However, any

facts about the material plant, for example, the fact that it exists, are of no interest to the phenomenologist, although they are of central interest to the botanist. For the phenomenologist, there is no difference in procedure for examining real plants or hallucinated plants; thus the empiricism of phenomenology is of a very different sort than the empirical inquiry indigenous to the 'natural' sciences.

This is still insufficient, however, for phenomenology as an examination of consciousness looks dangerously similar to the psychologistic methods against which Husserl's phenomenology is a reaction. The "description of consciousness" would also serve as a characterization of the approach to philosophy and psychology adopted by Locke, Hume, Brentano, Stumpf, and Wundt. We would, therefore, expect that Husserl has taken great pains to distinguish his descriptions of consciousness from those of the psychologists. The distinction between empirical psychology and phenomenology is one of the all-pervasive themes of Husserl's writings, and some of Husserl's most critical doctrines are directed at firmly maintaining this distinction. What lies at the basis of the psychology-phenomenology dichotomy is, of course, the distinction between *empirical* and *necessary truth*. The principles Husserl insists on deriving from his phenomenology are necessarily true. Any simple appeal to experience, as one finds in "naive" psychology, could not give us such principles. What we require is a *special way* of observing and describing our experiences such that we can glean from it knowledge of necessary truths. Husserl's technique for doing this involves what he calls *"reflection"*. We do not simply have and describe experiences, as a psychologist would, but we *reflect* upon our having these experiences. Thus, Husserl's method involves the sort of self-observation, "transcendental" self-observation, which we found in Kant's Transcendental Deduction. For Husserl, as for Kant, the deduction of "the possibility of the 'I Think' accompanying all my experiences" is the first principle of every philosophical inquiry. We do not examine simply the objects of our experience, but we examine the entire complex of my consciousness-of-objects which constitutes experience.

The intentional neglect of the worldly existence of the objects for consciousness coupled with this reflective attitude leads Husserl to describe phenomenology as "the suspension of the natural standpoint." This is the 'radical' beginning so often spoken of by Husserl. It means that the phenomenologist differs from all other scientists in that the subject of his examination is the autonomous and independent workings of consciousness. Unlike the biologist or the chemist, he is not concerned with objects except as they appear to consciousness. Unlike the psychologist, he is not concerned with the *cause* of an object's conscious appearance, but only with the *essential* nature of that appearance. For Husserl, consciousness is a separate 'realm', a 'world' of its own. In Husserl's terms, consciousness, *viewed from the phenomenological standpoint*, is a realm of *pure meanings* or *sense*. What the phenomenologist describes, therefore, is not facts about consciousness, but the *meaning* or *essence* of consciousness.

We have mentioned these notions of "meaning" and "essence" several times as central to Husserl's philosophy. Aristotle famously distinguished between the *"essence"* or *essential properties* of a thing and the *accidents* or *accidental properties* of a thing. The essential properties are "defining characteristics" which make some particular object a member of a species of objects. For example, the greenness of an emerald is an essential property, if it is a necessary truth that all emeralds are green. Similarly, the rationality of Socrates is an essential property of Socrates if it is a necessary truth that "all men are rational." We should recognize Kant's "analytic-synthetic" distinction at work here, and one might even apply his characterization of "one concept's containing another." *P* is an essential property of *X* if "X is P" is a necessary truth. (Alternatively, *P* is an essence [of *X*] if "X is P" is a necessary truth.) An accident or an accidental property is a property which is not essential. The size of an emerald is an 'accident', and the intelligence of a man is also 'accidental'.

Husserl is interested in *essences* (*Wesen*) or *meanings* (*Sinn*). He would not agree with the direction of our initial characterization above, however, because he would disagree that our talk of "necessary truth" is the defining trait of essences. Conversely, he will argue that the notion of necessary truth makes sense only because of essences. The problem, therefore, is to give an adequate analysis of and description of essences.

What has been described in as jargon-free a manner as possible in the past few pages is a brief outline of a method and philosophy which it takes Husserl over 50,000 pages to present and clarify. The outline should be already clear to us: phenomenology is the description of consciousness as a special realm of meaning or essences, and by examining this realm independently of any presupposed theories about the world or consciousness, we can derive necessary truths which will serve as foundations for mathematics, natural science, and human knowledge in general. The method of phenomenology is to *reduce* these experiences to *essential experiences* which are the subject matter of such a description. Phenomenology does not try to *explain* its findings, or even give us a philosophical theory about them (although, to be sure, Husserl sometimes cannot avoid this). The business of phenomenology is simply to get us to *"see"* that our consciousness is of such and such an essential nature.

The whole of Husserl's 'radical empiricism' is a set of techniques for *reducing* consciousness and its objects to a peculiarly phenomenological status. To so reduce our experiences, it is necessary to view them from a special reflective or phenomenological standpoint. This standpoint, however, is not simply one 'perspective' among others, as Nietzsche suggests, nor is it simply an alternative to the 'natural' standpoint of the 'naive' sciences. The phenomenological viewpoint is the only viewpoint that will allow us to obtain philosophical truth, and all other truths ultimately rest on philosophy. Consequently, phenomenology is not only a new way of viewing 'things' according to Husserl, it is the only *true* way of viewing things. All other viewpoints, including the 'natural viewpoint', are derivative of this primitive perspective. Thus, we must take Husserl's well-known rallying call, *Zu den Sachen Selbst* ("To the Things Themselves") very seriously. He is not simply giving us a new way of viewing philosophy; he claims to be giving us a technique for viewing ourselves and the world in a way undistorted by philosophical theories which have taken control over our perceptual and conceptual faculties.

All of this is still terribly vague, of course. How can we examine the objects of consciousness without examining at the same time the objects of the natural world? How is consciousness to be treated as a special autonomous "realm of Being," as opposed to one more set of facts about the world (that is, about human beings in the world)? How can an examination of consciousness give us necessary truths? Looking over our characterization of Husserl's phenomenology thus far, we are not even clear what it is that is to be looked at. What is an *experience*? What is a reflected-upon experience? What is an essential experience?

The Object of
Phenomenological Investigation

Husserl's phenomenology shares a central purpose with Kant's critical philosophy, the search for necessary truths that will serve as a foundation for mathematics, natural science, and knowledge in general. Husserl's affinity to Kant runs much deeper than this mutual interest, however, for Husserl views Kant's "transcendental method" as a half-conscious forerunner of the phenomenological approach to philosophy.[32] For Husserl, as for Kant, the business of philosophy is the examination of the immediate data of consciousness, or *phenomena,* and the result of such an examination shall yield certain necessary truths based on necessary structures of consciousness ("the essence of consciousness").[33]

Thus we might apply to our discussion of Husserl the opening sentence of Kant's *Critique of Pure Reason.* "There can be no doubt that all our knowledge begins with experience . . . (But though all our knowledge begins with experience, it does not follow that it all arises out of experience").[34] Like Kant, Husserl hastily moves from general talk of "experience," with its strong connotations of strictly empirical knowledge, to talk of "intuition" (*Anschauung*):

In whatever manner and by whatever means a mode of knowledge may relate to objects, intuition is that through which it is in immediate relation to them, and to which all thought as a means is directed. But intuition takes place only in so far as the object is given to us. This again is only possible, to man at least, in so far as the mind is affected in a certain way.[35]

The fundamental defect of the empiricists' argument lies in this, that the basic

requirement of a return to the 'facts themselves' is identified or confused with the requirement that all knowledge shall be grounded in experience. . . . Thus for 'experience' (Erfahrung) *we substitute the more general 'intuition' . . .*[36]

Unlike Kant, Husserl explicitly distinguishes between two very different notions of "intuition," only one of which is the equivalent of "experience" *(Erfahrung)* or Kant's "sensibility." The second sort of intuition, with which phenomenology and all philosophy is properly and uniquely concerned, is the sort of intuition which can provide us with nonempirical, "essential" insights. One can interpret Kant's doctrines such that our knowledge of the 'a priori *forms* of intuition' (including mathematics and geometry) is based upon such "intuition." Kant's "intuition" does not, in general correspond to Husserl's "essential" *(fidetic)* intuition. Closer to Husserl's notion would be the classical Greek conception of *Nous,* or the "intellectual intuition" which Kant allows only to God, or the same notion as it is used by Fichte and Schelling (and repudiated by Hegel in the Preface to the Phenomenology). These "essential intuitions" are capable of giving us necessary truths, and give us *Evidenz* on which all knowledge must be based. (This *Evidenz* in Husserl must be sharply distinguished from the more everyday notion of "evidence" which can give us only a certain degree of confirmation for empirical generalizations. "Adequate Evidenz" gives us necessary truth. "Adequate Evidence" gives us, at best, a reasonable but always limited warrant for accepting an always tentative empirical proposition.)

The 'given' for phenomenology is introduced by Husserl as *Primordial Dator Intuition (Primordial Dator Consciousness,* or *Primordial Dator Act*). The 'radical empiricism' we introduced is an exclusive appeal to the Primordial Dator Intuition/Consciousness/Act;

that very primordial dator intuition is a source of authority for knowledge, that whatever presents itself in 'intuition' in primordial form (as it were in its bodily reality) is simply to be accepted as it gives itself out to be, though only within the limits in which it then presents itself.[37]

Husserl calls this his "first Principle" or his "Principle of All Principles."[38] "Primordial Dator Intuition (Consciousness/

Act)" is used by Husserl both to refer to essential intuition and to refer to intuition in general. In *Ideas* (I), we find primordial dator consciousness to be a genus of which sensory experience and essential intuition are species:

Immediate seeing (Sehen) *not merely the sensory seeing of experiences but seeing in general as primordial dator consciousness of any kind whatsoever, is the ultimate source of justification for all rational statements.*[39]

Throughout his prolific career, Husserl is concerned with both essential and 'sensory' primordial dator intuition. He insists, however, that his interests in sensory intuition are also nonempirical interests in the "essence" of sensory intuition;

the pure phenomenology of experiences in general . . . has to do with the experiences that can be grasped and analyzed in intuition in their essential generality, but not with empirically apperceived experiences as real matters of fact . . . The essences directly grasped in essential intuition and the connections based solely upon the essences, are brought to expression descriptively in concepts of essence and lawful statements of essence. Every such statement is an a priori one in the best sense of the term.[40]

Husserl, like Kant, seeks the a priori conditions for all experience and knowledge. His interest in sensory experience is not an interest in particular 'contents', but an interest in the essential *forms* of that experience and the knowledge based on it. Husserl attempts to find these essential forms by "insight" into "thought-and-knowledge-experiences."[41] For Husserl, all philosophical investigation depends on essential insight into essential intuition and the essential forms of intuition in general.

What is intuition? Husserl tells us, as Kant had told us, that intuition is "that through which objects are immediately given." These objects, in turn, are called *phenomena*. Phenomenology is the study of whatever is immediately given in consciousness. Husserl does not present the concept of "phenomenon" in contrast to a concept of "noumenon" or "things-in-themselves": quite to the contrary, it is one of the central theses of his philosophy that *phenomena are the things themselves.*

Furthermore, Husserl rejects the distinction between the "faculties of sense and understanding" which is at the basis of Kant's account of phenomena. He takes Kant's "faculty view" as one of those unfortunate "presuppositions" which have corrupted the sound philosophical endeavors of the past. Thus, "phenomenon" for Husserl does not refer to the product of the "employment of the categories of the understanding to the manifold of intuition (given in sense)," but refers *simply* to the 'given' intuitions. For Husserl there is no distinction to be made a priori between those elements of intuition which are 'given' and those which are 'constituted'. This distinction, if it can be made out at all, must be made *on the basis of* the examination of phenomena, not as a presupposition of this examination. Thus Husserl includes in his notion of "intuition" *both* the products of Kant's *sensibility* and *understanding*. This has important philosophical consequences. Kant had identified the understanding as the primary source of a priori knowledge. Husserl claims that all necessary truths are given in intuition. Thus we might say that where Kant attempted to demonstrate the transcendental necessity of certain rules ("concepts") of the faculty of understanding, Husserl attempts to show that all such necessities are (like Kant's space and time) a piori forms or contents of intuition. In strictly Kantian terms, we might say that Husserl differs from Kant in eliminating all talk of the Understanding, equating *phenomenon* with the *given* in Intuition, and rewriting the entire *Critique of Pure Reason* as a modified *Transcendental Aesthetic*. (We shall see, however, that Husserl's problematic notion of "constitution" will render such an account one-sided.)

The various terms "intuition," "phenomenon," "Primordial Dator Intuition/Consciousness/Act," "seeing," and "given" are introduced in a system of mutually dependent characterizations; *phenomenon* is whatever is *given* in *intuition; intuition* is whatever is *given* to *consciousness; Primordial Dator . . .* is whatever is *given* in an immediate *'seeing'; 'seeing'* is 'grasping' what is in *intuition; Consciousness* is what is *given;* what is *given,* finally, is what can be immediately *'seen'* or *intuited*. Our understanding of these basic notions thus remains inadequate until we can break out of this circle. Husserl's persistent attempts to do this culminate in his phenomenological *reductions,* which we have yet to discuss. However, the notion of *reduction*, and what is reduced to what, can be clarified only by appeal back to these basic notions of "phenomenon," "intuition," "what is given," and so forth. We can now appreciate the seriousness of the methodological circle we spoke of earlier. Husserl will struggle throughout his entire career in the attempt to clarify these basic notions, and his characterizations, and thus his entire philosophy, will undergo serious modifications.

We can at least approach this family of terms by appealing to the initial demand which Husserl places on philosophy. The demand that philosophy must be presuppositionless and purely descriptive gives us a clue that the *given* (intuition or phenomena) are not theoretical or abstract entities[42] and are not an *interpretation* of anything, but are whatever can be simply described. *"Phenomena are given in intuition"* means that there is something which can be described apart from any theoretical or interpretive considerations. We still are not very clear what a phenomenon is, therefore, or whether there actually is anything which can be described without a theoretical framework or an interpretation. (Nietzsche and Hegel would both flatly deny the possibility of any such pretheoretical or preinterpretive structures. Nietzsche tells us that "there are no facts, there are only interpretations."[43] Hegel repeatedly insists on the need for the *Concept,* and his *"Phenomenology"* never pretends to be a pure description of consciousness apart from any theory of consciousness. It is rather a sequence of descriptions of various theories of consciousness, it being made very clear to us from the outset—for example, in the Preface to the *Phenomenology*—that there can be no description of consciousness which does not presuppose a theory about consciousness. What is this *given* in consciousness? and does it make sense to suppose that there could be any such givens? Again we shall find that Husserl has established, or reestablished, a central philosophical problem which he himself never satisfactorily solves.

We can move closer to Husserl's thinking by outlining some of the things which phenomena clearly are *not*. First, a phenomenon is nothing 'outside of' consciousness ("transcendent"). We have already mentioned that Husserl does not even accept Kant's notion of "noumenon" (which

Husserl calls "absurd"), and that a phenomenon therefore is roughly equivalent to what Kant called "that which appears." However, phenomena are not 'outside of' consciousness; in another, more interesting sense, phenomena are not *natural objects*. Husserl insists that consciousness (as viewed in phenomenology) is an 'ideal timeless realm', and not part of the 'natural' world of objects in space and time. Thus, the phenomenon (of) the tree which I intuit is the tree as it appears or "presents itself" to me. This phenomenal tree is not a natural object, it does not have spacio-temporal location as such, it does not have weight, is not made of wood, is not living, is not even 'real' (as opposed to imaginary or a picture of a tree). What is true of the tree as phenomenon is what is true of the tree as it appears. This distinction between the tree as phenomenon and the tree as a natural object is not Kant's distinction between the phenomenal and noumenal tree. Neither is Husserl claiming that there is *both* a natural tree and a phenomenal tree. He is not saying, as the traditional empiricists had said, that there is the object tree and my impressions (experience, "sense-data") of the tree. What makes Husserl's doctrine of perception so bizarre to philosophical tradition is that his concept of "phenomena" is not contrasted either with things-in-themselves or with the 'real' things 'behind' appearances. The absence of such a contrast makes a simple description of Husserl's doctrines unavoidably clumsy, for Husserl's rejection of these traditional distinctions leaves us without our traditional vocabulary for talking about "appearance," "reality," and the "things themselves." (Husserl's own use of this traditional terminology only increases confusion, which is why he attempts to avoid it as much as possible.) The contrast between the tree as phenomenon and the tree-in-itself, we shall see, is not a contrast between experience and something else, but rather a relationship between a single experience and a *system* of experiences. Husserl will teach us that our experiences of objects (in-themselves) are *constituted* —that is, constructed as complexes out of simple elements—out of experience. We may remind ourselves of Hegel's "absolute" destruction of the traditional subject-object distinction and his claims that there is no distinction between the objects and our experiences (knowledge) of objects. Husserl similarly argues the invalidity of this traditional epistemological distinction, and his famous *epoche* or "bracketing of existence" will not be designed to separate appearances and reality but rather to demonstrate to us the absurdity of making any such distinction.

The objects of phenomenological investigation are phenomena given in intuition. The task of phenomenology is to characterize the essences of various given phenomena and the essential form of intuition in general. Husserl's phenomenology becomes concerned with two inseparable traditional philosophical problems as this description is attempted. First, there is the problem already encountered, "How does consciousness reach beyond itself to grasp its object?" This problem of perception reduces to the problem of accurately describing the forms of intuition in which we experience objects and the essential forms of those objects themselves. It is in answer to this problem of perception that Husserl introduces his important notion of the perceptual "noema" and its relationship to our perception of objects.[44] Secondly, there is a problem of knowledge and truth which parallels the problem of perception. Husserl confronts the skeptic who doubts that we really know what we think we know, and who claims that the truth is unfathomable. Husserl wishes to object that the truth can be known and that we can really know that we know the truth. His campaign against skepticism leads him to claim that the truth is timeless, and that we can know it through insight into essential intuition. We can know the truth because we can examine *essences,* a priori structures of consciousness. The search for the truth—absolute and necessary truth—becomes a search for essences in our intuitions.

These two problems run together in Husserl's writings, and both are characterized as a demand for "objective truth." The problem of perception is, "Can we know objects?" The problem of knowledge and truth is, "Can we know the truth?" The former question thus becomes a special instance of the latter. One kind of knowledge (empirical knowledge) is knowledge of objects. Like Kant, Husserl wishes to challenge the skeptic's doubts that we can ever know objects in themselves and not just mere appearances. There are other kinds of knowledge, for example, knowledge of mathematics and

logic, which are different in kind from perceptual knowledge. In addition to the demonstration that perceptual knowledge is possible, Husserl must prove that nonsensory knowledge is also possible. His task is very close to that confronting the Logical Positivists who were to write several decades later (and many vocal "positivists," of his own time, including all those who referred to themselves as "empiricists" [Locke, Hume, Mill, and Brentano]), to show how our knowledge of the world could be based on experience and how we could know the eternal truths of mathematics and logic. Husserl's answers to these problems differ dramatically from the positivists, however, The positivists are to contend that our knowledge of the world is founded on a *causal* relationship between the world and our experience; Husserl insists that such a causal theory is incomprehensible. The positivists claim that we can know necessary truths because they are analytic. Husserl insists that analytic truths are trivial and that the a priori truths in question are synthetic. Both the positivists and Husserl place a high premium on experience, but the positivists limit experience to sensory experience and restrict meaningful nonempirical discourse to analytic truths. Husserl attacks positivism as a return to the old skepticism, not because their theories fail to give the certainty that philosophy demands, but rather because their *starting point* makes philosophical success impossible. Husserl argues that all forms of positivism begin from what he calls "the natural standpoint." It is to show what is wrong with this "natural standpoint" that Husserl introduces his *epoche.* The first step in solving the traditional problems of perception and truth is to destroy the traditional framework within which these problems are approached.

The Natural Standpoint
and Its Suspension: The *Epoche*

We have mentioned several times that Husserl insists that philosophy must begin by rejecting the 'natural standpoint' which is the starting point of the 'special' or natural sciences. However, although we have given slight indication that this standpoint involves presupposing what the philosopher must establish, for example, the independent existence of a 'real' or 'external' world and the sufficiency of causal explanations, we have neither indicated what the natural standpoint is, or why it should be suspended or abandoned or how it would be possible to suspend or abandon it. Furthermore, we have not put ourselves in a position to appreciate the 'radical' nature of Husserl's claim until we have seen just how far this 'natural standpoint' has permeated our philosophical thinking and how the acceptance of this standpoint involves all such philosophies in "demonstrable absurdities."[45]

Naturalism, properly conceived, is;

a phenomenon consequent on the discovery of nature, which is to say, nature considered as the unity of spacio-temporal being subject to laws of nature.[46]

Thus the 'naturalist' "has the tendency to look upon everything as nature, . . . (and) sees everything as nature, primarily physical nature."[47] The 'natural' world is identified by its 'externality,' its being 'out there' in space and time;

I find myself continually present and standing over against me the one spacio-temporal fact-world to which I myself belong, as do all other men found in it and related the same way to it. This 'fact-world' as the word already tells us, I find to be out there, *and also take it just as it gives itself to me as something that exists out there.*[48]

This given world, then, is the "spaciotemporal world of bodies in nature,"[49] and the key to the natural standpoint is the presumption that the existence of this world is totally independent of me. I might change the world in many ways, of course, but were I not 'here', the world would exist nevertheless;

The world and its property, "in and for itself" exists as it exists, whether I or we happen or not to be conscious of it.[50]

This *given* world is not only a world of physical objects. It is also a world in which there are other conscious beings:

animals, and perhaps also men are immediately there for me.[51]

Moreover, the natural world is not just a world of *facts,* but also a world in which I am *given* values;

world of goods, a practical world. Without further effort on my part, I find the things before me furnished not only with the qualities that befit their positive nature, but with value characters such as beautiful or ugly, agreeable and disagreeable, pleasant or unpleasant, and so forth. (Similarly for men and animals,) "they are my 'friends' or my 'foes,' my 'servants' or my 'superiors,' 'strangers' or 'relatives' and so forth.[52]

This thesis that values are 'in the natural world' would be acceptable to only a few Anglo-American philosophers of recent years (G. E. Moore's "intuitionism" would be one of the few ethical theories compatible with it, although *goodness,* for him, is still a 'non-natural property'). We have seen that Nietzsche sharply denies the existence of such 'moral facts' and Kant, Hegel and Kierkegaard, in various ways, make the same denial.[53] This thesis of value will become a central problem for the existentialist phenomenologists, notably Heidegger and Sartre.

The basic tenet of naturalism is that the world we perceive and know (and in which we value and act) is simply *given* to us as is. We might doubt or reject one datum or another, for example when we learn to recognize illusions, hallucinations, and perceptual errors, but,

all doubting and rejecting of the data of the natural world leaves standing the general thesis of the natural standpoint.[54]

Some entities may be "struck out of it (the world)," but "the 'it' remains forever."[55]

This presupposition of the existence of the world leads us to a remarkable philosophical realization; the givenness of the 'external' world is so basic to our knowledge that to question the existence of this world borders on nonsense. The natural standpoint (this acceptance of the world as given) provides us with the concepts of "existence" and "reality" ("real"). Thus we can question the reality or existence of a hallucinated centaur because we accept the natural standpoint. However, because it is the natural standpoint which provides these terms with significance, it makes little sense to question the existence or reality of nature (the world) itself. (One might compare this to our attempting to question whether the standard measure for one gram in Paris itself weighs exactly one gram.) Thus, 'the world' is that which provides the conceptual framework for making all judgments about existence; it, therefore, cannot be judged to exist or not to exist itself.

The general thesis according to which the real world about me is at all times known . . . as a fact world that has its being out there, does not consist, of course, in an act proper, in an articulated judgment about existence. It is and remains something all the time the standpoint that is adopted . . .[56]

The 'givenness' of the world is not the only feature of this natural standpoint. Of equal importance is that feature of the natural standpoint such that the world consists of objects which behave according to *universal laws;*

The World is the totality of objects that can be known through experience, known in terms of orderly theoretical thought on the basis of direct present experience.[57]

Every corporeal being is subject to laws of possible changes, and these laws concern the identical, the thing, not by itself but in the unified, actual, and possible totality of one nature.[58]

The study of the natural world (from the natural standpoint) gives us the various "Sciences of the World,"[59] which includes all the physical and, more broadly, the natural sciences. The natural science which Husserl is concerned to distinguish from philosophy is not limited to the sciences of nature, insofar as nature is limited to the totality of "material things," but to the study of any subject matter which adopts the natural standpoint. Thus, the sciences of psychology, sociology, and anthropology, although not normally classified as 'natural' sciences, are naturalistic in Husserl's sense. Furthermore, since values and the like are given in the natural standpoint as well as facts, these traditional studies of values which treat values as given are also natural sciences. Thus, all empirical approaches to value theory have been naturalistic. Notably, Nietzsche's "Genealogy of Morals" would be (by his own insistence) a naturalistic study.[60] Thus, for Husserl,

ethics, history, and the "cultural sciences" are natural sciences in just the same way as physics, chemistry, and biology. They assume the givenness of the world 'out there' as a totality of objects of possible experience interrelated by universal causal laws.

The attack on naturalism is in fact a general attack on philosophy with unquestioned yet debatable presuppositions. Thus Husserl's antinaturalism includes an attack on many doctrines and methods which would not normally be considered 'naturalistic'. This is true in part because 'naturalism' for Husserl refers to the 'standpoint' of an investigation as well as its subject matter, as we discussed above. It is sometimes the case that philosophies are rejected as 'naturalistic' because of very different kinds of presuppositions. For example, Husserl attacks the British empiricists for their *naturalism,* part of which involves a heavy reliance on a theory of *meaning* as a basis for their philosophy. Similarly, Husserl levies a heavy attack on historicism—the view that a proposition is necessary (or true) only within the context of a particular culture or conceptual scheme.[61] Historicism, because it adopts a type of psychologistic approach to the interpretation of necessary truth, falls within easy range of the key objections to all forms of naturalism. Naturalism cannot possibly, because of its own presupposition of the natural standpoint, give us philosophical certainty and necessary truth.

It must be clear that Husserl is not against naturalism *as such,* but only against naturalism as a *philosophical* approach. Key to such naturalism in philosophy is the "naturalizing of consciousness";

Characteristic of all forms of extreme and consistent naturalism. . . . is on one hand the naturalizing of consciousness . . . and on the other the naturalizing of ideas and consequently of all absolute ideals and norms.[62]

In other words, naturalism is a general form of Husserl's early psychologism. It is the attempt to apply the techniques of natural science to the problems of the a priori disciplines of mathematics, logic, and philosophy, and reduce all necessary truths to well-confirmed empirical generalizations. In his mature philosophy, Husserl has come to identify consciousness as the realm of ideal (a priori) laws rather than causal (natural) laws. Thus the naturalistic, as opposed to the phenomenological study of consciousness, is the fatal step to the naturalizing (psychologizing) of principles which can only adequately be interpreted as necessary or a priori truths.

To naturalize consciousness is to break it into mental *entities*—peculiar natural objects with causal relationships to each other and "as bound to certain physical things called bodies."[63] Consciousness is treated as one more object in the world, and the "stream of consciousness" is literally a flowing sequence of peculiar natural objects in a peculiar multidimensional field. The 'contents' of a naturalized consciousness can be identified only with reference to the 'external world', and every idea, perception, calculation, or feeling is interpreted as a different worldly object. Now much of this may be a caricature of considerably more sophisticated naturalistic views of consciousness. Husserl yet insists that the basic tenets of naturalism, the treatment of every object as a natural object determined by universal natural laws, is basic to every form of naturalism in philosophy;

From our point of view, there is no essential alteration in this interpretation [of naturalism as psychophysical nature, determined by rigid law] when in the positivistic sense (whether it be a positivism that bases itself on a naturalistically interpreted Kant or one that renews and consistently develops Hume) physical nature is sensually broken up into complexes of sensations, into colours, sounds, pressures, etc. and in the same way the so-called 'psychical' is broken up into complementary complexes of the same or still other sensations.[64]

The resulting "sense-datum" theory and the 'naturalizing of consciousness' had secure origins in Western philosophy long before the German psychologists. Husserl traces it back to a perversion of Descartes by the English philosopher John Locke, in his "plain historical method" (see Chapter 1);

The Cartesian transcendental 'mens' became the "human mind" which Locke undertook to explore; and Locke's exploration turned into a psychology of the internal experience. And since

Locke thought his psychology could embrace the transcendental problems, in whose interest he had begun his work, he became the founder of a false psychologistical philosophy. . .[65]

Far from being totally critical of the intent of Locke's philosophy, however, Husserl is quick to defend Locke and his successors;

Empiricistic naturalism springs from the most praiseworthy motives. It is an intellectually practical radicalism, which in opposition to all 'idols', to the powers of tradition and superstition, to crude and refined prejudices of every kind, seeks to establish the right of self-governing reason to be the only authority in matters that concern truth.[66]

In fact, this naturalistic empiricism has close similarities to Husserl's own philosophical approach,

Now to pass rational or scientific judgments on facts means being guided by the facts themselves, getting away from talk and opinion back to the facts, questioning them in their self-givenness, and laying aside all prejudices alien to their nature.[67]

It is the naturalism that bothers Husserl, the attempt to explain,

cognition as a fact of nature . . . a psychological fact, . . . (and) as any psychological fact, it can be described according to its kinds and internal connections and its genetic relations to be investigated.[68]

His attack on naturalism becomes a more generalized attack than that of the *Logical Investigations*, against, not only psychologism, but all forms of philosophy and (a priori science) which take up the natural standpoint.

What is wrong with naturalism? It seems only reasonable that the

victorious advance of the natural sciences . . . has favoured philosophical empiricism, and has made it the dominating, and indeed in the circles of empirical science almost exclusively dominating, conviction.[69]

Can philosophy thus follow the natural sciences? The problem of philosophy is the defense of the *validity of the natural standpoint*: How are we justified in accepting the world as given, in accepting the world with a Principle of Universal Causation, in accepting the propositions of mathematics as necessarily true of this world? Husserl denies that mathematics and necessary truth can be validated by appeal to the natural standpoint. Conversely, since the validity of the natural standpoint itself presupposes the validity of certain necessary truths, we have to ask whether these particular necessary truths can be justified independently of the natural standpoint. Thus we have two questions; the latter concerning the validity of those necessary truths which are statements of the natural standpoint (Kant's Categories), and the other concerning the validity of necessary truths which are not statements of the natural standpoint (but may nevertheless be applicable to this standpoint). Husserl does *not* accept Kant's reduction of mathematics and geometry to a priori propositions about the nature of space and time.[70]

We have already discussed in some detail the inadequacy of naturalistic accounts of necessary truths in our discussion of Husserl's encounters and battles with psychologism. Naturalism fails because it cannot give certainty to truths which are certainly true. The truths of mathematics cannot be justified by appeal to naturalism because certain or necessary truth cannot be established by the techniques of natural science. Thus the natural world and the natural standpoint are irrelevant to the establishment of necessary truths.

Now it may be evident that the natural standpoint is relevant to those truths which are themselves statements of the natural standpoint; for example, the 'given' existence or reality of the world, the universality of causal laws among events in that world. However, it should also be evident why these truths cannot be established by appeal to the natural standpoint. If it is the natural standpoint itself we are calling into question in our philosophical investigations, we cannot use this same standpoint to justify itself. One is reminded of Hume's argument against any attempts to prove the principle of induction (one tenet of the natural standpoint) by appealing to its suc-

cessful uses in the past; one cannot validly demonstrate a principle by invoking the authority of that very principle. Hume's argument here can be extended to the *set* of principles which define the natural standpoint. The Principle of Universal Causation cannot be established by appealing to certain causal necessities; the existence of the world 'out there' cannot be established by pointing 'out there'.

In perception the perceived thing is believed to be directly given. Before my perceiving eyes stands the thing. I see it, and I grasp it. Yet the perceiving is simply a mental act of mine, of the perceiving subject. . . . How do I, the cognizing subject, know if I can ever really know, that there exist not only my own mental processes in these acts of cognizing but also that which they apprehend?[71]

The natural standpoint cannot be called upon to testify in its own behalf.

To expect from natural science itself the solution of any of the problems inherent in it as such . . . or even merely to suppose that it could contribute to the solution of such a problem any premises whatsoever, is to be involved in a vicious circle.[72]

In short, what is in question is cognition itself (the *possibility* of knowing natural objects), not the *fact* of cognition (whether we actually know objects correctly), for we are yet (philosophically) unsure whether there is any such operation. Philosophy is first and foremost concerned with the validity of cognition, but by definition,

The natural attitude of mind is as yet unconcerned with the Critique of cognition.[73]

what is taken for granted *in natural thinking is the possibility of cognition.*[74]

Natural science, therefore, is philosophically impotent;

All natural science is naive in regard to its point of departure. The nature that it will investigate is for it simply there . . .

*Natural science, then, simply follows
consistently the sense of what the
thing so to speak pretends to be as
experienced.*[75]

The 'special' (natural) sciences simply
assume the validity of those truths we
wish to validate. The validity of all these
sciences, therefore (all human knowledge), is dependent on the success of
philosophy to establish their foundations
in an investigation of cognition in general.

While Husserl retains strong affinities
with traditional empiricism, it is this same
empiricism which remains his foremost
antagonist. What is basically wrong with
the empiricist philosophy is that it is
circular, in that it assumes what it tries to
demonstrate and that it attempts to establish necessary truths by inductive (empirical) procedures. The empiricist gets
into this "radical absurdity," according to
Husserl, because he fails to distinguish
two distinct philosophical concepts, and
thus fails to distinguish two very different
methodological claims. First, there is the
claim, accepted by Husserl as well as the
empiricists, that philosophy must return
"to the facts themselves" (*Zu den Sachen
Selbst*). Secondly, there is a claim, treated
by the traditional empiricists as equivalent
to this first one, that all (nonanalytic)
knowledge is founded upon *sensual
experience*;

*The fundamental defect of the
empiricist's argument lies in this, that
the basic requirement of a return to
the 'facts themselves' is identified or
confused with the requirement that all
knowledge shall be grounded in
experience.*[76]

According to Husserl, all that is given in
consciousness (that is, in primordial dator
consciousness/intuition) is not derived
from sense-experience. Notably, our
knowledge of geometrical truths is not so
derived. A return to the 'facts' of consciousness is a very different claim from
a restricted return to the experience of the
senses. This difference makes all the difference between the success of the central
phenomenological claim—that essences
are intuited—and the reduction of this
same proposition to utter meaninglessness.
Husserl distinguished between two kinds
of intuition, those which do simply give
us the products of sensory awareness, but

also those which give us essences,
"eidetic intuitions." Correspondingly,
there are 'facts of experience', 'sciences of
experience' (natural science), 'eidetic experience', and 'eidetic science'. It is the
latter which can provide us, supposedly,
with necessary truths.

Empiricism's failing, one which Husserl
studiously seeks to avoid himself, is ultimately a failure to question one's own
methodological principles and concepts.

*To maintain straight away that all
judgments permit of being grounded
in experience and even demand such
grounding, without previously submitting
to study the essential nature of
judgments with due regard to their
fundamentally different types [i.e.,
necessary vs. empirical] . . . that is a
'speculative construction a priori', which is
none the better for proceeding in this
instance from the empiricist side.*[77]

It is such failure which makes any philosophy "unscientific," and Husserl's own
conscientiousness and concern for 'pure
scientific' philosophy explain his own intense concern with clarification of method.
Against one who insists from the outset
that all (nonanalytic) knowledge is
grounded in experience, there might be
no successful refutation; against Hume's
skepticism, Husserl argues:

*Prejudices blind, and one who sees
only empirical facts and grants intrinsic
validity only to empirical science will
not be particularly disturbed by absurd
consequences that cannot be proved
empirically to contradict facts of
nature.*[78]

Skepticism is an intolerable alternative to
Husserl, and a skeptical conclusion to any
argument does not establish a conclusion,
but constitutes an indication that something has gone wrong. Husserl often aligns
himself with Hume's conclusions to present his own problems. For example,

*Shall I, with Hume, reduce all
transcendent objectivity to fictions
lending themselves to psychological
explanation but to no rational
justification?*[79]

The answer to this rhetorical question is
assuredly "No!" for it is the "absurdity"

of such conclusions which has resulted in Husserl's philosophical "crisis." Skepticism is not a solution, and the fact that Hume's empiricism leads us to it is sufficient grounds for giving up Hume's (Locke's, et al.) empiricism. We are in need of a new, nonnatural, peculiarly philosophical starting point,

a phenomenology of consciousness as opposed to a natural science about consciousness.[80]

The naturalist standpoint, Husserl argues, is not confined to traditional empiricism. What makes it such a source of danger to philosophical thinking is its current subversion of even those philosophies which do not accept empiricism. Historicism, for example, in all its forms (but Husserl primarily had in mind the work of Dilthey) accepts enough of the naturalist standpoint to invalidate its results. A philosophy that so clearly denies the possibility of justifying the necessity of any proposition outside the context of a particular historical society depends only on the presuppositions of naturalism, for it is but a generalized empiricism; philosophical truths are abstractions within a particular society. More importantly, and more dramatically, the fallacy of naturalism enters even into the seemingly secure camp of the idealists. Idealists, like the empiricists, fail to realize that,

Every process of insight involving judgment, *and in particular the insight into unconditionally* universal *truths, falls* under the concept "dator intuition", which has indeed differentiations of different sorts, *above all, those* that run parallel to the logical categories.[81]

Whereas the empiricists err by denying the possibility of universal and necessary nonanalytic truths, the idealists err by denying that these can be founded on intuition. Both commit the same error, according to Husserl, they fail to appreciate the possibility of *eidetic intuition.* This in itself does not commit the idealists to naturalism; what does commit them is their attempts to explain the origins of our knowledge of necessary truth. Descartes formulated several criteria for necessary or *'apodeictic'* truth; necessary truths were those seen by the "natural light of rea-

son," and those ideas which were "clear and distinct." Most generally, there was the notion of 'self-evident truth', which remained a central concept of subsequent rationalism. The problem with this, according to Husserl, is its "obscurity," first of all, but, when clarified, the notion of "self-evidence" can be seen to be a covertly *psychological* notion;

These so-called feelings of self-evidence, of intellectual necessity and however they may otherwise be called, are just theoretically invented feelings.[82]

Husserl claims that even Kant, the most sophisticated of the idealists and the idealist closest to Husserl's own "transcendental idealism," accepted dangerously naturalistic presuppositions. Kant did not use naturalist techniques and concepts in his philosophy, Husserl grants, but he did incorporate many positions inherent in naturalism to his own philosophy when he accepted the then fashionable "faculty" model of mind, a model which is clearly indefensible within Kant's own first *Critique* and just as clearly a piece of psychological theorizing rather than an established doctrine of the transcendental philosophy:

It also becomes clear that just as every scientific, so every prescientific application of nature must in principle remain excluded in a theory of knowledge that is to retain its univocal sense. So too must all expressions that imply thetic existential positings of things in the framework of space, time, causality, etc. This obviously applies also to all existential positings with regard to the empirical being of the investigator, of his psychical faculties, and the like.*[83]

Philosophy cannot begin within the natural standpoint;

Philosophy lies in a wholly new dimension. It needs an entirely new point of departure and an entirely new method of distinguishing it in principle from any 'natural' science.[84]

In phenomenology,

in addition to all other adjustments a new way of looking at things *is necessary, one that contrasts at every point with the natural attitude of experience and thought.*[85]

This new standpoint can be achieved, according to Husserl, by a "radical alteration of the natural thesis,"[86] by the first "phenomenological reduction" or *epoche.*[87]

The natural standpoint, while we are 'under' it, is naturally never made explicit, so that we do not 'judge' the existence of the (spacio-temporal) world at all. ("We cannot doubt under the natural standpoint.") However, in philosophical reflection,

We can treat the potential and unexpressed thesis exactly as we do the thesis of the explicit judgment. A procedure of this sort, possible at any time, is, for instance, the attempt to doubt everything which Descartes . . . undertook to carry through.[88]

It is in philosophical reflection (and only in philosophical reflection) that this method of universal doubt is appropriate and even desirable as a starting point;

We can attempt to doubt anything and everything, however convinced we may be concerning what we doubt, even though the evidence which seals our assurance is completely adequate.[89]

We should not be surprised, therefore, to find Husserl proclaim himself in the methodological company of Descartes, whom he lauds as the progenitor of transcendental phenomenological philosophy:

The fundamental thought of Descartes in its wonderful profundity is already pressing towards it (phenomenology),[90]

and later, in a book entitled *Cartesian Meditations;*

Rene Descartes gave transcendental phenomenology new impulses through his Meditations; their study acted quite directly on the transformation of an already developing phenomenology into a new kind of transcendental philosophy. [Husserl is here talking about his own development and not the history of philosophy into which Descartes directly intruded.] Accordingly, one might almost call

transcendental phenomenology a neo-Cartesianism, even though it is obliged . . . to reject nearly all the well-known doctrinal content of Cartesian philosophy.[91]

However, we do not truly *doubt* the existence of the world for Husserl as for Descartes, we rather "suspend judgments about its existence," "put it in brackets," "abstain" from accepting it (the literal translation of *'epoche'*).

We do not abandon the thesis we have adopted, we make no change in our conviction. . . . *And yet the thesis undergoes a modification—while remaining in itself what it is, we set it as it were "out of action," we "disconnect it," "bracket it." . . . We can also say, The thesis is experienced as lived, but we make 'no use' of it. . .*[92]

The disagreement with Descartes, as Husserl presents it, is a disagreement between the need to *doubt* the natural standpoint ("We add the supposition of non-being")[93] and the need only to suspend judgment (to "use the *epoche* which bars me completely from using any judgment that concerns spacio-temporal existence (*Dasein*)").[94] The difference between Descartes and Husserl, then, is that Descartes thinks it to be clearly intelligible that we suppose that our belief in an external world is false, while Husserl maintains only that we ought not to assume it as true;

With Descartes, this is so markedly the case that one can say that his universal attempt to doubt is just an attempt at universal denial.[95]

This difference seems trivial only if we insist that every proposition which is not true is false. The possibility of the *falsity* of the natural thesis is simply not considered in Husserl's philosophy. This means that we "suspend" all natural science, but we do not suppose that it might be (that is, its most abstract principles might be) false. With the abstention from judgments concerning 'objectivity.

every thesis related to this objectivity must be disconnected and changed into its bracketed counterpart.[96]

What is this difference between Husserl and Descartes? Both men can allow themselves to accept only propositions which are apodeictic or certainly true, and for both men, such judgments are only those which concern themselves with "immediate knowledge" (more properly, intuition). Notably excluded are any judgments about the natural world (including the now-explicit judgment that there is such a world), for we could be wrong in any such judgment (we could be hallucinating or dreaming according to traditional arguments). Then, Descartes adds the problematic supposition that there is no such external world, that there might be an "evil demon" fooling him into thinking that there is such a world. Descartes tries to argue out of this supposition to re-establish an 'objective' world of which we can be certain. Husserl, on the other hand, does not even suppose that there might not be an external world, does not suppose that we might (generally) be fooled about it, and makes no attempt, therefore, to circumvent these suppositions to establish the 'real' existence of such a world. Unlike Descartes, Husserl does not suggest that we suspend all judgment, but only those judgments which constitute the natural standpoint; and, Husserl tells us not to *doubt* the natural standpoint, but only not to make use of it;

We limit the universality of this epoche.
. . . We put out of action the general thesis which belongs to the essence of the natural standpoint, *we place in brackets whatever it includes respecting the nature of Being:* this entire natural world therefore *which is continually "there for us", "present to our hand" and will ever remain there, is a "fact-world" of which we continue to be conscious, even though it pleases us to put it in brackets.*[97]

The *epoche* is not Descartes' universal doubt, but, rather,

a certain refraining from judgment which is compatible and unshakeable because self-evidencing conviction of the Truth.[98]

How is it possible that the *epoche* involves a *suspension* of the natural standpoint, but yet need not and does not entail at least the entertaining of the possibility that the thesis of the natural standpoint

is false? A different way of stating the same thesis is to recast the *epoche,* not in the image of Descartes' doubt, but in the more approximate resemblance of Kant's transcendental deduction. The philosopher, after performing the *epoche,* does not talk about *things* (objects), but speaks only about his knowledge and experience of things. In other words, the *epoche* is purely a technique for reflection; in fact, it is the technique which puts us into the philosophical (reflective) attitude.[99] In reflection, consciousness "turns upon itself." The *epoche* is a technique for assuring ourselves of the phenomenological standpoint. Any judgment about a relationship between consciousness and anything else is a return to the psycho-physics against which Husserl is campaigning. In phenomenology, we can consider propositions about consciousness and nothing other than consciousness; all other considerations are *bracketed.* This does not mean that they are false, or even possibly false. It is more like the sort of mental 'bracketing' I perform when I study philosophy. It is not the case that the inane chores and nuisances of everyday life are denied by me or supposed possibly not to exist, but yet I effectively put them out of my thinking entirely, in the sense that they have no relevance to what I am doing. What is bracketed is not considered to be even possibly false; it is not considered relevant to the investigation at present. In the case of phenomenological investigation, the investigation is the reflective examination of consciousness. What concerns me is the way I experience things, the way I know things. Whether or not there is anything known in fact does not trouble me, for it is simply consciousness itself I am attempting to describe. Thus, in the example given at the end of the preceding section, the phenomenological investigation of my perception of the tree concerns itself only with how I perceive the tree, without (*prima facie*) regard for the actual existence of the tree. I do not deny the tree's existence, or, for the moment, even consider whether or not it exists. I bracket the natural world, and with it the natural tree, and I now ask (whether or not this is 'real', or a picture, or a hallucination), what is it for me to be conscious of a tree-phenomenon?

We have yet to see how such an *epoche* is possible, and how it avoids the sort of skepticism we find in Hume. Is there anything remaining after we suspend our belief in the natural world? Once we have suspended our belief in the natural standpoint, is there any way of regaining that belief without perverting our philosophy? How is Husserl not in the same unfortunate position as every other Cartesian, beginning with the reflective search for philosophical certainty and ending up with the admission that one can never achieve objective knowledge from a subjective starting point?

Husserl attempts to solve all of these problems in a typically phenomenological way. Rather than attempt to give us a priori arguments for the possibility of objective knowledge, he simply turns to consciousness itself, and attempts to *show* us what is essential to knowledge, what is essential to perception, what is essential to consciousness in general. This investigation of consciousness plays a peculiar central role in Husserl's philosophy. On the one hand, it is the subject matter for study by the phenomenologist after the *epoche* has been performed. Yet it is also, we must not forget, necessary for the very defense of the possibility of the *epoche*. What must consciousness be like (a very Kantian question) in order for the reduction of consciousness to be possible (a very un-Kantian question)? Thus, the most important *essence* to be investigated will be the essence of consciousness, just in order to find out how it is possible to know any essences at all.

Intentionality, Objects, and Acts of Consciousness

What is left—what is this phenomenological residuum—after we have performed the *epoche*? Very simply, what is left is consciousness, but what is this? If we look to the empiricists for their description of this consciousness, we find that it is simply a collection of "experiences," ordered in time, a "stream of consciousness." Hume, the most thoroughgoing of the British empiricists, states this most clearly in his classic rejection of the earlier (Locke's) notion of self-identity:

What must become of all our particular perceptions upon this hypothesis (that there is a unifying self)? All these are different and distinguishable and separate from each other, and may be separately considered and may exist

separately, and have no need of anything to support their existence. . . . I never catch myself at any time with a perception, and never can observe anything but the perception. . . .[100]

Such a view of consciousness is unwarranted by careful observation, Husserl tells us, and empiricism fails, in spite of its correct approach, because it presupposes an incorrect theory of consciousness and therefore neglects to give an adequate description of consciousness.

What will an adequate description disclose to us? We have already seen that Husserl insists that there are two very distinct kinds of intuition, of which "empirical intuition" or "experience" is the less philosophically important. We also intuit essences, and the intuition itself is of a distinct sort, an *eidetic* intuition as opposed to a mere "experiencing." But a careful description of a 'reduced' consciousness discloses to us far more than two kinds of intuitions. An accurate description of consciousness discloses to us a remarkable *structure* which previous philosophers have neglected at their peril. The thesis that consciousness is a stream of experiences (intuitions) on which so many philosophies have been based, is shown by Husserl to be simple-minded. Like Kant, he sets out to show us that consciousness is much more than 'atomic' intuitions; it has structures, and these structures can and must be described independently of any particular experiences. A central inquiry of Husserl's phenomenology, therefore, is the examination of the "essence of consciousness."

Husserl's 'philosophy of mind' is largely derived from the 'empirical psychology' of his teacher, Franz Brentano. From Brentano, Husserl inherits his two central contrasts between consciousness and physical objects: (1) consciousness consists, not in passive reception of sensory data (as we find in the British empiricists for example), but of *acts* of consciousness; (2) consciousness is *intentional*. This latter thesis, in a phrase, tells us that consciousness always takes an *object*.

Everything, although not in the same way, contains something as object in itself. In the idea something is ideated, in judgment something is acknowledged or denied, in love loved, in hate hated, in desire desired, etc.[101]

Conscious processes are also called intentional; *to be conscious of something; as a* cogito *to bear within itself its* cogitatum.[102]

An act of consciousness is always *directed* towards something. When we love, we love something; when we are afraid, we are afraid of something; and when we perceive, we perceive something. However, this object of an act of consciousness need not be an existent or real object. I can be afraid of demons, although there are no demons; I can imagine a ten-finger human hand, although there is no such thing; I can hallucinate a golden mountain ahead of us on the highway, although there is no golden mountain present. This peculiar sort of object, which is an object *for* or *of* consciousness but need not be a real object, is most evident in certain sorts of mental acts (philosophers after Frege refer to them as "propositional attitudes") of belief, assertion, and the like. For example, we might say that "Husserl believed that essences could be intuited," or "Frege asserted that Kerry[103] was confused." What is the object of belief or assertion in these sentences? It is not essences or Kerry. Rather, what is believed or asserted is whatever is the object of belief (namely, *that* essences could be intuited, or *that* Kerry was confused). These objects hold a special place of great importance in philosophy, for their nature has long been a source of puzzlement.

Brentano's theory of intentionality states that an act of consciousness is intentional even if not directed to a real object ("even if a fiction"). In other words, I can be afraid of something that does not exist, but my fear must be fear of *something.* Brentano thus characterizes all conscious (psychic) acts,

by what the scholastics of the Middle Ages referred to as the intentional (also the mental) inexistence of the object, and what we . . . would call relation to a content, direction upon an object (which is not here to be understood as a reality) or immanent objectivity.[104]

Similarly, Austrian philosopher Alexius von Meinong (1853–1920) introduced a 'Theory of Objects" in which he gives a detailed account of the *subsistence,* as opposed to actual or real *existence,* of such objects. The objects of most con-scious acts, for example, fearing, loving, perceiving, imagining, hallucinating, and the like, he simply calls "objects," whether or not these actually exist. In his most famous example, he queries how it is possible to talk about, question the existence of, and even falsely maintain the existence of such nonexistent objects as *The Golden Mountain.* Meinong replies that we must delineate a realm of objects whose existence is purely mental, whether or not they have actually existing correlates. Every psychological act is directed towards an *object* whether or not there is any such *real* object. Meinong isolates a specific kind of "ideal object" which he calls an *"objective"*: an objective is the object of believing, knowing, asserting, doubting, and the like; it is what many contemporary philosophers would call a *proposition.* It is not a sentence, or a state of affairs, but a peculiar entity that gives *meaning* to what we say, believe, know, assert, doubt, etc.

In Husserl, this notion of an 'object of consciousness' which may or may not have *real* existence is of central importance. The *epoche* has insured us that we remain unconcerned with the real existence of objects and concerned only with consciousness itself. We asked, "What is left when we reduce everything to consciousness"? We now see that a great deal is left over —the intentional counterparts of all the reduced objects remain, along with a great many other intentional objects which have no *real* counterparts. Phenomenology, therefore, is the study of the objects of consciousness, whether or not there are any real objects corresponding to them.

This notion of intentionality gives Husserl a mighty weapon against the simplistic philosophy of mind of the early empiricists. They had been inclined (after Descartes) to distinguish simply between *immanence* and *transcendence,* between consciousness itself and the object 'outside of' consciousness. Husserl points out,[105] however, that there is serious confusion residing in this distinction, because it fails to recognize another, more philosophically important distinction between the *immanence (reelle Immanenz)* of that which is an act of consciousness—and the matter *(hyle)* of consciousness—and the transcendence of that which is an *object* for consciousness ("self-givenness as constituted in *Evidence"*). This second distinction between "immanence" and "transcendence," however, is within the scope of "immanence" in the first, and transcendent objects (in the second sense) remain after the *epoche.*

Formerly philosophers had simply distinguished between the "content of consciousness" or what is (immanent) "in consciousness" and what is "outside of consciousness" or "in-itself." Husserl (who accepts a form of the same metaphor of consciousness as a quasi-spacial "realm") claims that there are two distinctions hidden here; first, there is the distinction between objects as they are known and objects as they are in themselves apart from any possible knowledge of them (Kant's distinction between phenomena and noumena; Locke's distinction between "ideas" and "substance"). It is this distinction which Husserl wishes to reject as meaningless. One can draw a distinction, however, between consciousness and its objects in another sense. The object of consciousness can be said to be "transcendent" whether it is perceived, dreamt, hallucinated, or imagined, insofar as it is an *object* at all. To say that something is an object is to say that it is perceived (or imagined) as something which can be characterized without reference to the subject. For example, I may see or hallucinate a *centaur,* and I can describe this centaur without raising any question as to whether it exists or not (that is, whether I am perceiving or hallucinating). In either case, the centaur appears to be eighteen feet long, horse-tailed, bushy bearded, and smiling. The centaur is a transcendent object in this second sense because it can be characterized in this way and an endless number of details can be provided.[106] A transcendent object, on this characterization, is whatever can be described without any reference to the perceiving (hallucinating) subject. In this sense, Brentano's and Meinong's "objects of consciousness" are transcendent whether or not they exist as 'real' (natural) objects. Contrasted with this sense of "transcendent" is a sense of "immanent" which is limited to acts of consciousness (acts of the Ego, in Husserl's later works) and to that conscious matter (*hyle*) which cannot be described in detail as an object (for example, formless color flashes or ringing in the ears). When Husserl speaks of "transcendence" and "immanence," he is distinguishing between the independently describable object of consciousness (the *noema*) and the act of consciousness (noesis) and what is not characterizable as an object.

This is so important to an understanding of Husserl's view of perception (and, we must add, to the views of Bolzano, Meinong, and Brentano) that it would be worth our while to consider an example in detail.

Let us suppose that we are looking with pleasure in a garden at a blossoming apple-tree . . . From the natural standpoint the apple-tree is something that exists in the transcendent reality of space, and the perception as well as the pleasure of a psychical state which we enjoy as real human beings. . . . Let us now pass over to the phenomenological standpoint. The transcendent world enters its 'bracket'; in respect of its real being we use the disconnecting epoche. . . . yet a relationship between perception and perceived. . . . is obviously left over, . . . everything remains . . . even the phenomenologically reduced perceptual experience is a perception of "this apple-tree in bloom, in this garden, and so forth."[107]

From the phenomenological standpoint, there is no immediate difference between perceiving a tree and hallucinating a tree. In phenomenology, we are concerned with this tree only as an object of consciousness, not as an object in the world. In this examination of *phenomena,* or "the thing as it appears as such,"[108] we are unconcerned with the *transcendent* insofar as this signifies objects independent of consciousness (Kant's *noumena*). In his earlier works (including, for the most part, *Ideas*), Husserl simply insists that the transcendent in this sense is not the *interest* of phenomenology. Later (*Cartesian Meditations*), we shall find that Husserl adopts the much stronger thesis that it makes *no sense* to speak of such transcendent objects. The foundation for this *idealism,*[109] however, is to be found in *Ideas,* for even there Husserl tells us that "All reality exists through (our) dispensing of meaning,"[110] and that to ascribe reality as taken "from the concept of natural reality is simply nonsense."[111] Yet he insists that his philosophy is "no subjective idealism." Husserl does not hold that we are aware "only of our own ideas."

The "essence of consciousness" is to *act* towards ("intentional") *objects,* which may themselves not be *real* objects. What then are these *objects* of consciousness, and do they have any relationship to objects in themselves? It is in this area that Husserl's careful drawing of distinctions becomes most valuable. His theory of perception is largely a reaction against the simplistic theory of the empiricists. According to them, we have experiences (impressions, images) and then, mysteriously, these become converted to ideas of objects. This is a passive mechanism, and, in Locke's metaphor, the mind is a blank tablet in which experiences leave their mark. The impressions are *caused* by the objects themselves; thus, we have a psychophysical or *causal* theory of perception. Physical objects *cause* our mind to have experiences of the objects. The theory, then, has two types of entities, a physical object and a mental impression of the object (which gives rise to an *idea*) in a causal relationship. A more sophisticated empiricism developed after Kant's *Critique of Pure Reason* drawing a distinction between the object in itself (Kant's *noumenon*), the experiences (presumably) caused by the object (the manifold of intuition) and the experiences of the object itself (*phenomena*).[112] This new intermediary gives us what many refer to as "sense-data," or "raw experience." Thus Russell, in his very important treatise on *Logical Atomism,* tells us that what we see immediately are sense-data, and that objects are 'logical constructions' out of sense data. This more sophisticated causal theory states that there are physical objects which cause us to have experiences which we interpret as experiences of objects. Perception of objects, on this account, is always mediated by sense-data, and is always problematic (since we have no way of knowing whether the physical objects are really there or not, or whether they are as we interpret them to be from sense-data or not).[113]

Husserl's theory departs from this sense-datum doctrine in several important respects. First, it dispenses with a causal theory, and rejects as "absurd" all talk of physical objects which cannot be immediately perceived. Secondly, it places its approximation of "sense-datum" (*hyle*) in

a relatively secondary role in the theory, and concentrates the analysis of perception on the notion of "constitution" (like Kant's "synthesis"). Thirdly, Husserl does not take this to be a passive process but a conscious *activity* of constitution. Fourthly, Husserl attempts to answer, as he claims the empiricists do not, how it is that hyle or sense-data, which are themselves uninterpreted or 'meaningless', can be understood or interpreted as experiences of objects.

The object of perception, for Husserl, is the object *itself;*

It is a fundamental error to suppose that perception (and every other type of intuition of things, each after its own manner) fails to come into contact with the thing itself.[114]

What things are, . . . they are as things of experience.[115]

An object that has being in itself is never such as to be out of relationship to consciousness and its ego.[116]

There is, therefore, no *mediated* perception of objects; we perceive objects *themselves,* not sense-data which are caused by objects and then interpreted as experiences of objects.[117]

How do we see objects? What is the object of perception if it is not a physical thing? According to Husserl, the empiricist creates problems for himself because he begins by supposing, after Descartes, that what we are immediately aware of are our own experiences and not objects, and then, of course, the existence of objects becomes problematic. Husserl says that what we are immediately aware of are objects, that the Cartesian starting point is really the result of careless phenomenological description. According to the Cartesian, we immediately 'see' experiences and then interpret them; according to Husserl, the process of seeing is already an interpretive process.

This idea of 'seeing' as an interpretive process does not square at all well with Husserl's methodological insistence on the need for pure description of experience. As we shall argue in the final section of this chapter, Husserl never does reconcile two opposing yet central ideas in his philosophy; phenomena are said to be *given* in intuition, yet phenomena are also said to be *constituted* (constructed). The conflict between 'seeing' as interpretive and the possibility for pure description of experience without theoretical prejudice is one manifestation of this general unresolved conflict. If all 'seeing' is theory-laden, then pure description of phenomena without theory is impossible. (This is not to say, however, that one might not give a pure phenomenological description of a theory which is already implicit in all conscious activity. Presumably Kant's description of the categories and principles of the understanding would be of this sort.) However, if phenomena are constituted by us, then it is easy to see why it is that we see objects instead of pure sense data, but it is not clear why we could not constitute objects in very different ways, or even constitute our experience without objects. We see here the very same sort of problem of 'constitution' according to 'rules' of consciousness which plagued Kant's first *Critique* and led Fichte to his Copernican counter-revolution. We shall see a similar 'counter-revolution' in the Existentialist revolt against Husserl. This is, of course, unintelligible if one begins by distinguishing the object itself from the object as it appears, and it is here, suggests Husserl, that every philosopher from Descartes to Kant through the turn of the century runs afoul. In our examination of the perceptual process, we reflect on (that is, Husserl tells us to reflect on) that which is immediately perceived. What is immediately perceived is not raw sense-experience, not is it the object-in-itself in either the noumenal sense or the sense that philosophers (e.g. Descartes) had thought perceptual judgments to be incorrigible. What we see is an object itself, but *in one and only one aspect*. The immediate perception, therefore, is neither uninterpreted sense datum nor a complete object; it is an *aspect of an object*. Husserl calls this "object of individual perception" or "individual perceptual presentation" a *noema* (plural, *"noemata"*); it serves as the central term in Husserl's theory of perception.

A noema is the immediate object of perception; it is the object of perception as a "partial presentation," or a "one-sided presentation." (There is some inconsistent terminology here; sometimes Husserl simply talks about the noema as the object of perception; elsewhere he talks of the noema as an aspect of the object or as "pointing to" the object. What is impor-

tant is that we keep in mind that the object of perception is the object itself, and the noema is the appearance of this object from 'one side' or in one 'aspect'.)

The unity of perception of an object is, as Kant said, a perception of a *synthetic unity*. Where does this unity come from? According to the empiricists, it remains a mystery. It is assumed that the unity of perception is caused by the unity of the object itself. However, this will not do, as Kant and Husserl both point out, because perception itself can never examine these alleged causal ties between the object itself and the object as it is experienced. Kant's solution to this dilemma was the supposition that the unity of apperception is contributed to intuition by the faculty of understanding. Husserl, however, in denying Kant's faculty view of consciousness, cannot accept this interpretation. For him, the unity of the perceived object is *given in intuition*. There is no extrinsic unification of experience; this unity is rather "itself an immediate phenomenal datum." The unity of the object is not, as Russell and so many others suggest, a construction out of experience. It is itself a fundamental given in experience. I do not have experiences and then interpret them as an apple tree; I have an experience of an apple tree.

Here again arises the conflict between Husserl's notions of the 'given' in intuition and constitution of objects. In *Ideas,* the central thesis is that stated here. In later works, Husserl moves closer to the thesis that all objects are interpreted (constituted) as such by us (see "The Transcendental Ego").

If the object of perception is given to us in one aspect by a noema, we can provide an account of our perceptions of objects in themselves which makes no reference to objects 'outside of' experience. The object-in-itself or "thing" perceived is a *system of noemata*. Every noema "refers itself to other noemata," and perception of an object is perception of noemata of a particular system. Let us refer back to Husserl's apple tree example. The object of immediate perception is the ('reduced') apple tree, but only from this particular viewpoint. Now we might ask why I take this particular perceptual *noema* to be an aspect of an apple tree, rather than an aspect of a cherry tree, or an aspect of a painting of an apple tree, or a hallucinated apple tree. This particular percep tion cannot assure me, or give me *Evidenz* (for Husserl *Evidenz* is assurance, not just a clue) that this is an apple tree, or a real apple tree, because this particular perception may be consistent with very different systems of noemata. However, the *noema,* as we just said, "refers itself" to other noemata. A simple way to put this is that every noema carries with it (in a *noematic nucleus)* an indefinitely large set of *expectations,* or a "*horizon.*" On my perception of this particular *noema,*—an apple tree from this perspective—I expect that I should experience the same noema if I were to blink my eyes and then open them. I expect that I should have appropriate noematic experiences if I should move to the right or the left, or circle 'around' the tree.[118] I expect that 'the tree' would resist a hard kick, and that I should be able to climb it, and that it will still be there in two days. I should expect that apples will appear on its branches and not cherries. These expectations (and there are as many expectations as there are 'aspects' of the tree) are all *fulfillable* in noemata or perceptions of the tree from different perspectives (we are not limiting ourselves to *visual* perspectives here). The feel of the trunk, the sound of the wind through leaves, the pain in my leg after kicking the roots, are all perceptions of the tree from various perspectives, and thus various aspects of one and the same perceptual object, the apple tree. It is the fulfilling of the various noemata of a system which allows us to confidently assert that we perceive this particular object. The complete or adequate fulfillment of a system of noemata may be, of course, impossible. It is in *this sense,* and this sense only, that the tree is *transcendent* to all possible perceptions. Adequately perceiving the tree, that is, from every possible perspective, is an endless process and our perception of the tree is never completed. However, each noema, in its reference to other noemata, gives us an *Idea* (in Kant's sense of the *Transcendental Dialectic)* of the tree in its *totality,* as a *thing-in-itself.* It is in this sense that we cannot know things-in-themselves according to Husserl; we cannot actually experience every possible noema of the system. We do know of the system, and we can outline, at least, the noemata which must be fulfilled if one were to have complete or adequate knowledge. This ultimate unity of perception, however, can never

be experienced, but must remain an *ideal.* This ideal, for Husserl, is a thing's *essence,* the thing perceived from every possible standpoint. This notion of *essence,* however, as the thing-in-itself, is but one of several uses of this important concept in Husserl. In this sense, one must see *what* the essence of the object is, but cannot ever *fulfill* the expectations in that essence. In another sense, however, one which Husserl uses most often, to 'see' or to 'grasp' an essence is simply to see *what* a thing is,—that is—to see the kinds of noematic expectations that are required.

Perception of an object is 'immediate', in that we 'immediately' perceive the object itself from a particular perspective. The object as a coherent noematic system allows us to explain how it is, at one and the same time, we can immediately perceive objects but at the same time be wrong about them. For the empiricist, immediate perception is incorrigible perception, perception about which one cannot be wrong. For Husserl, immediate perception is the perception of a noema, but one can be wrong about the object perceived. To be wrong, the expectations of the noema must be unfulfilled. For example, I perceive an apple tree from *this* perspective and expect that this noema will refer me to others. If, however, I blink and open my eyes and I do not again perceive the apple tree, the noema *explodes,* the expectations are unfulfilled. If I kick the tree with my foot and feel and hear the tearing of canvas, and then perceive a patch of grass and fluttering colored sheet at the base of the 'tree', I also find my expectations unfulfilled. This position is most important as an alternative to empiricism. On the one hand, the noemata are not given to me uninterpreted, but they are given in a system of expectations or with a *horizon.* In other words, I perceive this as a tree immediately, but then it may turn out that I am wrong. According to the empiricist, I have experience (sense-data) and interpret them as experience of a tree, and then, when the system breaks down (the noemata unfulfilled) I decide that my *interpretation* was wrong. For Husserl, the noemata come with an interpretation (a noematic nucleus—this system of expectations). In retrospect, I can change my mind about the system, but that noema was *seen as a tree.* I may have been disappointed in my expectations, but I was not wrong in my perception as a perception of a tree. (This is *not* to say, we must insist, that the perceptual noema is a Cartesian incorrigible given. One can misperceive a noema as well as misconceive the noematic meaning.)

Because all perception is perception of an object from some aspect, one cannot talk about perception as one talks about objects themselves. One is inclined to describe experience as experience of objects *simpliciter* instead of experience of objects from some viewpoint. This is disastrous in cases in which noematic expectations are unfulfilled. I see a tree, and it disappears: what can I say about my original perception of the tree? It was not a perception of a tree after all? But that is misleading at best. What I saw was a tree, but it turned out that future perceptions have taught me that there was no tree there. One cannot say that there was a tree in the first perception but not in subsequent perceptions. This becomes a problem only so long as we talk about perception as we talk about physical objects. The first noema was a noema of a tree, a tree from one aspect; future noemata were not noemata of a tree.

This problem can be differently put if we adopt the modern notion of 'opaque contexts', and add perception to the list of predicates which introduce such contexts. "John believes that Cicero is evil" is not translatable into "John believes that Tully is evil," even though Cicero and Tully are the same person. The reasoning behind this is that we are talking about John's belief and not Cicero. Similarly, "John perceives the tree" must be construed not as a relationship between John and a physical tree, but as a relationship between John and the object of his experience. Thus, "John perceives a tree" ought to be construed as "John experienced (what he took to be) a tree." This is fully compatible with there not being a tree. Descriptions of what one perceives may thus be non-interchangeable. "John saw a painting" might be false, even though John did see a painting of a tree (he saw it as a tree).

Husserl does give us an equivalent of the empiricists "sense-data," what he calls the *matter* of perception or *hyle*. However, these are never uninterpreted or un-'synthesized', but are *given* as noemata, as significant or meaningful objects of experience. The noema is organized *hyle:* thus Husserl talks of the noema as the "mean-

ing of a perception." However, we must remember that an act of perception always has a *noema,* never simply *hyle; there are no uninterpreted (insignificant) perceptual acts.* (But there may be some uninterpreted and unintentional *hyle* [which are not given in *acts;* for example, pains, tickles].)

We have said that every perceptual (conscious) act has a noema, and that every object of perception has indefinitely many noemata. This leads us to the interesting view that, for Husserl, although it is the object (that is, one aspect of it) which is the immediate object of perception, we never perceive a material object as it is in-itself, that is, from all possible perspectives. We perceive objects as and only as noemata. It is in this sense in which objects are 'transcendent' but also the objects of 'immediate perception'.

Husserl's view of perception is, summarily, that every object of perception is 'immediately given' as a *noema,* which is a significant or organized *hyle,* which carries with it, in its noematic nucleus, a set of expectations for fulfillment in subsequent noemata: the object-itself (the 'essence of the object') is just this system of noemata. There are gaps in this account, however. We have insisted that the organization of *hyle* into noemata cannot be caused by an 'outside' physical object, but that this organization is in itself *given* as a phenomenal datum, that is, in intuition. However, Husserl does not leave us with this account of noematic unity as given, but adds to it an account of the source of this unity or *morphe,* in the act of perception itself, the perceptual *noesis.*

The act of perception (more generally, the act of consciousness) has played no role in our discussion of perception thus far. With its introduction, a curious duality (or perhaps, contradiction) appears in Husserl's account of perception. We have noted that the unity or meaning of noema is simply given in intuition but that this unity is *constituted* by *acts* (*noeses*) of *intending, objectification,* and *apperception.* In this theory of *constitution,* Husserl comes very nearly back to Kant's notion of the "synthetic unification of apperception" by the Understanding: in his doctrine of the 'given' intuition, because he rejects the causal theory of perception (that is, that physical objects cause sensations and their unity), Husserl is unable to explain how it is that experience is given as unified experience of an object. We shall return to this very serious problem in the final section of this chapter. For now, it will suffice to provide a brief examination of this *noesis* as it appears in *Ideas*.

Where the noema was tied to the content and object of consciousness, the *noesis* is an act of consciousness, that which *intends* or is directed towards an object (of consciousness). The central function of this intending is to provide a "formative synthesis to shape material elements (*hyle*) into intentional experiences."[119] In other words, the noesis is responsible for the organization of experience into experiences of objects. However, just as there are indefinitely many noema for any given object, there are indefinitely many noeses for every object. So far, we have spoken primarily of perception in this section. However, the perceptual act is only one of many acts which is directed toward objects. Among the *cognitive* acts of consciousness (those involved in *knowing* an object), there is also imagination, doubting, judging, asserting, attending, believing, knowing, questioning, and so forth. Some of these are more central acts than others (attending, judging), but all are different attitudes towards the objects of consciousness. One can perform different acts towards the same object; for example, I can judge about, doubt, question, assert, know, believe, refuse to believe, joke about, pretend not to understand, or try to forget about one and the same proposition. Similarly, I may see a tree, or may attend to, or study or imagine or remember or hallucinate the tree or I may "disbelieve my senses." I can adopt any number of different attitudes (that is, direct any number of acts) towards the same noema or the same perceptual object. Because it is the noesis which constitutes or forms the significance or meaning of the noema, the noesis and noema are *correlates,*

characters which we find *as inseparable features of the perceived, fancied, remembered etc. as such, of the meaning of perception, the meaning of fancy, the meaning of memory, and as necessarily belonging to these in correlation with the respective types of noetic experiences.*[120]

Thus we find Husserl often bypassing his own distinction by talking about "noetic-noematic structures" because of the "thor-ough-going correlation" between them. The noema which is given in intuition as (an aspect of) the object of consciousness is nevertheless *constituted* by the act of consciousness of which it is an object. We can understand this as we understand that the noematic nucleus—the set of expectations for other noemata—will be different depending upon the act. If I *perceive* a tree, I should expect to be able to climb it; if I hallucinate a tree, I should not expect to do so. Yet, although noesis and noema must always be 'correlated', particular noeses and noemata may vary vis-à-vis each other.

intuition and the intuited perception and the thing perceived, though essentially related to each other, are in principle and of necessity not really and essentially one and united.[121]

Husserl's student, A. Gurwitsch, has taken great pains to show that the noesis-noema 'correlation' is not a dualism.[122] Gurwitsch, who favors a strong idealist interpretation of Husserl, is particularly anxious to protect phenomenology from the traditional 'wedge' between act and object which leads idealism to skepticism. We can see the sense in which Gurwitsch is correct: A (particular) noema is independent of a (particular) noesis, but noeses and noemata, in general, cannot be abstracted from each other. This cementing of noesis and noema is not sufficient to protect Husserl from skepticism, as we shall see in the next section. What Gurwitsch's interpretation of Husserl does is to move both noesis and noema over to the idealist side in an analysis, which focuses upon the noema as a "perceptual Gestalt" that is given in consciousness. But this return to the noema-noesis as Cartesian given simply raises again Husserl's own question, "how is it possible for consciousness (here, the noetic act and the noema) to reach its object?" One might balance Gurwitsch's model with an interpretation which places less concern on the "dualism" of noesis and noema and more concern with the relationship of noema and object. The closer noema and object become, the less room for idealism and skepticism. Such an interpretation is found, for example, in the work of Dagfinn Føllesdal[123] who follows Husserl's analysis of the noema of *ideal* objects (for example, objects of mathematics). As such, the noema *is* a meaning (where Husserl says the noema *has* a meaning[124]). On this model, the noema is the meaning of an object. But then we seem to lose that essential part of Husserl's analysis in which the noema is "the perceived as such." In our analysis here, we have tried to maneuver in between these two authoritative but extreme interpretations. The noema points to its object through its noematic nucleus (its meaning). In the limiting case of an *ideal* object, the noema, the object, and the noematic nucleus coincide (as in Føllesdal's analysis).

There are noncognitive noeses as well as the cognitive noeses which occupy most of Husserl's attention. There are "affective, appetitive, and volitional noeses" which are also given in experience ("grounded in presentations"). I can, in addition to perceiving a tree, *enjoy* the perception. I can, in addition to perceiving an apple, *desire* to eat it. I can, in addition to surveying the tree, *attempt* to climb it. These various acts are also acts of consciousness, and (unlike Kant) all acts of one and the same consciousness from one and the same standpoint. These "value-laden" acts, which will so much occupy Heidegger and Sartre, play little part in Husserl's own investigations (until his very last works). In our study of Husserl's phenomenology, it will simply suffice to mention them.

Our survey of Husserl's theory of consciousness has shown us that consciousness consists in *acts* (*noeses*) and sensory matter (*hyle*) which together give us intentional *objects* (*noemata*) (or, more properly, which together give us *noemata* with their horizons which "point to" or are aspects of intentional and transcendent objects). One most important element has not been mentioned, the *agent* who performs these various acts. This, for Husserl as for Kant, is the *Transcendental Ego*, the *pure Ego*. It is here that the Cartesian *cogito* becomes the model form of the act of consciousness. According to Husserl (but not explicit in Descartes), this *cogito* is necessarily intentional, that is, thinking must always be thinking *of* something or other. However, the central import of Descartes' *Meditations* remains throughout Husserl, "the thesis of my pure Ego is necessary and plainly indubitable." In Husserl as in Descartes and Kant, we find that every *cogitatio* (thought) requires a *cogito!* "The 'I think' must be able to ac-

company all my presentations."[125] Furthermore, although it is 'behind' our every experience, the ego can be known only upon *reflection*. All consciousness consists of acts of a pure ego towards its objects, which it is responsible for constituting.

The Transcendental Ego and Our Knowledge of Objects: An Unresolved Problem

In our examination of Husserl's theory of consciousness, we have seen that consciousness consists of acts of a pure *cogito* or *Ego* directed towards its objects or *noemata*. We have said little about this Ego, for its role in Husserl's philosophy is varied and problematic. On the one hand, Husserl's *Ego* is described as "absolute": this Ego is *discovered* in reflection and constitutes its objects which are therefore dependent on it for their existence. On the other hand, Husserl speaks of the Ego as dependent upon its objects (not 'absolute') and itself 'constituted in reflection'.

The problem of formulating an acceptable doctrine of the Ego is now a familiar problem for us. Descartes had 'discovered' this Ego as the indubitable subject of all thinking. He clearly saw that the Ego was not a *person* but only that which did the thinking, and consequently he called the ego a "thinking *substance*." Philosophers of various persuasions adopted derivative views of self-identity, (for example, Leibniz' monads; Locke's empirically discoverable mental self). Hume denied that there was any such mental substance to be discovered through experience or reason, but even he could not avoid referring to him*self* when attempting to state his thesis ("*I* cannot catch my*self* . . .") Kant's "I Think" is a reply to both Hume and Descartes, an attempt to provide a notion of "self" which is nonempirical but which captures the insight of the *cogito*. Husserl once again (as Wittgenstein just after him) attempts to introduce a transcendental subject, a "nonpsychological I," into philosophy and describe it in detail. As we noted with Kant, however, once one has introduced an Ego that is the subject of every experience and the object of no possible experience, there is nothing which can be *described*. Since Husserl insists that phenomenology must restrict itself to pure description, we can easily see why the notion of the *Ego* will give him such trouble.

In the *Logical Investigations*, Husserl remains faithful to his 'pure description' demand (even though he has not fully formulated it yet) and rejects the concept of a Transcendental Ego. There is little discussion of any concept of Ego or Self and there is an argument reminiscent of Hume's attack on Descartes' *cogito* (and surprisingly like Sartre's critique of Husserl's *Ego* in *Transcendence of the Ego*). Husserl identifies consciousness simply as a "bundle" of acts; there is no need of a "referential center."

The *cogito* appears early in *Ideas*[126] and is introduced in Cartesian fashion as "necessary." When the *epoche* is performed, the *cogito* remains "unbracketable," and we are told that it is "the ego and its experiences" on which we reflect in phenomenology. Yet *Ideas I* makes little use of this *cogito* and its role in that work is little more than that of a necessary truth which can be conveniently ignored while the business of phenomenological inquiry is carried through. The role of the Ego in perception and in phenomenological reflection is left unexamined. The Ego itself is not described; in fact, Husserl still maintains the rigorous empiricism of *Logical Investigations* and insists that the *Ego* cannot be described;

The experiencing ego is still nothing that might be taken for itself and made into an object of inquiry on its own account. Apart from its "ways of being related" or "ways of behaving", it is completely empty of essential components, it has no content that could be unravelled, it is in and for itself indescribable: pure Ego and nothing further.[127]

In *Ideas II*, Husserl turns to the neglected Ego and describes it as a "soul" (*Seele*) which is "passive" for the most part. The Ego is described as a "functional center" (compare the rejected notion of the "referential center" in *Logical Investigations*) and as a "polarity" to which intuition "happens." In *Ideas II*, the Ego "constitutes itself," a claim which is reiterated in the fourth *Cartesian Meditation*.

If we were to focus our study of Husserl on just the earlier writings, we should be able to formulate a reasonably coherent picture of the role of the Ego in acts of consciousness. The insistence that the Ego is a "center" and mostly "passive" and "constitutes itself" would seem to bring Husserl's early conception of the Ego in line with Kant's theory of the "I Think." This Ego is not a substance, not describable apart from its necessary role in perception, and it is as necessary for the existence of (its) objects as (its) objects are necessary for it. The picture we get from the early writings of Husserl's theory of consciousness is very similar to the picture Kant gives us in the "Refutation of Idealism" in the first *Critique*. The Ego and (its) objects are "polarities" each necessary to the other. The Ego has a decided role in knowledge of these objects, in that it is this Ego which provides the forms of intuition and Categories of Understanding within which objects can be known. Yet this Ego is passive so far as intuition is concerned and cannot be said to "create" its objects in any meaningful sense. Of course, there is an unresolved ambiguity in Kant as well as in Husserl on this point; it is unclear to what extent the contribution of the Understanding (or of "constitution" by the Ego) is truly a "productive" as opposed to a "reproductive" process.[128] Here, this ambiguity is not nearly so serious as it becomes in Husserl's later writings.

In the writings of the period represented by the *Cartesian Meditations* and *Formal and Transcendental Logic* the *cogito* regains its status as the Archimedean point of philosophical investigation. Husserl continuously talks about the Ego as "absolute," meaning that all objects exist only by relation to it but that it exists independently of its objects. In several curious early passages, he maintains that the Ego would survive even a "total destruction of the world." The *Meditations* refers to the *Ego* as a "monad," marking the striking resemblance between Husserl's conception of the absolutely independent Ego viewing *its* entire world from its own vantage point and Leibniz' model of the "windowless" absolute perceiver. We are told that

the monadically concrete ego includes also the whole of actual and potential conscious life, . . . Consequently the phenomenology of this self-constitution coincides with phenomenology as a whole (including objects).[129]

and that,

Objects exist for me, and are for me what they are, only as objects of actual and possible consciousness.[130]

In this later period, a more general change occurs in Husserl's philosophy as a result of (or as a cause of) the change in conception of the Ego. In *Ideas I* and *II*, the "phenomenological reduction" referred to the *epoche* and the suspension of the natural standpoint. Moreover, this *epoche* was a methodological principle, a technique for assuring us of a "presuppositionless" philosophy. In the *Cartesian Meditations* there is a *transcendental reduction* which is also referred to alternatively as the "phenomenological reduction." Both these reductions are accompanied by the "eidetic reduction" of intuition to *essential* intuition. In *Cartesian Meditations* and other works of the period, a variety of terms are introduced, for example, "the transcendental-phenomenological reduction" and the "transcendental *epoche*." This unfortunate terminological smoke screen hides some most radical changes in Husserl's conception of his method. In the *Ideas I* and *II*, reference is made to a "realm of *Ideas*" and to "the phenomenological realm," but these expressions are best interpreted metaphorically. The "realm" discovered by the methodological *epoche* is the natural world "reduced"; it is not a different world at all. Husserl repeatedly redescribes his quest in *Ideas* as a quest for understanding of our knowledge of the natural world; this quest could not be accomplished through an examination of some other world. In *Cartesian Meditations*, however, it becomes increasingly clear that our introduction to the *transcendental realm* is not intended as a metaphor or as a methodological ploy. The transcendental reduction of the *Meditations* does not simply assure us of proper phenomenological reflection; it teaches us that "all true knowledge is a knowledge of transcendental subjectivity":

It is not a temporary, but a permanent deliberate abstention from belief in the existence of the world, an abstention which I, as phenomenologist, am bound to observe permanently.[131]

The changes are particularly dramatic with reference to the place of the Ego in these reductions. In all cases, the Ego remains "unbracketable." The early *epoche* effected a reduction to *pure consciousness* in which the Ego is a necessary inhabitant; the transcendental reduction of the *Meditations* is a reduction to the *pure (transcendental) Ego*. The attempt to retain the same terminology throughout these changes tends to hide them from the casual reader. However, these changes are far from negligible, and we shall soon see that the changes in the conception of the Ego and the reductions manifests a serious and perhaps fatal problem that Husserl never succeeded in resolving.

Husserl is never very secure with this conception of an Absolute Ego; presumably he never lost the suspicions he held against such a conception in *Logical Investigations*. Consequently, Husserl's conception of the Ego in the writings of 1928–1932 shows the signs of strain between his Cartesian preoccupation with the necessity of the *cogito* and his radical empiricist demand for pure description. In earlier discussions, we saw that Husserl reacts viscerally to skepticism and that one of the enemies to be crushed by his philosophy is the skeptic who claims we cannot know anything except our own "subjectivity." However, the doctrine of the Absolute Ego threatens Husserl with this same skepticism, for the doctrines that everything is relative to the Ego and that "all knowledge is knowledge of transcendental subjectivity" entails the skeptic's conclusion that we cannot know anything except our own subjectivity. In reaction to his perilous position, Husserl often throws himself into the "realist" camp and demands that he is not committed to this unwanted position. Realism here is the doctrine that objects (the natural world) exist independently of any consciousness of those objects (of that world). For example, we are told

The world and its property, "in and for itself" exists as it exists whether I or we happen or not to be conscious of it.[132]

But to deny that one holds a solipsistic doctrine is not to prove that one's thesis does not commit him to solipsism. Husserl struggles to save both his absolute Ego and his realism, an impossible contest. In the 1931 Preface to the English translation of *Ideas I*, we find this attempt to squeeze between the horns of his dilemma:

the result of the phenomenological clarification of meaning of the manner of existence of the real world . . . is that only transcendental subjectivity has ontologically the meaning of Absolute Being, that it only is non-relative, that is, relative only to itself; whereas the real world indeed exists, but in respect of essence is relative to transcendental subjectivity, and in such a way that it can have its meaning as existing reality only as the intentional meaning-product of transcendental subjectivity.[133]

In the earlier writings, the introduction of the Ego as an active agent in the knowledge of objects raised the problem of how much the Ego is responsible for producing its objects in addition to simply knowing them. As the tendency to interpret the *Ego* as absolute becomes more marked in the later writings, this ambiguity becomes a tragic flaw. As the *cogito* changes from a necessary but negligible principle to the basic premise of all philosophy, Husserl finds himself facing the same skeptical attacks that plagued Descartes. Where Descartes was rescued by his belief in God's beneficence, Husserl can allow himself no such transcendent (as opposed to transcendental) luxury. Once the Absolute Ego is introduced, the committment to solipsism seems unavoidable. ("The 'way in' to consciousness having been outlined, the interest now turns to the 'way out' or to the consideration of the constitutive problem of truth and reality.")[134]

If the Ego *constitutes* its objects, what phenomenological grounds could there be for supposing that the world has any existence apart from its creation by the Ego; in other words, what defense does Husserl have against skepticism? Do objects have only 'constitutional' existence depending on the Ego? Or are they independently existing and *"given in intuition"* (Primordial Dator Intuition) as we are told in *Ideas I?* Moreover, what is the role of phenomenological reflection in all of this? Husserl usually talks as if the structures described by the phenomenologist are waiting there to be discovered. What if some of the structures 'discovered' by reflection are rather created in reflection? For example, it may be that the Ego is not discovered in consciousness at all but is produced by the reflective act of the *cogito;* in other words, the Cartesian "I think, therefore I am" is not a description of a structure of consciousness at all but

an act or "performance" in which the "I" is created. This thesis is argued by such very different philosophers as Jean-Paul Sartre[135] and the logician Jaako Hintikka.[136]

In our discussion of Husserl, we have already suspected that there are two divergent tendencies threatening to wrench his phenomenology apart. Even in *Ideas I,* the introduction of the concepts of "intuition" and "constitution" and the notions of "noema" and "noesis" gave rise to two very different accounts of the relationship between consciousness and its objects. On the one hand, an object is described as a system of noemata whose unity is *given in intuition.* Accordingly, phenomenology is the description of this unity as it is given and phenomenological reflection itself contributes nothing to this unity and maintains its "presuppositionless" philosophical stance. It is this view of consciousness as described by phenomenology which we find in *Logical Investigations* and in much of *Ideas I.* However, there is a second picture emerging from *Ideas I* and becoming more evident in later writings; we introduced the notion of "constitution of objects" as a kind of "construction of a complex from simple parts" and found that Husserl's theory of knowledge had much to say of the "constitution of objects by consciousness" and "by the ego." The role of the noesis or noetic act in perception is that of "signifying" and "constituting" the unity of the object by giving it meaning (*Sinn*). In later writings, this second picture becomes the very strong claim that objects exist only as objects constituted by the absolute ego. It is this account which drives Husserl towards solipsism.

We can now see that the varied conceptions of the Ego are a result as well as cause of these overall tensions in Husserl's thought. As the emphasis is on pure description of what is given in consciousness, the Ego, insofar as it need be mentioned at all, plays a passive role and need not be distinguished from consciousness. As attention turns to the active contribution of consciousness to understanding its objects, the Ego as an agent is introduced. As more stress is placed on the dependency of objects on the acts of the Ego and as the Kantian concept of a "polarity" of mutual dependency is neglected, the Ego is consequently conceived of more as an Absolute. As the Ego and its "transcendental realm" become more central to

Husserl's phenomenology, the danger of solipsism increases.

How can Husserl defend his phenomenology from unwanted commitment to solipsism? To do so, he must show that his theory of consciousness is not committed to the position that objects exist only insofar as they are perceived (that is, the subjective idealist position of Berkeley's *esse est percipi*). To do this by exorcising the theory of constitutional acts of consciousness would be to sacrifice what Husserl himself considers a main theme of his philosophy.[137] The problem is to interpret Husserl's conception of "the constitution of objects" in such a way that solipsism is not entailed by his theory and such that it is possible to maintain the demand that phenomenology concern itself with "pure description." The problem can be stated simply enough; Husserl is committed to a method which demands that we limit ourselves to descriptions of objects *given* in experience; yet a major doctrine of Husserl's theory of experience is that the objects of experience are *constituted* by consciousness. Is this method compatible with this doctrine?[138]

The ambiguity in Husserl which forces us to confuse his notion of the given and the constituted in consciousness might be traced to a feature of his philosophy which we discussed at the very beginning of our discussion. Husserl's phenomenology is often understood as a philosophical method as well as a kind of philosophical doctrine. We recall that Hegel criticized Kant for failing to realize the inseparability of his critique of knowledge and his use of that same knowledge. Husserl, in spite of his own equation of philosophy and method, falls into the same trap as Kant and falls under Hegel's critique, applied skillfully in this case by Sartre. Husserl fails to realize to what extent his own investigations determine the subject matter of those investigations. Husserl often talks as if conscious self-reflection does not alter consciousness at all, but Hegel's argument is that any reflection of consciousness on itself necessarily changes consciousness. Sartre's argument, as we have anticipated it, is that there is no Ego as Husserl believes, in consciousness, it is the act of reflection that *creates* the Ego. How much of phenomenological 'description' is truly description? How much is a reflective creation of conscious structures which were not there before?

This confusion of method and subject matter is nowhere more manifest in Husserl's works than in his changing conception of the role of the phenomenological reductions. Apart from the changes in the reductions themselves, we find a serious change from the use of the reduction as a methodological device to the conception of the reduction as a philosophical truth itself.

Husserl introduces the *epoche* as a methodological necessity, as a technique for assuring us that our phenomenological description of consciousness will not be contaminated with prejudices from the natural standpoint. The phenomenological standpoint does not give us a *true* picture of the world while the natural standpoint gives us a *false* one. The purpose of the *epoche* is to allow us to *justify* the natural standpoint from the unbiased phenomenological standpoint. With this interpretation of the *epoche*, we might make the equivocation of "constitution" and "clarification" legitimate by insisting that the notion of "constitution" applies only in that peculiar situation in which one looks at the world after the *epoche*. As such, the "constitution of objects" is a phenomenon described only from the phenomenological standpoint and is therefore a part of and only a part of the philosopher's inquiry; it is a temporary abstention and not a normal feature of consciousness. This interpretation is brought forth in Husserl's lectures on *The Phenomenology of Internal Time-Consciousness*[139] where he stresses that "objects are not constituted, only cognition is."

Expressions like "origin-analysis" and "genetic account" can be found from *Logical Investigations* all the way through *Formal and Transcendental Logic,* and *Experience and Judgment.* Such expressions point to Husserl's insistence that phenomenology describes the basic units of intuition and then accounts for the fact that we see a world of objects. "Constitution" might then be restricted to that process by which consciousness is seen to construct objects out of these basic perceptual units *without making any claims at all about the nature of the objects themselves.* Thus we might interpret Husserl's phenomenology as making a much less 'radical' claim than we originally supposed. He still rejects a causal account of knowledge (that is, things-themselves *cause* impressions in us), but his insistence on the illegitimacy of the distinction between objects themselves and objects of consciousness can no longer rely on his equation of objects and objects of cognition. On this interpretation, Husserl's theory is a theory of how consciousness creates a unity out of its perceptions and thus perceives objects. This interpretation can say nothing whatsoever about the possibility that there might be objects other than those perceived by us. The phenomenological reductions assure us that we shall describe the cognitive process with reference only to consciousness itself, but this methodological restriction guarantees the phenomenological propriety of the resultant philosophical description only at the expense of reintroducing skepticism once again. To see this, we need only notice how nearly identical this interpretation of Husserl is to Kant's transcendental idealism. The phenomenological *epoche* performs the same function as Kant's 'Copernican revolution' and produces a theory of cognition from the "subjective" standpoint only at the expense of ignoring the "thing-in-itself" and allowing it to be a constant plague to philosophy. On this interpretation, Husserl gives us a theory of cognition but not a theory of objects. This agrees well with some of his pronouncements but not with others (particularly with the strong idealist claims of *Cartesian Meditations*). It succeeds in achieving a radical empiricism and a "pure description of consciousness," but it fails to give us the absolute foundation Husserl promised us. This interpretation is objectionable to Husserl's vanity if not his philosophy, for it barely distinguishes Husserl from Kant.[140]

To be sure, the above interpretation of Husserl's theory of consciousness is too Kantian and does not account for many of his philosophical demands, for example, that philosophy must give us absolute foundations and provide us with knowledge of things-in-themselves. It is illuminating to see that the above interpretation is coherent even if one-sided, and that the very nature of the position (that is, the start from the first-person standpoint) seems to commit us to acknowledging the impossibility of ever knowing things-in-themselves. Husserl will not acknowledge this, and his philosophy from *Ideas I* onward is a struggle to break out of this Kantian position and consistently argue both that we constitute the objects of our experience and that we know objects as they are in-themselves. It should be evident that the claim that we do know the things-themselves becomes more definitive as more stress is placed on the role of constitution; if objects exist *only* insofar as we constitute them (the position of *Cartesian Meditations),* then clearly the objects we know are the objects-in-themselves. This stress on constitution leads to the confrontation with solipsism, and to avoid solipsism, it is necessary to shift the theoretical stress to the claims that objects have existence independent of our being conscious of them and that our consciousness of them is not (wholly) a matter of our constitution of objects but also a matter of their being *given* to us (and to any other consciousness) in intuition. Here again is the crux of the problem for Husserl; to make his anti-Kantian claim good that we can know things-in-themselves, he must face the charge of solipsism; to save himself from solipsism, he must give up the philosophical security which assures him that there are no objects other than the objects we know.

We may recall that Hegel also started from a Kantian position and made the same demands for absolute truth and for knowledge of things-in-themselves. Hegel's philosophy managed to fill these demands by making two major changes (among others) in Kant's first *Critique;* he changed Kant's theory of the role of the understanding in conceptualizing objects to a theory in which it is *Reason* that does this work; and he changed the Kantian personal transcendental Ego to a public Ego or *Spirit*. In spite of Husserl's intense dislike for Hegel, we find him making precisely the same moves in order to fulfill his philosophical demands. As early as the last part of *Ideas I,* he begins to shift the emphasis from intuition to *Reason*. In his later works, the individual thinking Ego becomes replaced by a Transcendental community Ego, and the world of knowledge is replaced by an interpersonal cultural life world.

In *Ideas I,* Husserl tells us that "a complete phenomenology of Reason coincides with phenomenology generally,"[141] and that the characterization of "rationality," of "constitution of objects," and of "consciousness" would be ultimately the same phenomenological project. Reason is characterized by Husserl as the "source of necessity" and "a priori conditions of possible experience." In other words, Husserl's notion of Reason replaces Kant's notion of Understanding (as we found in Hegel's *Phenomenology*). Reason is not to be contrasted with intuition here (for Reason and Eidetic intuition are identical), but contrasted with contingent or individual intuition only. Reason carries with it the demand for *necessity,* by which Husserl intends that the constitution of the objects for consciousness proceeds in such a manner that any alternative constitution is impossible. Thus, Husserl's "Reason" is a compromise between Kant's Understanding and Hegel's "Reason." The necessity we find in Husserl is the same 'transcendental necessity' we found in Kant. Like Hegel, Husserl insists that the objects of consciousness are the things themselves. What Husserl is tacitly insisting in his use of "Reason" is that the consciousness of objects is *both* the intuition of things themselves and the constitution of objects by Reason.

The use of the notion of "Reason" carries with it the idea that we know things-in-themselves, but the question still remains (as it did for Kant) whether the things we know have independent existence or not. Hegel claimed only to be interested in "the Concept" and not in the existence of objects, but it is this "negative" aspect of his philosophy that brings down the existential wrath of Schelling and Kierkegaard. We may interpret Husserl as interested in cognition rather than existence (he states so many times);[142] but then he also claims to be interested in the possible *existence* of things-in-themselves apart from our knowledge of them. To *call* the things of our experience "things-in-themselves" is again to simply gloss over a tremendous problem. As one of Husserl's most sympathetic commentators states,

nor will he (Husserl) accept Kant's limitation of science, according to which a being is recognized which can be thought of but which cannot be scientifically known. Husserl's ideal is a universal science, and he will retain the ideal even if the price he has to pay is the complete subjectivizing of all objectivity and the simple identification of being with what can be scientifically known.[143]

Complete subjectivizing of all objectivity" is a polite way of saying that Husserl has found himself committed to solipsism. If we take the notion of "constitution of objects" in Husserl as some form of active synthesis, then we do seem committed to solipsism. (Sartre and Heidegger will both make this charge against Husserl and use it as a basis for their rejection of the entire "transcendental" enterprise.) If we take the notion "constitution of objects" to be simply an unfortunate expression for "intuition of objects," then phenomenology, although it will be more faithful to its original ideal of "pure description," will find itself incapable of providing us with the "transcendental necessity" and "rationality" (imposition of such necessity) which Husserl takes as his ideal.

In Husserl's last years (1934–1937), he once again approached this problem and virtually revised his entire philosophy in order to meet it. His last work, *Crisis of European Philosophy,* is almost embarrassingly Hegelian. *Crisis* is a *historical* work, redeveloping phenomenology as an "intentional history." The book replaces the personal Ego with a community Ego and stresses the *social* nature of cognition. The concept of "truth" is lifted beyond its epistemological status to cover all forms of human activity.

"Intersubjectivity" is said to be one of the necessary conditions for any consciousness whatever. We may recall that *publicity* has been a criterion for objectivity for both Kant and Hegel (and obliquely, for Kierkegaard and Nietzsche also). In *Cartesian Meditations,* Husserl first explains our constitution of the personal Ego, and then goes on to establish the constitution of others. It is important to note that Husserl does not attempt a *proof* of the existence of others, and he sees (as Sartre and many 'analytic' philosophers after Wittgenstein will see) that there can be no such 'proof'. Husserl answers the question, "What is it to perceive another person?" but not the skeptical question, "How can I justify my belief that there are other persons?" As we found in Kant, the demarcation between exposition and 'proof' is blurred here, but what does differentiate Husserl's "exposition" from the many attempts to prove the existence of others is the fact that he is not interested in proving the existence of others so much as he is interested merely in the concept of the *possibility* of others. In other words, his "transcendental community" does not consist of other persons as such, but of an "all-embracing unity" which transcends individuals.[144] The role of "intersubjectivity" in Husserl has little to do with the question of "other minds"; it has more to do with Husserl's "transcendental problem of ideal objectivities." Husserl's concept would remain essential to his philosophy even if there were *in fact* no other people.

In *Crisis,* this community Ego is the starting point. There is no attempt to clarify the existence of others *after* the discussion of "the constitution of myself" (as in *Cartesian Meditations*); in *Crisis* our knowledge of the existence of others and of ourselves is one and the same. To know of the world *we* perceive is already to know of the existence of others in the world with me. (This strong concept of intersubjectivity is to become a central feature of the Christian Existential Phenomenologists, for example, Gabriel Marcel, who begins his philosophy with a concept of community like the one presented by Husserl.)

The force of solipsism is the charge that the world and its objects exist only *for me;* this force is expelled if it can be shown that the world and its objects exist not only for me but for any possible perceiver. The notion of a transcendental *community,* such as we find in Husserl (and Hegel), assures us that this publicity of objects will always be the case. Thus, Husserl attempts to save his philosophy from solipsism while maintaining his strong sense of "constitution" by insisting that it is *everybody* who does the constituting and that consequently there is no danger that objects exist only for me. Of course, one can restate the solipsistic objection by noting that one is committed to the position that there are no objects apart from the existence of some *possible* perceiver. However, this is solipsism with its teeth pulled—it did not bother Hegel and it does not bother Husserl. So long as there is a single "Objective" (that is, public) world for all of us, solipsism is not a problem.

Phenomenological explication does nothing but explicate the sense this world has for us all, prior to any philosophizing . . . a sense which philosophy can uncover but never alter.[145]

This very Hegelian interpretation assures us that we know things-themselves.

The concept of an intersubjective community leaves problematic the most important starting point of Husserl's phenomenology, the insistence that phenomenology proceed with a pure description of the contents of consciousness and its essential structure. What descriptive ground can the phenomenologist give for supposing *from the outset* that the consciousness he describes is the Ego of a community. This may well be one of the conclusions to be drawn from a nonphenomenological sociology, but it is difficult to see how this Hegelian thesis can be defended as a *datum.*

Although the phenomenological foundations of the intersubjective Ego may be unclear, the purpose of insisting upon such an Ego is evident. We recall that Hegel utilized his twin notions of *Spirit* and *The Idea* in order to stop talking about individual consciousness and talk rather about the *Concept.* Hegel's *Logic* talks about concepts and not about people having concepts. Similarly in this century, Gottlob Frege has talked about "The Thought" which is independent of being 'had' as an "Idea" by any particular person (compare *"The* Pythagorean theorem" with *"His* idea of the Pythagorean theorem"). Such talk about concepts rather than a person's having concepts is the best possible insurance against the threat of psychologism. This is what has appealed to Husserl since his early *Investigations,* talk of a "timeless realm of ideas" apart from the particular ideas of persons. The phenomenological accounts of the individual Ego inevitably leave us with the uncomfortable suspicion that we may not be talking about these timeless Ideas but only about our own ideas. Intersubjectivity surmounts this problem by building the notion of a universal consciousness directly into the notion of consciousness. It then follows that phenomenology and examination of universal consciousness are one and the same. The problem remains for Husserl, as for Hegel, to defend a coherent *phenomenological* account of intersubjectivity. Husserl attempts to show (in *Cartesian Meditations*) that phenomenology can explain intersubjectivity, but he does not and perhaps cannot justify accepting this intersubjectivity as a *starting point* for phenomenology.

In the final analysis, it would be rash to claim that we have gained from Husserl a new ready-to-apply method for dealing with traditional philosophical puzzles. It would be more appropriate to conclude that we have gained a new tangle of traditional problems, tied together with some original insights and an unflinching demand for rigor and lack of bias. Husserl demands everything of philosophy, and the result is that philosophy finds itself unable to deliver. Husserl insists that philosophy restrict itself to description of experience, but he also begins by insisting that the result of this investigation will be essential truth and an unshakable foundation for all knowledge. Why should we suppose that this unshakable foundation can be discovered in experience? Husserl demands that we perform an *epoche* to rid ourselves of all naturalistic prejudice, but he also expects that we shall be able to establish the absolute validity of naturalism as a result of this *epoche*. Why should we suppose that we shall be able to 'retrieve' the existence of objects after we have 'bracketed' them? Husserl insists that we restrict our examination to consciousness, but then he supposes that what we shall find will be truths concerning all consciousnesses. How do we know that each of us is not conscious in very peculiar ways? How do we know that our descriptions of consciousness refer to the same structures? How much is what we know truly given to us in intuition? Is there no account we can give of *why* we intuit objects? Husserl forbids us such accounts with the *epoche*. How much do we contribute to the objects we perceive? Do we create them? If not, what is the difference between perceptual constitution of objects and imaginative constitution of objects? Can we constitute objects as we will, or is the 'constitution' of objects given to us? (Does this question even make sense?) All of this depends upon a more adequate account (and less sympathetic account) of the *epoche* and the concepts of "intuition" and "constitution."

This welter of confusions must not make us lose sight of Husserl's prominence in twentieth-century philosophy. It is unfortunate that his demands for his work and his and his students' overbearing praise for their own accomplishments should make the actual results of phenomenology appear more than they are. Husserl did succeed in inspiring a philosophical fervor on the continent second, perhaps, only to the enthusiastic 'new metaphysics' inspired by Kant. Husserl's conception of a "presuppositionless" philosophy basing itself on an examination of intuition has dominated the European philosophical scene for half a century. There are many philosophers who have closely followed Husserl and maintained a "transcendental" approach to phenomenology basing itself on such works as *Cartesian Meditations*. The doctrines of the "transcendental Ego," the "transcendental reduction," the "transcendental realm," and "constitution" and "subjectivity" weigh heavily in these accounts. The threat of solipsism does not please the transcendental phenomenologists any more than it pleased Husserl, but many of them continue to celebrate phenomenology as a "triumph of subjectivity" and as the only alternative to naturalism and skepticism.[146]

Ironically, Husserl's antiontological phenomenology inspired an enthusiasm for a new ontology just as Kant's antimetaphysical *Dialectic* inspired a new metaphysics in Fichte and Hegel. That heretic brand of phenomenology which calls itself "existential" attempts to provide us with a "phenomenological ontology." Martin Heidegger, Jean-Paul Sartre, and Maurice Merleau-Ponty are the most distinguished members of this movement. We shall study their departure from Husserl in the following chapters.

Bibliography
Husserl's Works in English

Logical Investigations. Translated by J. N. Findlay. New York, 1970.

The Idea of Phenomenology. Translated by W. Alston and G. Nakhnikian. The Hague, 1964.

"Philosophy as a Rigorous Science" and "Philosophy and the Crisis of European Man." Translated by Lauer. In *Phenomenology and the Crisis of Philosophy.* New York, 1965.

Ideas: General Introduction to Pure Phenomenology. Translated by W. R. Boyce Gibson. New York, 1931.

Phenomenology of Internal Time-Consciousness. Edited by M. Heidegger. Translated by J. Churchill. Bloomington, Ind., 1964.

"Phenomenology." In the *Encyclopedia Britannica*. 14th ed. Reprinted in *Realism and the Background of Phenomenology*. Edited by Chisholm. New York, 1960.

Formal and Transcendental Logic. Translated by D. Cairns. The Hague, 1970.

Cartesian Meditations. Translated by D. Cairns. The Hague, 1960.

The Paris Lectures. Translated by P. Koestenbaum. The Hague, 1964.

The Crisis of European Sciences and Transcendental Philosophy. Translated by D. Carr. Evanston, Ill., 1970.

Books about Husserl's Philosophy

Chrisholm, R., ed. "Introduction." In *Realism and the Background of Phenomenology*. New York, 1960.

Edie, J., ed. *An Invitation to Phenomenology*. Chicago, 1967.

———. *Phenomenology in America*. Chicago, 1969.

———. *New Essays in Phenomenology*. Chicago, 1969.

Farber, M. *The Aims of Phenomenology*. New York, 1966.

———. *The Foundations of Phenom-* York, 1966.

———, ed. *Philosophical Essays in Memory of Edmund Husserl*. Cambridge, Mass., 1940.

Findlay. "Phenomenology." In the *Encyclopedia Britannica*. Chicago, 1964.

Gurwitsch, A. *The Field of Consciousness*. Pittsburgh, 1964.

———. *Studies in Phenomenology and Psychology*. Evanston, Ill., 1966.

Kockelmans, J., ed. *Phenomenology*. New York, 1967.

Lauer, Q. *Phenomenology: Its Genesis and Prospect*. New York, 1958.

Natanson, M., ed. *Essays in Phenomenology*. The Hague, 1966.

Natanson, M., Edie, J. and Tillman, F. "Phenomenology as a Rigorous Science." Symposium for American Philosophical Association, 1966. In *International Philosophical Quarterly*. Vol. VII, No. 1, March 1967.

Ricouer, P. *Husserl: An Examination of His Philosophy*. Evanston, Ill., 1967.

Ryle, G. "Phenomenology." *Proceedings Aristotelian Society Supplement*. Vol. 11, 1932.

Schlick, M. "Is There a Factual A Priori?" In *Readings in Philosophical Analysis*. Edited by Feigl and Sellars. New York, 1949.

Schmitt, R. "Husserl's Transcendental-Phenomenological Reduction." In *Phenomenology*. Edited by Kockelmans. New York, 1967.

———. "Phenomenology" and "Edmund Husserl." In *The Encyclopedia of Philosophy*. Edited by P. Edwards. New York, 1967.

———. "Transcendental Phenomenology: Muddle of Mystery." *British Society for Phenomenological Research,* 1971.

Solomon, R. C. ed. *Phenomenology and Existentialism*. New York, 1972.

Spiegleberg, H. *The Phenomenological Movement*. Vol. I. The Hague, 1960. A classic study.

Spiegleberg, H., Chisholm, R., and Chappell, V. "The Concept of a Person,' symposium in *The Monist*. Vol. 49, 1965 With several other articles on phenomenology.

Tillman, F. "Phenomenology and Philosophical Analysis." In *International Philosophical Quarterly*. Vol. VI, No. 3, September 1966.

Zaner, R. M. *The Way of Phenomenology*. New York, 1970.

Martin Heidegger:
Being and
Being Human
CHAPTER 6

Existentialism is well known for the eccentricity of its practitioners, but perhaps there is no more peculiar figure in twentieth-century philosophy than Martin Heidegger. His obscurity and penchant for creating new words and stating simple propositions in nearly incomprehensible prose betters that of Husserl and Hegel. He has forcefully dissociated himself from every philosophical school or movement (as he has several times repudiated the very idea of a 'school' of philosophy). He broke firmly away from his teacher, Edmund Husserl, with his first major publication, *Being and Time* (*Sein und Zeit*)[1] and publicly rejected the label "existentialist" although he himself is often credited with initiating that 'movement' in its twentieth-century form. Most unfortunately, however, Heidegger has made himself a reputation as a Nazi, and it is for this that many philosophers who might otherwise be sympathetic and even enthusiastic about his work have viciously attacked him. We have seen these "Nazi" charges against German philosophers before, of course. Nietzsche is often so accused, so that it becomes almost a personal obligation of any Nietzsche commentator to show how violently Nietzsche differed from that most antiphilosophical movement. Similarly, Hegel has been so accused, but, though he might have had considerably more sympathy for Fascism than Nietzsche, the claim is still clearly unsubstantiatable and a product of uncritical criticism rather than historical fact. Heidegger's relationship with Nazism is far from speculative, and his influence is much more than the alleged 'philosophical influence' of which these other German thinkers stand accused. In 1933, Heidegger accepted the rectorship of the University of Freiburg under the newly inaugurated Hitler regime and welcomed his new post with an inaugural address which is still used as conclusive evidence of the complete and total collaboration of Heidegger with his government. In this terrifying speech, academic freedom is sacrificed, or simply slaughtered, for the purpose of national unity and philosophical thought is reduced to *staat*-edification. In fact, Heidegger gave up his government post only one year later and it is not unreasonable to infer that the entire episode might have been as much foolishness as fascism. But it is insisted by his critics that he never actually renounced Nazism. In a 1953 publication, these critics seized on a now famous claim which is alleged to show that Heidegger still held a Nazi philosophy, and had differed with the Hitler regime only on matters of execution;

The works that are being peddled about nowadays as the philosophy of National Socialism but have nothing whatever to do with the inner truth and greatness of this movement (namely the encounter between global technology and modern man)—have all been written by men fishing in the troubled waters of "values" and "totalities."[2]

Heidegger's short public display of enthusiasm took a tragic toll in the reception of his philosophy, which was most often criticized simply on the supposition that whatever it said was either based on or a basis for Fascism. It thus became much easier to dismiss Heidegger on the basis of a few newspaper comments than to discuss his very hard-to-read works. Heidegger has spent much of his "retirement" (he is now in his eighties) in seclusion in the Black

Forest, rarely lecturing publicly and only occasionally discussing philosophy with his students or with visitors.

Enough of Heidegger's unpretty life, for we are interested in his philosophy. His philosophy is indeed a remarkable historical phenomenon; it signals a major breach within the phenomenological movement which has not been healed today. It marks the beginning of existentialism as a serious philosophical movement, and it is at least reasonable to suggest that Sartre could never have written *Being and Nothingness* had he not first been made familiar with Heidegger's *Sein und Zeit* (in a concentration camp during the war). Furthermore, Heidegger has had a welcome effect in bringing into the mainstream of philosophy such isolated figures as Nietzsche, Kierkegaard, and the poets Hölderlin and Rilke. Many philosophers do not look on this as a contribution, but it is clear that the line of demarcation between philosophy 'proper' and literature has been smeared past recognition in the philosophy of Heidegger. As we shall see, this is not the only time-honored distinction which will be all but obliterated by Heidegger.

Heidegger, more than any philosopher we have studied except Hegel, is extremely historically minded, and philosophy and the history of philosophy have an intimate association in his works. Unlike Hegel, however, Heidegger is not willing to ignore the disagreeable points of historical philosophies, and much of his historical thinking is harshly critical. In fact, he argues that the whole of Western philosophy since Plato has rested on a single mistake that is not only the result of bad philosophical thinking, but a manifestation of a cowardice which is common to all men, not only philosophers. Yet his treatment of historical figures, although sometimes horribly distorted, is not always unsympathetic. In *Sein und Zeit,* Kierkegaard is clearly admired and taken up as the very basis of Heidegger's philosophy. In his later works, Heidegger presents a sympathetic (but very controversial) account of Kant's first *Critique,* an enormous work, also very sympathetic, on Nietzsche, whom he dubiously interprets as primarily a metaphysician, and essays on Plato, Hegel, Hölderlin, and the pre-Socratic philosophers, which also attempt to give a sympathetic reading to history. As a student of Husserl, Heidegger was thoroughly educated and evidently quite gifted in Husserl's particular brand of phenomenology.

Like Kierkegaard, Heidegger was brought up religiously and early directed himself towards a life in the ministry. He gave up this ambition, but, although he remained virtually an atheist throughout his career, the Kierkegaardian influence—even the Kierkegaardian religious influence—continues to be pronounced throughout his philosophy. We may recall how Kierkegaard reacts to Hegel's heavy emphasis on 'the Concept' and puts a new stress on the 'ethical reality of the individual'. If we consider the similarities between Hegel and Husserl, particularly their mutual concern with *essences,* we may already extrapolate an understanding of the direction of Heidegger's new "existentialist" philosophy. Heidegger complains that Husserl's phenomenology similarly neglects individual *Existenz.* Heidegger, like both Kierkegaard and Husserl, argues that conceptual analysis is not sufficient to give us knowledge of what actually exists and what does not. Unlike Husserl, Heidegger refuses to "neglect being" by 'bracketing' existence and by concerning himself with essences.

In spite of an obvious difference in style between Kierkegaard and Heidegger, we shall find a great many of Kierkegaard's central ideas expanded in the heavy academic formulations of *Sein und Zeit.* Both have the aforementioned concern with individual human existence. This leads both of them into an attack on conceptual analysis-particular analyses of 'human nature'. They both maintain that the "real self" is "ethical, not cognitive." They both turn to the more morbid aspects of individual human existence—death *Angst*—to give an analysis of human being as Freedom. In his later writings, we shall see that Heidegger even introduces a notion of 'Being' into his seemingly atheistic philosophy which is very much like the "Mystery" of Kierkegaard's Christian God.

We shall focus our efforts on Heidegger's first great "existentialist" work, *Being and Time.* It is this work which influenced Sartre and Merleau-Ponty, and it is this work which introduces most of Heidegger's most influential ideas. It is also the work most often cited as the reason for Heidegger's prominence in philosophy, and this praise is often followed by a regret that he began to err so soon afterwards. This erring, however, does not refer to Heidegger's previously mentioned political follies, but to the fact that his later works drift continuously further from both the substance and the inspiration of *Sein und Zeit*. There is an open debate which continues as to whether these later works ought even be considered the work of the same thinker, and whether the program stated and introduced in *Sein und Zeit* is continued or rejected in subsequent works. Heidegger himself claims that the project of *Sein und Zeit* remains his central concern, but certain inadequacies in the method of *Sein und Zeit* have caused him to approach the problem differently. Many prominent commentators support this, for example, King and Langan, but most do not, for example, Waelhans, Löwith, Versenyi, Richardson, and Heinemann.[3] We find references to two (or even three) different Heideggers. In support of this extreme contention, it is argued that Heidegger's own retroactive interpretation of *Sein und Zeit* is purposively distorted and unfaithful. This claim, understandably, has generated considerable anger among those 'faithful' commentators who maintain the unity and integrity of Heidegger's work.

The central theme, or a central theme, of *Sein und Zeit* is the *problem of Being,* with a preliminary analysis of *human being.* We shall not discuss the post *Sein und Zeit* works sufficiently to prove that there is or is not a decided continuity in Heidegger's overall philosophy. However, we shall suggest that there is a continuity in the central *problem* of all his works, and as such, we shall side with those commentators who maintain the unity of project. We shall also find, however, that the approach to this problem, and even the presentation of the problem—the "problem of Being"—changes so drastically from *Sein und Zeit* to the most recent works that there is good ground as well for the claim that the continuity of project in Heidegger's philosophy is a nominal continuity only.

What is Philosophy?

In each of the authors we have studied thus far, we have seen that a concern for the nature of the philosophical enterprise stands as the basis for his philosophy. Kant begins with a "Critique" of traditional conceptions of and approaches to metaphysics; Hegel begins in turn by criticizing Kant's approach; Kierkegaard and Nietzsche begin by criticizing 'systematic' philosophy in general and all philosophy which does not take *practical* concerns as central; and in Husserl, we see the concern for philosophical methodology encompass the totality of his philosophical efforts. We have seen that the emphasis a philosopher puts on theory as opposed to practice, the emphasis on empirical and scientific observation as opposed to the paradigms of mathematics and necessary truth, and his choice of a piecemeal as opposed to a systematic approach to philosophical problems determine much of how his philosophy will develop.

Heidegger has read and absorbed the great authors we have studied and has assimilated many of their very disparate ideas into his own unique and powerful conception of philosophy. He is at once both a systematic and an 'individual' thinker; he is concerned with the most abstract theoretical and practical moral problems at one and the same time. He rejects nearly all the methodologies of the past, insisting that the necessary truths of philosophy can be obtained neither by empirical scientific study, nor by 'reason,' nor through the phenomenological reductions. Heidegger accepts a version of philosophy which is similar yet strange to the conceptual analysis of analytic philosophy, but at the same time he both affiliates and distinguishes himself from the 'speculative' systematic philosophies of nineteenth-century Germany. Philosophy, according to Heidegger, is very much concerned with language and concepts; it is also closely akin to poetry. Philosophy is the study of the most abstract problems, but it is also concerned with the basic problems of how a man should live his life.

In the introductory chapters of *Sein und Zeit,* it becomes clear that Heidegger's concern with *Being* is at least in part a concern for the concept of "Being" and the meaning of the German word *"Sein."* He also makes it clear, however, that what is to be involved in answering the question of Being is not simply an analysis of *"Sein,"* for our obtaining a "conceptual grasp"[4] of Being first involves obtaining a "proper set of concepts"[5] for talking about Being and formulating the problem of Being. According to Heidegger, we have not previously asked the question of Being properly, because we have not had the concepts with which to express either the question or the answer. We need a new philosophical vocabulary to talk about what we have confusedly and improperly been calling "Being," and, Heidegger stresses, "we not only lack the words needed but also the grammar."[6] Being, that is, talk about Being, requires "its own conceptual scheme."[7] Heidegger's concern for an understanding of Being is closely tied to our gaining an adequate *conception* of Being, but this conception is not to be obtained through analysis of our ordinary concept of "Being."

This interpretation of Heidegger as a philosopher of the *concept* of "Being" is at odds with any interpretation which focuses on the later works and stresses Heidegger's total divorce from conceptual concerns. In the later works, it becomes clear that Heidegger is concerned with *Being* and not with "Being" *("Sein")*. In *Sein und Zeit,* however, it is clear that Heidegger is very concerned with concepts and language. The introduction to *Sein und Zeit* is riddled with talk about "concepts," and his work in general is centrally concerned with linguistic considerations. In *Sein und Zeit* he tells us that "speech (as) an existential condition of the openness of Dasein is constitutive of its essence."[8] In *Introduction to Metaphysics*, the analysis of Being begins with a study of the etymology and grammar of the word "Sein." Even in a later article on the poet Hölderlin, Heidegger tells us that "we are what we say to one another." Consequently, there is a defensible and plausible interpretation of Heidegger's (early) thought (contra-Heidegger's Kierkegaardian influence), which claims that Heidegger is primarily concerned with *concepts* of "Being." Frederick Olafson[9] has thus analyzed Heidegger's central notions into conceptions of analytic philosophy in such a way that he claims that Heidegger has misleadingly or confusedly expressed conceptual considerations as 'ontological' ones. When Heidegger says he is talking about Being, he is really talking about "Being"; when Heidegger talks of "possibility", he is really talking about "capability of using certain concepts."[10] Similarly, Richard Schmitt[11] notes his general agreement with Olafson and claims that Heidegger's analysis of Being is essentially an analysis of "Being." What Heidegger calls "ontology," according to both commentators, could just as well, and less confusingly, be called "conceptual analysis."

Much of what is obscure in Heidegger's ontology' can be clarified by understanding that he is making *conceptual* claims.

However, we must guard ourselves against disvaluing Heidegger by saying he is doing obscure conceptual analysis: he is not. First, we must remember that Heidegger sometimes really is talking about the *meaning of Being* as well as the *meaning of "Being,"* and that these two are very different. The first, unlike the second, does not openly commit itself to analysis of the *concept* of "Being" in any particular language. More importantly, however, Heidegger is not doing an *analysis* of concepts we use, that is, "no dissection of mere words,"[12] but is attempting to formulate *new* concepts. This makes what he is doing very different from what now is called "conceptual analysis." The whole business of philosophy is concerned with concepts, but with *new* concepts. Thus Heidegger's philosophy is neither conceptual analysis nor simple ontology (description of beings). He is trying to get a new language in which to express insights concerning Being.

In *Individuals,* P. F. Strawson distinguishes between 'descriptive' metaphysics, the examination and analysis of the language in which we do talk about the world, and 'prescriptive' metaphysics, which suggests *new* languages for describing the world. It is tempting to classify Heidegger's enterprise as 'prescriptive' metaphysics, and thus distinguish it from the 'descriptive' enterprise which more 'analytically' minded philosophers attempt. However, there is a problem with 'prescriptive' metaphysics which is noteworthy, for it is often used (if implicitly) to dismiss the entire 'ontological' enterprise practiced by continental philosophers; descriptive analyses can be shown to be 'correct' by demonstrating their faithfulness to everyday usage. It is manifest that 'prescriptive' metaphysics has no such court of appeal because its avowed purpose is to *replace* ordinary language. The problem then becomes whether any prescriptive metaphysics is as good or as valid or as true as any other.

What must be urged in Heidegger's defense is that the alleged distinction between "new meaning" and "old meaning" of a term is not all so clear and that the distinction between two sorts of metaphysics can be no more clear than this. We shall not find it a simple matter, for example, to determine whether a philosophical doctrine's fidelity to 'common sense' is a valid—much less the only—

reason for accepting it. According to Heidegger, this is a notably bad reason for acceptance. The evaluation of a philosophical theory, therefore, should not rely simply on this descriptive-prescriptive distinction, but upon a more basic foundation, the adequacy of a system of thought or language to describe the world. The nature of this criterion will unfold in this section and throughout this chapter.

In this chapter, we shall come to understand *why* Heidegger is so insistent on avoiding traditional philosophical and everyday terminology; he believes that it is just this sort of speech which has generated the philosophical problems and inadequacies which philosophers are attempting to resolve. However, we shall also come to see that it is not just the fault of language (as we come to suspect in Wittgenstein's assault on philosophical "puzzles" resulting from "language going on a holiday"), but a fault of human 'nature' itself that causes us to make philosophical mistakes. Philosophy or 'ontology', according to Heidegger, is nothing other than a verbal (conceptual) expression of certain *ontical* or preverbal structures. Philosophical 'mistakes,' therefore, are expressions of certain *ontical* or preverbal failings in the philosopher *as a man*. In Heidegger, we shall find a remarkable intimacy between questions about *things* (including humans) and questions about concepts; concepts give us the *ontological manifestation of ontical structures*. The distinction between 'ontology' (study of beings) and 'conceptual analysis' is of little help in understanding Heidegger's philosophy.

Because Heidegger is concerned to formulate a new grammar and vocabulary for philosophy, we may well expect that he will not take a piecemeal approach to philosophical problems. He openly rejects Husserl's call for "back to the things themselves," and he insists, with Hegel, that studies of conceptual matters must always be *systematic*. There can be no isolated treatment of this or that philosophical problem, and, as we shall see, even the broadest distinctions between philosophical disciplines are denied. The distinction between theoretical and practical pursuits, so important in Kant and in Kierkegaard, is strictly denied in Heidegger. Like Fichte and Hegel, Heidegger refuses to draw a distinction between metaphysics and ethics. We shall see that the philoso-phy of *Sein und Zeit* clearly does both.

Because Heidegger insists that the traditional language we use to speak about philosophical matters is inadequate, we may also expect that philosophy must show little regard to 'common sense':

But what philosophy is in the estimation of sound common sense . . . does not affect its essence.[13]

Philosophy, however, can never refute common sense since common sense is deaf to the language of philosophy. Nor may it even wish to do so, since common sense is blind to the things which philosophy sees before her essence-seeking eyes.[14]

According to common sense, the ordinary everyday way of 'thinking', philosophy will always have a sense of the 'ridiculous' to it.

To philosophize is to inquire into the extra-ordinary. . . . This questioning does not lie along the way so that we bump into it one day unexpectedly. Nor is it a part of everyday life: there is no requirement or regulation that forces us into it: it gratifies no urgent or prevailing need. The questioning itself is "out of order."[15]

The rejection of philosophy by common sense cannot be a ground for rejection of philosophy, for the very business of philosophy is to transcend the prejudices of common sense. If a philosopher tells us that "all men are selfish," it will not suffice to refute him by relying on our common sense intuitions that Jones did a kind deed yesterday. Then, on the other hand, it is incorrect to suppose that 'common sense' is a completely formed set of ideas, in fact a philosophy itself, before it has been challenged by a philosophical thesis:

at that moment in the world when philosophy came to birth there also began, and not before, the express domination of common sense. (Sophism) Unlike 'common sense', philosophy can "admit no outside authority."[16]

Heidegger praisingly cites Kant:

In this position philosophy has to demonstrate its sincerity as the keeper of its own laws which ingrained sense or

*some kind of guardian nature whispers
in its ear.*[17]

Thus, the entire philosophical enterprise is
essentially a rejection of the platitudes of
the 'common sense' of the times:

*Philosophy is essentially untimely because
it is one of those few things that can never
find an immediate echo in the present.
When such an echo seems to occur, when
a philosophy becomes fashionable, either
it is no real philosophy or it has been
misinterpreted and misused for ephemeral
and extraneous purposes.*[18]

Furthermore, we must not suppose that philosophy is a general technique or exercise
which will help us in more practical everyday matters. It is not, as so many teachers
of philosophy emphasize, to introduce philosophy to the 'practical' student, an exercise to help one think more clearly or
quicken his mind.

*Philosophy is expected to promote and
even to accelerate—to make easier as it
were—the practical and technical business
of culture. But it is in the very nature of
philosophy never to make things easier
but only more difficult.*[19]

We must not suppose that philosophy and
common sense—everyday practical concerns—will ever reside together peace-
fully. Philosophy is not only impractical,
it is essentially *anti*practical. It opens up
for us, as we shall see, questions and paths
and directions which make practical living
impossible. Heidegger quotes Nietzsche,
"Philosophy is a voluntary living amid ice
and mountain heights."[20] We must never
suppose, therefore, that philosophy "leads
to nothing." It is true, Heidegger insists,
that "you can't do anything with
philosophy":

*It is only wrong to suppose that this is the
last word on philosophy. For the rejoinder
imposes itself: Granted that we cannot do
anything with philosophy, might not
philosophy, if we concern ourselves with it,
do something with us?*[21]

Like his teacher Husserl, Heidegger
opposes all doctrines of *historicism*, the
thesis which asserts that philosophical
truth is relative to a culture and that a
'necessary truth' is necessary only for that
particular culture. We must be careful not
to confuse this thesis of "historicism,"
which Heidegger rejects, with the thesis
of "historicity," which he accepts. When
Heidegger emphasizes man's *historicity*,
he is talking about the fact that man exists
in time (which he later goes on to say is
the very essence of man). Historicity has
nothing to do with Dilthey and Spengler's
doctrine of historicism. Historicism might
seem to hold true for the dictates of common sense, since common sense varies
freely from culture to culture. However,
Heidegger's radical separation of philosophy and common sense allows him to insist that philosophical truth differs from
truths of common sense precisely in their
timelessness. (It is here that Heidegger
remains most faithful to Husserl.) If philosophy is essentially 'untimely', then philosophy cannot be a mere expression of
a culture, that is, the expression of the
common sense of a culture. It is the business of philosophy to "keep its own laws"
and relate us to "the original truth of what
is-as-such." So philosophy cannot be tied
to a particular way of thinking. Against
historicism, Heidegger objects that,

the most helpless (enslavement of
philosophy) *is to be found in the
subterfuge of letting philosophy assert
itself merely as an 'expression' of 'culture'
*(Spengler), *as the ornament of creative
humanity.*[22]

What makes philosophy so opposed to
common sense, and *vice versa*, is that
philosophy always attempts to seek out
the roots of common sense and display
them as unfounded prejudices. As we
have already mentioned, the roots of these
prejudices may themselves be embedded
in the very language of everyday discourse, and at this juncture, it becomes
necessary for philosophy to create a new
language in order to get the unprejudiced
perspective it requires. Philosophy must
also, for the same reason, be 'unreasonable' or even *against reason* and *logic*, for
these also may have absorbed and retained the structure of the commonsense
prejudices which it is the philosopher's
business to destroy. So, the philosophical
enterprise becomes the most difficult
enterprise of all, the attempt to create
new, more pure or 'primitive' or 'original'
perspectives by creating a new language
in which we are capable of truly *"think-*

ing." It even requires a new way of thinking, against reason and logic.

If philosophy is the creation and re-structuring of language even against logic and reason in order to furnish us with new, more pure perspectives, then the philosopher has an ally in his work—the poet. It is in his drawing together of philosophy and poetry that Heidegger's view on philosophy may sound most bizarre to the 'scientific' minded philosopher. We are so used to thinking of poetry as being virtually devoid of cognitive content—so much the antithesis of philosophy—that it is shocking to see them joined in the philosophical enterprise. Plato warned us against the "enticements of poets, who could not distinguish truth from error." Nietzsche chastised the poets for present-ing their ideas on a "carriage of rhythm, because they were too weak to walk." Now Heidegger tells us that poetry is *akin* to philosophy:

Only poetry stands in the same order as philosophy and its thinking.[23]

In the opening of his famous essay on the German poet Hölderlin (the friend of the young Hegel) Heidegger offers us the quotation:

Therefore has language, most dangerous of possessions, been given to man . . . so that he may affirm what he is . . .[24]

In the text of the same essay, Heidegger tells us that "our existence is funda-mentally poetic."[25] Poetry, Heidegger ar-gues, is a kind of "seeing" (compare Husserl's use of the same term *"Sehen"*), a 'primitive', 'innocent', 'original' kind of seeing that escapes the prejudices philoso-phy wishes to seek out and destroy. Heidegger again quotes Hölderlin, who says that the writing of poetry is "the most innocent of all occupations."[26] "Innocent" here ought to be taken in much the same way that Husserl insists that his phenome-nology be "pure" and "unprejudiced." The poet, Heidegger tells us, is "present" and "earthy," he sees things without preju-dices; he sees things as they *really* are. It is thus the poet who will show us the way in philosophy.

With Heidegger, the paradigm of phi-losophy takes a major shift from venera-tion of the sciences to emulation of the arts. It perhaps is here that the continen-tal conception of philosophy has been most repugnant to the 'scientific' minded philosophers of twentieth-century England and America. It is obvious that Heidegger is open to the objection that poets, who do not often care about finding a *true* per-spective as much as finding an interesting or shocking or bizarre or simply beautiful perspective, do not give us a way of dis-cerning philosophical poetic insights from very unphilosophical poetic creations. Rather than harp on this obvious criticism, it would be helpful to see how much in-sight there is in Heidegger's bringing to-gether of philosophy and poetry.

Heidegger continuously insists that our ontology is determined by the language we speak; what we believe to exist de-pends on the kinds of entities we can refer to:

Language is the house of Being.[27]

Ordinary language and ordinary ways of thinking, including everyday logic and rea-son, are permeated with philosophical prej-udices. Traditional everyday language, and traditional philosophical language as well, are inadequate to capture the philosophical truths Heidegger seeks. In its search for truth, therefore, philosophy must become inventor of language, and here the affinity with poetry is clear. Where the two differ, clearly, is that philosophy seeks a *single* true language—the best language for pro-viding us with an original view of Being. Poetry, because it does not seek this truth, can content itself with the arbitrary inven-tion of languages and perspectives for very unphilosophical reasons.

When Heidegger claims to be against logic and reason, however, this does not mean that he will countenance straight-forward contradictions in his writings, nor does it even mean that he attempts to break the rules of logic or will he allow himself to do so. Although Heidegger often overstates his opposition to logic and reason, what he does mean is quite clear. Let us not begin by presupposing the rul s of logic or the validity of inference which most men would consider 'reasonable'. Like Husserl, Heidegger insists that phi-losophy must begin without presupposi-tions (although Husserlian phenomenol-ogists are quick to insist that Heidegger has failed here in an almost grotesque manner), and therefore he proposes not to accept even the most obvious dictates of common sense until they have been proven phenomenologically. Thus, the *Reason* rejected is not the use of careful critical thought, but only a kind of cleverness or structured thought which has not examined its own principles. What is rejected is not *logic,* but only the mechanical application of rules of inference which have not been subjected to philosophical scrutiny. Although Heidegger is not particularly concerned with logic in *Sein und Zeit,* he quite clearly does not reject most of the fundamental laws of 'logical' thinking. (Some of his latest writings appear to bring this into question: see last two sections of this chapter.)

To stress his departure from traditional philosophical thinking, with its allegedly uncritical acceptance and employment of traditional logic and 'reasoning,' Heidegger often refers to his own endeavor as "Thinking" (*Denken*). By this general term, he wishes to stress the unprejudiced and broad scope of his philosophy. Thinking, for Heidegger, is the search for unprejudiced truth, specifically, unprejudiced truth about Being. This kind of thinking, Heidegger stresses, is a special sort of activity, and not the sort of 'thinking' we do about a mathematics problem or the problem of buying a new car. This sort of thinking about Being has yet to be accomplished, in fact:

The most thought-provoking thing in our thought-provoking age is that we still are not thinking.[28]

The Problem of Being
The stated problem of Heidegger's life work in philosophy, and of *Sein und Zeit* in particular, is the *problem of Being.* This problem receives various formulations, remarkably different in appearance; it is most often asked as straightforward if not easily interpretable queries, "What is Being?" and "What is the Being (*Sein*) of entities (*Seindes*)?"[29] We are led to ask, "What is the meaning of Being?"[30] and, seemingly very differently, "What is the meaning of the expression 'being'?"[31] In *Introduction to Metaphysics* (which Heidegger began to write just after *Sein und Zeit* although it was not to be revised and published for twenty-five years after *Sein und Zeit*), the question becomes, "Why are there entities rather than nothing?"[32] and this question is in turn reinterpreted as,

Why, that is to say, on what ground? from what source does the being derive? On what ground does it stand?[33]

and later,

We are asking for the ground of the being; that it is and is what it is, and that there is not rather nothing.[34]

and "How stands it with Being?" as a preliminary to "Why is there something rather than nothing?"[35] We may thus distinguish several 'problems of Being' which concern Heidegger (although we shall see as we proceed how very interconnected they become);

1. The analytic question: "What is the meaning (in English/German) of the expression, 'Being' (*Sein*)?"
2. The metaphysical question: "What is Being?" Or, "What is the ground of Being?"
3. The theological question: "Why is there Being (rather than nothing at all)?"

The first of these questions is the most straightforward, the simplest to answer directly, and that which is most in accordance with questions asked by most philosophers of the Western tradition. It asks, "What are we saying of a thing (anything) when we assert that it exists?" Presumably, what we would like in answer to this question is a set of criteria of some sort for determining whether or not a thing exists, regardless of what particular thing or type of thing it is. The second question is much more perturbing. It may be and Heidegger often suggests that it is the case that the expressions we use to discuss Being do not faithfully capture the *correct* concept of Being. If this is so, then a "mere dissection of words"[36] will not suffice to help us understand being. We should have to go beyond our present language to develop a better language for capturing certain philosophical insights. Heidegger does believe this, and so it becomes his task to give us a language which can capture these truths. It is this development of a new un-German (un-English) language which, in part, makes understanding Heidegger's writings so very difficult. In his later writings, the thesis that our everyday language cannot capture essential truths about Being becomes generalized to the thesis that language cannot capture these truths. At this point, we shall see, Heidegger's philosophy moves away from the sort of linguistic-ontological concern of *Sein und Zeit* and moves to a bizarre form of non-theological mysticism.

The third question, which I have taken the liberty of calling "theological," is the most perplexing of all and that which has turned away many novice readers of Heidegger's popular *Introduction to Metaphysics*. The question, "Why are there beings?" sounds very much like a quest for an explanation, or even a justification for there being beings. It is the sort of question theologians are prone to ask, "Why did God create anything?" but it has the not unimportant complication that Heidegger himself is an atheist:

Anyone for whom the Bible is divine revelation and truth has the answer to the question "Why are there beings rather than nothing?" even before it is asked: everything that is, except God himself, has been created by Him. God himself, the increate creator, "is." One who holds to such faith can in a way participate in the asking of our question, but he cannot really question without ceasing to be a believer and taking all the consequences of such a step. He will only be able to act 'as if'. . . .[37]

The third question, "Why is there Being rather than nothing?" may be interpreted as a reiteration of the second question, and it is sometimes clear that Heidegger so intends it. The question "Why . . .?" in this interpretation, is simply the question for an explanation of *what* it is for something to exist, and not a quest for an explanation of why it *ought* to exist. We must not suppose that the 'theological' question is absent from Heidegger's thought. The question, "Why . . .?" is also a quest for *meaning* and *justification* for Being (particularly *human* Being), and the answer to this question is of importance far beyond the confines of academic philosophy;

Philosophy always aims at the first and last grounds of the being, with particular emphasis on man himself and on the meaning and goals of human being-there.[38]

This question of *goals* turns out to be one with the question "Why . . . ?" and thus this question is to be assimilated less to

the sort of meanderings we encountered in Kant's first *Critique* (which is about the *Being* of phenomena) than to Kierkegaard's neurotic despair over the "leap of faith" his thought required;

We find out that this privileged question "Why" has its ground in a leap through which man thrusts away all the previous security, whether real or imagined, of his life. The question is asked only in this leap; it is *the leap; without it there is no asking.[39]*

Moreover, this question of Being, because of this third interpretation, is of profound importance in all human culture, and the neglect of the question, and subsequent "falling away from Being" is responsible not only for the disreputable state of metaphysics (as Kant had complained), but of a decline of culture in general;

What if it were possible that man, that nations in their greatest movements and traditions, are linked to Being and yet had long fallen out of Being, without knowing it, and that this was the most powerful and most central cause of their decline?[40]

Strangely enough, the question of Being allows Heidegger to make all sorts of political evaluations on metaphysical grounds;

From a metaphysical point of view, Russia and America are the same; the same dreary technological frenzy, the same unrestricted organization of the average man.[41]

We (Germans) are caught in a pincers. Situated in the center, our nation incurs the severest pressure. It is the nation with the most neighbors and hence the most endangered. With all this, it is the most metaphysical of nations. We are certain of this vocation . . . All this implies that this nation as a historical nation must move itself and thereby the history of the West beyond the center of their future 'happening', and into the primordial realm of the powers of being.[42]

If it seems strange to us that abstract metaphysics allows itself to be so specifically evaluative, we shall have to keep in mind that the third 'theological' question is always interlaced with the first two, and that all philosophical questions (that is, all questions about Being) will commit themselves to a statement about the meaning or goals involved in Being. Thus there will be no divorcing metaphysics from ethics in Heidegger's philosophy, even though, as we shall see, Heidegger himself claims to have no interest in ethics whatsoever.

The Fallenness from Being

The problem of Being, according to what we have said above, is a problem central not only to philosophy but vital to all human culture. Men, not just philosophers, have "fallen out of Being." But what is this "fallenness"? Dubiously, it is the failure to ask a very abstract metaphysical question that threatens human culture as a whole. But is this charge of neglect true of philosophers? What sort of justification can be given to the claim that philosophers have not recognized this problem and even made it the center of their inquiry? And, looking ahead to Heidegger's own analysis of *Being,* how ought we take up this problem?

Philosophers have always been concerned with metaphysics, the concern with what *is*. Heidegger frequently distinguishes among "metaphysics," "ontology," and "the study of Being." His usage is not consistent. It is the study of Being that interests him, of course, but sometimes he uses "metaphysics" to refer to this study and other times he does not. Sometimes the problem of Being is the fundamental question of metaphysics; elsewhere philosophy must go "beyond Metaphysics"; similarly, "ontology" is sometimes the name for the inadequate philosophical concern of previous philosophers who have "forgotten Being"; but "ontology," in *Sein und Zeit,* for example, is used as a blanket term to designate all investigations of Being. For simplicity, we shall continue to employ the term "metaphysics" to refer to the study of Being, and restrict "ontology" to its special use in *Sein und Zeit.* The common distinction between "metaphysics" as the study of Being and "ontology" as the study of entities will not be employed here.

Here we must distinguish two very different sorts of metaphysical questions. We may ask whether a particular entity exists (whether some proper name has a denotation); for example, "Is there a God?" "Is there a Santa Claus?" "Was there an Odysseus?" or whether a particular *type* of entity exists (whether there are members of a certain class or whether there are instances manifesting a certain description); for example, "Are there centaurs?" or "Are there intelligent creatures which are not of humanoid form?" Secondly, we may ask what it is that is being asked in all such questions, that is, what it is for anything to *be*. It is the second question which Heidegger wishes to ask; it is the first question which has concerned previous philosophers. What is the difference? The first question already presumes an answer to the second. To ask whether a particular entity exists presupposes that we already understand what it is to exist and that it makes sense to speak in general of "existence." Philosophers have "fallen out of being", forgotten the question of being, insofar as they have asked only the first question (about 'entities') instead of the second question (about "the Being of entities"). Being (*Sein*) is the problem, the existence of particular entities must await an answer to this fundamental problem.

In Sein und Zeit *the question of the meaning of Being is raised and developed* as a question *for the first time in the history of philosophy.*[43]

"Being has become hidden (or concealed) from us," Heidegger often complains. We cannot see Being for the entities; we no longer consider it a problem that we say of everything that "it exists" but are unable to say by virtue of what 'it' exists. We say that elephants exist, feelings exist, ideas exist, prime numbers exist. Do we want to say that they all have something in common, namely Being, by virtue of which they exist? What do elephants have in common with prime numbers? Perhaps, philosophers might suppose, there is something dreadfully wrong with the question. Indeed, philosophers have argued just this. Most notable among such arguments is the thesis promoted by Kant in his refutation of the 'ontological proof' of God's existence. Existence is not a property of any kind and "exists" is not a predicate of any kind. What Kant wishes to prove is that any statement of the form "X exists" is necessarily synthetic. His proof, however, revolves about the claim that,

'Being' *is obviously not a real predicate; that is, it is not a concept of something which could be added to the concept of a thing. It is merely the positing of a thing, or of certain determinations, as existing in themselves. Logically, it is merely the copula of a judgment. . . . By whatever and by however many predicates we may think a thing—even if we completely determine it—we do not make the least addition to the thing when we further declare that this thing is.*[44]

In other words, "existence" is not a concept; it is the fulfilling of "the context of experience as a whole" conforming to "the *universal conditions* of possible empirical knowledge in general."[45] Hegel does treat Being as a concept, but adds that it is the 'emptiest' of all concepts. Similarly, Aristotle, in his *Metaphysics,* argued that Being is the most universal of all concepts.[46] Modern logicians, similarly, agree that existence must be introduced into quantificational logics not as a predicate but as a quantifier. In other words, "Unicorns do not exist" must be formulated as "there does not exist anything which has the properties of being a unicorn" rather than "there is nothing that is both a unicorn and exists." All of these theses have in common the supposition that there is no possible illuminating philosophical exploration of "existence" or Being itself. To say that Being is the 'emptiest' or 'most universal' of concepts is to say that Being promiscuously attaches itself to *everything,* so that there is nothing which everything that is has in common. To say that Being is not a predicate or a concept at all is to claim, even more strongly, that there is nothing to be looked for as the 'ground' or 'meaning' of Being. Entities *are.* Some possible entities are *not.* Philosophers, however, refuse to see that there are serious philosophical problems lurking here; this is what constitutes their "fallenness from Being" according to Heidegger.

Philosophers have not always been so "fallen," and Heidegger's philosophy comes to pay increasing attention to the pre-Socratic philosophers, who are said to have faced the problem of Being. Plato, and everyone after him, we are to find, escaped the problem, and turned to other concerns. There have been moments in which the *"disclosure of Being"* ("the unlocking of what forgetfulness of Being closes and hides")[47] has been approached, most notably, in the German idealism initiated by Kant, Fichte, and Schelling, culminating in Hegel, but which "collapsed" in the middle of the nineteenth century. However,

it was not German idealism that collapsed; rather, the age was no longer strong enough to stand up to the greatness, breadth, and originality of that spiritual world, i.e., truly to realize it, for to realize a philosophy means something very different from applying theorems and insights.[48]

The culmination of the forgetfulness of or fallenness out of Being occurs in the philosophy of Nietzsche, who does not simply neglect the question, but boldly asserts that the question does not signify anything. "Being" is not only an empty word, it is not even a word. Heidegger apprehensively quotes Nietzsche from his *Twilight of the Idols;*

[*Could it be that*] *in the last analysis Nietzsche was perfectly right in calling such "highest concepts" as Being "the last cloudy streak of evaporating reality." . . . Nothing indeed has exercised a more simple power of persuasion than the error of being.*[49]

Heidegger goes so far, in his early work as well as in his later two-volume work on Nietzsche, to interpret Nietzsche as fundamentally concerned with the denial of this problem of Being:

What Nietzsche says here of Being is no random remark thrown out in the frenzy of preparation for his central never finished work. No, this was his guiding view of being from the earliest days of his philosophical effort. It is the fundamental support and determinant of his philosophy.[50]

Against all such historical 'fallen' positions, Heidegger asserts that the understanding of Being—of what it is for anything to exist—is the basic problem of not only philosophy but of all human fields of endeavor and all human being in general. Philosophy can make no claims to having completed its search for *foundations* so long as the most basic concept, Being, remains the "darkest concept of all."[51] Furthermore, the problems of the *foundations* of other disciplines, for example, foundations of mathematics (which so worried Frege and Husserl), the disputes between classical and Einsteinian physics, and the controversy in biology between vitalism and mechanism are all based on the problem of Being. As we have seen, Heidegger believes that the basic tensions of modern culture are themselves based on failure to apprehend the problem of Being;

the world is darkening. The essential episodes of this darkening are: the flight of the gods, the destruction of the earth, the standardization of man, the preeminence of the mediocre. . . . Darkening the world means emasculation of the spirit, the disintegration, wasting away, repression, and misinterpretation of the spirit.[52]

Heidegger insists that the prejudices (*Vorurteil*) or 'presuppositions' that insist that Being is the most 'universal," 'most empty," and "most self-evident" of all concepts[53] are all based on serious misunderstandings as well as important insights. What is valuable in these suggestions is the recognition that Being is not a 'genus' or 'class-name', and does not just designate some genus or class of individuals, but designates all individuals indiscriminately. It also recognizes that existence is not a *property of* things which things may or may not have, and so it recognizes that "X exists", in Kant's words, "adds nothing to the concept of 'X'." It furthermore recognizes that we do, in fact, find ourselves able to quite thoroughly determine whether things or kinds of things do exist or not, showing that we have considerable prephilosophical ability at handling the concept of "Being". We are capable of determining whether there *is* a table in front of us or not, or whether there *is* a prime number greater than seven and less than thirteen, or whether there *is* any nation with a population greater than one billion persons. Those cases in which we are not quite sure whether to attribute existence or not, for example, to the objects of religion and mythology, or to the theoretical 'entities' postulated by the abstract sciences, are simply the proof that we generally know how to ascribe existence. In this sense, Being is self-evident. We all know, to a remarkable degree, how to tell whether entities exist or not.

These "presuppositions" really are misleading 'prejudices' if they are interpreted to signify that the problem of Being as set forth by Heidegger does not make sense. Being may not be a class or genus-name, and it may not be the name of an entity or refer to any particular property and thus not be a normal predicate, but this does not mean that there is no describable difference between that which exists and that which does not. The fact that we do discern the existing from the nonexisting is ample evidence that we do have at our (prephilosophical) disposal a set of criteria for ascertaining existence, and we do, therefore, have a concept of existence which is subject to illuminating philosophical analysis. As for the claim that the meaning of this concept is 'self-evident', that is simply false if it is interpreted to mean that we can provide such an *analysis* self-evidently. To the contrary, it is the failure to provide such an analysis, and the refusal to even attempt to provide one, which constitutes our 'fallenness from Being'. It is one thing to be able to recognize things as existing; it is something very different to recognize *what it is for something to exist.*

Basically, all ontology, no matter how rich and firmly compacted a system of categories it has at its disposal, remains blind and perverted from its ownmost aim, if it has not first adequately clarified the meaning of Being, and conceived this clarification as its fundamental task.[54]

Heidegger, Husserl, and Phenomenology

We have already mentioned that Heidegger studied with Husserl (Husserl considered him one of his most promising students) and wrote *Sein und Zeit* well versed in Husserl's phenomenological method (the book is dedicated to him). The method of *Sein und Zeit* is the phenomenological method, and we must, therefore, interpret its findings as the result of this methodology. Where Heidegger's philosophy differs from that of Husserl (as it does radically on some central issues), we must distinguish where this is a difference in the employment of the phenomenological method and where this is a difference based on radically different conceptions of that method itself.

There is no need for us to repeat those essential features of phenomenological research which Heidegger takes more or less directly from Husserl. For Heidegger, "the expression 'phenomenology' signifies primarily a *methodological conception.* This expression does not characterize the *what* of the objects of philosophical research as subject matter, but rather the *how* of that research."⁵⁵

*Thus the term 'phenomenology' expresses a maxim which can be formulated as 'To the Things themselves'. It is opposed to all free-floating constructions and accidental findings; it is opposed to taking over any conceptions which only seem to have been demonstrated; it is opposed to those pseudo-questions which parade themselves as 'problems', often for generations at a time.*⁵⁶

Phenomenology is "the *science of phenomena*"; a *phenomenon* is simply "that which shows itself," but this "showing itself" must be sharply distinguished from the traditional notion of "appearance." "Phenomenon"

*has nothing at all to do with what is called an 'appearance' or still less a 'mere appearance.'*⁵⁷

The purpose of this last move is evident enough—to avoid the move from "appearance" to a distinction between the "mere appearance" of a thing and the thing-in-itself which plagued Kant and so many other philosophers.

"Phenomenon," *the showing-itself-in-itself, signifies a distinctive way in which something can be encountered. . . . If in taking the concept of "phenomenon" in this way, we leave indefinite which entities we consider as "phenomena," and leave it open whether what shows itself is an entity or rather some characteristic which an entity may have in its Being . . . then we have arrived at the* formal conception *of "phenomenon" (as opposed to the* ordinary conception—an occurrence in *space and time).*⁵⁸

Phenomenology is the *description* of phenomena, which is also an *interpretation* or (when applied to the peculiar phenomenon of *human being*) a *hermeneutic*. Heidegger's philosophy, like Husserl's, is the careful (hopefully) description-interpretation of "the things themselves" or "that which presents itself" (intuition).

*The following investigation would not have been possible if the ground had not been prepared by Edmund Husserl.*⁵⁹

This totally unprejudiced, presuppositionless 'seeing' of *phenomena* is called "primitive" or "original."

*The main thing is not to let ourselves be led astray by over-hasty theories, but to experience things as they are on the basis of the first thing that comes to hand.*⁶⁰

Yet, in spite of Heidegger's enormous philosophical debt to Husserl, the student is not hesitant to accuse his teacher of having "fallen out of Being" along with other philosophers. His conception of method, however brilliant, did not suffice to allow Husserl to recognize the problem of Being. Rather, Husserl explicitly began his researches by distinguishing between phenomenology and 'ontology' or metaphysics, thereby presupposing that the phenomena encountered in the one were different from the entities encountered in the other. This is already to lay the ground for the suggestion that entities-in-themselves are not the entities that appear to us as phenomena. Of course, Husserl intends to reject this conclusion, and argue that, through the "transcendental constitution" of objects, the things that appear to us are the things themselves (see Chapter 5). Heidegger challenges, is it possible to begin by distinguishing phenomenology from the study of Being and then to bring them together again? We have already seen how acutely Husserl felt this problem, but it is Heidegger who suggests that it is the very *starting point* of Husserl's phenomenology which makes this discomfort necessary. Once we have distinguished between phenomenology and the study of entities or distinguished *beings* from *phenomena*, we are trapped in the skepticism Husserl so very much wishes to avoid. "Why should we believe that the objects of our experience correspond to objects as they are in themselves?"

We find that Heidegger, although he accepts Husserl's method, challenges Husserl's starting point in employing that method. Both agree that philosophy must examine phenomena, but they sharply differ as to how these phenomena are to be encountered. Husserl began his entire philosophy with a phenomenological *epoche*, a "bracketing of the natural standpoint." Within this new perspective, we suspend judgment concerning existence, and we inquire into essences (see Chapter

5), but this is to say that phenomenology is not concerned with *existence* at all. According to Heidegger, existence is not to be so neglected, for the problem of Being—what is it for a thing to exist—is *the* problem of philosophy. Granted that Husserl hopes to establish that objects are constituted, and thus to show that the natural standpoint is derivative of the phenomenological standpoint, but Heidegger shall claim that this is a meaningless hope. Once one has performed the phenomenological *epoche*, this "bracketing of the world" (as Husserl himself claims in his *Encyclopedia* article) is permanent. Against Husserl, therefore, Heidegger rejects the methodological step of "bracketing," and with it, the phenomenological standpoint;

our treatise does not subscribe to a 'standpoint' or represent any special 'direction'; for phenomenology is nothing of either sort, nor can it become so long as it understands itself.[61]

Being simply cannot be bracketed. It is not our choice, our adoption of a 'standpoint' which presents entities (Husserl's *objects*) to us:

The entity is. *It is given, it confronts us; accordingly it* is *to be found at any time, and it is, in certain realms, known to us.*[62]

Our "primitive" view of the world (our unprejudiced examination of it), according to Heidegger, is not an experience of entities (objects) which can be so 'bracketed'. Husserl's supposedly 'presuppositionless' philosophy begins by presupposing that our familiarity with entities in the world is itself a philosophical theory which has been imposed on us. However, Heidegger tells us, our belief in the existence of entities and a *world* in general, is not a philosophical imposition, but an essential aspect of our most 'primitive' experience.

Furthermore, Heidegger rejects Husserl's famous catchphrase, quoted at the beginning of this section, "To the things themselves";

"Away from this empty word 'being': go to the particular entities" proves to be not only a hasty but also a highly questionable counsel.[63]

On the one hand, Heidegger does accept Husserl's direct appeal to phenomena; on the other hand, he rejects Husserl's appeal to particular *objects* (entities). The difference between the two is that Heidegger has already maintained that no understanding of Being, which is his goal, can ever be derived from any knowledge, no matter how direct, of particular beings:

How are we going to find our famous particulars, the individual trees as such, as trees; how shall we be able even to look *for trees, unless the representation of what a tree in general is shines before us? . . . Unless we are guided by a developed knowledge of treeness . . . we can look over thousands and thousands of trees in vain—we shall not see the tree for the trees.*[64]

Thus, phenomenological investigation for Heidegger will not be an examination of individual objects but an examination of the phenomenon of Being as such. The piecemeal investigation encouraged and practiced by Husserl will not have any place in Heidegger's philosophy. Moreover, "the World" will not simply be a totality of objects, but a peculiarly independent object for examination apart from any and all entities in it.

Husserl thought he had solved the problem of our knowledge of objects by arguing that there is a transcendental constitution of objects by the 'pure' or 'transcendental ego'. An object is constituted by this ego (through its noetic acts) as a system of noemata: intuitions and expectations of intuitions; each noema is a different "aspect" of that object. Heidegger retains large segments of Husserl's theory of perception, particularly his theory of constitution of objects out of various aspects ("noemata"),

the main thing is to impress it on our experience that we cannot immediately grasp the Being of the entity itself . . . we get only aspects.[65]

However, the all-important difference between Heidegger's theory and Husserl's is that *it is not an Ego that constitutes the world*.

In *Ideas I*, Husserl had argued, with Descartes, that the *cogito* or "I Think" remained after every doubting or 'reduction', and that it is the 'pure ego' which performs the acts of constitution which yield 'the World'. In his later writings, Husserl introduced an explicitly 'transcendental reduction', which reduced all objects of intuition to products of this ego. There is perhaps no thesis more antithetical to Heidegger than this reduction to the 'pure ego', and it is on this point that Heidegger makes his most radical break with the philosophers of the past (of the traditions we have been exploring). There is, to be sure, an important grammatical necessity for self-reference when talking about experiences of the world. We have a grammar which distinguishes subjects from predicates, and thus the language of perception necessarily speaks of a perceiver-subject and a perceived-object. Why should we accept this distinction, grammatically necessary or not? Why must we suppose that the necessity of referring to a subject is any sort of necessity other than grammatical necessity? Why need we postulate a "thinking substance" or "ego" as this subject, as Descartes did? Or, why should we even accept this notion of 'I Think' as a necessary condition or a 'unifying principle' for knowledge, as Kant did? Why should we accept the host of metaphors, accepted by Husserl as well as by Descartes and Kant, to the effect that there is an 'inside' and an 'outside' to consciousness (compare the notions of 'immanent', 'transcendent', 'subjective', 'objective', 'mental *contents'*, and 'in my mind'). Why do we accept the notion of "the *'external'* world" (usually with quotation marks) as a sensible expression, much less as a serious problem? In short, why do we accept a distinction between *subject* and *object*? Heidegger suggests nothing less radical than the rejection of this most basic common sense distinction, and with it, the rejection of the myriad of epistemological problems which have plagued modern philosophy. According to Heidegger, there is no ego, there is simply "Being-in-the-world." The world is no more 'bracketable' than the ego is necessary. Once we rid ourselves of the ego, we save ourselves from philosophical skepticism as well. It is here that Heidegger splits the "phenomenological movement" in two, and establishes "existential phenomenology" (not so called by Heidegger) as an effective threat to Husserl's entire enterprise, even among his own followers.

Dasein as Being-in-the-World

Although the stated concern of Heidegger's philosophy is the problem of Being, the problems of ethics and the study of a particular kind of Being—human being— occupy the bulk of *Sein und Zeit:*

It is noteworthy that in this questioning one kind of being persists in coming to the fore, namely the men who ask the question.[66]

Heidegger calls this special being-human being-*Dasein* (literally translated "Being-there"):

Dasein is an entity which does not just occur among other entities. Rather it is distinguished by the fact that, in its very Being, that Being is an issue for it. . . . It is peculiar to this entity that with and through its Being, this Being is disclosed to it. Understanding of Being is itself a definite characteristic of Dasein's Being.[67]

Dasein has "being in such a way that one has an understanding of Being."[68] Because of this *essential* relationship of Dasein (human being) to Being, the problem of Being must be approached through an investigation of Dasein;

Therefore, fundamental ontology, from which alone all other ontologies can take their rise, must be sought in the existential analytic of Dasein.[69]

If to interpret the meaning of Being becomes our task, Dasein is not only the primary entity to be interrogated; it is also that entity which already comports itself, in its Being, towards what we are asking about when we ask this question.[70]

The claim that we may come to understand Being (or "Being") through an analysis of Dasein looks dangerously similar to the traditional Cartesian approach to philosophy. Descartes wanted to capture (necessary) truths about the world (Being), and began with the 'discovery' and analysis of the subject, the *cogito,* of experience and knowledge. Similarly, Kant approached his theory of knowledge by examining the subjective or a priori conditions for experience and knowledge, and Husserl began his phenomenological investigations with an examination of the reduced 'pure' ego. Now, in spite of his departure from these philosophers, it might appear that Heidegger is also beginning his investigation with an examination of the *subject* of experience and knowledge, for the analysis of Dasein is explicitly presented as an answer to the traditional metaphysical question of self-identity.

It is of the utmost necessity, therefore, that we understand that the analysis of Dasein for Heidegger is not the examination of a *subject,* or an ego, or consciousness, and that the "self-identity" which becomes a problem in the question "Who is Dasein?" is a very different problem than it becomes for Descartes, Kant, and Husserl. The nature of Dasein thus becomes the focal point of *Sein und Zeit,* for it is with this strange new conception of human being that Heidegger intends to defend his attacks on Husserl's conception of phenomenology, to commence his answer to the "problem of Being," and to attack virtually the whole of Western philosophy as misguided. Heidegger is quick to point out that the question "Who is Dasein?" ("Who am I?") looks deceptively elementary, and we must not be misled into underestimating our ignorance on the subject just because that 'subject' happens to be ourselves. Contrary to Descartes' starting point, we do not know ourselves best and foremost: rather,

We say 'I am'. Each man can assert the being here intended only for himself: my being. Wherein does it consist and where does it reside? Seemingly this is what should be easiest for us to bring to light, for to no being are we so close as to what we ourselves are . . . And yet the truth is that everyone is remotest from himself, as remote as the I from the you in 'You are'.[71]

It could be that the 'who' of everyday Dasein just is not the 'I myself'.[72]

We have repeatedly encountered a distinction between two different "egos" or "selves" in past chapters. There is an *empirical ego,* which is that 'self' which can be cut by a razor, studied by a psychoanalyst or a sociologist, which is subject to laws of nature and which is a kind of natural 'object'; and there is a *transcendental* or *pure ego,* which can never be an object of experience, but which 'lies behind' or 'has' all experiences.[73] We may state at the outset that Heidegger's analysis of Dasein is similar to neither of these notions, and undercuts the basis for making this well-entrenched distinction between 'egos'. Heidegger rejects the notion of a philosophical or 'transcendental' subject altogether, and, with this rejection,

the notion of a 'subject' which can be treated as a natural 'object' becomes indefensible. The 'real self' is Dasein, but Dasein is neither subject nor natural object, and neither transcendental nor empirical.

In the analysis of Dasein, two very important distinctions are introduced (but not defined in the text), between *ontic* and *ontological,* and between *existential* and *existentielle.* The two distinctions are closely related, as they are related to several important distinctions in traditional philosophy. "Ontic" is an adjectival form of "existence," and might be interpreted as "having to do with existence" or "by virtue of existing" or simply "existent." For example, in a quote above (p. 198), we deleted (with dots) a use of "ontic" in which Heidegger speaks of Dasein as "ontically distinguished by Being being an issue for it." (The phrase "being-ontical" which occasionally occurs in *Sein und Zeit* [for example, p. 12] is redundant.) Contrasted with "ontic" is "ontological," which means "the study of being." An ontological investigation is one which asks the question of Being. Heidegger tells us that Dasein is essentially ontological, which means that Dasein necessarily asks about Being. This is stated as,

Dasein is ontically distinctive in that it is ontological.[74]

Only Dasein is ontological, although everything that exists is ontic. "Dasein's ontological structure" refers to the particular characteristic of Dasein such that it asks questions about Being.

From what has been said of "ontic" and "ontological," it should be evident that the distinction is approximate to the distinction between "reflexive" and "prereflexive" and "philosophical" and "prephilosophical" which occurs in other authors (for example, Kant, Hegel, and Husserl). Thus, Heidegger tells us that "ontically, we are Dasein, each one of us," but that "ontologically, we are farthest [from ourselves]."[75] Thus we are ourselves, that is a simple logical truth, but we do not *know* ourselves, that is, we cannot give an adequate analysis of ourselves. Ontology makes explicit ontic (or *preontological*) truths.

This characterization should lead us to see a link between the above distinction and the traditional empirical, a priori distinction of which we have had much to say. When Heidegger talks of "the ontical sciences" or "ontic truth," he is referring to "empirical truth." An ontological truth is a necessary truth. There are problems with this equivalence, however. Heidegger sometimes speaks of "ontic necessity," which shows that "ontic" sometimes can refer to necessities (for example, when Dasein is characterized as "ontically ontological"). Secondly, and more important philosophically, is the fact that the traditional empirical a priori distinction was employed with reference to *conceptual* knowledge, and one spoke of empirically and a priori true *propositions* (judgments). As we shall soon see, Heidegger very much wishes to expand his theory of 'knowledge' beyond conceptual knowledge, and so "ontic" and "ontological" will be applied to attitudes, actions, states-of-affairs, and properties, and will be used in other contexts in which the traditional empirical a priori distinction would not be used. We have already warned ourselves about Heidegger's manufacture of language. This is one of those cases in which a deviation from traditional terminology encompasses a marked change in philosophical viewpoint.

The second distinction, between "existentielle" and "existential" can now be quickly introduced. "Existentielle," is related to "ontical," and is the specific application of "ontical" to Dasein. Thus we can speak of the ontical structures of a tree, but can speak of existentielle structures of only Dasein. "Existentielle" when applied to Dasein, always refers to the nonessential. A statement about the existentielle structure of Dasein (for example, that human beings tend to worry about weight-gain) are always empirical statements. "Existential," on the other hand, is "ontological" applied specifically to Dasein. An "existential structure" of Dasein is an essential structure; all statements about Dasein's existential structures (or *existentialia*) are a priori (for example, that Dasein is "in-the-world"). Ontological (a priori) features of all other entities are called "categories" (after Kant).

With these distinctions at our disposal, we may now approach Heidegger's analysis of Dasein by stating that this analysis is itself an *existential* analysis—searching for the a priori structures of Dasein. These structures are preontological, but are explicated ontologically. The problem of finding these structures is therefore the problem of correctly describing (ontologically) these necessary structures. To do so, we adopt Husserl's method of phenomenological investigation, and attempt to arrive at a "primitive" or "original" (that is, unprejudiced or presuppositionless) view of ourselves in relation to the world. Husserl suggests that the first truth of the application of this method is the distinction between subject and object ("immanent" and "transcendent," *cogito* and *cogitatio*). Heidegger, we have suggested but not yet argued, maintains that the first truth of phenomenology ought to be the absence of any such distinction.

Dasein is not a subject but undermines the traditional distinction between "subject" and "object" because Dasein is introduced and defined as *"being-in-the-world."* Dasein cannot be distinguished, even in logic, from its existence in the world. Therefore, it makes no sense to suppose that we know ourselves better than we know the world, and it makes no sense to say that we know about ourselves in a different way than we know about the world. We do not know ourselves 'immediately' and certainly and 'know' the world only 'mediately' and always with a certain skepticism. We know ourselves and the world identically, for ourselves (as Dasein) and the world constitute a single phenomenon:

The compound expression 'Being-in-the-world' indicates in the very way we have coined it, that it stands for a unitary phenomenon.[76]

Let us refamiliarize ourselves with a move against Kant in Hegel's philosophy. Kant begins his philosophy with a sharp subject-object dichotomy, resulting in the problematic distinction between phenomena (objects as they appear to the subject) and *noumena* (objects as they exist in themselves). Hegel complains that the very drawing of this distinction leads one to an ultimate skepticism, never knowing whether one really knows things as they are or not. In response to Kant, Hegel introduces his notion of 'Geist' (and the notion of 'the Idea' in the *Logics*) which is "subject and substance as well." Spirit or the Idea is neither subject nor object, and this avoidance of the subject-object distinction allows Hegel to claim access to 'absolute knowledge'. We may look at Heidegger's move against Husserl (in particular) as a similar attempt to avoid the skepticism which the latter has made the unwanted (but unrefuted) consequence of his philosophy. To begin by 'bracketing' the world is to commit oneself to skepticism from the outset. Thus, Heidegger rejects the phenomenological *epoche* as the greatest danger to Husserl's own goals. The world cannot be bracketed or doubted, for the ego or consciousness, the Archimedian point from which all such bracketing or doubting takes place, is a philosophical illusion. There is no subject distinguishable and therefore separable from the world; there is simply Dasein, Being-in-the-world. It makes no sense, therefore, to ask how Dasein could "reach beyond itself to grasp the world," or to suppose that Dasein is dreaming of a world but not part of it. "Dasein" and "Being-in-the-world" are inseparable, they are (defined as) the same phenomenon.

We may grant that the skepticism arising from this subject-object distinction has been a constant source of philosophical perplexity in 'modern' Western philosophy. However, has Heidegger done more for us than *define* the problem out of existence? Is not the "subject-object" distinction at the basis of common sense? Is it not even at the very foundation of our language? Could we dispense with the distinction without giving up the subject-predicate grammar which is the basis of English (and German)? Has Heidegger 'solved' the most pressing problem of knowledge by simply defining a new term in which that problem cannot be stated? It is as if one were to solve the quasi-philosophical question, "Were there eggs before chickens or chickens before eggs?" by introducing a term "cheg," which signifies indiscriminately both chickens and eggs, and thereby declared the problem solved, seeing how one need not ask whether there were *chegs* before there were *chegs*.

This is not the sort of arbitrary problem-busting which is performed by Heidegger. He has introduced a new terminology and a new starting point for philosophical investigation, but neither is arbitrary. We must remember that Heidegger is doing phenomenology, and that justification for his starting point as well as his terminology must be its accuracy of description of "primitive" experience. The justification for the rejection of the

subject-object distinction and the resultant substitution of "Dasein" in place of the very different traditional concepts of "ego," "consciousness," and "subject" must be defended by phenomenological inquiry. This inquiry will show us, according to Heidegger, two fundamental mistakes in traditional philosophy and in Husserl's philosophy in particular; first, the identification of the ego or consciousness is not founded on phenomenological *Evidenz* (cf. p. 154); and second, there is a distinction between *the world* and the *objects in the world* to which former philosophers have not paid sufficient attention.

The first point is not new, but Heidegger will make brilliantly new uses of it. The rejection of the ego as a phenomenological datum was ably presented by David Hume (quoted in Chapter 1, p. 22), who claimed that among his various 'impressions,' there was nothing which corresponded to him*Self*. Husserl had told us to go "back to the things themselves," and then begins himself by talking about an *ego* which, by its very nature, cannot be defended by phenomenology. Heidegger is making a basically Humean point—there is no experience which can justify talk about an ego or consciousness, and, because of the rigorous restrictions on phenomenological research, such talk cannot be initiated apart from its foundation in phenomenology itself. There is, therefore, no subject, no ego, and an accurate, 'primitive' view of our experience of the world cannot describe this experience as an experience *of* an ego. It cannot even say with Hume that there are experiences (or "thoughts" after Descartes), for this description leads us back to the notion of a "subject" that 'has' experiences. There is simply, according to Heidegger's analysis, Being-in-the-world.

Why have philosophers been so misled so consistently? They have been misled by grammar, and have interpreted a grammatical necessity for an ontological (metaphysical) one. The famous *cogito* of Descartes, the 'I Think' of Kant, and the 'pure ego' of Husserl, these are only exaggerated recognitions of a grammar which forces us to use the expression 'I'. This is *only* a grammatical necessity, it does not refer us to any special substance, or even to a unifying principle of consciousness. It has no ontological significance whatsoever;

*The word 'I' is to be understood only
in the sense of a noncommittal formal
indicator, . . .*[77]

There is, therefore, no 'I' which can be
substantially distinguished from the world
in general, and there can be no bracketing
or doubting of things 'outside of' consciousness. Once we have given up the
notion of an indubitable 'primitive' ego
and the resultant metaphors ("contents
of consciousness," the "external world"),
traditional epistemological problems cannot be raised.

The second point raised against Husserl
is more complicated and equally askew
with our common sense and traditional
philosophical 'prejudices'. Descartes
moved from the observation that he was
aware of sometimes being fooled by his
senses to the skeptical conclusion that perhaps he was always fooled by his senses.
In other words, Descartes found himself
able to justifiably doubt his knowledge regarding particular objects and began to
suspect that he could with equal justification doubt the world as a whole. The
world as a whole, of course, is all objects,
and so it is characterized, innocently
enough, by most philosophers. Some will
say that the world is the "totality of
facts,"[78] others that the world is the
"totality of objects that can be known
through experience."[79] All such characterizations of the world are naive and insidious, according to Heidegger. *The world*
is something different from entities-in-the-
world, and, as we found that we could
not understand *Being* through an investigation of *entities* (p. 193), we now find that
we cannot understand *the world* through an
understanding of a 'totality' of entities:

*Neither the ontical depiction of entities
within-the-world nor the ontological
interpretation of their Being is such as to
reach the phenomenon of the 'world'.*[80]

"The World," in this special sense, is an
essential characteristic or structure (an
existential) of Dasein. It is an "onto-
logico-existential concept."[81] In this context, Heidegger speaks of the "worldhood
of the world."[82] We can doubt the existence of any and even all particular objects within-the-world, but we cannot
doubt (or 'bracket') the world itself. In
linguistic terminology, "the world" is not

an *extensional* concept—a concept denoting a set—here an indefinitely large set
of existing objects, but rather an *intentional* concept, a concept whose meaning
is distinct from whatever objects, to which
it might be used to refer. Even if the
world were totally different, it would still
be the *same* world, and this world could
even be devoid of objects. The world is
composed of entities, but it is not constituted by those entities. To relate this to
a familiar mathematical analog, we may
wish to speak about sets and their properties differently than we would speak
about members of sets and their properties.
There can be, and we can characterize in detail, sets which have no members. Heidegger is telling us that our conception of the world is like a conception of
a set; it is not the composite conception
of the various subsets and members.

What is it for Dasein to Be-in-the-world,
if it is not to be one among indefinitely
many entities? We must understand that
the *'in'* in the expression 'in-the-world'
when applied to Dasein is a very special
sense of 'in'. Dasein is not *in* the world as
a prisoner is *in* the stockade, for Dasein
is not simply an entity among entities in
space. Space, like the world, is one of
Dasein's structures. We tend to think of
ourselves as *in* space in the usual sense of
'in' only because we are able to give our
bodies a spatial (and temporal) location
in a worldly (that is, ontic) coordinate
system and we naively think of our Selves
as 'in' our bodies;

*the naive supposition that man is, in the
first instance, a spiritual thing which
subsequently gets misplaced 'into'
a space.*[83]

Like Kant's 'a priori forms of intuition',
space for Heidegger is projected by
Dasein; it is one of its essential structures.
For Heidegger, unlike Kant, it is not a
subject that constitutes this spatial structure 'in' the world, but it is a structure
constituted *as* Dasein. As we cannot stress
enough, Dasein and the world are logically inseparable, and it is the "unitary
structure" of *Being-in-the-world* which has
the world, spatiality, as one of its essential structures. For Heidegger, the "phenomenological standpoint" and "the natural standpoint" cannot be distinguished
by the *epoche*. Being-in-the-world is the

only possible standpoint, the only *logically* possible standpoint (we might well refuse to call it a 'standpoint' at all). There can be no talk of Dasein apart from its Being-in-the-world, and no sense to talk about 'the World' apart from Dasein. Here we can see a new realization of Husserl's ambition to go beyond *both* traditional idealism and realism. Heidegger's philosophy rejects idealism, because it rejects the self or consciousness to which all 'reality' belongs according to idealism; it also rejects realism, however, for it makes no sense to suppose that there might be a world apart from Dasein. Dasein is not simply one more entity within the world.

We have indicated that Heidegger accepts an equivalent of Husserl's notion of 'transcendental constitution' but rejects the notion of 'transcendental constitution *by the subject*'. This should raise no problems if we avoid thinking of *constitution* as an activity performed by an agent on some object. "The World is constituted by Dasein and Dasein is constituted by the world" means simply that there is no sense to any reference *beyond* Dasein and no sense to separating Dasein from the world. Space, for example, is constituted by Dasein as one of its structures. The World, according to Heidegger, is the realm of *meanings* (as consciousness is described by Husserl); *the world,* which is an existential of Dasein, is a space-oriented conceptual framework in which there are entities and other Daseins. It makes no sense to ask, therefore, if there are things *outside* of this world. There is simply no way to make sense out of this "outside of." Heidegger tells us that "the world *belongs to* Dasein"; this is not a restatement of idealism but a reminder that there can be no intelligible distinction between *Dasein* and the *World.*

All of this so far is intended primarily to establish an essentially negative point, that it is a mistake to distinguish the world from that which perceives and knows the world, and all subsequent discussion must embark from a position in which this mistake is avoided. To avoid this mistake, Heidegger borrows Husserl's 'radical empiricism' as well as his basic 'prejudices' against skepticism and any notion which would make sense of a "world outside of our own" and argues that philosophy must begin with the special conception of Dasein, with which

all doubts concerning our knowledge of the world-in-itself cannot arise.

The World as Equipment
Our starting point in the formulation of our 'primitive' or 'natural viewpoint of the world' is Dasein as Being-in-the-world. The world is an essential structure of Dasein, but particular entities in the world to which Dasein relates are not essential structures or existentialia of Dasein. Consequently, there are necessary connections between Dasein and the world, but not between Dasein and entities in the world. The entities we confront might be different (there might not be any entities). We can talk of the absence of particular entities, but not intelligibly talk of the absence of the world (as in Cartesian doubt). It is with reference to entities, not the world, that we can begin to speak of a distinction between subject and object. However, we have yet to examine the primitive relationship between Dasein and particular entities.

In traditional philosophy, for example, in the philosophies of Descartes, Kant, and Husserl, this relationship is one of *knowing,* and the entities known are *things* or *objects:*

The phenomenon of Being-in has for the most part been represented exclusively by a single exemplar—knowing the world. This has not only been the case in epistemology; for even practical behavior has been understood as behavior which is 'non-theoretical' and 'atheoretical'.[84]

We now ask which entities shall be taken as our preliminary theme and established as the pre-phenomenal basis for our study. . . . One may answer: "Things." But with this obvious answer we have perhaps already missed the pre-phenomenal basis we are seeking. For in addressing these entities as Things, we have tacitly anticipated their ontological character.[85]

This emphasis on *knowing things* has 'concealed' from us our 'primitive' or 'natural' viewpoint;

Because knowing has been given this priority, our understanding of its own-most kind of being gets led astray.[86]

It has been the traditional mistake of philosophers to suppose that our *conscious-*

ness of the world is primarily a knowing of the world (compare Descartes, Kant, and Husserl), but

the 'commercium' of the subject with a world does not get created for the first time by knowing, nor does it arise from some way in which the world acts upon the subject [compare Husserl's uncomfortable dualism between 'intuition' of objects and 'constitution' of objects]. Knowing as a mode of Dasein founded upon Being-in-the-world, as a basic state, must be interpreted beforehand.[87]

What is this basic state if it is not a knowledge of things?

The Being of those entities which we encounter as closest to us can be exhibited phenomenologically if we take as our clue our everyday Being-in-the-world, which we also call our "dealings" in the world and with entities in-the-world. Such dealings have already dispersed themselves into manifold ways of concern. This kind of dealing which is closest to us is . . . not a bare perceptual cognition, but rather that kind of concern which manipulates things and puts them to use; and this has its own kind of "knowledge."[88]

In Husserlian terminology, there are many intentional (noetic) acts one can perform towards objects, but Husserl took all of these to be related to a narrow paradigm of *knowing*—the sort of theoretical or descriptive knowledge of the scientist in careful detached reflection. According to Heidegger, this sort of knowing is not our 'original' encounter with the world, but derivative of more practical relationships, for example,

having to do with something, producing something, attending to something and looking after it, making use of something, giving something up and letting it go, undertaking, accomplishing, evincing, interrogating, considering, discussing, determining . . .[89]

Heidegger characterizes these general 'practical' attitudes as *concern* (*Besorge*). Being-in-the-world is primarily *using* entities, and the entities thus encountered are not *things*:[90]

We shall call those entities which we encounter in concern "equipment."[91]

It would seem to be a point unworthy of a central position in Heidegger's philosophy that we use entities as well as know them, but the claim we find in Heidegger is much more radical than that. Heidegger is denying a proposition that most philosophers would consider as analytically true, "the world is full of things." We do not first recognize things and then find uses for them; we use entities before we can recognize them as things. The notion of *thinghood* is a derivative concept, derivative of the concept of *equipment*.

What is *equipment* as opposed to *things*? Things are characterized *ontologically* in the familiar terms of "substantiality, materiality, extension, contiguity."[92] To say that an entity is a thing is to say that it takes up space, that it has substance, that it enters into causal relationships with other things, that it can (in principle) be moved from one location to another. In familiar philosophical terms, to recognize an entity as a thing is to apply the Kantian Categories (and forms of intuition) of the Understanding to 'it'. On this viewpoint, the World is the totality of things, spacially extended, substantial, and knowable.

Equipment is not *categorized* in this way, and the world as a totality of equipment is not so categorized either. This is not to say that a hammer, a book, and a pen are not material objects or not spacially extended, of course, but as equipment they are not so viewed. In using a hammer, for example,

an entity of this kind is not grasped thematically (that is, known theoretically) as an occurring thing, nor is the equipment-structure known as such ever in the using. The hammerer does not simply have knowledge about the hammer's character as equipment, but it has appropriated this equipment in a way which could not possibly be more suitable. In dealings such as this, where something is put to use, our concern subordinates itself to the "in-order-to" which is constitutive for the equipment we are employing at the time; the less we just stare at the hammer-Thing, and the more we seize hold of it and use it, the more primordial does our relationship to it become, and the more unveiledly is it encountered as that which it is—as equipment.[93]

There is a distinction between *things* and *equipment* which is not simply a distinction between things we can use and things for which we have no use. We look at ('stare at') things; our 'knowledge' of entities of use is not a 'looking at' at all. An everyday observation may help clarify this difference: A violinist who knows how to play a difficult passage begins to fumble when he attempts to 'observe' his fingers; a cyclist who 'knows' his cycle is prone to spills as soon as he begins to theorize about his riding; there is a parable of the centipede who when asked how he so admirably coordinated his many legs found himself unable to walk at all. This empirical observation already indicates that there are two very different activities of "knowing" involved in observing and in using. Heidegger tells us that these two sorts of knowing, "knowing how" and "knowing that," are correlated with two different ways of encountering entities—equipment and things.

Consider the strange experience we have when we notice a part of our bodies, which is equipment in this sense, as a thing (for example, when we see a detached hand, or "notice" our hands dangling from the ends of our wrists). What makes this experience bizarre is the fact that our hands are never considered by us as things, but as equipment. We do not think of them as 'material objects' (not that they cannot always be correctly so considered) but as a constantly usable set of tools. Hands in a thing-context are something strange. (In this light, we may recall G. E. Moore's famous 'refutation' of idealism, "I have two thumbs. Thumbs are material objects. *Ergo,* there are material objects.")

Our understanding of an entity as equipment, or of what it is for an entity to be equipment, in general, is never reducible to our understanding of things:

No matter how sharply we just look at the 'outward appearance' of Things in whatever form this takes, we cannot discover anything ready-to-hand. If we look at things just 'theoretically', we can get along without understanding readiness-to-hand [zuhanden]; *of tools and equipment.*[94]

Equipment is not a thing with a use, but not a thing at all. A thing has properties, causal relationships, a location in space; a tool has a use, is employed in a project, occurs in a total tool-context. Things can be isolated, a hammer-Thing remains a

thing wherever we might encounter it. It is a thing which can be useless, thrown into the outer reaches of space, destroyed as a tool and still remain a thing. The hammer as a thing is context independent. The hammer-tool, on the contrary, is always dependent on an equipment context. A hammer is not a (tool-)hammer where there can be no hammering:

Taken strictly, there 'is' no such thing as an equipment. To the Being of any equipment there always belongs a totality of equipment, in which it can be this equipment that it is.[95]

Equipment—in accordance with its equipmentality—always is in terms of its belonging to other equipment: inkstand pen, ink, paper, blotting pad, table, lamp, furniture, windows, doors, room. . . . Out of this the 'arrangement' emerges and it is in this that any 'individual' item of equipment shows itself. Before it does so, a totality of equipment has already been discovered.[96]

We now see why equipment is not things; our *concern* for equipment is inseparably tied to a total context of a task-to-be-done-here. We do not notice individual things, therefore, but only the entire context;

Dealings with equipment subordinate themselves to the manifold assignments of 'in-order-to'. And the sight with which they thus accommodate themselves is circumspection.[97]

The context of equipment is lit up, not as something

never seen before, but as a totality constantly sighted beforehand in circumspection. With this totality, however, the world announces itself.[98]

It is not to be thought that the distinction between things and equipment (and between two correlated kinds of knowing) entails that there can be no knowledge in equipment contexts. To the contrary, the purpose of this exposition is to stress the primacy of *knowing how* and to unseat the time-honored priority of conceptual *knowing that.* Knowing how to use a hammer is true knowledge, even if one is incapable of verbalizing this knowledge. (Consider the absurdity of "I know how to play the violin." "How do you?")

Practical behavior has its own sort of knowledge of which conceptual or theoretical knowledge is derivative:

The way it [practical behavior] differs from theoretical behavior does not lie simply in that fact that in theoretical behavior one observes while in practical behavior one acts, and that action must employ theoretical cognition if it is not to become blind. . . . action has its own kind of sight. Theoretical behavior is just looking, without circumspection. But the fact that this looking is non-circumspective does not mean that it follows no rules; it constructs a canon for itself in the form of method.[99]

We have claimed that there is a distinct difference between equipment and things and two ways of 'knowing', but we have also claimed (that is, Heidegger has claimed) that equipment and 'knowing how' are primitive, while things and 'knowing that' are derivative. The argument for this is brief[100] as there is considerable attention given to the mode of derivation of things from equipment, but little argument that the derivation could not be argued conversely. The claim, clearly enough, is that one can derive a thing view from an equipment concern, but one cannot derive an equipment concern from a thing view.

How is a thing view derived from an equipment concern? It has probably struck the reader as palpably false that tools are always in a tool context, for it is evident that tools can be misplaced, or unusable for any number of reasons. Heidegger does not deny this, rather he uses this as his key to introducing our derivation of "thinghood." We might bring up another everyday observation: we do not notice tools which are totally dependably ready-at-hand. We rarely notice our hands, for example, as we probably would not notice our pen if we always had it present. If our fingers were numb from the cold, they would become a source of irritation and be noticed. If our pen was broken or missing, it would then come to our attention. This everyday observation is mirrored in an important philosophical thesis, that the 'primitive' view of the world as totality of equipment depends on a certain dependable order, what Heidegger calls "the whole workshop." When tools become unuseful, then we begin to look at them as opposed to simply using them:

When we concern ourselves with something, the entities which are most closely ready-to-hand may be met as something unusable, not properly adapted for the use we have decided upon. The tool turns out to be damaged, or the material unsuitable. In each of these cases equipment is here, ready-to-hand. We discover its unusability, however, not by looking at it and establishing its properties, but rather by the circumspection of the dealings in which we use it. When its unusability is thus discovered, equipment becomes conspicuous. This conspicuousness presents the ready-to-hand equipment as in a certain unreadiness-to-hand. But this implies that what cannot be used just lies there; it shows itself as an equipment-Thing which looks so-and-so, and which, in its readiness-to-hand as looking that way, has constantly been present-at-hand too. Pure presence-at-hand announces itself in such equipment.[101]

Heidegger distinguishes three categories of disruptions in our equipment world which lead us to look at our equipment as things, as equipment items become conspicuous. Through damage, a tool may become unusable, and becomes *conspicuous* through its failure to perform. We notice our pen, instead of the work we are writing, when the pen leaks or fails to write. We notice a part of our automobile only when it causes the car to malfunction. We notice our lack of physical strength when we find ourselves unable to lift something. Secondly, we may reach for a tool and find it is missing; thus we first think of the pen as a thing instead of a tool when we cannot find it and have to look for it. We do not think of the pen as having shape and color when we are writing, but these features become all-important when we begin our search for it. Heidegger calls this *obtrusiveness*. Finally, our equipment may not work well or be ready for us, but items of our equipment world may actually block our progress. Thus, we do not notice the books on our typing table until they block the movement of the carriage; this *obstinacy* then brings these books to our attention. These disruptions are responsible for our coming to view entities as things rather than as mere equipment:

The modes of conspicuousness,

obtrusiveness, and obstinacy all have the
function of bringing to the fore the
characteristic of presence-at-hand in
what is ready-to-hand.[102]

If our equipment world were always to
function smoothly, we could never come
to have a conception of *things.* Knowledge
of the world (knowledge that) is a
product of disaster on this theory (although very minor disasters will suffice).

We have seen how several of the philosophers we have studied concern themselves with the traditional theory-practice
distinction. Some maintain it (Kant),
some deny it (Fichte and Hegel), some
maintain it but heavily stress one side of
it (Kierkegaard). Nietzsche attacks the
distinction, but for the most part, he
simply limits his interests to practical concerns, not denying the possibility of theory
but simply considering theory as it relates
to practice. Conversely, Husserl acknowledges the reality of values, but treats
value and practice only so far as they
enter into his interests in knowledge. (In
his last work, *Crisis of European Philosophy,* Husserl adopts Heidegger's 'pragmatic' picture in his characterization of
a *Lebenswelt.* There, Knowledge is secondary to "living".) Heidegger, however,
provides us with the first thorough analysis of this theoretical-practical distinction. He does not deny the distinction
as such, but does maintain that all theoretical concerns are derivative of practical
ones. This does not commit him to the
position that all theoretical concerns are
practical concerns, for it is possible that
the offspring of practical concern may become independent of its pragmatic
parentage. In fact, this is the case, and
Heidegger does not claim that there are
no impractical theoretical pursuits. On the
contrary, we have seen that Heidegger's
view of philosophy commits him to saying
that there is at least one discipline which
is essentially impractical. We shall see,
however, that the impracticality of philosophy does not entail that philosophy
makes no difference. The analysis of
Dasein, notably, will yield 'ontological' results which cannot possibly be interpreted
with 'detached' theoretical interest.

Care

In *Being and Time,* Dasein is further defined as *care (Sorge);* all other structures
of Dasein are introduced as structures of
care. Care is a generalized structure of the
concern *(Besorge)* which we encountered
earlier. *Care* in Heidegger plays much the
same role as "intentionality" in the philosophy of Husserl. However, we have already seen that Heidegger objects to
Husserl's overemphasis on the intentional
acts of knowing, believing, asserting, judging, and his almost total neglect of more
'practical' intentional acts, such as 'using',
'taking advantage of', 'despising', 'wanting
to eat', 'looking for', and so on. Dasein's
structure as care is parallel to Husserl's
thesis that the structure of consciousness
is *intentionality.* It is the nature of
Dasein/consciousness to always be
Dasein-in-the-world/consciousness of objects. The very nature of Dasein/con-
sciousness is such that Dasein/conscious-
ness must always find itself confronting
an object. Of course, as we have repeatedly insisted, the *object* has a very different ontological status in the philosophies
of Husserl and Heidegger (as Dasein is
radically different from 'consciousness').
Care is intentionality, but with a new emphasis on the more 'practical' and 'noncognitive' acts which were neglected by Husserl. It is easy to feel the influence of
Kierkegaard here:

The real subject is not the cognitive
subject . . . the real subject is the ethically
existing subject. The only reality that exists
for the existing individual is his own
ethical reality. [103]

In an earlier section, we saw that Heidegger argues that our 'primitive' encounter
with the world is not *cognitive*—is not
knowing the world—and we do not 'primitively' confront *things.* Rather, our relationship to the world is 'originally' practical, and the objects we confront are first
of all equipment or tools. In this context,
we said that our primitive attitude to the
world is not one of knowledge, but one of
concern. In concern, we see a tool as part
of a totality of equipment; we see the
world as this totality of equipment. Man's
concerns are not limited to his concern to
get a task completed, to use a tool to do
a job; man is ultimately concerned about
himself, and it is this ultimate concern
which is *care.* Dasein (care) is essentially
self-concern. This is not to be interpreted
in the vulgar sense in which it is said that
man is essentially selfish. Dasein is not
self-concerned in the "nasty brutish short"
manner of Hobbes' presocietal man, but

he is concerned for himself in a primarily *philosophical* way. He is not only concerned to obtain food, territory, sexual gratification for himself, he is concerned to gain philosophical enlightenment. The concern for himself is basically the concern to find out *who he is.* Care is the search for self-identity (compare Nietzsche's *Übermensch* and his striving for power in Chapter 4).

We have already noted that Heidegger characterizes Dasein as that Being such that "in its very being, Being is an issue for it." and that "in Dasein's being, its being is in question."[104] We may now relate this "ontological character" of Dasein to the basic existential structure of Care; Dasein is essentially that which seeks self-identity;

In its very being this being relates to its being. As a being of this kind it is entrusted to its own being.[105]

It is by virtue of this concern for self-identity that Dasein relates to other persons, to objects, and even to oneself. The fascinating thesis here is that all human endeavors are ultimately directed towards self-recognition, towards the defining of oneself. The "mineness" we mentioned already is thus the focus of Dasein as well as its central attribute. Descartes' *cogito,* on this account, is not a fundamental philosophical truth so much as an articulated symbol of the central goal of Dasein. However, it is not enough to simply recognize that one exists; one must appreciate and understand the nature of this existence. Thus Heidegger's philosophy is a working out of this essential human quest, finding out what (who) we are.

Again we must emphasize that this search for self-identity is not a peculiarly philosophical enterprise, a task which confronts only philosophers. Everyman is Dasein, and everyman asks this same question. Ontologically, it is the philosophers who are most explicitly concerned with the question, but philosophers have no privileged position, and often (Heidegger points out frequently) the 'schoolishness' of professional philosophy leaves the 'philosopher' less capable of answering or even recognizing the question of self-identity than other men. However, every time a man asks what he is doing with his life, or contemplates suicide, or considers his impending death, or asks why he was

born or why he must die, he is manifesting this basic self-questioning structure of Dasein.

The essential structure of *care* as this self-questioning is not, however, sufficient to insure that all men do so question all the time. To the contrary, Heidegger admits that men rarely question, and the "fallenness from Being" of our age is due to our forgetting how to ask such questions. The existential (essential) structures disclosed by Heidegger yield human (Dasein) potentialities, but not necessities. Thus, the thesis that man (Dasein) is essentially ontological—self-questioning—does not mean that all men do ask questions, but only that it is possible for them to do so at any time. We shall later see that the *necessity* of asking questions arises only in order for Dasein to live *authentically.* It is also possible for Dasein to live inauthentically and suppress these questions. This too is one of the 'existential' structures of Dasein.

This brings up a most difficult point of interpretation for us; Heidegger tells us that this 'essential' characteristic of man is nevertheless one which most men fail to fulfill. He also tells us that the failure to fulfill it is one more essential characteristic of Dasein. If it is not necessary that men *do* question, what is the status of the expectation that they will question their identity. A most plausible suggestion is that man *ought* to question his own Being by virtue of his own nature. Heidegger, however, rejects this interpretation, and without it we are somewhat at a loss to explain in what sense men essentially are or ought to be *ontological.*

A partial answer to this dilemma, which will be examined for most of the remainder of this chapter, is given by the fact that Dasein has 'in itself' no fixed specific qualities—life styles, goals, or values—but that these are created by Dasein;

Dasein decides its existence, whether it does so by taking hold or by neglecting.[106]

This is to say that every Dasein does provide an answer to the question of self-identity in choosing a life for himself. Many people choose, however, by neglect, by simply accepting a *given* way of life. They face the question of being, but not articulately, and without giving serious consideration to all of the alternatives. In other words, all men face and provide their answer to the question of (their) Being, but most men face the question only on an *ontic* level, prereflectively, and answer the question simply by accepting a given way of life. Although this is, as we shall see, the paradigm of *inauthenticity,* it is nevertheless a recognition (and suppression) of the question of Being. Authenticity does not differ from inauthenticity in the recognition of the question, therefore, but differs in the explicitness of its confrontation. The authentic Dasein makes the question articulate and does not suppress it but recognizes the radical nature and extent of the choices of his *Existenz* offered him. To ask the question of Being, of self-identity, is therefore an essential structure of all men, and all men do ask this question, but some explicitly and with an honest recognition of the range of answers (authenticity) although most men simply suppress the question as soon as they recognize it and rely on a ready-made answer provided by others (inauthenticity).

What does or should one recognize when he asks the question, "Who am I?" One should and will recognize in himself three existential (essential) structures, which Heidegger calls *Existenz, Facticity,* and *Fallenness.* Of course, every man cannot be expected to know before reading Heidegger these fanciful names for these structures, but everyman in his self-examination nevertheless recognizes them whether he chooses to face them honestly (in authenticity) or to suppress this recognition (in inauthenticity). These three structures are called *existentialia* or sometimes *existentials* as well as "existential structures." They are a priori characteristics of Dasein; they are not to be confused with *categories* which are also a priori characteristics but which apply to objects or entities within the world other than Dasein. We have already discussed in detail the first existential structure of Dasein—its Being-in-the-world. However, we have also discussed, or at least been introduced to, many other existentialia as well; "*Being-in*" is listed as an existential —that is, in Kantian terms, the constitution of space. We have also seen that man's 'primitive' attitude towards the world as equipment is an existential and the characterization of Dasein as the Being who questions its own Being is an existential. The necessity of referring to Dasein with a first-person pronoun is an-

other existentialia of great significance. Dasein's concern towards the world is another; Dasein's *possibility* for *choosing* is an existential, as is his tendency to live an inauthentic given life. We shall also find that *death* constitutes an existential, as do those philosophically significant experiences discussed by Kierkegaard as *dread, guilt,* and *resolution. Freedom* in Kierkegaard becomes another structure of Dasein, and, consequently and of the greatest importance for Sartre and Merleau-Ponty, the possibility of *authenticity* and *inauthenticity* are existentialia.

If this is an ominous list of a priori structures, we might begin by noting that they are all interrelated, and we might even say, as Heidegger sometimes leads us to say, that they are all derivative of the central characterization of Dasein's existence as ontological (self-questioning) being-in-the-world. Heidegger, unlike Kant, does not give us a single neat table of existentialia. Perhaps this gives him a freedom from "schematizing formalism" (Hegel's complaint against Schelling) which closes itself off from an open analysis; but it makes it difficult for an interpreter who must organize these into a pattern. Perhaps the simplest way is to follow the pattern of *Sein und Zeit* itself, which is, although it begins with the question of Being, a long analysis of the a priori structures—*existentialia*—of Dasein.

Authentic living, or authentic self-recognition, is the recognition of the three existential structures of *Existenz, Facticity,* and *Fallenness. Existenz*[107] is defined in terms of *possibility* and *understanding.* Dasein as *Existenz* is the projection of possibilities by the understanding (*Verstehen*). We shall see that Heidegger's concept of "understanding" here is very much like Kant's concept of "reason in its practical employment." Dasein's facticity (*Facticität*) is "Dasein's finding himself already in the world" (*Befindlichkeit*):

The concept of "facticity" implies that
an entity 'within-the-world' has
Being-in-the-world in such a way that it
can understand itself as bound up in its
'destiny' with the Being of those entities
which it encounters within its own
world.[108]

Facticity is the *fact* that Dasein exists, and exists in a *particular* world (for example, twentieth-century America, born on this date from these parents. . .). (This notion of "facticity" is lifted by Sartre, for whom it also becomes a basic structure of being-human.) We have encountered the concept of "fallenness" already. "Fallenness from Being" is failure to ask the question of Being and failure to question one's own being in particular. Fallenness is "falling captive to the world." It is to 'forget' (or refuse to recognize) one's true existential nature as all three structures, including possibilities and 'given' facts, and to lose all perspective and involve oneself with the petty tasks of the present as they 'present' themselves. It is this structure of Dasein which manifests itself in inauthenticity. The tendency to fallenness threatens all of us all of the time, and most of us yield to it, according to Heidegger, most of the time. *Average Everydayness,* the normal lot of man, is a state of fallenness.

The first definition of *care* provided for us by Heidegger is in fact a restatement of Dasein as these three structures. Care is the "unity" of these structures; *care* is, by definition,

ahead-of-itself- already-being-in (the-world-) as being-near-to (beings encountered within the world).[109]

The first part of this formula ("ahead-of-itself") refers to Dasein's *Existenz* or projection of possibilities; the second part ("already-being-in-the-world") refers to Facticity of Dasein's already finding himself in the world; and the last part refers to man's tendency to fallenness, the "falling captive to the world."

Existenz: Possibility and Understanding
The concept of *Existenz* refers to that a priori or existential structure of Dasein that is a "projection of possibilities." This very special notion of *Existenz* has its ancestry in Kierkegaard's writings, where he separates those "truly existing human beings" who recognize their possibilities from those 'men' with "so-called existence" who do not. Heidegger, like Kierkegaard, insists that freedom of choice and recognition of this freedom is the very essence of *Existenz;*

The 'essence' of Dasein consists of its Existenz.[110]

Dasein is mine to be in one way or another. Dasein has always made some sort of

decision as to the way in which it is in each case mine. That entity which in its being has this very being as an issue, comports itself towards its Being as its ownmost possibility.[111]

Existenz (Ek-sistenz—"standing-out") is the projection of possibilities, so we must inquire into the nature of these possibilities and the nature of this projection.

In each case Dasein is its possibility, and it 'has' this possibility, but not just as a property as something present at hand would. And because Dasein is in each case essentially its own possibility, it can, in its very being, 'choose 'itself and win itself; it can also lose itself and never win itself; or it can only 'seem' to do so.[112]

It is most important that Heidegger insists that *Existenz is* possibility and does not simply say that *Existenz has* possibilities (compare Kierkegaard's "Human being *is* freedom"). *Existenz* does not have possibilities as an acorn has the possibility of becoming an oak tree; one can give independent characterization of the acorn. One cannot give any independent characterization of *Existenz.* We shall see that this characterization of *Existenz* as possibility instead of as something with possibilities shall be a central theme in both Heidegger and Sartre.

Dasein is ("in each case," that is, for each person) "its own possibility." This means that we should not expect to find a general set of potentialities or capacities for all human beings. This warning, so typical of the existentialists, can easily become confusing. It is not to say that we cannot give a general biological specification of what will count as *homo sapiens* and what will not; nor is it even to say that certain generalizations as to what people value and how they behave are not in order and will not be empirically accurate. It is rather the claim, reminiscent of Nietzsche particularly, that we should not expect any a priori characterization of human projects, goals, and values. According to Heidegger, there is no 'human nature', and there are, therefore, no given human endeavors. Kant, in his characterization of rationality, has told us that man can postulate any end he chooses, whether in accordance with his 'nature' or desires or not. Heidegger echoes this capacity of man, and adds, *contra* Kant, that there is no a priori justification for his choosing one end over another, and no a priori reason for expecting that men will *in fact* tend to choose (by virtue of the nature of their will) one end over another. "Dasein in each case having its own possibility" is the insistence that while Dasein (because of *Existenz*) always has possibilities, these possibilities may be as varied as the number of human beings.

The famous slogan of Sartre "Existence precedes essence" is taken from Heidegger's insistence that "the essence of Dasein is its Existenz." Heidegger has objected (in his *Letter on Humanism*) that Sartre uses the notion of "existence" in the traditional sense in which it applies to objects, whereas *Existenz* clearly has special meaning. In Heidegger, "The *Existenz* of man is his essence" is somewhat of an analytic truth. The correlative statement in Sartre surely is not. Moreover, the sense of "before" in "existence precedes essence" as Sartre espouses the principle in some of his popular writings looks like a straightforward temporal "before." This is surely nothing like the 'ontological truth' Heidegger has in mind. For Heidegger, the priority of *Existenz* over essence (Being) is an *epistemological* priority; we must know about human being (*Existenz*) before we can know about Being (essence). In the next chapter, we shall examine Sartre's slogan in detail, and go back into a comparison between Heidegger and Sartre (and Merleau-Ponty), after we have had a chance to examine both doctrines in more detail.

In spite of the indefinitely large number of possibilities available to Dasein (which are Dasein's *Existenz*), these possibilities are based on a single pair of possibilities, the possibility of being authentic ("winning oneself") and the possibility of being inauthentic ("losing oneself"). These possibilities are of a very different nature the various 'possibilities' or goals on which men may disagree. These later possibilities, the choice of the life of an artist, or the life of a musician, or the life of a political figure or a revolutionary, or the life of a religious figure or a good citizen, or the life of a Don Juan or of a Dostoevsky, these are all relatively specific choices which are open to a man, but one can easily neglect any number of these. The possibilities of authenticity and inauthenticity are not so negligible, however, and there is no room for men to disagree about them or refuse to recognize them.

These possibilities are essential to Dasein's *Existenz*—they are the very nature of *Existenz*. Authenticity and inauthenticity are possibilities concerning the manner of Dasein's choosing among possibilities in general (compare Kierkegaard's notion of "existential values"). The explicit and honest recognition of the necessity of making choices is authenticity; the refusal to recognize one's choices (as one's own) is inauthenticity. *Existenz* is possibility, and therefore the one 'possibility' which is not open to Dasein is to give up his possibilities;

We have defined the idea of Existenz as a potentiality-for-Being—a potentiality which understands, and for which its own being is an issue.[113]

Existenz is also defined as "*Seinkönnen*," "the possibility of being or not being our own self." *Existenz* is the possibility and necessity of "choosing oneself," of formulating a conception of oneself and a set of projects, goals, and values for oneself. To say that Dasein is his *Existenz* is to say that to be human is to have free choices. To say that man *is* his possibilities (or is freedom), as we find in Heidegger, in Sartre, in Kierkegaard, in Hegel, and Kant, is to stress the radical difference between man (Dasein) and every other sort of Being.

Philosophers have long been concerned with establishing human freedom of choice and action for the sake of certain moral considerations. Kant introduced the peculiar expression of human being as freedom in his ethics with the intention of sharply distinguishing man as a moral creature from all considerations of man as an object of nature. Kierkegaard repeats this equation as do Heidegger and Sartre for much the same reasons. However, it must be seriously questioned whether this obscure equivalence does anything to settle the celebrated free will problem except to enforce artificially a rigid distinction between talk about human freedom and talk about natural law and causation. We shall have more to say of this in the following chapter. Of greater importance for our understanding of Heidegger is the recognition that he, like Kierkegaard, is relatively unconcerned with freedom of *action*. He is rather concerned with freedom of *choice*, and on this issue he is not so much an ally of Kant as much as his greatest opposition.

Kant argued for human freedom of action, but insisted that human choice was dictated by certain rational guidelines. Of central importance to Heidegger (and Kierkegaard and Nietzsche) is the rejection of such "rational guidelines" and the insistence that there are no (a priori) grounds for making one choice over another. Heidegger, again like Kierkegaard, is not so much concerned with very specific choices (the choice of this automobile over that one; the choice of this career over that one) but only with the most general choices—choices of general life styles—choices of ultimate evaluative criteria. Heidegger thus stresses the extent to which every life style—every set of evaluative criteria—is not based upon rational justification but is always based on a personal *decision* or *choice;*

Dasein always understands itself in terms of its Existenz—*in terms of a possibility of itself: to be itself or not itself. Dasein has either chosen these possibilities itself, or got itself into them, or grown up in them already. Only the particular Dasein decides its* Existenz, *whether it does so by taking hold or by neglecting. The question of existing never gets straightened out except through existing itself.*[114]

"To be itself," to "decide *Existenz* by . . . taking hold," to "choose one's possibilities" is to live *authentically.* "To not be itself," to "not have chosen one's possibilities but to have got oneself into them, or grown up in them already," or "to neglect one's *Existenz"* is to live *inauthentically.* To *exist* is to make decisions and choices; "through existing itself" thus means "making decisions." The question "Who am I?" can never be answered except through a *decision* as to what I intend to make of myself.

What is a *possibility?* From what we have said above, it is evident that a possibility is a choice; it is an alternative which can be chosen by Dasein. Yet, this is too simple. A possibility need not present us with a choice as such, as we can see from some of Heidegger's examples. He speaks, for example, of "possible" and "impossible possibilities,"[115] as well as of "necessary possibilities." If a possibility is *necessary,* we cannot have a choice as to whether we shall adopt it or not, but *death* is such a necessary possibility.

Death is Dasein's ultimate and 'ownmost' possibility, as we shall see, but it is also necessary—we cannot choose whether to die or not. We must conclude, therefore, that "possibility" does not simply mean "something which can be chosen or not by Dasein." Similarly, there are "impossible possibilities," for example, the impossibility of immortality, or the impossibility in our wish to be God. We cannot choose to be immortal or to be God. Yet it is one of our possibilities in the requisite sense. We must further inquire into this sense of "possibility."

Kant had introduced his Categories (and concepts in general) as "possibilities." By this, he meant *rules* that might be employed in the synthesis of experience into objects. Yet he did not mean and harshly rejected any notion (such as that made by Fichte) that these rules were left to our choice. The categories—that very special set of a priori concepts—applied necessarily to every experience. Yet they could be characterized as possibilities because they applied to every possible experience and were thus logically prior (more 'primitive') than any actual objects. A possibility, for Kant, was thus a rule which could be instantiated; whether it was instantiated or not, whether it was necessarily instantiated by any conscious creature, or whether it could not be instantiated, was of little difference. Categories (concepts in general) were always possibilities. Heidegger's notion of possibility can be taken from this use of "possibility" in Kant. A possibility for Heidegger is any structure of the world, a *horizon* (a term borrowed directly from Husserl), a set of "limiting images." Kant's concepts are of strictly cognitive significance. For Heidegger, possibilities are not just possibilities for experience or possibilities for knowing. There are also possibilities for actions, possibilities for moods, attitudes, and feelings. Possibilities are possible structures of Being-in-the-world, and these are possible simply by virtue of the fact that they can be conceived of by Dasein. Possibility, for Heidegger, is any envisionable structure for Being-in-the-world. Because of the peculiar structure of Dasein as being-in-the-world, any structure of Being-in-the-world is a structure of Dasein itself. In less Heideggerian language, all understanding or conceiving of the world is at one and the same time an understanding or conceiving of oneself. One's conception of the world and one's conception of oneself are inseparable; these conceptions are (Dasein's) possibilities.

We might wish to think of possibilities for Heidegger as any conceivable goals or projects we wish to envision. This is a helpful formulation, and there is good reason to think of possibilities in terms of posited values or projects or goals, as Sartre will do later. Heidegger, however, is very much against any such ethical or evaluative interpretation of his thesis, as we shall soon see.

A projection of a possibility is not a *prediction* about a future state of affairs (as when we say that the acorn has the possibility of growing into an oak tree); this is to neglect the very practical or 'concerned' nature of Dasein. Projection of possibilities is the project, or design (*entwurf*) of a structure of the world. It is what many other philosophers, with less obscurity and fanfare, have referred to as an *intention* (not in Husserl's sense), a *plan* to change the world, a *design* on one's world. "*Existenz* as possibility" means that a human being (Dasein) is an essentially "foreward projecting" creature, who does not just know the world, nor does he unknowingly act in the world. What characterizes Dasein is his laying of plans to change the world and his attempting to carry these out. Animals can change the world (as can earthquakes and volcanos) but they cannot design these changes. Husserl's vision of man is such that he can know about the world, but he is in no position to change it.

Like Kant, Heidegger gives a central place in his philosophy to the concept of 'understanding' (Heidegger generally avoids the Kantian notion of 'faculty'). We have seen how Heidegger generally takes Kant and Husserl's strictly cognitive notions and expands them to include practical concerns. So it is also with the concept of 'understanding'. It is through understanding that Dasein projects its possibilities. Understanding manipulates possibilities (as Kant's understanding manipulated concepts). Understanding is the projection of fundamental possibilities into the future, the laying of plans and designs. Understanding of the world is thus a thinking of the world in terms of one's structuring and restructuring of it; it is also a thinking of oneself and of structuring and restructuring oneself.

Understanding, for Heidegger (unlike for Kant and Husserl) is not always a self-conscious or reflective activity. This does not mean that understanding is not always self-understanding in the above-mentioned sense of a projection of future possibilities. It does mean that this understanding is not always articulated or *conceptualized* (that is, '*ontological*'). Thus understanding is not primarily a knowledge of things, or a knowledge of oneself as an entity, nor is it a knowledge which need be articulated. One manifests understanding when he employs a tool, or when he solicits help from other people, or when he treats himself in certain ways. One has *preconceptual* ('preontological') understanding which precedes articulation and the sort of explicit understanding which is the special skill of the philosopher. Thus, the structures of Dasein which we are enumerating will now be only thought of by most readers as Heidegger expounds their nature. Nevertheless, Heidegger would argue that we may have a prearticulated knowledge of these structures even before we are given the philosophical sophistication to recognize them. This relationship between the preconceptual (ontic) understanding of ourselves and articulated (ontological) understanding of ourselves will become very important for our understanding of Heidegger's 'ethical' views.

Facticity and "Being Tuned"

The existential structure of Dasein which Heidegger refers to as "facticity" is a direct consequence of the definition of Dasein as "Being-in-the-world." Dasein 'lives' in a world, in some particular world, in some place, at some time, for some duration of time. According to Heidegger, we can never simply recognize our own existence (much less the alleged necessity of our own existence) without also recognizing our existence in a particular world. Husserl has pointed this out in one of his central 'discoveries' as he told us that the *cogito* always finds itself confronting an *object* (a *cogitatio*). As we have seen, Heidegger firmly rejects the Cartesian doctrine of the 'self-evidence' of the *cogito* and dubitable existence of 'the World'. We have also seen that he rejects Husserl's interpretation of the *cogitatio* or objects confronting the *cogito* as 'reduced' or 'bracketed' objects *of consciousness*. Dasein *necessarily* finds himself in a particular, irreducible, unbracketable world of real objects.

The importance of this discovery for the traditional philosophical problems of knowledge has already been discussed. Because our knowledge of our own existence (in the *cogito*) and our knowledge of our existence in a world are inseparable, there can be no 'problem of knowledge'. We have only shown the significance of Dasein's Being-in-the-world, however, and have not said anything about the particular world of objects in which Dasein finds himself. Dasein does not, of course, simply find himself in a world, but finds himself in a world of twentieth-century America, or Germany, born of these parents, with this body, and in these social environments. Such *facts* about Dasein are not part of his *Existenz*, for these are not *chosen* by Dasein. Dasein finds himself already in such and such a situation. In Heidegger's dramatic phraseology, Dasein finds himself *thrown* into a particular world. "Facticity" is thus equivalent to what Heidegger calls "thrownness" (*(Geworfenheit)*. I find myself living in middle-class America, with traits inherited from my parents, with a personality partially determined by my early childhood, facing responsibilities and expectations thrust on me by my 'station in life'. My entire *past* is my facticity, for it is a set of *facts* about which I have no choices. My bodily presence in the world is part of my facticity; I can leave this place, this country, even this planet, but I am stuck with my body. For Heidegger (as for Sartre, who employs the same term) facticity is the set of all those 'givens' which I must encounter in my *Existenz*. I am not, of course, determined to react or respond to these 'givens'. My *Existenz* always forces me to *choose* my attitudes and projects concerning these givens. I find myself with this body, but I may choose to worship it, to degrade and despise it, to treat it as a tool for carrying out more spiritual tasks, or treat it as a curious 'thing'. Similarly, I find myself born into middle-class America, but I may choose to become middle class myself, or an American chauvinist, or a traitor to this country, or to simply ignore it altogether. My circumstances, my facticity, are always determined, given to me. I am 'thrown' into them, but my attitudes and plans for confronting these circumstances are always undetermined. My *Existenz* is always a range of possibilities regarding facticity. What evidence (*Evidenz*) is there that *facticity* is one of our existential structures? ("How is facticity disclosed to us?") To show the a priority of facticity, Heidegger's phenomenology must demonstrate to us the 'intuitions' which yield this 'essential' insight. These are to be found in "being-tuned" (*Gestimmtsein*), in the *moods* we experience finding ourselves in the world. Mood is not a continuous experience, which we experience all the time, nor need it be a particularly exciting experience such as that which arises in the famous existential traumas so well described by Camus and Sartre. Mood, to the contrary, is a product of "being tuned" to 'everyday' routine, and the mood which yields this great philosophical insight is better characterized by the bourgeois businessman's *Weltanschauung* on a rainy Monday morning than by any of the more exciting examples of the French existentialists. In fact, Heidegger is very concerned with the dreariness of everyday existence, and this is even to be raised, as we shall see, to one of the essential structures of Dasein—as "fallenness"—this tendency to experience life as a burden that has been foisted on us.

It is wrong to think of mood or being-tuned as a specifically directed feeling. The bourgeois Monday morning mood is not simply directed at the cold or the rain outside, or at the headache, or the prospect of going to work at a routine and uninspiring job, or facing one's family, or co-workers, or breakfast. Mood, as distinct from specific feelings of revulsion, nausea, pain, annoyance, indifference, or unsociability, is a general attitude towards *the world* rather than towards any particular objects in the world. We shall see that existentialists are fond of pointing out the philosophical significance of such 'objectless' experiences. Kierkegaard's *dread* is the prototype of a host of such feelings. Mood is the experience which "discloses concrete being overall" to us. It is this mood which discloses the everydayness of the world.

Not all moods are as dismal as Monday morning drearies, but these certainly receive the most attention from Heidegger. There is a spectrum of moods, from utter boredom and ennui with everything, which "makes all things and other human beings and myself fuse into a colorless indifference," to the occasional joy we feel towards the world as a whole when, for example, we find ourselves in love. Again, the philosophical significance of these moods is taken to be very great. My feeling towards another human being in love is not so important as the accompanying mood I have towards the world. It is this general mood, without a particular object, which 'discloses' to me my being in the world, my facticity. From this latter example, it is clear that facticity need not be considered as an onus. Yet it is well known that that is the picture we often get from the existentialists (it is facticity which produces the ontologically significant experience of *nausea* in Roquentin).

The most important mood for Heidegger, as for Kierkegaard, is the mood of dread or *Angst*. Like the mood of boredom, it discloses overall concrete being, and like other moods, it does not take a particular object. Dread is an ontologically significant version of fear (Heidegger would say that fear is ontic, dread is ontological). Dread is not fear of this or that object, or this or that possible future occurrence. "Dread is a fear of *nothing*." It is this experience which discloses to us man's *Existenz*. It is the counterpart of moods which disclose to us facticity. We shall have more to say of this shortly.

Average Everydayness:
Fallenness and *das Man*

Although *Existenz* or possibility is one of the existential structures of Dasein, it is possible that Dasein may fail to recognize this *Existenz,* and fail to recognize his various possibilities. In fact, the third existential structure of Dasein, which Heidegger characterizes as *Fallenness,* is just this tendency to neglect one's *Existenz.* In fact, Heidegger argues that, although *Existenz* and *Fallenness* are both a priori capabilities of Dasein, men rarely come to grips with their *Existenz,* but nearly always fall to the temptations of *Fallenness.* Man in his "average everydayness" or "everyday Dasein" is in a state of fallenness. He is so preoccupied with the petty tasks and concerns of everyday life that he spares no time for reflection on his *Existenz.* As we shall see, this 'fallen' neglect of *Existenz* is the heart of the inauthentic life.

Man's 'primitive' attitude towards the world is neither authentic (explicit recognition of his *Existenz*) nor is it essentially inauthentic (the refusal to come to grips with *Existenz*). Man's primitive mode of being is what Heidegger calls "undifferentiated primitive everydayness." It is "average everydayness" in which man is Dasein in the world of equipment, in the world of petty tasks and everyday chores. This undifferentiated everydayness is characterized by the fact that it is unreflective. Man has not yet raised the question of being, he has not yet considered his possibilities. As average everydayness, man does not define himself uniquely, but he defines himself as part of a *public.* (Once again Heidegger borrows both the idea and the term from Kierkegaard; see Chapter 3.) Man in this 'primitive' state defines himself, or lets himself be defined, in terms of a general concept of mentogether (*Mitsein*), in which everyman is a manifestation of average man, or man in general.

It is this average everydayness which forms the basis for Heidegger's "preliminary analysis of Dasein," and man is first to be disclosed to us insofar as he is simply *"das Man,"* this undifferentiated man who is not yet a real (authentic) human being, but neither is he an inauthentic being. We have already seen how Heidegger interprets primitive Being-in-the-world in terms of the totality of equipment of the world of everyday purposes. Undifferentiated average everyday man belongs 'in' this practical world, in which there are not things and causal relationships and substance but rather tools and jobs-to-be-done. We have seen that all conceptions of things and "the world" as a totality of objects, causal relationships, space, and time are concepts derivative from the conception of the world as totality of tools. Primitively, and for most men most of their lives, Dasein exists in this average everyday manner, taking care of the tasks of his world as they present themselves.

What is philosophically important about this everyday Being-in-the-world is not only Dasein's relation to *equipment.* As a mere user of tools, it is reasonable to suppose that Dasein could not be reflective, could not inquire into its own being, and could not formulate an image of *himself.* The formulation of a self-image, or self-consciousness, is a problem we have encountered before, notably in Hegel's 'phenomenological' discussion of the master-slave relationship. There is indication, we argued, that Hegel considers self-consciousness to arise only in inter-action with other self-consciousnesses. In Husserl, we saw a similar thesis, again not very thoroughly argued, in his discussion of the intersubjective community in *Cartesian Meditations* and *Crisis* (see Chapter 5, last section). Now, in Heidegger, we find this thesis argued in some detail. In *Sein und Zeit,* Heidegger maintains that man's consciousness of himself arises in the context of mutual recognition in a community of Daseins. To find out 'who' Dasein is, we must inquire into the 'primitive' relations between Daseins, and Dasein's recognition of the others. It is on the basis of the study of Being-with-others that Heidegger and the French existialists he influenced are said to lay great stress on man's solitude, the isolation and loneliness of individual man. In fact, Heidegger's thesis is just the contrary, man is primarily ('primitively') a social being, a Being-with-others. The problem of existentialism is not man's loneliness, but the restrictive inauthentic ties he forms with others. The thrust of Heidegger's existentialism is to force us to break some of those ties with others. Man is first the good citizen, the average 'guy', the everyday Dasein, the establishment: the task of existential questioning is to pry him loose from this social framework and allow him to find his "ownmost possibilities," or his "authentic self."

In the chapter on Husserl, we mentioned that there is little of the interest in the "problem of other minds" on the continent that we find in the last twenty years of American and British philosophy (Chapter 5, last section). With Heidegger, however (as with Sartre and Husserl in *Cartesian Meditations*), this is not merely a matter of neglect. According to Heidegger, the problem, "How do I know that others have minds?" is not a real problem at all but a source of tremendous confusion. It assumes that we begin with a concept of self and self-consciousness and then attempt to argue that there are others who are also self-conscious. How could such an argument proceed? Traditionally (for example, in the philosophy of John Stuart Mill), it has been argued that we infer *by analogy* that other Beings who behave as we do must have minds as we do. At one point Husserl accepted this argument, but augmented it with the claim that we know of others by means of *empathy (einfühlung).* Heidegger asks

how can I feel empathy with a Being whom I do not already know to be conscious?[116] Heidegger argues that if we do not *begin* by knowing of the existence of others, we will never be able to argue *to* that conclusion by means of inference or empathy. It is wrong to start from the assumption that I know of my own existence *before* (ontologically before) I know of the existence of others. My very knowledge of my own existence already presupposed that I know there are others; my knowledge of my own Being presupposed my Being-with-Others.[117]

Our initial experience of others is not an experience of things (for example, bodies moving in certain ways, as Mill and other philosophers have made the first step of the argument by analogy); but neither do we first encounter the other as a person (compare Husserl, Chapter 5, last section, and Sartre, Chapter 7, "Being-for-others"). Rather, our first encounter with an other is much like our 'primitive' encounter with the world as equipment. Others are to be employed to serve purposes. However, one cannot manipulate an other as one does a tool, rather our initial management of the other is through *soliciting (Fürsorge).* Soliciting may simply consist in requesting, demanding, and the like. Or, soliciting may take on a 'negative' form, an indifference to others, as when we ignore them, or leave them. Or, soliciting may be 'positive' manipulation of the person, as in punishment, or commanding. One can make other people dependent on oneself through solicitude and even make slaves of others; one can have very respectful 'authentic' relations with others, much as those formulated in the categorical imperative by Kant. Heidegger does not go into these various interpersonal relations, however; this is to be carried through by Heidegger's illustrious French 'student', Jean-Paul Sartre. In our discussion of Sartre, we shall find this abbreviated portion of Heidegger's philosophy developed into a fascinating theory of interpersonal relationships, borrowing heavily from Heidegger, but also from Hegel, Kierkegaard, and Nietzsche.

The error in traditional approaches to the understanding of self-identity, according to Heidegger, is the supposition that we already know 'who' Dasein is; it is 'I myself'. This becomes clear from what we have already seen, that "Dasein is an entity which is in each case I myself."[118]

The assertion that it is I who in each Dasein is, is ontically obvious; but this must not mislead us into supposing that the route for an ontological interpretation of what is 'given' in this way has been unmistakably prescribed.[119]

This is again something we have seen before, even in Descartes' reflection on the *cogito;* it is one thing to recognize the 'necessity' of the *cogito;* it is something else to say what this *I* identified is. It is normally supposed that this *I* which is found in philosophical (ontological) reflection is one with the 'I' belonging to everyday Dasein. But,

It could be that 'who' of everyday Dasein just is not the 'I myself'.[120]

The philosophical 'I', according to Heidegger, is only a

"non-committal formal indicator."[121]

The 'who' of everyday life, however, must not be assumed to be this formal indicator, but we are interested in "that kind of being in which Dasein maintains itself proximally and for the most part."[122] The answer to this problem is that *I* is not given first as set off from the others we encounter in our everyday world; rather, the myself conception arises from my recognition of all of us;

in characterizing the encountering of others, one is again still oriented by that Dasein which is in each case one's own. But even in this characterization does one not start by marking out and isolating the 'I' so that one must then seek some way of getting over to the others from this isolated subject? To avoid this misunderstanding, we must notice in what sense we are talking about 'the others'. By 'others' we do not mean everyone else but me—those over against whom the 'I' stands out. They are rather those from whom, for the most part, one does not *distinguish oneself— those among whom one is too.*[123]

What must be stressed in this analysis is that Being-with-others, which is another existential (a priori) structure of Dasein, does not consist of the *fact* that we happen to inhabit a world with other people:

Being-with is an existential characteristic of Dasein even when factically no other

is present at hand or perceived. Even Dasein's Being-alone is Being-with in the world. The other can be missing only in and for a Being-with. [124]

Our conception of ourselves is dependent on the conception of ourselves as Being-in-the-world-with-others, and thus the traditional arguments from my knowledge of myself to my knowledge of the existence of others is both invalid and based on the false supposition we can know ourselves before we can know others.

This argument has its equally famous analog—briefly argued—in the writings of the philosopher Ludwig Wittgenstein. Wittgenstein was also concerned with the supposition that we know other consciousnesses "from our own cases," and one of the famous arguments—or rather hints towards an argument—in his later writings argues similarly that there can be no self-knowledge independently of knowledge of others. One of the most important consequences of this sequence of thoughts in Wittgenstein is flatly rejected by Heidegger; Wittgenstein briefly argues (and many of his disciples have argued) on the basis of this general argument concerning self-knowledge that there can be no formulation of a private language, a language based on the mental goings-on of one person. One of Heidegger's complaints about everyday Dasein, we shall see, is that the language which is formulated for everydayness is *not* a private language.

Thus, as Being-with, Dasein 'is' essentially for the sake of others.[125]

Now the question becomes, what is the character of Dasein insofar as it is Being-with-others? The answer to that question is that Dasein is characterized with the others as inseparable from the others. Dasein in his everydayness is "self-forgetful." He has only the self of others. The identity of Dasein becomes the identity of the others; to know 'who' Dasein is, we have to ask 'who' the others are. Heidegger tells us:

they are what they do (sie sind das, was sie betreiben).[126]

This important claim is not elaborated in *Sein und Zeit,* but it is clear enough what Heidegger is pointing out. Dasein, as Being-with is a part of the *public*, has his identity in his social *roles;* he *is* a college professor, a medical student, a nobody (*does* nothing *for* society). These social roles are defined, not by the individual, but by the public itself. We have already seen that Dasein has, as one of its existential characteristics, *Existenz*, or possibilities. As Being-with, as one of the public, Dasein resigns *his* right to project these possibilities for himself;

Dasein's everyday possibilities of Being are for others to dispose of as they please.[127]

These possibilities, because they are 'disposed of' by the public instead of by oneself, no longer become one's *own* responsibility, except insofar as "One belongs to the others oneself and enhances their power."[128] The power to determine what Dasein is belongs not to oneself, and thus the self of Dasein is not a personal self but the self of the anonymous public, the others. However, "these others are not definite others";[129]

The "who" is not this one, not that one, not oneself, not some people, and not the sum of them all. "The who" is the neuter, das Man.[130]

As *das Man*, Dasein's understanding of his own possibilities is restricted to the standards of success and failure which are imposed by *das Man*, by no one in particular. This reduces all individual differences to mere differences of "distance," more or less satisfaction of these impersonal standards. The goal of *das Man* is thus to be *average;*

Being-with-one-another concerns itself as such with averageness, *which is an existential characteristic of* das Man. *Das Man, in its being, essentially makes an issue out of this. Thus* das Man *maintains itself factically in the averageness of that which belongs to it, of that which it regards as value and that which it does not, and of that to which it grants success and that to which it denies it.*[131]

Again we can see Heidegger giving an academic exposition of a point originally raised in bitter dispute by Kierkegaard;

This care of averageness reveals in turn an essential tendency of Dasein which we call the "leveling down" (Einebnung) *of all possibilities of Being.*[132]

By publicness everything gets obscured, and what has thus been covered up gets passed off as something familiar and accessible to everyone.[133]

All things sank to the same level, a surface resembling a blind mirror that no longer reflects . . . The prevailing dimension became that of extension and number. Intelligence no longer meant a wealth of talent, lavishly spent, and the command of energies, but only what could be learned by everyone, the practice of a routine, always associated with a certain amount of sweat and a certain amount of show.[134]

Dasein, as *das Man*, is "disburdened," is relieved of the responsibility of setting its own standards of success, and, because the standards of *das Man* are directed towards averageness (mediocrity), Dasein as *das Man* can "take things easily and make them easy."[135]

Everyone is the other, and no one is himself. Das Man, which supplies the answer to the question of the 'who' of everyday Dasein, is the 'nobody' to whom every Dasein has already surrendered itself in Being-among-one-another.[136]

Das Man makes life easy for Dasein; in *das Man*, the everyday self of Dasein finds "stability." Thus Dasein is tempted to remain in the mode of *Existenz* dictated by *das Man*, although,

it is not 'I,' in the sense of my own self, that 'am' but rather the others, whose way is that of das Man.[137]

This temptation to remain as *das Man* is fallenness, and this is also the basis of the inauthentic self;

The Self of everyday is das Man-self, *which we distinguish from the* authentic Self—*that is, from the Self which has been taken hold of in its own way. As* das Man-self, *the particular Dasein has been dispersed into* das Man, *and must first find itself. This dispersal characterized the 'subject' of that kind of Being which we know as concernful absorption in the world we encounter as closest to us.*[138]

Authenticity, Inauthenticity, Fallenness, and *Angst*
Heidegger tells us that there are two 'modes' of existing as *Dasein* (apart from

the "undifferentiatedness" of 'primitive' Dasein); *authenticity* and *inauthenticity* (*Eigentlichkeit*, *Uneigentlichkeit*), also translatable as "ownness" "disownness" (for example, by King).[139] Authenticity and inauthenticity refer to "a man's relationship to himself." The authentic man thinks and acts in terms of an adequate understanding 'who' he is; the inauthentic man, because of an enforced refusal to see himself as he really is, acts "blindly," substituting means for ends. Both authenticity and inauthenticity are every Dasein's possibilities; it is not the case that some men are 'naturally' authentic and others are not. Moreover, Heidegger insists that authenticity and inauthenticity are ontologically basic to Dasein, they are both existentialia; authenticity depends on an adequate ontological recognition of one's *Existenz,* facticity, and fallenness. Inauthenticity neglects *Existenz* and lives in fallenness. It is clear that authenticity is something to be striven for, in spite of its 'ontological' status. However, Heidegger warns us that authenticity can only be an *ideal* for us. Everyman is structured by the tendency towards fallenness, and every action will be tinged with inauthenticity.

Although authenticity is the goal, Heidegger stresses that most people strive *against* it; their fundamental tendency is to refuse to recognize themselves 'for what they are' (that is, what *Sein und Zeit* says they are) and turn to 'self-forgetful' preoccupation in tasks and "endless" chores ('endless' both in the sense of 'continual' and in the sense of 'without ultimate purpose') with other self-forgetful people. Man strives to be *das Man.* The undifferentiated everydayness which is 'primitive' to Dasein becomes the goal for lifelong activity. Thus the difference between undifferentiated everydayness and inauthentic 'fallen' existence seems to be a *refusal* to come to grips with one's "ownmost" possibilities in the latter case. These two are closely related, but it is only the latter referred to by "man has *forgotten* Being" (that is, *repressed* Being, in Freud's sense) and "man has *refused* to ask the question of Being" in the Introduction to *Sein und Zeit.* To refuse to ask the question is to be inauthentic, to simply not ask it, because one is too immature or unsophisticated, is mere undifferentiated everydayness.

What is Dasein's *self* that the authentic Dasein is supposed to recognize and act in accordance with? We have seen that

Dasein is structured by *Existenz,* facticity, and fallenness; to be authentic is to always act with a view to this as the nature of Dasein. The 'enemy' of authenticity is, we can guess, *das Man. Das Man* is the paradigm of inauthenticity; none of his actions are his own, none of his values are his own, not even his conception of himself is his own. He does, of course, have a conception of himself as *das Man* and as having succeeded or failed by the anonymous 'leveling' standards of *das Man,* but this conception is not one which he has created in accordance with his *Existenz* and understanding—the capability of projecting possibilities of his own and choosing them. The standards according to which *das Man* succeeds or fails, therefore, are not his own choice either. Inauthenticity, in its commonest forms is the blind acceptance of *public* conceptions and standards, and the failure or refusal to consider this acceptance as a choice of one among a number of alternative modes of existence.

Heidegger characterizes authentic existence by three "modes of comportment towards the world"; discovery of oneself as already in the world (*Befindlichkeit*) which is the recognition of one's *facticity,* understanding (*Verstehen*) which is the projection of possibilities regarding one's attitudes and projects towards the world in which he has discovered himself (*Existenz*), and finally there is *discourse* (*Rede*). *Rede* here is not speech, but an underlying structure which makes speech possible.[140] Discourse is the capacity to articulate what "tuning-in" and the Understanding disclose to us. Heidegger's claim for language is a remarkably strong one, particularly in view of Heidegger's later 'mystical' approach to philosophy; whatever can be understood can be articulated in speech. We have seen that this claim in effect is one of the presuppositions of Heidegger's philosophy. It is speech which discloses to us the nature of Being. Ontology thus consists of the study of language in order to understand the structures disclosed by language.

These three characteristics of authenticity have their counterparts in the characterization of inauthenticity. The inauthentic man does not 'discover himself already in the world', but rather finds himself in a state of *ambiguity* (*Zweideutigkeit*), caught up in a *whirlpool* (*Wirhen*) of daily "endless" (meaningless) activity. In this inauthentic *Existenz,* the Understanding cannot function, for the inauthentic man cannot distinguish between what he understands and what he inherits from *das Man*. Understanding thus degenerates from questioning one's own *Existenz* and possibilities to a *curiosity* (*Neugier*) about things. Curiosity need not be stupid; on the contrary, curiosity often manifests itself as 'cleverness' and 'calculation'. The curious man may be a brilliant accountant, or student, or scholar, or even scientist. What is crucial to curiosity is that it will not let itself ask itself *fundamental* questions, that is, questions about oneself (except insofar as these are also nonfundamental, as might be asked by a physiologist or a psychiatrist who is applying theories to 'a case' rather than truly examining himself). The curious man operates within a framework ("horizon") established by others (by *das Man*), but within this framework, he may be very 'intelligent' or 'clever' indeed. What the curious man will not do—what makes him inauthentic—is that he will never push a problem far enough to touch his own *Existenz*.

The discourse that expresses understanding for the authentic man thus cannot function for the inauthentic man, for his understanding has been preempted by his curiosity. What replaces discourse in inauthenticity is *prattle* or *chatter* (*Gerede*). Prattle is speech, but it is speech which says nothing, that is, it says nothing about the fundamental issues of 'who' we are. Prattle is an effective tool for conveying the produce of curiosity, but prattle cannot express ontological truths. Prattle, everyday talk, is an effective block to true discourse and understanding, for prattle catches us up and preoccupies us with trivia in such a way that we cannot employ our understanding. Thus cocktail conversation, as all talk, a mere exchange of 'curiosities' (where it may include even the most sophisticated scientific theories), is one of the essential structures of inauthenticity. As much as most of us would like to think that such prattle occupies only a small part of our speech activities, Heidegger discomforts us with the thought that most men speak nothing but prattle.

The importance of speech as discourse or prattle cannot be underestimated in Heidegger. In the early parts of this chapter, we emphasized how language is the key to philosophy and ontological inquiry.

It would follow that it is also the key to authentic and inauthentic existence. It is in speech, in writing and talking, that we best understand our possibilities. Our speech can work as an effective preventive from such understanding, preoccupying us with trivia to avoid hard ontological thinking. Poetry, Heidegger suggests, is exemplary as a use of speech in authentic existence, for it is poetry which best shows us the various possibilities of *Existenz*. On the other side, speech may consist of mere parroting or copying of what others have said. Even when the 'original' is itself a brilliant piece of authentic discourse, however, the parroting or copying is inauthentic and a block to authenticity just by virtue of the fact that it is a copy or a parroting. One does not become authentic, for example, by reading or reiterating Heidegger. To the contrary, Heidegger would say, the time spent doing a commentary on Heidegger is, in effect, a block to the author's working out his "ownmost possibilities."

Heidegger has a more detailed discussion of inauthentic speech which is scattered throughout his works. It is a fascinating suggestion, to be found in Nietzsche as well, to the effect that everyday language is itself a product of *das Man* with its consequent leveling effect, such that one cannot, in ordinary language, express anything that is *one's own*.[141] This is, of course, why both Nietzsche and Heidegger place so much stress on poetry, with its conscientious deviance from everyday speech. Heidegger often tells us that it is the grammar of everyday speech and of traditional philosophical discourse which is parasitic upon everyday speech that tangles us in philosophical dilemmas. For example, the subject-predicate form of our grammar is responsible, Heidegger thinks, for our blind acceptance of the subject-object distinction in epistemology[142] (a point that occupies Hegel's attention in the Preface to the *Phenomenology* as well). Similarly, Nietzsche argues that "we shall believe in God because we still believe in grammar."[143] Everyday speech is formulated by *das Man* as an impersonal, superficial, and unprofound organ like everything else created by *das Man*. This impersonal, public language is therefore inadequate to express philosophical truths. We must have recourse to a more poetic language, an essentially *private* language, in which philosophical truths, personal truths, can be expressed.

Clearly, there are problems with this view. First, there is the obvious problem of how a strictly private language could ever be used to communicate with anyone else. In a relatively unsophisticated objection, we might argue that such a language, once formulated, would be utterly useless, since one could not speak it with anyone else. More sophisticatedly, and more problematically, one might argue, after Wittgenstein and many of his followers, that there could not even be the formulation of such a private language for oneself.

According to this objection in its most standard form, any language requires rules which are based on public criteria: there could be no language which only one person could understand. This objection has seen many variations. Some would qualify the conclusion to read "there can be no language which only one person *in principle* can understand." Others would weaken it to claim that there could be no language which derives its meaning from entities (for example, thoughts, sensations, images) to which only one person "has access."[144] The working through of these arguments has been the interesting study of many books, but it is clearly far afield from our interest in Heidegger, since he does not argue against them (antedating them by twenty years). Heidegger simply denies, in *Sein und Zeit,* all such arguments, and true discourse, for him, will have to be a language based on personal rules, personal criteria and essentially fully understandable by nobody else. Heidegger does not make it clear to what extent a private language might be shared with others. If he allows that each person's language must be private only in the sense that he derives it himself but always on the basis of certain *common* ontological structures, he might be interpreted very much like Chomsky (cf. #140 n.). In any case, this receives inadequate treatment in *Sein und Zeit.* In *Introduction to Metaphysics* and other works of the "middle period" (for example, *ET*), Heidegger seems to assume that a public ontologically adequate language is possible. In his late works, he argues that *all language* is inauthentic. It is interesting, however, that Heidegger eventually rejects private language not because such a language fails to capture private truths but because there is an increasing suspicion on his part of the possibility of ever capturing the truth about *Being* (that is nonprivate "universal" truth) in any language at all, particularly a private language. He then turns, as we shall see, to the view that Being can never be truly understood, and thus we can never have an adequate solution to the question of Being, and the reason for this is that language itself is incapable of capturing such truths. Insofar as a language is the public language of *das Man,* it cannot capture the existential perspective on Being. But even the most personal poetry, insofar as it is publicly comprehensible, cannot be an expression of Being either. We shall see that Heidegger seems to move significantly away from his *Sein und Zeit* philosophy towards an increasingly obscure mystical approach to Being.

This discussion of authenticity and inauthenticity may be cast in a slightly different way, which will become the core of Jean-Paul Sartre's variation on the same theme. The stress on the personal nature of discovering one's facticity, understanding, and discourse is a rejection of traditional philosophical efforts to find a universal abstract characterization of the essence of all men. Insofar as we do find some sort of universal factor, Heidegger argues, all we can come up with is *das Man.* Aristotle's talk of "human function" is such a concept, as is all talk of "human nature." Heidegger takes special pains to distinguish his theory of the 'authentic self' from all previous attempts to find the true self-human nature, whether this lies in the egoism of Hobbes' 'natural' man, the rational subject of the moral law of Kant, the spiritual nature of Hegel, or even the self-reflective nature of Descartes and almost everyone else. The being of Dasein, Heidegger tells us, is possibility (*Existenz*). The existential structures he lists for us are also possibilities which can be realized or neglected. Some men may choose to be authentic, and consequently make all subsequent choices in view of all of their possibilities. Or, a man may choose to be inauthentic, and blindly follow the dictates of the public and the demands of "endless" necessities of everyday life. Man has no universal nature, but man has possibilities. In another of Sartre's popular slogans, "Man Makes Himself." Authentic life is the recognition of this responsibility and the open-ended range of choices one always has concerning his own "mode of existence." Inauthentic life is the refusal to recognize this responsibility and one's choices. The inauthentic life is the life of *das Man,* who has his alternatives handed to him and his responsibility taken away from him.

Why do men become inauthentic?— first, because it is easy. One is in average everydayness in his 'primitive' encounter with the world, and voluntarily remaining in this anonymous world is more manageable than taking the difficult step towards authenticity. The public world is always "seductive" (*Versucherisch*) and "reassuring" (*Beruhigung*). However, it is not to be thought that the initial ease, lack of responsibility for oneself, and consoling mediocrity of the life of *das Man* will remain the peaceful Utopia of Nietzsche's "Last Man." We already warned that man can never totally become authentic because 'fallenness' always retains its grip as a structure of Dasein. One can never succeed in becoming totally inauthentic either, for *Existenz* maintains the same unyielding hold, interfering with total inauthenticity just as fallenness interrupts authenticity. As one's *Existenz* peeks through the fog of inauthenticity, the life of *das Man* is recognized as an escape from one's true self, and one becomes less and less satisfied with the anonymity and mediocrity of average everydayness. This is a state with which we have long been familiar, man's separation from himself. We find it in Hegel as "disharmony" in the "unhappy consciousness," and all through the *Phenomenology.* We find the same notion in Marx as 'alienation', here with a specifically materialistic interpretation. It appears again in Nietzsche and Kierkegaard in various forms of frenzy and despair. In Heidegger, it is called *estrangement* (*Entfremdung*). It results in an extreme frenzy of self-analysis, in which man becomes totally tangled in himself (*Verfangnis*). But this self-examination by the inauthentic man is not sufficient to make him become authentic. His lack of *understanding* seeks refuge in curiosity, and his self-examination degenerates into one more form of inauthenticity. Psychoanalysis, a favorite enemy of Sartre, is a presently popular inauthentic mode of self-examination. One is greatly concerned about oneself, but becomes so blocked by theories and relations with the analyst and the like that he fails to really examine himself. Thus the inauthentic life is not necessarily a happy life. However, we have yet to see why anyone would choose the authentic life, or how he would even see that there is such a possible mode of existence unless he has read Heidegger.

Our introduction to the authentic life comes about through a very special mood (or tuning-in) towards the world, the mood of *Angst* or *dread.* We have already argued that *Angst* differs from ordinary fear in that it does not take on a particular object; it is dread towards Being-in-the-world-in-general. Specifically, it is dread of *nothingness.* This is given two very different interpretations; first, dread is dread of *death* (we shall discuss that in a subsequent section); secondly, dread is dread of one's *Existenz,* of the open-ended range of possibilities which one has projected for himself. Dread comes about in a period of trauma, one of those incidents which force us to reevaluate our most fundamental desires, interests, and values. Of course, facing death is foremost among such traumas, and thus the experience of dread is most often dread facing death (compare Meursault in Camus' *Stranger,* who receives his introduction to authenticity while awaiting execution in prison. We shall discuss this more fully in the following chapter). Apart from facing death, however, simply the extreme estrangement and guilt of the inauthentic life may force us to face the dread of nothingness, and this is a source of dread which very much concerns Heidegger.

We have said that fear takes an object, whereas dread is directed at Being-in-the-world-in-general. A different way of putting this is to say that dread is "man's attempt to flee from *himself.*" Inauthenticity is initially seductive and reassuring, we argued, but it is so as an escape from the dreadful recognition of *Existenz* involved in authentic living. Dread is the mood of recognition of the open-endedness and personal responsibility for one's own possibilities. Dread is the fear of Being-in-the-world as such. What is dreadful is the utter meaninglessness of human life, the lack of given directions, given standards and values, and a given conception of oneself. It is to escape this nothingness that Dasein tends to retreat into inauthenticity. Dread makes everything insignificant, for it sees that one can always simply choose to make anything significant. This seeing everything as insignificant but by one's own choice is equivalent to the recognition of one's *Existenz,* and therefore seeing the possibility for authentic *Existenz.* Dread shows us that we do not derive our meaning from the world (there is no human *nature),* but rather than the world derives its meaning from us. It is interesting to see how differently Heidegger makes the same point as Husserl here. Husserl also maintains that we "constitute the significance of the world," but this is a disinterested and certainly not dreadful philosophical truth for him. For Heidegger, this recognition is a shaking of the foundations of our very lives. Dread makes the world unfamiliar, or as Heidegger puts it, it destroys our "taken-for-granted-at-homeness" in the world and substitutes for it an uncanny "not-at-home";

The not-at-home must be grasped as the more original phenomenon in the existential-ontological sense.[145]

It is this peculiar feeling of dread which introduces us to the authentic mode of existence. But why should we choose to become authentic? Heidegger really has no full answer to why we *should* choose the authentic life. What he gives us is a theory as to why we are pushed by ourselves to choose it. There is a "call of conscience,"[146] a call never "planned, prepared, or willingly accomplished by ourselves," a call that "falls on us." It is *conscience* that pushes us toward the authentic life, but this is not a *justification* for the authentic life, and this, we shall find, is something Heidegger does not give us. On the contrary, we shall see that his philosophy is such that any urging towards a way of life is out of place, even an urging towards the authentic life.

Dasein and
Temporarily: Being-unto-Death
Although we have said little of *time* in our discussion of *Being and Time* thus far, this is clearly one of the central concepts of Heidegger's philosophy. The analysis of Dasein that we have so far discussed (drawn mainly from Division I of *Sein und Zeit*) is treated by Heidegger as a *preliminary* study. It is the study of Dasein and temporality which completes the analysis of human Being, readying us,

purportedly, for the investigation of Being.

According to Heidegger, *Dasein is temporality.* There could be no time except for Dasein; conversely, there can be no Dasein without there being time. Just as Dasein is essentially 'in' space, Dasein is essentially 'in' time. This 'in', as we have seen, is not the same concept as utilized when we say that the inkwell is *in* the drawer or that the Crimean War was *in* the nineteenth century. Dasein constitutes or *projects* temporality. Time is "originally with" Dasein. Heidegger's thesis regarding time is essentially close to that of Kant in the *Critique of Pure Reason.* For Heidegger, time is an a priori condition for Being-in-the-world. Time does not exist apart from human consciousness or Dasein, and all 'objective' time is based on this "subjective condition." Heidegger, of course, does not agree with Kant's use of 'subjective' and 'objective', for reasons which we have argued repeatedly, but he adopts the essence of Kant's thesis that Dasein and temporality are ontologically dependent on one another.

Heidegger does not place space and time on an equal footing. Space is one of Dasein's existentialia, but time or temporality *is* Dasein. Furthermore, in his analysis of Kant,[147] Heidegger argues that this central role of time is the core of Kant's thought as well. According to Heidegger, all Being-in-the-world is grounded in Dasein as temporality, and all the concepts we have introduced thus far must be reintroduced as *temporal* concepts. The initial characterization of Dasein as "an entity in whose being its being is in question" is thus recast as a characterization of *Being-in-time,* with time as the unity of being, time as the "horizon of the Understanding" and "time as that which makes understanding of being possible."

In our earlier discussion, we learned that Heidegger's Dasein is defined as "Being-in-the-world". We now find that Dasein is defined as "primarily historical"[148] and the "horizon" we spoke of earlier now become the temporal horizon of Dasein's projection of itself (its possibilities) into the future. We have already seen that Dasein is our approach to Being and the 'problem of Being'; now we find that time is the unity of Being as such, as well as 'the unity of Dasein'. In the temporal conception of Dasein, Dasein is not primarily Being-in-the-world, but Being-in-time.

We have already seen that the unity of Dasein has been defined in terms of care (*Sorge*). Thus we may suppose that care will also be redefined in terms of temporality. Care is projection into the future, and it is defined now in terms of the unity of time. Care unifies *past, present,* and *future.* We have learned that care is the unity of *Existenz, facticity,* and *fallenness,* and so we find that these three existential structures of Dasein are each equated with a temporal (*ek-static*) structure. *Existenz* corresponds to the future; *Existenz* is possibilities projected into the future. Facticity corresponds to the past; facticity is Dasein's *"already* being-in-the-world."* Fallenness corresponds to the present; fallenness is the preoccupation with the everyday concerns of the 'now.' Accordingly, authenticity and inauthenticity must also be reoriented to this temporal mode of thinking. Inauthenticity, like fallenness, will be characterized by its preoccupation with the present. Authenticity will be characterized by its unified view of past, and future, the present being "the offspring of future and past."

The specific modes of existence, both authentic and inauthentic, are also reinterpreted temporally. *Befindlichkeit,* or discovering oneself already in the world, is the discovery that one's "situation is rooted in the past." *Existenz* is "tuned in" to what has been already: moods are directed at a state of the world as it is found to already be. *Understanding* (*Verstehen*) becomes projection into the future on the basis of knowledge about the past. *Discourse* (*Rede*) becomes the discussion of possibilities for the future. *Ambiguity* and *curiosity,* on the other hand, become preoccupation with the present, "seeking neither origins nor destinies." *Prattle,* contrasted with discourse, is only to 'occupy' time, or, at best, an expression of present preoccupations. Inauthentic existence (not *Existenz*) is reinterpreted after the 'everyday' cliché, "only the present is real." This inauthentic view of time, Heidegger assures us, is not the 'original' phenomenon of time which is "manifest to us in our own Being." The 'original' conception of time is the authentic conception. The inauthentic 'everyday' conception of time is grounded in this original authentic

conception, but is an inauthentic modification of this original phenomenon. Our 'everyday' conception of time, according to Heidegger, is a 'vulgar' conception derived from our busy dealings in the company of others, and not based on an authentic conception of ourselves as the "origin of temporality."

This everyday conception of time is based, as we have said, on the *present.* It is a succession of instants, a "following of now-points (*Jetzt-Punkt*)." This 'vulgar' conception of 'everyday' time Heidegger identifies as *Weltzeit,* or world-time, and it is this concept of time which has preoccupied 'worldly' philosophy since the ancients. Aristotle characterized time as "the measure of motion according to the before and after."[149] This presumes, Heidegger argues, the 'everyday' commonsense notion of time as an infinite succession of instants. Such a conception is convenient because it allows us to measure 'objective' time, a succession of calculated instants according to a *public* standard, and this in turn allows us to make our appointments with others and cooperate in our everyday tasks with them. Such an 'objective' view of time is most convenient and even necessary for everyday business, but it forgets, according to Heidegger, the true "existential-ontological structure of time," namely, that *We* are the source of all time, that temporality is imposed upon the world *by us.* The time imposed on us by the public, by *das Man,* is not our time at all, it is not authentic time. However convenient the 'everyday' concept of *Weltzeit* may be for everyday purposes, it is not the business of philosophy to make things more convenient for us. The original phenomenon of time, we are reminded, is the authentic phenomenon of time. This time is *our own.* Inauthentic or everyday world-time is a succession of present instants from the past into the future. As such, time continues infinitely 'back' and infinitely 'forward'. Of course, all of this is, in an important sense, metaphorical, for we cannot intelligibly say that time goes infinitely far back 'in time' and infinitely far forward 'in time'. Yet some such notion seems to be central to the characterization of world-time, and it is such problems of clarifying the metaphorical expressions "back in"/"forward in time" that generate philosophical puzzles about time.[150] These are puzzles which Heidegger has no interest in resolving, for they are based on a derivative and in-authentic picture of time. Authentic time is not a succession of instants, but is a "unity of past and future in the 'now.'" The present is not a mere 'now-point', but it is a moment (*Augenblick*) in the fashion of all time. Dasein is not 'in' time, but Dasein originates time. Dasein as temporality is living with a constant eye towards goals and origins. It is not being captured by the present, but always having a view towards both the future and the past. In this sense, authentic time differs from everyday time seemingly not so much in its conception of time, but in its view of the importance of the future and the past. The authentic Dasein does not live in the present, tackling whatever task presents itself to him; he rather always sees these tasks in the context of his entire life.[151] He is continuously projecting and acting on possibilities for his *entire* future, and viewing his past not as something over and done with, but as something constraining his alternative possibilities and restricting the range of his *Existenz*. It is easy enough to think of this as an ethical prescription, that one should not lose oneself in the moment but always keep his perspective of long-term goals and established handicaps. We must remember that Heidegger presents this thesis as an *ontological* thesis, and it is intended, therefore, as a thesis about the nature of time. Therefore, the concept of authentic existence does not primarily give us an ideal about how to live 'in' time; it gives us a theory about the concept of 'time'. Time is not composed of instants each one of which "is a now sometime." Time is the projection of Dasein's possibilities and the facticity of his origins.

Time is conceived of in terms of the projects we make for ourselves. It is difficult to see this point as long as we think of time in terms of derivative world-time and not 'primitive' personal time. Perhaps an example will help to clarify this crucial difference. I sit in a room with my eyes closed thinking about a problem; the clock in the next room says I have been sitting there for twenty minutes, but I *seem* to be sitting there for an hour. Now suppose we ask how we come to have the general categories of "lasting twenty minutes" and "seems to be one hour." Philosophers who take world-time as time would say that we first come to have concepts, such as 'lasting twenty minutes' and then, through our

inability to accurately estimate time, we come to have concepts like 'seems to last one hour'. According to Heidegger, just the reverse is the truth. 'Clock-time' or 'world-time' is based on concepts such as 'seeming to last one hour'. The basis of the latter concepts is not a faulty estimate of publicly measured clock time, but a measure of our own projection of temporality. Thus, the basis of our 'seeming to last so long' is ultimately our impatience to get to work, our concern with the future, our anxiety of 'lack of time'. Of course, the concept of a 'minute' or an 'hour' is solely dependent on public time. Here the general idea of temporality, of spending time, spending too much time, or not having enough time are more primitive than all concepts of clock time. It is on the basis of our experiences of waiting, expecting, striving, not having enough time, and the like, that we get a notion of time, a personal notion of time. Public time is simply the imposition of a public measuring system on this personal time.

This example should give some idea of the very difficult thesis Heidegger is attempting to argue. The thesis is that public time is dependent on a personal (existential) notion of time, and not the other way around. One might be left with the impression that this dispute is academic, that even if Heidegger's position is intelligible and plausible, it makes little difference to his overall project of analyzing Dasein (with a view to the analysis of Being). This impression can be corrected when we consider the most important consequence of the analysis of time as an "existential-ontological structure of Dasein" instead of public or world-time. According to the public view of time, time is infinite. However, according to Heidegger's analysis of time, it turns out that time is finite, not infinite, and that Dasein's projection of possibilities, unlike world-time, has its end. That end is *death*.

What is death? This question had occupied Kierkegaard, and he had answered it by distinguishing between my biological or 'objective' death—my heart's no longer beating, my lack of bodily response—and my ontological or 'subjective' death. The first is something which we all understand, but the second is an absolute 'uncertainty', something which we cannot understand at all. I can understand what it means for an organism to die, but I cannot personally grasp the *significance* of *my own* death. The *existential* problem, for Kierke-gaard, is the problem of how to approach death;

is it the case that the living individual is absolutely excluded from the possibility of approaching death in any sense whatever, since he cannot experimentally come near enough without comically sacrificing himself upon the altar of his own experiment, and since he cannot experientially restrain the experiment, and so learns nothing from it.[152]

But the fact of my own death is not for me by any means such a something in general, although for others the fact of my death may indeed be something of that sort.[153]

The problem of the uncertainty of death is its influence on life. We should like to ignore our impending death altogether and make a "resolution for life", but:

This is essentially to forget the uncertainty of death, since otherwise the enthusiastic resolve for the whole of life must be made commensurable with the uncertainty of death.[154]

The uncertainty of death, for the subjec-tive thinker, becomes more and more of a problem:

It thus becomes more and more important for me to think it in connection with every factor and phase of my life.[155]

For Heidegger also, death is an unap-preciated but centrally important problem for the existential. Dasein is defined as possibilities (his *Existenz*) and death is Dasein's "innermost possibility." It is a possibility moreover, which reveals itself as a necessity, as an existential structure of Dasein, as a 'phenomenon of life'. Death is said to be Dasein's "extreme possibility" and the "limit of Dasein's possibilities." It is said to be "the end of Dasein's pos-sibilities." Dasein is dying as long as he lives, even from birth. It is the one possi-bility of all men, of which men have no choice. It is what makes Dasein's tempo-rality finite, for Dasein's possibilities are limited by his death. Dasein is, therefore, *Being-unto-death* (*Sein-zum-Tode*), and everything we have understood so far

must be understood now in terms of Dasein's imminent death.

It is death, or the threat of death, which makes authenticity possible. Authenticity is fundamentally facing and enduring death as one's own possibility. For Hei-degger, as for Kierkegaard, death per-meates all of life, and it is death which forces us to see our 'true' selves. Death limits my possibilities by limiting my time; if I had infinite time (or pretended I did), I could simply wait to do everything. With the knowledge of death, life be-comes more urgent, and time becomes meaningful. Knowing of impending death gives meaning to life, a meaning which would not be had by an eternally living creature. It is my individual death which exposes the "nakedness of my personal *Existenz*." (In spite of Heidegger's athe-ism, his emphasis on death is explicitly *not* a denial of an afterlife.)[156]

For Heidegger, as for Kierkegaard, the central problem of death is that we cannot understand it. Death "reveals itself as something that knows no measure."[157] Death is for us a simple "nothing," it is simply not existing, but we can have no conception of non-*Existenz*. As Freud (about the same time) said of death,

One's own death is unimaginable, since we all think of ourselves surviving as spectators.[158]

The uncertainty of death makes an au-thentic attitude towards death a "fantastic requirement."[159] Authentic living, living with a constant view as to what one really is, must keep itself constantly aware of ap-proaching death. It is this incomprehensi-ble 'end of our possibilities' which ulti-mately makes life meaningful. The 'end' here is purposively ambiguous; on the one hand, death is (temporally) the end of life, but sometimes it seems that death is also the 'goal' of life. This ambiguity con-tinues through *Sein und Zeit,* but in his later writings, death really becomes the goal of life, and not just a threat which makes all living more urgent.

It is the dread of death which is ulti-mately responsible for the "call of con-science" to be authentic, to break away from the public and its preoccupation with the present, to examine our lives as a projected whole. It is foreknowledge of immanent death which forces man to "take hold of his destiny." Of extreme phil-osophical importance for Heidegger is the near-trivial truth, "I can die only *my* death." Death always claims the individual, not *das Man,* and it is, therefore, the threat of death which forces Dasein to see himself as something apart from *das Man.* Death is the greatest enemy of the *public;* and the public (*das Man*) protects itself by hiding the fact of death. It does this by reducing death to an anonymous, biological occurrence; it treats death as subject to be avoided. It invents euphemisms to make death seem unreal (for example, "Passing on"). It presents death so frequently and so insignificantly that it allows people to be aware of death in the most trivial way, not a personal way at all (for example, in novels, movies, television). The "call of conscience" announces personal death nevertheless, and it is this "call" which brings man to realize his "true essence as Being-unto-death." The prospect of death gives us a most important choice, the choice to be authentic or not. The prospect of death raises in us a tremendous *guilt* (*Schuld*) of what we have not done, of what we have not tried to do, and raises in us a *resolve* (*Entschlossenkeit*), a resolution to be authentic. Resolve is "Dasein's coming face to face with death as his own inevitable, inalienable, extreme possibility." Resolve is a "choice of this choice, the decision for being able to be oneself on one's own."[160] It is dread of death that shows a man what he really is, that which gets him to appreciate the existential structure which we have described thus far.

All of this is terribly depressing philosophy it would seem, and Heidegger is often criticized for his gloomy view of human existence as "Being-unto-death." However, it is important to distinguish Heidegger's view of facing death with the sort of gloomy anguish so often exemplified in the French existentialist novels about impending death. The recognition of death is a bright prospect for Heidegger. In one sense, it signals the end of our *Existenz,* but it also frees us from the tyranny of *das Man.* It is recognition of death which lets us truly (authentically) live. The prospect of this freedom is not a gloomy prospect at all (as it often becomes for Camus and Sartre), but is much more like Nietzsche's celebration of the 'awful truth' that "God is dead."

Along with sober anguish, which brings [Dasein] up before the reality of his

central existential possibility, goes a supporting joy over this very possibility. In [grasping this possibility] Dasein becomes free from the "accidents" of subsistence problems which arise out of the goings-on in the world of a life of busy curiosity.[161]

Heidegger does not say, however, that death is a *good* thing for Dasein, for he conscientiously refrains from making value judgments, restricts himself to setting forth an *ontology,* a purely descriptive philosophy. Yet it is clear enough that the discussions of death and authenticity contain within them some revolutionary ethical commands. Heidegger would never consider himself a moral philosopher, but we have already indicated that ontology for him is scarcely distinguishable from ethics, since he ultimately rejects the distinctions between practical and theoretical, value and fact. It is necessary then, that we attempt to extract some of these ethical commands before we move beyond *Sein und Zeit* to his later works.

Heidegger's Ethics

In our discussion of Dasein, it has become evident that Heidegger pursues a campaign which is largely directed against the traditional philosophical distinction between 'practice' and 'theory'. He thus rejects the notion of 'things' as our primitive conception of entities in the world and replaces it with a notion of 'equipment'. He rejects the Cartesian *cogito* as the starting point of phenomenological investigation and substitutes for it "Being-in-the-world," a notion which does not pretend to restrict its scope to cognitive matters. Thus, the notion of 'intentionality' in Husserl, which so often appears as a cognitive attitude towards objects, is replaced by 'care' which has clear practical connotations; "knowledge of the world" is moved to a secondary position in Heidegger's philosophy while involvement, design, utility, moods, and concern become primitive human attitudes towards the world. With this breakdown in the distinction between 'theory' and 'practice', we must expect a parallel breakdown between the traditional philosophical categories of metaphysics and ethics. If there is no clear distinction between knowledge and practice, between what the world is and what we aspire to make of it, then these two traditionally very different philosophical enterprises, the search for truth and the search for values, are indistinguishable. Therefore, we must now ask what sort of ethical recommendations are to be found in the 'ontology' of *Sein und Zeit.*

A discussion of Heidegger's ethics is made unnecessarily difficult from the start by the fact that Heidegger repeatedly insists that he is not doing ethics, that philosophy has no room for ethics, and that his concepts are purely 'descriptive' and contain no moralizing criticism or negative value judgments. In *Sein und Zeit,* we are told that ethical matters are *existentielle* or *ontic* matters, and that they, therefore, have no place in philosophy (*ontology*). In a later comment on the contents of *Sein und Zeit,* Heidegger again chastises the many readers who have 'misunderstood' him. If one takes *Sein and Zeit,*

in spite of all expressly given warnings not to take it as an ontic characterization of man—as a philosophy of life or an ethics which appraises "human life" then everything will be thrown into confusion.[162]

These insistences recur in Heidegger's most recent works, most notably in his "Letter on Humanism," in which he sharply distinguishes his own philosophy from the more explicitly value-laden 'ontology' of Sartre. This rejection of the ethical import of his treatise has generated untold confusion among those who wish to give fair interpretation of Heidegger's early philosophy. Further complicating Heidegger's proclaimed rejection of ethics as philosophically irrelevant is his own disastrous flirtation and endorsement of the National Socialist Party in his inaugural address (as Rector of the University of Freiburg) in 1933, only six years after *Sein und Zeit* was published. Heidegger's most embittered personal critics claim that his philosophy was such that it allowed him to accept any evaluative position, even the most despicable one. Others argue that the rejection of ethics as a part of philosophy and emphasis on the 'thrownness' of Dasein has allowed Heidegger to simply accept whatever evaluations are current in the *Zeitgeist.* Both of these attempts to explain Heidegger's Nazi leanings are unfair, but they reflect a most serious problem in Heidegger interpretation. To what extent do the ontological formulations of *Sein und Zeit* raise ethical

problems, and to what extent do they commit us to moral (or immoral) positions? The breakdown between practical and theoretical would seem to entail that Heidegger's heavily practical conceptions as to what it is to be a human being would commit him to some practical demands as to how human beings ought to behave. For example, if it is the very nature of Dasein to "question its own being," why is it not some sort of *obligation* of Dasein to ask this question? Heidegger surely does consider our "falling from being" a *failing,* and one which he seeks to *correct.* Why is Heidegger hesitant to say that this is one of the *values*—the value of self-examination—which is entailed by the ontological formulations of *Sein und Zeit?* If men are, for the most part, inauthentic, is that not something for us to strive to overcome? Is not the central ethical commitment of Heidegger's philosophy of being human the prescription that we *ought* to strive for authenticity? [The terms "authentic" and "inauthentic" are themselves clearly morally 'loaded' terms. However, this does not show that Heidegger's claims that they are not evaluative is 'most implausible' as argued in passing by Warnock (*Existentialist Ethics*) and other unsympathetic commentators. Recall that the original German translates as "ownness" and "disownness," terms which are not clearly evaluative.]

Commentators have not been agreed as to how heavily to stress, or whether to mention, Heidegger's 'ethics' as a part of his philosophy. Many commentators attempt to remain faithful to Heidegger's own denials of ethical import and restrict themselves to discussions of his ontology (for example, Langan, Versenyi, King, and Heinemann).[163] A few recent commentators have reinterpreted Heidegger's 'ontology' as a primarily ethical theory (Olafson and Warnock).[164] However, as an interpretation of a philosopher whose central theme is the breakdown of those distinctions which mark the boundaries between ontology and ethics, all such approaches must be misleading. For to maintain that Heidegger is doing or not doing ethics in his ontology is to already reinstitute the same distinction which he has rejected. It must be admitted that Heidegger himself makes this mistake and fails to recognize that the whole of *Sein und Zeit* with its notably value-laden terminology commits him to a very definite, even though quite abstract, moral philosophy. The nature of the ethics of *Sein und Zeit* is not less complex than the treatise as a whole.

Heidegger's dismissal of ethics as philosophically (ontologically) irrelevant seems implausible at first: how can philosophy not concern itself with ethics? To understand Heidegger's position, let us remind ourselves of Husserl's attitude towards values and value theory. For Husserl, all consciousness is some form of *knowing* based on intuition. Values, therefore, are *objects of knowledge* intuited in much the same way that 'facts' of nature are intuited. We have quoted some of the few passages in which Husserl puts forward this claim (p. 158). Husserl's general lack of concern with every field which was not concerned most centrally with knowledge could not allow him to pursue this thesis. In one of Husserl's more gifted students, however, Max Scheler (1874–1928), this theory is worked out in considerable detail.[165] His 'intuitionist' thesis of ethics—that values are intuited—is presented in direct opposition to all theories of ethics which present values as evolutionary or utilitarian products, for example, the various Darwinian ethics (Spengler, Spencer, Hegel to some extent, Marx, and Nietzsche with some reservations), and the many utility-directed "shopkeeper" moralities of the British. Scheler also opposed all formalist ethics, primarily that of Kant, against whom he wrote many pages of objections. According to Scheler's development of the germ of ethical theory in Husserl, all evaluation is a special kind of knowing, involving a special sort of intuition, the intuition of values. When we evaluate 'x' as good, according to him, we are not instantiating some more general-universal-ethical principle, nor are we stating a historical fact or a fact about pleasure/pain or expected pleasure/pain, nor are we making a prediction about consequences in general. We are primarily stating an intuited fact; values, according to Husserl and Scheler, are *in the world*. We do not perceive a thing/state-of-affairs and then attach a value to it. We perceive the thing/state-of-affairs as already valuable.

This intuitionist theory in Germany was paralleled by a similar theory in England, most prominently argued by G. E. Moore. The core of both theses, although argued very differently, was the rejection of all ethical theories which took knowledge of good/bad/right/wrong to be derivative of other kinds of knowledge (for example, knowledge of pleasure and pain, and knowledge of historical origins), and the setting apart of knowledge of values as an autonomous way of knowing through intuition. Moore stressed the first part of this thesis, and spent much of his time arguing against "naturalists" who insisted on reducing evaluations to some set of 'natural facts.' Scheler spent most of his polemic against Kantians and others who agreed that values were not reducible to natural facts, but yet would not allow that values were, therefore, something which could be *known*.

Heidegger's reaction to this theory ought to be easily predictable from his general approach to Husserl—all consciousness is *not a form of knowing*. Evaluation, specifically, is not a kind of knowing, at least not a kind of knowing anything like the knowledge we receive through an *intuition* of *things*. Husserl and Scheler made the mistake, Heidegger thinks, of construing all consciousness (all intentional acts) on the model of scientific or mathematical knowledge. *Sein und Zeit* has argued that our 'primitive' relationship to the world is not one of knowing, but one of *concern*.

At this point, we wish to argue that Heidegger has grossly misunderstood his own enterprise. Basing his criticism on the fruits of *Sein und Zeit*, he has done well to point out that Husserl and Scheler have misinterpreted the nature of evaluation because of their preoccupation with a single sort of intentional act. Here, if he consistently followed *Sein und Zeit*, Heidegger ought to have argued that evaluation is more 'primitive' than knowing, that knowing is derived from evaluating, but that ultimately the two are inseparably connected.[166] However, this is not his argument, and the doctrine against ethics he does give us does not tell us that evaluation is 'primitive', but that evaluation has no place in our ontological investigations at all. He tells us that values are of strictly *ontic* concern, and that ontology has nothing to say about what ought to be done. Heidegger thus tells us that we do not *know* values at all, either on the basis of 'natural facts' or on the basis of specifically evaluative intuitions. Values, according to Heidegger are creations of "human subjectivity," and are mere "objectifications of individual wants." It is curious that Heidegger should take recourse in the 'subjective-objective' distinction he so much rejects, but it is even more surprising that a philosophy which places so much 'value' on individual authenticity should reject out of hand all consideration of individual human wants and 'subjective creations.' In his book on Plato, this attack on values continues in an even more bizarre direction;

It is high time to understand that through the characterization as 'value' the valued object is deprived of its dignity. This means that through the evaluation of something as value, the value is merely admitted as an object of human valuation. But whatever is, is not exhausted qua being in its being an object, especially not if this objectivity has the character of value. . . . Thinking in values is here, as always, the greatest possible blasphemy in the face of Being. To think against values does not therefore mean raising one's voice for the worthlessness and nullity of Being, on the contrary it implies, in opposition to the subjective transformation of being into a mere object, bringing the light of the truth of being before our thought.[167]

This relatively late work (1942) shows just how extreme the antihumanistic tendency of Heidegger's philosophy will go. The 'primitive' practical human elements which played such an important part in *Sein und Zeit* are now rejected out of hand to maintain the 'dignity' of Being. One ought to wonder how 'dignity' can be spelled out without an appeal to values, and one can only be surprised by Heidegger's central claim here, which not only throws evaluation out of philosophy, but attempts to reject evaluation as an 'authentic' human activity altogether. Philosophers like Kierkegaard and Nietzsche have attempted extreme "revaluations of values," but neither of them went so far as Heidegger does now, attempting to get rid of not this set of values in favor of that one but to get rid of *all* values.

Olafson[168] has suggested that the reaction of Heidegger (and Sartre) to Husserl and Scheler remarkably parallels the rejection of Moore's intuitionism by Charles Stevenson and R. N. Hare in Anglo-American philosophy. This parallelism shows a most important tendency in twentieth-century ethics which seems to have developed independently in Britain, America, and Germany. Heidegger, like Stevenson and Hare, rejects the notion of 'evaluative facts' and the 'intuition' of these 'facts.' Values, for Heidegger as for Stevenson and Hare, are merely 'subjective', and are not to be likened to objects of cognition, beliefs, and the like. Values are mere expressions of attitude, or 'subjectivity,' and as such have no place in philosophy which deals only with what can be established 'objectively.' However, it must be stressed that Heidegger goes far beyond the British "emotivists" in his rejection of values altogether. Stevenson et al. will gladly admit that evaluation is a *bona fide* human activity. It is simply not an activity in which philosophers can take an active part *qua* philosophers (their role is simply to explain how it is that such evaluation takes place). Heidegger not only adopts a "meta-ethical" stance, refusing to allow himself *qua* philosopher to participate in evaluating, he refuses to allow himself as an authentic human being to participate in valuing as well. Of course, it is clearly not the case that Heidegger the man has abstained from making evaluations, but the suggestion that one *ought* to abstain from valuing, in addition to being an evaluation about proper human activity itself, seems to require something absurd of us.

This absurd demand to reject values is clearly not the last word on Heidegger's ethics. Contrary to his insistence, we have maintained that *Sein und Zeit* is as much a treatise on human values (the truth of *Existenz*) as a treatise on ontology, and that the products of *Sein und Zeit* are not only descriptions of Dasein, but instructions for Dasein. The primary instruction, of course, is that we should strive to be authentic. Inauthenticity or fallenness is to be fought against and overcome. Of course, Heidegger stresses that, because Dasein existentially has tendencies to both authenticity and inauthenticity, no one could ever attain complete authenticity, nor could anyone 'fall' to complete inauthenticity. The demands of every day and the public will always cause a certain amount of inauthenticity and failure to treat oneself according to one's *Existenz*. Similarly, the approach of death and the *Angst* which is encountered in certain instances will jar even the most "average everyday'' man out of his inauthenticity to a shocking recognition of his own true individuality. The ethics of *Sein und Zeit* can thus be simply stated; one must strive to be authentic, and to be authentic is to ask the question of Being regarding oneself, to accept Heidegger's analysis of the nature of Dasein as *Existenz*, facticity, fallenness (as care), and strive to act accordingly. What is it to act accordingly? It is here that Heidegger's critics, and the critics of existentialism generally, attack this philosophy for its failure to provide any concrete proposals for action. If we accept *Sein und Zeit*'s demand that we strive for authenticity, should we all become Nazis, or Communists, or Democrats, and should we get married, write philosophy, or accept a job which will force us to concern ourselves with small tasks? What does Heidegger tell us about what we ought to do in order to be authentic?

It is here that Heidegger refuses, and rightly refuses, to give us an ethics. From our discussion of Kierkegaard, it should be evident why he must refuse and why all existentialists who turn from universal ethics in favor of an ethics of 'authenticity' must also refuse to give us a specific life-program or life-style. It is the nature of these philosophies that "becoming authentic" essentially requires that we each give up the quest for a set of 'given' values, whether these be given from God, from society (*das Man*), or from philosophers. Kierkegaard's separation of the three 'spheres of existence' serves us well here to illustrate this point. Each sphere dictates its own life-style, but authenticity, the 'existential value', depends on an 'arbitrary' or 'irrational' choice of spheres. Similarly for Heidegger, who does not attempt to distinguish distinct life styles, it is impossible for the philosopher to give a criterion for the correct choice of a way of life, for any such criterion would directly violate the basic 'existential' principle that Dasein must choose his own mode of existence. The ethics of *Sein und Zeit,* therefore, is necessarily incomplete; it must be more of an antiethics. This does not signify the rejection of values as such, as Heidegger later indicates, it only indicates the rejection of universal values, values imposed on Dasein by others.

Heidegger's ethics is thus much less promising as a source of guidance than we may come to expect of an ethics. How-

ever, as we have seen in the philosophies of Kierkegaard and Nietzsche, to whom the later existentialists are in heavy debt, any philosophy which so heavily stresses individual autonomy of choice will find itself forced to be noncommittal as to correct life-programs. It is *in spite of* this ethics of authenticity that Heidegger turns to National Socialism as a 'correct' moral choice, as it is *in spite of* his similar philosophy that Sartre defends Communism. The choice of a specific ethical position is, of course, open to these existentialists, and even necessary for them, but there is no possible defense as to the correctness of their choice. It must be lamented that the backsliding into 'objectivist' ethics is one of the persistent personal dangers for these thinkers.

A full discussion of twentieth-century 'existentialist' ethics will be postponed until our treatment of Sartre and his contemporaries, Camus, Simone De Beauvoir, and Merleau-Ponty. However, there is one more peculiarly existentialist theme which ought to be reintroduced here, for it is one of the peculiarities of existentialism which has sharply set it off temperamentally from many other philosophies. We have seen how both Kierkegaard and Nietzsche criticize other philosophers on a very personal basis instead of criticizing detached and impersonal ideas. Such ad hominem critiques are generally frowned on by the scholarly community, but it is necessary that we seriously consider the truth of such a position, that philosophical mistakes are a symptom of some more personal failing. Kierkegaard and Nietzsche make this claim, but certainly do not advance a theory to support it. Heidegger, on the other hand, does give us a theory to the effect that philosophical doctrines are inseparably a product of the philosopher who creates them, and that philosophical mistakes cannot be isolated from certain personal failings of the philosopher.

We have alrea seen the great importance Heidegger attributes to the distinction between 'ontic' and 'ontological' and to the two corresponding very different kinds of knowledge. Ontological knowledge is conceptual, verbal, philosophical knowledge; ontic 'knowledge' is preconceptual, preverbal, prephilosophical, and manifests itself in knowing *how* to do things, in actions. Thus it is possible for a man to 'know' himself in two very different ways; he may have a conception about himself, write a philosophy of human nature, and thus have (existential) ontological knowledge about himself. A man can also have ontic (existential-ontic) knowledge about himself, he may treat himself in certain ways and act towards himself in certain ways. Clearly our ontic 'knowledge' of ourselves is the temporally prior of the two. Ontological knowledge is a verbal expression or conceptualization of our ontic knowledge of ourselves. One's ontological knowledge of himself is derivative of his preontological understanding of himself, however, and this means that a philosophy—a person's ontological conception of himself—is a reflection of his ontic understanding of himself. Philosophy is, therefore, the expression of the person himself, and not simply an impersonal manipulation of ideas. Furthermore, philosophical errors reflect a personal failing, and not simply careless thinking.

"Fallenness" (and "fallenness from Being") is not simply a failure of philosophers to ask certain questions; it is a failure of men "to be what they are," a personal weakness rather than philosophical neglect. Fallenness is primarily a pre-ontological or ontic misunderstanding of oneself. Specifically, fallenness is the 'primitive' attitudes towards oneself as *das Man* in average everydayness; this itself is not a philosophical mistake, it is personal failure to treat oneself and to act as a being with *Existenz* (possibilities). Philosophies which remain within the inauthentic attitude of average everydayness are not simply bad characterizations of what it is to be a human being, they are expressions of men who are themselves in this inauthentic attitude. Inauthenticity is not primarily a philosophical mistake, it is a failure to live correctly which is expressed (unwittingly) in inauthentic philosophies.

All of this raises a serious problem for Heidegger's ethics and his ontology as a whole.[169] If philosophy (ontology) is always a reflection of preontological understanding of ourselves, how is it possible to understand an authentic ontology unless one is already an authentic person (ontically)? Furthermore, how is it possible to suggest that one should strive for authenticity if one cannot even understand the concept of 'authenticity' unless he already is authentic? Heidegger's answer to this is that philosophical mis-

takes are not simply human inadequacies which manifest themselves in ontology, but they are conscientious *refusals* to recognize oneself for what one really is. In other words, we all have some kind of pre-ontological recognition of ourselves, but we actively refuse to come to grips with this recognition, even in our ontic understanding of ourselves. Fallenness — and inauthenticity are thus purposive self-deceptions ("concealment from self"), the knowing and yet refusing to admit that one has the freedom of possibility of *Existenz*. Thus Heidegger echos another of the indictments against philosophers heralded by Kierkegaard and Nietzsche; their mistakes are not simply bad thinking or even personal failings as much as *cowardice*, a refusal to face what one knows to be the case about *oneself*. The 'ethics' of *Sein und Zeit* thus has a most difficult task; to force its readers to face their own nature as Dasein, and overcome their cowardice, their refusal to see themselves as they really are. Clearly the writing style of *Sein und Zeit* is hardly the vehicle to carry out this task, and Heidegger's later writings seem to have lost the urgency for this self-realization. The attack on self-deception, therefore, will have to await the redoing of Heidegger's 'existentialist' philosophy in the hands of the French.

Being and Truth

Let us now return to the stated theme of Heidegger's inquiry, the problem of Being. How has our investigation of Dasein helped us to approach this fundamental metaphysical problem?

Ultimately, the problem of Being is referred to the problem of temporality, but not worked out, as *Sein und Zeit* ends;

The existential-ontological constitution of Dasein's totality is grounded in temporality. Hence the ecstatical [that is temporal] projection of Being must be made possible by some primordial way in which ecstatical temporality temporalizes. How is this mode of the temporalizing of temporality to be interpreted? Is there a way which leads from primordial time to the meaning of Being? Does time itself manifest itself as the horizon of Being?[170]

This open ending has generated considerable confusion in the interpretation of Heidegger's philosophy. *Sein und Zeit* is clearly not intended as a finished treatise. Its 'design' prepares us for the third division of Sein und Zeit, "Time and Being," which has never appeared, as well as an entire second part on "the phenomenological destruction of the history of ontology, with the problematic of temporality as our clue". Some of this has appeared, but without any attempt to incorporate it into the project of Sein und Zeit.[171] Moreover, Heidegger comes explicitly to reject certain key theses in Sein und Zeit shortly after its publication, most importantly, the notion that human understanding can allow us to disclose Being for ourselves. This has led many readers to sharply distinguish the early Heidegger from the later Heidegger (sometimes distinguishing a middle period as well). Although there clearly is a marked change in direction after Sein und Zeit, it seems quite pointless for us to argue that Heidegger has or has not 'totally' changed his philosophy, since the "problem and disclosure of Being" remains its central theme from Sein und Zeit to the most recent writings. After Sein und Zeit, Heidegger published his well-known and often-disputed interpretation of Kant und das Problem der Metaphysik, an essay on "The Essence of Foundations" (Vom Wesen des Grundes),[172] and a very important essay, Was ist Metaphysik? During the long period of Nazi rise to power and Heidegger's own political involvements and embarrassments, only a single major work was published, the essay on Hölderlin (quoted in the section on "What Is Philosophy?"). During the war, Heidegger wrote an article, "On the Essence of Truth" (Vom Wesen der Wahrheit) which we shall discuss in this section. The essay on "Plato's Theory of Truth" (Platons Lehre von der Wahreit) with the "Letter on Humanism" (Humanismusbrief) in which Heidegger divorces himself from Sartre's philosophy was published in 1947. Since 1950, Heidegger has been very productive, publishing a set of essays as Holzwege (on Nietzsche, Hegel, the pre-Socratics, and poetry), and publishing a two-volume interpretation of Nietzsche's 'metaphysics' (1961). His very important Introduction to Metaphysics (Einführung in die Metaphysik) to which we have referred frequently, was originally written as a lecture shortly after the publication of Sein und Zeit. It was rewritten after the war and was not published until 1953. In 1953, he published two essays on "Think-

ing" (Was ist Denken? and Aus der Erfahrung des Denkens), and several essays on old topics, "What Is Philosophy?" (1956) and a new essay on the question of Being (Zur Seinfrage) (1956). He has written dozens of less-known articles and essays since 1950 and is still actively writing.

Although we shall avoid all attempts to decide on the basis of our brief discussion whether it is justifiable to speak of Heidegger's 'abandonment' of Sein und Zeit, we shall be able to characterize a number of marked changes in emphasis from Sein und Zeit through later works. First, and most famously, the discussion turns from a heavy emphasis on Dasein back to the problem of Being itself. (This does not warrant the conclusion that Heidegger has changed projects however, since it was announced in Sein und Zeit that the investigation of Dasein was only a preliminary to the problem of Being.) Secondly, Heidegger's views on language and philosophy become increasingly radical: in Sein und Zeit, traditional language was insufficient; in later writings, only Greek is truly adequate to the task (for example, in "What Is Philosophy?") and ultimately all conceptual language is incapable of grasping Being and Truth (for example in What Is Thinking?). Philosophy moves from creating new ('ideal') languages to ancient Greek etymology to poetry to mysticism. Thirdly, there is the transition from disclosure of Being as a function of human (Dasein) understanding to the reception of this disclosure of Being in a special nonconceptual insight. (Thus, 'ontology', which plays so great a role in Sein und Zeit, gradually fades in importance in later writings.) Fourthly, there is an increased emphasis on the role of nothing in the analysis of Being. This notion of 'nothing' and the 'not' appears in Sein und Zeit, but becomes central to philosophy in the essay on Kant and in "What Is Metaphysics?" With this emphasis, an increased Kierkegaardian development of an attack on reason and logic also occurs. We cannot trace these developments in detail, but we can summarize them in order to see how far Heidegger has turned from his analysis in Sein und Zeit, and why his "existentialist" influence has not been based on his later works.

We have seen that the question of Being arises through the Being (Existenz) of

Dasein, and that the world cannot be distinguished from Dasein (Being-in-the-world). From these discussions, we may gather that Heidegger is going to reject the oldest and most commonsensical interpretation of Being and truth—the thesis that "Being is apart from our encounters with Being" and that "the truth is what is the case." In traditional philosophy, Being is simply *there,* whether or not we know it, doubt it, 'bracket it', or cannot know it at all. This Being-in-itself is also said to be the *truth* or the *true,* and we derivatively say that our ideas or judgments are true if they *correspond* to the truth or Being or "the way it really is." According to Heidegger, such theories arise from a wrong start as exemplified in Descartes—the sharp distinction between the subject and the objects known. This same distinction has permeated philosophy since Plato and has secured itself in the very grammar we use to talk about Being. Once we have given up this theory, however, we cease to look at the *truth* as an unknown with which our ideas, perceptions, judgments 'match up' and begin to see Truth as *disclosure;*

'Disclose' and 'disclosedness' will be used as technical terms in the passages that follow, and shall signify 'to lay open' and 'the character of having been laid open'. Thus 'to disclose' never means anything like 'to obtain indirectly through inference'.[173]

Being (not entities) is something which 'there is' only in so far as truth is. And truth is only in so far as and as long as Dasein is. Being and truth 'are' equiprimordially.[174]

Dasein only 'has' meaning, so far as the disclosedness of Being-in-the-world can be 'filled-in' by the entities discoverable in that disclosedness.[175]

The Being of truth is connected primordially with Dasein. And only because Dasein is as constituted by disclosedness (that is, by understanding), can anything like Being be understood; only so is it possible to understand Being.[176]

Disclosure, like "understanding" and many of the concepts we have encountered in Heidegger, does not apply to only conceptual processes,

Being has been disclosed in a preliminary way, though non-conceptually; and this makes it possible for Dasein as existent Being-in-the-world to comport itself towards entities—*towards those which it encounters within-the-world as well as towards itself as existent.*[177]

Even in *Sein und Zeit,* Heidegger's primary antagonist is all theories which suggest a 'transcendent' or 'external' reality to which objects of our experience correspond. *Disclosure* of truth signifies that our discovery of the truth (Being) does not consist in our inferring a correspondence between what we (think we) know and what *really* is the case, but rather it is a discovery of what we know, a discovery of Being *qua* Being. In *Sein und Zeit,* the argument against the correspondence theory of truth (although not presented as such) is the entire working through of the conception of *Dasein.* Our 'primitive' encounter with the world cannot be accounted for in terms of correspondence theory because there is no distinction between objects of consciousness and objects-in-themselves on which to base the correspondence. Furthermore, this is true, as we have seen, because our 'primitive' encounter with the world is not essentially *cognitive* and not related to *things.* Our primitive encounter is a *practical* encounter, and truth or *disclosure* must include these practical concerns as well as the well-trodden problems concerning the truth of propositions.

In later writings, this argument remains constant. In the essay on "The Essence of Truth," Heidegger begins by reminding us that

The question as to the nature of truth is not concerned with whether truth is the truth of practical experience or economic calculation, whether it is the truth of a technical consideration or of political shrewdness, or, more particularly, the truth of scientific research or of art, or even the truth of contemplative thought or of religious belief. The essential question disregards all this and fixes its attention on the one thing that is the mark of 'truth' of every kind.[178]

We may thus compare Heidegger's broad notion of 'truth' to the equally broad notion we encountered in Hegel; there is *truth* in every human endeavor, and not just the truth of assertive speech. Like Hegel, Heidegger wishes to claim that the correspondence theory of truth is not *false* itself, but simply overextends itself from contexts in which it does adequately account for our use of 'truth' to areas for which it cannot account. The correspondence theory does well as an account of our notion of 'truth' in straightforward empirical descriptions; for example, "The cat is on the mat" is true if and only if there is a state-of-affairs such that the cat is on the mat. Even this 'ordinary' (and 'traditional philosophical') notion of 'truth' does not represent primarily *propositional* truth, but a more general correspondence notion which has propositional correspondence, that is, the correspondence of a proposition or judgment to a state-of-affairs as a special instance.

What do we ordinarily understand by "truth"? This exalted but at the same time overworked and almost exhausted word "truth" means: that which makes something true into a truth. . . . The True is the Real . . . we speak of "true coin" as distinct from false . . . Genuine coin is that real thing whose reality agrees with what we always and in advance 'really' mean by "coin."[179]

We call "true" not only . . . genuine coin and all actualities of that sort, we also and principally call "true" or "false" our statements concerning such actualities as are themselves true or false in their kind, which may be thus or thus in their reality. A statement is true when what it means and says agrees with the thing of which it speaks.[180]

Thus, *correspondence* is a broader notion than correspondence between propositions and things. Philosophers have often treated propositional truth as the paradigm of truth and treated such expressions as "a true man" as parasitic deviant usage. Heidegger claims, to the contrary, that it is the application of truth to things which is the paradigm of truth as correspondence:

The True, then, be it a true thing or a true proposition, is that which is right, which corresponds. Being true and truth here mean correspondence, and that in a double sense: firstly, the correspondence of a thing with the idea of it as conceived in advance, and secondly, the correspondence of

that which is intended by the statement with the thing itself.[181]

Ordinary-traditional or not, the correspondence theory of truth is not an adequate theory. This is not to say that the theory is *false,* but only that it cannot adequately account for all truth. The correspondence theory works well within most everyday contexts in talking about and evaluating *things.* We have already seen that 'thing' is not a primitive notion, and thus an account of 'truth' which relies on our notion of 'thing' will not give us an account of our primitive notion of 'truth'. The correspondence theory cannot explain the notion of 'truth' in practical or 'equipment' contexts (where there are no *things*), nor can it account for the sorts of truths which are expressed in the a priori propositions of an ontology (for example, "Dasein is Being-in-the-world"). Correspondence must be recognized as a limited and derivative notion of truth, and correspondence theory can be accepted as an accurate account of this limited and derivative notion. However, correspondence is not truth as such, and correspondence theory does not account for truth as such.

As we ought to expect, Heidegger's theory of truth presents us with a primarily *practical* conception of truth, one which is inseparably tied to human behavior in general and not only to human speech and conceptual knowledge;

Rightness (truth) of statement is only made possible by the overt character of behavior.[182]

It is behavior which gives us a "criterion, a possibility" for obtaining the truth, and not speech. This behavior is itself grounded in the being of Dasein, specifically, in *freedom;*

The overt character of behavior in the sense that it makes rightness (truth) a possibility, is grounded in freedom. The essence of truth is freedom.[183]

This is not to say, however, that truth is arbitrary;

But to turn truth into freedom—is that not to abandon truth to the caprice of man?[184]

Rather, it stresses for us that truth does not refer to some *thing beyond* human being (Dasein), but

truth is brought down to the subjective level of the human subject. Even if this subject can attain to some kind of objectivity, it still remains human in its subjectivity and subject to human control.[185]

(The reemergence of the forbidden notions of 'subject-subjectivity', 'object-objectivity' is a mark of Heidegger's later writings.)

Once again we encounter the familiar yet obscure notion of 'freedom' at the very foundation of a philosophy of human being (as we did in Kant, Fichte, Hegel, and Kierkegaard). What is this *freedom?* Heidegger makes it quite clear to us that it is not simply the "random ability to do as we please, to go this way or that in our choice."[186]

Freedom is not license in what we do or do not do. Nor, on the other hand, is freedom a mere readiness to do something requisite and necessary . . . Over and above all this ["negative" and "positive" freedom] freedom is a participation in the disclosure of what-is-as-such.[187]

"Freedom" is rather identified—primitively described—as "letting-be." Freedom reveals itself as the "letting-be" of what-is.[188] This "letting-be" is, in turn, analyzed not as "indifference" or "neglect," but rather

To let something be is in fact to have something to do with it. . . . To let what-is be what it is means participating in something overt and its overtness, in which everything that 'is' takes up its position and which entails such overtness.[189]

Here we find ourselves back before our 'primitive' encounter with the world as a totality not of things but of equipment. To let something be, to manifest our freedom, is to act towards the world, to "participate in something overt." Truth is, therefore, disclosure in the sense that truth is primarily our overt behavior toward the world, not our asserting correct propositions about things in the world;

Freedom, so understood as the letting-be of what-is, fulfils and perfects the nature

of truth in the sense that truth is the unconcealment and revealment [Disclosure] of what-is. "Truth" is not the mark of some correct proposition made by a human "subject" in respect of an "object" and which then—in precisely what sphere we do not know—counts as "true"; truth is rather the revelation of what-is, a revelation through which something "overt" comes into force. All human behavior is an exposition into that overtness.[190]

What is *truth* for Heidegger, then? We may perhaps direct our understanding of his theory to two quite familiar theories of truth in modern philosophy. Philosophers who have rejected the correspondence theory of truth as a general account of truth because of its failure to account for a priori truth, have often turned to a *coherence* theory of truth.[191] Propositions of mathematics, for example, cannot be said to be true by virtue of their "agreement with the world," for it is the nature of mathematics to give us *necessary* truth —"truth independent of any and all states of affairs in the world" (compare Husserl, Chapter 5). Similarly, analytic truths, truths "by linguistic convention," cannot be accounted for on a correspondence theory, so philosophers have suggested that the truth of such propositions must lie not in their relationship to the world but in their relationship to each other. Analytic truths are true, consequently, through their coherence with all other propositions in the language; truths of mathematics are true because they "hang together" in a system of mathematical truths. A statement cannot be said to be true out of the context of some particular language; a mathematical proposition cannot be said to be true outside the context of a particular system of mathematical truths. Truth is determined by coherence —the coherence of a given proposition with other propositions of the same system of propositions.

Heidegger's view clearly has strong affinities for this theory, particularly in the rejection of the correspondence theory. The coherence theory, however, suffers, like the opposing correspondence theory, from the error of interpreting a notion of 'truth' which applies to a restricted kind of truth and overextends this notion to all truth. Coherence theory applies well to analytic and certain a priori propositions; it fares badly as an analysis of straight-

forward descriptive (empirical) propositions. It is implausible to maintain that the
truth of "the cat is on the mat" has nothing to do with the state of affairs that the
cat is on the mat. Furthermore, the coherence theory of truth is a theory about
the truth of *propositions,* and we have
already seen this is but one narrow conception of truth. Heidegger's theory of
truth obtains not only for true (and false)
propositions, but for truths pertaining to
our preverbal encounter with the world
as well.

We may still maintain that Heidegger
has offered us a coherence theory of truth,
one which accounts for empirical descriptions as well, if we keep in mind that it
is not only propositions which must "hang
together" coherently, but all human activity. Truth is determined by what we say
and, primarily, what we do; truth is fundamentally *pragmatic* truth (although Heidegger would not favor this term). Truth
is determined by our *moods* (our "being
tuned") as well as what we assert; it
is determined by our dread of death as
well as whatever science may tell us
about death. Man is "in error" ("He is in
error always because, by ex-sisting, he insists and is thus already in error") not because he *says* what is *false,* but because
he *acts falsely.* Most importantly, men err
towards themselves not only in what they
say about themselves (their ontology),
but in the way they act towards themselves ('ontically'). This is, as we have
seen, man's 'fallenness,' which is not only
an occasional and avoidable error, but
"part of the inner structure of *Dasein.*"[192]
The basic truth, therefore, is truth about
ourselves (Dasein)—what we are. It is
this truth which is the special concern of
philosophy (ontology is not mentioned in
this later essay); this is "original truth,"
the basis of all truth.

What is Being, then, given that truth
is the disclosure of Being? Being is not
beyond Dasein, but is a structure of
Dasein as "Being-in-the-world." Being is
whatever exists *for* Dasein; it cannot be
what corresponds to Dasein's ideas, experiences, or ideas. Being is whatever is
encountered by Dasein, and verbal description is but one way in which Dasein
encounters his world. "A being asserts
itself, it has authority."[193] Being is always essentially "Being-for-Dasein"; "Being" and "Dasein" are inseparable, just as
we maintain "Dasein" and "the World"
are inseparable.

We began this chapter by asking the
"question of Being" and claiming that it
was wrong to maintain that "Being is just
an empty word" on the grounds that we
do distinguish things that are from nothing. We must now reformulate this problem, for after *Sein und Zeit,* Heidegger
has moved us to a position where this
formulation of the problem is no longer
adequate. *Entities* (beings) are distinguished from *nothing,* and it is with
reference to *entities* that we ask, *"Why is
there something rather than nothing?"*[194]

Being itself is not distinguished from
nothing (we shall soon see that *nothing*
turns out to be a species of Being). Our
traditional notion of 'Being' is rather delineated in four different ways: Being is
distinguished from (1) becoming, (2) appearance, (3) thinking, (4) the 'ought'
(value).[195] Distinctions (2) and (3) are
crucial, and it is these distinctions which
have given rise to the correspondence
theory of truth which is the manifestation
of the 'fallenness' of Western man. We
distinguish between being and appearance, because we insist that there must
be something behind the appearances.
Heidegger traces this error to Plato, who
postulated *ideas* or *forms* in a realm of
Being 'above' the appearances of this
realm of *Becoming.* Subsequently, "appearance" degenerated to "mere appearance" and philosophy became caught, as
we have seen, in the problem of moving
from these "mere appearances" to the
things-themselves. Christian thought with
its transcendent God became simply one
more manifestation of this same error;

*Nietzsche was right in saying that
Christianity is Platonism for the people.*[196]

The error reaches ultimate confusion in
Kant, who uses "Being" to refer both to
objects as they appear (*phenomena*) and
to objects-in-themselves (*noumena*).

Similarly, philosophy since Plato has
come to distinguish *logos,* Thinking, from
Being, the former dealing with universals,
the latter pertaining only to particular
beings. Philosophers thus come to distinguish objects of thought from true Being.
Again, Heidegger argues that the distinction is an error, an error based on the failure to distinguish entities (beings) from
Being, and that Thinking and Being were
inseparable, just as Dasein and the world
are inseparable. The distinction between
Thinking and Being is based on (is identi-

cal to) the distinction between object and subject (thinking subject). We have seen that this distinction is a fundamental error and so must be the 'thinking-being' distinction. The problem of Being is not, therefore, the problem of inferring Being (and beings) from appearances and Thinking; it is the demand for analysis of how Being is Being, for Dasein. Heidegger insists that Nietzsche's radical claim that Being is just appearance and Thinking (that is, "our impressing order on chaos") is not an answer to this problem of Being (no matter how much Nietzsche's 'pragmatic' theory of truth would seem to anticipate Heidegger), but simply an inversion, in essence identical with Plato's theory of forms. Philosophy must move beyond the distinction between subject-object, and with this reject questions about the relation between subject (objects as they appear or are thought by the subject) and objects (in-themselves). It is for this reason that Heidegger asserts, in *Introduction to Metaphysics,* that *Sein und Zeit* asks the question of Being "for the first time."

Logic, Language, and Nothing
Throughout our discussion of Heidegger, we have emphasized his central concern with language. In *Sein und Zeit,* it is the stated business of philosophy to provide us with a new vocabulary and even a new grammar to talk about (and disclose) Being. In *Introduction to Metaphysics,* the question of Being commences with an investigation into the etymology and grammar of Being. We are told that "language is the house of Being," and that ontological errors (errors of verbal expression) are expressions of "fallenness from Being." However, the emphasis on language is not an emphasis on *ordinary* language, and Heidegger is quick to point out to us that we have no assurance that our word "Being" (*Sein*) adequately expresses Being. To the contrary,

in the course of time language has produced a blunted indefinite meaning of this word.[197]

We must, therefore, go beyond this word itself and return to the "primitive phenomenon" of Being, by-passing all philosophical prejudices, many of which are already structured in language. Ordinary and traditional philosophical language clearly will not do. However, as Heidegger's thinking develops, it becomes increasingly clear that Germanic-derived language will not suffice either. In his *Letter on Humanism,* he complains that the language of *Sein und Zeit* was "too metaphysical" to express truths about Being. In later writings, he turns increasingly toward an adaptation of ancient Greek, claiming that it better suffices to capture the metaphysical insights in the answer to the problem of Being. Soon this return is not sufficient either, and, during the war, we find Heidegger turning more toward the metaphysical expressiveness of poetry. Poetry, although assuredly not identical with philosophy, shares its goal, the expression of Being and the escape from the 'fallenness' which is already built into everyday speech. In his most recent writings,[198] Heidegger distinguishes between all human languages and *the Word* or *the Message,* the language which "Being itself speaks to Itself." It then becomes a serious question whether men can understand this language of Being, and Heidegger's most recent position seems to be that no human language can express Being.

The movement to this farfetched endpoint is of great philosophical significance, however, and we can see, in Heidegger's move towards mysticism, important and often unappreciated philosophical 'presuppositions' being systematically uprooted. Most importantly, Heidegger argues that philosophical discourse (ontology) must go beyond all prejudices, including those most basic prejudices built into language. We have already stressed the importance of the 'subject-object' distinction (and the correlated 'subject-predicate' distinction in language) in this regard, but there are more basic prejudices than that to be exhumed. Most notably, all logic and grammar are philosophical prejudices although they have been rarely recognized as such. We think of logic as the basis of all 'clear and careful thinking'; in fact, logic is one rigid form of thought which true philosophical (that is, presuppositionless) thinking must go beyond;

Logic is the science of thinking, the doctrine of the rules of thinking and the forms of thought. Moreover, it is the one philosophical discipline in which views of the world, the trends of Weltanschauung, play little or no part. Furthermore, logic passes as a secure and reliable science. It

has taught the same thing from time
immemorial. . . . Logic relieves us of the
need for any troublesome inquiry into the
essence of thinking.[199]

Thinking, Heidegger emphasizes, is not
the same as making statements in a language, even though (and Heidegger never
denies this) it may be the case that there
can be no thinking without language. We
can understand this by recalling his distinction between authentic *discourse*
(*Rede*) and inauthentic *prattle* (*Gerede*).
Both of these involve making statements,
but only the former is an expression of
thinking ("Thinking" in later writings
takes on the praiseworthy status of "understanding" in *Sein und Zeit* as authentic
human intellectual grappling with Being).
Inauthentic prattle may be logical, that
does not make it thinking. Authentic discourse expressing true thinking may be
nonlogical, but this does not invalidate it,
since the business of such thinking is,
among other tasks, to establish a foundation for logic (compare Husserl, Chapter
5, "Phenomenology and Foundations of
Philosophy");

Logic itself is in need of an explanation
and foundation in regard to its own origin
and its claim to provide the authoritative
interpretation of thinking.[200]

The superlogical thinking, however, is not
thereby *illogical;* it simply is a questioning
that includes in its scrutiny the principles
of logic; it is metalogical;

To surpass the traditional logic does not
mean elimination of thought and the
domination of sheer feeling; it means
more radical, stricter thinking, a thinking
that is part and parcel of being.[201]

"Logical thinking" is the basis of every
rationalism, the philosophical emphasis of
thinking (*logic*) over *Being* (*physis*).
Since Heidegger wishes to bring together
thinking and Being, he must similarly reject rationalism. It is thus that he makes
his well-known and rarely understood
attack on *Reason.* Heidegger, however, is
not an *irrationalist,* for irrationalism is to
make the same error of separating thinking and being, but change the emphasis
to Being.

Irrationalism is only the obvious weakness
and failure of rationalism and hence itself

a kind of rationalism. Irrationalism is a way
out of rationalism, an escape which does
not lead us into the open but merely
tangles us more in rationalism. . . .[202]

Thus it is the business of philosophy to
not assume the principles of logic to be
true, to recognize there is nothing to be
gained for philosophy in the further working out of logic;

For despite Kant and Hegel, logic has not
made a single advance in the essential and
initial questions. The only possible step
that remains is to stand on the very ground
from which logic rose and to overturn it
[as the dominant perspective for the
interpretation of Being].[203]

This rejection of logic involves the rejection of virtually every 'natural' language.
Given this as a necessary starting point for
asking the question of Being, we can
easily see how Heidegger slowly comes
to conclude that the question of Being
cannot be answered by (human) language at all.

Perhaps the whole body of logic as it is
known to us, perhaps all that we treat as
a gift from heaven, is grounded in a
very definite answer to the question about
Being; perhaps, in consequence, all
thinking which solely follows the laws of
thought prescribed by traditional logic
is incapable from the very start of even
understanding the question of being by its
own resources, let alone actually
unfolding the question and guiding it
towards an answer.[204]

The liberation of language from grammar,
. . . is reserved for thought and poetry.[205]

The blade with which traditional logic
is cut down is the concept of *the nothing.*
In one formulation of the problem of Being
(in *Introduction to Metaphysics*), Heidegger
asks, "Why there are beings *rather than
nothing?*" and then asks whether this last
phrase is not superfluous to the question;

Nothing is simply nothing. Here there is
nothing more to inquire about. And above
all, in talking about nothing or nothingness,
we are not making the slightest advance
toward the knowledge of being.

He who speaks of nothing does not know
what he is doing. In speaking of nothing

he makes it into a something. . . . He contradicts himself. But discourse that contradicts itself offends against the fundamental rule of logos, against "logic". To speak of nothing is illogical.[206]

The *"rather than nothing"* is essential to the question of being, for every being might not be;

True, the being remains manifested to us. But it cannot slough off the problematic fact that it might also not be what it is and as it is.[207]

The contrast between "beings" and "nothing" then turns and remains as a contrast of two kinds of Being;

Everything that is not simply nothing is, and for us even nothing "belongs" to "being."[208]

The atrocity of talking about nothing as 'a something' is anathema to science and logic;

To speak of nothing will always remain a horror and an absurdity for science.[209]

Authentic speaking about nothing will always remain extraordinary. It cannot be vulgarized. It dissolves if it is placed in the cheap acid of a merely logical intelligence.[210]

In principle, nothingness remains inaccessible to science.[211] However, despite this 'horror' which has been so often criticized by philosophers who lack tolerance with such metaphysical juggling (most famously, Rudolph Carnap has attacked Heidegger's thesis of the *nothing* on two separate occasions), there is an important point to be made here. Science, Heidegger tells us, deals only with the real world; philosophy deals with all possible worlds. The existence of things is always contingent; this is a very old philosophical point. Husserl distinguished between the researches of the natural scientist and the researches of the geometrician (who seeks *essences*) by noting that the scientist deals only with the factual world, the geometer deals with imagination and all possible worlds. Heidegger is making the same point, but with one very clever and extremely important switch. What is the contingency of objects? It is the possibility that they *might not be* (or might not be

as they are). This possibility, Heidegger tells us, is not something imposed on objects by us (that is, possibility is not a *modality*—a metalinguistic consideration),[212] rather the possibility of being nothing is in the phenomena themselves:

We do not experience this possibility as something that we add to the being by thinking; rather the being itself elicits this possibility, and in this possibility reveals itself.[213]

In other words, the contingency of objects is not something which we think about objects, we do not see an object and then ask whether or not it is contingent, but we actually experience (intuit) the contingency, the possibility of its not being. Now the problem becomes, how is this experience to be described? Husserl had not described contingency and possibility for us, although he employed both notions frequently. Husserl, Heidegger claims, restricted himself to *science*, and thereby refused himself access to the notion of contingency and possibility, which involve the antiscientific concept of 'nothing'. Heidegger now tells us that nothing itself is a sort of Being, and in his writings after *Sein und Zeit* he often talks of "The Nothing." We are reminded of the pair of exchanges with the metaphysically inept White King in *Through the Looking Glass;*

"I see nobody on the road," said Alice. "I only wish I had such eyes," the King remarked in a fretful tone. "To be able to see Nobody! and at that distance too."

"Who did you pass on the road?" the King went on. "Nobody," said the Messenger. "Quite right," said the King. "This young lady saw him too. So, of course Nobody walks slower than you." "I do my best," the Messenger said in a sullen tone. "I'm sure nobody walks much faster than I do!" "He can't do that," said the King, "or else he'd have been here first."[214]

What about Nothing?[215]

Philosophers have often claimed that the sort of paradox exploited in the Lewis Carroll passage can be avoided as soon as we realize that 'nothing' does not *name* anything, but rather rests on a familiar linguistic transformation process called "negation." We use names to denote *things* and learn to deny the existence of things by applying "not" to their names ("It is not an *x*"; "it is a not-*x*"). This is what Heidegger denies, and the basis of his repudiation of logic and science on the basis of *nothing* is really a denial of only a single traditional claim, that the concept of 'nothing' can be explained solely by appeal to the linguistic process of *negation*.

"Nothing is more original than the not and negation."[216] *Nothing,* according to Heidegger, *is,* it is based on *experience* and can be found *in phenomena* through phenomenological inquiry, through a search for "experience of Nothing."[217]

Our familiarity with Heidegger's philosophy already tells us where to look for the 'primitive' experience of nothing, not in the theoretical concerns of logic but in everyday *activities:* refusing and detesting; and in everyday *moods:* finding repulsive, hating, and detesting. Most importantly, there is a single mood which reveals 'nothing' most dramatically, in which "we are brought face to face with Nothing itself."[218] This is the familiar mood of *Angst,* or *dread,* which is interpreted as a direct confrontation with nothing.

"Dread reveals nothing."[219] What is this nothing?

"Nothing" is revealed in dread, but not as something that "is." Neither can it be taken as an object. Dread is not an apprehension of Nothing. All the same, Nothing is revealed in and through dread, yet not, again, in the sense that Nothing appears as if detached and apart from what-is-in-totality when we have that 'uncanny' feeling. We would say rather: in dread Nothing functions as if at one with what-is-in-totality. . . . In dread what-is-in-totality becomes untenable. . . . What-is is not annihilated by dread, so as to leave Nothing over. . . . Nothing shows itself as belonging essentially to what-is while this is slipping away in totality.[220]

This complex description of our dreadful encounter with nothing makes the important claim that nothing is not the result of an annihilation of things (everything), but an essential part of our experience of things (everything). Nothing is a *repulsion,* a *nihilation:*

ın dread there is a retreat from something . . . . This "retreat from" has its source in

Nothing. The latter does not attract; its nature is to repel.[221]

How are we to describe our experience of nothing? It is to be described by Heidegger's famous catch phrase, "Nothing nothings" (*Das Nichts nichtet*). This is not so mysterious as it is usually interpreted to be; simply stated, it means that we sometimes *experience* repulsion, and that occasionally, in moments of *Angst,* this repulsion does not limit itself to one or a few objects in our environment, but extends itself to the world as a whole. We see the contingency of everything (ultimately, we see this in our own Being-unto-death), and the world thus repulses us. We see the ultimate lack of justification of all values (which is the key to *Angst* for Kierkegaard, only implicit in Heidegger), and all actions and attitudes seem equally arbitrary, equally nothing. "Nothing" is the name for that sort of experience; it does not name an object as such, but it does name a definite phenomenon. Nothing is, in this sense, 'a something,' and the logical process of negation is possible because of the experience of this 'something'.

This proof does not suffice, it should be evident, to establish the radical conclusion that philosophical *thinking* must go beyond logic and science. However, the argument for the phenomenal nature of nothing had great influence on Sartre, who made the notion of "Nothingness" the key to his philosophy in *Being and Nothingness;* and the attack on logic, while not substantiated by the argument that the experience of nothing precedes and is the foundation for negation, has other sources from which to draw its support. In his constant concern with language, Heidegger formulates a general objection to all 'natural' languages; they all, by virtue of grammar, are "metaphysical" and commit us to talking about the *Being of entities* (as in *Sein und Zeit*). In Heidegger's later writings, he wishes to "go beyond metaphysics" and talk about *Being as such.* It is thus that the enterprise of *Sein und Zeit,* with its emphasis on human being and the being of entities, is abandoned, and with it the appeal to all 'natural' language in which philosophical discourse has traditionally taken place.

Beyond Metaphysics: Godless Theology

The transition from *Sein und Zeit* to Heidegger's latest works is marked (as one would expect of a creative thinker) by several contrasts.[222] Central to all of these, however, is a shift from the study of the Being of particular entities (including Human Being) to an attempt to come to grips with *Being itself*. Traditional language—including the not-so-traditional language of *Sein und Zeit*—can only express answers to the first 'problem of Being.' So, we have already mentioned several times, that Heidegger turns increasingly to poetry as a kin of philosophy;

Only poetry stands in the same order of philosophy and its thinking, though poetry and thought are not the same thing.[223]

Thinking is . . . poetizing. . . . The thinking of Being is the fundamental manner of poetizing.[224]

The search for an unmetaphysical language, a language which is thereby 'nonconceptual', leads him to the poetry, philosophy of the pre-Socraties ("Letter on Humanism"), and the poetry of Hölderlin. Ultimately, however, the search for an unprejudiced language to express Being itself carries Heidegger away from even these quasi-philosophical enterprises to a bizarre sort of mysticism, in which the philosopher no longer 'ontologizes' or attempts to 'disclose truth', but simply *waits* patiently and passively for 'the Word', not of God, but of Being itself.

In looking back at *Sein und Zeit*, Heidegger despairs at his earlier commitment to humanism, that is, the thesis that Being has its ground in man (Dasein); in the first volume on Nietzsche, Heidegger complains,

With all his representation, intuition and definition of what is, man is always forced into the impasse of his own humanity.[225]

It thus becomes necessary to escape this "inescapable humanization" if we are to understand Being itself, and this requires giving up the notion that Dasein himself discloses the truth of Being to himself. In these later writings, *disclosure* is not carried out by Dasein (as in *Sein und Zeit*), but is "granted" or "given" to Dasein by Being itself. This disclosure, or gift of Being, is no longer based on Dasein, but on an *original mystery*. Being no longer is for Dasein, but Dasein is for the sake of Being!

Man is only the persona, *the mask of Being.*[226]

Being needs *and* uses *the essence of man.*[227]

This switch from Being as disclosed by man for himself to Being disclosing itself to man is already foreshadowed in the discussion of the pre-Socratic notion of *physis* in *Introduction to Metaphysics*, in which "Being unfolds itself." In the later writings, it becomes quite clear that *Being* has taken the place of the traditional transcendent Christian God and man is a vehicle for the self-revelation of Being in much the same manner as Hegel's conception of individual man as a manifestation of spirit served as a formulation of an (immanent) Christian God. Being becomes grossly personified, and man's attitude towards Being becomes more like worship of God than the asking of a philosophical question;

Being is the mission of thought.[228]

Thought is the devotion to Being, nothing else.[229]

The need is: to preserve the truth of Being no matter what may happen to man and everything that 'is'.[230]

In sacrifice there is expressed that hidden thanking which alone does homage to the grace wherewith Being has endowed the nature of man, in order that he may take over, in his relationship to Being the guardianship of Being.[231]

Man's relationship to Being is likened to the 'shepherd' function of the early Christian leaders, and man attempts to "win for himself to the preservation of the dignity of Being" through "the spirit of sacrifice ready prepared for dread, which takes upon itself kinship with the imperishable."[232] The concern for the ability of language to express Being turns from man's use of language to hold discourse about Being to 'the Word' which is spoken *by* Being to man;

Obedient to the voice of Being, thought seeks the Word through which the truth of Being may be expressed.[233]

It is clear that this language is not a 'natural' language, and the preparation for the truth of Being consists not in careful preparing or 'thinking' in any normal sense of that term, but

Out of long-guarded speechlessness and the careful clarification of the field thus cleared, comes the utterance of the thinker . . . poetry and thinking are most purely alike in their care of the word, . . . The thinker utters Being. The poet names what is holy.[234]

In this later work, it is Being that constitutes Dasein, and not the other way around. The 'original' or 'essential' thought of the truth of Being is "given to man" from "transcendent origins":

standing within disclosure of Being, that is what I call the existence of man.[235]

We earlier encountered the phrase "language is the house of Being." This no longer means that man uses language to understand and express Being, but that "the Word gives . . . language uses man." We "get the message from Being," and "Being discloses itself to itself," and disclosure to man is a 'gift' for which we are to patiently wait and be thankful. Philosophy, as we have conceived it in its broadest outlines, is thus no longer relevant to this new 'theology.' Being becomes, not a philosophical problem, but *the mystery.* Heidegger complains that we are "too late for the Gods and too early for Being"; this is no longer a philosophy, or a theology, which we can recognize.

Heidegger is still awaiting the word from Being, but continental philosophy is not waiting with him. The Heidegger who has so enormously influenced the course of twentieth-century philosophy is still to be found in *Sein und Zeit* and those works completed before Heidegger's unfortunate and evidently traumatic encounter with Nazism in the early thirties. The theological aspects of this late philosophy, however, have not gone without influence of their own. The rise of "religious existentialism" owes a heavy, though often unacknowledged debt to this strange Godless theology of the late Heidegger. Tillich, Buber, Barth, and Bultmann, among others, capture some of the essential notions of the late Heidegger, although it must be admitted that the similarities are often due to their mutual source in Kierkegaard rather than reliance on Heidegger. However, we shall abandon this tradition in our study, and restrict our attentions to the nonreligious, even antireligious, humanistic existentialism which grew from Heidegger's work on the Nazi-occupied soil of France.

Bibliography
Heidegger's Works in English
Being and Time. Translated by MacQuarrie and Robinson. New York, 1962.
The most important work.
Introduction to Metaphysics. Translated by R. Manheim. New Haven, 1958.
Kant and the Problem of Metaphysics. Translated by J. Churchill. Bloomington, Ind., 1962.
"What Is Metaphysics?" and "On the Essence of Truth." Translated by A. Crick and R. F. C. Hull. In *Existence and Being*. Edited by W. Brock. Chicago, 1949.
"Letter on Humanism." Translated by E. Lohner In *Twentieth Century Philosophy*. Vol. II. Edited by H. Aiken and W. Barrett. New York, 1962.
What Is Called Thinking? New York, 1968.
What Is Philosophy? Translated by Khublack and Wilde. New York, 1958.
The Question of Being. Translated by Khublack and Wilde. New York, 1958.

"The Way Back into the Ground of Metaphysics." Translated by W. Kaufmann. In *Existentialism from Dostoyevsky to Sartre*. Edited by Kaufmann. New York, 1956.
Discourse on Thinking. Translated by J. Anderson and E. H. Freund. New York, 1966.
Hegel's Concept of Existence. New York, 1970.

Books about Heidegger's Philosophy
Barrett, W. *Irrational Man*. New York, 1958.
Greene, M. *Martin Heidegger*. London, 1957.
Heinemann, F. H. *Existentialism and the Modern Predicament*. New York, 1953.
King, M. *Heidegger's Philosophy*. New York, 1964.
Langan, T. *The Meaning of Heidegger*. New York, 1959.
Macomber, H. *The Anatomy of Disillusion*. Evanston, Ill., 1967.

Olafson, F. *Principles and Persons*. Baltimore, 1967.
An excellent analysis and defense of the ethics of Heidegger and Sartre.

Richardson, W. *Heidegger: Through Phenomenology to Thought*. The Hague, 1963.

Schmitt, R. *Martin Heidegger on Being Human*. New York, 1969.
The best book on Heidegger's philosophy, in my opinion.

Spiegelberg, H. *The Phenomenological Movement*. Vol. II. The Hague, 1962.

Versenyi, L. *Heidegger, Being and Truth*. New Haven, 1965.

Vycinas. *Earth and Gods*. The Hague, 1961.

Warnock, M. *Existentialist Ethics*. New York, 1967.

Wyschogrod, M. *Kierkegaard and Heidegger: The Ontology of Existence*. London, 1954.

Jean-Paul Sartre and French Existentialism
CHAPTER 7

The fashionable epithet "existentialism" is inextricably coupled with a group of French philosophers whose personal as well as philosophical intimacy grew from a deep involvement in the social-political turmoil of war-torn Europe in the 1940s. It is this deep philosophical-personal commitment to social-political issues which perhaps most markedly distinguishes Jean-Paul Sartre, Maurice Merleau-Ponty, Albert Camus, and Simone De Beauvoir from Kierkegaard, Nietzsche, and Heidegger, who in retrospect have been identified as part of the "existentialist movement." Kierkegaard and Nietzsche looked on all politics as a degradation of the individual; socialistic and democratic sociopolitical institutions were particularly contemptuous. Heidegger bent to Nazi rule in Germany without resistance, and his philosophy says little of politics; in his later writings he rejects all political involvement and all ethics as well. In contrast, Sartre, Merleau-Ponty, Camus, and De Beauvoir have been continuously engaged and outspoken in both French and international politics since their fight in the Resistance against Nazi occupation armies. All four have spent great portions of their considerable literary talents in political-social polemics. Sartre and Merleau-Ponty have long been active in formulating and proselytizing an up-to-date and existentially sound Marxist ideology; Camus was a revolutionary if sometimes confused social democrat. Simone De Beauvoir has contributed enormously to contemporary women's liberation movements as well as to contemporary moral-social thought.

The central figure of French existentialism who has given the movement both its definitive expression and its name is Jean-Paul Sartre. Our study of French existen-

tialism will focus on his work. Albert Camus is best known for his philosophical novels, but his philosophical essays have caused his name to be one of the first mentioned in discussions of "existentialism" (although he himself has rejected this affiliation). Simone De Beauvoir is also best known as a novelist, but her two theoretical works in existentialist theory, including the only explicit formulation of existentialist ethics within the movement, demonstrate her confessed allegiance to Sartre's philosophy. Least known outside of philosophical-political circles is Maurice Merleau-Ponty, but he is perhaps the most philosophically gifted writer of the group.

This list is not exhaustive, to be sure. In the period immediately following the war, "existentialist" was as generously applied by French intellectuals to themselves as "Communist" had been applied to political opposition since the mid-nineteenth century.[1] It was not long after "existentialism" was introduced in philosophical discussions that the term became honorifically or critically applied to almost every philosopher or *littérateur* who had anything to say about the individual, and in France, naturally, that included almost everybody. "Existentialism" became employed to celebrate almost every French author, but a variety of such names as André Gide, Samuel Beckett, André Malraux, and Alain Robbe-Grillet, and in retrospect, Kafka, Dostoevsky, and Rilke became known as existentialists. In politics, anyone who committed himself to a 'cause' earned the title of "existentialist." An important school of anti-Freudian psychology grew from the writings of Heidegger and Sartre, and spread the term "existentialism" into the social sciences from philosophy and literature.[2] The meaning of "existentialism," as we might expect, was lost in such extensive application. We shall get little help in understanding this philosophical movement if we begin by asking what those figures and schools of thought which have been called "existentialist" have in common.

Of course, there are many figures with close philosophical ties to Sartre who deserve to be included in this movement in even the very narrow interpretation we choose to give it here. Jean Wahl and Paul Ricoeur, for example, are both first-rate exponents of French existential phenomenology who are active in France today. Also missing from our list is Gabriel Marcel, whose existentialism differs from that of Sartre in one central aspect, he is a *Christian* existentialist and his commitments to religion carry him far afield from the doctrines of "atheism" and "nihilism" that are central to Sartre, et al. Marcel's social-religious existentialism parallels that of the German self-avowed existentialist Karl Jaspers, and both trace their work back to Kierkegaard. Marcel is also related to Husserl, however, which distinguishes him from Jaspers who was little influenced by phenomenology. We have neglected this religious direction of European thought which derives from Kierkegaard's view of the "religious mode of life" and theory of "existential commitment." If we were to study this religious development, we should have to consider such important figures as Tillich, Buber, Barth, and Bultmann as well as Marcel and Jaspers. In our treatment of French atheistic existentialism, however, we shall mention these figures only in passing.

Our discussion will focus upon those writings published by Sartre, Merleau-Ponty, and Camus prior to 1945. The writings of all three authors have dramatically changed their complexion since the end of the war. Sartre's writings have become increasingly political, often to the sacrifice of the existentialism that made him famous. Merleau-Ponty moved increasingly away from Sartre after 1950, and his thought deflected again in a radically new direction just before his untimely death in 1961. Camus's essay on *The Rebel* in 1952 marks an equally sharp move in his thought, also considerably more political than in his earlier writings. Our study of existentialism prior to 1945 is still very much within the scope of our treatment of Kant, Hegel, Kierkegaard, Nietzsche, Husserl, and Heidegger. A study of existentialism after 1945 would have to focus its attention on political problems we have neglected in this book. The dominant historical figures in that study would not be Kant or Nietzsche or Kierkegaard, but Proudhon, Marx, and Lenin, and the problems would not be the problems of self-identity, free will, and the justification of values, but rather the means and ends to establish Socialism in bourgeois Western Europe and the place of nationalist movements in the development of international Communism.

Our study of Sartre will concentrate on his central 'existentialist' treatise. *L'être et le néant.* (*Being and Nothingness*),[3] and the essays and literary works of the same period. Similarly, our discussion of Merleau-Ponty will focus upon his two early works, *La structure du comportement*[4] (*The Structure of Behavior*) and *Phénoménologie de la perception*[5] (*The Phenomenology of Perception*). The works of Camus[6] and De Beauvoir[7] will generally be mentioned only in comparison and contrast with Sartre's philosophy.

These four philosophers had several intimate and politically volatile relationships among them; Simone De Beauvoir and Jean-Paul Sartre were and still are lovers. Sartre and Merleau-Ponty were close friends from their school days at the École Normale Supérieure in Paris and founded the still very influential journal, *Le Temps Modernes,* together after the war. Sartre and Camus were close 'professional' friends for many years, but the deep political ties and interests which brought these friends together were also to force them apart. Sartre's long closeness with Merleau-Ponty dissolved over a dispute over Communist policies during the Korean War. His friendship with Camus publically ruptured as the result of a long and sometimes bitter disagreement over Sartre's sympathies with world Communism— reaching a final schism in a debate over the relative importance of means and ends in politics—centering on Camus's book *The Rebel,* in 1952. Sartre's Communism itself was sufficiently unorthodox and his allegiance to Marxism sufficiently eccentric, however, that he never became a member of the French Communist party, but founded (with Merleau-Ponty) a short-lived 'socialist alliance' in 1948. His position in the world of politics remains notoriously individualistic; he openly attacked Moscow Communism after the invasion of Hungary in 1956, but he has continued a long personal polemic against the politics of 'the West'. In 1964, he was offered the Nobel prize in literature and spectacularly rejected it. (Camus had been given the prize in 1957.) Most recently, he helped to organize (with Bertrand Russell) a "War Crimes Tribunal" directed against the abortive American involvement in Southeast Asian politics.

Accordingly, we would expect that the literature which has been produced by the "existentialists" would reflect these political disputes. Sartre's novels and plays are often heavily political, for example, the trilogy *Chemins de la Liberté, Les Mains sales (Dirty Hands),* and *Les séquestres d'Altone (The Condemned of Altoona).* De Beauvoir's prize-winning novel, *The Mandarins,* is similarly based on people in politics. Even where their writings are not openly political, however, the problems of interpersonal relations are a French existentialist preoccupation. Where Kierkegaard and Nietzsche speak almost exclusively of the socially isolated individual and Heidegger dismisses the *Mitsein* after a dozen pages to return to the problem of the authentic nonpublic self, Sartre and Merleau-Ponty spend the bulk of their 'ontologies' studying *Being-for-others.* A central problem of their philosophy will not be the *Angst* of personal isolation and 'abandonment' as much as the guilt before and concern for other persons. The degradation of social commitment in the earlier existentialists will become their salvation.

The French existentialists have also distinguished themselves as a philosophical movement in literature; it is existentialism that has become the prime modern example of the expression of philosophy in literary form; or, more accurately, it has broken down the mutual antipathy between academic philosophy and literature. "Existentialism" is more often than not understood on the basis of Sartre's, Camus's and De Beauvoir's novels than through the difficult tracts of *Being and Nothingness* or *The Phenomenology of Perception.* Because existentialist philosophy and literature are inextricably connected, it is not coincidental that the questions "What is literature?" and "Why should one write?" become burning questions for all these authors. Of course, *Be-*

ing and Nothingness is much more similar to Hegel's *Phenomenology* or Heidegger's *Being and Time* than to the short piercing novels of Camus (*The Stranger* and *The Fall*), and some of Sartre's early stories ("The Wall") contain little explicit philosophical insight (whether or not these stories might be retroactively reinterpreted in light of subsequent philosophical writings). Even these heavy works show the closeness of the philosophical and literary enterprises. The examples in *Being and Nothingness* are often drawn from or appear later in Sartre's literature, as the (prereflective) philosophical stance of Ibbieta in "The Wall" will be the subject of explanation in later writings. The plays *No Exit (Huis Clos)* and the *Flies (Les Mouches)* and his first novel, *Nausea,* more clearly exemplify the mutual dependence of literary expression and philosophical reflection. In *Nausea,* for example, the line separating philosophy and literature is blurred beyond recognition. De Beauvoir similarly exemplifies in her novels what she theorizes in her essays; Camus published *The Stranger* and his philosophical essay *Myth of Sisyphus* as a matched pair, the latter as an 'explanation' of the former. In our discussion of these authors, therefore, we shall not attempt to distinguish between their 'serious philosophy' and their literary creations. Of course, we will have to distinguish doctrines affirmed by fictional characters from the philosophical beliefs of the author, but we may yet use these same characters to illustrate or even to exemplify the author's philosophy. There is always the temptation to turn to the literature as the *primary* source of existentialist philosophy. Perhaps it is this temptation which has led to such widespread misunderstanding and oversimplification of this school of thought. We shall focus our attention on *Being and Nothingness* and bring in suggestions from literary works only where they illuminate this central work. Existentialism is serious philosophy; there is no 'easy' way to approach it. The popularity of this movement ought not mislead us into expecting a readily digestible set of doctrines; on the contrary, it may become more difficult to understand Sartre's thought because of the popularized misrepresentations of it.

It is curious that Sartre is best known for his work in ethics, since he has never written a work on ethics. At the close of *Being and Nothingness,* he promises to write such a work, but it has not yet appeared. There is a foundation for an "existentialist ethics" in *Being and Nothingness,* but Sartre's only major attempt to explicate this foundation is in a grossly popularized lecture called "Existentialism Is a Humanism" which he himself repudiated as a "mistake" afterwards. *Being and Nothingness* is a work more similar to recent German metaphysics than to Kierkegaard and Nietzsche, with whom he is most often grouped in anthologies. The two most influential sources for *Being and Nothingness* were (by Sartre's admission) Hegel's *Phenomenology* and Heidegger's *Being and Time* (with which we have already compared it). Sartre is an ontologist, a phenomenologist, a philosophical psychologist, before he is a moralist.

The central tenet of Sartre's existentialism is the *freedom of human consciousness,* freedom to act, freedom to value, and freedom to "make itself." For Sartre, human being (consciousness) *is* freedom, as it is for Kant, for Kierkegaard, for Heidegger. Unlike Kant and Kierkegaard, however, Sartre does not leave this freedom as an unanalyzed presupposition of human action and ethics; it is argued to be inherent in the conditions of human existence. From Husserl and Heidegger, Sartre inherits the means of establishing this thesis—a phenomenology of consciousness—a detailed 'unprejudiced' descriptive analysis of human experience. Both Sartre and Merleau-Ponty are unabashedly phenomenologists.

In spite of the dominant German influences and overtones in their work, Sartre and Merleau-Ponty are still markedly French. The problems of their philosophies may be similar to those of Kant, but they are taken directly and explicitly from Descartes—the problems of perception, of the nature of the *cogito,* and of human freedom. The traditional doctrines they seek to destroy are clothed in the terminology and methodology of Husserl, but they are Cartesian doctrines. Sartre's initial favors lie towards the side of Heidegger, and the dominant theme in *Being and Nothingness* is man's "Being-in-the-world," but the explicit starting point of the investigation of *Being and Nothingness* is nevertheless Descartes' *cogito.* Similarly, Merleau-Ponty draws heavily from Husserl and Heidegger, but the first philosopher referred to in his first book, *The Structure of Behavior,* is Descartes. Both

Being and Nothingness and *The Phenomenology of Perception,* their twentieth-century and Germanic appearance aside, can be viewed as modern French attempts to rethink Descartes' *Meditations.*

The Phenomenological Pursuit of Being

Sartre and Merleau-Ponty are phenomenologists; both had studied Husserl and Heidegger and found themselves occupied by those problems generated in the attempt to go beyond the natural attitude. In the split between Husserl and Heidegger on such central matters as the possibility of the phenomenological reduction or the phenomenological status of the Ego or subject, Sartre explicitly sides with Heidegger. In substance, Mereau-Ponty also rejects Husserl's 'transcendental idealism' in favor of Heidegger's 'existential' phenomenology, but his manner of doing so is not to attack Husserl but rather to *reinterpret* him as an existentialist. (He uses Husserl's last works, esp. *Crisis,* as support.)[8] We may expect to find that Sartre and Merleau-Ponty are very close in their agreement with Heidegger's approach to phenomenology. [In later writings, after their personal falling out, Merleau-Ponty becomes more sharply critical and further removed from Sartre's phenomenology, which is then said to return unwittingly to classical (pre-Heideggerian) 'subject-object' dualism.]

The predominant problem of phenomenology for Heidegger is the problem of *Being* (see Chapter 6), a problem which Husserl allegedly neglected through his employment of the *epoche.* According to Husserl, phenomenological investigation must begin by 'bracketing' the world and the 'real' objects in the world and focus its attention solely on the *phenomenon* of the world and its objects as they appear to consciousness. According to Heidegger, this *epoche* and the presuppositions which support it (for example, the traditional 'subject-object' dualism) can only carry us to philosophical disaster. Heidegger insists that man's "Being-in-the-world" is (onto-)logically primitive. There can be no Cartesian doubt, no Husserlian bracketing, and no separation of man (Dasein) from the world in which he 'lives'. Both Sartre and Merleau-Ponty agree with this rejection of the phenomenological *epoche,* and both agree with Heidegger that there can be no valid distinction between phenomenology and ontology. Sartre subtitles

Being and Nothingness as "An Essay in Phenomenological Ontology" and the work begins with an introduction called "The Pursuit of Being." Merleau-Ponty's *Phenomenology of Perception* similarly begins with a brilliant discussion of the nature of phenomenology and its function of disclosing for us, not simply phenomena, but the world. Both Sartre and Merleau-Ponty argue that phenomena and things-in-themselves ("essences" for Sartre) cannot be distinguished, even in a tentative preliminary *epoche* which will later give way to a theory of the *constitution* of the world from these phenomena. It is misleading to think of the epistemology of Sartre and Merleau-Ponty as a reaction only to Husserl, of course. Their opposition is an entire movement of philosophy from Kant (and before) which distinguishes appearances from reality in itself and the products of the 'senses' from the concepts of understanding which 'synthesize' these. Husserl, of course, ultimately holds such a view. In France, the philosopher Leon Brunschvicg held such a position and became a dominating negative influence on the French existentialists.

Before we delve into these matters, it may be prudent to stress one often publicized 'difference' between Husserl's phenomenology and existentialism which is not a subject of more-than-verbal disagreement between them. Husserl refers to his phenomenology as a *rationalism* and tells us that its business is to give us a rationalization of experience;[9] Sartre and Merleau-Ponty avoid the concepts of Reason and rationality, but it must not therefore be supposed that their 'existentialism' is a sort of *irrationalism*. (Camus, the most notorious 'irrationalist', continuously appeals to 'human reason' and 'logic' in his "absurd" argument.)[10] It is true that Sartre, for example, spends an extraordinary amount of attention on the more "emotive" aspects of human existence, as Merleau-Ponty and Heidegger spend a great deal of time concerning 'life' and practical everyday endeavors. It is also true that they reject 'rationalism', 'objectivism', and even 'science' *as a basis for philosophy*. However, philosophy remains for them an attempt to gain a conceptual unification of the varieties of human experience—this is *raitonalism* in Hegel's sense, which Merleau-Ponty freely praises as the precursor of all modern philosophy

(*Sense and Nonsense,* in "L'existentialisme chez Hegel"). If Husserl chooses to call the systematic descriptive results of phenomenology a rationalism and these other authors do not, and if Husserl (overly) concentrates on the 'intellectual' or 'cognitive' aspects of human experience and these other authors do not, this is not yet any justification for supposing existential phenomenology to be irrational or even nonrational. As we found with Kierkegaard and again with Nietzsche and Heidegger, the identification of existentialism with 'irrationalism' can only lead to a total misunderstanding of the nature of this philosophy.

Soon after the publication of his *Being and Time,* as the depth of the disagreement between Husserl and himself became evident, Heidegger ceased to refer to his own philosophy as "phenomenology." Among the French phenomenologists, however, notably Sartre and Merleau-Ponty, the disagreements between Husserl and Heidegger were never considered so serious as to constitute a break from phenomenology or even a serious split within phenomenology. Sartre and Merleau-Ponty both considered themselves phenomenologists in the very same sense as Husserl, and it may be argued that, if anything, both sometimes underestimated the severity of the differences between Husserl's philosophy and their own.

The focal point of this difference, of course, is the *epoche,* and the Cartesian distinction between the being of consciousness (which knows itself immediately and 'apodeictically') and the being of the perceived object (or the world in general), which is known only mediately (through the senses) and never with certainty. Both Sartre and Merleau-Ponty accept Heidegger's primitive notion of "Being-in-the-world," and the *epoche* becomes impossible for them:

Truth does not 'inhabit' only the 'inner man', or more accurately, there is no inner man, man is in the world, and only in the world does he know himself. When I return to myself from an excursion into the realm of dogmatic common sense or of science, I find, not a source of intrinsic truth, but a subject destined to be in the world.[11]

Husserl performs the *epoche* with the expectation that he will be able to reintroduce the world as constituted by consciousness. Merleau-Ponty characteristically interprets this move of Husserl's nonliterally and writes as if Husserl never conceived of the world as 'bracketed' at all:

> [Phenomenology] is also a philosophy for which the world is always 'already there' before reflection begins—as an inalienable presence; and all its efforts are concentrated upon reachieving a direct and primitive contact with the world, and endowing that contact with philosophical status.[12]

Sartre is not so kind, and clearly interprets Husserl's conception of the epoche as a literal neglect of the existence of the world. As such, it is impossible, Sartre maintains, to expect to 'found' this bracketed world on the constituting acts of consciousness:

> It is futile by a sleight of hand to attempt to found the reality of the object on the subjective plenitude of impressions and its objectivity on non-being; the objective will never come out of the subjective nor the transcendent from immanence, nor being from non-being.[13]

Sartre agrees with Heidegger that this initial distinction between acts of consciousness and objects (of consciousness) is not only philosophically disastrous, but even unfaithful to the phenomenological method itself:

> But, we are told, Husserl defines consciousness precisely as a transcendence. In truth he does. This is what he posits. This is his essential discovery. But from the moment that he makes of the noema an unreal, a correlate of the noesis, a noema whose esse is percipi, he is totally unfaithful to his principle.[14]

Husserl had introduced the subject and the object as polarities (as had Kant in his "Refutation of Idealism"). The cogito and the cogitatio—the knower and the known—were ontologically dependent on each other. There could be no cogito without a world; there could be no world without a cogito. Husserl took this polarity and distorted it by emphasizing the dependence of the world on the subject. As a result, he becomes, of necessity, an ideal-

ist. But why emphasize the dependency of the object on the subject?

Heidegger's concept of "Being-in-the-world" restores the balance of this mutual dependence. The same balance is adopted by Merleau-Ponty, who chastises philosophers (notably not Husserl) for neglecting this mutuality:

> Descartes and particularly Kant detached the subject, or consciousness, by showing that I could not possibly apprehend anything as existing unless I first of all experienced myself as existing in the act of apprehending it. They presented consciousness, the absolute certainty of my existence for myself, as the condition of there being anything at all. . . . But the relations between subject and world are not strictly bilateral; if they were, the certainty of the world would, in Descartes, be immediately given with that of the Cogito, and Kant would not have talked about his "Copernican revolution."[15]

Sartre, however, shifts the balance in the opposite direction and stresses the dependence of the subject on the object:

> Consciousness of consciousness of something. This means that transcendence is the constitutive structure of consciousness; that is, that consciousness is born supported by a being which is not itself.[16]

From this passage, it must be evident that Sartre's notion of 'transcendence' (in this context) does not refer to that which lies 'beyond' or 'behind' consciousness or to the objects of consciousness, but simply to the objects themselves. There will be no distinction, for Sartre, between 'object' and 'object of (for) consciousness'. Objects ("Beings-in-themselves") simply are ("Being is. Being is in-itself. Being is what it is").[17] Therefore, the problem for Sartre is not the constitution of objects by consciousness (as it was for Husserl), but the peculiar nature of consciousness, which is dependent for its existence on the objects of which it is conscious.

Merleau-Ponty does not launch such a frontal attack on Husserl's subject-object distinction and epoche, but attempts to show that Husserl in fact did not disagree with Sartre (and Merleau-Ponty);

> Far from being, as has been thought, a procedure of idealistic philosophy,

phenomenological reduction belongs to existential philosophy; Heidegger's 'Being-in-the-world' appears only against the background of the phenomenological reduction.[18]

In order to show this, the *epoche* or reduction is sympathetically reinterpreted not as a 'bracketing' but simply as a reexamination of our experiences of the world:

It is because we are through and through compounded of relationships with the world that for us the only way to become aware of the fact is to suspend the resultant activity, . . . to put it 'out of play.' Not because we reject the certainties of common sense and a natural attitude to things—they are, in the contrary, the constant theme of philosophy—but because, being the presupposed basis of any thought, they are taken for granted, and go unnoticed, and because in order to arouse them and bring them to view, we have to suspend for a moment our recognition of them. . . . Reflection does not withdraw from the world towards the unity of consciousness as the world's basis; it steps back to watch the forms of transcendence fly up like sparks from a fire; it slackens the intentional threads which attach us to the world and thus brings them to our notice; it alone is consciousness of the world because it reveals that world as strange and paradoxical.[19]

As a result, Merleau-Ponty leaves us with the impression that Husserl's phenomenology itself shows us the impossibility of the *epoche;*

The most important lesson which the reduction teaches us is the impossibility of a complete reduction. This is why Husserl is constantly reexamining the possibility of the reduction.[20]

Thus, for both Sartre and Merleau-Ponty, there can be no bracketing of the world, no separation of subject and object or of object and object of consciousness. To do phenomenology is to give descriptions of *phenomena* or *appearances* (Sartre does not distinguish these as Heidegger does), and *ipso facto* to give descriptions of our Being-in-the-world. Phenomenology is emphatically a "matter of describing, not explaining or analyzing" (Merleau-Ponty), but a description

of *things* as well as *experiences*. Phenomenology and ontology are the same enterprise, and distinct from all enterprises which foolishly attempt to go 'behind' things as they appear to us or experiences —which Sartre refers to as "metaphysics." Any attempt to *explain* the world by appeal to superphenomenal (noumenal) beings is excluded from philosophy by all phenomenologists, who agree that phenomenology must appeal only to 'the things (of experience) themselves.' (In spite of the very different use of the term "metaphysics" in different authors, this point remains central for all of them.)

What are these 'things themselves'? It is clear that they are not to be distinguished from 'things as experienced', and so the traditional dualisms between phenomena and noumena—objects of experience and objects in themselves, appearance and reality—find no place in existentialist phenomenology. The thing or phenomenon is just as it appears—is "*absolutely indicative of itself*":

But if we once get away from what Nietzsche called "the illusion of worlds-behind-the scene," and if we no longer believe in the being-behind-the-appearance, then the appearance becomes full positivity: its essence is an 'appearing' which is no longer opposed to being but on the contrary is the measure of it. For the being of an existent is exactly what it appears. *Thus we arrive at the idea of the phenomenon such as we can find, for example, in the "phenomenology" of Husserl or of Heidegger—the phenomenon or the relative-absolute. Relative the phenomenon remains, for 'to appear' supposes in essence somebody to whom to appear. But it does not have the double relativity of Kant's* Erscheinung *(appearance). It does not point over its shoulder to a true being which would be, for it, absolute. What it is, it is absolutely, for it reveals itself as it is. The phenomenon can be studied and described as such, for it is* absolutely indicative of itself.[21]

That is why we can equally reject the dualism of appearance and essence. The appearance does not hide the essence, it reveals it; it is the essence.[22]

If there is no distinction between object and experience, reality and appearance, then how are we to distinguish essences (things-themselves) from *mere* appearances or from aspects (*noemata*)? According to Sartre,

the essence is no longer a property sunk in the cavity of this existent; it is the manifest law which presides over the succession of its appearances, it is the principle of the series.[23]
The phenomenal being manifests itself; it manifests its essence as well as its existence, and it is nothing but the well connected series of its manifestations.[24]

There is, therefore, no distinction between the chair as I perceive it and the chair itself; there is only a distinction between any number of appearances of the chair and the infinite series of all possible appearances of the chair. To explain the object as 'nothing but' the sum of its possible appearances is to undercut the need for any 'real' chair 'behind' the chair I perceive:

For the moment, the first consequence of the "theory of the phenomenon" is that the appearance does not refer to being as Kant's phenomenon refers to noumenon. Since there is nothing behind the appearance, and since it indicates only itself (and the total series of appearances), it can not be supported by any being other than its own.[25]

This view borrows heavily from Husserl's theory of *noemata*[26] but it is even more radical than Husserl's theory in denying *from the outset* any possibility of postulating a being (a 'real' object) 'behind' the phenomenon. Similarly, Merleau-Ponty rejects all Cartesian attempts to doubt or 'bracket' the world. The world is simply *what* we perceive, and the distinction between perception and nonperceptual appearances (images) *precedes* philosophical analysis:

if I tried to distinguish my perceptions from my dreams with the aid of 'criteria', I should overlook the phenomenon of the world. . . . this distinction is already made before any analysis; it is because I have an experience of the real as of the imaginary, and the problem then becomes not one of asking how critical thought can provide for itself secondary equivalents of this distinction, but of making explicit our
primordial knowledge of the 'real', of describing our perception of the world as that upon which our idea of truth is forever based. We must not, therefore, wonder whether we really perceive a world, we must instead say: the world is what we perceive.[27]

The attack on Husserl's *epoche* and subject-object dualism is nowhere better executed than in Sartre's early essays and, surprisingly enough, in his first novel. In two early essays on the imagination,[28] Sartre argued that Husserl's *epoche* ignored the crucial difference between *perception* and *imagination*, between those phenomena which are passively received and those which we actively originate or "spontaneously call up." According to Husserl's phenomenology, all phenomena are, after 'bracketing', demonstrated to be *constituted* by consciousness. Consequently, no distinction between perception and imagination seems possible. It is this problem which seems to have first marked the breach between Husserl and Sartre (before Sartre had read Heidegger). According to both Sartre and Husserl, the *object* perceived and the *object* imagined cannot be distinguished.[29]

Whether I perceive or imagine this chair, the object of my perception and that of my image are identical; it is this wicker chair on which I am sitting.[30]

This claim is in marked contrast to traditional attempts to distinguish perceptions from imaginings on the basis of their 'force' and the like (cf. Hume, distinguishing *impressions* and *ideas*):

Those perceptions which enter with most force and violence, we may name impressions . . . by ideas I mean the faint images of these in thinking and reasoning.[31]

There is no difference between the perceived and the imagined objects. As Sartre states this conclusion, the difference between them is *nothing*. This "nothing" has a special significance for Sartre as for Heidegger, and "nothing" will turn out to be equivalent to the all-important concept of 'freedom'. The difference between perception and imagination, we then find, is just this difference between the freedom of imagination and the lack of freedom of perception. This is not a difference in the objects (of consciousness) but in the *acts* of consciousness. The act of imagining involves a special act of *nihilation*, "the ability of consciousness to destroy, or ignore, or 'go beyond' its objects":

I can say that the image includes a certain nothingness . . . however lively, touching or strong an image may be, it gives its object as not being.[32]

I have a freedom (the object has a certain 'nothingness') in imagination which is not present in acts of perception. In perception (which is our central concern), the object is characterized by its *obtrusiveness*—its resistance to nihilation. (Cf. the American pragmatist, Charles Peirce, who argues that imagination is distinguished by the *indeterminateness* of the object.) It is this obtrusiveness which makes a 'bracketing' of existence impossible in the case of perception. It is just the possibility of bracketing, or 'nihilating,' that characterizes imagination. A universal *epoche*, as defended by Husserl, is therefore impossible.

This obtrusiveness is dramatically presented, and with it an argument against the Husserlian *epoche*. In Sartre's early novel, *Nausea*,[33] the antihero, Antoine Roquentin, has a 'nauseating' encounter with an object, the root of a chestnut tree. However brilliant the Husserlian conception of the *epoche*, it becomes unintelligible when we attempt to apply it to a concrete situation:

I was in the park just now. The roots of the chestnut tree were sunk in the ground just under my bench. I couldn't remember it was a root any more. The words had vanished and with them the significance of things, their methods of use, and the feeble points of reference which men have traced on alone in front of this black, knotty mass, entirely beastly, which frightened me. Then I had this vision.

It left me breathless. Never, until these last few days, had I understood the meaning of "existence." I was like the others, like the ones walking along the seashore, all dressed in their spring finery. I said, like them, "the ocean is green; that white speck up there is a seagull," but I didn't feel that it existed or that the seagull was an "existing seagull," usually existence hides itself. It is there, around us, in us, it is us, you can't say two words without mentioning it, but you can never touch it. When I believed I was thinking about it, I must believe that I was thinking nothing, my head was empty, or there was just one word in my head, the word "to be." Or else I was thinking . . . how can I explain it? I was thinking of belonging, I was telling myself that the sea belonged to the class of green objects, or that the green was a part of the duality of the sea. Even when I looked at things, I was miles from dreaming that they existed: they looked like scenery to me. I picked them up in my hands, they served me as tools, I foresaw their resistance. But that all happened on the surface. If anyone had asked me what existence was, I would have answered in good faith, that it was nothing, simply an empty form which was added to external things without changing anything in their nature. And then, all of a sudden, there it was, clear as day: existence had suddenly unveiled itself. It had lost the harmless look of an abstract category: it was the very paste of things, this root was kneaded into existence . . . existed in a way that I could not explain it.

. . . In vain to repeat: "This is a root" —it didn't work any more. I saw clearly that you could not pass from its function as a root, as a breathing pump, to that, to this hard and compact skin of a sea lion, to this oily, callous, headstrong look. The function explained nothing: it allowed you to understand generally that it was a root, but not that one at all. This root, with its colour, shape, its congealed movement, was . . . below all explanation. . . . To exist is simply to be there. . . .[34]

Camus refers to the same argument in abbreviated form,

And here are trees and I know their gnarled surface, water and I feel its taste. The scents of grass and stars at night, certain evenings when the heart relaxes—how shall I negate this world whose power and strength I feel.[35]

Although the rejection of the *epoche* lies at the heart of the "existentialist" break from Husserl's phenomenology, there are other differences of great importance. Husserl had introduced the *cogito* —reflective consciousness—as the Cartesian starting point of his philosophy. In the study of this *cogito*, it is discovered that consciousness (the *cogito*) is *intentional* and always takes some object. However, we have seen that Husserl places heavy emphasis on the *cognitive* or *knowing* acts of consciousness and neglects those preconceptual aspects of human consciousness which are given attention in Heidegger. This neglect is also compensated for by Sartre and Merleau-Ponty, who, like Heidegger, stress practical and preconceptual ('preontological') Being-in-the-world more than the various reflective ways in which we *know* the world. In his early essay on "the emotions,"[36] Sartre argues that the business of phenomenology is to determine the "significance of phenomena as goal-directed ways of behavior (*conduites*)." Human behavior, and not human knowledge, is of ultimate interest for him. In *Being and Nothingness*, Sartre tells us that

"Having," "doing," and "being": are the cardinal categories of human reality. Under them are subsumed all types of human conduct. Knowing, for example, is a modality of having.[37]

It is clear that "having" (including *knowing*) is the least important of the three;

Is the supreme value of human activity a doing *or a* being? *And whichever solution we adopt, what is to become of* having?[38]

Similarly, Merleau-Ponty tells us that:

the world is not what I think but what I live through.

Unlike what classical idealism thought, the relationship of subject and object is no longer that cognitive relationship in which the object always appears as constructed by the subject, but is a relationship of being, through which, to use a paradox, the subject is his body, his world, his situation, and, in a certain sense, enters into interaction with it.[39]

We can see the extensive similarity between Merleau-Ponty's conception of man-in-the-world and Heidegger's *Dasein* from this description. According to Merleau-Ponty, consciousness "is not originally 'I think' but 'I am able to'."[40] In Heidegger's *Being and Time*, we were told of the 'primitive' or 'original' importance of the practical preontological aspects of human

Existenz, but these were not examined in any detail. In the French phenomenologists, these preconceptual aspects are studied in marvelous detail. Sartre's study of the emotions, of the preverbal aspects of our relationships with other people, and Merleau-Ponty's extensive studies of human behavior advance Heidegger's thesis, but go far beyond it in giving us an understanding of our 'original' encounters with the world and other people. In their examination, we find that traditional problems concerning articulated or conceptual or scientific knowledge will play only a minor role.[41]

This emphasis on the behavioral-emotional aspects of our experience leads Sartre and Merleau-Ponty to introduce a distinction between two different sorts of consciousness or intentionality into their studies, again drawn from Heidegger's *Being and Time*. Husserl, like Descartes and Kant, took the *cogito* to be purely *reflective*, and then interpreted consciousness itself as necessarily reflective. However, all consciousness is not reflective, and Heidegger had pointed out the many sorts of encounters with the world (as equipment) which were not reflective or conceptual at all. Sartre and Merleau-Ponty similarly recognize the many preconceptual activities which are presupposed by the reflective activities carried on by the philosopher. Heidegger had captured this difference in his distinction between ontic and ontological.[42] Sartre distinguishes between prereflective and reflective consciousness, or between a positional ("thetic") and a nonpositional ("nonthetic") consciousness. The prereflective or positional consciousness is the consciousness of 'selfless' activity. As we found in Heidegger, this sort of 'consciousness' (Heidegger does not call it this) is not self-conscious, but simply conscious of its immediate tasks and equipment. Similarly, Merleau-Ponty distinguishes between preconscious intentionality and conscious intentionality. Only the latter is reflective or explicitly self-conscious. "Preconscious intentionality" is also said to be "preobjective"; not only is there no 'self' at one 'pole' of this intentional relationship, but there is no *object* either (just as the entities encountered in the primitive world of equipment for Heidegger are not *'things'*). Phenomenology, according to Merleau-Ponty, is the description of this preconscious, preobjective landscape, this "operative intentionality," which produces the *natural or ante-predicative unity of the world and of our life, being apparent in our desires, our evaluations and in the landscape we see, more clearly than in objective knowledge, and furnishing the text which our knowledge tries to translate into precise language.*[43]

Phenomenology is an attempt to disclose *meanings* to us, not just of words but of things as well;

in the silence of primary consciousness can be seen appearing not only what words mean, but also what things mean: the core of primary meaning round which the acts of naming and expression take shape.[44]

This disclosure of essences is not "the end, but the means" of phenomenology,

But it is clear that the essence is here not the end, but a means, that our effective involvement in the world is precisely what has to be understood and made amenable to conceptualization.[45]

Both Heidegger and Sartre avoid Husserl's heavy emphasis upon *essences* (Sartre uses "essence" in a very limited employment): it is Merleau-Ponty who explicitly denies *essences* their privileged Husserlian role. There is no necessary and universal essential nucleus to phenomena; essences arise through language in our attempts to understand our reality. There can be no sharp distinction, therefore, between matters of 'fact' or 'individual intuitions' and 'truths of reason' or 'eidetic intuitions'. Similarly, there can be no distinction between *intuition* and *constitution,* thus eliminating the major problem of Husserl's "transcendental" phenomenology. Consequently, there can be no distinction between psychology and phenomenology of consciousness. We must not be surprised, therefore, that doctrines and concerns often considered 'psychological' or 'empirical' find a central place in Sartre's and Merleau-Ponty's phenomenology. This denial of the fact-essence distinction has an even more important consequence, unacknowledged in Heidegger and left implicit in Sartre but argued openly by Merleau-Ponty: there can be no eidetic reduction to essences (as in Husserl), and no search for absolute essential truth. There can be no definitive form of philosophical thought, but always a "dialogue with the world" in as many languages

as possible. There are no essences, and thus no final truths in philosophy.

In particular, there is no *human essence* —no essence of human consciousness. Heidegger has already told us that human being (Dasein) is structured as *Existenz,* and, as such, cannot be characterized as other entities can be characterized. Sartre has most famously captured this claim in his slogans "[human] existence precedes essence" and "man makes himself" and his less-known but more important characterization of human consciousness as "nothingness." Merleau-Ponty similarly tells us that there is only a human *Gestalt* —an interconnection of typically human characteristics, but no 'fixed essence.'

Accordingly, a human being receives a special position in all of these philosophies: we have already seen how radically this is so in Heidegger's *Being and Time.* Similarly, Sartre distinguishes a special category of Being that includes only human consciousness: Merleau-Ponty summarizes this special place for man—common to Descartes and Kant and Husserl as well as the existentialists:

I am not the outcome or meeting-point of numerous causal agencies which determine my bodily or psychological make-up. I cannot conceive of myself as nothing but a bit of the world, a mere object of biological, psychological, or sociological investigation. All my knowledge, even my scientific knowledge, is gained from my own particular point of view. . . . I am not a 'living creature' nor even a 'man', nor again even 'a consciousness' endowed with all the characteristics which zoology, social anatomy, or inductive psychology recognize in these various products of the natural or historical process—I am the absolute source, my existence does not stem from my antecedents, from my physical and social environment; instead it moves out towards them and sustains them. . . .[46]

We might easily guess that the bulk of existentialist writing in France will be preoccupied with the nature of human being and human consciousness. (We might note that Sartre and Merleau-Ponty, in spite of their substantial agreements with Heidegger, reintroduce the concept of "consciousness" into their writings.) Of the utmost importance is the understanding of *self-identity.* Reality and appearance are the same, according to Sartre, but appearance *to whom?* Is there an ego, as Descartes, Kant, and Husserl suggest, which is the ultimate source of all knowledge? Or, is there an Absolute subject approachable only through mystical intuition, as in Fichte and Schelling? Or, is there no ego at all, as in Heidegger? We shall see that the French phenomenologists reject the transcendental ego as an essential perversion of phenomenology. The *cogito* or *Self* or *I*, we find, is encountered only in reflective consciousness and then not as a *subject* but as "an object in the world."

The Transcendence of the Ego

Heidegger has already argued for us that the ego 'discovered' in the Cartesian *cogito* is not a substantial self, but only a 'formal indicator' that does not commit us to postulating any entity called 'the self.' The *self* is rather a conception imposed on us by the public—it is not something discovered 'in' ourselves—it is something learned from others. This same thesis is argued by Sartre in an early essay, "The Transcendence of the Ego" ("*La transcendence de l'ego*"), *Recherches philosophiques* (1936),[47] which similarly denies the ego its 'primitive' status, either as discovered in the *cogito* or as disclosed in phenomenological analysis;

For most philosophers the ego is an 'inhabitant' of consciousness. Some affirm its formal presence at the heart of Erlebnisse, as an empty principle of unification. Others—psychologists for the most part—claim to discover its material presence, as the center of desires and acts, in each moment of our psychic life. We should like to show here that the ego is neither formally nor materially in consciousness: it is outside, in the world. It is a being of the world, like the ego of another.[48]

Against the 'formal' conception of the Ego, Sartre argues that there is no reason for thinking that an 'I' gives unity to consciousness. Even the *cogito* does not succeed in establishing this; it proves only that "the representations of a consciousness must be united and articulated in such a way that it is always possible in their regard to note an 'I think.'"[49] In other words, the fact that consciousness is unified (allowing us to derive the

cogito) does not suffice to prove that the *I* gives this unification. The opponent in this argument is Descartes, primarily, but it is Kant who gives Sartre his path around the 'necessity' of the *cogito:*

It must be conceded to Kant that the 'I think' must be able to accompany all our representations. But need we then conclude that an I in fact inhabits all our states of consciousness and actually effects the supreme synthesis of our experience? . . . Kant says nothing concerning the actual existence of the 'I Think.' On the contrary, he seems to have seen perfectly well that there are moments of consciousness without the I, for he says "must be able to accompany."[50]

Thus the argument of Kant's *Transcendental Deduction* establishes only that "I can always regard my perception as mine." It does not establish that this 'I' actually does accompany every experience nor that there is some substantial or transcendental 'I' which is *responsible* for this possibility.

The opponent for the second part of the argument—the demonstration that the 'I' is not a *material I* 'inhabiting' every conscious act—is Husserl. Sartre interprets Husserl as claiming to discover that *cogito* is "a fact which is absolute"[51] and not, as in Kant, a "set of logical conditions." (Our discussion of Husserl's concept(s) of the ego[52] should throw some suspicion on this interpretation.) This 'fact' is rejected by Sartre. He distinguishes between the 'I' and the 'me', the latter being the empirical ego we have discussed previously; then,

Like Husserl, we are persuaded that our psychic and psycho-physical me is a transcendent object which must fall before the epoche. But we raise the following question: is not this psychic and psycho-physical me enough? Need one double it with a transcendental I, a structure of absolute consciousness?[53]

This is inadequate in light of Sartre's later works, since he there no longer accepts the *epoche*. However, he does claim throughout his works that the *only* ego is what here is referred to as the *me*, namely, that self which can be characterized by physiology and psychology. Like

Heidegger, who is often much clearer on this point, Sartre believes that the transcendental 'I' of the *cogito* is neither the name of an underlying mental substance, a 'unifying principle' nor consciousness itself. Of course, it cannot be denied that I do refer to *myself,* but this 'I'

can evidently be only an expression *(rather than a condition) of this incommunicability and inwardness of consciousness. Consequently we may reply without hesitation: the phenomenological conception of consciousness renders the unifying and individualizing role of the I totally useless. It is consciousness, on the contrary, which makes possible the unity and the personality of my I. The transcendental I, therefore,* has no raison d'etre.[54]

This argument as stated is much weaker, however, than the argument which emerges throughout the first part of the essay. Heidegger had claimed, but not argued, that the *I* was not to be found in phenomena and thus constituted a *failure* in Husserl's application of his own method. This is argued in detail by Sartre, who gives us a clear picture of *prereflective* consciousness, in which there is no *I*. When I am *involved* in tasks, I have no experience of my*self:*

When I run after a street-car, . . . there is no I. There is consciousness of the street-car-having-*to-be overtaken.*[55]

It is therefore false that every act (or state) of consciousness is 'inhabited' by an *I*. Furthermore, Sartre argues,[56] the *cogito*—the *I*—emerges only with *reflective* consciousness and does not then refer us to or indicate an underlying *self* which remained hidden in prereflective activity. The *I* expresses only the unity of prereflective consciousness itself. In a phrase borrowed from Descartes, Sartre tells us that the *cogito* is the "reflection of consciousness *on consciousness."* Contrary to Descartes" however, these two "consciousnesses" do not have the same referent. Sartre has distinguished a *reflected* (that is, prereflective) and a *reflecting* (that is, reflective) consciousness. *Neither of these is or 'contains' the I* of Descartes:

there was no I in the unreflected consciousness[57]

Thus the consciousness that says I Think is precisely not the consciousness that thinks.[58]

The *I* of the reflecting consciousness is not an *object* discovered in the *reflected* consciousness nor is it consciousness itself:

Let us note that the I Think does not appear to reflection as the reflected consciousness: it is given through reflected consciousness. To be sure, it is apprehended by intuition and is an object grasped with evidence. . . . it is only too certain that the I of the I Think is an object grasped with neither apodictic nor adequate evidence. The evidence is not apodictic since by saying I we affirm far more than we know. It is not adequate, for the I is presented as an opaque reality whose content would have to be unfolded.[59]

Furthermore, Sartre recoils from the suggestion that there is more than one *I,* and therefore rejects the traditional duality of a transcendental and an empirical ego as well as "the *I* of the reflected consciousness,"[60] and any number of other *I*'s that might be postulated. There is only one self, and any distinction among *I*'s or even between the *I* and the *me* is unacceptable.

Sartre's reply to this problem as it emerges in this essay is to introduce prereflective consciousness as impersonal ("without an *I*"), and to maintain with Heidegger the 'public' origin of the 'I', but then only on the reflective level of consciousness. Again with Heidegger, Sartre maintains that 'public' reflection is actually distorting and "modifies the spontaneous consciousness."[61] Moreover, the *I* is not distinct from the *me,* but "is only one aspect of the *me,* the active aspect."

"For Kant and for Husserl the I is a formal structure of consciousness. We have tried to show that an I is never purely formal, that it is always, even when conceived abstractly, an infinite contraction of the material me."[62]

I and me are only one. . . . The I is the ego as the unity of actions. The me is the ego as the unity of states or qualities. The distinction one makes between these two aspects of one and the same reality seems to us simply functional, not to say grammatical.[63]

We may wonder, on this account, how it is possible for us to talk about our*selves* as personalities at all. Sartre's answer is bluntly that all such talk about personality is talk about the public *me* and not about the *I* of the *cogito* at all:

It is ordinarily thought that the existence of a transcendental I may be justified by the need that consciousness has for unity and individuality. . . . It is because I can say my consciousness and because Peter and Paul can also speak of their consciousnesses that these consciousnesses distinguish themselves from each other.[64]

One may ask if personality (even the abstract personality of an I) is a necessary accompaniment of a consciousness, if one cannot conceive of absolutely impersonal consciousness.[65]

We have seen such an impersonal consciousness—at least a superpersonal consciousness—in Hegel's concept of *Geist* ("Spirit"), and in Husserl's early and last published works;[66] we may also find such a conception in Merleau-Ponty:

Insofar as I am a consciousness, that is, insofar as something has meaning for me, I am neither here nor there, neither Peter nor Paul; I am in no way distinguishable from an 'Other' consciousness, . . .[67]

This 'extermination' of the *I* 'behind' consciousness shall have most important philosophical consequences. First of all, it makes my*self* not a special object known certainly, leaving knowledge of other *selves* a problem:

My I, in effect, is no more certain for consciousness than the I of other men. It is only more intimate.[68]

There is no difficulty in understanding how I can conceive the Other, because I and consequently the Other are not conceived as part of the woven stuff of phenomena; they have validity rather than existence. There is nothing hidden behind these faces and gestures, no domain to which I have no access. . . . I must be the exterior that I present to others, and the body of the other must be the other himself.[69]

Secondly, the understanding of one*self* as the *me* is no longer a special phenomenological reflective activity, but it becomes the study of one more (peculiar, to be sure) *object* in the world. We shall not be able to appreciate how very important this strange doctrine shall become until we have had a chance to investigate Sartre's mature theory of consciousness and the ego in *Being and Nothingness*. We may, however, anticipate this importance by noting that Sartre like Heidegger destroys the conception of the ego-subject in order to further destroy all traditional dualisms between subject and object. We have seen the bold claims made by Heidegger on the strength of this position. We shall see that Sartre, like Heidegger, attributes most traditional philosophical problems to this single distinction, and with Merleau-Ponty goes far beyond Heidegger in drawing out the implications of this 'egoless' notion of consciousness for human interpersonal relationships and conceptions of oneself. We shall also find, however, that Sartre, unlike Heidegger and Merleau-Ponty, reestablished a dualism very similar to traditional Cartesian dualism.

Consciousness: "Being-for-Itself"

In previous chapters, we have referred indiscriminately to the *subject*, the *ego*, and *consciousness*, separating them only metaphorically, as when we introduced the notion of an ego 'behind' consciousness. In our discussion of Heidegger, we found that both notions of 'consciousness' and 'ego' fell with the denial of the transcendental subject, as we found in Kant, Hegel, and Husserl (all after Descartes) that the affirmation of the *cogito* was at the same time an affirmation of both the existence of consciousness and the ego. We have seen that Sartre (and Merleau-Ponty) have eliminated the (transcendental) ego from phenomenology; however, they do not eliminate the notion of 'consciousness' (although it must be emphasized that Merleau-Ponty avoids this notion as much as possible); Sartre, in particular, takes the existence of consciousness as his beginning. His denial of the ego is not a denial of consciousness. The acts of consciousness provide us with a describable starting point; there are no acts of an 'underlying' or *transcendental ego*.

Consciousness is analyzed, in the phenomenologies of Sartre and Merleau-

Ponty, not as a knowing consciousness or as a primarily reflecting consciousness, but rather as an active, 'living' consciousness. Where Descartes, Kant, and Husserl took thinking and knowing as the essential conscious acts, Sartre and Merleau-Ponty argue that consciousness is first of all a perceiving, feeling, motile consciousness. Consciousness is first of all a *practical* consciousness, a 'prereflective' consciousness. Following Heidegger, Sartre and Merleau-Ponty insist that practical or 'ontic' acts are more 'primitive' or 'original' than acts of 'ontological' cognition. In Merleau-Ponty, this insistence on precognitive intentional acts is carried through consistently and persuasively; in his analysis, the traditional dualisms between mind and body, subject and object are discarded in favor of the Heideggerian conception of man in the world. The Husserlian concept of 'intentionality' is stripped of its heavily cognitive connotations and becomes equivalent to the concept of 'motility'. Man is conscious, not *of* his body, but *through* his body. The paradigm of an intentional act is not "I think" or "I know," but "I can."

Sartre also strains to follow Husserl in his analysis of consciousness, but he constantly falls back into traditional subject-object language.[70] Although he intends to support Heidegger in his rejection of Cartesianism, the dualism between consciousness and one's own body is never rejected, even though he insists that one's body is not simply "another object." In spite of his rejection of Husserl's transcendental ego and his *epoche,* Sartre never succeeds in purging himself of those Cartesian elements which he most needs to reject according to his own methodological demands.

Perception need not be analyzed as a primarily cognitive notion (as we found in Husserl). Perception may be viewed more broadly as the general "relations of consciousness and nature"[71] or as "the original relation of consciousness to being."[72] Accordingly both Sartre and Merleau-Ponty take the problem of perception to be equivalent to the problems of phenomenology as a whole, and take perception as the basic activity of consciousness. Merleau-Ponty insists that "all consciousness is, to some extent, perceptual consciousness." Furthermore, we are told quite outright that perception is to be analyzed as 'primitive', and other modes of consciousness may be analyzed

derivatively. Sartre, on the other hand, largely ignores the analysis of perception as such, seeming to rest content with the reinterpretation of Husserl's noematic theory as a theory about *unreduced* objects.[73] For this reason, Sartre gives us little help on traditional problems of perception as such. However, it must be evident that, insofar as Sartre and Merleau-Ponty agree on basics (as they do prior to 1950), they form an unmatchable complementary pair. From Merleau-Ponty, we have a most complete and exemplary presentation of a phenomenology of perceptual consciousness. From Sartre, we have an equally complete and equally exemplary disclosing of those 'structures' of consciousness which are not foremost concerned with perception.

Both Merleau-Ponty and Sartre begin with the Husserlian dictum that "All consciousness is consciousness of something,"[74] and both also begin with the Cartesian doctrine that the existence of consciousness itself is known simply by virtue of its existence. We have already seen what Sartre and Merleau-Ponty make of this latter doctrine; this self-knowledge is *not* the defining characteristic of consciousness, for it ignores the 'prereflexive consciousness' or 'preconscious intentionality'. The *cogito* is true and necessary only on a reflective, articulate 'level' of consciousness. The definition of "consciousness" thus focuses on the *intentionality* of consciousness—its always being directed towards an object. According to these authors, consciousness is *nothing but* this intentional activity; it is not an object itself or an object for itself. Sartre dramatizes this by noting that consciousness is *nothing*. For Sartre, this leads to a distinction between two very different kinds of Being—the being of objects for consciousness (*Beings-in-themselves*) and the being of consciousness (*Being-for-itself*). Consciousness, as we have already seen, is said to be dependent on its objects for its own existence, and, to avoid any postulation of consciousness as an object of some sort distinct from its objects, Sartre introduces a convention of parenthesizing the "of" in the expression "consciousness (of) . . ." This locution is similar to Heidegger's characterization of "Being-in-the-world." In both cases, the point of the linguistic innovation is to prevent us from separating different *components* of the expression, specifically, from attempting to logically distinguish consciousness (or Dasein) from its objects (the world). "Consciousness (of) objects" is thus to be taken as a primitive for Sartre just as "Being-in-the-world" is a primitive for Heidegger. Both expressions carry enormous philosophical thrust, for they are basic rejections of Husserl's basic distinctions between *cogito* and *cogitatio, noetic act* and *noema*, subject and object.

On the basis of this characterization of consciousness as intentionality, it is now possible to recharacterize the sense in which consciousness is self-knowing, is Being-for-itself. Consciousness is essentially aware of itself, but *not as an ego.* Consciousness is necessarily conscious of itself as consciousness (of) an object.[75] According to Sartre, this is even a necessary ('ontological') feature of consciousness. It is not to be confused with the reflexivity of the Cartesian *cogito*. There is no self in this consciousness (of) an object, and all of this is still prereflective. The *cogito* is based on this 'second-order' consciousness (the term comes from Merleau-Ponty), but it is only a "necessary possibility" as we have seen in the previous section. Consciousness can then be characterized as "Being-for-itself" because its existence consists in its dependency on objects, its (*preflective*) knowledge of its own dependency on objects, and the possibility of explicit recognition of itself in the Cartesian *cogito*. Much of the characterization of Being-for-itself, however, must be made in contrast to Being-in-itself. Key to the distinction between the two kinds of being is the centrally important recognition that Being-for-itself can never be an object of itself. (This is the importance of the notation, "consciousness (of) itself".) In reflection, we have seen that it is a *different* consciousness which reflects from that which is reflected. The classic metaphor of reflection as a "turning of the mind on itself" (Locke, Descartes, and Kant) is thus rejected. The nature of consciousness, of these two consciousnesses, thus becomes a central problem for Sartre, and this problem may all be traced to the claim that consciousness cannot be an object for itself.

Merleau-Ponty's views on the concept of "consciousness" are much more difficult to summarize, largely because he avoids the term as much as possible, usually using "conscious" as an equivalent of "knowing" or "reflective" (compare his

notion of "preconscious intentionality" with Sartre's notion of "prereflective consciousness"). His views on consciousness can only be made fully explicit in an analysis of his overall theory of perception, but it is already clear to what extent he is in agreement with Sartre. He does not, even in his early work, make much use of Sartre's distinction between two kinds of Being (he does occasionally employ the terms "in-itself" and "for-itself"),[76] although he does not explicitly and totally reject this distinction until many years later (1955). He does, however, accept Sartre's notion of 'consciousness' (without distinguishing consciousness as a separate sort of Being);

In the final analysis, consciousness is defined by the possession of an object of thought or by transparence to itself.[77]

He similarly rejects the traditional Cartesian definition of consciousness as immediate self-knowledge; we must stop "defining consciousness by knowledge of self."[78] Their mutual acceptance of the Husserlian characterization of consciousness as intentionality and mutual rejection of the Husserlian doctrines of the *epoche* and the transcendental ego bring Sartre and Merleau-Ponty sufficiently close together so that we may, for the present, center the core of our discussion on Sartre's theory of consciousness as presented in *Being and Nothingness*. We shall indicate the differences where particularly remarkable, but the primary differences lie in the application and in the consistency of application of this theory; in Sartre's *Being and Nothingness* the analysis of Being-for-itself quickly shifts to problems of interpersonal relations and self-recognition. In Merleau-Ponty's *Phenomenology of Perception,* the discussion of consciousness is concerned with the problem of perception and introduces the Sartrian problem of human *freedom* only in the concluding chapter. In Merleau-Ponty, the attack on Cartesian dualism is persistent: in Sartre, it soon degenerates into only a shift of emphasis. However, the route that both philosophers take in their analysis of human being as a whole is very similar, but brilliantly original with each. Both find the key to their problems of self-recognition and interpersonal relations in the study of the human *body,* a topic of frequent neglect in 'spiritually' centered philosophical discussions.

From the foregoing discussions, some central features of *consciousness,* as analyzed by Sartre and Merleau-Ponty, have become evident. Consciousness is necessarily consciousness (of) objects; consciousness is *dependent* on its objects; there is a prereflective consciousness which is not 'inhabited' by an ego; yet consciousness is necessarily self-conscious, it is consciousness (of) being conscious (of) objects; prereflective consciousness is not primarily a knowing consciousness but a 'living' experiencing consciousness; consciousness is not to be consciousness; consciousness is not to be separated, even in logic, from the world (and its objects) of which it is conscious. Consequently, both Sartre and Merleau-Ponty join Heidegger in rejecting the traditional subject-object dualism which has allegedly been responsible for so much philosophical confusion. It is now time to begin investigation of these themes in detail.

In understanding these sometimes peculiar theories of consciousness, we must never forget that all of this investigation is being carried out from within the "phenomenological standpoint" (even though certain basic features of this standpoint, for example, the *epoche,* have been eliminated from Husserl's introduction of this standpoint). From this viewpoint, consciousness can never be treated as a natural object or as an object of any kind and cannot be 'reduced' to any complex of natural phenomena (to behavior of the 'conscious organism').

I am, not a 'living creature', nor even a 'man', nor again even 'a consciousness' endowed with all the characteristics which zoology, anatomy or inductive psychology recognize in these various products of the natural or historical process—I am the absolute source, my existence does not stem from my antecedents, from my physical or social environment; instead it moves out towards them and sustains them . . .[79]

From this phenomenological (or "first-person") standpoint, it may be shown that all consciousness is necessarily consciousness (of) objects, that there can be no consciousness apart from such consciousness (of) objects. In the analyses of Sartre, Heidegger, and Merleau-Ponty, this commits us to a primitive notion of "Being-in-the-world" such that there can be no intelligible separation of consciousness (or Dasein) and existence *'in'* a world. It may thus be said that consciousness is (ontologically) dependent on its objects insofar as it could not exist without them. In the formulation common to both Sartre and Merleau-Ponty, to be conscious is to be conscious (of) objects *by definition.* However, Sartre goes yet further and stresses that consciousness is absolutely *nothing* apart from its consciousness of objects, and that objects 'present themselves' as independent and 'fulfilled' or 'complete' in-themselves while consciousness (properly viewed) always presents itself as dependent, as 'unfulfilled', as 'incomplete' (a "decompression of Being"). (Merleau-Ponty does not place this inordinate stress on the dependency of consciousness on objects over the dependency of objects on consciousness.) This leads Sartre to maintain, with Heidegger and Merleau-Ponty, that consciousness can have no 'contents'[80] and can have no independent existence, no existence apart from its world. It would further follow that there can be no intelligible thesis of idealism, which relies on the independence of consciousness and the dependence of objects on consciousness (and its 'contents'), as it would follow that there could be no intelligible notion of *constitution* of objects (as in Husserl), since objects are encountered as independent ('in-themselves'), and it is consciousness whose existence and nature become a philosophical dilemma, not these objects.

With this analysis, the traditional notion of *subject* is altered radically. First, we have already seen how Sartre wishes to argue that there is no *ego* 'in' or 'behind' consciousness; the subject is simply consciousness itself:

Subject is not relative to experience, but it is this experience.[81]

Consciousness is

no longer the subject in Kant's meaning of the term, it is subjectivity itself, the immanence of self in self.[82]

This relationship of "self to self" is cited by both Sartre and Merleau-Ponty (as well as by many traditional thinkers) as one of the defining characteristics of consciousness. In one formulation, this relationship to self is called "transparency" or "translucence" and it is discussed by both authors:

the type of existence of consciousness is to be conscious of itself . . . All is therefore clear and lucid in consciousness . . . It is all lightness, all translucence.[63]

Every conscious existence exists as consciousness of existing.[64]

In the final analysis, consciousness is defined by the possession of an object of thought or by transparence to itself:[65]

The being of consciousness consists in appearing to itself.[66]

Self-knowledge becomes one of the central, perhaps the central, problem for Sartre, for whom the Cartesian *cogito* becomes not only a philosophical confusion, but a personal attempt at self-deception (like Heidegger's *inauthenticity*). It is clear enough that consciousness does have a peculiar relationship to itself, but this relationship is not primarily one of *knowing* itself; it is

an immediate, non-cognitive relation of the self to itself.[87]

It must not be thought, however, that this "relation to itself" is a characteristic of consciousness distinct from its characteristic consciousness (of) objects. The latter depends on the former;

The necessary and sufficient condition for a knowing consciousness to be knowledge of its object, is that it be consciousness of itself as being that knowledge.[88]

The act whereby I am conscious of something must itself be apprehended at the very moment at which it is carried out, otherwise it would collapse.[89]

Because we have already been told by both authors that the *cogito* is not primitively 'in' consciousness, that is, prereflective consciousness, we may already surmise that this consciousness (of) consciousness is not yet the Cartesian *cogito*, but that it is itself still prereflective. It is a *prereflective cogito:*

The first condition for all reflection is a preflective cogito. *This* cogito *to be sure does not posit an object; it remains within consciousness. But it is nonetheless homologous with the reflective* cogito *since it appears as the first necessity for the non-reflective consciousness to be seen by itself.*[90]

Prereflective consciousness is self-consciousness.[91]

Behind the spoken (reflective) cogito, *the one which is converted into discourse and into essential truth, there lies a tacit* cogito, *myself experienced by myself. . . . The tacit* cogito, *the presence of oneself to oneself, being no less than existence, is anterior to any philosophy, and knows itself only in those extreme situations in which it is under threat; for example, in the dread of death or of another's gaze upon me. . . . this silent consciousness grasps itself only as a generalized "I Think" in the face of a confused world 'to be thought about'. . . . The tacit* cogito *is a* cogito *only when it has found expression for itself.*[92]

This prereflective *cogito* is not a knowing cogito—a reflective cogito:

I am a field, an experience, . . . a possibility of situations.[93]

Merleau-Ponty tells us that Descartes' *cogito* is a "merely verbal *cogito.*"[94] The prereflective *cogito* is already familiar to us from Heidegger's discussion of Dasein's 'primitive' world of equipment.[95] Merleau-Ponty clearly echoes Heidegger's insight with approval; we must

stop defining consciousness by knowledge of self and . . . introduce the notion of a life of consciousness which goes beyond its explicit knowledge of itself. But something further . . . [would be] necessary: to describe the structures of action and knowledge in which consciousness is engaged. . .[96]

Merleau-Ponty complains that it is necessary to provide such a description in detail and of specific actions and bits of knowledge. Heidegger deals only with "the concrete in general." *The Structure of Behavior* is an attempt to correct this neglect, and *Phenomenology of Percep-*

tion is also primarily occupied with 'preconscious intentionality', the *prereflective cogito* which has not yet been "expressed" as the Cartesian (reflective) *cogito.*

Sartre similarly tells us to "abandon the primacy of knowledge"[97] and turn to the analysis of prereflective consciousness. One of the greatest difficulties in understanding the details of Sartre's theory of consciousness, however, is the enormous complexity of his description of the relation between prereflective and reflective consciousness. In *The Transcendence of the Ego,* it often sounds as if there are literally two consciousnesses being described, for example, when Sartre tells us that

my reflecting [reflective] consciousness does not take itself for an object when I reflect the Cogito. *What it affirms concerns the reflected [prereflective] consciousness.*[98]

In *Being and Nothingness,* the talk of reflective and prereflective consciousness also appears to be talk of two consciousnesses, one of which takes the other as an object:

The reflecting [reflective] consciousness posits the consciousness reflected-on [prereflective] as its object. In the act of reflecting I pass judgment on the consciousness reflected-on; I am ashamed of it, I am proud of it . . .[99]

In Sartre's ontology, it never does become clear to what extent we are to think literally of two consciousnesses, to what extent we are to think of two 'modes' of one consciousness, and to what extent there is simply one consciousness both of self and object.

All that there is of intention in my actual consciousness is directed toward the outside, toward the world. . . . every positional [reflective] consciousness of an object is at the same time a non-positional [prereflective] consciousness of itself.[100]

From what has been said (and from the last quotation in particular), it should be clear that the distinction between reflective and prereflective consciousness cannot be a difference in *self-consciousness.* The fact that Sartre insists that self-*knowledge* and the *ego* appear only with reflective consciousness does not entail that *self-*

consciousness or a *cogito* of sorts is peculiar to reflection. On the contrary, Sartre insists that *all* consciousness, prereflective as well as reflective, is self-consciousness. The reflective *cogito* of Descartes has a prereflective analog. Only the reflective *cogito* constitutes self-*knowledge* (knowledge for Sartre is essentially reflective); but prereflective consciousness has its own [prereflective] *cogito;* it is also self-consciousness. Although reflective consciousness takes prereflective consciousness as its object in the (reflective) *cogito,* prereflective consciousness, according to Sartre, simply *is* self-consciousness; it does not take itself as an object:

Consciousness of self is not dual.[101] *Every conscious existence exists as consciousness of existing. We understand now why the first consciousness of consciousness is not positional; it is because it is one with the consciousness of which it is conscious.*[102]

This self-consciousness we ought to consider not as a new consciousness, but as the only mode of existence which is possible for a consciousness of something.[103]

Merleau-Ponty defends the same thesis:

All consciousness is at the same time self-consciousness . . . self-consciousness is the very being of the mind in action.[104]

Merleau-Ponty is quite explicit about the relation between prereflective and reflective consciousness (preconscious and conscious intentionality). Reflection is the *expression* of prereflective consciousness and the reflective *cogito* is the *expression* of a prereflective self-consciousness. In this characterization of two kinds of self-consciousness, we must remind ourselves of Heidegger's distinction between *ontic* (preconceptual) self-recognition as manifested in our actions and attitudes towards ourselves and *ontological* (conceptual) self-recognition, in which we actually verbalize this conception.

In Sartre, however, this never becomes so clear. He surely does agree with Heidegger and Merleau-Ponty that there is a vital distinction between reflection and prereflective consciousness and a distinction between reflective self-*knowledge* (the Cartesian *cogito)* and prereflective self-consciousness.

Of course consciousness can know and know itself. But it is in itself something other than a knowledge turned back on itself.[105]

It is sufficiently clear in what the reflective *cogito* consists (although the problems surrounding the alleged 'necessity' of this *cogito* are not at all clear), and, from our discussion of Heidegger, it is evident that prereflective consciousness consists in being 'engaged' or 'involved' in an activity or task. But if there is no *self* or *ego* in prereflective consciousness, how can there be self-consciousness in any sense?

Sartre's two illustrations of this prereflective self-consciousness give us a feeling for the thesis he is grasping towards, but certainly no clarification. While counting the number of cigarettes in a case,

it is very possible I have no positional [reflective] consciousness of counting them. Then I do not know myself as counting . . . Yet at the moment when these cigarettes are revealed to me as a dozen, I have a non-thetic [prereflective] consciousness of my adding activity. If anyone questioned me . . . I should reply at once, "I am counting."[106]

There is the difference between engaging in the activity of counting and reflecting on that activity, but Sartre wants to claim that there is a sort of self-conscious activity even in the prereflective engagement. If we were not so conscious, Sartre wishes to argue, it would not make sense to say that we were conscious at all. Every conscious act involves the consciousness that one is performing that act, although the reflective consciousness (knowledge) of that performance is peculiar to only some acts. In the same vein, Sartre tells us that

pleasure cannot be distinguished, even logically, from consciousness of pleasure.[107]

Again we wish to distinguish between simply enjoying an activity and reflecting on our enjoyment and to insist that even the simple enjoyment is, in a special 'non-cognitive' sense, self-conscious enjoyment. But it is not clear what is 'added' to the prereflective consciousness of counting which allows me to make the reply, "I am counting." Neither is it clear in what sense my 'non-thetic' consciousness is self-con-

sciousness *apart from* my ability to reflect upon it. Similarly, it is not clear from Sartre's brief analysis of pleasure how "consciousness of pleasure" is also self-consciousness.

This complex and not sufficiently clear relationship between prereflexive and reflexive consciousness and self-consciousness lies at the very foundation of Sartre's philosophy. Specifically, his theory of *nothingness* and human *freedom,* is based on a description of prereflective consciousness. Freedom, we shall be told, exists on the prereflective level (it *is* prereflective consciousness), but it can be recognized as such only reflectively. It is on the basis of this freedom that we shall ultimately be able to characterize the difference between Being-in-itself and human Being-for-itself.

Our discussion of Being-in-itself in the last section instructed us that such beings or objects are characterized by their "completeness" and their determinacy: "Being is. Being is in-itself. Being is what it is."[108] Objects simply "present themselves" or "are given" to consciousness. Consciousness or Being-for-itself, on the other hand, is characterized, paradoxically, as "not being what it is and being what it is not."[109] In other words, what it thinks of itself is a determinant of what it is; "it *determines itself.*" Prereflective consciousness is simply (self-)consciousness of its objects, but it itself is *nothing.* This means, first of all, that it is not an *object* for itself. More importantly, however, it means that it cannot be characterized as objects are characterized, as given as such, or as having such and such fixed characteristics:

"The being of consciousness does not coincide with itself in a full equivalence."[110]

Being-for-itself is not what it is; its conception of itself is not, conversely, determined by what it is. This is one of several interpretations of Sartre's slogan, "Existence precedes essence"; consciousness is self-determining. This talk of indeterminacy, however, will remain an obscure formula until we have studied the sophisticated apparatus by which consciousness secures this 'indeterminacy.' By way of preview, we may remind ourselves that Heidegger also held such a theory regarding human being. Sartre's theory of the indeterminacy of human consciousness becomes equivalent to the Heideggerian claim that it is man who asks the "question of being":

consciousness is a being such that in its being, its being is in question insofar as this being implies a being other than itself.[111]

Consequently, we may expect that human consciousness will be characterized in terms of "possibility," thus accounting for its indeterminacy:

Since consciousness is not possible *before being [in-itself] but since its being is the source and condition of all possibility its existence implies its essence.*[112]

(Notice that the "existence implies . . . essence" above verbally contradicts the popular slogan. Sartre is unforgivably inconsistent in his usage of such key technical terms.)

Central to this theory of the indeterminacy of consciousness is the theory of (acts of) consciousness which relates to its objects and to itself in such a way as to "create a distance between itself and its objects." For Merleau-Ponty, all acts of consciousness create such a distance by acting to change the world and myself: "an act is a violent transition . . . from what I am now to what I want to be." For Sartre, the indeterminacy of consciousness and this important 'distance' is due to a special kind of act—an act of *nihilation*—an act which creates a *nothingness.*

Nothingness

The concepts of *nothing* and *nothingness* have been recurrent in our discussions of Heidegger and Sartre. "The nothing" came to occupy an increasingly important role in Heidegger's later philosophy, and it is at the very heart of Sartre's thought. However, it is easy to see how these concepts could have been unfairly ridiculed by critics who have not understood their special role in phenomenology. The phenomenological conceptions of nothing and nothingness are not commonsense conceptions (although, to be sure, they do signify experiences which are not uncommon).

To begin with, we have already introduced a reasonably 'innocent' interpretation of nothingness when we claimed that "consciousness is nothing" for Sartre. This means that consciousness is not an object (for consciousness). However, the phe-

nomenological concept of nothingness is not to be limited to this 'innocent' interpretation, and it is unfortunate that so many critics have blindly criticized Sartre's (and Heidegger's) employment of the term as only so many grammatical diversions over an obscurely stated but ultimately simple-minded thesis.[113] The concept of nothingness is not ill-cast as the focal point of *Being and Nothingness* (the discussion of *Being* confined mostly to the introduction), and the obscure grammatical formulations are attempts to express a sophisticated phenomenological theory. This is not to deny that Sartre all too readily yields to the temptation to pun on "nothing," but we must not forget that "nothingness" is equivalent to the obviously important notion of 'freedom', and as such is the key to French existentialism.

With respect to the 'innocent' interpretation of consciousness as nothing, we might remind ourselves that this is not a new philosophical thesis in spite of its new expression. We may well interpret Hume's rejection of Locke's *self* 'in' consciousness as the thesis that the *ego* is nothing. William James similarly tells us that "consciousness does not exist," and Wittgenstein, in the *Tractatus,* tells us "the thinking presenting subject—there is no such thing."[114] Closest to Sartre on this point is Nietzsche, who several times attacks the notion of the 'inner' ego as an insidious philosophical myth. So much for this innocent interpretation of the *nothing* of consciousness; the less innocent interpretations have far less historical support.

Closely tied to the concepts of *nothing* and *nothingness* is the concept of *nihilation.* Nihilation is an activity of consciousness and is responsible for the existence of nothingness 'in the world.' Furthermore, consciousness itself is said to be nothingness, not only in the innocent sense above, but in the sense that it is responsible for producing nothingness:

The being by which nothingness comes into the world must be its own nothingness.[115]

"Nihilation" is introduced in the essays on the imagination to refer to the reflective knowledge of the unreality of objects of imagination. In *Being and Nothingness,* we find that it is (prereflective) consciousness itself which is responsible for nihilation of objects, including objects of imagination. Furthermore, in both the essays on imagination and in *Being and Nothingness,* it is evident that nothingness is a component of our experience—it is 'in the world'. According to the phenomenological characterization of Being as an object of consciousness, therefore, we may even say that *nothingness* 'is a species of Being.' Thus we may distinguish two non-innocent characterizations of nothingness. It is an object of our experience, and it is produced by consciousness in the activity of nihilation. This peculiar object and this productive activity are least manifest in perception, most manifest in imagination, but we shall see that nothingness and nihilation pervade all of human conscious activities and, ultimately, distinguish man from all other beings. Most importantly, it is through nihilation and nothingness that human freedom is introduced into Sartre's phenomenology.

Let us first examine the claim that nothingness is an object of our experience—is 'in the world'. Common sense would seem to claim that we never see nothing (the very expression strikes us as ungrammatical) but always see something. Our consciousness of the world, according to this 'theory', is a consciousness of real objects in the world. Of course, consciousness of imagined objects then becomes a serious problem, but one which rarely leads to a rejection of the commonsense theory which has determined the epistemology of most traditional philosophies. Most immediately, Husserl's theory of perception left no room for nothing, and agreed with common sense that we see only something (objects) not nothing. Why should Sartre wish to disagree with this?

Do we only see something (leaving aside various colloquialisms like "What are you looking at?" "Nothing.")? Sartre's answer is that we do not just see 'somethings,' but, even in perception, see nothings. To use clear nonparadoxical English, we are not only conscious of the *presence* of objects in our world; we are also conscious of their *absence.* Thus, to borrow Sartre's example, I may have an experience of my friend Peter—he may be an object for me—but the *absence of Peter* may also be an object for me. If I walk into a cafe looking for Peter, I do not only see tables, chairs, glasses, and other people (but not Peter). I also see the absence of Peter, in fact, that may be the defining 'object' in my environment, the object to

which my attention is totally devoted. Similarly, when I am expecting a friend to drop by my house, or waiting for a phone call, I am not only conscious of the presence of the door, the telephone, and the other objects about me, I am primarily aware, frustratingly aware, of the *lack* of the knock on the door and the *failure* of the telephone to ring. Nothingness, the lack or absence of something rather than the presence of something, is definitive of my situation.[116] Sartre calls such experiences *négatités,* experiences of our environment as inhabited by nothingness.

Even our 'ordinary' language reflects these experiences or *négatités.* For example, the concept of "destruction" does not apply to the existence of an object, but to the lack of existence of an object which once existed. Of course, it is true that something else exists in the place of the destroyed object, but this is not what we are referring to when talking about the destruction. Furthermore, the nonexistence of some object does not constitute destruction. It must have once existed and it must have been made to go out of existence, but even then we do not wish to say that an object has been destroyed if it simply ceases to exist. There must be some value placed on the object as existing, so that its nonexistence is *experienced* as a loss. Destruction is not equivalent to nonexistence or disappearance, it essentially involves a *négatité,* an experience of absence.

It may be challenged that the above examples can be dealt with without reference to experience of nothingness by appeal to the logical function of judgments of *negation* in language. According to this very widespread argument, it is the concepts of negation and the possibility of constructing sentences with negatives ("not") that allow us to talk of, and thus to experience, such *négatités.* The dispute here becomes central to all of philosophy, namely, whether ontology determines our language or whether language determines our ontology. The prejudice of recent philosophy has frequently moved towards the latter. The positions of phenomenologists on this issue has not been entirely clear. Husserl, while emphasizing the underlying essences which language 'expresses' nevertheless refused to commit himself to the thesis that verbal expression was not in some way responsible for these essences. Similarly, we have seen that

Heidegger leans heavily on the thesis that our ontology is structured or misstructured by the language we speak, and he too, while stressing (in his later philosophy) the independence of Being from man, does not commit himself to the thesis that our ontology precedes and determines our language. Sartre clearly states the primacy of ontology:

Consciousness cannot produce a negation except in the form of consciousness of negation.[117]

With regard to negation and the experience of nothingness, we have seen a similar thesis argued in Heidegger's "What Is Metaphysics?" Heidegger, however, does not tell us in what this experience consists, and it is the virtue of Sartre's analysis that he gives us a reasonably clear picture of that to which the difficult concept 'experience of nothingness' refers. Nothingness is experienced in experiences of absence of objects, and, as an object of experience, nothingness is itself a sort of Being.

It is not correct, however, to say that Being and Nothingness are two kinds of Being on equal ontological footing. Hegel, for example, had argued that "Being and non-Being are logically contemporary," and Heidegger at one time ("What Is Metaphysics?") had similarly defended an ontologically independent *nothing* (*das Nichts nichtet*). Sartre insists that

Non-Being exists only on the surface of being.[118]

Emptiness is emptiness of something.[119]

In other words, there must be objects before we can experience the lack of objects. Imagination, of course, is simply a special case of the experience of nothingness. We experience an object and with it experience that it is not really there. We can see that the active imagination of a fantasy-painter and the dull thwarted expectation of my finding Peter in the cafe are closely related, both involve an experience of nothingness. Equally important, however, is that both involve a projection of a possibility which is not actualized—the projection of a fantasy which remains unreal or the expectation of finding Peter and not finding him. This brings us to the second characterization of nothingness, that it is

an object of experience which is produced by conscious activity of nihilation. Nothingness always requires an activity of ours, an expectation, a desire, an imagining. Being-in-itself is introduced as independent of us, as given to our consciousness. Nothingness is also 'given' in experience, but we find on analysis that it is ultimately *produced* in experience by ourselves.

We experience nothingness because of certain sorts of acts of consciousness, acts which will not simply accept what is given in consciousness (for example, simple observing or attending to), but which have certain expectations (for example, looking for, hoping, or desiring). Ultimately, however, we will see that virtually all acts of consciousness are of the second type. Husserl's analysis of the noematic expectations involved in perception—accepted in some form or other by Heidegger, Sartre, and Merleau-Ponty—would entail that every act of consciousness involves expectations and thus the possibility of nothingness (cf. Husserl's notion of an "explosion of noemata"). Consciousness is not a passive receiver (the picture we get from many empiricists), but makes active demands on its experiences which can be fulfilled or not fulfilled:

it is evident that non-being always appears within the limits of human expectation.[120]

Here we encounter a problem of interpretation, which we have already introduced in the last section. Is nothingness (which is produced by us in expectation) prereflective or uniquely reflective? On the one hand, we may argue that it *must* be prereflective for Sartre (as for Heidegger) or else their argument that the ontological experience of nothingness precedes the logical or reflective act of negation falls apart. Sometimes Sartre bears this out;

Negation is not only a quality of judgment —it is a prejudicative[i.e. prereflective] attitude.[121]

He also gives many indications that nothingness is not a mere object for prereflective consciousness, but rather, because nothingness is somehow 'produced' by us, it requires reflection;

The world does not disclose its non-beings to one who has not first postulated them as possibilities.[122]

Similarly, we are told that

by questioning the prereflective cogito . . . *we could not find nothingness anywhere.*[123]

and

nothingness is the putting into question of being by being—that is precisely consciousness of for-itself.[124]

In *Being and Nothingness,* Sartre tells us that "in anguish man gets consciousness of his freedom,"[125] but it remains a serious question whether Sartre consistently maintains that this consciousness of freedom is reflective or prereflective (freedom is nothingness). It sometimes seems, particularly in Sartre's examples (for example, in "Bad Faith"), that it is only through reflective acts of nihilation that freedom or nothingness arises. Other parts of Sartre's thesis, for example, his entire theory that "consciousness is nothingness is freedom," would require that nothingness exists in (and exists as) prereflective consciousness. Further evidence of this central confusion can be discovered in Sartre's repeated insistence on the uniqueness of nothingness as a *human* experience ("it is through man that nothingness comes into the world").[126] Of course, we might partially explain the neglect of intelligent animal consciousnesses by citing Sartre's dominating interest in humanism and the Cartesian prejudice that animals simply are to be considered as mechanisms. However, animals do seem to experience disappointments, frustrations, surprises as do humans, and we must ask whether Sartre perhaps neglects this because he is not certain of the correct status of nothingness himself. If nothingness is prereflective, then it would make perfectly good sense to suggest that nonself-conscious beings could nonetheless experience nothingness. On the other hand, if nothingness is strictly human because strictly reflective, then very serious problems arise for the whole of Sartre's philosophy. For it is one of Sartre's central theses that freedom (and therefore nothingness) exists in *prereflective* consciousness and not only with (philosophical) reflection.

What is an *act of nihilation?* We may simply characterize it by referring back to Heidegger's characterization of Dasein as the "projection of possibilities." An act of nihilation is a conscious (not to say reflective) act of 'going beyond' the actuality of a state of affairs. It is the attitude which is reflectively manifested in Husserl's *epoche* (Sartre stresses that the *epoche* can only arise through reflection) and takes an extreme form in the general question of Being in Heidegger, "Why is there something rather than nothing?" (which both Sartre and Merleau-Ponty reject as unanswerable). It is an intentional act which is performed in every act of doubt, in every question ("every question demands the possibility of a negative reply"), in every hope, in every desire, in every expectation. Because we have seen that every conscious act involves expectations (the *noematic system*), every conscious act involves an act of nihilation. This is to say that every act of consciousness includes within the "possibility of nothingness," that is, the consciousness that the object of that act might in fact be different. For example, my imagination of the presence of Nietzsche in this chair beside me is clearly accompanied by the consciousness that he is not really here beside me, but my perception of the portrait of Nietzsche in front of me similarly is accompanied by an act of nihilation—my wondering whether any such man truly existed, my faint philosophical doubt that perhaps I have not yet awakened and may be dreaming. Every postulation, no matter how fanciful or speculative, of a 'possible world' different from *this* actual world involves an act of nihilation—consciousness that things might be different than they are. The thesis that these acts of nihilation are involved in every conscious act and that consequently the experience of nothingness is (at least potentially) involved in every experience is a thesis which had been argued by Heidegger in "What Is Metaphysics?" where he tells us that every Being contains within it the possibility of non-Being. Sartre dramatically accepts this suggestion and tells us, "*nothingness haunts being.*"[127]

Nothingness lies coiled in the heart of Being, like a worm.[128]

Every human experience involves nothingness and every conscious act includes an act of nihilation. It is necessary that nihilation be a primarily *prereflective* act on this account (even if Sartre does not state this), and those acts which are reflective acts of nihilation are but a special case of conscious acts of nihilation in general. In other words, all human consciousness is filled with expectations, expectations that can at any time be thwarted (by a noematic 'explosion', for example), and human existence is thereby something essentially open to frustration, disappointment, despair, all of which are experiences of nothingness involving acts of nihilation. Frustration, for example, is the result of nonfulfilled expectations, the experience of not doing or not having what one wants. This leads to a remarkable thesis which permeates much of Sartre's philosophy—"man's desire to be God." God is defined (after Hegel's definition in the *Phenomenology*) as a Being in and for itself. Being-in-itself, we have been instructed, is 'complete' or 'fulfilled' and 'has no possibilities,' that is, sees no possibilities for itself and has no expectations. Being-for-itself, on the contrary, is all possibilities and all expectations. Being-in-itself cannot be frustrated or disappointed because it expects nothing of the world. Being-for-itself is constantly threatened by nothingness, for its very nature is to project possibilities, to expect things of the world. To be God would be to project infinite possibilities and have infinite expectations for oneself, but it would also be complete or 'fulfilled' and beyond the possibility of disappointment. In his search to escape frustration and nothingness in general, man seeks to be in-itself, complete and determined so that his future is not an open question, a series of possibilities and expectations many of which will be frustrated. Yet man also wishes to remain free, to continue to hope and plan for the future, to expect things of the future. Man's "impossible ideal" is to be both 'complete' (determined) and free—to be in-and-for-himself—to be God. This ideal, although unavoidable, is impossible because freedom and 'completeness' are incompatible. To be 'complete' or determined is to have no possibilities; to be free is to be 'incomplete'. The concept of God, therefore, the ideal of man, is an "ontological contradiction." Nothing can be both in and for itself. Yet it is easy to understand why man should take God as an ideal. If the nature of man (that is, the nature of human consciousness) is

such as to be essentially nihilating, to be essentially looking 'beyond' being (in-itself) as it appears toward *possible* (and more or less desirable) states of affairs, then human existence is bound to be plagued with the negative experiences called "nothingness." The escape from nothingness is the search for complete 'fulfillment' of one's expectations. However, it is in the very nature of an expectation that it can be frustrated, and it is therefore impossible that one could have expectations (hopes, desires) without the threat of failure, disappointment, or frustration. [Sartre makes little use of the notion of a generalized experience of nothingness—directed to the world as a whole, its meaninglessness or 'absurdity.' The notions of "dread" and "absurdity" do not play the central role in Sartre that they play in Kierkegaard, Heidegger, and Camus. *"Angoisse"* is a specific experience of anxiety toward self, not toward the world, and 'absurdity,' for Sartre, becomes a manifestation of 'bad faith'.]

The above characterization of God is not at all new to Western thought, of course. The medievals had worried at great lengths about a seeming 'ontological' contradiction in the nature of God as being both infinitely free (to choose and do as he wished) and infinitely knowing ('omniscient'). If he were free to choose, it must be without the knowledge that the future has been already determined, but if he were omniscient, he would already know everything that would happen in the future. His 'choice' therefore could not be a choice, or his knowledge could not possibly be complete. It is this traditional 'paradox' that is reformulated by Sartre. Sartre's solution to it, of course, is not one readily acceptable by the medievals—the dismissal of the ideal of God as 'impossible'.

An act of nihilation is a denial, of one sort or another, of the 'givenness' of Being-in-itself. It is a hope that things can be different, the desire to make things different, the skeptical doubt that things are not as they seem, the effort of imagination to shift one's attention away from the world as it presents itself to us. Acts of nihilation are not only so 'outwardly' directed towards Being-in-itself; acts of nihilation are also directed at Being-for-itself—at consciousness itself. Being-for-itself has already been introduced as a *nothingness*. We now find that the central nihilating activity of consciousness is the nihilation of its own being.

Sartre argues that the experience of nothingness requires an act of nihilation. He then argues that the act of nihilation must itself be 'performed' by a consciousness which is itself nothingness. We have already seen one (the 'innocent') sense in which consciousness is nothing; it is not an object for itself as other objects. The argument for the self-nihilation and nothingness of consciousness goes far deeper than this 'innocent' interpretation. It is, in fact, the core of Sartre's theory of freedom. The analysis of consciousness now turns from what consciousness is *not* (that is, it is not an object) to what consciousness is. We are told that consciousness *is this act of self-nihilation*. (It is evident that consciousness is many other things as well, for example, the consciousness of objects and the peculiar self-knowledge discussed in the previous section. Sartre's oversimplified equivalence here is exemplary of a tendency to misleading overstatement to be found throughout his works.)

Why must consciousness itself be nothingness? A pair of related arguments to this conclusion are remarkably similar to the transcendental arguments we studied in Kant's philosophy. An argument is made from our actual experiences (specifically experiences of nothingness) to the necessary ("transcendental") structure of consciousness:

It [consciousness] must necessarily be conscious of this cleavage in being [i.e. Being and Nothingness] but not as a phenomenon which it experiences rather as a structure of consciousness which it is.[129]

Sartre has already argued that nothingness comes about through an act of nihilation, but now an embarrassingly Cartesian prejudice comes to the surface. Who performs this act of nihilation? Sartre gives consideration to Heidegger's suggestion that "nothingness nihilates itself"[130] and rejects it:

if Nothingness can be conceived neither outside of Being nor in terms of Being, and if, on the other hand, since it is non-Being, it cannot derive from itself the necessary force to "nihilate itself," where does Nothingness come from?[131]

It must be that consciousness performs this act, and that consciousness itself is, therefore, nothingness:

The being by which Nothingness comes into the world must be its own Nothingness.[132]

Why is this? We have already seen that consciousness could not have expectations if it were determined by its consciousness of the actual world; all hoping, desiring, waiting, and even perceiving requires a *withdrawal* from the world, a "wrenching away from Being," a vision of possible but nonactual worlds. If I were simply a passive perceiver determined in my 'thoughts' by the world, I could not envision such possible worlds for I would be 'caught in reality.' In order to envision possible worlds—an ideal society towards which to work, or a new perspective on this object of perception—man must be able to negate (nihilate) the actual world:

This means that by a double movement of nihilation, he nihilates the thing questioned in relation to himself by placing it in a neutral state, between being and non-being [cf. Husserl's epoche] and that he nihilates himself in relation to the thing questioned by wrenching himself away from being in order to be able to bring out of himself the possibility of non-being.[133]

The necessity of this "wrenching away from Being" is also familiar to us from Kant's philosophy. The nature of human reason, we are told in the second *Critique,* is such that it is capable of postulating any end whatsoever, and it is so capable by virtue of the fact that man as a rational moral agent is free from determination by nature, by his environment, and by his own natural inclinations (human nature). In Sartre, the argument that consciousness itself must be nothingness ultimately relies on this Kantian insight. If man is part of the causal world, it is nonsense to suppose that he is capable of envisioning possible but nonactual worlds (as "ends"); the vision itself would be nothing but a product of the actual world. If man is a causal part of the world, there would be only one possible world—the actual world. The fact that man would not know beforehand how this world was determined does not offset the argument that he has no choice, no freedom, and, in Sartre's sense, no possibilities if he cannot separate himself from this causal world:

It is essential therefore that the questioner have the permanent possibility of dissociating himself from the causal series which constitutes being and which can produce only being. If we admitted that the question is determined in the questioner by universal determinism, the question would thereby become unintelligible and even inconceivable . . . Thus insofar as the questioner must be able to effect in relation to the questioned a kind of nihilating withdrawal, he is not subject to the causal order of the world.[134]

Sartre approves of Heidegger's characterization of man as "a being of distances,"[135] and the nature of man thus becomes *nothingness*. To be a man is to be capable of *withdrawing* or *wrenching away from* Being (the actual world) in order to conceive of possibilities, but this possibility of withdrawing in turn depends on man being outside of the causal order of the world. Sartre thus argues that the first act of nihilation must be directed toward man himself to effect this separation. Being-in-itself, we have been told, simply *is there*. Man (Being-for-itself), on the contrary, is a being of possibilities:

The for-itself is nothing but the pure nihilation of the in-itself.[136]

Man's relation with being is that he can modify it.[137]

Thus, by a very Kantian argument, human consciousness (the for-itself) is shown to be nothingness, an act of self-nihilation. If consciousness were something, it would be part of the causal order, in which case it would be wholly determined (for Sartre, contrary to his 'libertarian' image, does accept the Kantian Principle of Universal Causation, that every event, *in nature,* has sufficient natural cause). If consciousness were so determined by what is actually the case, it would be incapable of postulating possibilities—counterfactual states of affairs —except insofar as the idea of such possibilities was itself caused in consciousness. Of course, it is the motivating force behind the whole of Sartre's phenomenology to deny this causal status of consciousness. Experiences of nothingness, Sartre argues, are possible only because consciousness is not causally determined by the actual world. Therefore, consciousness must be outside the causal order of the world, it must nihilate itself as well as the actual

world. In other words, consciousness must be nothingness, it must be "the nothingness of being and the nihilating power both together."[138]

We have already indicated that this concept of *nothingness* will be equivalent to the very 'existentialist' notion of *freedom*. Freedom is the ability of consciousness to withdraw or 'wrench away from' the actual world:

Descartes following the Stoics has given a name to this possibility which human reality has to secrete a nothingness which isolates it—it is freedom.[139]

Sartre emphasizes, as did Kant, Hegel, Kierkegaard, and Heidegger, that this freedom is not merely a "faculty of the human soul,"[140] a *property* of human being, but man *is* freedom:

the essence of human being is suspended in his freedom. What we call freedom is impossible to distinguish from the being *of "human reality." Man does not exist* first *in order to be free subsequently; there is no difference between the being of man and his* being-free.[141]

Freedom is nothingness and is "the essential structure of the for-itself." The discussion of nothingness is thus going to allow Sartre to explain and defend a central existentialist (but not only existentialist) theme which Kierkegaard only asserts— that human existence is freedom. From this 'existentialist' starting point, it follows that man is free to choose and is thus *responsible for* his every action, his every intention. What differentiates man from all other beings, therefore, is this freedom, and with this freedom (self-nihilation as well as nihilation of Being) man and only man can question (nihilate) himself:

The being by which Nothingness arrives in the world is a being such that, in its being, the Nothingness of its being is in question.[142]

It is from the discussion of nothingness that the familiar doctrines of 'existentialism' take form. An act of nihilation will allow man to "put his past out of play."[143] The recognition of this freedom will cause *anguish;* the attempt to escape anguish leads to the denial of freedom and resultant self-deception or *bad faith*. This bad faith manifests itself in the attempt to give oneself a *Self*, a fixed characterization (like a Being-in-itself) and the attempt to give man in general an *'essence'*—a fixed nature. It is these famous doctrines to which we must now turn our attention.

Facticity and Transcendence:
Absurdity and Value
In our discussion of "Being-for-itself" and "Being-in-itself," we have rather glibly equated the former with human consciousness or human being. It is because of this equivalence that Sartre is able to say that man is *absolutely free,* and the radical existentialist theory of *absolute responsibility* follows from this. However, these doctrines are open to misinterpretation if we fail to see that this absolute freedom (and responsibility) exists only within a framework limited by one's *situation.* For example, Sartre would say that a young soldier on the battlefield or a young writer facing occupying Nazi troops is absolutely free to approach the situation as he chooses, but he is not at all free not to be there in that situation in which he must choose. In other words, the absolute choice, which is central to Sartre's existentialism, is itself subject to a kind of determination, the restriction of the range of alternatives by the situation in which the choice must be made.

A different way of putting this is to reject the original equation of Being-for-itself and human being, and replace it with the doctrine that man's being is *ambiguous.* Although Sartre does not make use of this term, it becomes a favorite vocabulary for DeBeauvoir (*Ethics of Ambiguity*) and Merleau-Ponty. (Heidegger has also used it in a special context.[144]) Man is both Being-in-itself and Being-for-itself. He is both a physical and biological organism in a particular situation in the world, and he is conscious and free. Man is thus a most peculiar entry in our ontology. He is both Being and nothingness, both bound by and free from his world. He can be viewed *both* as a free agent and as a victim of causal circumstance.

This 'ambiguous' picture of man is not at all new to us; it is Kant's two-standpoints view, Kierkegaard's subjective versus objective truth, and Husserl's natural versus phenomenological standpoint. Kant had held the two-standpoints to be equal in validity. Each standpoint— man as object, man as agent—was absolutely correct, and the 'antinomy' to which

this dualism gave rise was tolerated by Kant (and 'synthesized' by Hegel) because it was so very central to his philosophy. Kierkegaard, on the other hand, has no reservations about overstating the merits of the subjective viewpoint. Similarly, but with much more philosophical sophistication, Husserl argues that the phenomenological viewpoint is the correct one and the natural standpoint must be derivative of it. In a Kierkegaardian way, Sartre rejects a two-equivalent-standpoints view in favor of a one-standpoint view which degrades the natural or 'objective' or 'scientific' viewpoint and places before it a special first-person phenomenological stance. Similarly, Merleau-Ponty insists on the correctness of the first-person view,

I am not the outcome or the meeting point of the numerous causal agencies which determine my bodily or psychological make-up. I cannot conceive of myself as nothing but a bit of the world. . . . All my knowledge of the world, even my scientific knowledge, is gained from my own particular point of view . . . [145]

Merleau-Ponty, more than perhaps any other philosopher on the Continent (outside the Vienna circle at any rate), is centrally concerned with integrating the natural and 'social' sciences into his philosophical works. Thus, in our study of Sartre and Merleau-Ponty (as of all phenomenologists), we must keep in mind a vital, critical question—How much do their results depend on the peculiar phenomenological viewpoint they adopt? And, how much can these same truths be defended from another viewpoint, for example, the natural viewpoint? Behind this question, there is the overriding metaphilosophical question about the relative merits and competition among philosophical viewpoints. Does it make sense to claim that one viewpoint, for example, the phenomenological viewpoint, is the 'correct' one? We surely cannot attempt to provide an answer to this most important question in this study, but it is necessary to keep the question in mind as we proceed to discuss Sartre's very radical doctrine of human freedom and responsibility.

Sartre and Merleau-Ponty do not debate this question, but simply begin within the phenomenological position and do not attempt to look beyond it or move beyond its peculiar perspective. Therefore, their strong claims for the peculiar viewpoint of man as 'outside' the world order must always be tempered with the realization that this claim is made from *within* the phenomenological standpoint. At any rate, it is clear that, from this viewpoint, both Sartre and Merleau-Ponty are strongly anti-Kantian. There is no choice of views of man as determined object and as free agent. Man is necessarily free by virtue of the structures or 'condition' of Being-for-itself (both Sartre and Merleau-Ponty conscientiously avoid use of the standard notions of 'nature' and 'essence' in this context for reasons which will become evident throughout this chapter). The 'natural' view of man as an object of knowledge is a perversion of our 'primitive' view of man from a first-person standpoint. Furthermore, we have seen that even the view of man as *knower* is a view based on an inadequate analysis of human being. Man is first of all a *doer,* an agent who is involved or 'engaged' in the tasks of his practically demanding world.

Yet, in spite of this single standpoint within which man is necessarily free (because he, through acts of nihilation, is 'outside' of the causal determinations of the world), we have said that man is determined in very definite ways by his situation. A soldier may be free to fight or desert or commit suicide, but he is not free not to have been a soldier. The wish to have been in a different situation can never be more than empty because impossible. It can never be an intention, a plan of possible action. One's past is determinate—one's present situation is determined by that past. Human freedom must operate within the bounds of the facts of one's situation. Thus, even within Sartre's theory of absolute freedom, we must ask in which ways man is free and which ways he is not. A man is not free to do anything, for he is always restricted in his choices by certain facts. He cannot decide to walk in the grass because he is in prison; he cannot decide to desert because he is not in the army; he cannot marry the girl he loves because she will not have him. Thus, even for Sartre, we must distinguish those choices which are open to a man from those facts which are determined for him. Sartre's absolute freedom is therefore much less than overenthusiastic but ill-informed 'existentialists' would claim for it. It is not the ability "to do anything you want to do"; it is the restricted freedom (and necessity) within a situation to make choices.

Within Sartre's 'one-standpoint' view, however, two different perspectives towards oneself are discovered, and then even a third standpoint arises. This third standpoint, given little attention by Sartre (considerably more by Merleau-Ponty), is what Kant or Kierkegaard would refer to as the view of man as a physical natural object, as a physiological body. For Sartre, however, this is an essential perversion of our view of human beings, not the 'correct' or 'primitive' view of them at all. From his hasty dismissal of this 'physiological viewpoint,' we may already suspect that Sartre's attitude towards traditional Cartesian metaphysics which treats the human body as isolatable (in theory) from the human consciousness is considerably less than agreeable. Merleau-Ponty shares these views, but with much more concern for the proper place of the 'physiological' viewpoint. This "level of analysis," as he calls it, is valid so long as we realize its peculiarly derivative position in our conception of man. It is an incorrect view, he argues, only so long as we take this as *basic* knowledge of human being.

The first two perspectives mentioned are far more important for our understanding of human being. First, there is the 'primitive' or 'correct' view of oneself by oneself which forms the basis for the phenomenological and existential theory of man, but it is also possible to view ourselves from the standpoint of another person, to "see ourselves as others see us." Sartre and Merleau-Ponty agree that this is a viewpoint which is somehow philosophically inferior, but they are not anxious to dismiss it out of hand. It is important to see the difference between this third-person viewpoint and the perverted 'physiological' viewpoint. Looking at oneself as another is not equivalent to looking at oneself as a physical body. It is looking at oneself as another *person,* and this difference is all-important for the existentialists. Other persons have intentions and are conscious—bodies do not. To look at oneself as another person is not to look at oneself as an object.

What makes this second viewpoint so important is that it is the viewpoint adopted by most people and most philosophers most of the time. It is the viewpoint which Heidegger takes in his 'primitive' analysis of human *Existenz* as the view of oneself as an indistinguishable member of a *comraderie*—a *Mitsein*—and as an equally indistinguishable member of the *public*—*das Man*. It is, furthermore, the origin of the *self* in reflective consciousness for Sartre. It is only looking at ourselves as others see us that we attribute selfhood to ourselves. It is this view of oneself as another which will form one of the foundations of *bad faith*. It is Sartre's explicit task in philosophy (as it was Heidegger's nonexplicit task) to allow us to break out of this perspective of oneself as another and allow us to see ourselves as ourselves (that is, 'authentically' or 'sincerely').

It is only from the 'correct' *first-person* viewpoint that it becomes evident that we are both free within our situation but yet restricted by it. We are, therefore, both free to choose among alternatives within the situation, but not free to choose the situation itself. Insofar as we are free to choose, Sartre tells us that we have *transcendence;* insofar as we are determined by our situation, Sartre tells us we have *facticity.* Transcendence is based on our consciousness as freedom or Being-for-itself. Facticity is based on the determinacy of Being-in-itself. The term *facticity* (*facticität, facticité*), of course, comes directly from Heidegger's *Being and Time.* Transcendence (*La transcendance*) is a coinage by Sartre, but not an entirely fortunate one. We have seen several uses of similar terms in our studies thus far with which it can easily be confused. (Moreover, Sartre himself uses the term 'Transcendence' in the Husserlian context of talking about the objects of consciousness being 'outside' of consciousness. This cannot help but confuse a beginning reader.) *Facticity* and *transcendence* are parallel to Heidegger's "existential structures of Dasein"—*facticity* and *Existenz.* Heidegger's notion of *fallenness* has clear analogs in Sartre but is not elevated to a 'structure' equivalent in 'primitiveness' to these others.

Facticity is that set of *facts* about oneself which defines his *situation.* The "facts" that I am tall, Jewish, bald, French, an only child, living in the twentieth century, living in occupied France, are all part of my facticity. I may have an operation to shorten my legs, decide to escape from occupied France and give up my French citizenship, decide to renounce Judaism and convert to another faith, but these decisions are founded on the fact that I now find myself as tall, a Frenchman in occupied France, and Jewish. *Facticity* is "what makes a man what he is." All of one's past, therefore, is part of his facticity (Sartre sometimes tells us that a man's past *is* his facticity). One can act to change his present situation, and his future is 'open to him', but his past is simply there, as something of which to be ashamed, proud, inconvenienced, or used as a base for future exploits. The facts are there and not subject to my choices. Facticity, my situation, is simply *there* as *given* to me. It can be interpreted or given significance as I choose, but the facts remain. I may look at my past action of escaping from occupied France as an act of heroism and discretion, or I may view it as an act of cowardice, or I may view it simply as 'something that happened,' but I cannot wish it out of my past. It is a fixed part of me, regardless of how I attempt to capitalize on it, hide it from others, or suppress it from myself:

This inapprehensible fact of my condition . . . is the reason that the for-itself, while choosing the meaning of its situation and while constituting itself as the foundation of itself in situation, does not choose its position.[146]

Facticity is Heidegger's *thrownness*, man's simply finding himself in a particular situation which is not his choosing. Sartre expresses this same idea with his equally dramatic notion of *abandonment* (*délaissement*). He continuously insists that Being-in-itself which we confront is *de trop* or 'gratuitous'. It is unexplainable, that is, the entire situation is unexplainable; this is not to deny that particular parts of the situation can be explained in terms of other parts of that situation. For example, I cannot explain the existence of the world in general or everything in the world (as asked by Heidegger's 'question of being'), but I can explain the existence of my little brother by citing previous activities of my parents together with a large set of 'natural' laws. It is also unjustifiable; we can give no reason or defense of the situation (again as a whole, not simply one aspect of it). Yet Sartre wants to say that we are absolutely responsible for ourselves in that *de trop* situation:

This part of my condition [that I choose within my situation but do not choose it] is what causes me to apprehend myself as totally responsible for my being . . . and yet as totally unjustifiable.[147]

If Sartre argues that man is free but also determined, why should his philosophy be thought to be so very radical? The answer to this lies not in 'absolute freedom' in the popular sense which is close to human omnipotence, but in the extent to which he argues that we are free *within the situation.* For example, there are many 'facts' about ourselves which we would readily incorporate into our facticity which Sartre argues are not *facts* at all but conscious *choices* which are made in *bad faith.* Most important among these are those peculiar 'states' or events which philosophers have traditionally grouped together as the *passions.* There is a long-standing respectable philosophical and commonsense antagonism between Reason (and the ego), which is the 'real' us, and the passions, which act against reason and *happen to us.* We are overwhelmed by joy, overcome by sadness, struck by jealousy, incapacitated by anger, and we fall in love, are carried away by fear, are dumbstruck by terror, and float away in ecstasy. Passions are not ours, they are not chosen by us, but they are, according to this view, opponents of rational choice processes. One who is passionate is *ipso facto* said to be less "in control of himself." Sartre argues, first in his early essay on the *Emotions* and throughout *Being and Nothingness,* that this dichotomy is ill-founded, and that these so-called passions are not facts about us but conscious choices we make about our attitudes towards the world.

Similarly, traditional philosophy and common sense have been fond of speaking about the *facts* pertaining to a person's *personality* and *character.* It is a 'fact' about Garcin that he is a coward; it is a 'fact' about Daniel that he is a homosexual; it is a 'fact' about Meursault that he is insensitive. These facts are again not a choice of the person but simply part of what he is. As such, they are as if foreign determinants of his state of mind and his behavior. It is easy to see how traditional theories of the *determinism* of human behavior found a convenient take-off point from such 'facts.' Again, Sartre will argue that these are not facts at all, but consciously chosen projects.

This attempt to characterize people by the 'facts' concerning their emotional structure and temperament and personality has its most serious consequence in the attempt to ascribe such 'facts' to oneself. This attempt most often manifests itself in the attempt to describe one's *Self* or *ego* as the unity of these fixed facts about oneself, and it is here that we find the most pervasive instance of *bad faith.* On a more general basis, the attempt to define human *nature* or *essence* is but a more sophisticated way of defining one's own Self. Instead of simply characterizing a fixed set of 'facts' regarding oneself, one creates such a set of fictitious 'facts' about all men, applying this to oneself as a specific instance of *man.* This too is *bad faith,* and we are now prepared for an initial characterization of *bad faith* as the conscious refusal, the "mistake," of treating one's transcendence as facticity, of treating one's own choices as if they were facts imposed on one. The whole of deterministic psychology is primarily in *bad faith* as are all attempts to derive a *Self* for oneself. They are all attempts to find *excuses* for one's actions, to blame them on one's situation instead of taking responsibility for them. The radicalness of Sartre's philosophy does not lie in the phrase "absolute freedom," it lies in his often brilliant arguments to the effect that many of the alleged 'facts' we 'discover' about ourselves are in fact conscious choices. These choices—our interpretation of our situation—so deeply penetrate our facticity that it is not even possible to isolate a pure 'nude' fact:

It is impossible to grasp facticity in its brute nudity, since all that we will find of it is already recovered and freely constructed.[148]

A different way of characterizing the distinction between facticity and transcendence is by reference to the traditional distinction between *facts* and *values.* We have seen that Being-in-itself (and our *situation*) is characterized as that which presents itself, that which can be simply described as it is. As such, we have said that Being-in-itself or our situation presents itself as a set of *facts.* Being-for-itself or human consciousness has been characterized (somewhat opaquely) as "being what it is not and not being what it is"; in other words, consciousness cannot describe itself but must *prescribe* what it is *going to be*. Being-in-itself simply presents itself as is. Being-for-itself projects various possibilities for itself and places a value on these different alternatives. Value is "the beyond and the *for* of transcendence."[149] Transcendence is to be understood not as a detached consideration of possible courses of action, but as a concerned (even 'anguished') search for a value for these imminent possibilities. Again we find Sartre reacting to the traditional Cartesian-Husserlian overemphasis on knowledge. It is the practical evaluation of engagement in possible worlds, not the mere knowledge of them, which is central to acts of consciousness.

The characterization of the transcendence of the for-itself as the projection of possibilities and the "positing of values" leads us an important step closer to an understanding of Sartre's doctrine of freedom and its connection with the analysis of *nothingness* in the last section. We have already been told that Being-for-itself *is* nothingness and *is* freedom. Now we are told that Being-for-itself also *is* "being-for-value,"[150] and "both is and is not its own possibilities."[151] Thus we may see how this network of key concepts interrelates to form our conception of "human reality." Man is free to act as he chooses and he chooses according to his evaluations of various possible states of affairs—more accurately, possible situations for him—and he does so by virtue of the fact that consciousness is really nothingness. This *nothingness,* however, as forbidding as it sounds, is in turn analyzed in terms of *acts of nihilation.* The nothingness of consciousness is the ability to "wrench oneself away" from the real world and envision and evaluate possibilities for modifying that world. To say that man is "Being-for-value" is to stress simply one element of this complex equivalence (as Sartre is prone to do with each of the terms of this formula). The picture of human consciousness which we now begin to understand is a picture of a consciousness actively evaluating all possible situations, preparing itself to "modify the world" (and only occasionally reflecting on these conscious activities).

Values are "the beyond and the *for* of transcendence"; it is value that provides the direction in which consciousness attempts to "be itself." Now we encounter a familiar and vital feature of all existentialist thought. We have already begun to

argue that man as agent is 'outside' of the causal order of the world, and we have found that such diverse figures as Kant, Kierkegaard, and Sartre accept this thesis. However, Kant, although defending freedom of *action,* refused to defend freedom of rational *choice* regarding values. A man was free not to act according to the categorical imperative, but his act was *wrong* if he did so. In other words, Kant allowed that a man was free to act in any way he chose but was not free to act *correctly* in any way he chose. In Kierkegaard, we find an obvious contrast to this Kantian thesis; there is no correct "sphere of existence," and there is thus the 'freedom' to choose any among the three equally incorrect, equally correct value systems which he delineates. Sartre clearly sides with Kierkegaard on this issue, and maintains that human freedom entails freedom from 'rational' restrictions on choice as well as freedom from causal restrictions on choice. (At risk of becoming repetitious, we must again insist that the antirationality here is directed against Kant's peculiar notion of reason, and not against clear, careful, consistent, and coherent thinking.) There is no given morality or given values because there is no given human nature or given meaning or significance in any situation. Sartre, here going far beyond Kierkegaard in philosophical acuity, argues with Nietzsche that "there are no moral facts," and maintains (with many positivists) that there can be no *knowledge* of values. According to Sartre, values are posited by human beings; values are imposed on situations by consciousness. In a formula we have seen many times before, Sartre tells us that "it is only through human consciousness that value comes into the world."

The theory of value briefly argued by Sartre in *Being and Nothingness* is distinct from both the positivistic insistence that values are not known but are simply products of personal attitudes, and the naturalist thesis that values are a special kind of facts. According to Sartre, values are imposed on the world by human consciousness, yet they are to be found *'in the world.'* This thesis might well have seemed bizarre to us earlier, but we now find that it is simply a restatement of the analysis Sartre has given us for *nothingness. Nothingness* is experienced in the world but originates in conscious acts of nihilation. Similarly, values are located 'in the world' but originate in acts of evaluation by consciousness.

This thesis may be exemplified by Sartre's analysis of *desire*, a particular sort of evaluation. Desire is analyzed in terms of a *lack*, and here we find a convening point for many of the theses we have encountered earlier. First, we are reminded that conscious acts of nihilation necessarily turn to consciousness itself.

The for-itself cannot sustain nihilation without determining itself as a lack *of being.*[152]

It is this notion of a 'lack of being,' in turn, which forms the basis of the analysis of desire and, which in turn, forms the basis of the analysis of all human transcendence:

Of all internal negations, the one which penetrates most deeply into being . . . this negation is lack. . . . It appears in the world only with the upsurge of human reality. It is only in the human world that there can be lacks.[153]

In parallel with his argument from the human origins of nothingness to the nothingness of human consciousness, Sartre tells us that,

Human reality by which lack appears in the world must itself be a lack. . . . The existence of desire as a human fact is sufficient to prove that human reality is a lack.[154]

What is lacking, we are later told, is the being of Being-in-itself. In other words, consciousness is indeterminate, it lacks a fixed nature, and all desire is directed towards making itself determinate:

We have seen that human reality as for-itself is a lack and that what it lacks is a certain coincidence with itself.[155]

This determinacy towards which Being-for-itself strives is the *Self* or *ego;* all possibilities—desires specifically—are directed towards this Self:

The possible is the something which the for-itself lacks in order to be itself.[156]

Sartre's analysis of desire is notably similar to the analysis Hegel provides for us in the *Phenomenology.* Desire is the link between mere consciousness of the world and *Self*-consciousness of the world.[157] Desire is not a 'psychic state or a physical force' nor is it a 'fact about the world'. Our desires are recognitions of a certain lack (a failing, a dissatisfaction, a nothingness) in the world, but it is only our expectations of what the world *ought* to be like which allows us to perceive such lacks. We can see that Sartre's analysis of desire thus provides us with the way of maintaining, with regard to value in general, that values are both in the world (for example, experienced by us as lacks in the world) and yet that values have their origins in human consciousness. It is because we expect the world to be such-and-such that we experience the world as lacking. Ultimately, of course, all lacks are said to be lacks in human consciousness itself, since all expectations arise from the peculiar condition of consciousness as indeterminate.

What the for-itself lacks is the self, or itself as in-itself.[158] This lack can never be fulfilled; human beings cannot have all their desires satiated nor can they have all values fulfilled. This is for Hegel the "endless infinite movement" of desire ("life"), and it is what Sartre refers to as "man's impossible wish to be God." The transcendence of human reality is a continual "surpassing" or desire to actualize ("realize") its (indefinitely many) possibilities,

Human reality is a perpetual surpassing toward a coincidence with itself which is never given.[159]

Because this "coincidence with itself" is an ('onto')logical impossibility, human reality is said to be "by nature an unhappy consciousness with no possibility of surpassing its unhappy state."[160] It is thus that man strives to be God, and thus that God is an impossible ideal. We may now go beyond our former presentation of this problem by adding that the attempt to be God is commensurate to the attempt to be one's Self. The Self, like God, is both free and determinate, both in and for-itself; ultimately,

it is the individual completion of the self which haunts the for-itself.[161]

The search for a Self—the project of self-realization—is the attempt of man to be in-himself, to be pure facticity. The fact of consciousness, man's transcendence, makes such Being-in-itself impossible. At every point in a man's life, we can point to his transcendence—the possibilities open to him for the future—as well as identifying his facticity—the facts about his life which determine his present situation. Summarily, we have commented that a person's facticity is his *past* (as Heidegger's *facticität* is so interpreted) and a person's transcendence (Heidegger's *Existenz*) is his *future*. This allows us to explain a recurrent theme in Sartre's novels and plays as well as in *Being and Nothingness,* the doctrine that a man *is* the sum total of his past actions,

A man is nothing else but the sum of his actions, nothing else but what his life is . . . The genius of Proust is in the totality of the works of Proust.[162]

A man can be characterized as a Self (as an "essence") only with reference to his past; his future cannot be so characterized because it has yet to be determined what *Self* a man will strive to be ("a man is not what he is"). It is only at a man's death that we can say *what he is,* interpret the sum total of his actions thus far as the characterization ("essence") of the man. Thus, Garcin in *No Exit*[163] can be said to be a coward, irredeemably, because the sum total of his actions in life (he is now dead and in Hell) are cowardly actions. At no point within his life would this have been true of him. Death is the end of one's possibilities—the end of one's transcendence—and thus marks the point at which we can finally treat a man as a Being-in-himself. Of course, we can never treat ourselves as a Being-in-itself, because every moment we are alive offers us new choices and new possibilities. At death, we cannot treat ourselves as anything (thus the frustration of Garcin wishing to redeem himself while in Hell). Being-in-itself is pure "coincidence with itself," but by virtue of this "coincidence" it cannot be conscious of this; the life of a man is essentially dissatisfied and unfulfilled. Only his death satisfies and fulfills him, but not necessarily according to his own projects and goals for him-*Self.* (The satisfaction of death lies solely in man's final 'coincidence with himself," not in the fulfillment of any particular ideal for him-*Self.* Garcin desired to be heroic; his ful-

fillment at death completed his life as cowardly.)

The above discussion evidences a marked deviation from Heidegger's conception of Dasein as "Being-unto-death." For Heidegger, death is man's ultimate and 'ownmost' possibility. It is the "end" (goal as well as termination) of a man's life. Sartre clearly acknowledges the importance of death but denies its value as a goal in living. To be sure,

death haunts me at the very heart of each of my projects as their inevitable reverse side.[164]

Death is only a "boundary"[165] of human life, and it is not part of my life or part of my future or part of my possibilities at all. It is not

my possibility but . . . the possibility that there are for me no longer any possibilities . . . Death is not an obstacle to my projects. . . . Since death is always beyond my subjectivity, there is no place for it in my subjectivity.[166]

I may and probably must live with the knowledge that I am going to die, but I need not—Sartre at least implies that I *ought* not—take my death as any sort of goal. Death is simply the end of my possibilities; it is not one of my possibilities. Sartre's analysis of human reality as necessarily unfulfilling may be interestingly compared with the equally famous doctrine of "The Absurd" in the philosophy of Albert Camus. The tension between the for-itself and in-itself which makes the human 'condition' the impossible desire to be God (one-*Self*) is the same tension between the 'rational' and the 'irrational' in Camus that makes the human condition 'absurd.' Camus, unlike Sartre, is shamelessly *dis*interested in epistemology and ontology, and his philosophy of the 'absurd' is left without explanation or defense. There is the absurd, we are told, and that is the insight from which philosophy must *begin:*

the absurd, hitherto taken as a conclusion is considered in this essay as a starting point.[167]

My reasoning wants to be faithful to the evidence that aroused it. That evidence is the absurd. It is that divorce between the mind that desires and the world that disappoints, my nostalgia for unity, this fragmented universe and the contradiction that binds them together.[168]

The absurd is the world's noncooperation with basic human desires:

At this point of his effort man stands face to face with the irrational. He feels within him his longing for happiness and for reason. The absurd is born of this confrontation between the human need and the unreasonable silence of the world.[169]

the Absurd is not in man . . . nor in the world, but in their presence together. For the moment it is the only bond uniting them.[170]

The absurd is the failure of the world to satisfy human expectations of it, Sartre's for-itself struggling to become in-itself (that is, satisfied) but necessarily separated:

this mind and this world straining against each other without being able to embrace each other.[171]

For Camus as well as Sartre God becomes the necessary but 'impossible' ideal for man, but Sartre's God is the immanent satisfaction desired by man. Camus's God is clearly transcendent, a unifying personifying force which robs the world of its 'irrationality' (failure to satisfy our expectations of it). God is "the negation of human reason,"[172] and the 'leap of faith' to God by Kierkegaard is condemned by Camus (as "philosophical suicide"),[173] as a dishonest refusal to see the 'evidence' that the world is irrational and impersonal. Interestingly, Camus also considers Husserl's phenomenology a philosophy which begins with "absurd procedures" (by attempting to only describe and not explain the world), but culminates in philosophical suicide with unwarranted faith in "eternal Reason" and "essences";

From the abstract God of Husserl to the dazzling god of Kierkegaard the distance is not so great. Reason and the irrational lead to the same preaching. . . . The abstract philosopher and the religious philosopher start out from the same disorder and support each other in the same anxiety.[174]

We may appreciate how the very different philosophical temperaments of Camus and Sartre lead them from very different starting points—the problem of suicide for Camus, the phenomenology of Husserl for Sartre—to a remarkably similar doctrine. Man expects of the world what the world, because it is unresponsive ('irrational', 'silent', 'in-itself'), will not yield. To counteract this unhappy situation ("The Absurd"), man takes as his ideal a God for whom the world and man's desires are commensurate, a God who is 'in- and for-itself', but this ideal is impossible. For Camus, it is a "nostalgia" that overcomes reason; for Sartre, it is an ontologically contradictory notion, and so man is "abandoned" or "condemned" to be essentially dissatisfied, to face the absurd. The affinities between the two thinkers become much more pronounced as their differences become more spirited in the ethical consequences each attempts to draw from this 'ontological' starting point. We shall discuss this in a later section.

Existential Freedom:
Action, Intention, and Emotion

There is no concept more central to 'existentialist' thought than the concept of 'freedom'. Kierkegaard insisted that *human being, subjectivity,* and *freedom* were equivalent; Heidegger similarly interprets *Dasein* as *freedom.* Sartre makes the concept of *freedom* the defining 'structure' of the for-itself or human consciousness;

What is at the very heart and center of Existentialism is the absolute character of the free commitment, by which every man realizes himself. . . .[175]

Only freedom can account for man in his totality.[176]

Freedom is existence and in it existence precedes essence.[177]

Freedom is the recurrent theme in every author who is identified with this 'movement':

Once I am free, I am not to be counted among things, and I must then be uninterruptedly free.[178]

Every man is originally free, in the sense that he spontaneously casts himself into the world.[179]

Thinking of the future, establishing aims for oneself, having preferences—all this presupposes a belief in freedom.[180]

Thanks to freedom and Transcendence . . . (man's) finiteness is unique in comparison with other finite things in the world. . . .[181]

Man is essentially . . . 'freedom': freedom not in the sense of indeterminacy but in the sense of being able to determine himself through decisions in the center of his being.[182]

To be freed from belief that there is no freedom is indeed to be free.[183]

Freedom is also a key concept in the works of many obviously nonexistentialist thinkers, for example, Kant, Hegel, and Husserl. The doctrine that man is essentially *free* does not suffice to distinguish those philosophies which are peculiarly 'existentialist.'

Perhaps there is no single doctrine of human freedom which is common to Sartre, Merleau-Ponty, De Beauvoir, Camus, Marcel, Jaspers, Tillich, Buber, and other existentialists. However, certain peculiarly existentialist themes recur in their various philosophies: the doctrine that there is no human nature or 'essence', that "man makes himself"; and the thesis that human freedom entails not only freedom from causal determination but a freedom from rational, moral, divine, or 'naturalistic' imposition of values or goals. Both theses clearly distinguish the above figures from Kant, Hegel, and Husserl, who attempted to analyze the *essence* of human reality and who argued that human values and goals could be *objectively* or *rationally* validated. Existentialist *freedom* is both freedom from causal determination and from rational coercion.

We have already seen that Sartre's *absolute freedom* is not the exaggerated popular claim that "a man can do anything he wants to do," but rather that man is always free *within his situation to confer significance upon that situation.* Absolute freedom is thus freedom of *intention* (in the broad phenomenological sense as well as the more narrow sense in which we speak of behavioral intentions). Freedom is limited by one's situation, and freedom is absolute only within these limitations:

Our freedom does not destroy our situation, but gears itself to it.[184]

Man, as finite freedom, is free within the contingencies of his finitude.[185]

For example, I may today decide whether or not to volunteer for military service and, provided that I fulfill the physical and antispiritual requirements for acceptance, I have absolute freedom to volunteer or not. If I decide to volunteer today and two months hence I begin to reconsider my decision, my situation does not provide me with the freedom to choose simply, as I did before, whether to volunteer or not. My new situation demands that my decision, not to be in the military any longer, entails the most grave of alternatives. I may face prison or death as alternatives to continued service. I do not have the freedom to choose, as I once did, simply to be an uncommitted civilian. My absolute choice is now restricted by the fact that I am in the military.

The situation itself, while clearly restricting my choices in this way, does not *determine* my choice. The fact that I am committed to the military, for example, does not determine my continued loyal services. I can always decide that prison is preferable, or that the risk of death is worth the chance of escape. The situation is the *basis* for my choice (my already being in the military is the basis for my decision to desert or to remain there), but it is never a sufficient condition for my choice (it cannot compel me to desert or stay).

The choice we make within the situation depends on how we see that situation, how we interpret it, what significance we place on it. If I look at my position in the military as progress towards self-fulfillment, or if I interpret my service as an ideal sort of behavior, then my choice will be to remain in the military. However, if I see my membership in the military was an obstacle to my fulfillment of my life goals, or if I interpret my participation in the military as complicity in a national crime, then I shall choose to resist my military commitment. The significance we impose on our situation would thus seem to be the determinant of our choice within our situation. However, the significance we impose and the choices we make are inseparable. The situation itself, we have already noted, is already so permeated with interpretations and significances which we have posited in it that "nude facticity" is unavailable to us. Similarly,

The situation, *the common product of the contingency of the in-itself and of freedom, is an ambiguous phenomenon in which it is impossible for the for-itself to distinguish the contribution of freedom from that of the brute* existent.[186]

It is our ultimate choice of projects or ends which determines our view of the situation. There is no "brute existent" which presents itself to us for interpretation and subsequently as a basis for choice:

[*The*] *situation . . . is revealed to this freedom only as* already illuminated *by the end which freedom chooses.*[187]

Our situation is an interpreted text with goals and demands for action imposed on it by us. This interpreted situation is found by us as a complex of facticity and imposed possibilities. It makes no sense to say we are in an 'unfortunate' situation apart from any projects of our own which make this situation unfortunate for us, and it makes less sense to have projects in isolation from the situation in which these projects can be realized.

This understanding of absolute freedom as freedom within a situation will allow us to appreciate the difference between the bold and obviously false claim that human beings are absolutely free to do what they want and the more reasonable claim (made by Sartre) that human beings are absolutely free to choose their own projects and impose their own interpretations on the situation in which they find themselves (that is, in which they are "thrown" or "abandoned"). The first claim sounds ridiculously similar to a claim for human omnipotence, the ability to succeed at anything attempted, but failure is clearly possible on the more reasonable interpretation. I may freely choose to assassinate a tyrant, but be prevented from carrying out my plan by the tyrant's spies who capture me. Or, I may find the situation fully conducive to my assassination attempt, but fail simply because I am a terrible marksman. My choice has been free in any case; my action never succeeds in spite of my free choice. Absolute freedom is freedom of choice, freedom of intention,

or freedom of signification (these are ultimately equivalent) and not freedom of success in action;

"to be free" does not mean "to obtain what one has wished" but rather "by oneself to determine oneself to wish" (in the broad sense of choosing). In other words, success is not important to freedom.[188]

There is no denial that external circumstances may thwart action or cause actions to fumble, but Sartre does maintain that all such 'external circumstances' are such only in view of the goals we seek to achieve;

Human-reality everywhere encounters resistance and obstacles which it has not created, but these resistances and obstacles have meaning only in and through the free choice which human reality is.[189]

We may illustrate this with an example from Merleau-Ponty;

When I saw that this rock is unclimbable, it is certain that this attribute, like that of being big or little, straight and oblique, and indeed like all attributes in general, can be conferred upon it only by the project of climbing it, and by a human presence. It is, therefore, freedom which brings into being the obstacles to freedom, so that the latter can be set over against it as its bounds.[190]

If we were not intending to climb the rock, it would not be unclimbable for us, nor would its size and obliqueness present obstacles to us. It is only so far as we have expectations of success in climbing the rock that we find the rock to be an obstacle. The choice of the project of climbing or simply strolling by is entirely ours, but our success in climbing depends as much on the rock as it does on us. We are absolutely free to form the project and try to climb; we are not absolutely free to reach the top of the rock.

My success may be limited not only by obstacles in my way and by my own incompetence, but by unforeseen interferences which were not (for me) part of my choice situation at all. It may be that my decision to assassinate the tyrant took into account the many dangers of such a plan and the many chances for failure due to misfires, bad aim, premature discovery of the plot and so on, but I decide to attempt the assassination in the face of these obstacles. My plan fails because someone else assassinates the tyrant before I have my opportunity. From a third-person standpoint, we should wish to say that this sort of obstacle to success is in no way different from the foreseen obstacles, but it is here that the phenomenological standpoint makes a sharp difference. Foreseen obstacles are part of the situation, that is, always the situation *for the person,* and choices and interpretations are made taking these obstacles (which become obstacles only through these choices and interpretations) into account. However, unforeseen obstacles, because the person is ignorant of them, do not form part of his situation. I do not make a brave decision because I decide to drive my car across the bridge (not knowing that the bridge is about to collapse), and I am not a coward because I leave France *before* I hear that there has been a German invasion. My choice is free and I am responsible for it only as far as that choice was made in my situation.

Although Sartre's theory of human freedom is often interpreted in grossly implausible formulations which emphasize the concept of 'absolute freedom' and ignore the restrictions of the situation to which this notion is tied, we may find a close similarity between Sartre's notion of 'freedom' and a traditional conception of 'voluntary action' in Aristotle's *Nichomachean Ethics.* Aristotle instructs us that an action is involuntary if it is performed out of ignorance or has been determined by "external compulsion." An act is voluntary if it is performed knowingly and free of "external compulsion."[191] Sartre also allows that men are not always responsible for their actions, that is, the *success* of their actions, and that ignorant and contravening circumstances may absolve responsibility by restricting freedom (of success). Sartre allows no leniency with regard to responsibility for one's intentions and one's choices, for the freedom to intend and the freedom to choose is absolute.

Sartre does maintain that human beings have *freedom of action,* and it is necessary for us to distinguish a meaning for this claim which emerges only slowly from *Being and Nothingness* and is often neglected in more 'popular' writings. We

have said that the absolute freedom of which Sartre speaks is freedom of *intention,* both in the broad Husserlian sense in which an intention is any positing of significance and in the narrow ordinary sense in which an intention is an intention *to do* something. Sartre wishes to argue—along with an overwhelming number of British-American philosophers in a very different idiom—that intentions (to act) are inseparably tied to the actions themselves. To intend to act is to act, according to this argument, and freedom of intention must *ipso facto* be freedom of action. Does Sartre, therefore, wish to make the very strong claim for absolute freedom which we have interpreted as a ridiculous claim for human omnipotence?

We must distinguish, as Sartre does not, between different levels of action. We speak unphilosophically of my action of assassination or desertion or climbing the rock. Upon further analysis, however, we find this *action* may be broken up into indefinitely many actions. For example, we might claim that my action of assassinating the tyrant consists of my shooting my rifle and the resultant death of the tyrant. Or, we might claim that the action is my pulling the trigger and the resultant shooting of the tyrant by the rifle. Or, we might claim that the action is my moving my finger and the resultant firing of the rifle and so on. Furthermore, we might claim that my act was not an act of assassination at all but simply an act of murder. The assassination was not my action but the result of the murder plus a convention to the effect that murder of statesmen constitutes assassination. Or else, we might claim that I did not murder anybody but simply fired a bullet in a certain direction which subsequently passed through several objects. The murder of a man is the result of my firing the rifle plus a convention which calls the act of firing a bullet through an object which happens to be a man resulting in his death a "killing" and an additional law which makes such killings illegal and thereby a "murder." More problematically, we may wish to say that all of the above descriptions of the assassination are too remote from the 'original' action, the act of *willing* which initiated the finger movement, the trigger pulling and so on. Thus we may wish to say that the action for which I am absolutely responsible because I was absolutely free to choose it is only the first 'original' act of *willing.*

This thesis is to be clearly located in Kant's ethics, and it is because he considers all of the 'events' subsequent to the act of willing to be mere contingencies that he confines his attribution of responsibility and praise and blame to "the Will alone." We have already seen that Sartre denies the relevance of *success* to freedom, and we can conclude that it is not the act of assassination which we are absolutely free to *perform*. External circumstances may interfere with our 'action' at virtually any 'level'; the wound may not be fatal, the rifle may misfire, my finger may be paralyzed, and so we would not want to maintain absolute freedom to perform any of these 'actions' either, even the minimal action of moving my finger. Thus Sartre distinguishes between "freedom of choice" and "freedom of obtaining" (a distinction he attributes to Descartes),[192] and insists that it is only freedom of choice which he defends. Sartre avoids the Kantian idealist notion of "Willing," but his thesis approximates the Kantian focus on willing. It is in the formation of intentions, the making of choices in and interpretations of our situation, that we are free absolutely. Since every intention (to act) is already to act, the freedom to choose or intend is also the freedom to perform at least the most minimal action. This minimal action need not be the initiation of a bodily movement, for as we argued above, even such actions are open to failure. One might say that Sartre argues with Kant that we are always absolutely free to will whether or not any further 'action' results, but we may avoid the problematic notion of "Willing" altogether by restating the Sartrian thesis in humble everyday terms. One is always absolutely free *to try* to do whatever he chooses according to his fundamental choices of his projects and his interpretations of his situation.

It is in this sense that both Sartre and Merleau-Ponty can insist that freedom makes no sense unless there are obstacles —possibly overwhelming obstacles—to success, and because of this limited notion of 'absolute freedom' that Sartre, Merleau-Ponty, Camus, and De Beauvoir (as well as the 'religious' existentialists) bizarrely maintain that a slave or a prisoner is as free as a master or a "free" man:

When we declare that the slave is as free in his chains as his master, we do not speak of a freedom which would remain undetermined. The slave in chains is
free to break them; this means that the very meaning of his chains will appear to him in the light of the end which he will have chosen; to remain a slave or to risk the worst in order to get rid of his slavery. Of course, the slave will not be able to obtain the wealth and standard of living of his master; but these are not the objects of his projects. He can only dream of the possession of these treasures . . . it is necessary fundamentally to choose himself on the ground of slavery and thereby to give a meaning to this obscure constraint . . . just because the life of a slave who revolts and dies in the course of this revolt is a free life, . . . just because the urgent and principal problem of this life is "shall I attain my goal?" . . . the situation of the slave cannot be compared with that of the master.[193]

Absolute freedom thus refers us to choice, intention, 'trying', and 'adopting a conduct'. My freedom is my awareness "that *nothing* can compel me to adopt that (particular) conduct."[194] One choice of conduct which is almost always open to us, of course, is the choice of obliterating our situation by killing ourselves. Even such 'desperate' conduct is always a matter of choice and a matter of the projects we chose for our-*Selves:*

If nothing *compels me to save my life,* nothing *prevents me from precipitating myself into the abyss. The decisive conduct will emanate from a self which I am not yet.*[195]

It is the act of suicide which Camus (in a very different temperament but for very similar reasons to Heidegger's) considers to be the *ultimate* human choice. It is important to note that there is a fundamental difference in this choice between Camus and Sartre in spite of the superficial similarities between them. For Camus, the feeling of the absurd is 'given' to us or "strikes us in the face,"[196] and suicide is a response to this feeling. This feeling of the absurd, however, is not "brute existence" or facticity but an interpretation of the world as nonsatisfying which in turn depends on a set of demands which we have already placed before the world. What Camus is doing, therefore, is to take this interpretation of the world as something presented to us and he does not allow for the possibility of our conscious alteration of that interpretation. It is thus that Sartre does not commit himself to "keeping the absurd alive" with Camus, for he sees our absolute freedom to destroy the absurd, which is, after all, only one of our interpretations, and to replace it with an alternative interpretation and project. Our freedom in a situation does not compel us to view our situation as absurd because the absurd is our creation, a replaceable creation, in the first place.

We are already well informed of the origins of this freedom; it is in acts of nihilation, specifically, acts of self-nihilation in which human freedom is born. It is because consciousness—human reality —is *nothing* that he is 'outside' of the causal order of the world. Man is not an object in the world, Buber tells us several years before Sartre's writing of *Being and Nothingness*,

The unlimited reign of causality in the world of the it, *of fundamental importance for the scientific ordering of nature, does not weigh heavily on man, who is not limited to the world of the* it.[197]

The 'existentialist' theory of freedom is not limited to freedom from *causal* determination of choice. It also maintains freedom from rational or moral or divine or naturalistic coercion to accept any particular project or any particular interpretation of the world. This thesis is held even by those religious existentialists who wish to maintain belief in God as the ultimate "project." We may remind ourselves that Kierkegaard left the choice of the religious sphere open for us but he refused any arguments to the effect that such a choice would be 'rational' or 'correct'. Similarly for Jaspers, Marcel, Buber, Tillich, and other existentialists who wish to maintain their faith in God, God is a choice, a commitment, and not the correct or rational end of life. Freedom is free choice among equally correct (and equally incorrect) projects or styles of life.

Central to this notion of freedom from *rational* coercion is the doctrine that human beings have no *nature* or *essence;*

If man as the Existentialist sees him is not definable, it is because to begin with he is nothing. He will not be anything until later, and then he will be what he makes of himself.[198]

If this is taken literally, we may well wonder what Sartre has been attempting to describe throughout the many hundreds of pages of *Being and Nothingness*, which purportedly is an analysis of human reality, but we are told that,

although it is impossible to find in each and every man a universal essence that can be called human nature, there is nevertheless a human universality of condition . . . By this condition they [thinkers of today] understand, with more or less clarity, all the limitations which a priori define man's fundamental situation in the universe.[199]

Although there are clearly objections to this maneuver as nothing more than wordplay, the significance of this thesis becomes evident in the question of the correctness of any 'given' system of projects or values. The analysis of the human 'condition' as *nothing(ness)* carries with it the conclusion that there can be no a priori values for man and no naturalistic values as well. The first part of this thesis, the impossibility of a priori values, is familiar to us from Kierkegaard and from Nietzsche. However, both Kierkegaard and Nietzsche remained attached to naturalistic justifications for value; Kierkegaard in his subjective appeal to the passions for support, and Nietzsche, quite explicitly, in his appeal to the naturalistic hypothesis of the *Will to Power.* Sartre rejects not only all "rationalistic" criteria for values (for example, Kant's categorical imperative), but also all 'natural' criteria. If man is not part of the natural order, then there is no place for a natural theory of value. We have already seen that value, for Sartre, is essentially a product of human nihilating activity; values cannot, therefore, be simply given in our situation. In short, Sartre becomes a *Nihilist* considerably more radical than Nietzsche. There are no human values, no human goals or projects, other than those which men choose for themselves.

In his more popular writings, but not in *Being and Nothingness*, Sartre bases his nihilism on the rejection of the belief in God, much as Nietzsche does in his *Zarathustra.* Like Nietzsche, Sartre sees the incredible consequences of atheism, and, in *Existentialism Is a Humanism*, he reinterprets the concept of 'abandonment' as the doctrine of atheism (in *Being and*

Nothingness, it refers simply to the *de trop* character of our situation);

[by "abandonment"] we only mean to
say that God does not exist, and that it
is necessary to draw the consequences
of his absence right to the end . . .
Dostoyevsky once wrote, "if God did not
exist, everything would be permitted";
and that, for Existentialism, is the starting
point.[200]

It is with the disappearance of God that
we lose the possibility of the a priori values of Kant's ethics. The nonexistence of
God is not simply the dispensing of a
hypothesis which has been found to be
unnecessary and costly;

The existentialist, on the contrary, finds it
extremely embarrassing that God does not
exist, for there disappears with him all
possibility of finding values in an
intelligible heaven.[201]

We find this doctrine echoes in De
Beauvoir;

The genuine man will not agree to
recognize any foreign absolute . . . He
bears responsibility for a world which is
not the work of a strange power, but of
himself, where his defeats are inscribed,
and his victories as well.[202]

And in Camus,[203]

I don't know whether this world has a
meaning that transcends it. But I know
that I do not know that meaning and that
it is impossible for me just now to know it.
What can a meaning outside my condition
mean to me?[204]

It is on the basis of this absence of
transcendent meaning or value that existentialism becomes a form of nihilism, but
this nihilism is to be replaced by a new
source of values, as we found in
Nietzsche. For the existentialists, this new
source is human *freedom*. (The new
source for Nietzsche was human psychology, specifically the *Will to Power*.) We
shall treat "existentialist ethics" at greater
length in a subsequent section. For the
present, it will suffice to comment that the
ethics based on human freedom is an ethics of commitment and not an ethics of
whim or caprice;

Even if my choice is determined by no a
priori value whatever, it can have
nothing to do with caprice.[205]

Life has a meaning if we really wish to
give it one. First of all we must act, throw
ourselves into some enterprise. Then, if
later we reflect on it, the die is already
cast; we are committed.[206]

One can choose anything, but only if it
is upon the plane of free commitment.[207]

Similarly for Camus, the only meaning in
the world is due to human demand for
meanings;

I continue to believe that this world has
no higher meaning, But I know that
something in it has meaning and that is
man; for he is the one being to insist on
having a meaning.[208]

Thus again we may conclude that the
freedom at the basis of existentialism is
essentially freedom of *intention* (in Husserl's general sense), the freedom to interpret the world and assign values to it of
one's own choosing.

The freedom of which we have been
speaking is freedom of *prereflective* consciousness. Consciousness is freedom even
before it has been made (reflectively) aware
of its freedom. It is in *anguish* (*Angoisse*)
that man becomes conscious of his freedom.

It is in anguish that man becomes the
consciousness of his freedom, or if you
prefer, anguish is the mode of being
of freedom as consciousness of being; it
is in anguish that freedom is, in its being,
in question for itself.[209]

It is important to emphasize that the
experience of anguish depends upon
freedom and cannot be cited as a proof
of human freedom . . . anguish has not
appeared to us as a proof of human
freedom; the latter was given to us as the
necessary condition for the question.[210]

In other words, we must presuppose freedom in order to describe the feeling as
anguish:

We wished only to show that there is a
special consciousness of freedom, and we

wished to show that this consciousness is anguish.[211]

Sartre credits the centrality of this concept of *Angst* to Kierkegaard, who precedes him in "characterizing it as anguish in the face of freedom." He also notes that Heidegger's concept of *Angst* appears very different as the "apprehension of nothingness." Because Sartre has argued that freedom and nothingness are equivalent, he concludes that

these two descriptions of anguish do not appear to us as contradictory; on the contrary the one implied the other.[212]

Once again we may distinguish *anguish* from *fear* by noting that fear is fear of particular objects while *anguish* is, according to Kierkegaard, a "nameless dread." According to Sartre, fear is fear of "Beings-in-the-world";

anguish is anguish before myself. Vertigo is anguish to the extent that I am afraid not of falling over the precipice but of throwing myself over. A situation provokes fear if there is a possibility of my life being changed from without; my being provokes anguish to the extent that I distrust myself and my own reactions in that situation.[213]

Anguish occurs as we recognize our own responsibility—'causal' responsibility—for what we do and what we are. Anguish also occurs, however, at our own responsibility for our values and projects, and for the absence of such values as absolutes;

There is ethical anguish when I consider myself in my original relation to values. . . . It is the anguish before values which is the recognition of the ideality of values.[214]

This is not to deny, of course, that our everyday 'moral' and evaluative dealings are free from anguish and simply encounters with environmentally 'given' values:

In fact I am engaged in a world of values . . . The immediate is the world with its urgency. . . . Values are sown in my path as thousands of little real demands, like signs which order us to keep off the grass.[215]

What we might call everyday morality is exclusive of ethical anguish.[216]

The recognition of our freedom and responsibility—the recognition that these everyday values are not 'given' but willfully accepted for no reason at all—can initiate anguish as soon as we gain the perspective (Heidegger's "authentic view of time") to see our lives and our routines as a whole:

Rising, streetcar, four hours in the office or the factory, meal, streetcar, four hours of work, meal, sleep, and Monday, Tuesday, Wednesday, Thursday, Friday and Saturday according to the same rhythm—this path is easily followed most of the time. But one day the "why" arises and everything begins in that weariness tinged with amazement. . . . Mere "anxiety" as Heidegger calls it, is at the source of everything.[217]

Because anguish arises with (or *is*) the recognition of one's freedom, and because freedom is consciousness and consciousness always must have the ability to know itself, there can be no escape from the possibility of anguish. For Sartre, as for Kierkegaard and Heidegger, anguish is an essential characteristic of man. This is not to say that it is a constant experience. On the contrary. Sartre maintains that it is rare, but nearly all the existential philosophers we have been discussing agree that anguish is not simply one more human emotion, but a definitive structure of human being:

the anxiety which is despair is not always present. But the rare occasions on which it is present determine the interpretation of existence as a whole.[218]

For Heidegger, it is confrontation with the possibility of death which insures the manifestation of *Angst* even in the most rigidly inauthentic people. For Sartre, on the other hand, death plays little role in the recognition of freedom and the experience of anguish. Rather this recognition is forced upon us in any number of choice situations, situations in which our everyday routines will not suffice but which require a reconsideration of our entire perspective on our world. It is for this reason that Sartre's plays and novels so often take wartime situations as their setting, for it is in such extraordinary situations that we are forced into confrontation with ourselves.

The discomfort of anguish drives man to attempt to "flee from anguish," and it is in this flight that man searches for excuses for himself, interpretations of his situation (which are presented not as interpretations but as *facts*) which limit his freedom and responsibility. It is in this search for excuses that *bad faith* is born. Because the possibility of anguish is always with us, the tendency to bad faith is always with us as well. This "necessary possibility" of bad faith leads Sartre into some confusion we shall see, for he tends to conclude from the inevitable tendency to bad faith that bad faith is unavoidable. The attempted escape from anguish takes on the character of the attempt to see ourselves as things or to see ourselves not as ourselves but as an other would see us;

Thus we flee from anguish by attempting to apprehend ourselves from without as an Other or as a thing.[219]

According to the analysis of human reality in Sartre,

every event in the world can be revealed to me only as an opportunity . . . *or as a chance.*[220]

The accompanying anguish causes most of us most of the time "to flee anguish in bad faith." This flight takes on characteristic behaviors, most centrally the attempts to interpret one's possibilities as part of his facticity. All such attempts are attempts to give oneself a *Self* or *Ego*, to make oneself into a thing with fixed characteristics and projects. Every form of psychological determinism is such an escape from anguish through an attempt to turn oneself into a thing;

psychological determinism, before being a theoretical conception, is first an attitude of excuse, or, if you prefer, the basis of all attitudes of excuse. . . . Psychological determinism denies that transcendence of human reality which makes it emerge in anguish beyond its own essence.[221]

Among the theories of psychological determinism, Sartre is most concerned with psychoanalytic theory as taught by Freud. His theory of unconscious determination of consciousness is the most explicit and the most convincing of all such theories.

Whereas Sartre insists that an understanding of man relies primarily on the appreciation of the importance of future possibilities, psychoanalysis does not even recognize "the dimension of the future."[222] Similarly in ethics, we find traditional 'theories' of ethics primarily systems of excuses, attempts to deny or ignore the freedom of choice which is the 'condition' of man and posit values which are 'given' as absolutes. All theories of universalization, for example, Kant's categorical imperative, are such systems of excuses, for their purpose is to provide us with a decision mechanism which takes the burden of choice of values from our shoulders. In the same vein, Merleau-Ponty tells us that

the classical concept of deliberation is relevant only to a freedom in "bad faith."[223]

Deliberation already presupposes a fixed set of criteria according to which one deliberates. The only adequate ethics is an ethics which rejects all 'given' absolutes. All other ethics are attempts to escape responsibility and anguish. The nature of this flight from anguish in bad faith should now be reasonably evident. Bad faith is the attempt to take one's situation and one's reactions to it as pure facticity and deny one's own interpretive evaluative role in that situation. Causal determinism in general is the attempt to argue that everything about a man is pure facticity, that there is no possibility and no transcendence. Psychological determinism is the more specific thesis that there are sufficient antecedent causal factors to determine every feeling, every idea, every intention, and every choice. Traditional ethics is the similar attempts to argue that there are rational determinations of the 'correct' conception of oneself and the 'correct' projects for oneself. Every attempt to speak of one's *Self* and *ego* is primarily an attempt to interpret one's own actions, feelings, and decisions as matters of extrapersonal determination. All such attempts are really attempts to find excuses. However,

the peculiar character of human-reality is that it is without excuse.[224]

I am condemned to be free. This means that no limits to my freedom can be found except freedom itself or, if you prefer, that we are not free to cease being free.[225]

Bad Faith

Mauvaise Foi or *bad faith* is the attempt to flee the anguish of freedom and responsibility. Because human reality *is* freedom, the possibility of bad faith is an a priori feature of being human. We may thus compare Sartre's *bad faith* with Heidegger's 'existential structure' of *Fallenness,* which is also this necessary tendency to escape freedom ("what one truly —'authentically'—is"). In Heidegger's analysis, however, the discussion of fallenness and its derivative—inauthenticity—is left in the abstract. We are told that fallenness and everydayness are a retreat to the anonymous safety of *das Man* or the public, that it is busy concern with present "average everyday" tasks and chores, that it replaces human understanding and discourse with curiosity and prattle. The mechanisms of fallenness and inauthenticity are never given precise exemplification, and, characteristically, we shall find Sartre's philosophical genius best illustrated in his development of a detailed analysis based on Heidegger's abstract claims.

Sartre's conception of 'bad faith' is one of the better-known ideas of his philosophy, but it is too often misunderstood as either a purely ethical notion or as a specific problem which he employs as a foil against Freud. The former interpretation is easily rejected on the basis of everything we have discussed thus far. Sartre is fundamentally an ontologist-phenomenologist, only secondarily interested in an ethics (which he still has not given us). The notion of 'bad faith' is primarily a part of the ontology of *Being and Nothingness;* its ethical implications are secondary. The interpretation of Sartre's discussion of *bad faith* as an attack on Freud is furthered by the heavy emphasis on the argument against Freud in the second chapter of *Being and Nothingness* which is titled "Bad Faith." This chapter is only a small part of the discussion of bad faith, which permeates *Being and Nothingness* in its entirety and might even be said to be its central theme. The chapter on 'bad faith' is often extracted and reprinted separately, which has the disadvantage of giving the impression that 'bad faith' is an 'solated problem and is primarily a psychological thesis. (The quasi-translation of *mauvaise foi* as "self-deception"[226] adds

to this misimpression. Since the core of the argument is the thesis that there is no *Self* to be deceived, this replacement is singularly unfortunate. In addition, the evaluative overtones of 'bad faith' are surely not unintentional, and this literal translation saves the evaluative-descriptive ambiguity which is clearly present in the French.)

The problem of bad faith is the problem of describing what it is to be a human being (the human condition), and thus demonstrating the various modes of escape from what Sartre has already described as 'absolute freedom'. For Sartre, the phenomenon of bad faith is clearly present in most or even all human activities, and the problem, therefore, becomes a Kantian problem of explaining how such a phenomenon is *possible*. The actuality of such behavior is not questioned, but its description is problematic because it superficially seems to contradict other parts of Sartre's ontology. Specifically, consciousness has been described as *nothingness* and as "entirely translucent to itself": as such, how could it be possible for the phenomenon of bad faith to occur? If bad faith is a hiding of a truth from oneself (that is, 'self-deception'), then the whole of Sartre's ontology must collapse, for consciousness can no longer be "consciousness (of) consciousness" and man, in his ignorance even of what goes on 'in' his own mind, cannot possibly be said to have absolute freedom of choice and intention.

If we begin by describing the phenomenon of *bad faith* as 'self-deception', we may simply conceive of bad faith as a *lie to oneself;*[227] more specifically, a lie to oneself *about oneself.* Sartre offers us an example of a woman who consents to go out with a man whom she knows to have sexual intentions towards her:

She knows also that it will be necessary sooner or later for her to make a decision. But she does not want to realize the urgency: she concerns herself only with what is respectful and discreet in the attitude of her companion. She does not apprehend this conduct as an attempt to achieve what we call "the first approach."[228]

She interprets whatever her companion says as devoid of sexual suggestiveness, and even responds to his physical advances by denying their intentional import. He takes her hand and she simply divorces herself from it and ignores the fact that her hand is with him.

We shall say that this woman is in bad faith. . . . She has disarmed the actions of her companion by reducing them to being only what they are, that is, to existing in the mode of the in-itself.[229]

The woman is deceiving herself concerning the intentions of her companion, but Sartre does not want to say that she is simply deceiving herself about *him.* She is deceiving herself about her own desires and intentions as well as about her own sexual nature. She is pretending that she is not a sexual being, and she is pretending that her companion's advances do not have anything (sexual) to do with her. This woman is in bad faith primarily because she denies the necessity of her own *choice* in the situation. By treating herself as nonsexual (and subsequently interpreting her companion's actions as not directed towards her sexually), she has denied the situation in which she must choose to accept or reject her sexuality and her companion's advances.

To describe this incident as "self-deception" leads to the following glib interpretation. The woman lies to herself; she knows that she is being treated as a sexual object but will not allow herself to realize this. She knows the truth, on the one hand, but refuses to disclose it to herself on the other. A lie is, in general, knowing the truth but refusing to disclose it, presenting some other proposition which one knows to be false instead. A lie to oneself, self-deception, is knowing something and hiding it from oneself.

Sartre claims that,

A man does not lie about what he is ignorant of; he does not lie when he spreads an error of which he himself is the dupe; he does not lie when he is mistaken.[230]

[This characterization of lying has an interesting consequence in the interpretation of "The Wall" (*Le Mur*) in which Ibbietta tells the enemy what he thinks to be a lie which turns out to be the truth. According to the above characterization of "lying," Ibbietta does not 'lie' when he tells the police that his friend is hiding in the cemetery (which he is) when he believes that his friend is elsewhere. Does lying (for Sartre) entail knowing the truth and denying it or only denying what one believes to be the truth?]

Given the thesis of the translucency of consciousness which has been defended in *The Transcendence of the Ego* and *Being and Nothingness,* the nature of this 'hiding' is mysterious to say the least. *Where* 'in' consciousness is this truth to hide if there is no 'in', no *contents,* of consciousness? Furthermore, *who* is doing the hiding and *from whom?* We have already seen that there is no *Self* or ego 'in' consciousness and that the *Self* or ego only arrives with *reflective* consciousness. Sartre tells us that bad faith is a prereflective phenomenon (as evidenced that a person in bad faith need not and usually does not know that he is in bad faith). Thus, there is no self to "possess the truth" and no self to hide the truth. Furthermore, we have already seen that the *self* or *ego* in reflection is not a subject but a unity of one's actions and states of consciousness. There is no self which is a subject which could be deceived because the self is only an object for consciousness. Consequently, there is no self to do the deceiving or to be deceived. The "self" in "self-deception" cannot be more than grammatical; it misleads us into thinking that "self-deception" is a kind of lying to oneself. This characterization turns out to be meaningless. Yet the problem remains to give an adequate description of an evidently common human phenomenon.

Let us look at some other examples of bad faith. In a famous essay on anti-Semitism, Sartre describes the anti-Semite as a man in bad faith:

The anti-Semite has created the Jew from his need. Prejudice is not uninformed opinion. (Anti-Semitism) is an attitude totally and freely self-chosen, a global attitude which is adopted not only in regard to Jews but in regard to men in general . . . it is a passion and at the same time a concept of the world . . . He is a man who is afraid, . . . Not of the Jews, of course, but of himself, of his conscience, of his instincts, of his responsibilities, of solitude, of change, of society, and the world; of everything except the Jews. He is a coward who does not wish to admit his cowardice to himself; a murderer who represses and censures his penchant for murder without

*being able to restrain it and who
nevertheless does not dare to kill except
in effigy or in the anonymity of a mob;
a malcontent who dares not revolt for
fear of the consequences of his rebellion.
By adhering to anti-Semitism, he is not
only adopting an opinion, he is choosing
himself as a person. He is choosing
the permanence and the impenetrability
of rock, the total irresponsibility of the
warrior who obeys his leaders—and he
has no leader . . . He chooses finally,
that good be readymade, not in question,
out of reach; . . . The Jew is only a
pretext: elsewhere it will be the Negro,
the yellow race; the Jew's existence
simply allows the anti-Semite to nip his
anxieties in the bud by persuading himself
that his place has always been cut out
in the world. . . . Anti-Semitism, in a
word, is fear of man's fate. The
anti-Semite is the man who wants to be
pitiless stone, furious torrent, devastating
lightning: in short, everything but a man.*[231]

Similarly, Simone De Beauvoir points out
bad faith in women regarding their *humanity*—a woman treats herself as a sexual object (as a "woman") in order to
deny her freedom. De Beauvoir declares
that the common bad faith of woman is
her appeal to her 'feminine' nature:

*Woman is a female to the extent that
she feels herself as such . . . It is not
nature that defines woman, it is she who
defines herself.*[232]

Conversely, Sartre has cited the bad faith
of the woman who denies her sexuality.
People in bad faith permeate Sartre's novels and plays. In fact, it may be plausibly
argued that there is not a single character
in his works who escapes bad faith. Garcin of *No Exit* has already been accused
of bad faith for his refusal to face his own
cowardice; the remorse ('the flies') of
Orestes in *The Flies* is his bad faith;
Mathieu and Boris of *The Age of Reason*
reject their freedom in spite of (and
partly with the aid of) their continuous
insistence that they are free men; nearly
all of Sartre's women (Inez and Estelle
of *No Exit,* Electra of *The Flies,* Marcelle
of *Age of Reason,* Lizzie as *The Respectful
Prostitute,* Jessica of *Dirty Hands*) are in
bad faith by virtue of their sexuality. Recurrent through this literature is the person who interprets his role as definitive of

his actions (for example, the Nazi soldier
who defines himself as a soldier), the person who takes his own free choices of himself as his 'destiny' (as Sartre criticizes
Baudelaire, and as he explains the life
style of Jean Genet), the person who
maintains his freedom to such an extent
that he is oblivious to his situation (Mathieu in *Age of Reason*). What is common
to all of these examples of *bad faith* is
what might ordinarily be called "self-deception", but we have seen that this characterization of bad faith as a "lie to oneself" does not make sense. How then are
we to understand bad faith?

Twentieth-century thought has been
given a remarkable theory to explain the
phenomenon of bad faith (and many
other behavioral and 'mental' phenomena) in Freud's theory of the *unconscious*. This theory is particularly germane
to the problem of bad faith as it allows an
interpretation of bad faith as self-deception which makes sense of the deceiver-de-
ceived distinction implicit in the conception of a "lie to oneself." The theory of
the 'translucency' of consciousness renders
senseless the idea of consciousness hiding
a truth from itself. To escape these difficulties, people have rejected the 'translucency' thesis and turned to a theory of a
bifurcated mind—conscious and unconscious 'realms' of consciousness—an id
and an ego which are two different selves
which 'inhabit' consciousness. Freud
would explain bad faith as a literal lie to
oneself, but with the stipulation that there
are actually two different selves involved,
each 'hidden' from the other. Self-deception is the unconscious lying to the conscious mind—the id hiding the painful
truth from the ego.

Sartre rejects this analysis, of course,
and his defense of his "translucency theory" depends on his ability to give an adequate account without appeal to the
Freudian model of an 'opaque' or 'dual'
consciousness. It would suffice to simply
present the alternative account; the celebrated attack on Freud in *Being and
Nothingness* is somewhat inessential to the
project as a whole. However, Freud's
theory is too generally accepted and too
persuasive to simply ignore, and so Sartre
launches into an attack which has since
become a philosophical classic. This is
perhaps unfortunate, for the attack on
Freud's account of self-deception is possibly the most slovenly analysis in all of

Being and Nothingness. The argument is based on a most simple-minded characature of Freudian theory, ultimately reduces to a long-standing naive objection to Freud, and even then is formulated in an argument which is unforgivably invalid. We shall present Sartre's critique of Freud, therefore, partly in order to *minimize* its centrality to Sartre's ontology.

The assault on Freud's theory is not at first a frontal attack but rather a juxtaposition of two different 'ontologies.' Sartre has argued that consciousness is necessarily "unified" (in prereflective consciousness of objects) and "translucent" (or consciousness of itself). Freud argues that consciousness is essentially dual and "opaque." The differences run deep, for Sartre is arguing descriptively from a phenomenological standpoint while Freud is arguing a theoretical model for explaining human behavior from the natural standpoint. Freud's 'second' consciousness, the unconscious, is a postulate of a theory to explain certain behaviors which are unaccountable on standard mentalistic theories of behavior. As such, we might argue that Freud's starting point and purposes are so different from Sartre's starting point and interests that the two theories are not clearly incompatible: Sartre, of course, takes the Freudian model of consciousness as a direct threat to his ontology, and as a result argues from within his own ontology that the Freudian model is internally inconsistent and fails to account for the phenomenon of bad faith.

The argument that Freud is internally inconsistent is not original with Sartre, but is the oldest and least sophisticated of the arguments against the concept of the 'unconscious mind'. According to this criticism, there is a "logical mistake in cutting consciousness in two." In other words, the notion 'unconscious mind' is a contradiction in terms. Whether or not this criticism would be valid for the everyday notions of 'unconscious' and 'mind',[233] it is not legitimate for Sartre as he is clearly not concerned with the analysis of these everyday terms, but rather with the phenomenological description of consciousbased on a most simple-minded caricaemploying the notion of 'consciousness' ture of Freudian theory, ultimately reways, the simple argument that Freud's concepts are inconsistent on the basis of the concepts as they are used in Sartre's

ontology is clearly inadequate. If Freud is introducing a specialized mentalistic language into scientific discourse to provide a theory of human behavior and Sartre is introducing an equally specialized but very different language for a phenomenological description, then there is not the basis for comparison that Sartre assumes.

The second wave of Sartre's attack on Freud is more sophisticated but no more successful. Sartre quotes Stekel's claim that "whenever he had pursued his investigations far enough, the source of the psychosis was conscious."[234] It is argued more specifically that the theory of the unconscious cannot adequately explain the phenomenon of bad faith. It is here that Sartre relies on an almost children's book characterization of Freud's theory and raises an all too famous, but invalid, argument against Freud's analysis.

The Freudian model of bad faith as interpreted by Sartre takes the consciousness of which one is aware, the consciousness that "I am" as the *ego* and interprets the *id* as the unconscious "to which I hold no privileged position." The ego is the crude equivalent of Sartre's consciousness; the id is known to me only as it would be known to anybody else, by observation of my behavior.[235] Bad faith, in (Sartre's characterization of) Freud's analysis, is a lie to myself, a lie 'told' by the id to the ego. Thus, psychoanalytic theory

replaces the duality of the deceiver and the deceived, the essential condition of the lie, by that of 'id' and 'ego.'[236]

In addition to these two 'selves,' however, there is a mediating *censor*, which Sartre claims is

conceived as a line of demarcation with customs, passport division, currency control, etc.[237]

and it is this censor which is responsible for the 'opacity' of the unconscious and therefore the possibility of bad faith. [It is reasonable to object that Sartre has hypostatized and personified Freud's constructs beyond the limits of even the most metaphorical of the Freudian representations.]

It is the role of the censor which Sartre finds to be the defect of the theory. How is a piece of knowledge 'repressed,' or kept from the consciousness of the ego?

It cannot be repressed by the ego itself, Sartre argues for Freud, because it would itself have to know what it refuses to know; the problem of bad faith would remain intact. Neither can it be the id that does the repressing. The very foundation of Freudian theory is that the id seeks to express itself in consciousness but is frustrated;

The complex [the repressed piece of knowledge] as such is rather the collaborator of the psychoanalyst since it aims at expressing itself in clear consciousness, since it plays tricks on the censor and seeks to elude it.[238]

Sartre is here talking of the various techniques of sublimation, the expression of the unconscious content in disguised form and other 'ego-defense mechanisms', but why must it be disguised?

The only 'level' at which we can locate the source of 'repression' is that of the censor. Only the censor is the repressing agent, for the knowledge it represses must be completely hidden from the ego and the repression must be carried out against the demands of the id. In this role of the censor Sartre claims to discover a fatal flaw in the Freudian account of bad faith. It is argued that the censor, in order to carry on its role of repression, must know the content of the Id and know, by the needs and tolerances of the ego, that this content is to be repressed. According to Sartre's account of knowledge "all knowing entails consciousness of knowing."[239] The censor must be conscious of knowing the content of the id. From this step, however, Sartre unforgivably jumps to the conclusion that,

[The self-consciousness of the censor] must be the consciousness (of) being conscious of the drive to be repressed, but precisely, in order not to be conscious of it.[240]

From this, Sartre concludes that the censor must be in bad faith, and that

Psychoanalysis has not gained anything for us since in order to overcome bad faith, it has established between the unconscious and consciousness an autonomous consciousness in bad faith.

If we maintain the interpretation of the censor as an "autonomous consciousness,"

it is clear that we are nowhere required to conclude that the censor must repress anything from *itself*, and this is what would lead it into bad faith. If Sartre interprets the censor as separated from both ego and id, then there is no objection to a straightforward 'lying' relationship between censor and ego.

Because psychoanalysis "has merely localized this double activity (of deceiving and being deceived) on the level of the censor"[241] and appeals to 'magic' (symbolism) to explain away this remaining 'contradiction', Sartre concludes that proponents of Freudian theory "have hypostatized and 'reified' bad faith; they have not escaped it."[242] It is in this context that Sartre cites Stekel's alleged "departure from psychoanalytical tradition" and maintains that the phenomena (self-deception) which have been explained by appeal to the unconscious can always be explained by a theory of a unified 'translucent' consciousness. Sartre's argument against Freud is inadequate, and even if there is an alternative account for self-deception, Freud's theory has not been refuted. It has not been shown that Freud's "cutting consciousness in two" is unintelligible or unsatisfactory for explanations of behavior.

We have commented[243] that Freud and Sartre may not differ so radically as one might expect from Sartre's critique. The example which Sartre gives us to demonstrate the superiority of a *conscious* explanation of bad faith over an *unconscious* explanation is the case of the frigid woman who denies her sexuality:

Admissions which Stekel was able to draw out inform us that these pathologically frigid women apply themselves to becoming distracted in advance from the pleasure which they dread; many for example at the time of the sexual act, turn their thoughts away toward their daily occupations, make up their household accounts. Will anyone speak of an unconscious here?[244]

There is a distinction in Freud neglected by Sartre between *suppression* (which is conscious) and *repression* (which is unconscious). Sartre's example (and all of his examples of bad faith) are examples of *suppression*, and so compatible with Freud's analysis. There is no attempt by Sartre to deal with the cases which Freud classically cites as examples of patho-logical neurosis which involve *repression*. Hysteria, obsession and anxiety reactions, and the like are much less prone to Sartre's analysis than the case of the frigid woman. Sartre and Freud are thus inter-ested in different phenomena, and it is possible that the two theories might be reconciled if we take Sartre to be focusing his attention on suppression, which Freud agrees is due to conscious distraction of one's attention, and we take Freud to be focusing his attention on unconscious acts of repression. This is not to deny, of course, that Freud maintains that *every* conscious act, including acts of suppres-sion, involves unconscious determinants; nor is it to deny that Sartre's theory of existential psychoanalysis, as he comes to call it, might not be applicable, with im-portant qualifications, to various neurotic and even psychotic 'choices'. (Cf. R. D. Laing, *Politics of Experience*.)

The difference between Freud and Sartre is not simply a difference in ap-proaches and interests, of course. Under-lying Freud's psychoanalytic theory is a thesis of *psychic determinism*, and it is central to Sartre's ontology to deny any causal thesis having to do with conscious-ness. It is strange that he does not men-tion this disagreement in his attack on Freud in Chapter Two of *Being and Noth-ingness*, although he continuously raises the point elsewhere in *Being and Nothing-ness*.[245] Again, however, we must point out that the difference between Freud and Sartre is no more striking than the sim-ilarities. Freud's theory of psychotherapy is founded on the notion that bringing the 'contents' of the unconscious into con-sciousness *liberates* the person to freely deal with them. Apart from a difference in philosophical idiom (Freud is writing in nineteenth-century metaphysical lan-guage) the supposition central to both authors is the same, consciousness is free-dom. The unconscious bears on conscious-ness for Freud only so long as it is uncon-scious, and this thesis is not significantly different from Sartre's theory of bad faith. Sartre, in spite of himself, has constant recourse to the (Heideggerian as well as Freudian) idiom of 'hiding' and explains the hiding of knowledge in bad faith by appeal to a model not far removed from Freud's *pleasure principle* which keeps unconscious (through suppression or re-pression) what is unpleasant to us:

To be sure, the one who practices bad faith is hiding a displeasing truth or presenting as truth a pleasing untruth.[246]

Sartre's solution to the problem of bad faith is a careful phenomenological de-scription of the phenomena commonly called "self-deception" and the demonstra-tion that these phenomena can be ac-counted for by the theory of *absolute free-dom* of *Being and Nothingness* coupled with the observation that man tends to "flee this freedom," or, more accurately, flee the anguish of recognition of freedom by constructing *excuses* for himself and denying this freedom. Bad faith is a willful *refusal* to recognize oneself as both facticity and transcendence, as a man with a past and a future yet to be determined. The para-digm case of bad faith is thus the misin-terpretation of *choices* which one makes for himself as *facts* which determine one. Bad faith is flight from anguish in the face of freedom, a denial of transcendence and the attempt to look at oneself as a *thing*.

The paradigm of bad faith is "fleeing from my own freedom and possibilities." The characterization of bad faith, however, is not restricted to this paradigm case, and it is one of the weaknesses of Sartre's oth-erwise brilliant analysis of bad faith that he sometimes places inordinate stress on one kind of bad faith (particularly in the chapter of *Being and Nothingness* called "Bad Faith"). Bad faith is generally char-acterized as a "refusal to recognize what I am," namely, a being who is both facticity *and* transcendence. Thus, bad faith does not solely consist in denial of one's transcendence in order to flee an-guish; it may also consist of the denial of one's facticity and overemphasis on his transcendence. We shall see that some of our examples are illustrations of this sort of bad faith (notably, the examples of Mathieu in *Age of Reason*, Garcin in *No Exit*). Moreover, there is a third sort of bad faith, often neglected but equal in im-portance to these two: treating oneself as an *other* instead of treating oneself as one-self is also a form of bad faith, distinct al-though parallel to the first paradigm form of bad faith. To treat oneself as an other is to deny transcendence and turn oneself, not into a *thing* but nonetheless into pure facticity. Sartre argues that this third form of bad faith is the most 'primitive' (to bor-row Heidegger's term) of the three. It is through Being-with-others (Heidegger's

Mitsein) that we first learn to reflect on ourselves at all, and it is the resultant Being-for-others which forms the basis (but not the paradigm) of all bad faith. (Sartre begins his discussion of bad faith with a reference to Hegel's master-slave relationship, but it is Heidegger's discussion of *das Man* and inauthenticity which is closest to his own theses.)

The bad faith of denying transcendence is that form of bad faith which formulates excuses by treating oneself as a *thing* and interpreting one's *situation* as sufficient to determine the future. We have already introduced several such methods of bad faith; every attempt to discover an essence of man or a human nature is such a method. Accordingly, all traditional metaphysics and deterministic psychology are mechanisms of bad faith. Similarly every attempt to give a complete characterization of one-*Self* is in bad faith. Yet, we have to go into the details of such mechanisms of bad faith, and it is in these details that some of Sartre's most significant contributions are to be found.

We have already related (without criticism) Sartre's thesis that all actions are intentional and therefore 'absolutely free' and outside the causal world of Being-in-itself. In order to defend this thesis, Sartre joins with many contemporary Anglo-American philosophers in sharply distinguishing between the language in which we discuss human actions and the language in which we discuss events 'in-the-world' in general. Against this thesis, it has been maintained that there could still be a causal system of explanations for human actions so long as we restrict the causal factors to other action-related states, events, and entities. Thus, it could be denied that neural physiology could provide adequate explanations for human actions, but that these same actions could still be determined by motivation, by environmental stimuli, and by any of the variables currently cited by psychologists in deterministic explanations of behavior. Sartre must show, therefore, that there cannot be 'internal' causes sufficient to determine a man's behavior.

Among these internal causes, we find several recurrent in psychological and philosophical literature. Foremost among these are those behavioral determinants which are referred to as *motivation*—motives, desires, drives, and compulsions (intentions are often excluded from this list, occupying a unique place in explanations of actions). Secondly, *dispositions* and *traits*—personality characteristics, temperament, and 'character'—are cited as determinants of behavior which most conveniently allow for prediction of future actions. Thirdly, the *passions*—emotions, moods, attitudes, and feelings—are identified as recurrent but irregular determinants of future behavior. According to determinists, some or all of the above causal factors are always sufficient to completely determine future behavior, and therefore, since a man is what he has done, some or all of these causal factors are sufficient to determine what a man will *be*. Sartre has already asserted that human beings are absolutely free to become what they choose, and Sartre must therefore deny all such determinist theories. However, in showing such theories to be wrong (and we have already indicated the general arguments Sartre advances to prove this), Sartre is not simply accusing the defenders of these theories of being *mistaken;* he accuses them of being in *bad faith*. Since bad faith (of the first sort) is confusing one's choices (transcendence) for facts about oneself (facticity), all such theories are mechanisms of bad faith.

Against the thesis that motivational factors are sufficient causes of action, or causes of the intentions or choices to act, Sartre argues that all such theories of 'internal' causation depend on the rejected concept of a 'contents of consciousness'; and

as soon as we abandon the hypothesis of the contents of consciousness, we must recognize that there is never a motive in consciousness; motives are only for consciousness. And due to the fact that the motive can arise only as appearance, it constitutes itself as ineffective.[247]

The argument here is familiar; motives are part of my situation, they are the facts which are the *basis* but not the determination of my choices. Sartre tells us that the 'situation *is* our motivation,' and we have already seen that our situation is *never* a determinant of our choice but only a restriction of the range of our choices. Motives are therefore 'ineffective' because they are always open to interpretation in the light of our 'projects'. To choose a simple example, *hunger* is cited by most psychologists as a basic drive or motivating factor and therefore cited as a determinant of behavior. What is this motive? A feeling of some sort which is open to interpretation? If I am on a diet, the hunger will be interpreted as a threat to be conscientiously denied; if I have been working hard all day, I may view my hunger as a welcome opportunity to stop work and indulge myself; if I am in training for a religious sect which preaches abstinence or if I am on a hunger strike for political reasons, my hunger will be taken as a test of strength. My hunger does not determine me to eat, it only presents me with a situation in which I must choose whether or not to eat in view of my general projects and goals,

It is not because I am free that my act is not subject to the determination of motives; on the contrary, the structure of motives as ineffective is the condition of my freedom.[248]

Merleau-Ponty argues a similar thesis;

one cannot be to some extent free, and if, as is often said, motives incline me in a certain direction, one of two things happens: either they are strong enough to force me to act, in which case there is no freedom, or else they are not strong enough, and then freedom is complete, . . . We ought, therefore, to reject not only the idea of causality, but also that of motivation.[249]

For Merleau-Ponty, my motives do not determine my decisions, but "it is my secret decision which brings motives to light."[250] Merleau-Ponty and Sartre agree that motives do not determine our actions, but Merleau-Ponty departs from Sartre on a central issue—the *need* for motives in decision making. He tells us that "decisions give motives their force"[251] and that "motivation, of course, does not do away with freedom."[252] Here Sartre would imply that decisions can be made *in the absence of motivation,* and that only a decision is necessary to set up an 'existential project.' Merleau-Ponty violently reacts to this thesis, and insists that motivation and situation

are the virtues proper to action and commitment; at the outset, I am not an individual beyond class, I am situated in a social environment, and my freedom,

though it may have the power to commit me elsewhere, has not the power to transform me instantaneously into what I decide to be.[253]

Merleau-Ponty becomes deeply involved with the concepts and goals of 'class consciousness' (with Sartre) and argues that the Sartrian 'intellectual' would suggest that commitment to the Marxist 'cause' is simply a matter of decision, but

to make class consciousness the outcome of a decision and a choice is to say that problems are solved on the day they are posed, . . . In reality, the intellectual project and the positing of ends are merely the bringing to completion of an existential project.[254]

One can truly decide, Merleau-Ponty insists, only where his motivation can be given force by his decision. Sartre speaks as if the decision has its own force, but it is argued against him that decisions only have the force they share with motivation.

Now with the worker it is a fortiori *the case that his decision is elaborated in the course of his life.*[255]

It would follow that a man is not entirely free, for he is dependent on his motivation in order to make his free commitments.

The dispute between Sartre and Merleau-Ponty becomes a profound split within existentialism, for it is Sartre's absolute notion of freedom which so distinguishes his philosophy from traditional theories of 'soft determinism'. We may simply point out here, however, that Sartre's argument concerning the 'inefficacy' of motives can account for Merleau-Ponty's complaint by reminding us that motives are part of our situation, and that they limit our choices by his theory also. We cannot act in regard to a motive if we do not have that motive. It would follow, therefore, that the worker could not make the decision to join the 'movement' unless his situation was such that that was one of his 'possibilities'. Sartre is quite clear that motivation—intention—action form a complex and that there can be no action without motivation as well as intention (these are not to be confused—*motivation* is a function of our situation; *intention* is our choice of projects regarding that situation). The worker joins the movement only when his situation *motivates him* to join, that is, when reflection on his situation discloses to him the unsatisfactoriness of that situation and (through an act of nihilation) leads him to "throw his lot with the movement."[256] On the one hand, it might be thought that this weakens Sartre's radical position on freedom too much. It also shows that the concept of 'motivation' holds a very curious place in Sartre's discussion of human action. Although motivation is a function of or *is* our situation, it is clear that motivation is not simply a factual state;

No factual state, whatever it may be (the political and economic structure of society, the psychological "state" etc.) is capable by itself of motivating any act whatsoever.[257]

Yet Sartre does not wholly disagree with the "general consideration" that "the motive is a subjective fact." However, it is not simply a 'fact';

the motive is understood only by the end: that is, by the non-existent. It is therefore in-itself a-négatité.[258]

This means that the motive is chosen by us; it is not the situation but our interpretation of the situation in light of our projects. It is not yet the intention, which is specific to a single course of action (whereas motivation still leaves open a variety of courses of action), but it is not part of the uninterpreted situation (or brute 'nude' facticity). A situation, primarily those affective components of a situation like pleasure, suffering, and so on—is made into a motive in an act of nihilation:

This means evidently that it is by a pure wrenching away from himself and the world that the worker can posit his suffering as unbearable suffering and consequently make of it the motive for his revolutionary action.[259]

The dispute between Merleau-Ponty and Sartre is not as clear-cut as it may seem in its superficial summary, "Merleau-Ponty rejects Sartre's thesis of absolute freedom." Both agree that motives are created, not given, and both agree that motives are necessary for action. The difference then reduces to the question whether we can be held responsible for our motivation,

and because of the peculiar status of motivation for both Sartre and Merleau-Ponty, this question does not seem to admit of a simple answer either. Superficially, it would seem that Sartre maintains that we are responsible for our motives, and Merleau-Ponty maintains that we are not. From our brief discussion of motivation in these two authors, it hopefully is clear that such a simple answer will not do. For Sartre, motivation (the situation) retains its share of facticity; for Merleau-Ponty, motives "come to light" only by one's decisions.

If motives do not determine action, then appeal to motives as determinants of action is an act of bad faith. On this point, Sartre and Merleau-Ponty agree, and the conclusion is that motivation, although it may (and perhaps must) be a factor in our decisions to act is never a determinant to choose a particular course of action.

Sartre gives less attention to the second class of "causal determinants"—traits, dispositions, personality, and 'character'—but his position is clear from his discussion of motivation and psychological determinism. To say that Garcin is a coward or that Marcelle (or even women in general) is (are) weak seems to be the ascription of a causal factor of some sort which has determined, does determine, and will determine all of Garcin's or Marcelles's (or all women's) actions. Sartre argues that a dispositional statement does not have such causal import but is only a summary of actions completed *in the past*.[260] All statements about personality, 'character', and all ascriptions of traits and dispositions can only be a summary of past behavior which have no causal influence on future behavior. Of course, one can always take these statements as statements about determinants of his future behavior, and, when he does, he is in bad faith. Cowardice or weakness are not determinants of behavior but are *what one has been. You* may expect me to be a coward because I 'am' a coward, but *I* must choose my future without thinking of myself as a determined coward. You may say of me that I *am* a sexual pervert because of my past behavior, but I cannot (in good faith) say of myself that I *am* a sexual pervert in the sense that I consider myself to be a sexual pervert in the future. In general, one cannot *predict* his own behavior, such prediction is indicative of bad faith. No summary of my past behavior, past situations, environments, and 'influences' is sufficient to give *me* reason to believe that I am determined to act in certain ways. For me to believe so is for me to be in bad faith.

Dispositions and personality traits are a primary source of bad faith. Some such dispositions are attributed universally to all men, as human 'nature', and appealed to by the individual in bad faith. For example, the theory of psychological egoism —that all men act in their own self-interest—can be used as an *excuse* for selfish behavior. Similarly, the Freudian claim that all men hate their fathers can be used as an excuse for this man's hating his father. All such attempts at deriving a theory of human nature or a general theory of human behavior lend themselves to this sort of bad faith. In fact, such theories can only be summaries of the behavior of other men. As soon as I cite such a theory with reference to my own future, I am in bad faith.

The more usual application of this sort of bad faith is to individual dispositions, personality traits, and the like. Such attempts to escape recognition of one's freedom of choice give rise to rigid *Self-conceptions*—the postulation of a core *Self* for me:

This self *with its* a priori *and historical content is the essence of man.*[261]

Essence is everything in the human being which we can indicate by the words— that is.[262]

In bad faith, 'self-realization' is an escape from our freedom; it is the insistence that facts about ourselves have determined future actions and our statements about our own future are in no way essentially different from statements about our future made by anyone else.

A central theme in recent analytic philosophy of mind may help illustrate the asymmetry between my view of my own future and anyone else's view of my future. According to the man in bad faith, a prediction of my future actions and a statement of my intentions, if those intentions are relevant to the action at all, are equivalent. (If they are not equivalent, then it is maintained either that intentions were irrelevant to the determination of the action or else that those intentions were not the *true* intentions of the person; 'unconscious intentions' are often cited in this

regard.) However, predictions and statements of intention are very different sorts of pronouncements. The first are true or false depending on actual future behavior; the latter are themselves decisions to act, and are sincere or insincere rather than true or false. A prediction which itself effects that which it predicts is not merely a prediction. Predictions of one's own behavior always influence one's behavior, at least by adding a new dimension to one's intentions. (See, for example, Stuart Hampshire's *Thought and Action.*)

Kant said, "we cannot conceive of ourselves as other than free." In bad faith, however, one treats himself as determined, predicts his future actions, and denies the relevance of his decisions and intentions to his future behavior. For example, the German soldier who claims that "he cannot do otherwise" on the grounds that he is a German and a member of the army is in bad faith; he maintains, truly, that in his role as a German soldier, he is obligated to obey his orders. What he refuses to recognize is the fact that he is a German patriot and soldier *by choice,* and that he is always free to desert, to quit, to kill himself, to become a traitor. He is in bad faith in that he treats himself as determined by his past choices, his place of birth, the dictates of his country. He treats himself as a thing—as a German soldier—and not as a human being. Similarly, the man who provides a psychological characterization of himself, and uses this characterization as an *excuse* to absolve himself of responsibility for his actions is in bad faith. He may 'find' that he is lazy, and then attempt to excuse himself from work on the grounds that he is lazy; or he may characterize himself as stupid, and then excuse himself from thinking, or a man may, on the basis of a past of homosexual encounters, characterize himself as a homosexual, thus excusing himself from responsibility for future homosexual acts.[263] "After all," these people can all claim, "we are simply acting according to our 'psychological makeup', our own 'personalities' or 'natures'; accordingly, how can we be blamed for our actions? We could not act otherwise."

What these people *refuse* to recognize is that their past histories of laziness, stupidity, or homosexuality do not determine their intentions for the future. This does not mean, as Sartre is so often misunderstood to mean, that these people do not, in one sense, have 'personalities' or 'natures' or even 'compulsions' to perform certain actions. A man consistently stupid in the past will very likely be stupid in the future. It is *his* resignation that he will be stupid, his refusal even to bother to try or to intend to act intelligently, that characterizes his bad faith. Similarly, the homosexual will no doubt be troubled by sexual desires and even compulsions, but it is in his acceptance of his future as determined by these—his refusal to take these urges as something to be overcome—that he acts in bad faith. One's past behavior is the best possible grounds for someone else to predict what one shall do in the future. (Only where actions "far in the future" are concerned may I predict whether I shall then act or decide to act in such and such a way.) However, I cannot, although someone else may, take this past behavior as *sufficient* to say that I will do *x*. When I assert, "I will do *x*," I am not simply making a statement about the future—it is a statement about my present intentions —what I will *try* to do in the future. Facts never *determine* my future, I can always choose to 'revolt' against the *facts* (my 'situation'). No number of facts about me can make my decision or my intention *irrelevant* to what I do. I may, of course, *fail* to succeed and, in retrospect, see that the 'facts' about me were, after all, overwhelming. I cannot say this about my *future*, however, for my possibilities are always open for me. I cannot say "I will do *x*" as a prediction without formulating, to some degree, my intention to do *x*, or at least my lack of intention to resist *x*'s happening. The degree to which self-prediction hides intention, of course, varies from instance to instance. Sometimes (for example, "I will fail the test anyway so I need not even show up"), the prediction is totally self-confirming; the prediction itself suffices to frustrate any competing intentions. Other times (e.g., "I will probably panic at the moment of attack but I intend to make every effort to be brave"), the prediction may only weaken the intention so as to make it slightly less likely that it will be fully attempted. (In cases like this one, the prediction may even result in an added resoluteness which will make the prediction itself less likely to become fulfilled—a self-defeating prediction.) In every case in which one predicts his own future behavior, the prediction is a ready *excuse* for

failure to succeed and even for failure to try. My 'knowledge' that I am likely to panic is already at hand as an excuse when the moment of attack comes and is already an opportunity to give up my noble intention. The prediction will serve to excuse my action, and allow me to feel free from responsibility to perform an action from which I may be excused.

A man in bad faith *distracts* himself from the recognition of his freedom. The most common form of distraction is to be found in the notion of 'role-playing', or as Sartre characterizes it, "Being what I am not." In our discussion of facticity and the for-itself, we stressed the importance for Sartre (as for Heidegger), of a man's "being thrown into a situation" or abandonment. In any situation, a set of demands are placed on us, and our freedom consists in our giving significance to those demands, that is, accepting or rejecting them. I am born a Frenchman, and thus have a *prima facie* duty to fight in the army of France, to pay French taxes, or the like. My freedom consists of my ability to refuse to fight, pay taxes, and so on. In order to avoid the recognition of this freedom, however, I accept the *role* of Frenchman. This entails simply an unreflective acceptance of the demands placed upon me by 'France'. I pretend to *be* a Frenchman, and simply ignore the question of whether I *decide* to accept this role or not; I simply accept it, presumably "because I was born there." There is a conscientious effort to continually refuse to question the role; if the question does arise, there is an equally conscientious effort to find *excuses* for accepting the role —reasons why it is a *natural* role. For example, my being born in France makes me French; the question concerning the possibility of leaving France is simply avoided. When this question is asked, the next move is to excuse not leaving or even considering leaving by appeal to the natural human attachment for one's place of birth or being French 'by nature'. Bad faith is this accepting as 'natural' what ought to be decided by free and undetermined choice.

One is also in bad faith when he assumes a social role as *his* role and avoids questioning that role. Thus one pays attention to the details of his responsibilities and *distracts* himself from his freedom to accept or not accept those responsibilities. The most obvious example of such bad faith is the petty bureaucrat, who focuses his attention *ad ridiculosum* to petty rules and regulations and simply refuses to consider even the intentions and basic principles underlying those petty rules. Attention to one's 'duties' and social role as a form of bad faith is famously illustrated in Sartre's brilliant description of the cafe waiter;

His movement is quick and studied, a little too precise, a little too rapid. He comes toward the patrons with a step a little too quick. He bends forward a little too eagerly; his voice, his eyes express an interest a little too solicitous for the order of the customer. Finally there he returns, trying to imitate in his walk the inflexible stiffness of some kind of automaton while carrying his tray with the recklessness of a tightropewalker by putting it in a perpetually unstable, perpetually broken equilibrium which he perpetually re-establishes by a light movement of the arm and hand. All this behavior seems to us a game. He is trying to link his movements together as if they were mechanisms, the one regulating the other; . . . He is playing with himself. But what is he playing? We need not watch long before we can explain it; he is playing at being *a waiter in a cafe . . . The waiter in the cafe plays with his condition in order to* realize *it.*[264]

What the waiter attempts to be is a Being-in-itself; something which is only a waiter and could not be anything else. Accepting the role hides the possibility that one *could be* the rich businessman waited on; it is bad faith in that one denies that he could be anything other than a waiter. [James Baldwin gives us a similar description of the same phenomenon in his essay "Nobody Knows My Name." The waiter in Paris *is* a waiter. The waiter in America, on the other hand, is *not* a waiter and resents his customers for having realized what he believes to be *his* possibilities.]

According to Sartre, no statements about my past behavior, my tendencies to behave, my personality, my 'character', my 'nature' or 'essence', and no predictions about my future behavior or characterizations of my 'natural' or social roles are equivalent to or entail any statements about my present or future decisions or intentions to act. The analysis of consciousness has entailed the *absolute free-*

dom of consciousness from all such determination; to believe in such determination with reference to one's own decisions or intentions to act is not simply to be philosophically mistaken, it is to be in *bad faith.*

Sartre's theory of the passions can be briefly summarized on the basis of our past discussions. In a very early essay on the emotions, he hypothesized that emotions are "a magical transformation of the world" rather than states or events 'in' consciousness. In *Being and Nothingness*, this thesis is represented by the rejection of the idea that passions (emotions, moods, attitudes, and so on) are pure sensations or psychic 'givens' ('feelings' in one sense). He suggests that passions are feelings (in the above sense) which must be given a significance;

A feeling [i.e. a passion or an emotion] is a feeling in the presence of a norm.[265]

The Existentialist does not believe in the power of passion. He will never regard a grand passion as a destructive torrent upon which a man is swept into certain actions as by fate, and which, therefore, is an excuse for them.[266]

Shame, for example, is not merely a feeling, a sensation, but an evaluation of a feeling in a situation which one comes to regard as a shameful one. The situation is a shameful one not because I feel ashamed but because I evaluate it as a situation in which I am responsible for some disgraceful action. I feel ashamed only because I evaluate the situation as shameful: I do not think the situation shameful because I feel ashamed.[267]

A passion is what we make out of it. When one suffers, one would like to think that his suffering overwhelms him, but

One suffers and one suffers from not suffering enough. The suffering of which we speak is never exactly that which we feel. What we call 'noble' or 'good' or 'true' suffering and what moves us is the suffering which we read on the faces of others, better yet in portraits, in the face of a statue, in a tragic mask. It is a suffering which has being. . . . *The suffering which I experience, on the contrary, is never adequate suffering, . . . I cannot observe it as I observe the suffering of the statue, since I make my own suffering and since I know it. If I*

*should suffer, I should prefer that my
suffering would seize me and flow over me
like a storm, but instead I must raise it
into existence through my free spontaneity
[choice].*[268]

Since passions and feelings are not 'given'
in our situation, but 'made' by us in an interpretation or evaluation of that situation,
passions and feelings cannot be causal
determinants of our behavior. To attempt
to excuse one's actions by appealing to his
suffering, his shame, his being in love, his
intense hatred, his jealousy (or even, we
must add, his existential anguish), is always an act of bad faith, a denial of one's
free choice and a misinterpretation of
choice as given fact.

Our discussion has thus far limited itself
to that form of *bad faith* in which one
denies one's possibilities in order to avoid
the anguish of facing a choice or taking
responsibility for a previous choice. However much focus this paradigm of *bad
faith* has received, it is but one of several
varieties of this phenomenon. In bad faith,
one need not deny one's choices, he might
also deny certain facts about himself. The
woman in our initial example practices
this type of bad faith as well as the first;
she refuses to recognize the facts that she
has a woman's body, a woman's desires,
and that her partner intends to take full
advantage of both. "She realizes herself
as *not being* her own body." This denial
of facticity is also bad faith. Similarly,
Garcin, the antihero of *No Exit,* is a dramatic illustration of this sort of bad faith.
All his life he had been a coward, he has
performed cowardly actions, and his life
ends with a clownishly cowardly performance before the firing squad. Yet, in death
(with no possibilities left), he claims that
he is *not* a coward in spite of his past.
Since, in death, he *is* only his past, Garcin
in Hell practices a peculiar form of bad
faith. Garcin in death refuses to face his
facticity (in this case, his entire life).
Again, a painter may refuse to look at his
continuous failures and seemingly total
lack of talent and insist on maintaining
the fantastic ambition to become a great
painter. Up to a certain point, we might
wish to argue that the painter is simply
fighting to develop himself, but past that
point, we should feel convinced that his
ambition is hopeless. If the painter himself
realizes the hopelessness of such a case,
but continues to support his fantasy, he
is in bad faith.

It is easy to ignore this sort of bad faith
because Sartre is so often fighting the
battle against determinism. Here it is extremely important that we keep both
forms of bad faith in mind for one can be
in bad faith by ignoring his facticity
which makes it very clear that Sartre does
not intend his notion of 'absolute freedom'
to deny the relevance of the concrete situation to one's choices. One must look to
"what he is" and "what he has been" as
well as to his future ("what he is not").

Perhaps we may augment our discussion of bad faith by introducing an analogy[269] to Sartre's doctrine. The discussions of freedom and bad faith have been
based on a distinction between facticity
and transcendence, between what is
'given' and what is chosen. We have argued that man is free because he can *interpret* and *evaluate* the situation and
project his own possibilities ('projects')
on the basis of this interpretation. We
might compare this situation and interpretation of our situation to the problem of
the interpretation of a text, for example,
a Kafka parable. If one wishes to interpret
Kafka's *The Trial,* one must both remain
faithful to the text but yet go significantly
beyond it. There are any number of possible interpretations, of course, so that it
does not make sense to speak of the 'correct' interpretation. However, it does
make sense to speak of "extravagant" or
"profound" or "superficial" or "impossible" interpretations, and thus we would
not want to move from the claim that
there is no correct interpretation to the
claim that one interpretation is as good as
any other. A profound interpretation of
The Trial might be a commentary on the
psychology of religious guilt (although
this is by now a quite 'accepted' interpretation). An impossible interpretation
might be the thesis that *The Trial* is a
commentary on stock market practices in
eighteenth-century Germany. A superficial
interpretation might be the claim that the
story is about a man who is indicted for
an unnamed crime and put on trial under
bizarre circumstances. The profound and
superficial interpretations both correspond
to the text, but one goes far beyond the
text while the other simply paraphrases
the text and accepts it as completely
given. The impossible interpretation, regardless of the brilliance of its own theme,
is inadequate because it strays too far
from the text. Analogously, we may say
that our interpretation and evaluation of

our situation as a basis for our projects admits of any number of variations none of which are strictly 'correct' or 'incorrect'. Some interpretations will depart from the situation (the 'text') so that we shall feel the interpretation and projects based on it are too remote from the situation. Some interpretations will be correct but superficial, they rely too heavily on the situation. Other interpretations will remain faithful to the situation but will be profound and make much more of the situation than was originally given. Freedom, for Sartre, is the ability to formulate a variety of interpretations and corresponding projects based on our situation. Our freedom is restricted only by the details of the situation. Freedom is best realized in a profound interpretation of our situation (the 'text') which is aware of itself as only one of many possible interpretations. Freedom is denied when we give ourselves a superficial interpretation, one which takes the situation as given in-itself and denies that there are possibilities of interpretation other than a paraphrase. The superficial interpretation of our situation takes the text as determinant of the interpretation, and this is the *bad faith* of denying transcendence (possibilities of interpretation) and seeing only facticity (the 'text' as given). On the other hand, the impossible interpretation is parallel to the second kind of bad faith; it is ignoring our situation (the 'text') and formulating a fanciful story which only pretends to be an interpretation. One cannot interpret Kafka without paying strict attention to details, but neither can one interpret Kafka by refusing to go beyond what is written. Human reality is the same demand for profound yet faithful interpretation of our situation. Bad faith is "fallen into" by either straying away from the text of our life or timidly staying too close to it.

There is a third form of bad faith as well, one closely related to the first but sufficiently different to be treated separately. In addition to the denial of my ability to choose which results from my treating myself as a *thing* (Being-in-itself), a similar denial results from my treating myself as *another person*. We have already seen Sartre argue that I cannot predict my own actions as someone else can, because I can determine my actions in a manner in which no one else (logically) could. Consequently, we shall see Sartre argue that my *Being-for-others*

opens up new possibilities for bad faith as well as new possibilities for choice. Treating myself as another person is not, however, the same as treating myself as a *thing*. Furthermore, we shall see that our *Being-for-others* virtually always leads us to act in bad faith according to Sartre's theory of human relationships. We might even wish to delineate a fourth form of bad faith which emerges in some of Sartre's and Camus's literary works consisting in the refusal to recognize the importance of Being-for-others. This, we might argue, is another form of self-deception for Garcin in *No Exit* as for Meursault in *The Stranger*. (We shall focus our attention on Being-for-others in the following two sections.)

It ought to seem curious that we have spent so many pages talking about *bad faith* without devoting so much as a single paragraph to the concept of *good faith*. Good faith or *sincerity* is largely neglected in *Being and Nothingness,* and references to it are for the most part limited to footnoted comments referring us to future studies which have never been written. From our characterization of bad faith as the denial of what one is (namely, both facticity and transcendence), we ought to be able to surmise that good faith is the honest recognition of what one is, the recognition of one(self) as facticity and transcendence, as free and responsible. This characterization seems to give Sartre some difficulties in *Being and Nothingness*. At various points, he seems to alternatively indicate that it is necessary for consciousness to be sincere and impossible for consciousness to be sincere. Because consciousness is 'translucent', one's being in bad faith must itself be recognized as such:

That which affects itself with bad faith must be conscious (of) its bad faith since the being of consciousness is the consciousness of its being. It appears then that I must be in good faith at least to the extent that I am conscious of my bad faith.[270]

Sometimes sincerity is supposed to be *equivalent* to bad faith.[271] Sometimes sincerity is explicitly taken as an *ideal*:

in order for bad faith to be possible, sincerity itself must be in bad faith . . . here naturally Kant's 'You ought, therefore you can' is implicitly understood. I can become sincere; this is what my duty and my effort to achieve sincerity imply.[272]

The most consistent interpretation of the 'possibility of good faith', I believe, is parallel to Sartre's analysis of Kant's 'I think' in *Transcendence of the Ego.* Bad faith is "a permanent risk of consciousness," but this does not entail that one must always *be* in bad faith. The possibility of bad faith is a necessary and therefore ever-present threat. But one can, by being aware of this threat, struggle against it. This is not to say that Sartre ever gives us the encouragement to believe that attaining 'good faith' or 'sincerity' is humanly possible. Virtually none of his literary characters escape bad faith, although clearly there are degrees of good and bad faith. (Cf. Inez, Garcin, and Estelle of *No Exit.*) What becomes clear is that awareness of the tendency to bad faith is the first step in struggling against it. This is *not* to say with Camus in *The Myth of Sisyphus,* that one must merely recognize and accept *the absurd* and "keep it alive." For Sartre, the purpose of this recognition is to struggle against and overcome bad faith.

The real possibility of overcoming bad faith and becoming sincere is left something of a mystery in Sartre's ontological works. For an understanding of sincerity as an ideal, therefore (and, conversely, for an understanding of bad faith as a fault), we must turn to the few explicitly ethical works of the French existentialists, for example, De Beauvoir's *Ethics of Ambiguity* and Sartre's "unfortunate" essay, *Existentialism Is a Humanism.* Unfortunately, these have been few in number and are not nearly equal in quality to such serious 'ontological' works as *Being and Nothingness* and *Phenomenology of Perception.* In other works, the confusion surrounding the characterization of sincerity is simply ignored, and existentialist ethics bears a superficial charm of simplicity which is obviously lacking in the works we have been studying.

Being-for-Others

Thus far we have discussed Sartre's ontology with regard only to the solitary human consciousness and its relations to 'its' world. Sartre's ontology is not limited to my consciousness and the objects of which I am conscious; there are also other *people,* other consciousnesses. It might seem that this ought to be an obvious feature in any description of our world, but Sartre is not simply claiming that there are other people. He claims that our relations with other people cannot be explained as relations, no matter how complex, with things. *Being-for-others,* in other words, is not a category of human reality which is a special function of Being-in-itself and Being-for-itself. It is a "mode of being" of equal ontological status with these others. People are not things or objects, and our relations with people are of a very different kind than our relations with things. Furthermore, our relations with other people are an essential part of our 'primitive' experience of our world. We may recall how Heidegger also held that *Mitsein,* Being-with-others, was introduced as a part of the 'primitive' human world, and how he carefully distinguished—even in prereflective ('ontic') relations with others—between the 'concern' with which we related to the things (more accurately—equipment) in our world and the *solicitude* with which we related to others.

Sartre's model for our relations with other people does not come from Heidegger, however, and his comraderie of the *Mitsein,* but from the life and death struggle of the master-slave relationship in Hegel's *Phenomenology.* Our relations with others are a necessary foundation for any *Self-consciousness* whatever, but our relations with others are also based on a bitter struggle—not necessarily for each other's lives—but for the protection of our *freedom.*

The first step in the analysis of "Being-for-others" is the description of our knowledge that there are other people. This is, of course, an old philosophical problem: how can I know that there are other conscious beings and not mere humanoid figures which 'people' my world as peculiar objects? This problem of justifying our *knowledge* of others has become central to contemporary philosophy in America and Britain, but it has remained of passing interest to Continental philosophies. This can be explained, in part, by reminding ourselves of the very different starting points of the two 'schools' of philosophy. The tradional and analytic mode of introducing the "problem of other minds" is to ask how I can know that these particular objects (other human bodies) are conscious. In terms we have been using, the question is asked from the *natural standpoint,* and the required argument must then carry us from statements about objects in the (natural) world to statements about conscious being. Sartre (and Heidegger and Husserl before him, Merleau-Ponty after him) rejects this argument and the possibility of ever making such a move from objects to persons. According to Sartre, other people are experienced by us in a manner totally different from any of our experiences of objects. As such, one could never prove the existence of other conscious beings in the natural standpoint. In the phenomenological standpoint, however, this cannot be proved as such either; it can simply be described:

the metaphysical question no longer has meaning. We have encountered a fundamental contingency, and we can answer only by "So it is."[273]

The problem arises because of the traditional dualism between the subject and his body (which is treated as a particular instance of the subject-object distinction), and it is evident that, given this dichotomy, I can perceive the body of the other but I can never perceive him *as subject*. 'I know my own soul better than my own body', according to Descartes, but I can know only the body of the other:

If it is true that for a spiritual realism, the soul is easier to know than the body, still the body will be easier to know than the Other's soul.[274]

The answer to this traditional problem is a variety of arguments *by analogy,* arguments to the *best explanation* of the other's *behavior.* A more recent answer, favored by many phenomenologists (notably Husserl), is that we know of the other's existence by empathy (*Einfühlung*).

The problem with all arguments *by analogy* or induction from other humanoid bodies to human consciousnesses is that they begin with the supposition that there are two sorts of things (more properly, substances) which must somehow be "connected in thought." In the Cartesian tradition with which Sartre is most familiar (and which he is attacking here), the other minds problem reduces to the quest for an inference from my knowledge of material objects (that is, human bodies) to a more problematic but derivative knowledge of human souls. Against this claim,

Sartre wishes to argue, first, that my perception of other people is not first a perception of other bodies and then (by inference) a perception of persons. Second, he argues that my relations with other people are not founded on the *knowledge* that they exist. Thirdly, he argues that I do not perceive other *bodies* but other *persons*. And underlying all of these arguments is the thesis that the dualism which underlies all traditional arguments (as well as the problem itself) is untenable.

In recent attempts to close the 'gap' between 'analytic' and existential-phenomenological philosophies, the problem of other minds has rightfully been cited as one possible source of reconciliation. In spite of the different starting points, there is a marked similarity between Sartre's 'solution' to the other minds problem and certain solutions advanced by recent British analytic philosophers. This correspondence holds both in the negative arguments advanced *against* the arguments by analogy and sympathy as well as in the positive arguments for an alternative solution. The argument against the argument by analogy is customarily attributed to Wittgenstein (in his *Philosophical Investigations,* and earlier studies), but its defense is best presented in the writings of his followers. Notably, Norman Malcolm has forcefully maintained that the argument by analogy fails because it wrongly supposes that it is possible to argue from other people's behavior (that is, movement of their bodies) to the fact that they have minds, because it wrongly supposes that it is possible to have consciousness of oneself (knowledge of one's own mind) independently of knowledge of others, and because it ultimately leads us into the untenable position of solipsism.[275] From our above summary of Sartre's complaints, we can see the remarkable agreement in direction between these two very different philosophers.

The argument in Sartre's works (and in Malcolm's studies, couched in a very different philosophical idiom) is that it is a mistake to begin by supposing that there are two different substances, mind and body, which must be related:

The philosophy of the Nineteenth and Twentieth Centuries seems to have understood that once myself and the Other are considered as two separate substances, we cannot escape solipsism;

any union of these two substances must in fact be held to be impossible.[276]

Furthermore, the idea that the existence of other minds can be established as a *hypothesis*—as a piece of *knowledge*—implies that the other is to be argued to exist on the basis of *evidence* and his existence can only be *probable*. Sartre argues that the very nature of the problem is such that the other is not a possible object of my experience, and I cannot therefore have *evidence* for his existence at all. Since knowledge is based on evidence, we can have no knowledge of the existence of others. It also follows from this that it makes no sense to say that it is only *probable* that other people exist, for the notion of 'probability' is tied to the notions of 'knowledge' and 'evidence'. This is not to say, of course, that we cannot *doubt* the existence of other people. It is only to claim that the notion of 'probability' does not apply here.

Using these arguments, Sartre attacks Husserl's conception of our *knowledge* of other people (and also his own theses in *The Transcendence of the Ego*):

Because Husserl has reduced being to a series of meanings, the only connection which he has been able to establish between my being and that of the Other is a connection of knowledge. Therefore Husserl cannot escape solipsism any more than Kant could.[277]

Formerly I believed that I could escape solipsism by refuting Husserl's concept of the existence of the Transcendental "Ego". [TE 1937]. At that time I thought that since I had emptied my consciousness of its subject, nothing remained there which was privileged as compared to the Other. But actually although I am still persuaded that the hypothesis of a transcendental subject is useless and disastrous, abandoning it does not help one bit to solve the question of the existence of Others. Even if outside the empirical Ego there is nothing other than the consciousness of that Ego—that is a transcendental field without a subject—the fact remains that my affirmation of the Other demands and requires the existence beyond the world of a similar transcendental field.[278]

In the argument by analogy, why should we have any reason at all for sup-

posing that these other bodies 'have' minds? Again, in Husserl's theory of empathy, why should we *feel* ('intuit') that these other bodies have minds? Both theses assume that we have some sort of evidence on which to base such a hypothesis or feeling. It further assumes that my knowledge of others is of a radically different kind from my knowledge of myself. It still further assumes that other people are objects of a sort. The first step to the solution of the problem of other minds is to realize that

What I aim at in the Other is nothing more than what I find in myself. But these phenomena are radically distinct from all other phenomena.[279]

We do not see bodies and then infer that they are bodies of persons; we see persons. Sartre accuses traditional philosophy, particularly Kant, of ignoring the concept of a *person*. Sartre's solution to the other minds problem is to deny the Cartesian premise from which it begins, "I know other person's bodies directly but can never know their souls directly." To the contrary, we know neither their bodies nor their souls but simply know them as *persons*.

This positive solution has its marked parallel in British analytic philosophy. P. F. Strawson in *Individuals*[280] argues that the concept of 'person' must be a *primitive* and not derived from the traditional concepts of 'body' and 'mind'. Of course, Sartre is talking (phenomenologically) about our 'primitive' *experiences* of the other and Strawson is talking about the concepts of the English language which we use to talk about persons, but the marked similarity in argument shows just how close these different philosophical approaches can become. According to both philosophers, we must begin with a rejection of all arguments attempting to prove the existence of persons on the evidence derived from human bodies and their 'behavior' (that is, movement). On this basis, Sartre argues that we can give no *proof* of the existence of other persons at all:

Such a theory can not offer a new proof of the existence of others, or an argument better than any other against solipsism. Actually if solipsism is to be rejected, this cannot be because it is impossible, or if

you prefer, because nobody is truly solipsistic. The Other's existence will always be subject to doubt . . . the Other's existence cannot be a probability. Probability can concern only objects which appear in our experience . . . There is probability only if a validation or invalidation of it is at every moment possible.[281]

We must reject the view that the other is an object of my experience, that the other is a duality of mind and body, that the other is known in a way different from the way I know myself. We can see that Merleau-Ponty is in essential agreement with Sartre in this problem in spite of some differences in specifics (or at least in expression);

There is no difficulty in understanding how I can conceive the Other, because the I and consequently the other are not conceived as part of the woven stuff of phenomena; they have validity rather than existence. There is nothing hidden behind these faces and gestures, no domain to which I have no access, merely a little shadow which owes its very existence to the light. . . . If the Other is truly for himself alone, beyond his being for me, . . . He and I must have an outer appearance . . . in that case it is not I that the other would see, nor he that I should see.[282]

In a very different light, we see Camus illustrating (but not arguing) the same thesis:

A man is talking on the telephone behind a glass partition; we don't hear him, but we see his unintelligible dumb show; we wonder why he is alive.[283]

We cannot perceive others as if they were simply 'behaving' bodies of which we subsequently hypothesize that they are persons.

We have not yet seen of what our experience of the other consists; we have only been told from what it is not derived. Sartre traces his solution, his thesis that we 'primitively' experience persons, to Hegel's *Phenomenology*. It is in the apprehension of my-*Self* that I become conscious of the other as also a *Self;*

Hegel's brilliant intuition is to make me depend on the Other in my being. I am, he

said, a being-for-itself which is for-itself only through another. Therefore the Other penetrates me to the heart. I cannot doubt him without doubting myself since "self consciousness is real only in so far as it recognizes its echo (and its reflection) in another.[284]

The origin of Self- and other-consciousness is the *confrontation* with the Other,

The Other is the one who excludes me by being himself, the one whom I exclude by being myself.

Consciousnesses are directly supported by one another in a reciprocal imbrication of their being. This position allows us at the same time to define the way in which the Other appears to me: he is the one who is Other than I; therefore he is given as a non-essential object with a character of negativity.[285]

We may recall that Hegel's master-slave relationship, apart from its dramatization as a life-death struggle, is a struggle for mutual *recognition*. Similarly, the encounter with the other is a struggle for recognition, in particular (as for Hegel), recognition as *freedom*. The master and slave result from a struggle for *domination;* any two people perform the same battle in their every encounter for Sartre. The other attempts to 'reduce me to an object', to *define* me as a fixed Self; I try to do the same to the other. Thus we may easily see how Being-for-others leads us into the third (and fourth) forms of *bad faith* mentioned at the end of the previous section. Being-for-others is essentially a struggle to avoid Being-an-*object*-for-others. Human relationships, like human reality in general, are necessarily unhappy in Sartre's philosophy.

What is the peculiar set of experiences in which we are Being-for-others? It is exemplified by being *looked at* by another person. We do not experience other people as objects because essential to any such experience is the experience of being viewed by the other as I view him. It is this *look (le Regard)* which is the basis of my relations with other people. (It is not a *proof* of the existence of other people.) All attitudes of 'self-consciousness' presume such a *look* from others (where 'self-consciousness' here has the same ambiguity we discussed in Hegel's 'master-slave relationship').

We introduced a brief discussion of the emotion *shame* in the last section where we argued with Sartre that shame was not simply a feeling (a sensation) but involved an evaluation of the situation. We may now expand that analysis with the comment that this evaluation is one which is made in terms of the *look* of an *other*. I am ashamed of myself only insofar as I see myself being seen by another. When I am simply performing a disgraceful act, for example, looking through a keyhole, I am not self-conscious:

This means first of all that there is no self to inhabit my consciousness, nothing therefore to which I can refer my acts in order to qualify them. They are in no way known; I am my acts . . . I am a pure consciousness of things. This means that behind that door a spectacle is presented as "to be seen," a conversation as "to be heard." The door, the keyhole are at once both instruments and obstacles. . . . [286]

But all of a sudden I hear footsteps in the hall. Someone is looking at me! What does this mean? It means that I am suddenly affected in my being and that essential modifications appear in my structure— modifications which I can apprehend and fix conceptually by means of the reflective cogito. First of all I now exist as myself because somebody sees me—as it is usually expressed . . . here the self comes to haunt the unreflective consciousness. . . . I am for myself only as I am a pure reference to the Other. [287]

The shame consists, in part, of a feeling, of course, an "immediate shudder which rushes through me from head to foot without any discursive preparation," [288] but the shame is primarily recognition of myself as *being* as the other sees me;

By the mere appearance of the Other, I am put in the position of passing judgment on myself as an object, for it is as an object that I appear to the Other. [289]

(I am not strictly an object, because I give him a look, for example, a defensive look, and am another for him as well.) I am *fixed* by his *look,*

For the Other, I am leaning over the keyhole as this tree is bent by the wind. I have a nature. [290]

The other's *look* thus makes me see myself "as the other would see me," and I then see myself as a fixed set of properties and behaviors. In the other's eyes, I am a 'peeping Tom', a disgrace. For myself (unreflectively), there was simply the scene behind the door being viewed by me; now I see the entire situation of myself looking through the keyhole and I feel shame. I am *self-conscious* in that I take another's view of my behavior. I simplify myself, categorize myself, analyze myself into the crude fixations which I would never apply to myself alone. My vulgarity defines me, but, Sartre tells us, "Nobody can be vulgar all by himself." The *look* of the other turns me into a fixed personality, and what we have been calling "reflection" is possible only with this mutual recognition of others;

Contrary to the philosophy of Descartes, contrary to that of Kant, when we say "I Think" we are attaining to ourselves in the presence of the Other, and we are just as certain of the Other as we are of ourselves. Thus the man who discovers himself directly in the Cogito also discovers all the Others, and discovers them as the condition of his own existence. [291]

I cannot attain any truth about myself, except through the mediation of the Other. [292]

This theme permeates Sartre's novels and plays, and the complex relationships that quickly develop in his works are illustrations of the thesis that our conception of ourselves depends on what others think of us;

I no longer exist in myself, but only in him. [293]

In *St. Genet*, it is the *look* of an adult 'catching' ten-year-old Jean that moves him to think of himself as a thief and a pervert. In *No Exit*, Inez teases Estelle,

Suppose I covered my eyes and refused to look at you, all that loveliness of yours would be wasted on the desert air. [294]

and Estelle says of herself, after finding that there is no mirror in the room in Hell,

I feel so queer. (She pats herself.) Don't you ever feel that way too? When I can't

see myself I begin to wonder if I really exist, I pat myself just to make sure, but it doesn't help.[295]

Similarly, in *The Reprieve* (third novel of the *Le Chemins de Liberté* series), Daniel says,

"I think, therefore I am," which used to trouble me so sorely, for the more I thought the less I seemed to be; and I say, "I am seen, therefore I am" . . . he who sees me causes me to be; I am as he sees me.[296]

Again in *The Flies,* we find King Aegisthus remarking,

I have come to see myself only as they see me. . . . Am I anything more than the dread that others have of me?[297]

The concern for Being-for-others is captured by other French existentialists as well. De Beauvoir tells us, in *Ethics of Ambiguity,*

the individual defines himself only by his relation to the world and to other individuals.[298]

and Merleau-Ponty tells us,

The For-Themselves, me for myself and the other for himself—must stand out against a background of For Others—I for the Other and the Other for me. My life must have a significance which I do not constitute; there must strictly speaking be an intersubjectivity.[299]

We are involved in the world and with others in an inextricable tangle.[300]

Merleau-Ponty remakes Sartre's distinction between being-for-myself and Being-for-Others;

It is often a matter of surprise that the cripple or the invalid can put up with himself. The reason is that such people are not for themselves deformed or at death's door. . . . Consciousness can never objectify itself into invalid-consciousness or cripple-consciousness, and even if the old man complains of his age or the cripple of his deformity, they can do so only by comparing themselves

with others or seeing themselves through the eyes of others.[301]

Everything I 'am' in virtue of nature or history—hunchbacked, handsome, or Jewish—I never am completely for myself.[302]

Merleau-Ponty ends his *Philosophy of Phenomenology* with a quote from Saint-Exupéry:

Man is but a network of relationships, and these alone matter to him.[303]

In *The Rebel,* Camus demands, "I revolt, therefore we are," and his works are also heavily dependent on the peculiarity of the tensions between people which is given theoretical substance in Sartre. Clemence, the guilt-ridden ex-barrister of *The Fall,* is obsessed with the self-consciousness that comes from being constantly viewed by others as a noble man, a ladies' man, or a generous man, and acts on others by guilt, instilling the same morose self-consciousness in them. On the other hand, Meursault, *The Stranger,* is strange primarily in peculiar ability to escape the look of others;

he refuses to lie . . . Meursault, contrary to appearances, does not want to simplify life. He tells the truth, he refuses to exaggerate his feelings, and immediately, society feels threatened.[304]

The sudden change in Meursault's temperament towards the end of the book begins at his trial, the first time the opinions of others begin to affect him:

It was then that I noticed a row of faces opposite me. These people were staring hard at me . . . I had a foolish desire to burst into tears. For the first time I'd realized how all these people loathed me.[305]

The look is a *fixating look;* it denies our freedom to be what we wish and introduces an inescapable facticity to our conception of ourselves. I make a vulgar gesture in the privacy of my room and the fact that I made it can be neglected in all my future choices. I make the same gesture before others, and my actions are always considered in the light of my vulgarity, even by me.

It is the existence of the other and the effects of his view of me that is definitive to my Being-in-the-world. If we were to skeptically reject or doubt the existence of others, whole segments of our lives would be swept away. We would no longer be self-conscious, and, moreover, we would no longer be forced to see the world as a public world. Husserl had come to the insight late in life that it is only because of our cohabitation of our world with other people that we have 'objective' experience at all. Sartre sees this as well, and is willing to go so far as to say that our existence in the world ontologically depends on the existence of other people. Once again we may pardon Sartre's penchant for overstatement as we realize how much other people are neglected in traditional ontologies. Our 'human condition' is not founded upon our conscious relations with things. Most of our experiences would rather seem to fall under the heading of "Being-for-other."

My Body
One of the distinct features of the philosophy of Sartre and Merleau-Ponty is their emphasis on the analysis of the human body. From our discussion thus far, it should be evident why they think such an investigation is necessary. Traditional philosophers, Descartes for example, had simply distinguished material objects (substance) from consciousness (mental substance); my body was one among other material objects, although one of special interest to me. My body, according to the traditional thesis, was no different philosophically than the chair in which I sit. It is the dualism which we have seen attacked in this and the last chapter between mind and object (particularly mind and body) which is responsible for the apparent meaningfulness of expressions like "my body," or "I have a body." We ought to ask, "*Who* has this body?" and as soon as we do, we see that there is something very peculiar about thinking of my body as a physical object.

The peculiarity is initiated because I think "myself manifested to the other and the other manifested for me *as a body*":[306] We then tend to think of the body as,

a certain thing *having its own laws and capable of being defined from outside.*[30']

Obsessed with being, and forgetful of the perspectivism of my experience, I henceforth treat it as an object and deduce it from a relationship point of view upon the world, as one of the objects of the world.[308]

Once we think of the body as an object, as an object of physiology, for example, there are "insurmountable difficulties" in trying to 'reunite' consciousness with this physiological system. According to Sartre, I never "apprehend the contingency of my body as body for me." My body is not an object in the world. Furthermore, the body-mind distinction is simply untenable:

Being-for-itself must be wholly body and it must be wholly consciousness; it cannot be united with a body. Similarly, being-for-Others is wholly body; there are no 'psychic phenomena' there to be united with the body. There is nothing behind the body. But the body is wholly 'psychic'.[309]

The consciousness of the body invades the body, the soul spreads over all its parts, . . .[310]

If there is no distinction between mind and body *in my own case*, and if I can clearly view other bodies and even my own body as an object in special instances, what is my body?

According to Sartre, traditional thought has unwisely simplified the concept of 'my body' so that it becomes a kind of physical object which stands in a special set of causal relationships *to me*. My body, however, is primarily *me*, not an object *of mine*. My body is

an instrumental center of instrumental complexes, a point of view and a point of departure.[311]

My body is *"lived and not known":*[312]

the body is not distinct from the situation of the for-itself since the for-itself, to exist and to be situated are one and the same.[313]

I cannot understand the function of the living body except by enacting it myself, and except in so far as I am a body which rises towards the world.[314]

This is not the only 'perspective' (or 'level of conceptualization' in Merleau-Ponty) which I may take towards my body. I can look at my body as I look at others, as the cripple (who is not a cripple-consciousness prereflectively) sees himself as a cripple only by reference to what others can do that he cannot. Even in this 'perspective' towards the body, it must be made clear that the body is not an *object,* in the sense of mere Being-in-itself. In the discussion of *Being-for-others,* we insisted that the *look* of others turns us into an object. Now, it must be clear that to be turned into an object in this sense—because one is still viewed as a *person*—is not to be turned into a mere (physical) body;

I must apprehend the Other first as the one for whom I exist as an object; ... The Other exists for me first and I apprehend him in his body subsequently.[315]

We must distinguish between viewing a person ("through his body") and simply viewing a (physical) body; we can view a body of a person as a mere physical body; but this is a highly peculiar situation, and certainly not the way we usually view others. It is virtually never the way we view our own bodies. (In our discussion of Heidegger, we similarly claimed that one never sees his hand as a *thing,* but always as a part of his instrumentality.)[316] The anatomist-physiologist view of the body is not more 'basic' or 'primitive' than 'less scientific' views; it is highly derivative and even a perversion of these views.

If my body is not a material object, either for myself or for others, then we can extend some interesting theses encountered in our analysis of consciousness (and Heidegger's analysis of *Dasein*) as applicable to the body as well. For example, it does not make sense to say that our body is ('primitively') *in* space and time. Merleau-Ponty tells us that "it *inhabits* space and time."[317] Neither does it make sense to talk of the divisibility' of the body. According to Sartre, I "never perceive an arm raised alongside a motionless body. I perceive Pierre who raises his hand."[318] I do not see, even in others, parts of a body functioning together; I always see a body functioning. In my own case, this is even more clearly the case. I act through my body; I do not mysteriously organize various material objects

(the parts and organs of my body) into objects of which I can make use.

The body is to be compared, not to a physical object, but to a work of art. . . . It is a focal point of living meanings, not the function of a certain number of mutually variable terms.[319]

So conceived, our body is not delimited by the anatomist-physiologist's portrait of the human body. For Merleau-Ponty, for example, *habit* is a matter of 'enlarging' our body;

Habit expresses our power of dilating our being into the world, or changing our existence by appropriately fresh instruments. To get used to a hat, a car, or a stick is to be transplanted into them, or conversely to incorporate them into the bulk of our own body. . . . It is literally true that the subject who learns to type incorporates the key-blank space into his bodily space.[320]

We conclude that the body is not simply another object in the world to which I (that is, consciousness) am mysteriously attached; my body and I are indistinguishable:

[my body] is an object which does not leave me. But in that case is it still an object?[321]

I for-myself am both consciousness and body inseparably, as I for-others and others for-me are consciousness and body inseparably. We have already seen that my relations with others are always a struggle to preserve my freedom, especially to preserve it from the objectifying *looks* of others. To preserve my freedom, I attempt to change the other into an object-for-me (and, impossibly, to change him into an object even for-himself). First, my *looks* serve this purpose, but more dramatically, I can focus my and his attention on his body and attempt to reduce him to pure body. This is, of course, impossible, but the more 'physical' the other becomes, the more free I become from him. The means of creating such a focus of attention is *sex;* sex is not 'accidental' to human relationships, but is at the very core of our struggle with others. The brutal life-death struggle of Hegel's master-slave relationship is replaced in

Sartre by the sophisticated bodily clashes of the sexual encounter, for it is here that our attempts to objectify the other achieve their greatest success.

The key to sex is the notion of *'flesh'*; flesh is not mere material substance, but it is the living substance of an other. Our perception of flesh (like our perception of the other) is essentially different from our perception of all other things. This is not, as we often suppose, because we know that this fleshy material is permeated with sensory receptors which give pleasure (and pain) to the other, for we do not think so anatomically in our normal encounters with the other.

Sex is not mere genital contact, to be sure (Merleau-Ponty praises Freud for this insight), sex always involves the whole body (that is, the whole person). Sex is primarily a desire for power over the other, the master-slave relationship in the bedroom.

Saying that I have a body is thus another way of saying that I can be seen as an object and that I try to be seen as a subject—that another can be my master or slave, so that shame or shamelessness express the dialectic of the plurality of consciousness, and have a metaphysical significance. The same might be said of sexual desire: if it cannot accept the presence of a third party as witness, if it feels that too natural an attitude or over-casual remarks, on the part of the desired person are signs of hostility, this is because it seeks to fascinate, and because the observing third party or the person desired if he is too free in manner, escapes this fascination. . . . What we try to possess, then, is not just a body, but a body brought to life by consciousness.[322]

This purely sexual overpowering is still only a single aspect of the complex struggles with others. Philosophically, it is a more important aspect than has usually been allowed, but it is, as has been generally supposed, one of the less sophisticated aspects of human relationships. In the following section, we shall briefly discuss some of the more 'sophisticated' mechanisms of protecting ourselves from the other.

In closing this discussion of the body, it is worth commenting that Merleau-Ponty has turned these insights concerning the peculiar place of my body in the world into a basis for a theory of perception;

The theory of the body is already a theory of perception. One could not grasp the object without the mediation of bodily experience.[323]

External perception and the perception of one's own body vary in conjunction because they are two facets of one and the same act.[324]

This theory of bodily perception will allow an answer to a most puzzling question in Husserl.[325] When we speak of "looking at an object in its different aspects" and from different viewpoints, how are we to make sense of the notion of 'different aspects' and 'different viewpoints' after bracketing the world, including my own body? If my body is bracketed, what sense does it make to say that I 'walk around the object'? Merleau-Ponty has dispensed both with this problematic 'bracketing' of existence and rejected the claim that my own body is just another object. Thus he is able to assert that it is

by conceiving my body itself as a mobile object that I am able to interpret perceptual appearance and construct the cube [I am walking around] as it truly is.[326]

Relations with Other People
My relations with things in the world are not a threat to me. On the contrary, it is the *ability* I have to nihilate these things (my situation or facticity) and myself which is constitutive of my *freedom*. My relations with other people, however, do constitute a threat to my freedom, for the other has the ability to make me into an object. I also have the ability to turn him into an object, and thus become an equal threat to him. We have already seen that sex is a mechanism for reducing the other to flesh and escaping from his *look*. We may gather from this that human relationships in general will consist of the same sort of struggle and be essentially unhappy, unsatisfactory affairs. There may be a possibility of satisfactory human relationships (just as there may be some possibility of being in *good faith*). It is evident that such relationships are virtually nonexistent in Sartre's literary works. The general picture of 'primitive' human relationships he gives us in *Being and Nothingness* is that of a confrontation and

struggle between two subjects each wishing to escape the other's look.

We can see how very different Sartre's gloomy picture of interpersonal relationships is from Heidegger's portrait of the harmonious "Being-together" of his *Mitsein*. Sartre refers to such a group as a *crew* rather than a relationship, and objects that

The essence of the relation between consciousnesses is not the Mitsein; *it is conflict.*[327]

Sartre does not deny the possibility of a *Mitsein;* he denies only that it is a 'primitive' relationship between persons. He devotes an entire although brief section to the *Mitsein* in *Being and Nothingness,*[328] in order to explain the *derivation* of this attitude towards others. In his later, more political works, the *mitsein* of *class-consciousness* will become central; conflict relationships are no longer thought to be essential but only a product of capitalist social conditioning.

The weapons in the existentialist master-slave conflict need be no more than the person's eyes, but what one sees is always a person's body. Thus we found that human relations were *centrally* sexual; in fact, this is still too weak. Sartre wishes to claim that sex is the basic or 'primitive' form of every human relationship:

My original attempt to get hold of the Other's free subjectivity through his objectivity-for-me is sexual desire.[329]

In the discussion of the body, we treated sex as purely a bodily relation, albeit with the warning that the body is never merely a physical body. Now we must see that sex is not just bodily contact, and sexual desire is not desire for bodily contact or for 'sexual' (that is, physiological) *fulfillment*. Sex is not 'instinctual' or 'bodily' or 'physiological' in the least. No matter how often we speak of sex as 'natural' and as 'physical', it remains much more than that. Sex is often treated with hunger as a simple 'drive' (we have already commented that even hunger ought not be construed as a 'mere drive' but as an interpretation and evaluation of our situation). Sex is not directed towards some sexual object or other as hunger is directed toward any sort of food, and sexual satisfaction is clearly not simply defined by bodily 'fulfillment'. With Freud, Sartre assigns a role

to sexuality as a *general* personal characteristic, one that pervades all human endeavors. Whereas Freud links sex to the unconscious *libido*, however, Sartre insists that it is a conscious *project*. Sex is consciously attained *power*, and it should not surprise us that sexual relations permeate all of Sartre's literary works and is an explicitly power-seeking mechanism (compare the three way 'Hell' among Garcin, Inez (who is a Lesbian), and Estelle in *No Exit;* Daniel's conscious use of sex as a manipulative tool in *Age of Reason,* and even the debate between Zeus and Orestes in *The Flies*).

The purpose of sexual desire is to turn one's partner into a pure body. To this end, Sartre argues originally but dubiously, it is the most fleshy (that is, object-like) parts of the body which are primarily involved in sexual intercourse:

It is not by chance that [sexual] desire while aiming at the body as a whole attains it especially through masses of flesh which are very little differentiated, largely nerveless, hardly capable of spontaneous movement, through breasts, buttocks, thighs, stomach; these form an image of pure facticity.[330]

Against the commonsense notion of sex as a pleasurable activity, Sartre argues that pleasure is not even a desirable accompaniment to sexual intercourse:

Pleasure is the death and failure of [sexual] desire.[331]

Pleasure diverts one from the primary purpose of sexual encounter, power over the other. When one enjoys his sexual activity, he yields himself to the other and actually defeats his purpose. Perversion, on this account, is not using the pleasurable activities of sex to "one's own advantage"; it is conversely using the essentially conflict-centered activities of sex for one's pleasure.

There is not a single attitude towards sex and human relations, however, and there are two 'primitive' attitudes one may have towards the other (neither of which are conducive to harmonious or happy relationships). First, there is love, which is essentially masochistic. Second, there is hate and indifference, which are essentially sadistic. One may again wonder whether there is any room in this account for a satisfactory love affair. Simone De

Beauvoir claims (in her *Memoirs*) that Sartre intended to make the fourth book of the *Chemins de Liberté* series include a happy love between Mathieu and Odette; but the fact that Sartre gave up writing the book is in itself significant.

The fact that our 'primitive' confrontation with the other is born in conflict would not entail that all human relationships are based on such struggle. Yet, this is decidedly the picture of human relations which emerges from *Being and Nothingness*. It is true that we attempt to form harmonious relations with the other, and Sartre allows that our "first attitude" towards the other is that of *love*. But the attempt at love is essentially abortive, for the primitive structure of every human relation is already based on the other's attempts to reduce me to an object in his eyes. As an object, I cannot at the same time be viewed as a free subject, and, as I protect myself by attempting to objectify the other, I cannot view him at the same time as a free subject with whom I can have true contact. Love attempts to overcome this conflict by establishing a relationship between two subjects each completely respecting each other's freedom. According to Sartre, this attempt is doomed to failure. Sartre claims that love of an other is *possession* of that other and being possessed by the other. But only objects, not free subjects, can be possessed, and so Sartre concludes that love is impossible. Our possession of the other forbids us from respecting his freedom (he can have no freedom as an object for me); his possession of me limits my freedom insofar as I recognize myself as his possession. Consequently, love as such is a "contradictory effort."

It is this frustrated love that turns to masochism, which is not, according to Sartre, a perversion of love but its essential consequence. Masochism is the attempt to achieve a human relationship through the sacrifice of one's own freedom and offering oneself as the other's possession. Masochism is a paradigm of *bad faith*—the bad faith of looking at oneself simply as an object for the other. Because it is love that leads to this reduction of oneself to an object for the other, love is itself a paradigm of *bad faith*.

The basis of the love relationship is usually thought to be some form of communion or *Mitsein* in which personal interests and ego-images are sacrificed or at least suspended. Sartre, on the other hand, takes the basis of every human relationship, including love relationships, to be the retaining of my own freedom from others. Hegel had pointed out the most obvious way of maintaining one's freedom from the other, kill the other. Sartre sees that there are more subtle ways than murder, and follows Hegel's 'master-slave' conception as a resolution of conflict. Slavery attempts (but as we saw, fails) to reduce the other (the slave) to a mere object without will (freedom) of his own. Love attempts the same end, but within the bounds of societal restrictions. As to ultimate purpose, murder, slavery, and loving are on a par.

In love, I attempt to gain the respect of the other and in so doing retain my own self-respect and freedom. He expects the same of me; thus, the illusion (according to Sartre) arises that we have a cooperative endeavor of mutual respect. Because freedom requires possession, and possession can only take objects, there can be no respect for those we love. In other words, I am free only insofar as I am free to interpret the other as I choose, and insofar as I can escape his interpretation of me. He is free only insofar as he is free to interpret me as he chooses, and insofar as he is free from my interpretations of him. Consequently, love is impossible and most look elsewhere for human communion.

There are many efforts of *bad faith* which can be used to hide the failure of love. The 'lovers' may appeal to "transcendent meanings" ("You were meant for me" or "Marriages are made in Heaven"), or 'degrade' their failing relation to raw sex ("the contact of two epidermises"), or it can follow Kierkegaard's model for 'psychic love' which consists in a full commitment to the love. In any case, love must necessarily fail with every *look* at each other, and end in despair, in masochism.

Masochism is not the end of the attempt to form a human relationship in which one's own freedom is protected. It is only the end of the 'first attitude' of which love is the beginning. From love-masochism, one can attempt to regain full control over the other by reducing him to an object. Hate is this suppression of the other, and it, like love, attempts to proceed through mutual recognition with the other. Hate is identical to love in its purpose and its structure but differs only in the replacement of mutual respect by mutual urges to *destruction* of the other. Similarly, indifference is an attitude of *denial* of the other's existence. Hatred, however, is a failure just as love is a failure; either one succumbs to the other's hatred and becomes an object or one wins over the other and *ipso facto* loses the means for the recognition of his freedom by the other. We saw this argument in Hegel as the consequence of the master-slave relationship. It would appear to be less applicable here, insofar as the desire to eliminate the other and the desire to gain his recognition are different. We find that these two different desires are closely related; as love gives way to masochism, hatred gives way to sadism. It is in sadism that sex becomes basic, as one attempts to "trap the other in his own flesh." Sadistic sex is clearly not performed for pleasure, but for power. (We have seen that Sartre would disagree with those, for example, Nietzsche or, specific to this problem, the Marquis de Sade, who would maintain that pleasure is at least a common concomitant of the power.) *Obscenity* is an experience which is essentially tied to sadism; it is the *ungraceful* body of the suppressed other which is seen as an object, as *de trop*. It is the same experience which induced *nausea* in Roquentin in his encounter with the meaninglessness of the *things* in the world. The attempt of sadism to reduce the other to a mere body, a mere thing, a mere obscenity, is a failure as soon as the other *looks* at him, for this look, like all looks, counters the sadist by reestablishing the other *as* an other. At this point, the only way of eliminating the threat of the other—the *look* of the other—is to kill him. Sartre tells us even this is unsatisfactory. In our killing of the other, we cannot kill the fact that he has looked at us in the past and thus defined us as objects—as sadists, as murderers. The *look* remains even after the other has been murdered.

It would hardly be necessary to comment at this point that the resultant picture of human relationships is one of catastrophe. The seemingly well-intentioned efforts of love turn to masochism, masochism to hate, hate to sadism, sadism o attempted murder, and all of this in a necessary pattern. It would be easy enough to begin a pointed attack on this depressing progression, starting with Sartre's dubious characterization of love as possession, but we shall continue our policy to abstain as much as possible from criticism of these views in order to stress what is plausible in the analysis. It is all too easy to take "love" as an evidently possible and obviously desirable human relationship, to think of sex as a natural 'given' or a nonessential benefit of love, to interpret masochism and sadism as essentially perversions instead of considering their roles in human relationships. It is all too common in moral and social philosophy to begin with the supposition that membership in the *Mitsein* is the desirable and attainable goal of every human being. We have spoken throughout this book of men who have provided strong arguments for the separation of the individual from the public, the crowd, the herd, the others, and the consequence of this isolation of the individual cannot help but make such a supposition less palatable. It is often commented that existentialism is a "wrong" philosophy because it takes such a dim view, or a diminishing view of human relationships. It is important, however, to see just how much the existentialist starting point determines our view of relationships with others. Given this starting point, it just may be, as Sartre argues, that human relationships are *essentially* unhappy. We can hardly take ourselves seriously as philosophers if we do not accord this hopeless view the most serious consideration. We shall postpone a critique of it to a future study.[332]

"Existentialist Ethics"

Considering the popular opinion that existentialism is first of all an ethical code, it might be surprising that we have limited our study of Sartre's 'ethics' to a short concluding section. In a sense, however, there is nothing more to be said about Sartre's 'ethics'. He has never written a major work on ethics as such. At the end of *Being and Nothingness,* he promises such a work, but it has never appeared. The source of 'existentialist ethics' might be sought in the works of less central authors, e.g., in Simone De Beauvoir's *Ethics of Ambiguity* or Camus's *Myth of Sisyphus,* or in the works of the 'religious existentialists', Marcel, Jaspers, Tillich, Buber. Or, today, one might seek a characterization of what passes for 'existentialism' in the glorification of arbitrary action in

Norman Mailer's *The Presidential Papers.* But Sartre flatly states that *Being and Nothingness* is at most the foundation for an ethics and not a treatise in ethics.

Does Sartre's ontology give us an ethics? On the one hand, we might say that the central thesis of *Being and Nothingness,* that all values are authored in action by the individual, entails that Sartre cannot give us a set of values. Any claim he would make for the universal validity of any choice of actions would at worst be a brazen instance of 'bad faith', and at best, be autobiographical and not be binding on us. But on the other hand, Sartre's celebration of freedom, his analysis of human relationships, and his description of *bad faith* are clearly the basis for a set of values. In particular, Sartre's 'ontology' gives us a set of what Kierkegaard called "existential values," values that concern the person and the *manner* of making decisions rather than the specific choice.

One way of interpreting Sartre's denial that he is doing ethics is to invoke a distinction familiar in Anglo-American analytic philosophy between "normative ethics" and "meta-ethics". (F. Olafson has employed this distinction in this way in his *Principles and Persons.*)

Normative ethics provides us with concrete prescriptions and specific principles instructing us what we ought to do. Metaethics is the formulation of an ethical framework and the establishing of a logic and a discourse for delimiting the kinds of principles which are open to consideration and the kinds of arguments which are acceptable. (In analytic philosophy, metaethics is further restricted as a *description* of ethical discourse and logic and limited to second-level discussions about normative problems.) Metaethics is literally talk *about* ethics, but this need *not* imply that metaethics is normatively impotent: on the contrary, it is metaethical considerations which determine what our normative ethics will be like.[333] Thus Kant's ethics clearly is metaethical in its attempts to formulate the formal principles to which any moral judgment must conform, and even Nietzsche and Kierkegaard are doing metaethics and not normative ethics. Sartre, we may now see, is doing ethics in one sense and not doing it in another. He is setting up a framework within which we can make normative judgments, but he is not helping us to make those judgments. Sartre *cannot* give

us a normative ethics, because the metaethics, often explicit in *Being and Nothingness,* precludes any possible defense of a normative code of ethics. This metaethics is the same nihilism we have seen in Kierkegaard, Nietzsche, and Heidegger as well as in Sartre (and Camus and De Beauvoir). It is the thesis that there is no and can be no ultimate justification for normative ethics. Consequently, no existentialist can consistently present a normative ethics as correct.

Existentialist ethics centers itself on the doctrine that 'there can be no ethics'. If this proclamation seems contradictory, it is only because we have failed to distinguish the two very different senses of "ethics" used here. Sartre's neglect of 'ethics' in *Being and Nothingness* is a rejection of normative ethics. Similarly, Heidegger's outspoken attack on 'values' in general can be understood according to the same interpretation. Sartre recognizes, however, that such "existential values" do form an ethics of a sort. Heidegger does not:

In truth Heidegger's description [of authenticity and inauthenticity] shows all too clearly his anxiety to establish an ontological foundation for Ethics with which he claims not to be concerned, as also to reconcile his humanism with the religious sense of the transcendent.[334]

Existentialist ethics is based on nihilism (often with the Nietzsche-Dostoevskian argument that "If God does not exist, everything is permitted"). Freedom is the ontological heart of existentialism; it is also its ethical foundation. There is no criterion of normative ethics which can be defended as 'correct', but the principle of freedom is defended as 'correct' on a metaethical level. In other words, what normative system of values one chooses is not open to judgment, but whether or not he chooses it in freedom is open to judgment. A man cannot, therefore, make a wrong choice of values, but he can make his choice wrongly. We may remind ourselves of Kierkegaard's dictum, "it is not *what* you choose, but *how* you choose that is important." This same dictum forms the basis of modern existentialist ethics:

To will oneself moral and to will oneself free are one and the same decision.[335]

What is at the very heart and center of existentialism is the absolute character of

the free commitment by which every
man realizes himself.[336]

One can choose anything, but only if it
is upon the plane of free commitment.[337]

Existentialism, like Kantian ethics, evaluates the *person* as well as the act. To be a 'good' existentialist is to recognize one's freedom of commitment and thus to take *responsibility* for whatever one *does* or *is*:

He bears responsibility for a world which
is not the work of a strange power, but
of himself, where his defeats are
inscribed, and his victories as well.[338]

To be a 'bad' existentialist is to refuse to recognize one's freedom and responsibility: it is to be in 'bad faith'.

. . . it would be contradictory deliberately
to will oneself not free. But one can
choose not to will himself free, in
laziness, heedlessness, capriciousness,
cowardice, impatience. . . .[339]

It may be objected that existentialism "does not tell us what to do," but it must be obvious why this is so. It can, by its own principles, instruct us only to be free and choose freely, but this prescription cannot at the same time give us a specific course of action. However, this does not make the principle empty, for what we have said about freedom makes it clear that the ethical principle of freedom tells us not only that we are free, but that we must act—must commit ourselves:

One of the chief objections leveled
against existentialism is that the precept
"to will freedom" is only a hollow formula
and offers no concrete content for action.
But that is because one has begun by
emptying the word freedom of its concrete
meaning; we have already seen that
freedom realizes itself only by engaging
itself in the world: to such an extent that
man's project toward freedom is embodied
in him in definite acts of behavior.[340]

It would seem that existentialism ethics is such that it would be impossible to criticize another person's actions. It is true that we cannot criticize the specific course of action he chooses, but we can criticize his way of choosing:

People say to us, "you are unable to judge
others." This is true in one sense and
false in another. It is true in this sense,
that whenever a man chooses his purpose
and his commitment in all clearness and
in all sincerity, whatever that purpose
may be it is impossible for him to prefer
another. . . . We can judge nevertheless
. . . that in certain cases choice is founded
upon an error, and in others upon the
truth. One can judge a man by saying
that he deceives himself.[341]

In our discussion of freedom, we insisted that a man is *absolutely* free both in his freedom from causal determination of his intentions and decisions and in his freedom from 'outside authority' instructing him what course of action is correct. The belief in freedom from causal determination has been common to every philosopher discussed in this book (excepting perhaps only Nietzsche who does not talk about it). The insistence upon freedom from authority is what sharply distinguishes the existentialist from Kant, who taught that there clearly is a *rational* standard of behavior. Kant argued that men were causally free to choose but not rationally free to choose their own values ("posit their own ends"). Existentialism, however, teaches that there is no standard of correctness for one's choices. If reason is argued to be the ultimate justification of morality, one is free to be 'irrational'. If God is posited as the ultimate source of all true values, one is free to be irreverent; if patriotism is taken as the ultimate duty, one is free to be treasonably undutiful; and if human nature is cited as support for a principle, one is free to act 'unnaturally'. This is not to say, of course, that one is free from the consequences of his freedom to reject a value; the irreverent may still be damned, the treasonous may still be hanged, the 'unnatural' may become ill. One is always free to reject whatever values one chooses to reject, often with the understanding that his rejection will be met with disapproval or punishment from others. We might consider, in this context, Hermann Broch's distinction (in *The Sleepwalkers*) between the criminal and the traitor. The criminal accepts the value system of society and intentionally breaks what he recognizes to be a valid law. He therefore accepts his punishment as a fair and 'natural' consequence of his act. The traitor, on the other hand, rejects the values themselves. He need not break the laws which codify these values in order to be a traitor. If he does, he may be caught and punished, but he does not recognize their validity. The criminal may recognize himself as *caught;* the traitor can find only that his freedom is being interfered with by his punishment. Similarly, the student of the 1930s who 'misbehaves' in a spring riot is attacking an authority which he also respects: his 'punishment' must be seen as punishment. But the political activist of the 1960s challenges an authority which he refuses to accept. He cannot, therefore, be *punished* by their 'authority' even though he can be forced to endure the same inconveniences that would otherwise constitute his punishment.

It cannot be stressed too often that the 'absolute freedom' of Sartre's existentialism does not signify freedom to *do* whatever one wants or freedom from the consequences of one's actions or freedom from responsibility for those consequences. Sartre's freedom, in Husserl's terms, is always a 'freedom of intention—as an obstacle, or a challenge is one's own meaning in a situation. Whether painful experience or an inconvenience is constituted as a punishment, as a misfortune, as an obstacle or a challenge is one's own choice; but the experience itself may not be. A past act can be seen as a crime, as an embarrassment, as a revolutionary act, as a mistake; but one cannot choose not to have performed that act. Sartre's theory of value, and here the distinction between 'normative' and 'meta-ethics' begins to break down, is that what has value—all that has value—is a man and his manner of choosing. Not only is it through man that values enter the world; ultimately, it is only man that is valuable.

With Kant, Sartre teaches that "the only thing unqualifiedly good is a good will". For Sartre, the 'good will' is not one that makes correct (rational) choices; but one that sees itself as always making choices. A 'bad will' (or an act in bad faith) is not one that chooses incorrectly (irrationally), but one that does not see itself as a choice. However much Sartre insists that he is simply 'describing' the human condition, there can be no doubt that he believes bad faith to be *bad*, sincerity to be *good*. These 'existential values' carry with them—in any meaningful sense of the term—*moral* weight. In his

defense of the bourgeois morality that Sartre despises, Kant had written that the heart of morality lay in the responsible and freely chosen act. For Sartre as well, 'morality' can lie only in the act of free responsible choice, but such an insistence entails, for him, the destruction of the content of Kant's 'morality'. There is no point in talking of 'free responsible choice' if the values that are chosen are 'a priori given'. Always keeping this major reversal in mind, however, we can avoid many of the most common misinterpretations of Sartre's 'ethics' if we remember his close kinship with Kant. Sartre is a very 'Protestant' moral philosopher: he cares very much for the conceptions of 'good' and 'bad' (and 'good' and 'evil'), but seeks only to continue Kant's shift in the locus of these values from 'moral facts' to acts of choice. Like Kant's "morality", Sartre's 'ethics' is the very antithesis of an ethics of arbitrariness or irresponsibility. Everything a man does, even where we might sometimes say 'he had no choice', is his responsibility. And Sartre's neglect of the consequences of action as irrelevant to moral worth should not be construed as a condoning of action without regard for consequences. Again, the parallel with Kant will suffice to remind us that the purpose of such neglect of consequences serves only to eliminate grounds for excuse ("I couldn't help it, . . .") and further place the burden of responsibility on the choice itself, whatever its consequences.

It is worth our while to reintroduce a remarkable comparison between existentialist ethics and a powerfully influential school of moral philosophy in the analytic tradition. The metaethics of philosophers like C. L. Stevenson and R. N. Hare, on the basis of an attempted *description* of ordinary (*status quo*) ethics, argues that disagreements in ethics are not disagreements in belief or descriptions of states-of-affairs, but rather are differences in *attitude* or prescriptions. Their position, like that of the existentialists, does not allow them to present any normative position as 'correct' or 'true', for their thesis itself, although based upon very different grounds than existentialist nihilism, commits them to the view that moral principles are not 'true' or 'false' ('correct' or 'incorrect'). These philosophers end their moralizing with a refusal to moralize. They do not recognize the incredible normative implications of their view, for example, the demand that we no longer hold the proscriptions against genocide and mass rape as more valid than a 'morality' which actively encouraged these horrors. The existentialists must accept this consequence of their thought as well, but at least they fully recognize its nature, and bear full responsibility for it. This important difference permeates their morality as a whole in contrast to the meta-ethical analysts: Stevenson's *emotivism* or Hare's *prescriptivism* does not go so far as to claim that one is responsible for his attitudes, or that the *manner* of choice is open to criticism (apart from straightforward logical inconsistency).

The comparison with Stevenson and Hare might be used to point out an important difference between the 'ethics' of Sartre and the philosophies of Heidegger and Merleau-Ponty. We have commented elsewhere that Sartre often returns to traditional Cartesian dualism where Heidegger and Merleau-Ponty take the same dualism to be the source of traditional problems. Here, we find that Sartre freely accepts a relatively sharp distinction between facts and values, facticity and transcendence, everyday 'given' bourgeois values and existentially chosen values. Heidegger and Merleau-Ponty, on the other hand, argue at length that there are no such things as 'values' (or 'facts' either), because there is no viable distinction between 'fact' and 'value'. Heidegger's critique of 'values' occupies a central role in *Being and Time*, but it must not be supposed that he is attacking the idea of there being values as well as *facts*.[342] For Heidegger, Being-in-the-World does not involve both facts and values (any more than it involves consciousness and world). The very idea of his 'primitive' analysis of world as "equipment" is intended to destroy all such Cartesian (and Husserlian) dualisms. Merleau-Ponty attacks the dualism of fact and value by placing far more stress than Sartre on the notion of 'the situation'. Where Sartre is quick to degrade 'everyday' and 'given bourgeois' values, Merleau-Ponty sees that these values deserve the central place in our ontology—not strictly as moral facts, but not as 'chosen' values either. To be a worker, a bourgeois, French, Jewish, black, is already a source, not only of 'facticity' upon which we base our choices, but of intentions and interests and possibilities. Sartre

often writes as if, "I am a worker; now I have to freely decide whether to be a cooperative laborer or a revolutionary." But Merleau-Ponty sees that one's situation cannot be separated from his perceptions, and that one's choices cannot be separated from his interests. Finding myself as a worker is already finding myself 'thrown' into a set of choices and preferences. Everyday values are neither strictly 'given' (in the sense celebrated by Kant and attacked by Nietzsche), nor are they strictly chosen, since one is "thrown" into them before one has any chance to 'choose'. In a sense, Merleau-Ponty reintroduces Hegel's notion of *'Sittlichkeit'* as a substitute for both the notions of 'given values' (Kant's *'moralität'*) and Sartre's and Kierkegaard's exaggerated notion of existential choice. According to Merleau-Ponty, one cannot, in Sartre's terms, "wrench himself away" from his situation, but must always make his less-than-absolute choices within the limited perspective and the prejudicial atmosphere of his situation. Merleau-Ponty's arguments have had considerable influence on Sartre. In his more recent work, he has clearly given up the very strong notion of 'choice' he then accepted. In a recent interview, Sartre has said of his earlier ideas, "little by little, I found that the world was more complicated than that." In 1970, he finds it "absolutely incredible" that he believed that "whatever the circumstances, and whatever the site, a man is always free to choose to be a traitor or not. . . ."[343]

Kierkegaard and Nietzsche, Heidegger, Camus, Sartre, and Merleau-Ponty—each in his own way becomes an ethical 'radical', not only in the sense that each rejects the Kantian idea of a 'foundation' for morality, but also in the sense that each rejects in some way the *content* of Kant's bourgeois *'moralität'*. But, if existentialism is limited to evaluation of the manner of choosing and not the *what* of choice, how can such 'radicalism' be defended? One can, of course, criticize people who believe in morality (as opposed to morality itself) on existential grounds: thus Nietzsche's blasphemies against Christianity are directed against the false reasons people hold for their beliefs rather than the beliefs themselves. Nietzsche's own 'ideals' of the *Übermensch* and the eternal recurrence are notoriously devoid of specific content. Similarly, Kierkegaard's philosophy carefully avoids the claim that his chosen way of life (the religious life) is 'correct' and that alternative choices ('aesthetic' or 'ethical' existence) are 'incorrect'. Yet Kierkegaard's moral indignation does emerge against the 'public' and against the man 'in the crowd' who will not choose. In Sartre as well, the brunt of attack is on those who choose for insincere reasons or refuse to recognize their choices. Garcin of *No Exit* is condemned not for his cowardice but for his insincerity. In a strict sense, existentialism is a nihilism that has no 'content', and consequently cannot directly attack the 'contents' of 'morality' or other ethical codes. It can, however, attack and destroy the grounds upon which people base such codes. But this is not to say that existentialism is a purely destructive philosophy. We have many times pointed out that the existentialists themselves typically adopt a strong moral and radical stance. They differ from traditional moralists in being unwilling and incapable—by their own arguments—to give a rational justification for this stance.

A common argument against all forms of 'nihilism', of which existentialism is one, is that it opens the way of all sorts of horrors; it places rape and genocide on the same (a)moral plane as giving gifts and keeping promises. One of the traditional pragmatic arguments against all such philosophies of freedom of choice is the argument that chaos will break loose if people accept it. Existentialism has always been identified as the philosophy with the pessimistic view of man. But what must be evident here is that it is existentialism which places its highest confidence in humanity—that people will *choose* to be humane as well as human. It is just those philosophies and moralities that depend upon sanctions, authority, and 'given' values that presume man will naturally kill, plunder, pillage. Traditional Christianity is clearly degrading to man. It explicitly sees him as pathetically unable to resist temptation to 'evil' without the most horrid of threats. And British utilitarianism, with its 'happy' view of man, depends upon the idea of sanctions to make man's life more than 'nasty, brutish and short'. Even J. S. Mill feels it absolutely necessary to argue with men that it is *rational* to be moral. The existentialists argue that there can be no argument to that conclusion. Yet they do not look at their 'nihilism' as a gateway to disaster.

Some existentialists, of course, particularly Kierkegaard and Nietzsche, don't believe for a second that their ideas will spread beyond 'a few'. But all apparently believe that the freedom they seek will lead not to murder and chaos, but to artistic sensitivity, deeply felt religion, Socratic ethics, or new political and social conscience. Existentialism does not replace morality and humane values but places them on surer ground. To give up belief in 'morality' as a set of a priori or empirically practical principles is not to take the role of the 'fanatic'. It is to set aside invalid justifications and become moral for the right reasons—because one *commits* himself. Existentialism gives us perhaps the most optimistic view of man ever advanced in Western philosophy: man will, without being ordered, instructed, forced by man or nature, choose to be humane. Sartre's 'Existential hero' and Camus 'Absurd hero' are not madmen, and it is more than clear that Nietzsche's nihilist *Übermensch* is not a Nazi prototype. The existentialists may begin with Dostoevsky's concern, "If there is no God, all is permitted," but they soon leave Dostoevskian worries behind. Why should we suppose that man will do 'evil' if we remove the forces of authority of 'good'. Perhaps there is no reason, and the existentialists do not even argue the point. In every author, there is the optimistic and almost simple-minded presupposition that man's freedom is desirable without qualification. (This is not to say, however, that freedom is, for the existentialists, an 'end in itself'. It sometimes appears, in De Beauvoir's *Ethics of Ambiguity,* for example, that freedom is the end to which all actions are to be means. But this notion of freedom has no 'content' in precisely this sense; it cannot intelligibly function in an ends-means relationship with any particular choices. It is a description of the choice, not the object of the choice. In Sartre, freedom is consciousness, and just as consciousness "cannot be its own object," freedom cannot be its own object either.)

Yet each of our authors is a 'radical'. Kierkegaard rejects traditional Christianity to replace it with his own notion of 'becoming a Christian'. Nietzsche rejects the whole of Judeo-Christian morality to replace it with an ethic of "self-realization." Sartre and Merleau-Ponty become Marxists. In no case, however, is *morality* simply rejected, but reinterpreted in a personal and often more consistent way. Kierkegaard retains the moral side of Christianity, but makes personal commitment to God the defining mark of *his* moral life. Nietzsche brutally degrades 'morality', which he says is 'immoral', but retains the moral virtues of courage, loyalty, integrity. Sartre and Merleau-Ponty place politics and revolutionary necessities above everyday morality, but they do not simply reject morality out of hand. In each case, the existentialists reject the authority of 'morals', not to reject morality but to make it their own ethic. And, where there is a contradiction between their own morality and the old, the old morality is not simply dismissed, but necessarily recognized as an ever-present alternative choice;

If I occupy myself in treating as absolute ends certain chosen persons, my wife, my son, my friends, the poor man I meet on my way, if I wear myself out in fulfilling my duties towards them, I shall have to pass in silence over the injustices of the age, the class-struggle, anti-Semitism, etc. and finally I shall have to profit from oppression to do good. . . . But on the other hand, if I throw myself into a revolutionary enterprise, I take the risk of having no leisure for personal relations, and worse still of being brought by the logic of action to treat the greater part of men and even my comrades as means.[344]

From everything we have said thus far, the picture of the existential man is a picture of a man very much alone in the world. Kierkegaard and Nietzsche surely encourage this sort of portrait of their ideal in both their writings and in their own lives. Heidegger also insists that one break from the public or *Mitsein* and become "his own man"; and Heidegger's own life again exemplifies this 'existential solitude'. Camus's picture of the isolated Sisyphus also encourages this image, and Sartre's depressing picture of all human relationships as unhappy conflict gives us a very antisocial picture of existentialism indeed.

We should be surprised, therefore, to find that the existential ethics of Sartre, De Beauvoir, and Camus places a highest value on political and social commitment and principles of mutual respect and sociability.

When a man commits himself to anything, fully realizing that he is not only choosing what he will be, but is thereby at the same time a legislator deciding for the whole of mankind—in such a moment a man cannot escape from the sense of complete and profound responsibility.[345]

I revolt, therefore, we exist.[346]

We have said little of ethical *principles* in this discussion; we have spoken mostly of individual decisions to act. It must not be supposed, however, that existentialism has no room for action on universal principle. First, freedom itself yields a principle which is universal in scope.[347] All principles of action, however, apply not only to myself, but (at least implicitly) to all men. Every human action presupposes not only the principle of freedom but more specific normative principles as well. When I make a decision,

I am thereby committing not only myself, but humanity as a whole.[348]

Sartre even goes so far as to agree with Kant that

in truth, one ought always to ask oneself what would happen if everyone did as one is doing.[349]

The essential and very important difference between Kant and Sartre is that Kant believes that the principles of correct action can be justified independently of their application and exist prior to their application in any particular action. According to Sartre, however, the principle exists only insofar as it is applied in decisions to act, and more importantly, it does not have any justification other than the fact that it is chosen as a principle of action (in other words, it has no justification). Sartre's famous illustration for this theory of ethical principles[350] is his young student who must choose between staying with his mother (who has lost others in her family to the enemy) and joining the Free French forces. He is forced to choose between avenging his older brother and father who have been killed and comforting his despairing mother. Traditional ethics would insist that some principle must be sought which legislates the relative merits of the two choices and then apply the principle to this situation.

Sartre, on the contrary, denies the a priori relevance of any principle and denies that there are principles which could support either choice as opposed to the other. The problem of finding a principle is not that the situation is *unique,* as is so often argued. One might easily find that any number of relevantly similar situations have occurred. The problem is the absence of a criterion for identifying either relevant aspects of the situation or priority of competing general principles. The young man must choose his principle as he makes his decision. If he decides to stay with his mother, he has thereby legislated for all mankind the principle that one ought, in such cases, remain with one's mother.

Sartre's position must further be distinguished from Kant's universalizability principle (The Categorical Imperative) with which it bears a superficial resemblance. The extension of one's choice of action and principle to all mankind is not intended as an a priori test of the *correctness* of the choice, for there are no standards of correctness possible for free choice. The intention behind the universalization of principles in Sartre's philosophy must rather be referred back to his claims that "human beings have no essence." Because this is true of human beings, it is also true of *human being.* An individual man is what he chooses to be and what he actually does. Mankind as a whole is also what it chooses and what it does. As such, each action of each man contributes to this overall portrait of mankind:

Of all the actions a man may take in order
to create himself as he wills to be, there
is not one which is not creative at the
same time of an image of man such as he
believes he ought to be.[351]

I choose for all mankind in the sense that my choice presents an image of what I think all men should be. If I choose to act selfishly, I thereby choose an image for men in general as selfish. If I choose to act nobly, it is because I choose that men in general should act nobly. Of course, there is no reason to suppose that my choice will *in fact* have any effect on other men, and we have already rejected the claim that my choice of general principle (and an image for mankind) has any ultimate *justification.* Nevertheless, Sartre wants to insist that I always act for all mankind; my act is never *merely* the act of an individual.

The transition from individual freedom to collective and political freedom, from individual choice to morality, from existentialism to humanism, is never absent from French existentialism. Sartre's writings in and surrounding *Being and Nothingness* begin with the Kierkegaardian category of 'the individual', but never lose sight of the 'ontological necessity' of 'Being-for-Others! After the war, however, the focus of existentialism shifts from the individual to society. In the characterization of the German existentialist, Karl Jaspers;

Every man is free to the extent that
others are. Humanism can no longer
unfold in private. It is made subject to
political conditions, and above all to this
one alternative: freedom of the public
struggling spirit. . . .

In discussing the struggle for inner
independence we have been ultimately
concerned with the individual alone. Does
that not sound as though the individual
were everything? The opposite is true:
the individual is infinitesimal in the course
of events, and he is himself only to the
extent of his communication with other
selves and with the world as a whole.[352]

Jean-Paul Sartre becomes a Marxist. It is clear that there are heavy Marxist influences even in *Being and Nothingness*—at least to the extent that Hegel was the common ancestor of both Sartre and Marx. But Sartre's *Critique of Dialectical Reason* makes a clear and sharp move away from individualism and the 'Protestant' concern with personal salvation to the concern for "the group" and "universal good." Personal 'bad faith' becomes the collective problem of "serialization." The feeling of "being-with" (*Mitsein*) and the reciprocity of Kant's "Kingdom of Ends" which remain as unresolved dilemmas in *Being and Nothingness* become the starting point of the *Critique.* (We might remind ourselves that Hegel's dialectic took exactly this turn; and in a limited, strictly 'cognitive' way, Husserl's phenomenology takes the turn from individual cognition to community transcendental ego as well.)

The extent to which Sartre's Marxism is compatible with the 'existentialism' of

Being and Nothingness is hotly debated in contemporary literature. We can, however, avoid this discussion just as we avoided the similar dispute regarding the "two Heideggers." To suppose that a man ought—in any sense—argue compatible or identical theses at different times in his life is surely based upon a false conception of what it is to be a man: as if a man's ideas are a durable 'fact' about him of the same sort as his place of birth. The *Critique* is surely more than a shift in emphasis from the individual to society. Sartre himself has admitted[353] that his earlier notion of 'absolute freedom' was 'naive'! But Sartre's Marxism is unorthodox; it rejects the central 'Marxist' ideas of materialism and historical determinism; it retains the existentialist ideal of 'commitment' (now in the form of 'the pledge') and insists that membership in 'the Group' is never a matter of mere 'belonging' but always a matter of "renewing the pledge."

The move from *Being and Nothingness* to the *Critique* is not so abrupt as the superficial characterization of "from Existentialism to Marxism" would suggest. In his earlier work, Sartre argues that one must always *choose* his 'projects' and his actions and thereby his 'identity' or 'self'. But among these various projects—as an essential alternative—is always our relations to others and our membership in various groups. Even in *Being and Nothingness,* the available choices are frequently between the revolutionary class and the oppressor class, the resistance and the occupation forces, in other words, between groups. But then, to choose a 'project', a 'course of action' and an 'identity' is to *ipso facto* choose a group, a class, and a set of class interests, class values, class commitments. Of course, it is clear in *Being and Nothingness* that such choices are always *alliances* and not a literal 'belonging.' The group is a collection of individuals committed to the same ends. In the *Critique,* this distinction becomes blurred: it remains ambiguous to what extent one is 'free' to break the pledge and leave 'the group'. The fact that Sartre so often speaks of the 'terror' of the sanctions of the group would indicate that it is still the notion of 'alliance' rather than a stronger notion of 'belonging' that is operating here. And Sartre's own career of refusal to remain in revolutionary parties would serve as further evidence that it is still the

individual and not the group that serves as the locus of *choice*. The group, then, functions only as the focus of *projects*.

A major change from Sartre's early existentialism to the *Critique* is his change of attitude towards 'the existential hero'. As he has recently explained,

What the drama of the war gave me, as it did everyone else who participated in it, was the experience of heroism. Not my own, of course—all I did was a few errands. But the militant in the Resistance who was caught and tortured became a myth for us. Such militants existed, of course, but they represented a sort of personal myth as well. Would we be able to hold out against torture too? . . . This is what I mean by the experience of heroism, which is a false experience.

After the war came the true experience, that of society. But I think it was necessary for me to pass via the myth of heroism first.[354]

Even here, we can see that it is not a simple rejection of his earlier existentialism and an adoption of a new Marxism. What changes is not only Sartre's ideas, but the situation. Sartre sees that the pressures of wartime occupation create 'false' experiences which—in a phenomenologist—turn into a 'false' philosophy. But I think even the "false" here is out of place, and should be reinterpreted more in the way Hegel uses "false" to signify "one-sided" or "prejudiced." The experiences of the war were extreme experiences which made all choice situations into life-or-death choice situations. Thus we can understand Sartre's early degradation of bourgeois 'business as usual'. But we can also see that the revolutionary philosophy of the *Critique* will yield a more central place to everyday morality. During the war, bourgeois morality was usually a distraction and a temptation to bad faith; it led one away from the life-and-death issues of the war. But in his Marxism, partly from Merleau-Ponty's influence, Sartre sees that bourgeois 'business as usual' is one of the essential choices which is always facing us. In wartime, it is the constant instability and unpredictability of life that provide the source of the existential attitude. In everyday life, the foundation is stability and predictability ('seriality'), and it is the objective of the 'revolutionary consciousness' to upset just that foundation.

We might note that the change in situation from wartime France to postwar politics brings existentialism one small step closer to Anglo-American ethical analysis in the following sense: Sartre's early existentialism began with the idea that society was unstable, that moral institutions simply were not capable of supporting the sorts of choices that had to be made, and that the very sources of 'rationality'—the government and national institutions—were 'irrational'. Thus the paradigm of choice in Sartre's early work is the extreme situation in which there are no supports or criteria for choosing. After the war, however, 'society' presents itself as stable, legitimate, and the source of 'morality' and 'reason'. Accordingly, the presupposition of moral philosophy becomes the existence of moral institutions, and the problems of moral philosophy become the analysis and evaluation of those institutions. It is often commented, usually in a mocking tone, that the French existentialists were concerned with cases of life and death, anxiety-ridden choices between dangerous heroism and degrading cowardice, while the British moralists are concerned with the need to return books to the University library on time and the temptation to take more than their fair share at high table supper. But this difference in example is a natural consequence of the difference in the perspective on 'choice' within a situation where nothing can be taken as settled and a situation where everything is taken as settled. Sartre's early philosophy takes too little heed of the role of everyday duties and distractions in our conceptions of morality and choice. The British moralists take far too little heed of the ever-present possibilities for grand existential choices—the rejection of a moral institution as well as a well-defined choice *within* that institution. Sartre's recent revolutionary philosophy brings these extremes into perspective; both existential choices and everyday choices have their essential place in any adequate moral theory.

It would be impossible to present a fair overall evaluation of the existentialist philosophy that has emerged through these pages. I hope it is evident in the presentation that my own sympathies are deeply intertwined with the ideas of these seven great thinkers of the past century and a half. But it would be a mistake to think

that these agreements are simply the professional approval of a contemporary philosophy student for certain ideas of the past. Throughout this book, I have endorsed the Hegelian thesis that a philosophy is far more than a set of ideas detached from a historical social context. In Heidegger's terms, a philosophy always has its 'ontic' as well as its 'ontological' expressions. And so I view the existentialist attitudes as far more than a continuation of and a reaction to Kant's philosophy. Its attractiveness, I believe, is determined by the temperament of our society as well as the logic of ideas. What the authors in this book share is, above all else, a confidence in the free individual in the free society. What all these authors reject are those restrictions on our freedom which we ourselves have placed there. For some of the authors, modern technology and science in general are responsible for these restrictions. For others, it is a degrading view of ourselves that is responsible. But, in every case, these philosophers see that 'bad faith' in one form or another—a refusal to see oneself as free and responsible—is responsible for an uncomplimentary and self-imposed caricature of what it is to be a human being.

In an excellent commentary on contemporary American society, Philip Slater (*The Pursuit of Loneliness*) concludes by arguing that American individualism has been responsible for this degradation, and that the answer lies in the direction of an increased sense of 'community.' I hope I have made it evident that existentialism is not the same as "American individualism" and the existentialists—the French at least—are not in the least opposed to "community." But Slater urges that what is needed is a turn in emphasis from individualism to community. On the basis of the philosophy emerging from this book, I would want to urge a countereffort. What is still needed—what may always be needed—are philosophies that break us away from the 'crowd' and the 'herd' and the false "universal community of the bourgeoisie." Sartre has argued (in *Situations III*) that it is just such 'inauthentic' American collectivism that provides the basis for self-destructive American 'individualism'. Moreover, I would want to argue—after Kierkegaard and Sartre— that the adoption of a community is itself always an existential choice. I would wholly agree with Slater and the later Sartre that it is only through a radical communal approach to society and not through 'existential heroism' that one can make the necessary changes in society. But what will always be needed *first* is the rejection of our 'natural' tendency to accept without questioning, to see ourselves only 'from the outside' and to deny re-

sponsibility for what we are. And this is what existentialism is all about:

For the idea which I never have ceased to develop is that in the end one is always responsible for what is made of one. Even if one can do nothing else besides assume this responsibility.[355]

Bibliography
Sartre's Works in English

The Transcendence of the Ego. Translated by F. Williams. New York, 1957.

Imagination. Translated by F. Williams. Ann Arbor, Mich., 1962.

The Emotions: Outline of a Theory. Translated by B. Frechtman. New York, 1948.

Being and Nothingness. Translated by H. Barnes. New York, 1956.

"Existentialism As a Humanism." Translated by Mairet, *"Anti-Semite and Jew."* Translated by G. Becker. In *Existentialism from Dostoyevsky to Sartre.* Edited by W. Kaufmann.

Literary and Philosophical Essays. Translated by A. Michaelson. New York, 1962.

St. Genet: Actor and Martyr. Translated by B. Frechtman. New York, 1963.

Search for a Method. Translated by H. Barnes. New York, 1963.

Sartre's Novels and Plays of Philosophical Interest

Nausea. Translated by L. Alexander. New York, 1949.

"The Wall." Translated by L. Alexander. In *Existentialism from Dostoevsky to Sartre.* Edited by W. Kaufmann. New York, 1956.

"No Exit," "The Flies," "Dirty Hands." In *No Exit and Three Other Plays.* Trans. G. Steward and L. Abel. New York, 1947.

The Age of Reason and *The Reprieve.* Translated by E. Sutton. New York, 1947.

Troubled Sleep. Translated by G. Hopkins. New York, 1950. (Third novel of trilogy with *Age of Reason* and *The Reprieve.*)

The Devil and the Good Lord. Translated by K. Black. New York, 1960.

The Words: An Autobiography. Translated by B. Frechtman. New York, 1964.

"Sartre: An Interview." In *New York Review of Books.* March 26, 1970, vol. XIV, no. 6.

Books about Sartre's Philosophy

Cranston, M. *Jean-Paul Sartre.* New York, 1962.

Desan, W. *The Tragic Finale.* New York, 1960.

————. *The Marxism of Jean-Paul Sartre.* New York, 1965.

Fell, J. *Sartre's Theory of the Passions.* New York, 1962.

Hartmann, E. *Sartre's Ontology.* Evanston, Ill., 1966.

Manser, A. *Sartre: A Philosophical Study.* London, 1966.

Murdoch, I. *Sartre: Romantic Rationalist.* New Haven, 1953.

Natanson, M. *A Critique of Jean-Paul Sartre's Ontology.* Lincoln, Neb., 1951.

————. "Phenomenology and Existentialism, Husserl and Sartre on Intentionality." In *Phenomenology.* Edited by Kockelmans. New York, 1967.

Spiegelberg, H. *The Phenomenological Movement.* Vol. II. The Hague, 1962.

————. "Husserl's Phenomenology and Sartre's Existentialism." In *Phenomenology.* Edited by Kockelmans. New York, 1967.

Stern, A. *Sartre.* New York, 1953.

Warnock, M. *The Philosophy of Sartre.* London, 1965.

————. *Existentialism.* London, 1970.

Camus's Novels and Philosophical Essays

The Myth of Sisyphus. Translated by J. O'Brien. New York, 1955.

The Plague. Translated by S. Gilbert. New York, 1948.

The Rebel. Translated by A. Bower. New York, 1954.

The Fall. Translated by J. O'Brien. New York, 1957.

Resistance, Rebellion and Death. Translated by J. O'Brien. New York, 1961.

Works about Albert Camus
Bree, G. *Camus.* New Brunswick, N. J., 1961.
Cruickshank, J. A. *Camus and the Literature of Revolt.* London, 1959.
O'Brien, C. C. *Albert Camus.* New York, 1970.
Thody, P. *Camus: A Study of His Work.* London, 1957.

De Beauvoir's Works in English
The Ethics of Ambiguity. Translated by B. Frechtman. New York, '948.
The Second Sex. Translated by H. M. Parshley. New York, 1953.
The Mandarins. Translated by L. Friedman. Cleveland, 1956.
The Force of Circumstance. Translated by R. Howard. New York, 1965.

Merleau-Ponty's Works in English
The Structure of Behavior. Translated by A. Fisher. Boston, 1963.
The Phenomenology of Perception. Translated by C. Smith. London, 1962.
The Primacy of Perception. Edited by J. Edie. Evanston, Ill., 1964.
Themes from His Lectures, 1954–1960. Evanston, Ill., 1970.
Sense and Nonsense. Translated by H. and P. Dreyfus. Evanston, Ill., 1964.
Humanism and Terror. Translated by J. O'Neill. Boston, 1969.
Signs. Translated by R. McCleary. Evanston, Ill., 1964.
In Praise of Philosophy. Translated by Wild and Edie. Evanston, Ill., 1963.

Books about Merleau-Ponty
Kwant, R. *The Phenomenological Philosophy of Merleau-Ponty.* Pittsburgh, 1963.
Langan, T. *Merleau-Ponty's Critique of Reason.* New Haven, 1966.
Rabil, A. *Merleau-Ponty: Existentialist of the Social World.* New York, 1967.

Spiegelberg, H. *The Phenomenological Movement.* Vol. II. The Hague, 1962.

Marcel's Works in English
Metaphysical Journal. Translated by B. Woll. London, 1952.
Being and Having. Translated by K. Farrer. Boston, 1951.
Creative Fidelity. Translated by R. Rosthal. New York, 1964.
Homo Viator. Translated by E. Craufurd. Chicago, 1951.
The Philosophy of Existence. Translated by M. Harari. New York, 1949.
Mystery of Being. 2 vols. Translated by Frasar and Hauge. Chicago, 1951.

Books about Marcel
Cain, S. *Gabriel Marcel.* New York, 1963.
Gallagher, K. *The Philosophy of Gabriel Marcel.* New York, 1962.

Paul Ricoeur's Works in English
History and Truth. Translated by C. Kelbley. Evanston, Ill., 1965.
Freud and Philosophy. Translated by D. Savage. New Haven, 1970.
Fallible Man. Translated by C. Kelbley. Chicago, 1965.
Freedom and Nature: The Voluntary and the Involuntary. Translated by E. Kohak. Evanston, Ill., 1966.
Husserl. Translated by E. Ballard and L. Embree. Evanston, Ill., 1967.
The Philosophy of the Will (includes "Fallible Man"). Translated by C. Kelbley. Chicago, 1965.
The Religious Significance of Atheism. Translated by C. Kelbley and A. MacIntyre. Chicago, 1965.
The Symbolism of Evil. Translated by E. Buchanan. New York, 1967.

Works by Maritain
Degrees of Knowledge. Translated by Wall and Adams. New York, 1938.
Existence and the Existent. Translated by L. Galantiere. New York, 1966.
Introduction to Philosophy. Translated by E. Watkins. New York, 1931.

Footnotes

Chapter 1

1. H. Heine, *Germany, Works,* vol. V, p. 136. Reprinted in Aiken, *The Age of Ideology* (New York: Mentor, 1956), pp. 27–28.

2. See *The Philosophical Works of Descartes,* trans. Haldane and Ross, 2 vols. (New York: Dover, 1955); A. Kenny, *Descartes: A Study of His Philosophy* (New York: Random House, 1968); and B. Williams, "Descartes" in *The Encyclopedia of Philosophy* (New York: Macmillan, 1967), vol. 2, pp. 344–354.

3. The following are two useful studies of Newton's mechanics and its influences: A. R. Hall, *From Galileo to Newton* (New York: Harper & Row, 1963) and D. Shapere, "Newtonian Mechanics and Mechanical Explanation," in *The Encyclopedia of Philosophy, op. cit.,* vol. 5, pp. 491–496.

4. Brief surveys of this remarkable period are Manuel's *Age of Reason* (Ithaca, N.Y.: Cornell University Press, 1951) and *The Age of Reason,* Hampshire, ed. (New York: Mentor, 1956).

5. See, for example, John Stuart Mill, *Utilitarianism* (New York: Bobbs-Merrill, 1957) and David Hume, *Moral and Political Philosophy,* Aiken, ed. (New York: Hafner, 1948).

6. Immanuel Kant, *Prolegomena to Any Future Metaphysics,* trans. L. W. Beck (New York: Bobbs-Merrill, 1956), p. 8.

7. Although Kant spent most of his long life in philosophy, his important "critical" works were not written until he was in his late fifties. He then produced, in rapid succession, three magnificent critiques: the *Critique of Pure Reason (Kritik der reinen Vernunft),* 1781, second edition, 1787 (I shall follow conventional notation in referring to the first edition of the *Critique of*

Pure Reason as "A" and to the second as "B"); *The Critique of Practical Reason (Kritik der praktischen Vernunft),* 1788 (hereafter cited as "CPrR"); and the *Critique of Judgment (Kritik der Urteilskraft),* 1790, second edition, 1793. The very difficult first *Critique* explores the basic philosophical problems of mathematics, natural science, and metaphysics. It was supplemented by the *Prolegomena to Any Future Metaphysics (Prolegomena zu einer jeden kunftigen Metaphysik)* in 1793 (hereafter cited as *Prolegomena),* which presents the tortuous arguments of the first *Critique* in simplified form. The construction of Kant's own metaphysical system is found in outline in *The Metaphysical Foundations of Natural Science,* 1786. The *Critique of Practical Reason,* which contains Kant's ethical philosophy and his theological proofs, is preceded by the *Foundations of the Metaphysics of Morals (Grundlegung zur Metaphysik der Sitten),* 1785 (hereafter cited as "FMM"), and supplemented by the *Metaphysics of Morals (Metaphysik der Sitten)* in 1797. He published *Religion Within the Limits of Reason Alone (Religion Innerhalb der Grenzen der Blossen Vernunft)* in 1793 (with a second edition published the following year), in which he gives the most advanced statement of the religious aspects of his ethical writings. Kant's last writings, never published during his lifetime, have been recently edited by Erich Adickes (1936–1938). In addition to these central writings, Kant wrote essays on a variety of subjects, including discourses in aesthetics, anthropology, physical geography, history, comparative religion, ethics, theology, law, education, prospects for world peace, and cosmology.

8. A, p. xii. All translations of the *Critique of Pure Reason* (New York: Macmil-

lan, 1958) are by Norman Kemp Smith. Page numbers refer to the pagination of the original German text, A or B (marginal in Kemp Smith).

9. B xv
10. B 7
11. David Hume, *Enquiry Concerning Human Understanding*, XII, iii, La Salle, III.: Open Court, 1963, p. 173.
12. *Prolegomena*, p. 116.
13. Ibid., p. 4.
14. Ibid., p. 123n.
15. B 25
16. *Prolegomena*, p. 123n.
17. B 1
18. B 29
19. B 75
20. *Prolegomena*, p. 67.
21. A 106
22. A 126
23. Ibid.
24. B 33
25. Although Kant equated the problems of space and time with the problem of justifying the foundations of mathematics and geometry, most commentators prefer to keep these separate. In the *Prolegomena*, in the counterpart to the *Transcendental Aesthetic,* Kant raises the problem "How Is Pure Mathematics Possible?" and soon states (p. 30): "Now the intuitions which pure mathematics lays at the foundation of all its cognitions and judgments which appear at once apodictic and necessary are space and time." The first *Critique* itself has little to say of mathematics and geometry and is directed towards the analysis of space and time. the *Aesthetic* therefore is better considered apart from the justification of mathematics and geometry it is intended to support.
26. B 131–132
27. B 139
28. B 130
29. B 218
30. B 246
31. B 246–247
32. The best and most thorough attempt to display the logic of the *Critique's Transcendental Analytic* can be found in Robert Paul Wolff, *Kant's Theory of Mental Activity* (Cambridge, Mass.: Harvard University Press, 1963).
33. This oversimplified claim would require serious qualification for some of the rationalists. For example, Spinoza would refer to two "modes" rather than entities. Leibniz gives us an even more complex picture.
34. B 274–279, "The Refutation of Idealism."
35. *Prolegomena*, p. 46; B 126.
36. Ibid., p. 66.
37. Hume, *Treatise*, IV, Book I.
38. B 359

39. B 361
40. After Plato's "Ideas."
41. B 434
42. B 395n
43. We cannot possibly enter into an exposition of the many different presentations, defenses, and criticisms of these famous arguments. An excellent detailed discussion can be found in the articles collected by John Hicks, *The Existence of God* (New York: Collier-Macmillan, 1964). A brief introduction is in any standard introductory text. We shall provide some detail in later chapters.
44. B 454; B 462
45. B 472; B 480
46. B 395n
47. All translations of *The Critique of Practical Reason* (New York: Bobbs-Merrill, 1956) are by L. W. Beck. Page numbers refer to the pagination of the original German text (marginal in Beck).
48. All translations of the *Foundations* are from H. J. Paton, *The Moral Law* (London 1948), or *Groundwork of the Metaphysics of Morals* (New York: Harper & Row, 1964). Page numbers refer to the pagination of the original German text (marginal in Paton).
49. FMM 8–9
50. FMM 12
51. FMM 2
52. CPrR, Book II, Chap. 1.
53. CPrR, Chap. 11.
54. FMM 52; cf. CPrR 30.
55. FMM 52. Given Kant's rigid distinction between "will" and "nature", the universalization according to these two formulations is very different; one is *willed* universally, the other *caused* universally.
56. FMM 54–55
57. FMM 53–54
58. FMM 66–67. The number of formulations is a matter of controversy. The two different formulations of what we have called the "first" formulation, for example, must be dealt with separately. Similarly, it is not always clear whether the "kingdom of ends" is another formulation.
59. "Third Antinomy," A444–451, B472–479.
60. Kant, *Critique of Judgment,* trans. J C. Meredith (Oxford: Oxford University Press, 1928), p. 413.
61. FMM 98
62. FMM 97
63. FMM 97
64. FMM 97
65. FMM 99
66. FMM 100
67. FMM 106
68. FMM 107
69. FMM 115
70. FMM 114
71. FMM 119
72. FMM 120

73 FMM 125
74. Ibid.
75. FMM 128
76. FMM 109–110
77. CPrR, Book 1, p. 11.
78. *Opus Posthumum*, published posthumously by Adickes in 1929.
79. *Nichomachean Ethics*, p. 1102a5.
80. CPrR 113
81. FMM 114
82. FMM 115
83. FMM 4–8
84. Cf. Hegel on "Positive Religion," in Chap. 2, in "The Early Theological Writings."
85. CPrR 127–128
86. CPrR 125–126
87. CPrR 115

Chapter 2

1. Although Hegel is often considered a remarkably prolific writer, he published only four books in his lifetime: *The Phenomenology of Spirit (System der Wissenschaft; erster Teil. Die Phänomenologie des Geistes*, 1807), The *Science of Logic (Wissenschaft der Logik*, vol. 1, Pt. 1, 1812, vol. I, Pt. 2, 1813, vol. II, 1816), *The Encyclopedia of the Philosophical Sciences (Encyklopädie der philosophischen Wissenschaften im Grundrisse*, 1817; 2nd ed., 1827; 3rd ed., 1830), and the *Philosophy of Right (Grundlinien der Philosophie des Rechts*, 1821). *The Phenomenology of Spirit* will be hereafter cited as *Phenomenology. The Logic*, unless further specified, will refer indiscriminately to both the *Science of Logic* and the *Lesser Logic*, the first part of the *Encyclopedia*. Most of the Hegel volumes now in print consist of notes taken from his lectures and edited by his students. The importance of this lecture material and the great popularity of some of these (especially the lectures on history and aesthetics) make any discussion of Hegal bound to go beyond the works that Hegel himself wrote, a technique always to be regarded with suspicion.

2. Published as Hegel's *Theologische Jugendschriften* by H. Nohl (Tübingen, 1907), hereafter cited as "Nohl," and in English by T. M. Knox (Chicago, 1946), hereafter cited as "Knox." Translations by Walter Kaufmann in his essay "The Young Hegel and Religion" in *From Shakespeare to Existentialism* (New York: Anchor Books, 1960), Chap. 8, will be hereafter cited as "WK." My discussion of the first two essays is based upon Kaufmann's essay and lectures on the same by Frithjof Bergmann.

3. WK 133
4. Nohl 22f.; WK 134.
5. Nohl 34; WK 134–135.
6. Nohl 41

7. Nohl 153; Knox 58.
8. Nohl 155
9. Lessing, "The Education of Mankind" (1780), Preface, in W. Kaufmann, *Hegel: A Reinterpretation*, New York, 1962, pp. 41–42.
10. It is important to note that Kant certainly would not have agreed with this interpretation of his second *Critique*, for there he argues that both God and man, as rational creatures, are bound by the same moral law, and it is not, as Hegel suggests, that man is bound by God's law. However, if this claim is not taken as an interpretation of Kant's concept of the source of the moral law but as a necessary consequence of Kant's notion of the *Summum Bonum*, which does indeed require God to be the enforcer and provider of the moral law even if he is not its source, then Hegel's argument contains a sound criticism of Kant. Kant cannot on the one hand claim God as a necessary postulate of morality because of his reward-giving capacity (appealing to men's inclinations to entice them to be moral) and at the same time claim that morality consists of dictates of practical reason. According to Kant (and Hegel), reason *is* freedom, and only action in accordance with reason is free action. On the other hand, action in accordance with the inclinations is not free, and action so motivated cannot be moral. Insofar as man depends on God for the moral law, and its enforcement, therefore, he is not a moral creature, and the postulate of God is not a necessary, or even possible, postulate of morality or practical reason.
11. Nohl 161
12. Nohl 161–162; Knox 79–80.
13. Lasson, *Weltgeschichte*, p. 43.
14. Nohl 266; Knox 212.
15. Chap. 1, "Morality and Metaphysics."
16. W. Kaufmann, *Hegel*, p. 108.
17. Cf. the extreme illustration in the "Life of Jesus."
18. In a footnote in the *Science of Logic* (p. 44), Hegel states that,

it [Kant's philosophy] constitutes the basis and point of departure of the modern German philosophy.

(When Hegel speaks of "modern German philosophy," it is never without reference to his own philosophy.)
19. All references to this work are to the English edition, translated by J. B. Baillie, *The Phenomenology of Mind*. I have taken certain liberties with key terms where necessary (for example, with *Geist* in the title).
20. In this section, I am deeply indebted to I. Soll, who wrote his doctoral dissertation, "Hegel's Search for Absolute

Truth" (Princeton University, 1965) on this topic.

21. *Encyclopedia*, section x. Soll, trans.

22. *Phenomenology*, p. 133.

23. Ibid.

24. From the Preface to the *Phenomenology*, p. 81–82.

25. A modern sequel to this Kantian dilemma occurs in Wittgenstein's *Tractatus Logico-philosophicus*, and is solved, in an almost Hegelian way, by P. F. Strawson in "Persons" (chap. 3, of *Individuals*). There the distinction between a transcendental and empirical ego (or *consciousness* and a *person*) is also reduced to a "no-ownership theory" of consciousness. The important difference is that Strawson considers this as a *reductio ad absurdum*, while Hegel clearly considers it as an important advance.

26. I have argued this thesis in detail in an article, "Hegel's Concept of *Geist*," in the *Review of Metaphysics*, vol. 23, no. 4, June 1970.

27. For example, W. Kaufmann, *Hegel* and WK, p. 159.

28. Findlay, *Hegel*, p. 87.

29. *Phenomenology*, p. 149.

30. Ibid.

31. Ibid., p. 160.

32. Findlay, op. cit., Chap. 3.

33. Here, Baillie, in his introduction to perception in his translation of the *Phenomenology*, reiterates the standard interpretation that this inadequacy "compels the mind to adopt another cognitive attitude" (p. 16). But again, if this is taken to mean that the dialectic has given us a causal account of this movement, it is mistaken. Primarily, there is nothing in the section on perception that could allow for such development which is available only to the philosophical critic who is now looking *back* on such a proposed development.

34. *Phenomenology*, p. 204.

35. Ibid., p. 205.

36. The inclusion of the Roman philosophers (Epictetus, Marcus Aurelius, and the implicit references to medieval philosophy in the following section are clear proof that the stages of consciousness are not to be interpreted as a literal history of philosophical doctrines, but rather as a hierarchy of stages of consciousness, as they approach Hegel's notion of Absolute Truth. In this regard, Hegel considers Epictetus more mature than Kant's first *Critique*. This juxtaposition should also be sufficient to show us that place in the dialectic alone is not sufficient to show Regel's evaluation of the worth of some particular *philosopher or* school of thought.

37. *Phenomenology*, p. 226.

38. Ibid., p. 229.

39. Ibid., p. 233.

40. Ibid.

41. Ibid., p. 234.

42. Ibid., p. 235.

43. Ibid., p. 267.

44. Ibid., p. 617

45. Ibid., p. 620.

46. Hegel actually uses this term, indicating that he still interprets Kant as taking God to be the *source* of moral principles. We have seen that this is in error. Kant takes reason alone to be the source of morality, and God, like man, is a rational creature bound by this morality.

47. See note 1; Hegel wrote two Logics both of which will be discussed here: The *Science of Logic* (1812–1816), trans. Johnston and Struthers (London: Allen & Urwin, 1959) and the *"Lesser" Logic*, the first part of the *Encyclopedia*, trans. W. Wallace (Oxford: Clarendon, 1870).

48. See Chap. 1, "The Dialectic."

49. *Science of Logic*, Introduction.

50. Ibid.

51. Ibid.

52. See Chap. 5, "The Transcendental Ego and Our Knowledge of Objects."

53. *Sense and Sensibilia* (Oxford: Clarendon, 1963).

54. *Science of Logic*, Introduction.

55. See Chap. 3, "The Attack on Hegelianism."

56. *Science of Logic*, Introduction.

57. *Lesser Logic*, p. 107.

58. Hegel, *History of Philosophy*, Introduction.

Chapter 3

1. Kierkegaard, *The Present Age*, trans. A. Dru (New York: Harper & Row, 1962), p. 33.

2. Kierkegaard, *Concluding Unscientific Postscript* (Princeton: Princeton University Press, 1941), p. 33 (hereafter cited as "CUP"). All quotations in this chapter must be taken with reservations. It is not always clear when Kierkegaard is or is not to be identified with "the author." In *CUP*, e.g., the "author" is not Kierkegaard, yet many passages do clearly reflect his views.

3. *Present Age*, p. 59.

4. CUP 318

5. *Journals* translated and edited by A. Dru (N.Y.: Harper Torchbooks, 1948). Reference cited by date of origin, 1837.

6. In Auden, W. H. *The Living Thoughts of Kierkegaard*, Bloomington, Ind.: Indiana Univ. Press, 1952, p. 26.

7. *Journals*, 1835.

8. For example, *Phenomenology*, Part C, *AA (V), B–E*, "Realization of rational self-consciousness through itself," and especially *C*. "Individually" (pp. 413–453). See chap. II, section xiv; cf. *Philosophy of Right*, Introduction, section 7 (V) trans. Knox, p. 23f.

9. CUP 173

10. CUP 173–174

11. This characteristic individual subjectivity, however, is universally applicable (in different specific ways) to each and every individual. In other words, Kierkegaard is making a claim about *all* men, and his "autobiographical" philosophy makes a definite commitment about *human nature.*

12. Auden, op. cit., 29.

13. CUP 182

14. For example, 1835–1841, when Kierkegaard was in his early twenties.

15. Kierkegaard spread the "fragments" of his philosophy over nearly 30 books and several volumes of *Journals* entries, literary reviews, newspaper articles, and letters. His main works include: *The Concept of Irony* (1841), *Either/Or* (1843), *Repetition* (1843), *Fear and Trembling* (1843), *Philosophical Fragments* (1844), *The Concept of Dread* (1844), *Stages on Life's Way* (1845), *Concluding Unscientific Postscript* (1846), *The Present Age* (1846), *Sickness unto Death* (1849), *The Point of View of My Work as an Author* (1849), *Training in Christianity* (1850), *The Attack Upon "Christendom"* (1850). Many of these books were written pseudonymously (notably *Philosophical Fragments* and *Concluding Unscientific Postscript* by "Johannes Climacus"). All of the above-mentioned works have been translated into English.

16. In "The Moment No. 5," *Attack Upon Christendom,* trans. W. Lowrie (Princeton: Princeton University Press, 1944), p. 155.

17. *Papirer XI,* A 12.

18. *Journals,* 1847.

19. CUP 386ff.

20. In his earlier works (for example, *Fear and Trembling*), "inwardness" *is* faith; later, inward feeling is only a necessary, not a sufficient condition, for becoming a Christian.

21. *Attack Upon Christendom.* III.

22. "My Task" in *Attack Upon Christendom.*

23. CUP 326

24. *Journals,* 1848.

25. CUP 339

26. CUP 182 (quoted this chapter)

27. CUP 182

28. *Journals,* 1847.

29. L. Festinger's theory of "Cognitive Dissonance," the theory that inconsistent beliefs ("dissonant cognitive elements") cause changes in attitudes and behavior, would certainly support this psychological claim.

30. CUP 31; of Nietzsche: "A joke is an epigram on the death of a feeling." *Mixed Opinions* (HAHII) 202.

31. *Philosophical Fragments,* 2nd ed., trans. D. Swensen (Princeton: Princeton University Press, 1962), pp. 49–50.

32. Or, that there exists something which has the properties of being a thing of this sort. This metaphysical thesis is captured elegantly and formally in nearly all recent quantificational logics by denying "x exists" ("∃ x") the status of a well-formed formula and allowing only "There exists an x with property F" ("(∃ x) Fx").

33. CUP 485

34. *Philosophical Fragments,* pp. 46,

35. For example, in the *Philosophical Fragments.*

36. *Journals,* 1843.

37. Martensen was a Hegelian Christian who became a bishop of Denmark. He was often a target for Kierkegaard's attacks.

38. *Journals,* 1835.

39. *Journals,* 1843.

40. Cf. Heidegger, Chap. 6, "What Is Philosophy?"

41. *Journals,* 1835.

42. CUP 173

43. Ibid.

44. *How to Do Things with Words,* ed. J. O. Urmson (New York: Oxford University Press, 1962.)

45. *Phenomenology,* Preface.

46. *Either/Or,* II, 294.

47. Quite contrary to Kierkegaard's own alleged penchant for paradox, he has harsh words to say of Hegel's central notion of *aufheben* (Chap. 2, "Reason"):

I am well aware that the German
(word aufheben has various)
and even contradictory meanings: . . .
Whether it is a good trait in a
word to admit of contradictory
meanings, I do not know, but anyone
who desires to express himself with
precision will be disposed to avoid
the use of such a word. . . . (CUP 199)

Kierkegaard adds that the impossible tricks which speculative philosophy performs with this word are like "talking with one's mouth full of hot mush." (CUP 199)

48. CUP 324–25

49. *Journals,* 1841.

50. CUP 31

51. CUP 30

52. CUP 216

53. CUP 182

54. For example, in John Wild's well-known discussion of Kierkegaard in his *Challenge of Existentialism* (Bloomington, Ind.; Indiana University Press, 1955), p. 31f.

55. CUP 276

56. Ibid.

57. Kierkegaard only occasionally employs the notion of *authenticity:* this term (in English translation) becomes a watchword of existentialism only with the new Kierkegaardian philosophy of Martin

Heidegger (see Chap. 6, "Authenticity, Inauthenticity, Fallenness, and *Angst*").

58. CUP 281

59. CUP 293–294. "Idea" here clearly refers to Hegel's *Spirit*.

60. CUP 294

61. CUP 280

62. Descartes included all mental acts as "thinking," and the *cogito* takes account of willing, feeling, hoping, desiring, as well as abstract philosophical thinking. Similarly, we have seen that Hegel rejects the *theory-practice* distinction and so interprets spirit as "living" as well as a product of abstract thought. Kierkegaard's harsh distinction is, therefore, directed primarily at Kant, who perhaps least deserves to be indicted for failure to respect the 'ethical' in man.

63. CUP 281

64. Ibid.

65. CUP 296

66. CUP 281

67. CUP 292

68. CUP 306

69. It is clear how the line of argument here parallels G. E. Moore's "Open Question Argument." Moore argues that any definition of such evaluative terms as 'good' in 'naturalistic' (descriptive) terms (for example, 'red', 'heavy', 'pleasure-producing', 'contributing to the gross national product') can be successfully challenged by the question, "Yes, this is (red, heavy . . .), but is it good?" Kierkegaard argues that any evaluation may be similarly challenged by the question, "Why should that be good?" However, it is evident that Kierkegaard is not concerned with the *meaning* of terms, as is Moore, but with the possibility of justification of values by appeal to some 'natural' fact. And, where Moore does find a justification for moral values in *Utility*, Kierkegaard denies that any such justification can be found.

70. It is on this *need* to choose values to avoid the absurd (lack of ultimate justification for values) that marks Camus's departure from Kierkegaard and forms the basis for Camus's charge that Kierkegaard commits "philosophical suicide." Camus proposes an alternative to Kierkegaard's irrational 'leap of faith'—a refusal to recognize the validity of any mere commitment—which he describes as "keeping the absurd alive." *Myth of Sisyphus* (N.Y.: Vintage, 1955), p. 47. See Chap. 7, "Facticity and Transcendence; Absurdity and Value."

71. For example, *Stages on Life's Way*, trans. W. Lowrie (Princeton: Princeton University Press, 1940), p. 430.

72. *Journals*, 1850.

73. *Either/Or*, Vol. II, 141, Anchor, II, 171.

74. CUP 181; furthering our brief comparison between J. L. Austin and Kierkegaard, we may add that only 'objective truths' (descriptive statements) are *true* or *false;* subjective truths (performatives) are *performed well* or *poorly, sincerely, halfheartedly,* or *fraudulently.*

75. See "Diary of a Seducer" in *Either/Or*, Vol. I, pp. 297–442.

76. Div. *C, AA*, section *B.* "The Realization of the Rational Self-Consciousness Through Itself: "Pleasure and Necessity'."

77. There is a noteworthy similarity to Camus's analysis of Don Juan in *Myth of Sisyphus.* Kierkegaard's semiautobiographic *Johannes, the Seducer* is a philosophically articulate Don Juan.

78. "The Rotation Method," *Either/Or*, Vol. 1, pp. 279–296.

79. Auden, op. cit. 73.

80. *Fear and Trembling* (Princeton: Princeton University Press 1941), p. 64.

81. *Journals* (and *Attack on Christendom*).

82. See "Kierkegaard on Christianity."

83. CUP 327

84. CUP 288

85. Cf. Chap. 1, *"God and Immortality";* Chap. 2, "The Early Theological Writings."

86. *Philosophical Fragments*, p. 35.

87. Ibid., p. 16.

88. Ibid., p. 20.

89. *Fear and Trembling.*

90. *Sickness unto Death*, trans. Lowrie (London: Oxford University Press, 1941), p. 197.

91. *Fear and Trembling.* The Abraham story provides the theme of this work.

92. Ibid., Problem I.

93. Ibid., p. 77.

94. ". . . that which is suspended is not lost, but remains preserved." *Sickness unto Death*, p. 197.

95. Because the notion of "phenomenological analysis" has recently been taken as analysis yielding a kind of "necessary" truth, and because "phenomenology" for Kierkegaard referred to the Hegelian study of the forms of consciousness in order of their necessity, this term is best not applied to his analyses.

Chapter 4

1. For example, the *Gay Science*, section 377.

2. "I am just now having all anti-Semites shot." Letter to to his friend Overbeck, 1889; trans. by Kaufmann, *The Portable Nietzsche* (New York: Viking, 1954), p. 687; hereafter cited as "Kaufmann, *Viking*".

3. *Schopenhauer as Educator* ("Untimely" Meditation III), in Kaufmann, *Nietzsche: Philosopher, Psychologist, Anti-Christ*, 3rd ed. (New York: Vintage

Books, 1968) (original, 1950), p. 104; hereafter cited as "Kaufmann, *Nietzsche*." I have attempted to use Kaufmann's superb translations wherever possible.

4. A. Bäumler, *Nietzsche der Philosoph und Politiker* (Leipzig: Reclam, 1931). This work is extensively criticized in Kaufmann, *Nietzsche.*

5. The most extensive and authoritative demonstration against Nietzsche's alleged Nazi sympathies are to be found in Kaufmann, *Nietzsche;* especially Chap. 10.

6. "On the Three Metamorphoses," *Thus Spake Zarathustra,* trans. W. Kaufmann (New York: Viking-Compass, 1954), Part I, p. 25.

7. *Birth of tragedy,* trans. W. Kaufmann (New York: Vintage, 1967), hereafter cited as "BT."

8. BT 5; K 52, 24, 141; cf. WP 416–17.

9. BT, section 1, pp. 33–38.

10. BT 31–32, *Preface* (dedicated to Richard Wagner).

11. *Nietzsche Contra Wagner,* in Kaufmann, *Viking,* p. 683.

12. There are four *"Untimely" Meditations,* in volumes VI and VII of Musarion collected works, trans. in Levy, 18 vols. (New York; Macmillan, 1909–11). The essay on history is the second; the third is on *Schopenhauer as Educator,* and the fourth is about Wagner.

13. "On the Use and Disadvantage of History for Life," quoted in Kaufmann, *Nietzsche,* p. 149.

14. Cf. *Ecce Homo,* "How One Becomes What He Is."

15. All of these works have been translated in the Levy collected works. *Gay Science* has been translated and issued separately by Kurt F. Reinhardt as *Joyful Wisdom* (New York: Ungar, 1960). Selections from these works are translated in W. Kaufmann, *Viking* (hereafter, "HAH," "Dawn," respectively).

16. *Beyond Good and Evil* (hereafter cited as "BGE"), *The Genealogy of Morals* (hereafter cited as "GM"), *The Case of Wagner* (hereafter cited as "CW"), and *Twilight of the Idols* (hereafter cited as "Twilight") were translated by W. Kaufmann (New York: Vintage, 1967), and collected in *Nietzsche* (New York: Modern Library, 1968). *Twilight, Antichrist,* and *Nietzsche Contra Wagner* were translated by W. Kaufmann and appear in *The Viking Portable Nietzsche* (New York, 1964).

17. *Will to Power,* trans. Kaufmann and Hollingdale (New York: Random House, 1967), hereafter cited as "WP." Reference numbers are to sections, not to pages.

18. Letter to Overbeck, 1881, Kaufmann, *Viking,* p. 92.

19. Cf. "Error is cowardice," WP 1041; EH, V.

20. Musarion, *Gesammelt Werke,* XIV, *Nietzsche,* p. 80.

21. *Twilight,* "Maxims and Arrows," section 26, p. 470.

22. WP 410; cf ibid., p. 470.

23. Musarion, IV, 151, Kaufmann, *Nietzsche,* p. 80.

24. Ibid., XVI, 76, Kaufmann, *Nietzsche,* p. 80.

25. D 51; Kaufmann, *Nietzsche,* p. 89.

26. Arthur Danto has offered us a fascinating elaboration of this comparison in his *Nietzsche as Philosopher* (New York: Macmillan, 1965), hereafter cited as "Danto's *Nietzsche.*"

27. M. Schlick, "Meaning and Verification," in W. Alston and G. Nakhnikian, *Readings in Twentieth Century Philosophy* (New York: Free Press, 1963), p. 471.

28. Rudolph Carnap, "Philosophy and Logical Syntax," in Alston/Nakhnikian, ibid., V., p. 428.

29. Dewey, *Logic: The Theory of Inquiry* (New York: Henry Holt, 1938), p. 122.

30. Dewey, *Quest for Certainty* (New York: Minton, Bloch, 1929), Chap. 10.

31. D 547; Kaufman, *Nietzsche,* p. 86.

32. See Chap. 5.

33. *Twilight,* " 'Reason' in Philosophy," 5, p. 483.

34. BT 24, p. 141.

35. EH 335

36. WP 7

37. *Twilight,* ' 'Reason' in Philosophy," 2, p. 481.

38. WP 481

39. *Twilight,* "The 'True World'," 5, Kaufmann, *Nietzsche,* p. 485.

40. WP 507

41. WP 522

42. WP 558

43. WP 454

44. WP 540

45. WP 70

46. *Gay Science.* 265

47. WP 493

48. The falseness of a given judgment does not constitute an objection against it . . . The real question is how far a judgment furthers and maintains life . . . (BGE 4; cf. WP 507).

49. BGE 16

50. HAH 517

51. BGE 18

52. BGE 11

53. WP 278

54. WP 449

55. WP 458

56. BT; cf. Kierkegaard: "Live in such a way that if your life were to be put on the stage the audience would weep in ecstasy." *Journals,* 1847.

57. "There are no moral phenomena at all but only a moral interpretation of phenomena." (BGE 108)

58. In his discussion of Nietzsche, F. Olafson (*Principles and Persons)* Baltimore: Johns Hopkins Press, 1967), Chaps. 1, 2) credits Nietzsche with the most explicit modern thesis of philosophical voluntarianism—the thesis that moral judgments are neither true nor false. While this is correct, it is dangerously misleading, for it implies that Nietzsche thought that *some* propositions were properly true or false. However, as I have presented Nietzsche here, it should be clear that he did not contrast moral judgments with 'cognitive' judgments in this way, but rather maintained that all propositions are 'voluntaristic'. Nietzsche, so conceived, does not share with Hume the ancestry of 'noncognitivist' ethics.

59. Jaspers, K. *Nietzsche,* trans. Wallraff and Schmitz (Tucson: Arizona University Press, 1965; and Berlin: DeGruyter, 1936).

60. Bertram, E. *Nietzsches Versuch einer Mythologie* (Berlin: Bondi, 1918). Extensively discussed in Kaufmann, *Nietzsche.*

61. *Myth of Sisyphus* (New York: Vintage, 1955).

62. Morgan, G. A. *What Nietzsche Means* (Cambridge, Mass.: Harvard University Press, 1941).

63. Kaufmann, *Nietzsche.*

64. For example, *Gay Science,* 125; *Zarathustra,* Prologue 3. The phrase occurs in Heine and early Hegel before its celebrated appearance in Nietzsche.

65. *Gay Science,* 125; EH 107.

66. Kaufmann, *Nietzsche,* p. 98.

67. *Zarathustra,* 77

68. Morgan, op. cit., 36.

69. A 47

70. WP 462

71. BGE 212

72. *Zarathustra,* III 20 (p. 209).

73. Ibid. 7, 12 (p. 200).

74. *Dawn,* p. 556; compare these 'Christian' values with those of Bazarov, the conscientiously vulgar 'nihilist' in Turgenev's *Fathers and Sons.*

75. BGE 211

76. D 202; Kaufmann, *Viking.*

77. BGE 6

78. WP 40

79. WP 424

80. For example, he often criticizes "morality for being immoral": See, e.g., *Wanderer and His Shadow,* 19; WP 266; WP 461.

81. These three different "senses" of "morality" are also played against each other in a current debate concerning "morality." William Frankena has argued the formal criterion and Falk the social

criterion. They have claimed, however, that these are logically sufficient analyses of a single concept of "morality," and not different senses of an ambiguous term. See Castenada, Nakhnikian, eds., *Morality and the Language of Conduct* (Detroit: Wayne State University Press, 1965).

82. BGE 19

83. BGE 22

84. BGE 9

85. *Dawn* in Danto, p. 137.

86. "Happily it is too late to reverse the development of reason." HAH 11, Levy.

87. *Twilight,* "Problem of Socrates," 7–9.

88. *Twilight,* "Morality as Anti-Nature." I, p. 486.

89. *Twilight,* "Morality as Anti-Nature," 1.

90. WP 522

91. HAH 517

92. *Gay Science,* 2; in Kaufmann, *Nietzsche,* p. 230–231. This quotation ought to be contrasted with the more known quotes, for example, "Some still have a need for metaphysics. But also that violent *longing for certainty . . .* an instinct for weakness." (*Gay Science,* 347)

93. WP 387

94. Nietzsche's frequent anticipation of Freud, not only with the concept of sublimation and defense mechanisms in general but the notion of the unconscious, of repression, dreams, of a dynamic mental energy system, of 'psychic determinism', all are found in Nietzsche before Freud's writings. Rather than compile a long list of quotations to prove Nietzsche's astounding role as a precursor of psychoanalysis, we need only quote Freud himself: *"Nietzsche,* the other philosopher whose premonitions and insights often agree in the most amazing manner with the laborious results of psychoanalysis, I have long avoided for this very reason. After all, I was less concerned about any priority than about the preservation of my openmindedness." (*Collected Works,* Vol. XIV, p. 86, London 1948)

95. Reason and intellect are "the tools of Power," WP 480. Cf. Hume: "It [reason] cannot move us to act on anything." (*Treatise,* p. 7).

96. *Twilight,* "Morality as Anti-Nature," I.

97. *Antichrist* 47

98. WP 383

99. This interpretation has been extensively defended by Kaufmann (*Nietzsche,* Chap. 6 and ff), who presents the principle of the *Will to Power* as Nietzsche's "monism" (Chap. 8, ii) and the fundamental principle of his mature philosophy (p. 179). Our discussion follows Kaufmann's in this section.

100. *Zarathustra,* I, 15 (58).

101. We have noted that Nietzsche at one time intended to 'systematize' his thought into a single *magnum opus* under the title *The Will to Power;* the collection of notes published under this title (WP) is not in this opus.

102. BT, iii, 282.

103. HAH 135

104. IX 398, Kaufmann, *Nietzsche,* p. 186.

105. *The Genealogy of Morals,* II, p. 18.

106. Nietsche has many nasty things to say of the socialism and democracy encroaching upon Europe: "*Socialism* represents the logical conclusion of the *tyranny* of the least and the dumbest." (WP 125) Democracy represents the disbelief in great human beings and an elite society: "Everyone is equal to everyone else." "At bottom we are one and all self-seeking cattle and mob." (WP 752; cf. Kaufmann, *Nietzsche,* 187). "The arming of the people is ultimately the arming of the mob." (WP 754)

107. WP 488

108. BGE 21; WP 667.

109. WP 688; cf. 704: "even trees and plants."

110. *Beyond Good and Evil,* 14; cf. *Twilight,* "Skirmishes . . ." 14; WP 706. Cf. "Freud on Energy Catharsis," e.g., Vol. XXIII, pp. 141ff.

111. WP 689

112. Nietzsche had read Mill, but did not think highly of him, to say the least. "Against John Stuart Mill: I abhor his vulgarity . . ." WP 926 (1888).

113. Mill, *Utilitarianism;* LLA, p. 16.

114. Ibid., p. 44.

115. WP 688.

116. Ibid.

117. V, X2, 1172, *Nichomachean Ethics.*

118. NE X4 1175.

119. NE X5 1175.

120. It is only fair to add that Mill's inference is not so clearly fallacious as it seems at first blush. "The sole evidence it is possible to produce that anything is desirable is that people actually do desire it" is not a bald claim that whatever is desired is worthy of desire. Mill also argues (unfortunately in a different book, *System of Logic*) that something is desirable only if it "excites in the speaker's mind the feeling of approbation," a feeling which depends on the expectation of pleasure (happiness). Thus, only pleasurable things are desired and only pleasurable things are desirable. This is not to say that *all* desired things are desirable, but only that desire is the only evidence for desirability. I take this analysis from M. Stocker, "Mill on Desire and Desirability," *Journal of the History of Philosophy,* vol. 7, 2, April 1969, pp. 188, 199–201. See also J. B. Schneewind, ed. *Mill's Ethical Writings*

(New York: Colliers, 1965).

121. Op. cit., p. 6.

122. *Dawn,* 348.

123. *Utilitarianism,* p. 14.

124. But health is a necessary condition for excellence; cf. "Egoism is of as much value as the physiological value of him who possesses it." (WP 373)

125. *Dawn,* 113.

126. Ibid, 113.

127. Ibid., 113; Kaufmann *Nietzsche* 196.

128. BGE 9

129. *Dawn,* 548; Kaufmann, *Nietzsche* 197.

130. WP 644

131. See Kaufmann, *Nietzsche,* Chap. 6.

132. A 57

133. BGE 260; GM I; WP 268.

134. BGE 261

135. Cf. Fichte, Chap. 2, "The Phenomenology of Spirit."

136. WP 364

137. WP 362

138. WP 363

139. WP 706

140. WP 370

141. WP 371

142. NE IV

143. Nietzsche does not have in mind here any particular racially characterized society, but elitism permeates all of his writings and it is clear that he did believe, and took as the premise of his 'social' philosophy, that some men are much better endowed than others.

144. "I distinguish between a type of ascending life and another type of decay, disintegration, and weakness. Is it credible that the question of the relative rank of these two types still needs to be posed?"

145. Nietzsche is ambivalent on this point: cf. "The values of the weak prevail because the strong have taken them over as devices of leadership." (WP 863)

146. GM I.

147. GM II 19.

148. For example, "On the New Idol," *Zarathustra,* I, 11.

149. *Zarathustra,* Prologue 4, p. 14.

150. Ibid. *Prologue* 3, p. 12.

151. *Übermensch* and *Selbüberwindung* are intimately linked, making the common translation of "superman" misleading if not comical. "Overman" is more literally correct but offends the ear. Therefore, we have retained the German original. This expression is not original with Nietzsche, and is to be found in Goethe as well as classical sources.

152. Ibid., II 4. (93)

153. *Dawn,* p. 18; Kaufmann, *Nietzsche,* p. 245.

154. WP 1026

155. *Dawn,* p. 202.

156. X   413;   Kaufmann,   *Nietzsche,*
p. 252.
157. *Zarathustra,* Prologue 5, p. 17.
158. *Antichrist,* p. 3.
159. *Gay Science,* p. 341.
160. *Gay Science,* pp. 270–271.
161. Arthur Danto has given a remarkable exigesis, reconstruction, and criticism
of this argument in his *Nietzsche as Phi-
lospher,* op. cit., Chap. 7, pp. 195ff.
162. WP 55
163. WP 1053–1067
164. WP 647
165. *Case of Wagner,* 155
166. EH, "Why I Am a Destiny," p. 6.

Chapter 5
1. *General Introduction to Pure Phenomenology* (*Ideen zu einer reinen Phänomenologie   und   phänomenologischen
Philosophie.* Title translated from 3rd ed.,
1928). Originally published in the *Jahrbuch
für Philosophie and phänomenologische
Forschung, Freiburg* (Halle: Niemeyer,
1913).
2. *Ideas,* p. 166, 6:62. All references to
Ideas are to the first volume of *Ideen,*
translated by W.R.B. Gibson (New York:
Macmillan, 1931), and printed in paperback (New York: Collier-Macmillan, 1962).
All references are to this paperback edition. Page number is followed by chapter
and section numbers: *Ideas,* page 166,
chapter 6, section 62.
3. *Jahrbuch für Philosophie und Phänomenologie Forschung* (1911), 11 vols.
(Halle: Niemeyer, 1913–30).
4. "Philosophy as a Rigorous Science,"
trans. Lauer, in *Phenomenology and the
Crisis of Philosophy* (New York: Harper &
Row, 1965), hereafter cited as "PRS."
5. M. Farber, *The Aims of Phenomenology* (New York: Harper & Row, 1966),
p. 3.
6. Introduction to the *Encyclopedia.*
7. 2 vols., 8th ed., London, 1872.
8. Because of the metalinguistic interest of Husserl's writings, a more rigorous
convention of quotation marking must be
adopted than we used in past chapters.
Names of *words* will be in double quotes
("number"), names of *concepts* or *ideas*
will be in italics (*number*), single quotes
will be used for technical terminology
('analyze', 'reduce'). Italics will be used to
introduce special terminology only where
not confusing (for example, *epoche*).
9. *Philosophie der Arithmetik* (Halle:
Pfeffer, 1891), hereafter cited as PA.
10. PA 80–82
11. I borrow this example from Roderick
Chisholm's introduction to his *Realism and
the Background of Phenomenology* (New
York: Free Press, 1960), and from G.
Nakhnikian's Introduction to Husserl's *Idea
of Phenomenology,* trans. Alston and Nakh-

nikian (The Hague: Nijhoff, 1964), p. x ff.;
hereafter all future references to *Idea of
Phenomenology* refer to this translation and
edition.
12. Frege, *Grundlagen der Arithmetik*
(Halle, 1892): *The Fundamental Laws of
Arithmetic,* trans. J. L. Austin (New York:
Harper & Row, 1960).
13. Ibid., p. xvii.
14. Ibid., pp. xvii–xviii.
15. Ibid., p. xviii.
16. Ibid., p. 99.
17. In *Zeitschrift für Philosophie und
phil. Kritik,* vol. 103, pp. 313–332; trans.
M. Black and P. Geach, excerpts, pp. 79–
85, from *Philosophical Writings of Gottlob
Frege* (Oxford: Blackwell's, 1952), hereafter
cited as "Black and Geach, *Frege.*"
18. Ibid., p. 79.
19. Ibid., p. 85.
20. He begins his next book by quoting
Goethe:

*One is opposed to nothing more severely
than to errors recently laid aside.*

Quoted in the Preface to Vol. 1 of the
Logical Investigations.
21. *Logische Untersuchungen* (Halle:
Niemeyer, 1900–01), hereafter cited as
"LU." English translation by J. H. Findlay,
The Logical Investigations, New York: Humanities Press, 1970. The main content of
these *Investigations* is included in M. Farber, *The Foundation of Phenomenology*
(New York: Paine-Whitman, 1962) now in
paperback by State University of New York
Press. The "Attack on Psychologism" sections have also been translated by D. Wil-
lard and are included in R. C. Solomon,
ed., *Phenomenology and Existentialism,*
New York: Harper & Row, 1972.
22. Wilhelm Dilthey had proposed such
a historicist theory of truth and became a
dominant influence on Husserl during this
early "psychologistic" period. It is also
Dilthey whom Husserl singles out for criticism of historicism in PRS. Many other
names might be mentioned in the same
context, however: Troeltsch, Wildelband,
Ricket, Meineke, and Croce all contributed
to the very powerful nineteenth-century historicist movement in Germany. K. Mann-
heim's "sociology of knowledge" is a classic historicist notion. Today, historicism still
has able defenders, particularly in studies
in the philosophy of science; for example,
R. Kuhn, *The Structure of Scientific Revolutions* (Chicago: University of Chicago
Press, 1962), and P. Feyerabend, see his
contributions in Feigl and Maxwell, eds.,
*Current Issues in the Philosophy of Sci-
ence* (New York: Holt, Rinehart and Win-
ston, 1964). It must be noted that the concept of "historicism" as Husserl attacks it
has little to do with the historicism of Vico,

Marx, and Engels in which history is used as a basis for predicting the future.

23. *Ideen*, Vols. II and III, Biemel, ed. (The Hague: Nijhoff, 1952).

24. *Formale und transzendentale Logic* (Halle: Niemeyer, 1929), hereafter cited as "FTL."

25. *Cartesian Meditationen*, Strasser, ed. (The Hague: Nijhoff, 1950), trans. Cairns (The Hague, Nijhoff, 1960), hereafter cited as "CM."

26. *Erste Philosophie, Husserliana*, vols. 7 and 8 (The Hague: Nijhoff, 1956–59). *Phänomenologische Psychologie, Husserliana*, vol. 9, and *Erfahrung und Urteil*, Landgrebe, ed. (Prague: Academia Verlag, 1939).

27. *Die Krisis der Europaischen Wissenschaften und die Transzendentale Phänomenologie*, Biemel, ed. (The Hague: Nijhoff, 1954), English translation by D. Carr, Evanston, Ill.: Northwestern University Press, 1970.

28. In the Archives of Louvain under the editorship of H. Van Breda. These are being published in *Husserliana* (The Hague: Nijhoff, since 1960).

29. Admitted by Husserl in *Ideas*, p. 173–175, 7:65.

30. *Ideas*, p. 76, 2:19.

31. *Being and Time*, Part II, p. 35.

32. See quote, p. 143.

33. Cf. p. 15ff, 166ff.

34. B, Introduction.

35. A 19.

36. *Ideas*, pp. 75–76, 2:19–20.

37. Ibid., p. 83, 2:24.

38. Ibid., p. 83, 2:24.

39. Ibid., p. 75–76.

40. LU, 2nd ed., p. 2; in Farber, op. cit., p. 198.

41. LU, 2nd ed., p. 4, in Farber, op. cit.

42. Dagfinn Føllesdal, one of the best interpreter's of Husserl's philosophy, has argued that several terms closely related to "essence" in Husserl are names of abstract entities. Specifically, Føllesdal argues that *noema* (see pp. 173f) and *Sinn* are such abstractions. While this interpretation succeeds in clarifying several problems encountered in interpreting Husserl, it does not account for Husserl's insistence that essences are *intuited. Journal of Philosophy*, vol. 50, 1969.

43. Chap. 4, "Epistemological Nihilism."

44. "Intentionality and Acts of Consciousness."

45. *Ideas*, p. 76, 2:20.

46. PRS 79

47. Ibid.

48. *Ideas*, p. 96, 3:30.

49. PRS 103

50. "Phenomenology," *Encyclopedia Britannica*, 14th ed., trans. C. Solomon, in *Chisholm*, op. cit., p. 123.

51. Ibid., p. 95, 3:29.

52. Ibid., p. 93, 3:27.

53. Chap. 4, "Values and Nihilism", cf. his "naturalistic" basis for the 'revaluation' and Chap. 1, "Metaphysics and Morals," Chap. 2, "Ethics," Chap. 3, "The Existential Dialectic."

54. *Ideas*, p. 96, 3:38.

55. Ibid., p. 96, 2:30.

56. Ibid., p. 96, 3:31.

57. Ibid., p. 46, 1:11.

58. PRS 104

59. *Ideas*, p 46, 1:11.

60. In spite of his insistence that there are no 'moral facts'.

61. See this chap. "Phenomenology and Foundations of Philosophy."

62. PRS 80

63. PRS 86

64. PRS 80

65. "Phenomenology," in *Encyclopedia Britannica*, 14th ed., in Chisholm, p. 123.

66. *Ideas*, p. 74, 2:19.

67. Ibid.

69. *Ideas*, p. 73, 2:18.

69. *Ideas*, p. 73 2:18.

70. *Ideas* I, p. 94, 3:28. He even introduces an "arithmetical standpoint" which is distinct from the natural standpoint.

71. *Idea of Phenomenology*, Lec. I.

72. PRS 89

73. *Idea of Phenomenology*, Lec. I.

74. Ibid.

75. PRS 105

76. *Ideas*, p. 74–75, 2:19.

77. Ibid, p. 75, 2:19.

78. PRS 81–82

79. *Idea of Phenomenology*, Lec. I.

80. PRS 91

81. *Ideas*, p. 79, 2:21.

82. Ibid., p. 79, 2:21.

83. PRS 89

84. *Idea of Phenomenology*, Lec. I, last page.

85. *Ideas*. Introduction.

86. Ibid., p. 3, 31.96.

87. In his earlier writings, Husserl used the notion of a "transcendental phenomenological reduction" to account for several different reductions or several "levels of reduction" ("Idea of Phenomenology") which he is later to distinguish. In all accounts after the *Logical Investigations*, the suspension of the natural standpoint is referred to as the *epoche*. The term 'reduction' is later reserved for the eidetic reduction, in which intuitions are reduced to intuitions of essences, and for a 'transcendental reduction', in we "discover the absolute being of the transcendental ego." [Ibid. p. 72] The notion of *epoche* ($\epsilon\pi o\chi\eta$) as a suspension of belief occurs in the teachings of ancient skeptics and in Nietzsche. (WP 266)

88. Ibid., p. 97, 3:30.

89. Ibid., p. 97 3:30; cf. Kant's "Refutation of Idealism."

90. Ibid., p. 166, 6:62.

91. *Cartesian Meditations*, p. 1, sect. 1.

92. *Ideas*, p. 98, 3:31.

93. *Ideas*, p. 98.

94. Ibid., p. 100, 3:32.

95. Ibid., p. 98, 3:31.

96. Ibid., p. 99, 3:31.

97. Ibid., p. 99–100, 33:32.

98. Ibid., p. 98–99, 33:31.

99. Richard Schmitt, in a very clear analysis of Husserl's *epoche,* argues that the *epoche* is nothing but a technique for inducing the reflective attitude: "Husserl's Transcendental-Phenomenological Reduction," in *Philosophy and Phenomenological Research,* 20 (1959–60), pp. 238–245.

100. Hume, *Treatise,* IV, Book II.

101. F. Brentano, *Psychologie vom Empirischen Standpunkt* (Hamburg, 1874), p. 198.

102. *Cartesian Meditations,* p. 33, para. 14.

103. Bruno Kerry was a colleague and frequent reviewer of Frege. He is discussed in some detail in Frege's "On Conceptual Objects," in Black and Geach, *Frege,* pp. 42–55.

104. Franz Brentano, from *Psychologie,* p. 108. Reprinted in Chisholm, *Perceiving* (New York: Cornell University Press, 1957), pp. 168–169.

105. This distinction first arises in LU, but is best presented in his essay, *The Idea of Phenomenology,* 1907.

106. Sartre gives us a similar characterization of the objects of imagination. See Chap. 7, "The Pursuit of Being."

107. *Ideas,* p. 239, 9:88.

108. Ibid., p. 240, 9:88.

109. Cf. Kant's "Transcendental Idealism" in Chap. 1.

110. *Ideas,* p. 152, 5:55.

111. Ibid., p. 153, 5:55.

112. For example, Logical Atomism (Russell, Wittgenstein) and Logical Positivism (Carnap, Schlick). This is *not* a theory held by Kant, as we argued in Chap. 1.

113. Cf. Husserl's reference to Hume, *Ideas,* 166, 6:62 and in vol. 1 of LU.

114. *Ideas,* p. 122, 4:43.

115. Ibid., p. 133, 5:47.

116. Ibid., p. 134, 5:47.

117. Cf. J. L. Austin's argument against 'sense datum' theory in *Sense and Sensibilia.* He also insists that we see *objects* and not sense-data and that a causal theory of perception is unintelligible.

118. Since we have performed the *epoche* and cannot talk about the spaciotemporal world, the spelling out of the meaning of "moving left or right" or "circling around" becomes a serious problem which phenomenologists have often been slow to appreciate. Husserl's notion of "thetic" (adopted by Heidegger and Sartre) meaning "positional" only hides this problem.

119. *Ideas,* pp. 228–229, 8:85.

120. *Ideas,* p. 245, 9:91.

121. Ibid., p. 117, 4:41.

122. "On the Intentionality of Consciousness," in *Studies in Phenomenology and Psychology,* Evanston, Ill., 1966.

123. Føllesdal, op. cit.

124. *Ideas* p. 333, 11; 129.

125. *Ideas,* p. 156, 5:57. Quoted from Kant's *Critique of Pure Reason.*

126. *Ideas I,* 3:28

127. *Ideas,* p. 214, 8:80

128. Cf. *"existence is in principle the result of 'constitution' "* and the "Problem of the origin of the world," in Farber, op. cit., p. 546ff.

129. CM 68, para. 33.

130. CM 65, para. 30.

131. "Philosophy and Anthropology" (1931), reprinted in Chisholm, op. cit., p. 135.

132. "Phenomenology," reprinted in Chisholm, op. cit., p. 124.

133. *Ideas,* p. 14.

134. Farber, *Foundation,* op. cit., p. 529.

135. *Transcendence of the Ego* (New York: Noonday Press, 1957), see Chap. 7, "The Transcendence of the Ego."

136. "Cogito Ergo Sum, Inference or Performative," *Philosophical Review,* vol. 71 (January 1962), pp. 3–32.

137. See D. Cairns, "Some Results of Husserl's Investigations," in Kockelmans, ed., *Phenomenology* (New York: Doubleday, 1967).

138. Many of Husserl's attempts to reconcile this conflict appear to be no more than equivocations on crucial terms. For example, the concept of a "Primordial Dator Act" in *Ideas I,* the atrocious notion of "passive constitution" in *Ideas II,* and "constitution" defined as a "clarification" or "discovery" in *Ideas III* and *Cartesian Meditations,* all attempt to hide rather than resolve the conflict between the *given* ("dator," "passive," "discovery") and the *constituted.* There is considerable disagreement whether Husserl ever succeeds in resolving this dispute at all. Paul Ricoeur, probably the foremost phenomenologist active in Europe today, argues that Husserl never succeeds in resolving this conflict between consciousness as a passive receptor of intuitions and consciousness as an active constitutor of objects. (Ricoeur, *Husserl: Analysis of His Phenomenology* Evanston, Ill.: Northwestern University Press, 1967). Some philosophers have argued that Husserl is a realist (and thus ultimately stresses the role of intuition in perception); authors have more frequently

identified him as a firm idealist—as he does himself (CM 40–41)—because of his Cartesian insistence that all objects exist by virtue of their constitution by consciousness (cf. Farber quote, p. 176). The bizarre nature of this conflict among Husserl commentators is that the conflict does not remain unresolved because of lack of textual support for one position or another. The problem is rather that each side can be convincingly defended on the basis of Husserl's own remarks. This has led some sympathetic interpreters (notably Merleau-Ponty) to conclude that Husserl had in mind a theory of consciousness which bypassed the traditional distinctions of "realism" and "idealism." The same ambiguous texts would lead us to the alternative conclusion that Husserl's writing is simply confused. A brief summary and bibliography of this on-going dispute is available in Kockelmans, "Husserl's Transcendental Idealism," in *Phenomenology*, op. cit., pp. 183–193. Husserl himself and his closest followers (for example, M. Farber and E. Fink) tended to minimize the conflict between intuition and constitution. Our survey of Husserl thus far has attempted to minimize the conflict as well; in what follows, we can give only an abbreviated summary of Husserl's own attempts to make his philosophy coherent. For a more detailed account of this problem, the reader is referred to Ricoeur or Kockelmans.

139. 1905–1910, Martin Heidegger, ed. (Halle, 1928).

140. Cf. "even a cursory glance at his [Husserl's] works is sufficient to indicate that he was an antagonist of Kantianism in practically every respect . . ." E. Walsh, *Philosophy of Edmund Husserl* (New York: Octagon, 1965), p. 229. The almost fanatic attempt to prove the originality of Husserl's thought has led to some remarkably bad histories of philosophy as well as to serious obstacles both to understanding the extent of Husserl's historical debts and his true contributions to philosophy.

141. *Ideas*, p. 394, 13:153.

142. *Ideas I*, 4:46.

143. Q. Lauer, *Phenomenology* (New York: Harper & Row, 1965), p. 119.

144. CM 60

145. CM 151

146. Quentin Lauer, *The Triumph of Subjectivity* (New York: Fordham, 1958) and M. Farber, *Naturalism and Subjectivity* (Springfield, Ill.: Thomas, 1959). Other faithful adherents to Husserl's "transcendental" position would include M. Natanson, J. Edie, E. Fink, A. Gurwitsch, S. Strasser, D. Cairns, L. Landgrebe, and A. Schütz. There are many who follow Husserl as closely as possible, but there are sufficient differences among them to forbid any short and accurate group portrait.

Chapter 6

1. Martin Heidegger, *Being and Time*, Part I, Div. II, trans. John MacQuarrie and Edward Robinson (New York: Harper & Row, 1962), from *Sein und Zeit* in *Jahrbuch für Phänomenologie und phänomenologische Forschung*, Ed. Husserl, ed. (hereafter cited as "SZ"). Page numbers following SZ refer to "H" pagination in MacQuarrie and Robinson translation.

2. *Introduction to Metaphysics* (1953), trans. Manheim (New York: Doubleday-Anchor, 1961), p. 166 (hereafter cited as "IM").

3. See bibliography at end of this Chapter.

4. SZ 6

5. Ibid.

6. SZ 39

7. SZ 6

8. SZ 161

9. *Principles and Persons* (Baltimore: Johns Hopkins University Press, 1967), chap. 4.

10. Ibid., p. 100.

11. Richard Schmitt, *Heidegger on Being Human* (New York: Random House, 1968), Chap. 1.

12. IM 63

13. "On the Essence of Truth," *Existence and Being*, ed. Brock, trans. Hull and Crick (Chicago: Regnery, 1949), p. 348 (hereafter cited as "ET").

14. ET 320

15. IM 10–11

16. ET 348

17. ET 348–349

18. ET 348

19. ET 9

20. ET 10

21. IM 11

22. ET 349

23. IM 21; logical positivists, for example, A. J. Ayer and R. Carnap, have also called metaphysics "poetry," but by this they do not share Heidegger's praise for both poetry and metaphysics. Rather, they condemn both as *meaningless*.

24. "Hölderlin and the Essence of Poetry," trans. Scott, in Brock, op. cit., p. 306.

25. Ibid.

26. Ibid.

27. *Humanismusbrief,* cf. Hegel, *Logic,* Introduction; BGE 20; *Twilight* III: W.V.O. Quine, *Word and object,* and "On What There Is," in *Logical Point of View* (New York: Harper & Row, 1967), Chap. 1: "To be is to be the value of a variable (to be denoted by a term in a language)."

28. *What Is Called Thinking,* trans. Gray (New York: Harper & Row, 1968), p. 3.

29. Translations of *"Seindes"* vary greatly, from "beings" to "essents" to

"entitles." We shall follow MacQuarrie & Robinson in adopting "entities," *even where quotations are taken from translations which do not accept this convention.*
30. SZ 1
31. Ibid.
32. IM 1
33. IM 2
34. IM 26
35. IM 32
36. IM 43
37. IM 6
38. IM 8
39. IM 5
40. IM 30
41. IM 31
42. IM 31–32
43. IM 70
44. B 626–628
45. B 628
46. Aristotle, *Metaphysics,* B 4: 10014–10021
47. IM 16
48. IM 37
49. IM 30
50. Ibid.
51. SZ 3
52. IM 37
53. SZ 2–4, section I 1.
54. IM 11
55. SZ 27
56. SZ 27–28; cf. Chap. 5, "Phenomenology and the Foundations of Philosophy."
57. SZ 29
58. SZ 31
59. SZ 38
60. IM 24–25
61. SZ 27
62. IM 22
63. IM 67
64. Ibid.
65. IM 28
66. IM 3
67. SZ 12
68. Ibid.
69. SZ 13
70. SZ 14–15
71. IM 57–58
72. SZ 115
73. Cf. Chap. 1, "The Transcendental Ego"; Chap. 2, "Spirit"; Chap. 5, "The Transcendental Ego."
74. SZ 12
75. SZ 15
76. SZ 53; This expression should provide ample reason for the too often ridiculed continental penchant for hyphenated expressions. The hyphens, although clumsy, mark an expression which does not designate a conglomeration of components which may be factually or even logically distinguished.
77. SZ 116
78 Wittgenstein, *Tractatus Logico-Philosophicus,* 1.1.

79. Husserl, *Ideas I,* 46, 1:1.
80. SZ 64
81. SZ 65
82. SZ 63ff.
83. SZ 56
84. SZ 59
85. SZ 67–68
86. SZ 59
87. SZ 62
88. SZ 66–67
89. SZ 56
90. Heidegger makes use of a distinction between entities *zuhanden* ("ready-to-hand") and *vorhanden* ("present-at-hand"). These correspond to *equipment* and *things* respectively, and we shall employ only the latter terminology.
91. SZ 68
92. Ibid.
93. SZ 69
94. Ibid.
95. SZ 68
96. SZ 68–69
97. SZ 69
98. SZ 75
99. SZ 69
100. Richard Schmitt, in chap. 2 of his book (op. cit.) and in an article, "Heidegger's Analysis of 'Tool'," *The Monist* (1965), p. 49, has admirably attempted to supply these missing arguments.
101. SZ 73
102. SZ 74
103. CUP 281. See Chap. 3, "The Meaning of Existence."
104. SZ 12
105. SZ 41–42
106. SZ 12
107. We shall not translate this term to avoid confusion with the more ordinary notion of "existence" as it applies to any entity. *"Existenz"* applies *only* to Dasein, and to state some of Heidegger's claims without this understanding (as Sartre does in his famous slogan, "Existence precedes essence") can only lead to serious confusion.
108. SZ 56
109. SZ 192
110. SZ 42
111. Ibid.
112. Ibid.
113. SZ 232
114. SZ 12
115. SZ 342
116. In *Cartesian Meditations,* Husserl recognized that his theory of *empathy* could not constitute a *proof* that there are other persons.
117. SZ 117–125
118. SZ 42
119. SZ 115. Italics mine.
120. Ibid.
121. Ibid.
122. SZ 117
123. SZ 118

124. SZ 120
125. SZ 123
126. SZ 126
127. Ibid.
128. Ibid.
129. Ibid.
130. Ibid. "Das Man" is often translated as "they" to signify this impersonal anonymous no-one in particular. Such a use of "they" is evident in such slogans as, "they say that. . . ." Because there is no English expression which captures this impersonality so well as "das Man" and because this expression is already prominent in English literature, we shall simply leave it untranslated.
131. SZ 127
132. Ibid.
133. Ibid.
134. IM 38
135. SZ 127–128
136. SZ 128
137. SZ 129
138. Ibid.
139. M. King, *Heidegger's Philosophy,* New York, 1964.
140. One might interestingly compare Heidegger's view of *Rede* as an ontological structure that serves as a basis for all language with Noam Chomsky's notion of "deep structures" which serve as a psychological basis for all natural language. (See, for example, *Syntactic Structures* [The Hague: Nijhoff, 1962].) Chomsky holds that this deep structure is ultimately of subject-predicate form, however; Heidegger would reject this form as a derivative of inauthentic speech.
141. *Gay Science,* para. 354
142. For example, SZ, section 64; IM, Chap. 3.
143. Nietzsche, *Twilight,* III.
144. Although the "private language argument" is generally credited to Wittgenstein (*Philosophical Investigations*) and attributed to his reaction to his earlier *Tractatus Logico-Philosophicus,* the argument has only been worked out in detail by his interpreters. There is still a raging controversy over how the sparse passages in the *Investigations* are to be interpreted and a more fruitful controversy about whether and how the private language argument might be validly formulated. The argument is most frequently presented as a *reductio ad absurdum* argument showing that such statements as "I have a pain" cannot be learned by learning to name a private sensation (see N. Malcolm's review of the *Philosophical Investigations* in Chappell, *Philosophy of Mind,* Englewood Cliffs, N. J.: Prentice-Hall, 1962). The argument may be generalized to show that no language can be learned by learning to refer to mental entities of any kind. In some versions of the argument, it is concluded that no such private entities can exist. In weaker versions, it is concluded only that language cannot be learned by reference to such entities. Many critics of the argument insist that the supposed impossibility of *learning* a language by reference to mental entities might still allow for a language which does refer to such entities. (See Pitcher, ed., *Wittgenstein* (New York: Doubleday-Anchor, 1966).

It should be evident that the phenomenological investigation we have been discussing for two chapters involves examination of 'private' intuitions (whether these are essential or not) and thus depends upon the invalidity or unsoundness of the "private language argument." There has been no explicit attempt of a major phenomenologist to attack Wittgenstein's argument as such (to our knowledge to date), but rather phenomenologists, particularly Husserl and Heidegger, begin by rejecting behaviorism and with it serious consideration of those arguments which take behaviorism as its conclusion. (An important exception to this is Merleau-Ponty, who arranges a remarkable compromise between phenomenology and philosophical behaviorism.)
145. SZ 189
146. SZ 275
147. *Kant und das Problem der Metaphysik* (Bonn: Cohen, 1929), trans. J. Churchill, *Kant and the Problem of Metaphysics* (Bloomington, Ind.: Indiana University Press, 1962).
148. SZ 381
149. *Phys* D 11, 219b; quoted by Heidegger, SZ 421.
150. See, for example, J. J. C. Smart *Problems of Space and Time* (New York: Macmillan, 1964).
151. Cf. Nietzsche, "live your life as a work of art"; Kierkegaard, "live as if your life were to be put on the stage."
152. CUP 147
153. Ibid.
154. CUP 149
155. Ibid.
156. SZ 248
157. SZ 262
158. "Thoughts of the Times on War and Death," Part A.
159. Ibid., p. 266.
160. SZ 268
161. SZ 310
162. *Kant und das Problem der Metaphysik,* p. 213, in Schmitt, op. cit., p. 224.
163. See bibliography.
164. See bibliography.
165. Scheler, *Formalism in Ethics (Der Formalismus in de Ethik und die Materiale Wertethik* (Bern: Francke, 1954).

166. A position briefly considered in the short section "Being and the Ought," in IM 164–167.

167. *Platons Lehre von der Wahrheit,* p. 99, trans. and quoted by Heinemann, *Existentialism and the Modern Predicament* (New York: Harper & Row, 1953), p. 100.

168. Olafson, op. cit., p. 65.

169. Richard Schmitt has presented a thorough discussion of this objection in the Conclusion of *Heidegger on Being Human.*

170. SZ 437

171. SZ 39f.

172. Both in 1929—dates are completion dates, not necessarily publication dates.

173. SZ 75

174. SZ 230

175. SZ 151

176. SZ 75

177. SZ 438

178. ET 319

179. ET 321

180. ET 322

181. Ibid.

182. ET 329

183. ET 330

184. ET 331

185. Ibid.

186. ET 334

187. Ibid.; "disclosure" replaced by us for "revealment" (*Unverborgenheit*).

188. ET 333

189. Ibid.

190. ET 336

191. Correspondence theory has been rejected for many reasons other than its failure to serve as a *general* account of truth. Bertrand Russell struggled to formulate an adequate version of this theory since 1910. The problem is to provide a coherent account of what the correspondence is supposed to be between; that is, Russell [*An Inquiry into Meaning and Truth,* 1940] states the correspondence to be between *beliefs* and *facts.* The problems involved in analyzing these two elements and the purported relationship between them become extraordinarily difficult. A brief but informative account of these problems is available in A. N. Prior's article "The Correspondence Theory of Truth," in the *Encyclopedia of Philosophy,* op. cit., vol. 2, pp. 223–232.

192. SZ 345

193. IM 154

194. IM 1

195. IM 79–169

196. IM 90

197. IM 63

198. E.g., *Unterwegs zur Sprache,* 1959

199. IM 101

200. IM 102

201. IM 103

202. IM 150

203. IM 158

204. IM 20–21

205. *Letter on Humanism,* p. 54.

206. IM 19

207. IM 24

208. IM 71

209. IM 21

210. IM 22

211. IM 21

212. Cf. Kant's *Categories of Modality,* Chap. 1.

213. IM 24

214. Lewis Carroll, *Through the Looking Glass* (New York: Random House, 1946), pp. 105, 107.

215. *What Is Metaphysics?* in Brock, op. cit., p. 359 (hereafter cited as "WM").

216. WM 361

217. WM 363

218. WM 365

219. WM 366; cf. SZ 187, in which "Being-in-the-world" itself is that in the face of which anxiety (*Angst*) is anxious (*angstlich*).

220. WM 368

221. WM 369

222. An extensive discussion may be found in Laszlo Versenyi's *Heidegger, Being and Truth* (New Haven: Yale University Press, 1965), pp. 139–142.

223. IM 21

224. *Holzwege,* p. 303.

225. *Nietzsche,* I. p. 358

226. WT 28

227. *Nietzsche,* I. p. 100

228. *Letter on Humanism,* p. 46.

229. Ibid., p. 42.

230. WM 389, postscript.

231. WM 389

232. WM 390

233. WM 391

234. Ibid.

235. *Letter on Humanism,* p. 13.

Chapter 7

1. "Where is the party in opposition that has not been decried as communistic by its opponents in power? Where the opposition that has not hurled back the branding reproach of Communism . . . ?" Marx and Engels, *Manifesto of the Communist Party,* Introduction.

2. R. E. May, et al., eds., *Existence: A New Dimension in Psychiatry and Psychology* (New York: Basic Books, 1958).

3. *L'être et le néant: Essay d'ontologie phenomenologique* (Paris: Gallimard, 1943), trans. Hazel Barnes (New York; Philosophical Library, 1956, Washington Square paperback, 1966), hereafter cited as "BN." Page references are to the Washington Square paperback (1st printing).

4. *La structure du comportement* (Paris: Presses Universitaires de France,

1942), trans. Alden L. Fisher (Boston, Beacon Press, 1963, paperback 1967), hereafter cited as "SB." Page references are to the Beacon Press paperback.

5. *Phénoménologie de la perception* (Paris: Gallimard, 1945), trans. Colin Smith (London: Routledge & Kegan Paul, 1962, and New York: Humanities Press, 1962), hereafter cited as "PP." Page references are to the Routledge edition.

6. Especially, *Le Mythe de Sisyphe,* (Paris: Gallimard, 1942), trans. J. O'Brien, *Myth of Sisyphus* (New York: Vintage, 1955), and its companion novel, *L'Étranger* (Paris: Gallimard, 1942) trans. J. O'Brien, *The Stranger* (New York: Vintage, 1946).

7. Especially, De Beauvoir, *L' Ethic de Ambiguité.*

8. PP, preface.
9. *Ideas* I, Book IV.
10. For example, *Myth* 23, 24f. 37.
11. PP vi
12. PP viii
13. BN lxxiii
14. BN lxiii
15. PP ix
16. BN lxxiii
17. BN lxxix
18. PP xiv
19. PP xiii
20. PP xiv
21. BN liv
22. BN lv
23. BN lv
24. Ibid.
25. BN lvi–lvii
26. Chap. 5, "Intentionality and Acts of Consciousness."
27. PP xxi
28. *L'Imagination* (Paris: Alcan, 1936), trans. to English as *Imagination* by Williams (Ann Arbor: University of Michigan Press, 1962) and *L'Imaginaire* (Paris: Gallimard, 1940).

29. In his book on Sartre, *Sartre: A Philosophical Study* (London: Oxford University Press, 1967), Antony Manser has brought out the remarkable similarity between this argument and that offered by the American Wittgensteinian philosopher Norman Malcom. In his book *Dreaming,* Malcom comments that, "The brother in one's dream may be 'in no way different' from one's brother. . . . There is identity in the one case as much as in the other." Page 93, quoted by Manser, page 28.

30. *L'Imaginaire,* p. 17.
31. *Treatise on Human Nature,* I, i, i.
32. *L'Imaginaire,* p. 25.
33. *Nausea* (Paris: Gallimard, 1938), trans. Alexander (New York: New Directions, 1949).
34. *Nausea,* pp. 170–177.
35. *Myth,* p. 15

36. "The Emotions" (Paris, Hermann, 1939), trans. Frechtman (New York: Philosophical Library, 1948).
37. BN 527
38. BN 528
39. *Sense et Non-sense* (Paris: Nagel, 1948), trans. Dreyfus, *Sense and Non-sense* (Evanston: Northwestern University Press, 1964), pp. 143–144.
40. PP 160
41. Merleau-Ponty finds it in Husserl's later conception of *Lebenswelt* in *Crisis.*
42. See Chap. 6, "The Problem of Being."
43. PP xviii
44. PP xv
45. PP xiv
46. PP viii, ix
47. Trans. Williams (New York: Noonday Press, 1957).
48. TE 31
49. TE 34
50. TE 50
51. TE 35
52. Chap. 5, "The Transcendental Ego."
53. TE 36
54. TE 39–40
55. TE 49
56. TE I, B
57. TE 47
58. TE 45
59. TE 51
60. TE 52
61. TE 48
62. TE 54
63. TE 60
64. TE 38
65. TE 36–37
66. Chap. 5, "The Transcendental Ego." LU and *Crisis.* LU rejects the Ego: In *Crisis,* it is a *community* Ego.
67. PP cf. xi.
68. TE 104
69. PP xii
70. Sartre rejects Heidegger's primitive concept of *Dasein* because it "has from the start been deprived of the dimension of consciousness." (BN 89–90)
71. SB 3
72. BN 128
73. Presented summarily in the Introduction to BN.
74. Quoted by Sartre, BN lxi; and Merleau-Ponty, p. xvii.
75. BN lxi–lxii
76. PP 373
77. SB 164
78. Ibid.
79. PP ix
80. BN lxi
81. BN lxvii
82. Ibid.
83. TE 40, 42
84. BN lxiii
85. SB 164
86. PP 377

87. BN liii
88. BN lxi
89. PP 371–372
90. BN 91
91. BN 93
92. PP 403–404
93. PP 404
94. PP 400; cf. Heidegger's "formal indicator"; Chap. 3, "The Fallenness from Being."
95. Chap. 6, "The World as Equipment."
96. SB 164
97. BN lxvi
98. TE 44
99. BN lxii
100. BN lxiii
101. BN lxii
102. BN lxiii–lxiv
103. BN lxiv
104. PP 371
105. BN lxi
106. BN lxiii
107. BN lxiv
108. BN lxxix
109. BN 93f.
110. BN 90
111. BN lxxiv
112. BN lxv
113. One such critique by a noted analytic philosopher is A. J. Ayer, "Novelist-Philosophers: V-Jean-Paul Sartre"—Horizon XII, no. 67 (July 1945), esp. 18–19. A more humorous but equally unsympathetic critique of "nothingness" is P. Heath, "Nothing," Encyclopedia of Philosophy, P. Edwards, ed., op. cit.
114. Wittgenstein, op. cit., 5, 631.
115. BN 23
116. It is perhaps his obsession with something that leads Wittgenstein (in his Philosophical Investigations) to the absurd conclusion that expecting does not refer to any experience, only behavior.
117. BN 11
118. BN 16
119. BN 15
120. BN 7
121. BN 8
122. BN 7
123. BN 96
124. Ibid.
125. BN 35
126. BN 6ff., esp. 29.
127. BN 19
128. BN 26
129. BN 34
130. Das Nichts Nichtet; cf. BN 26ff.
131. BN 26
132. BN 27–28
133. BN 28
134. Ibid.
135. BN 21
136. BN 775–776
137. BN 29–30
138. BN 95

139. BN 30
140. Ibid.
141. Ibid.
142. BN 27; cf. Heidegger on Dasein, Chap. 6.
143. BN 34
144. Chap. 6, "Authenticity, Inauthenticity, Fallenness, and Angst."
145. PP viii
146. BN 101
147. Ibid.
148. BN 102
149. BN 114
150. BN 115
151. BN 118
152. BN 104
153. BN 105
154. BN 106
155. BN 117
156. BN 125
157. Phenomenology, B; IV; 3; trans. Baillie, pp. 208–226.
158. BN 108
159. BN 109
160. BN 110; cf. Hegel's "Unhappy Consciousness", and Kierkegaard's "Aesthetic Despair."
161. BN 111
162. Existentialisme est un Humanisme (Paris: Nagel, 1946), trans. Mairet, Existentialism is a Humanism (London: Methuen, 1948), pp. 41, 42 (hereafter cited as EH).
163. Huis Clos, trans. by S. Gilbert as No Exit, in No Exit and Other Plays (New York: Vintage, 1947), esp. pp. 38–41.
164. BN 670
165. BN 650
166. BN 67
167. BN 2
168. Myth, p. 37.
169. Ibid., p. 21.
170. Ibid., p. 23.
171. Ibid., p. 30.
172. "Reason" is used multiambiguously in Camus's writings. Most often it is a normative expression meaning something like "correct deep thinking"; it does not mean "reason" in the sence expressed by rationalists (and antirationalists) in our discussion. It is closest, perhaps, to Heidegger's very broad notion of philosophical Denken. When he argues against reason, he argues against a conception of the world itself as rational (as in Hegel or Kant). The world is irrational, Camus insists, because it is indifferent to our concerns. Occasionally, "rationality" refers to no more than man's having desires, and expectations that the world will fulfill these desires, for example, when he juxtaposes man's rationality and the world's irrationality.
173. Ibid., p. 35.
174. Ibid.
175. EH47

176. Sartre, *St. Genet: Actor and Martyr*, trans. Frechtman (New York: Braziller, 1963), p. 536.

177. BN 695

178. PP 435

179. *Ethics of Ambiguity*, p. 25.

180. *Myth*, p. 42.

181. Karl Jaspers, "A New Humanism," in *Existentialism and Humanism*, trans. Fischer, ed. Ashton (New York: Moore and Co., 1952), p. 72.

182. Paul Tillich, *The Courage to Be* (New Haven: Yale University Press, 1952), p. 48.

183. Martin Buber, *I and Thou* (New York: Scribners, 1958), p. 58.

184. PP 442

185. Tillich, op. cit., p. 48

186. BN 597

187. BN 596

188. BN 591

189. BN 599

190. PP 439

191. While Aristotle devotes a great amount of attention to the problem of ignorance (and the resulting 'Socratic problem' whether knowledge necessitates right action), he has virtually no analysis of the problem of 'free will' which plays such a central role in modern philosophy.

192. BN 592

193. BN 673

194. BN 38

195. BN 39

196. *Myth*, p. 9.

197. Buber, op. cit., p. 51.

198. EH 28

199. EH 46

200. EH 32–33

201. Ibid.

202. *Ethics of Ambiguity*, p. 14, 16.

203. Camus comes to differ from the standard existentialist (Sartrian) denial of human nature:
The analysis of the conduct of revolt leads us to the suspicion, at least, that there is a human nature, as the Greeks believed there was and contrary to the postulates of contemporary thought.
The Rebel, p. 28 (New York: Vintage, 1954). Partly with this in mind, Camus has denied that he is an "existentialist" (*Les Nouve les litteraires*, 1945).

204. *Myth*, p. 38.

205. EH 48

206. *Nausea*, 148

207. EH 212

208. Camus, "Letter to a German Friend," trans. J. O'Brien, in *Resistance, Rebellion and Death* (New York: Modern Library, 1961).

209. BN 35

210. BN 40

211. BN 40–41

212. BN 35

213. Ibid.

214. BN 46

215. BN 46, 47

216. BN 46

217. *Myth*, p. 10.

218. Tillich, op. cit., p. 51

219. BN 52

220. BN 681

221. BN 48–49

222. BN 580

223. PP 438

224. BN 679

225. BN 537

226. E.g., in Kaufmann, *Existentialism from Dostoyevski to Sartre* New York: Meridian Books, 1956, pp. 287–311.

227. BN 57

228. BN 66

229. BN 67

230. BN 57

231. "Portrait of the Anti-Semite," Becker (New York: Schocken Books, 1948), pp. 8, 26–27; *Refexions sur la question juive* (Paris: Mortinien, 1940).

232. *The Second Sex*, p. 38.

233. I have attempted to argue that such an objection is not valid in *Unconscious Motivation* (Ann Arbor, Mich.: University Microfilms, 1967).

234. BN 65; A check on the original claim in Steckel's *La Femme Frigide* (Paris: Gallimard, 1942) shows that this claim only points to the possibility of making a psychosis conscious after extensive analysis: Stekel does not deny the unconscious origins of mental 'illness' (frigidity is rarely a psychosis).

235. This characterization of id and ego suggests a way of reconciling Sartre and Freud. It may be that Freud's distinction between conscious and unconscious (which for him is *not* equivalent to the ego and the id) is not altogether different from Sartre's distinction between reflective and prereflective consciousness. There is a definite disagreement about the ability to reflect or to know what is in prereflective consciousness (the unconscious), but not a disagreement about the existence of nonconscious (nonreflective) mental phenomena.

236. BN 62

237. BN 60

238. BN 63

239. BN 163

240. BN 64

241. Ibid. 64

242. BN 65

243. See note 140.

244. BN 65; cf. note 239.

245. BN 560ff.

246. BN 59

247. BN 41

248. Ibid.

249. PP 435

250. Ibid.

251. Ibid.
252. PP 447
253. PP 447
254. PP 446–447
255. PP 447
256. BN 531ff.
257. BN 532
258. BN 534
259. BN 533
260. Cf.: A powerful trend in British "philosophy of mind" which takes dispositional statements about human behavior to be "inference tickets" to future behavior. This thesis is clearly present in Wittgenstein's *Philosophical Investigations* and constitutes the central argument of G. Ryle's *Concept of Mind* (New York: Barnes & Noble, 1949). Ryle argues that statements like "He has a foul temper" and "He is a coward" allow us to infer probable future behavior. Moreover, Ryle believes that this same analysis can be extended to all statements about the 'mind' of a person, for example, "He wants to go fishing" and "He is expecting a letter." It should be clear that this species of "philosophical behaviorism" is much at odds with the phenomenological analyses of Sartre et al. Yet there is a source of agreement between the two analyses which ought to be noted: the British behaviorist approach constitutes an attempt to eliminate all causal accounts of human behavior. Ryle wishes to argue, specifically, that there is no *mind* (no "ghost in the [body] machine") to cause bodily behavior and that there is no causal factor (that is, one's cowardice, one's desire, one's temper) which causes one to behave. We have seen that Sartre also wishes to eliminate all talk of the 'mind' ("consciousness is nothingness"), but we may now note that Sartre and Ryle also join efforts in attempting to get rid of all causal accounts of behavior by denying that statements like "He has a foul temper" refer to a causal determinant of behavior. This is not to claim that either member in this team would agree to a common effort. Sartre comments (in his autobiographical *The Words*) that he would rather read a bad detective story than read Wittgensteinian philosophy; and Ryle, in a well-known reply to Merleau-Ponty's query, "Is not our program the same?" answered, "I hope not" (Paris: *Quatrieme Colloque de Royaumont,* 1962).
261. BN 42
262. Ibid.
263. See BN 77ff.
264. BN 71–72
265. BN 111
266. EH 33
267. A similar point has been recently argued in analytic philosophy of mind; cf. Bedford, "Emotions" in Gustafson, ed., *Essays in Philosophical Psychology* (New York: Doubleday Anchor, 1965).
268. BN 111, 112
269. I am indebted to Frithjof Bergmann for his analogy and his analysis of Kafka.
270. BN 59
271. BN 77, 79, 80
272. BN 76, 82
273. BN 369. Cf. Husserl, Chap. 5, "The Transcendental Ego."
274. BN 274
275. "On Our Knowledge of Other Minds," reprinted in Chappell, *Philosophy of Mind,* op. cit.
276. BN 285
277. BN 288
278. Ibid.
279. BN 277
280. Strawson, op. cit., Chap. 3.
281. BN 307
282. PP xii
283. *Myth,* p. 29.
284. *Phénomenologie de l'ésprit,* Cosson, p. 148n; BN 291.
285. BN 289
286. 317–318
287. 319
288. 313
289. 319
290. 322
291. EH 45
292. Ibid.
293. *Nausea,* p. 131.
294. *No Exit,* p. 21.
295. Ibid., p. 19.
296. *The Reprieve* (New York: Bantam, 1947).
297. "The Flies," in *No Exit,* p. 103.
298. *Ethics of Ambiguity,* p. 218.
299. PP 448
300. PP 453
301. PP 434
302. PP 435
303. PP 456
304. Preface to *L'Étranger,* in *Nation,* 16 November 1957, p. 355.
305. *The Stranger,* trans. J. O'Brien (New York: Vintage, 1946, pp. 103, 112).
306. BN 370
307. BN 371
308. PP 70
309. BN 374
310. PP 75
311. BN 399–400
312. BN 397
313. BN 378
314. PP 75
315. BN 415–416
316. Chap. 6, "The World as Equipment."
317. PP 139
318. BN 424
319. PP 150
320. PP 145
321. PP 90

322. PP 167
323. PP 203
324. PP 205
325. Introduced parenthetically in Chap. 5, note 124.
326. PP 205
327. BN 525
328. Ibid., Part III, Chap. 3, Sect. III.
329. BN 467
330. BN 484
331. BN 485
332. A very different analytic study of this problem has been recently published by T. Nagel, "Sexual Perversion," *Journal of Philosophy* 16 January 1969, pp. 5–17. See also Freud's "Three Contributions to the Theory of Sex," Essay no. 1, in the *Standard Edition of the Collected Works*, Vol. VII.
333. The analytic restriction to description of normative ethics makes it appear as if analytic metaethics is normatively impotent. It may well be the case, however, that it is not impotent but only dishonest. If metaethics takes its *descriptions* of *status quo* ethics as a formulation of the correct forms of ethical principles and arguments then it has given full support to *status quo* morality under the pretense of being "normatively neutral." Because it sets up standards for correctness for normative ethics, metaethics can *never* be normatively neutral. I have argued this thesis at length in "Normative and Meta Ethics," in *Philosophy and Phenomenological Research* (September 1970), Vol. XXXI, No. 1.

334. BN 98
335. De Beauvoir, *Ethics of Ambiguity*, p. 24.
336. EH 42
337. Ibid., p. 48.
338. De Beauvoir, op. cit., p. 16.
339. Ibid., p. 25.
340. Ibid., p. 78.
341. EH 42
342. Olafson argues this interpretation in great detail in *Principles and Persons*. He is surely correct in taking Heidegger's 'critique of values' as central, but it too often appears that he is interpreting Heidegger as holding on to the traditional distinction between 'facts' and 'values'. See esp. Chap. VI.
343. In *The New York Review of Books* (NYRB), March 26, 1970, pp. 22 f.
344. Sartre, *Situations II,* translated in Manser, op. cit., p. 165.
345. EH 311
346. *The Rebel,* trans. Bower (New York: Vintage, 1956), p. 22.
347. De Beauvoir, op. cit., p. 23.
348. EH 30
349. EH 30
350. Ibid.
351. EH 29
352. Jaspers, "A New Humanism," in *Existentialism and Humanism* (New York: Moore and Co., 1952), pp. 78, 79, 97.
353. NYRB, op. cit, p. 22.
354. NYRB
355. NYRB, ibid.

INDEX